T0320842

The Dynamics of Broadband Markets in Europe

The European Commission's Digital Agenda for Europe sets the targets for broadband development by 2020, yet current broadband market outcomes vary widely amongst the EU Member States and the objectives seem challenging for many. In this book, a group of in-country experts follows a framework of qualitative and quantitative analysis to capture patterns, commonalities and differences between 12 different European countries, in terms of infrastructure endowments, institutional arrangements, time of joining the EU, behavior of market actors, personal interventions of regulators, the role of municipalities, and the role perception of governments. By exploring how the past explains present broadband market outcomes, these longitudinal country case studies look to how improvements can be made for the future. As the first in-depth study of broadband developments in Europe, this book will be invaluable to policy-makers, regulators, academic researchers, advisors, and consultants working in the fields of telecommunications, broadband development, technology and innovation.

WOLTER LEMSTRA is Senior Research Fellow at the Department of Technology, Policy and Management at the Delft University of Technology, The Netherlands, and Visiting Senior Research Fellow at the Centre for Communication, Media and Information Technologies at Aalborg University, Denmark. He has 25 years of experience in the telecom sector and has occupied senior management positions in various telecoms technology firms. His current research is focussed on telecommunication sector governance, industry structure developments, firm strategic behaviour and innovation trajectories.

WILLIAM H. MELODY is Guest Professor at the Center for Communication, Media and Information Technology (CMI), Aalborg University Copenhagen, Denmark. He is Emeritus Professor, Economics of Infrastructures at the Department of Technology, Policy and Management, Delft University of Technology, and Emeritus Director, Learning Initiatives on Reforms for Network Economies (LIRNE.NET). He has participated in telecom and ICT research and policy development in all regions of the world.

The Dynamics of Broadband Markets in Europe

Realizing the 2020 Digital Agenda

Edited by

WOLTER LEMSTRA
WILLIAM H. MELODY

CAMBRIDGE
UNIVERSITY PRESS

University Printing House, Cambridge CB2 8BS, United Kingdom

Cambridge University Press is part of the University of Cambridge.

It furthers the University's mission by disseminating knowledge in the pursuit of
education, learning and research at the highest international levels of excellence.

www.cambridge.org
Information on this title: www.cambridge.org/9781107073586

First published 2015

Printed in the United Kingdom by Clays, St Ives plc

A catalogue record for this publication is available from the British Library

Library of Congress Cataloging-in-Publication Data
The Dynamics of broadband markets in Europe: realizing the 2020 digital agenda / edited by Wolter Lemstra
and William H. Melody.
     pages   cm
ISBN 978-1-107-07358-6 (Hardback)
1. Telecommunication–Europe.   2. Digital communications–Europe.   3. Broadband communication
systems–Europe.   4. Telecommunication policy–Europe.   5. Information technology–Government policy–Europe.
I. Lemstra, W. (Wolter) II. Melody, William H.
HE8084.D96 2014
384′.041094–dc23   2014014331

ISBN 978-1-107-07358-6 Hardback

To Jens C. Arnbak, A leader in telecom reform in Europe; colleague and friend to the editors and several authors in this book.

As a professor at the Delft University of Technology, the Netherlands, from 1986 he initiated research and training programs, and advised government bodies, industry and international agencies. He was the first Chair of OPTA, the independent Post and Telecom authority in the Netherlands, 1997-2005; the first Chair of the new European Telecommunication Regulators Group (ERG), as of 2002; and frequent adviser to the new national telecom regulators being appointed throughout Europe and attempting to find effective ways to implement EU telecom policies.

Contents

Figures

Tables

Contributors

Editors/authors

WOLTER LEMSTRA is Senior Research Fellow, Economics of Infrastructures, Department of Technology, Policy and Management, Delft University of Technology and Visiting Senior Research Fellow at the Center for Communications, Media and Information Technologies (CMI), Aalborg University, Copenhagen, Denmark, and was Vice-President, Business Development and Marketing at Lucent Technologies.

WILLIAM H. MELODY is Emeritus Director of LIRNE-NET, Emeritus Professor, Economics of Infrastructures, Department of Technology, Policy and Management, Delft University of Technology, and Guest Professor, Aalborg University, Copenhagen, Denmark.

Authors

OLGA BATURA defended her PhD thesis on the topic of universal service regulation in September 2013 at the Collaborative Research Center 597 'Transformations of the State' at the University of Bremen, Germany. She is also a visiting lecturer for European law at the European Humanities University in Exile, Vilnius, Lithuania.

RICHARD CADMAN is Director of SPC Network Ltd, a telecom regulation and economics consultancy, and PhD researcher at the ESRC Centre for Competition Policy at the University of East Anglia, Norwich, UK.

RICHARD CAWLEY is at the Directorate-General for Research and Innovation, the European Commission; Research Associate, Delft University of Technology; and Fellow of the Centre for Science and Policy, University of Cambridge.

ANASTASIA CONSTANTELOU is Assistant Professor of Innovation Management, University of the Aegean, Department of Financial and Management Engineering, Greece.

RAFAEL COOMONTE is Senior Researcher at the Centre for Applied ICTs of the Technical University of Madrid.

MORTEN FALCH is Associate Professor at the Center for Communications, Media and Information technologies (CMI), Aalborg University, Copenhagen, Denmark. He holds a bachelor degree in Mathematics, a masters in Economics and a PhD. Since 1988 he has specialized in economic and policy issues related to information and communication technologies.

CLAUDIO FEIJÓO is Professor, Faculty of Telecommunications Engineering, Technical University, Madrid, and was Senior Researcher at the Institute for Prospective Technological Studies, European Commission.

MARCO FORZATI is Senior Researcher and project manager at Acreo Swedish ICT, where he is coordinating the topic area 'Broadband Business and Society'.

DAVIDE GALLINO is Head of unit, Equivalence and access to digital platforms, networks and services – Electronic Communications Directorate, at the Italian national regulatory authority for telecoms and media (AGCOM).

JOSÉ LUIS GÓMEZ-BARROSO is Associate Professor, Faculty of Economics and Business Administration, National Distance Education University – UNED, Spain.

ANDERS HENTEN is Professor at the Center for Communications, Media and Information technologies (CMI) at the Department of Electronic Systems, Aalborg University, Copenhagen, Denmark. He is a graduate in communications and international development studies from Roskilde University, Denmark (1989) and holds a PhD from the Technical University of Denmark (1995).

EDVINS KARNITIS is Leading Researcher, Faculty of Computing, University of Latvia and was Commissioner, Public Utilities Commission of Latvia and is now Adviser to the Chairman of the Commission.

PIOTR ŁADNY is Assistant Professor at the Department of Innovation Effectiveness, Faculty of Management and Economics of Services, Szczecin University, Poland. He holds a PhD in Economics from Szczecin University, Poland (2003).

REINHARD LAROY is at the Belgian Institute for Postal Services and Telecommunications (BIPT) and affiliated to KU Leuven/HU Brussels, as a lecturer in the Advanced Masters in Intellectual Property Rights.

CLAUDIO LEPORELLI is Professor of Economics and Management of Technology, Department of Computer, Control, and Management Engineering, La Sapienza University of Rome, Italy.

AUDREY LORIDAN-BAUDRIER is Deputy Director for Research at the Institut Mines-Télécom. Formerly, she held several positions as Senior Economist for the National Spectrum Agency (ANFR), President of the ITU-D Study Group 1 and Deputy Chief for International Affairs at the French Telecommunications and Posts Regulator (ARCEP). She was Associate Professor in Economics at the Paris-Sud University. She holds a doctorate in Economics from the Paris 1 Panthéon-Sorbonne University and a masters degree from the University of Ottawa.

CRISTER MATTSSON is Senior Advisor at Acreo Swedish ICT where he is coordinating the topic area 'Broadband Business and Society'.

ALBERTO NUCCIARELLI is Research Fellow at the Faculty of Management, Cass Business School, City University, London. He previously worked at the Eindhoven University of Technology and Philips Research on ICT economics and policy, business models in the digital industry, public-private interplay in municipal broadband projects, and health economics.

SERGIO RAMOS is Associate Lecturer, Faculty of Economics and Business Administration, National Distance Education University – UNED, Spain, and Partner and Co-Founder at Noon Venture Consulting.

JUAN RENDON SCHNEIR is Financial and Regulatory Manager at the headquarters of Huawei for Western Europe in Düsseldorf and is Assistant Professor on leave from the Department of Information and Communications Technologies at Pompeu Fabra University, Barcelona, Spain. He was Senior Consultant in the Cost Modeling and Internet Economics Department at WIK-Consult in Germany.

SOFIE VERBRUGGE is Postdoctoral researcher at the Department of Information Technology, Ghent University – iMinds, Ghent, Belgium.

ANDRIS VIRTMANIS is Associate Professor, Faculty of Electronics and Telecommunications, Riga Technical University and Director, Department of Electronic Communications and Post, Public Utilities Commission of Latvia and was Director, Department of Informatics at the Ministry of Transport of Latvia.

MARLIES VAN DER WEE is a PhD researcher on social cost-benefit analysis of FttH deployments in a multi-actor setting at the Department of Information Technology, Ghent University – iMinds, Ghent, Belgium.

IWONA WINDEKILDE is Assistant Professor at the Center for Communications, Media and Information technologies (CMI), Department of Electronic Systems, Aalborg University, Copenhagen, Denmark. She holds a PhD in Economics from Szczecin University, Poland (2002).

Foreword

It has been recognized around the world that broadband telecommunication infrastructures will be necessary to support the information society objectives of nearly all countries. With each passing year broadband developments, and in particular the services and applications enabled by broadband, are linked more closely with economic growth and development. The European Union (EU), OECD, ITU and other international organizations have programmes that document progress, identify common barriers and best practices, and facilitate the development of broadband infrastructures.

A major focus is national government policies and regulations that play key roles in stimulating, directing or restricting broadband development within dynamic markets characterized by rapidly improving technologies and enhanced digital services. The research and analysis in this important book document and compare the responses to the broadband targets and objectives of the EU Digital Agenda 2020 in a widely diversified group of twelve EU countries.

Until recently, the most effective way for countries to foster telecommunication and information/communication technology (ICT) infrastructure development was to liberalize markets and promote competitive opportunities for new players through national regulatory authorities (NRAs). But for broadband infrastructure and digital economy development, it is being recognized that governments may need to play additional roles to stimulate the desired broadband investment, especially in relation to public services and achieving social goals.

Identifying the most effective roles that governments can play in this next stage of ICT-sector reform and digital-economy development is a much more challenging task than highlighting the successful practices of the leaders. It relies on building an evidence base, with harmonized metrics across different countries, to understand the foundations for policy and regulation and tools that enable greater consumer empowerment. On the one hand, it will enable a more comprehensive analysis of government policy options and, on the other, a more detailed analysis of the specific, often unique conditions in different countries. Wealthy countries have different options than poor ones; countries with universal fixed network penetration have different options than those that are dependent on mobile; countries with strong and effective public institutions have different options than those with a strong tradition of private market solutions. In some countries, sector-specific regulation works well; in others, much less so.

One of the most important messages from the research in this book is that for the next stage of broadband infrastructure and digital-economy development, there is no single policy pathway to success. Each country's unique legacy may be the most important factor in determining the set of policies and practices necessary to meet the EU Digital Agenda objectives. A common model of policy reform, such as the liberalization model that has been widely applied with significant success in the past, is no longer sufficient. The most important determinants of success will be government policies and industry investment programs that build on each country's historical and cultural development and its current economic and governmental structure.

More generally, maximizing the benefits for economic and social development, enabled by broadband and an open Internet, requires the launch of a range of complementary policy initiatives. One is to ensure that broadband networks are widespread, of high quality, available at competitive prices and attract sufficient investment. There is a critical need to reform policy and regulation to take advantage of the new opportunities enabled by the convergence of communication networks, technologies and services, to ensure greater choices for consumers and to enable platforms for innovation to flourish. But policies to improve high-speed infrastructures – 'fat pipes' – need to operate hand in hand with policies that stimulate the creation of content, services and applications which will create a demand that can justify investing in 'fat pipes'. The latter, together with the free flow of information, are essential to spur new business models and services across the economy from e-commerce to scientific collaboration to health and the environment.

Also essential are policies to build trust among citizens and businesses in the resilience and security of the infrastructure and the economic and social services that rely on it, as well as to strengthen user confidence that privacy and consumer rights are protected online. Finally, to be successful, the above policies need to be supplemented by efforts to equip users with the necessary ICT skills and literacy to take full advantage of ICTs, broadband and the Internet.

This book provides a refreshing focus on the dynamic dimensions of broadband markets and the roles that a new set of market entrants and government actors already are playing in twelve countries across the EU in implementing its Digital Agenda 2020. Although the differences between the old and new EU countries may be the most obvious, even those among the countries currently leading the broadband league tables are striking. The many useful insights generated here will enrich the understanding of everyone with an interest in the next stage of broadband and digital economy development.

Jørgen Abild Andersen,
Chairman, OECD Committee on
Digital Economy Policy;
Director General, National IT and
Telecom Agency,
Denmark (1991–2011).

Preface

The genesis of this book can be traced back to January 2009 when the working paper 'Do we need Policy 3.0 for Telecom 3.0?' by Professor Eli Noam of Columbia University was the subject of a lively debate at a seminar organized by the Ministry of Economic Affairs of the Netherlands. Dr Paul de Bijl, Head of the Department of Competition & Regulation at CPB – the Dutch public think-tank for economic policy research – had taken the initiative to organize the seminar and I had the honour of being invited as discussant. The question being addressed was: 'What are the policy implications of the transition to a new generation of telecommunications networks?'

Considering that from 2005 onward the Netherlands had featured in the Top-3 of the OECD broadband league tables, the market appeared to be performing very well. However, despite early trials, fibre to the home (FttH) deployments were lagging and municipalities had started to take the initiative, for instance in Amsterdam. Following other FttH initiatives by housing corporations, the copper cable-based duopoly was challenged by Reggefiber, a civil engineering company deploying open access fibre networks. In response, OPTA – the national regulatory authorithy (NRA) updated the wholesale access regulation, taking account of what was needed to create a viable business case for fibre deployments. In 2008 there followed a strategic move by KPN, the PSTN-incumbent, taking a 41 per cent share in Reggefiber. As a result, KPN was in a better position to counter the competitive pressure from CATV providers UPC and Ziggo who were providing 'fibre power' on their HFC-networks, with data rates up to 120 Mbit/s. Hence, the conclusion of my presentation was that, in the case of the Netherlands, the broadband market was sufficiently dynamic that Telecom 3.0 would not need Policy 3.0 but only

an extension of Policy 2.0. On Professor Noam's second question: 'Have we come full circle?...Is Telecom 3.0 merely a high-speed version of the original system Telecom 1.0, extended across the borders of countries and media, and supplemented by oligopoly, at best?' I responded with a 'maybe'.

Triggered by the interests of the seminar participants and stimulated by their valuable feedback, a paper was proposed and accepted for the Telecommunication Policy Research Conference (TPRC) held in September 2009 at George Mason University, Arlington, Virginia, USA. Following positive feedback at TPRC, the question was raised: 'How unique is the case of the Netherlands and what lessons can be learned?' Subsequent discussions with colleagues and friends, including Dr Richard Cawley, official at the European Commission (formerly with the Directorate-General – Information Society and currently with the Directorate-General – Research and Innovation), led to the belief that obtaining deeper insights into the dynamics of broadband markets across Europe would be a very meaningful research project and its outcome considered as highly valuable for the process of achieving the Digital Agenda targets. This led to the research-annex-book project on the dynamics of broadband markets in Europe. From the initial case study on the Netherlands, it became clear that obtaining these deep insights would require local experts to contribute to the project.

This book is the tangible outcome of a long period of collaboration involving experts at universities and research institutes in twelve countries across Europe and at the European Commission. I am deeply grateful for their time and efforts to make this research project a success. This also applies to the contributions by co-editor Professor William H. Melody at Aalborg University and the editorial support by Vic Hayes at the Delft

University of Technology (TUDelft). Moreover, I would like to acknowledge the support provided by the Delft University of Technology's Department of Technology, Policy and Management and Aalborg University's Center for Communications, Media and Information technologies.

Our collective aim has been to provide an accurate account of broadband market dynamics in Europe; where we have fallen short of this objective, the responsibility remains with the authors. The usual disclaimers also apply.

Wolter Lemstra,
Delft/Copenhagen, August 2014.

Introduction

WOLTER LEMSTRA AND WILLIAM H. MELODY

1.1 The dynamics of broadband markets

The importance of ubiquitous telecommunications services for economic development is widely recognized.[1] In the early days the objective was to have every home and enterprise connected to the public switched telephone network (PSTN). In the 1990s the introduction of GSM (originally Groupe Spéciale Mobile, later standing for Global System for Mobile Communications) allowed every person to be connected to the network – at any time and at any place – and within a decade mobile penetration exceeded fixed line penetration. In the mid-1990s the attention shifted to the emerging Internet. Today, the focus is on the availability, accessibility and affordability of broadband – fixed as well as mobile – at ever-increasing data rates in support of electronically mediated economic and social activity.

1.1.1 The Digital Agenda for Europe

The realization of a ubiquitous broadband infrastructure has become part of the economic and social policy agenda agreed between the European Commission and the European Union (EU) member states in 2000, as part of the so-called 'Lisbon Agenda' (EC, 2000).[2] These plans evolved through eEurope2002, eEurope 2005 and i2010. Today, the broadband objectives are part of the 'Digital Agenda for Europe' (EC, 2010)[3], and can be summarized as follows:

By 2013:

- Bringing basic broadband[4] to all Europeans;

By 2020:

- Ensuring that all Europeans will have access to the Internet with data rates above 30 Mbit/s, and
- 50% or more of European households will have subscribed to Internet access with data rates above 100 Mbit/s.

However, meeting these ambitious policy goals requires willing participation of two key intermediating actors: suppliers of broadband services and buyers of broadband services.

---

[1] Early publications on the relationship between telecommunications and economic growth include Hardy (1980) and Saunders, Warford and Wellenius (1994). More recent studies on the role of ICTs and growth include Röller and Waverman (2001) and Gruber and Koutroumpis (2011). The link between investment in broadband and economic growth is the subject of papers by, for instance, Crandall and Singer, 2009 and Czernich, Falck, Kretschmer and Woessmann (2009); see also Van Gorp et al. (2011).

[2] The EU ambition formulated in the 'Lisbon Agenda' was: "to become the most competitive and dynamic knowledge-based economy in the world by 2010." The major policy goals were: (1) to establish an inclusive, dynamic and knowledge-based economy; (2) to produce accelerated and sustained economic growth; (3) to restore full employment as the key objective of economic and social policy; and (4) to modernize our social protection systems. The eEurope Action Plan included establishing an ubiquitous broadband infrastructure. (EC, 2000)

At that time other countries and regions had plans addressing similar issues: e!Japan launched in 2001; eKorea Vision in 2002; Hong Kong: Digital 21 Strategy; USA: Information Super Highway in 2000.

[3] The Digital Agenda includes six pillars: Pillar I: Digital Single Market; Pillar II: Interoperability and Standards; Pillar III: Trust and Security; Pillar IV: Fast and ultra-fast Internet access; Pillar V: Research and innovation; Pillar VI: Enhancing digital literacy, skills and inclusion. The broadband targets are related to Pillar IV. (EC, 2010)

[4] Basic broadband is generally understood as 2 Mbit/s downstream.

Following the telecommunications[5] reform initiated in Europe in 1987 (EC, 1987), telecom markets have been liberalized and the degree to which broadband is made available to the public and enterprises is largely the result of the decisions taken by the private sector, by the service providers. These service providers exploit their legacy infrastructure and explore new technologies in the pursuit of new market opportunities while being subject to national policies and regulations.

As such, the availability of broadband is the aggregate outcome of investment decisions made by private firms operating in competitive markets and some additional contributions from the public sector, mostly to complete basic universal service. Expectations regarding end-user demand and willingness and ability to pay drive the income side of the business case. On the cost side, population density, equipment costs and the costs of deployment are the main factors. As such, entrepreneurs take calculated business decisions aimed at making future profits. Uncertainties regarding future policies and regulation are an important risk factor in the decision-making process.

Ultimately, it is the end-user's response to the various broadband offerings – infrastructure access and content – that determines the uptake of broadband and its use. In this setting, broad, intense and innovative forms of competition are important to increase end-user choices, improve service quality and reduce prices.

In such an environment, government policies and regulation are not realized through their enactment but through the actions of the market players, the telecom entrepreneurs at large. It is through the individual and collective actions of these entrepreneurs that policies and regulations are effectuated. Generally, effectiveness or ineffectiveness of policies and regulations becomes apparent through the results of the actions or inactions of the market actors.

This implies that a quest for understanding broadband performance – or an assessment of the achievement of the Digital Agenda targets – and any attempt to improve the level of performance require a deep understanding of broadband market dynamics. This is the core topic of this book.

With markets at its centre, this study is foremost an industry analysis. But, as markets are conditioned by policy and regulation, it includes policy analysis.

While broadband markets are largely national in scope[6], within the EU we share common institutional arrangements as to the development of e-communications infrastructure and services. We share a common regulatory framework for electronic communications.[7]

Implementation of the directives constituting the regulatory framework and shared objectives is delegated to the EU member states.[8] Each member state has the responsibility to transpose the EU-level directives into national laws, to be enforced by the national regulatory authorities.[9] Moreover,

---

[5] In this book we use telecommunications to denote the communication services having been provided over the PSTN for many years, such as telephony, facsimile, and in-band data communication. The term e-communications is used to denote all communication and distribution services provided over todays converged digital infrastructures.

The term 'telecommunications/e-communications sector' is used to denote the services side of the industry. The industry is understood to include the services sector as well as the infrastructure equipment with the related software and services, and the terminal equipment. The e-communication industry includes in addition the media and content services sectors and the related equipment, software platforms and services.

[6] On the one hand, fixed broadband evolved from narrowband, which was provided using the national PTSN infrastructure. On the other hand, it evolved from local and regional RTV-networks being upgraded to provide two-way communication services. Mobile broadband, 3G and 4G, evolved from narrowband 2G cellular networks; they are all operated based on radio spectrum licenses which are national in scope.

[7] EU regulatory framework for electronic communications, available at http://europa.eu/legislation_summaries/information_society/legislative_framework/l24216a_en.htm.

[8] Subsidiarity is an organizing principle of decentralization, which implies that a matter ought to be handled by the smallest, lowest, or least centralized authority capable of addressing that matter effectively.

[9] Market analysis is subject to common practice and remedies are reviewed at the EU level to assure harmonization. For more details, see Chapter 3 'The influence of European Union policies and regulation'. In this process the Body of European Regulators for Electronic Communications (BEREC, http://berec.europa.eu/) plays an important role.

the Digital Agenda for Europe must be translated into national plans for achieving the EU objectives at the national level.

Recognizing that each member state is different, for instance in terms of historical developments, institutional arrangements, time of joining the EU, market structure and political realities, the approach towards achieving the broadband objectives differs among member states and thus the market outcomes vary. As of January 2013, in the EU league table of fixed broadband subscriptions per hundred inhabitants, the Netherlands occupies first place with 40.2 per cent, while Romania is twenty-seventh with 16.6 per cent (EC, 2013). Even member states with similar rankings, such as the Netherlands (first) and Denmark (second) have distinctly different market structures and market dynamics.

So, should we conclude that every broadband market is unique and very little can be learned and shared across member states in pursuing our common objectives?

To the contrary, the contributors to this book believe that understanding the strategic behaviour of the principle actors – the e-communication services providers – will provide deep insights into the dynamics of broadband markets on both national and European levels, which in turn will provide valuable inputs into the policy and regulatory debate on how to stimulate broadband developments leading to achievement of the Digital Agenda targets. These insights may allow for a more ready acceptance of differences among member states and, hence, support for different developmental trajectories to reach a shared objective.

As the research was aimed at capturing the dynamics of broadband markets in Europe, and given that the situation in each member state has unique features, the research was performed through the development of a set of twelve longitudinal country case studies.

Through application of a common structure and a common framework of analysis, comparisons can be made and deep strategic insights can be obtained from these case studies. The purpose is to use these insights into the dynamics of broadband markets to complement the current policy and regulatory debate and to contribute to an accelerated development of

these individual markets towards achieving the shared broadband objectives and beyond.

Through the use of country-level case studies, the research presented in this book fills a void in the analysis of broadband developments in Europe, which for the most part remained generic – non country specific. The research provides the empirical and analytical basis for formulation of policies and regulations enabling the next stage of broadband and Internet developments. It provides the basis for response to the broader policy question of whether different programmes are needed for different circumstances: e.g., more generally, between developed and developing countries and, more specifically, within Europe between member states that joined early and those that joined more recently. Moreover, the research provides wide-ranging evidence on how broadband may be deployed in rural areas to close the digital divide.

Of particular interest in the development of broadband markets is the transition toward a new generation of access infrastructure that requires major investments. The need for these investments may run counter to the (short-run) business imperatives of private firms operating in competitive markets. One may also assert that the current regulatory regime is best suited for stable markets, not markets that are facing a major transition in the underlying technologies. In observing the current outcome of the forces operating in broadband markets, the league table of broadband penetration appears to be led by countries with a high degree of competition between infrastructures, PSTN-copper with (V)DSL on the one hand and RTV-cable with DOCSIS modems on the other. At the same time it appears that this competition hinders the transition towards fibre-based next-generation access networks, as the incumbent operators continue to exploit their installed bases through evolutionary upgrades of their legacy networks. So, will today's leaders become tomorrow's laggards? We respond to this question in the chapters that follow.

In member states with a lower degree of competition or no competition at all between PSTN and the RTV-cable network, the broadband development trajectories are different, as are the transitions to next-generation broadband networks. Moreover, in new member states the development of mobile and fibre access has become a substitute for the development of the PSTN, while RTV-cable penetration is relatively low. Hence, broadband development again follows a different trajectory, as will the transition to next-generation broadband networks. As the case studies show, operators in the new member states have the opportunity to leapfrog in technology.

The development of different broadband trajectories and the implications for the transition to next-generation access are the focus for the research reported in this book. Hence, two sets of related issues or research questions are of prime interest: the first set looks at the past to explain the current situation; the second looks at the current situation to explore the future of broadband.

- *Set 1*: What were the trajectories for broadband development (fixed and/or mobile)? Which actors have been instrumental in these broadband developments and how? To what degree have competition in and regulation of broadband markets played a role in the provision and uptake of broadband?
- *Set 2*: What are the (anticipated) trajectories toward the next generation of broadband networking (fixed and/or mobile) and achievement of the Digital Agenda targets? Which actors are instrumental in the transition and how will they act? To what degree should competition between infrastructures and the regulation of infrastructures play a role in the provision and uptake of next generation broadband?[10]

In this context, trajectories are considered to be the cumulative outcomes of strategies that were or are being pursued by the actors in the markets considered.

1.2 The case study approach

The broadband developments and market dynamics in twelve EU member states are captured in twelve longitudinal[11] case studies. The case study period starts with the introduction of broadband, around the year 2000, and runs until the year 2013. Overall benchmarks are provided at the beginning and at the end of the case study period, covering general country statistics, communication statistics and major events in relation to joining the EU and implementation of market liberalization. See Tables 1.2 and 1.3 at the end of this chapter.

As the case study period represents a 'snapshot' in the development of e-communication services, and as broadband follows from narrowband, which is an evolution based on the (existing) PSTN and CATV cable networks, a summary of historical developments is provided as part of each case study. The extent to which the history is captured has been the choice of the case author and depends on its relevance for explaining the developments of today.

1.2.1 Structure of the case studies

To facilitate cross-case comparison and analysis, each of the country case studies follows a common framing:

- *Introduction*: providing the historical highlights of telecommunications sector developments leading up to the period of broadband service provision, including information on the legacy market structure, role of the government,

---

[10] In the case descriptions and the subsequent analysis we should recognize that the PSTN and the RTV-Cable networks are not only different in the technological dimension but also with respect to content and content regulation. For the PSTN the core value was the reliable transfer of information with protection of the integrity of the content. In relation to the RTV-Cable networks, governments have been concerned with pluriformity of information supply, must-carry obligations, the role of advertizing, etc. As the telecom markets are converging, the tradition of linking content regulation to dedicated networks cannot be continued. In broadband and in the transition towards FttH open access, content is expected to play an important role which extends beyond the 'network neutrality' debate. Where the content dimension intersects with the infrastructure transition, this dimension is captured in the country case studies.

[11] A longitudinal study is defined as a correlational research study that involves repeated observations of the same variables over long periods of time, often many decades. It is a type of observational study. In our context, the term longitudinal case study is used to denote the developments over time of the same variables in qualitative terms.

introduction of Internet into the country and development of narrowband service provision;[12]

- *Case description*: providing the case description of the broadband market dynamics over time, with a focus on the strategies and execution thereof by the key actors: firms, regulators, and policy makers;
- *Case focus (where applicable; either embedded in the case description or as a separate section)*: providing specific information on the relevant actors, their strategies and the outcomes that have influenced the course of events in an important way;
- *Within-case analysis*: explaining the market outcomes over time with reference to the case description, indicating the alignment with prevailing theories and concepts, exploring and explaining the 'surprising events';
- *Conclusions*: summarizing the case; highlighting those insights that are of particular relevance for the key actors in the broadband market: in particular, those that will affect the achievement of the Digital Agenda targets and those that are considered worth recommending to others (do's and don'ts); the special features of the country case;
- *Reflections*: on the limitations of the case study and recommendations for follow-up research.

While the case studies are all longitudinal and cover common aspects, the case authors have been invited to focus on the salient developments. Hence, each case shows a different emphasis. Some cases focus on competition between incumbents and entrants; others emphasize broadband development from a public policy perspective, or the role of regulation to foster competition and investment. Still others place more emphasis on the role of non-traditional telecom actors, such as construction companies and housing corporations, while in some cases the role of municipalities appears to be important to broadband development.

All case studies include a reflection on the achievement of the Digital Agenda targets;

broadband performance at the end of the study period is presented in detail. Moreover, the case authors have been challenged to move beyond 2020 in their assessments of future developments. In the concluding sections the authors analyse the country case studies and highlight the lessons learned.

1.2.2 Selection of the case studies

The selection of the case studies is the result of a pragmatic approach by the editors, the goal being to have a representative set of cases across the EU, including: large, medium and small countries in terms of landmass and population; coverage of countries in Northern, Mid- and Southern Europe; longtime member states and those that recently joined the Union; diversity in infrastructure endowments, with different emphasis on the role of fixed versus mobile broadband; and diversity in perception of the role of government: i.e., the regulatory versus the developmental state.[13] The final selection has been determined by the availability of expert authors and their willingness to put a significant amount of time and effort into this project. The case study countries are Belgium, Denmark, France, Germany Greece, Spain, Italy, Latvia, the Netherlands, Poland, Sweden and the UK. Table 1.1. provides an overview of the broad characteristics of the country case studies.

1.2.3 Sequence of the case studies

As this research project was triggered by broadband developments in the Netherlands, this case study opens the series of twelve studies. In this case the academic network plays an important role in the development of the Internet and broadband. In addition to intense infrastructure-based competition, this case shows an important role for municipalities and a 'third actor' in fibre deployments. It is followed by the case study on Belgium, more specifically on Flanders, which provided for a first cross-case analysis.[14] Flanders shows an important

---

[12] Narrowband is defined in the context of this book as data rates below 2 Mbit/s, which includes dial-up Internet access using 56 kbit/s modems and ISDN at 144 kbit/s, basic broadband starts at 2 Mbit/s, with the application of ADSL and DOCSIS 1.0.

[13] See Chapter 2 Research context and perspective for a discussion.

[14] The initial explorations as part of the development of the case on the Netherlands led to a collaborative effort with

Table 1.1 Overview of country case studies

Cty	Cty/pop size S/M/L	Europe N/M/S	Member State E/R	Industry profile	Government/third actor role
BE	S/S	M	E	PSTN⇔RTV	Federal state, two regions
DE	L/L	M	E	PSTN(+RTV)	Federal; industry policy; *Stadtwerke*
DK	S/M	N	E	PSTN+RTV+FIBRE	Private equity case
EL	M/M	S	E	PSTN+MOBILE	Government programs
ES	L/L	S	E	PSTN(+RTV)	Autonomous regions
FR	L/L	M	E	PSTN(+RTV)	Visible hand, industrial policy, detailed fibre regulation
IT	L/L	S	E	PSTN(+FIBRE)	Visible hand, industry policy/functional separation
LV	S/S	N	R	PSTN+MOBILE +FIBRE	Regulatory intervention, bottom-up initiatives by alternative providers,
NL	S/M	M	E	PSTN⇔RTV	Municipalities, housing corporations, third actor
PL	L/L	M	R	PSTN(+RTV)+ MOBILE	Regulatory intervention, catch-up
SE	L/M	N	E	PSTN+RTV+FIBRE	Municipalities in fibre
UK	L/L	M	E	PSTN(+RTV)	Invisible hand; functional separation

Legend: Cty: country; Pop: population; S: small; M: medium; L: large; N: north; M: middle; S: south; E: early; R: recent.
Source: Author.

role for the regional government in orchestrating consolidation of the CATV networks into Telenet, an important competitor to the PSTN incumbent Belgacom.

Denmark follows as another small EU country with similar circumstances and similar level of broadband performance but a totally different market structure and a different role of the regulator. Sweden follows next, with special emphasis on the role of municipalities in 'fibre to the home' (FttH) development.

Subsequently we turn to the large countries, with Germany examined next. This case emphasizes the role of government in broadband development, at both the federal and the *Länder* levels. The case on the United Kingdom is next, with the

emphasis on functional separation of BT as the incumbent operator to improve access conditions for alternative operators.

The case of Italy addresses functional separation as an obligation imposed on Telecom Italia. Its salient features are the lack of CATV networks and the very early deployment of fibre to the home.

The case of France reflects a deep understanding of the challenges operators face in deploying ultra-fast broadband outside the major cities. The case features a strong role of government, including guidance on coordination and collaboration between public and private actors at the local level.

The case of Spain reflects the differences in challenges between urban and rural areas: i.e., the difficulties of achieving universal broadband. The case of Greece shows the challenges associated with the highlands and islands, as well as the impact of the financial crisis. The case of Poland reflects the importance of mobile in closing the 'digital divide', as well as the importance of the personality of the regulator in creating a level playing field. Finally, the case of Latvia concludes

researchers at Ghent University, Belgium, to compare more structurally the case of the Netherlands with that of Flanders. These efforts have proven to be a great lead into the larger broadband-research-book project. The results have been presented at ITS, Vienna (Van der Wee, Verbrugge and Lemstra, 2012).

Table 1.2 Key statistics at the beginning of the case study period, ~2000

	Year	Belgium BE	Denmark DK	France FR	Germany DE	Greece EL	Italy IT	Latvia LV	Netherlands NL	Poland PL	Spain ES	Sweden SE	United Kingdom UK
Country statistics													
Population	2000[B]	10,239,085	5,330,020	60,545,022	82,163,475	10,903,757	56,923,524	2,381,715	15,863,950	38,263,303	40,049,708	8,861,426	58,785,246
Area (km²)	2012[C]	30,528	42,915	551,695	357,021	131,940	301,338	64,569	37,357	312,679	505,968	449,964	243,610
Population density (p/km²)	2000[C]	339.0	123.9	96.0	230.3	83.5	193.0	38.1	470.2	122.4	79.6	21.6	241.5
Members per household	1999[C]	2.49	2.14	2.42	2.16	2.82	2.62	3	2.26	3.17	3.24	2.17	2.31
GDP (€ mln)	2000[C]	252,543	173,597	1,439,603	2,047,500	137,930	1,198,291	8,433	417,960	185,713	629,907	268,252	1,619,641
Per capita (€)	2000[C]	24,600	32,500	23,700	24,900	12,600	21,000	3,600	26,300	4,900	15,600	30,200	27,500
Communications statistics:													
Fixed telephone access paths[3]	2000[B]	4,475,000	3,202,000	29,597,000	39,666,000	5,760,000	24,494,000	735,000	8,174,000	9,615,000	17,748,000	6,053,000	31,823,000
Per capita (%)	2000[B]	43.7	60.0	48.9	48.3	52.8	43.0	30.8	51.5	25.1	44.3	68.3	54.1
ISDN channels (64 kbit/s)	2000[B]	1,017,000	958,084	4,300,000	17,300,000	312,324	5,666,100	19,600	3,288,778	2,235,780	1,674,100	944,700	3,170,00
Mobile phone subscribers	2000[B]	5,629,000	3,3636,552	29,613,764	48,202,000	5,932,403	42,200,000	401,000	11,000,000	6,747,000	23,938,970	6,369,000	43,452,000
Per capita (%)	2000[B]	54.9	63.0	50.3	58.6	56.0	73.8	16.8	69.1	17.5	60.0	71.8	72.7
TV households	2000[B]	4,026,000	2,349,000	22,724,000	35,887,000	3,500,000	20,660,000	1,027,000	6,600,000	12,113,000	13,200,000	4,045,000	23,400,000
Cable TV HH passed (%)	2001[A]	112	65	39	70	0	1	50	94	32	71	63	60
Cable TV per HH (%)	2001[A]	85	58	11	53	0	0	10.5	94	32	15	54	13
Satellite TV per HH (%)	2001[A]	2	22	18	32	0	9	8.8	5	19	13	19	20
Internet users percent pop.[1]	2000[A]	26	58	19	23	6	18	6.3	40	9	11	58	32

Table 1.2 (cont.)

	Year	Belgium BE	Denmark DK	France FR	Germany DE	Greece EL	Italy IT	Latvia LV	Netherlands NL	Poland PL	Spain ES	Sweden SE	United Kingdom UK
Broadband lines, DSL	2000[B]	43,000	26,399	64,000	162,000	72	114,900	0	10,000	0	44,956	49,000	38,000
Broadband lines, Cable	2000[B]	102,013	41,000	121,911	25,000	0	0	0	320,000	0	13,459	56,300	19,693
Broadband per capita (%)	2000[B]	1.4	1.3	0.3	0.2	0	0.2	0	2.1	0	0.1	1.2	0.1
Services revenues (€ bln)	2000[A]	5.1	3.4	29.5	41.9	4.3	29.0	0.25	9.2	7.2	18.7	5.0	30.4
Major events:													
Date of joining EEC/EU		1957	1973	1957	1957	1981	1957	2004	1951	2004	1986	1995	1973
Introduction of €		2002	na	1999	1999	2002	1999	2014	1999	na	1999	na	na
NRA established		BIPT: 1991	Tele-styrelsen: 1990	ART: 1997	RegTP: 1998	EETT: 1995	AGCOM: 1998	PUC: 2001	OPTA: 1997	URT: 2001	CMT: 1996	PTS: 1994	Oftel: 1984
Telecom services market liberalization (full)		1998	1996	1998	1998	2001	1998	2003	1998	2003	1998	1993	1984

Legend: [A] EC Sixth and Seventh Implementation Report COM(2000)814 and COM(2001)706, respectively; [B] OECD Communications Outlook 2003/2013; [C] Eurostat 2013-12; [D] Wikipedia country data; [1] User is a person having Internet access at home, workplace or school (indicative estimate); [2] Source authors; [3] Analogue plus ISDN lines.

Table 1.3 Key statistics at the end of the case study period, ~2013

	Year	Belgium BE	Denmark DK	France FR	Germany DE	Greece EL	Italy IT	Latvia LV	Netherlands NL	Poland PL	Spain ES	Sweden SE	United Kingdom UK
Country statistics													
Population	2013-01[C]	11,161,642	5,602,628	65,633,194	80,523,746	11,062,508	59,685,227	2,023,825	16,779,575	38,533,299	46,704,308	9,555,893	63,887,988
Population density (p/km^2)	2011[C]	364.3	129.7	103.0	229.0	86.4	201.5	33.1	494.5	123.2	92.0	23.0	256.8[4]
Members per household	2005[C]	2.44	2.1	2.39	2.11	2.73	2.5	2.55	2.27	2.83	2.94	2.15	2.36
GDP (€ mln)	2012[C]	375,881	245,252	2,032,296	2,666,400	193,749	1,567,010	22,256	599,338	381,204	1,029,002	407,820	1,929,580
Per capita (€)	2012[C]	34,000	43,900	31,100	32,600	17,200	25,700	10,900	35,800	9,900	22,300	42,800	30,500
Purchasing power standard	2012[C]	120	126	109	123	75	101	64	128	67	96	126	106
Communications statistics:													
Fixed telephone access paths[5]	2011[B]	3,787,000	1,227,000	15,900,000	28,629,000	5,076,000	22,023,000	516,000[3]	3,556,000	6,853,000	19,867,000	3,167,000	30,225,000
Per capita (%)	2011[B]	34.5	22.0	24.4	35.0	44.9	36.3	25.4[3]	21.3	17.8	43.1	33.5	48.2
Mobile phone subscribers	2012-10[A]	13,104,323	8,459,636	69,209,505	101,657,000	13,342,500	97,539,960	3,880,779	20,622,284	50,519,353	57,137,919	13,694,000	87,021,613
Per capita (%)	2012-10[A]	118.7	151.6	105.8	124.2	118.2	160.4	190.1	123.3	131.1	123.7	144.4	138.2
TV households	2011[B]	4,568,000	2,847,000	26,790,000	39,311,000	3,920,000	24,525,000	1,003,000[3]	7,270,000	12,959,000	16,377,000	4,900,000	26,109,000
Cable TV per HH (%)	2012-07[A]	69.6	76.8	9.4	42.6	0.0	0.0	38.5	69.0	28.0	7.6	758.8	13.5
Satellite TV per HH (%)	2012-07[A]	.	8.9	24.0	44.1	8.3	19.5	12.2	9.9[3]	47.6	10.0	14.2	34.6
IPTV per HH (%)	2012-07[A]	21.4	3.7	42.5	3.5	1.6	1.2	13.5	13.9[3]	1.4	5.0	13.1	2.8
Fixed broadband lines	2013-01[A]	3,692,009	2,218,719	24,032,000	27,960,396	2,689,428	13,675,231	472,039	6,730,985	7,240,401	11,460,342	3,104,757	21,179,609
Per capita (%)	2013-01[A]	33.4	39.8	36.7	34.2	23.8	22.5	23.1	40.2	18.8	24.8	32.7	33.6

Table 1.3 (*cont.*)

	Year	Belgium BE	Denmark DK	France FR	Germany DE	Greece EL	Italy IT	Latvia LV	Netherlands NL	Poland PL	Spain ES	Sweden SE	United Kingdom UK
Data rates 30-99 Mbit/s (%)	2013-01[A]	46.2	13.5	2.9	10.9	0.1	0.1	22.9	30.9	10.2	8.3	4.0	14.5
Data rates ≥100+ Mbit/s (%)	2013-01[A]	12.2	1.1	4.0	1.2	0.0	0.0	20.5	4.1	1.3	1.9	24.6	0.9
Broadband lines DSL	2011-06[B]	1,857,523	1,190,954	21,481,000	23,476,720	2,554,689	13,145,926	152,000[3]	3,347,000	3,158,944	9,023,365	1,470,000	16,297666
Broadband lines Cable	2011-06[B]	1,723,796	592,816	1,440,000	3,952,000	0	0	19,000[3]	2,924,000	1,653,339	2,103,880	593,000	4,168,129
Broadband lines Fibre	2011-06[B]	3,271	335,908	246,000	178,800	3,902	290,039	225,000[3]	302,000	162,953	245,062	977,000	582,829
Mobile broadband	2013-01[A]	3,638,434	5,427,417	28,400,000	33,617,141	5,079,260	31,556,471	891,387	10,248,800	28,287,157	24,974,417	9,973,000	52,436,585
Per capita (%)	2013-01[A]	33.3	97.6	43.6	41.1	44.8	52.1	40.0	61.5	74.1	54.1	105.9	84.0
Services revenues (€ bln)[1]	2011[A]	8,684	4,233	52,074	57,900	6,436	43,623	0.581	13,475	10,175	35,732	8,063	46,731
Major events:													
Date of joining EEC/EU		1957	1973	1957	1957	1981	1957	2004	1951	2004	1986	1995	1973
Introduction of €		2002	na	1999	1999	2002	1999	2014	1999	na	1999	na	na
NRA established		BIPT: 1991	Telestyrelsen: 1990	ART: 1997 ARCEP: 2005	RegTP: 1998 BNetzA: 2005	EETT: 1995	AGCOM: 1998	PUC: 2001	OPTA: 1997 ACM: 2013	URT: 2001 URTiP: 2002 UKE: 2006	CMT: 1996	PTS: 1994	Oftel: 1984 Ofcom: 2004
Market liberalization (full)		1998	1996	1998	1998	2001	1998	2003	1998	2003	1998	1993	1984

Legend: [A] EC Digital Agenda Scoreboard 2013; [B] OECD Communications Outlook 2013; [C] Eurostat 2013-12; [D] Wikipedia country data; [1] Electronic communications sector revenues, including mobile, fixed, pay TV, other; [2] Estimate based on KPN information Oct. 2013; [3] Source authors; [4] 2010; Plus 627,044 other technologies; [5] Analogue plus ISDN lines.

the series of case studies. As one of the new member states, it shows a remarkable catch-up and achievement in ultra-fast broadband.

1.2.4 The EU policy and regulatory context

As all market actors operate within the EU policy and regulatory framework, the series of case studies is preceded by a chapter dedicated to the policy and regulatory developments at the EU level in relation to broadband investment. These developments impact different countries in different ways and sometimes have different effects than the EU anticipated. Moreover the evolution of EU policies over time reflects a learning process with each new round of policy development. This chapter provides insights with respect to the EU policy dynamics that have shaped broadband development. The individual case studies reveal how the EU policies and regulations, which are necessarily general in nature, are translated into national-level policies and regulations and how they have affected broadband development.

1.2.5 The cross-case analysis

The concluding chapter provides a comparative analysis by the editors, aimed at identifying the emerging patterns in broadband development across the case studies: the commonalities, differences and innovations. The analysis provides a response to the two sets of research questions posed above. The implications of the country-level developments are assessed in the light of the evolving EU policies and programmes. Lessons learned from the collective research effort that might provide useful guidance to the players and policymakers are identified.

1.2.6 Common reference data

The tables on pages 7 through 10 provide the common reference data for the country chapters to follow. They are presented here to facilitate country comparisons and the consistent use of the same data sources for the common indicators identified in the tables. Table 1.2 provides the picture at the beginning of the study period and Table 1.3 the picture at the end.

References

Crandall, R. W. and H. J. Singer (2009). 'The economic impact of broadband investment.' Retrieved 2011-04-15, from www.ncta.com/DocumentBinary.aspx?id=880.

Czernich, N., O. Falck, T. Kretschmer and L. Woessmann (2009). Broadband infrastructure and economic growth. CESIFO Working Paper No. 2861, Category 6: Fiscal Policy, Macroeconomics and Growth.

EC (1987). COM(87)2 290: Green paper on the development of the common market for telecommunications services and equipment. Brussels: European Commission.

(2000). DOC/00/7: The Lisbon Council – An agenda of economic and social renewal for Europe. Brussels: European Commission.

(2010). COM(2010) 245 A digital agenda for Europe. Brussels: European Commission.

(2013). 'Digital Agenda Scoreboard.' Retrieved 2013-12-09, from http://ec.europa.eu/digital-agenda/en/scoreboard.

Gruber, H. and P. Koutroumpis (2011). 'Mobile telecommunications and the impact on economic development.' *Economic Policy* **26**(67): 387–426.

Hardy, A. P. (1980). 'The role of the telephone in economic development.' *Telecommunications Policy* **4**(4): 278–286.

Röller, L. H. and L. Waverman (2001). 'Telecommunications infrastructure and economic development: a simultaneous approach.' *American Economic Review*: 909–923.

Saunders, R. J., J. J. Warford and B. Wellenius (1994). *Telecommunication and economic development*. Baltimore: Johns Hopkins University Press.

Van der Wee, M., S. Verbrugge and W. Lemstra (2012). Understanding the dynamics of broadband markets: a comparative case study of Flanders and the Netherlands. Vienna: ITS Europe.

Van Gorp, N., M. Canoy, E. Canton, L. Meindert, B. Volkerink, W. Lemstra, and H. Stokking (2011). Steps towards a truly Internal Market for e-communications in the run-up to 2020. Brussels: European Commission: 206.

Research context and perspective

WOLTER LEMSTRA AND WILLIAM H. MELODY

2.1 Introduction

The research reported in this book is aimed at capturing, exploring and explaining the dynamics of broadband markets and their outcomes in Europe. By providing an understanding of these dynamics the authors intend to contribute valuable inputs to the realization of the Digital Agenda targets: i.e., the desired broadband market outcomes. To accomplish this objective, an appropriate research approach and methodology was needed. This is the subject of this chapter.

We first explore – at a high level – the challenges ahead and the meaning of market dynamics in the context of this research project. Then we review the selection of the research approach and the design of the longitudinal case studies. Finally we present a summary of the analytical frameworks applied.

2.2 Initial research findings

Following an initial write-up of developments in the telecommunications sector in the Netherlands[1], the OECD league table on (fixed) broadband penetration was consulted to identify countries with similar market outcomes. Denmark appeared to lead the league table (#1), followed by the Netherlands (#2) (OECD, 2011). An initial investigation showed that similar rankings were the result of totally different market dynamics.

In the Netherlands the outcome is considered to be the result of fierce competition between the PSTN-incumbent, the access-based operators and the two major RTV-cable incumbents, complemented by

influential third parties – municipalities and housing corporations – taking initiatives in fibre deployments. In Denmark the broadband market is dominated by the PSTN-incumbent, which also runs the major part of the RTV-cable network infrastructure and has acquired the largest share of the existing fibre infrastructure. In Denmark infrastructure-based competition does not appear to be a significant explanatory factor for the broadband market outcome.

The next exploratory step was a comparison between the Netherlands and Belgium, more specifically the Flanders region. Belgium was ranked #13 in the OECD league table. Given the historical unity of the Northern and Southern Netherlands, many similarities were expected. Indeed, in both cases we can observe very strong competition between the PSTN-based and RTV-based incumbents. However, in Flanders the government triggered the consolidation of the cable sector. Moreover, fibre deployments are absent. There are no housing corporations, nor have municipalities taken initiatives in fibre deployment. Also the National Regulatory Authorities (NRAs) – BIPT and OPTA, respectively – have followed different strategies.

It appears that different trajectories can lead to similar outcomes, and similar endowments may lead to different outcomes. It was concluded that a collaborative effort by local experts would be required to move beyond simple inferences to a more substantive explanation of the broadband market dynamics and their outcomes in Europe.[2]

---

[1] See the Preface and Chapter 1 Introduction.

[2] These initial explorations led to a collaborative effort with researchers at Ghent University, Belgium, to compare the case of The Netherlands more structurally with the case of Flanders. These efforts have proven to be a great lead into the larger broadband research-project. Initial results were

In terms of market dynamics, we need to recognize that since the introduction of the telecommunications reform process in the mid 1980s, e-communications services – which include broadband services – are provided primarily by private firms operating in competitive markets.[3] These firms use strategy and entrepreneurship to expand their markets and to obtain favourable positions vis-à-vis the competition. In this process they are both enabled and constrained by regulation. Government policy goals may be achieved indirectly through their actions but governments no longer have managerial control over the telecommunications operators. Hence, these firms are considered the primary actors in explaining the dynamics of broadband markets. The regulators and policy makers are now secondary actors that can influence market conditions to a degree, but cannot determine market outcomes.

However, if the market is perceived to fail in delivering the outcomes that are deemed to be of public interest, the secondary actors may become primary actors by taking over the entrepreneurial role in providing broadband services to the public, as some municipalities and regional governments have done. Or, alternatively, regulation – primarily aimed at assuring a more effective functioning of competitive markets – may be used as a tool of policy by attempting to guide the behaviour of the firms to achieve a particular market outcome.

Another factor influencing market dynamics is technology. For the entrepreneurial firms,

technology is a means to an end. However, for the incumbent broadband suppliers technology is not a free choice but a legacy, a result of choices made in an earlier period. The PSTN incumbent is exploiting an access network of twisted copper pairs; the RTV-cable incumbent is exploiting a coax-based distribution network; and the mobile/wireless services incumbent is exploiting a 3G (third generation) digital network which leverages the infrastructure built to supply 2G services. The heavy investment required to transition to a newer network technology and the ease of migrating existing customers to the new network strongly influence broadband market dynamics.

While entrants into the broadband infrastructure market are largely free to adopt the latest available technology, they lack the income stream from existing customers and face the challenge of acquiring customers rather than migrating existing ones. The transition to next-generation broadband networks – Fibre to the Business (FttB), large-scale Fibre to the Home (FttH) deployments and All-IP mobile/wireless infrastructure – represents major challenges that will influence the market dynamics in both the short and the long run.

And then there is the issue of content. In the early days access and backbone networks were designed and optimized to provide a single service: the PSTN to provide telephone service, the RTV-cable network to distribute radio and television signals. Consumers subscribed to a network to receive a particular service. Digitalization introduced in the 1970s and 1980s allowed networks to become general conveyers of information of all types: voice, data, image and video. This process of convergence enabled different infrastructures to compete in the provision of the same type of services.

The introduction of the TCP/IP protocol stack as part of the public Internet in the 1990s effectively decoupled the services from the underlying infrastructure. Technical convergence enabled greater consumer choice of infrastructure and services suppliers and changed the structure of markets and the nature of competition, fundamentally affecting broadband market dynamics. These are now driven by firms able to bundle services, up to and including quadruple-play: a combination of fixed and

presented at ITS, Vienna (Van der Wee, Verbrugge and Lemstra, 2012).

[3] On 30 June 2012, we commemorated the start of the telecommunications reform process in Europe as it linked to the publication of the 'Green Paper'. The full title of the Green Paper is: *Towards a Dynamic European Economy: Green Paper on the Development of the Common Market for Telecommunications Services and Equipment* (EC 1987). The creation of a common market for telecommunications service and equipment is directly linked with the liberalization of the telecommunications market. This dual objective distinguishes the telecommunications reform process in Europe from the reform processes in other regions, notably the United States, where the reform can be traced back to the landmark *Carterfone* decision in 1968, triggering the formulation of market entry policies starting with the customer terminal market (Melody, 2002).

mobile telephony, internet access and radio/television. More recently, 'Over-the-Top' services and operating system platforms have become increasingly important in driving competition in services and applications.

In short, broadband market dynamics reflect the interplay between supply and demand in a market environment subject to continuing, and often unexpected, changes, enabled by both past and new investments in technologies and assets, and conditioned by policy and regulation. The research challenge is how best to capture these market dynamics for subsequent analysis?

2.3 The research approach

Based on the high-level overview of the relevant market dynamics provided above, the research approach aimed at capturing the actions of the key players and the outcomes of these actions over time, hence, needs first of all to be descriptive. To allow the subsequent steps of exploring and explaining, we needed to capture the (potential) explanatory variables in these descriptions – for instance the motivations of the actors, the market structure, the distribution of market power, the regulations – as well as the market outcomes.[4] As such, the research aimed at investigating contemporary developments in a socio-technological setting, whereby questions of 'how 'and 'why' were pursued in a real-life context. This suggested the application of a longitudinal case study approach (Eisenhardt, 1989; Yin, 1989; Thietart et. al., 2001).

Recognizing that the broadband markets under consideration are essentially national in scope, a country-level case study approach was deemed appropriate. Having a set of case studies structured in terms of a common framework allowed a comparative research approach to be applied.

2.3.1 The country case study design

The scope of this research includes both fixed and mobile/wireless broadband. Achievement of the high-end data rate target of the Digital Agenda is to a large extent dependent on the deployment of fibre in the access network (fibre to the curb and to the last amplifier, as well as fibre to the business and to the home). As this transition to fibre is a major economic, regulatory and political challenge, the focus in most country case studies is on the developments in the market for fixed broadband. Nonetheless, as the Digital Agenda is also concerned with the provision of broadband to the population at large – including sparsely populated areas – mobile/wireless broadband is a major feature, for instance in the case studies covering the new member states.[5]

Our hypothesis was that broadband market dynamics are determined by a combination of factors, to be assessed in terms of their importance through the case study research, including:

- geography and demography;
- historical infrastructure developments;
- institutional arrangements;
- time of joining the EU;
- market structure;
- distribution of market power;
- firm ownership;
- position and role of the regulator;
- political priorities and preferences; and
- the industrial setting.

The units of analysis are the actions of the key actors operating in the broadband market and their outcomes. The key actors identified upfront are:

- the operators providing broadband services;
- the government, policy makers and legislators affecting operating conditions in the broadband market; and

---

[4]   In terms of the potential explanatory variables we build on general management literature (e.g., Porter, 1980, 1985; Normann and Ramirez, 1994; Porter, 2001; Besanko et al., 2004; De Wit and Meyer, 2010) and industry specific literature (e.g., Newbery, 1999; Boyland, 2000; Aalbers, et al., 2002; Spiller and Tommasi, 2005; Lemstra, 2006; Cawley, 2007; De Bijl and Peitz, 2008).

[5]   The Digital Agenda targets are set by population. We may infer that this will include the provision of broadband to small and medium size enterprises (SMEs). The broadband needs of the larger enterprises are considered to be provided for in the current market setting.

- regulators, enforcing the laws and regulations applicable to broadband.

The case studies reveal which 'third actors' have influenced the market dynamics to a significant extent and, hence, are included in the explanation of the broadband market outcomes. These actors include local and regional governments; housing corporations; citizen collectives; market entrants from outside the sector, etc.

The explanations of market outcomes by the authors of the case studies are based largely on the strategies firms apply in competitive markets, evaluating internal and external environment, market opportunities and threats against the company's strengths and weaknesses, as advised by a range of authors, from Porter (1980) to De Wit and Meyer (2010).[6] Research studies with a special emphasis on strategizing in network industries include Katz and Shapiro (1985, 1994); Economides (1996); Shy (2001); Gottinger (2003); Economides (2005), and more recently with respect to the information economy e.g.: Evans and Wurster (1997); Shapiro and Varian (1999); Porter (2001).

In their analyses of the market dynamics and their explanations of the market outcomes the case study researchers address the following issues:

(1) the market structure and its evolution, covering the infrastructure and services dimension and capturing the degree of entry and exit;
(2) the type of competition, e.g., price or functionality based, and the intensity of competition;
(3) the role of regulation, e.g., through local loop unbundling;
(4) the role of fixed versus mobile broadband[7];
(5) the investment pattern, privately or publicly driven;

(6) the role of innovation.

The market outcomes considered as the dependent variables are the uptake of broadband, the data rates and the prices. Each of the case studies concludes with the author's outlook on achievement of the Digital Agenda targets set for 2020.[8] The criteria for the interpretation of the case findings (e.g., in terms of intensity and degree) are largely a judgment call by the case researchers, leveraging their extensive experience in the field.

A recurring issue in interpreting the various approaches and outcomes in historical research is the lack of the counterfactual. In our research, the broad set of twelve comparable country-level case studies, capturing very diverse developments and market outcomes, is expected to compensate for the lack of a counterfactual in each case. A critical analysis of the similarities and differences in the settings of the cases allows for meaningful comparisons to be made and relevant patterns to be discerned (Diesing, 1971; Wilber and Harrison, 1978).

A comparative analysis constitutes the main body of the concluding chapter – the cross-case study analysis. From this analysis follows the identification of the emerging patterns (the commonalities across the case studies) and the salient phenomena (the unique features described in a case; the innovations). The case study outcomes are – at the summary level – compared with the outcomes predicted by the applicable theories, concepts and models. In particular, we evaluate

(1) the role of infrastructure-based versus services-based competition in explaining the market outcomes;
(2) explore the validity of the 'ladder of investment' concept;
(3) examine the role of fixed versus mobile; and
(4) assess the relationship between competition and innovation.

To this end we combine the largely qualitative information from the case studies with quantitative

---

[6] See also Normann and Ramirez (1994); Courtney et al. (1997); Pettigrew et al. (2002); Besanko et al. (2004); Mahoney (2005).

[7] Also of interest in this context is the way indoor traffic will be served in the future. Two principle options are emerging: (1) outdoor base stations (implying that in the competitive game the mobile operator beats the fixed operator); and (2) indoor base stations (which would imply that the fixed operator beats the mobile operator).

[8] This outlook to be reflected against the national broadband plans, as being requested by the European Commission in 2003.

information derived from a parallel research project into the performance of broadband markets in the EU.[9] In addition, we use the findings from a related study on local loop unbundling (Lemstra and Van Gorp, 2013).

A methodological difficulty is that the strategies of private actors are not necessarily in the public domain and hence must often be inferred in hindsight or established once the outcomes have become apparent, an issue that applies to a far lesser degree to public policy making. Hence, the capturing of motivations and the strategic analysis applied by these actors had to come from interactions of the case authors with these actors and from their insights into the (typical) strategic behaviour of these actors. These interactions were necessarily limited in number but considered sufficient for an appropriate interpretation of the case study materials, as the developments of broadband markets are (mostly) determined by only a few major actors.

In the design and the execution of the research, the researchers have paid due attention to assuring construct validity by using (to the extent possible) multiple sources of evidence, establishing chains of evidence and making these explicit. Where possible, local experts (e.g., fellow academics, regulators) have reviewed the case study data, analysis and conclusions. As the cases are largely built from literature and only a selective use of interviews, the reliability of the case studies is strengthened through detailed referencing.

In this multi-case-study research assuring the internal and external validity have gone hand-in-hand through the application of pattern recognition and pattern matching, the cross-validation of explanation building, the testing of rival explanations, and the validation of the replication logic across the multiple cases.

To facilitate the cross-case comparison, and thereby the testing of the replication logic, each of the country case studies follows the same framing of: Introduction; Case description; Case focus; Within-case analysis; Conclusions; and Reflections. The cross-case study analysis is also facilitated by the summary tables of statistical data at the beginning and end of the case study period – Tables 1.2 and 1.3 in Chapter 1, Introduction.

2.4 The case analysis

In our exploratory efforts we follow the methodological lead provided by Lawson in *Economics and Reality* (1997, p282–9): 'Social explanation, appropriately conceived, is not the attempted deduction of events from sets of individual conditions and constant-conjunction 'laws', but the identification and illumination of structures and/or mechanisms responsible for producing, or facilitating, social phenomena of interest'; or in other words, '...[T]he primary aim of science is not the illumination or prediction of events...but the identification and comprehension of the structures, powers, mechanisms and tendencies which produce or facilitate them. And this understanding is all that is required for policy analysis and (where feasible) effective action.'

As the market developments are an interplay between technological progress, entrepreneurial activity to exploit the new technological capabilities, and governments safeguarding the public interests and public values, the case studies highlight the policy dimension.

In the historical framing of the case descriptions we use the periodization used by Noam of in his discussion paper 'Policy 3.0 for Telecom 3.0' (Noam, 2008).[10] Telecom 1.0 and Policy 1.0 refer to the early period in which the telephone network was built; Telecom and Policy 2.0 start with the introduction of telecom reform and include the emergence of the Internet and the development of

---

[9] This quantitative analysis derives from a research project aimed at explaining broadband performance in the EU member states executed at the Delft University of Technology in collaboration with Ecorys, an economics research institute, and co-funded by ECTA, the European Competitive Telecommunications operators Association.

[10] The working paper was the basis of the publication in 2010 of 'Regulation 3.0 for telecom 3.0' (Noam, 2010).

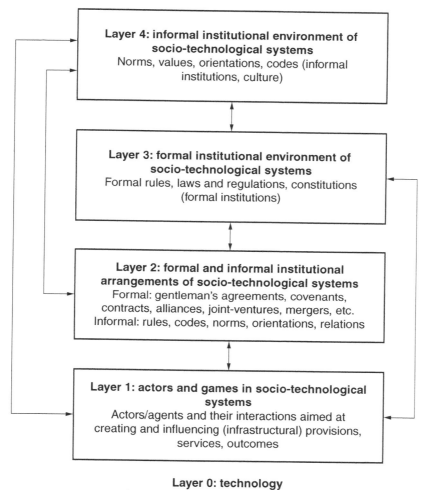

Figure 2.1 Five layer model – levels of institutional analysis, technology enabled
Source: Adapted from Koppenjan and Groenewegen, 2005.

broadband; Telecom 3.0 starts with the introduction of Fibre-to-the-Home.

2.4.1 The analysis of socio-technical systems

For the explanation of broadband market dynamics and market outcomes, we follow a general framework for the analysis of socio-technological systems,

see Figure 2.1. This framework was developed by Groenewegen and Koppenjan (2005), extended by Lemstra, and is based on the work by Williamson (1998) on transaction cost economics.

The exploration and analysis of broadband markets is necessarily of an historical nature and includes a variety of explanatory variables such as technology, laws and regulations, strategies of the firms, values and norms, etc. The behaviour of the actors concerning broadband service provisioning is largely conditioned by the institutional structures in their environment, such as laws and regulations. On the other hand, these actors have a certain degree of autonomy in realizing their own objectives, to explore new ways and to change the institutional structures around them. Moreover, actors interact not only with the institutional structures in their environment but also with one another. In doing so, they share ideas, they learn, but they also compete and try to control the behaviour of others. To explore and analyse the dynamics of broadband markets we need to understand the behaviour of the different actors involved.

Figure 2.1 reflects the different layers that can be distinguished in the institutional environment of the actors, with the arrows indicating the interactions. In conceptualizing institutions we follow North in his definition of institutions as 'humanly devised constraints that structure political, economic, and social interactions'; and 'institutions consist of a set of moral, ethical, behavioural norms which define the contours and that constrain the way in which the rules and regulations are specified and enforcement is carried out' (North, 1990).

At the top of Figure 2.1 in Layer 4 are the so-called informal institutions that influence – mostly implicitly – the behaviour of actors. This is the cultural embedding of the key actors involved in the provision of broadband services, which has an impact on the motivation of these actors and on their expectations of how the other (private and public) actors will behave. Our ideas about human rights and equity belong at this level.

While there are many similarities across Europe in norms and values, there are also cultural differences that will play-out at the lower levels. At Layer 3 we show the so-called formal institutions that influence the behaviour of the actors more explicitly. Here are located the laws about, for instance, competition and corporate governance, the EU Regulatory Framework for e-communications, the national telecom laws and regulations. These are examples of explicit institutions that have an impact on the behaviour of the industry actors.

Layer 3 is typically the working domain of public actors, such as the parliament, ministries and public agencies. At Layer 2 formal and informal institutional arrangements are identified, including the institutions that private actors create to coordinate the transactions between them. A distinction is made between the institutions that private actors purposefully create, such as contracts and organizations, and the ones that informally evolve, such as norms shared among the actors involved. Examples of purposeful institutions in our context are the GSM Association, the 3GPP, RIPE, and public-private partnerships.

At Layer 1 are the firm actors with their day-to-day routines, in our case operating in the competitive market place providing broadband service. These same actors, often in different roles and capacities, create and modify the institutional structures at the higher layers while at the same time being constrained by them. Examples of such efforts are the lobby groups of operators active at the European level, such as ETNO, ECTA and Cable Europe.

These interactive relationships are reflected by the arrows between the different layers. As the higher layers condition the actions at the lower layers, the institutional formation represented by these interactive relationships is an important aspect to be considered in explaining the dynamics of broadband markets. At the lower layers these relationships may be more explicit and traceable, while at the higher layers they are more diffuse and difficult to capture.

Technology plays an important role in the development of broadband. Hence, the model has been extended to reflect technology at Layer 0, which suggest linkages to all other layers. Technology is considered to be developed by actors/agents in Layer 1: i.e., as man-made. In its application it impacts Layers 2 through 4; in turn, technology is shaped through these interactions.

Because of the variety of explanatory variables involved at different levels of analysis, our case studies are clearly of a multi-disciplinary nature. At Layer 4 the disciplines of history, anthropology and sociology are relevant. Layer 3 is the domain of political science and law as well as of economics (e.g., property rights). For the analysis of the institutional arrangements at Layer 2, we consider institutional economics as particularly relevant, while for the analysis of the interactions between the layers we make use of the insights from evolutionary economics. Consequently, understanding, analysing and explaining the development process of broadband market dynamics and their outcomes is a multi-disciplinary affair in which different theories, concepts and models are applied within the broader framework of a country case study. The choice and rationalization thereof reside with the particular case study researcher.

2.4.2 Role perception of governments

Groenewegen provided a synthesis of the literature on the regulatory and developmental state into a framework which is useful for capturing the differences in the roles assumed by governments by relating these roles to the principle of operation of the market economy.[11] We summarize the discussion provided in *Markets and public values* (Lemstra and Groenewegen, 2009).

Economies are systems in which social systems, judicial systems, political systems, and economic systems are interrelated and form a consistent whole. Market economies differ in terms of the value system, the role of private and public actors, and the type of laws and regulations. A general characteristic of a market economy is decentralized decision-making. In the Anglo-Saxon perception of markets the grounding is in the individualistic values of freedom, individual responsibility and accountability. Those values relate to the norm of competition as the right mechanism to allocate scarce resources. When information and knowledge are diffused among individuals, competitive markets are considered to be adequate governance structures to coordinate transactions. Related to these individualistic values is the tenet that decisions should be made, costs borne and benefits received at the most decentralized level, motivating the actors to seek the most efficient means for production, distribution and consumption. In the value system that supports decentralized allocation

in markets, it is believed that those efficient private decisions will add up to the best possible public benefits. Prices that consumers pay reflect the costs of the inputs. Firms aim at profit maximization, or an increase of market share, innovative products, etc. When things go wrong this is reflected in prices and will initiate private actors to correct their decisions at the decentralized level. Therefore markets must be transparent, neutral and flexible. The market may also be assisted by government so it can perform even better. This takes us into the area of indicative planning, in which the supply of additional information as a public good is central.

To analyse the role of governments, Groenewegen (1989) defined a spectrum between two extremes in perceptions of the role of governments: the regulatory state and the developmental state.

Within the regulatory state, the government operates at a distance and plays the role of the 'watchdog'. Such a government is small and above all a facilitator of 'what society wants'. In terms of information production and diffusion, it is the 'lender of last resort'. After all other options have been tried, the state plays the role that remains. It monitors events; if it discovers inconsistencies, it does not intervene but feeds information back into the system. The regulatory state is strong in maintaining the rules of the game, supervising the free market and intervening strongly to enforce strict rules of competition.

In the 'developmental state' the government develops, a vision of the desired future, with or without consulting the private actors. The state defines the objectives and the instruments to be used to realize the vision. Such a state is well informed, is an authority in society, and is usually well respected because of its power to guide and direct structural developments.

2.4.3 Industrial analysis

For the industrial analysis reference is made to the Five Forces analysis framework introduced by Porter (1980) aimed at assessing the profitability of an industry. This framework is complemented by the SEPT framework based on Wheelen and Hunger (1983) reflecting the embedding of the industry in the socio-economic, political

[11] Examples of literature underpinning the framework are Johnson (1982, 1999); Groenewegen (1989); Majone (2010); and Levi-Faur (2011).

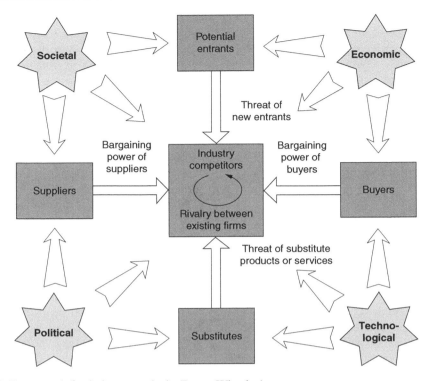

Figure 2.2 Framework for industry analysis (Porter-Wheelen)
Source: Adapted from Porter, 1980; Wheelen and Hunger, 1983.

and regulatory, and technological environment. See Figure 2.2.[12]

2.4.4 *The entrepreneur centre stage*

When considering the role of the e-communications entrepreneur in economic terms, we can refer to the 'production function' and to economic activity aimed at adding value. A firm combines various inputs – capital, labour, knowledge – to produce outputs – products and services. In the case of an e-communications service provider special inputs are required, such as rights-of-way and, for providing mobile services, radio frequency spectrum usage rights. For the e-communications firm, the broadband infrastructure is a 'means of production', equivalent to a factory. See Figure 2.3.

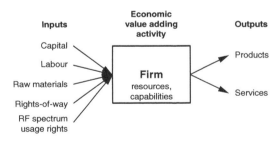

Figure 2.3 Production function

In general, firms will only invest in new products and/or services if they can expect a future return. These investment decisions are driven by four major considerations:

(1) the prospective demand and willingness to pay for new products and/or services;
(2) the magnitude of the investments required;
(3) the strategies of the competition; and

---

[12] For a further discussion and application in the field of business strategy see De Wit and Meyer (2010).

(4) the degree of risk or uncertainty involved, including regulatory uncertainty.

The business case, in terms of depth of investment and the recovery period required, will influence the ability to obtain the necessary (external) funding. As such, the business case is especially challenging for communication services provisioning that requires an associated infrastructure roll-out such as Fibre-to-the-Home or, in the case of mobile broadband, the acquisition of the right to exploit the radio spectrum. A long period to exploit the investments will contribute to the willingness of entrepreneurs to invest, as it will make the broadband business case more viable.

2.4.5 Selecting the appropriate context and perspectives

This chapter reviewed the range of contexts and perspectives that have informed the various studies reported in this book. Aware of the diversity of approaches, the author(s) of each study have selected and applied the frameworks, theoretical grounding and perspective(s) that provided the best explanation for the developments being studied. In this way, we attempted to capture benefits not only from the commonalities in methodology applied across all the studies, but also the diversity in considering the variety of analytical perspectives that may strengthen our understanding of the evolution of broadband in light of the EU 2020 objectives.

References

Aalbers, R. F. T., E. Dijkgraaf, M. Varkevisser and H. R. J. Vollebregh (2002). Welvaart en de regulering van netwerksectoren (Welfare and the regulation of network sectors). The Hague, The Netherlands: Ministry of Economic Affairs.

Besanko, D., D. Dranove, M. Shanley and S. Schaeffer (2004). *Economics of strategy.* Hoboken, NJ: Wiley.

Boyland, O., and G. Nicoletti (2000). Regulation, market structure and performance in telecommunications. Economics department working papers. Paris: OECD.

Cawley, R. A. (2007). The new EU approach to sector regulation in the network infrastructure industries. Dissertation: Faculty of Technology, Policy and Management. Delft, the Netherlands: TUDelft. p 552.

Courtney, H., J. Kirkland and P. Viguerie (1997). Strategy under uncertainty *Harvard Business Review* Vol. Nov.-Dec.: p 67–79.

De Bijl, P. W. J. and M. Peitz (2008). Innovation, convergence and the role of regulation in the Netherlands and beyond. *Telecommunications Policy* **32**: 744–754.

De Wit, B. and R. Meyer (2010). *Strategy: Process, content, context – An international perspective* (4th Edition). Andover, UK: South-Western Cengage Learning.

Diesing, P. (1971). *Patterns of discovery in the social sciences.* Chicago: Aldine Atherton Inc.

Economides, N. (1996). The economics of networks. *International Journal of Industrial Organization* **14**(2).

Economides, N. (2005). Networks, telecommunications economics and strategic issues in digital convergence. Retrieved 2005-04-11, from www.stern.nyu.edu/networks/market_structure_slides_2005.pdf.

Eisenhardt, K. M. (1989). Building theories from case study research. *Academy of Management Review* **14**(4): 532–550.

Evans, P. B. and T. S. Wurster (1997). Strategy and the new economics of information. *Harvard Business Review* Vol. Sept.-Oct.: p 71–82.

Gottinger, H.-W. (2003). *Economies of network industries.* London: Routledge.

Groenewegen, J. P. M. (1989). Planning in een markteconomie. (Dissertation.) Delft: Eburon. p 365.

Johnson, C. A. (1982). *MiTi and the Japanese miracle: The growth of industrial policy: 1925–1975.* Stanford: Stanford University Press. (1999). The Developmental State: Odyssey of a concept. In *The developmental state.* M. Woo-Cumings (ed.). Ithaca, NY: Cornell University Press.

Katz, M. L. and C. Shapiro (1985). Network externalities, competition, and compatibility. *American Economic Review* **75**: 424–440. (1994). Systems competition and network effects. *Journal of economic perspectives* **40**: 93–115.

Koppenjan, J. F. M. and J. P. M. Groenewegen (2005). Institutional design for complex technological systems. *Int. Journal Technology, Policy and Management* **5**(3): 240–257.

Lawson, T. (1997). *Economics and reality*. London: Routledge.

Lemstra, W. (2006). The Internet bubble and the impact on the development path of the telecommunication sector. Dissertation. Department of Technology, Policy and Management. Delft, The Netherlands: TUDelft. p 460.

Lemstra, W. and J. P. M. Groenewegen (2009). Markets and public values – The potential effects of Private Equity Leveraged Buyouts on the safeguarding of public values in the telecommunications sector. Delft, The Netherlands: TUDelft.

Lemstra, W. and N. van Gorp (2013). Unbundling: Regulation is a necessary, but not sufficient conditions to reach the final rung of the investment ladder. Second Annual Conference on the Regulation of Infrastructure Industries in an Age of Convergence. Florence, Italy: Florence School of Regulation.

Levi-Faur, D. (2011). The Odessey of the regulatory state – Episode One: The rescue of the welfare state. Jerusalem Papers in Regulation & Governance. Jerusalem, Israel: The Hebrew University.

Mahoney, J. T. (2005). *Economic foundations of strategy*. Thousand Oaks, CA: Sage Publications.

Majone, G. (2010). The transformation of the regulatory State: Osservatorio sull'Analisi di Impatto della Regolazione.

Melody, W. H. (2002). Designing utility regulation for 21st century markets. *The institutionalist approach to public utility regulation*. E. S. Miller and W. J. Samuels (eds.). East Lansing, MI: Michigan State University Press.

Newbery, D. M. (1999). *Privatization, restructuring, and regulation of network utilities*. Cambridge, MA: MIT Press.

Noam, E. M. (2008). Policy 3.0 for Telecom 3.0. New York: Columbia University.

Noam, E. M. (2010). Regulation 3.0 for telecom 3.0 *Telecommunications Policy* **34**(1–2): 4–10.

Normann, R. and R. Ramirez (1994). *Designing interactive strategy, from value chain to value constellation*. Chichester, UK: Wiley.

North, D. C. (1990). *Institutions, institutional change and economic performance*. Cambridge: Cambridge University Press.

OECD (2011). Communications Outlook 2011. Paris: Organisation for Economic Co-operation and Development.

Pettigrew, A., H. Thomas and R. Whittington (2002). *Handbook of strategy and management*. London: Sage.

Porter, M. E. (1980). *Competitive strategy – Techniques for Analyzing Industries and Competitors*. New York: The Free Press.
  (1985). Competitive advantage – Creating and sustaining superior performance. New York: The Free Press.
  (2001). Strategy and the internet. *Harvard Business Review* Vol. March: 63–78.

Shapiro, C. and H. R. Varian (1999). *Information Rules – A strategic guide to the network economy*. Boston: Harvard Business School Press.

Shy, O. (2001). *The economics of network industries*. Cambridge, UK: Cambridge University Press.

Spiller, P. T. and M. Tommasi (2005). The institutions of regulation: An application to public utilities. *Handbook of New Institutional Economics*. In: C. Menard and M. M. Shirley (eds.). Dordrecht, the Netherlands: Springer.

Thietart, R.-A. (2001). *Doing management research – a comprehensive guide*. London: SAGE Publications Ltd.

Van der Wee, M., S. Verbrugge and W. Lemstra (2012). Understanding the dynamics of broadband markets: A comparative case study of Flanders and the Netherlands. Vienna: ITS Europe.

Wheelen, T. L. and D. J. Hunger (1983). *Strategic management and business policy*. Reading, MA: Addison-Wesley Publishing.

Wilber, C. K. and R. S. Harrison (1978). The methodological basis of institutional economics: pattern model, storytelling and holism. *Journal of Economic Issues* **12**: 61–89.

Williamson, O. E. (1998). Transaction cost economics: How it works; where it is headed. *De Economist* **146**(1): 23–58.

Yin, R. K. (1989). *Case study research – Design and methods*. Newbury Park, UK: Sage.

PART 1

European Union context

The influence of European Union policies and regulation

RICHARD CAWLEY

3.1 Introduction

Investments in broadband networks in Europe have occurred in the context of more than two decades of legal and institutional change, which have introduced competition and sought to harmonise regulatory rules and practice across the member states of the European Union.[1]

In the early stages of introducing competition and seeking to create a single European telecommunications market, the EU policy focus was relatively broad in scope. It sought to lift impediments to competition and change across all market segments. That included mobile and wireless communications (with a view to promoting the development of pan-European services based on competitive licensing within harmonised frequency bands) as well as any kind of fixed networks and services. By 1998, all restrictions on building competing fixed networks had been lifted.[2] Regulation (at both EU and member-state level) then came to be increasingly focused on the design of the detailed access and interconnection rules that enabled entrants to compete against the incumbent operators using combinations of their own investments and rented assets.

The introduction of (regulated) competition (with safeguards for universal service) was relatively successful in terms of lowering prices, improving choice, facilitating entry and stimulating investment.

However, the market shares of incumbent operators for fixed access and services have remained high in many EU member states. Consequently, the way in which broadband services have developed (in terms of coverage, quality and data rates) has often depended on the business plans of the incumbent, particularly where competition has been predominantly service-based (i.e., dependent on the incumbent's network rather than an alternative infrastructure).

The policy and regulatory approach has been influenced by what has become known as the 'ladder of investment' concept[3]. Under this approach, an entrant combines its own inputs with those of the incumbent's network that are more difficult to replicate, the latter being made available via access conditions imposed by the national regulator. Over time, it was argued, the entrant could invest in assets that were more difficult to replicate and use the regulated access inputs as stepping stones or rungs of a ladder towards full facilities-based entry.

The evidence as to whether or not regulation has helped entrants climb the ladder towards facilities-based entry is mixed (as Section 3.4 indicates). In some countries or regions, alternative operators have used unbundled loops to build a sufficiently large customer base to begin investing themselves in new broadband networks. But many entrants have continued to use regulated inputs to basically re-sell the services of incumbents (under their own brand-name) and some have subsequently exited the market if they could not obtain sufficient market share or if margins became too narrow.

---

[1] See for example the *Green Paper on the development of the common market for telecommunications services and equipment*, COM(87)290, June 1987, and *Directive 2002/21/EC*, March 2002, on a common regulatory framework for electronic communications networks and services (the Framework Directive).

[2] The lifting of restrictions was subject to the transposition of EU regulation into national law and some member states were granted a delay in the enforcement date.

[3] Originally due to Cave (2004a) and known in the USA as the 'stepping stones approach'.

Experience has therefore shown that where regulation is based on the principle of not expecting much competition (so that access inputs are made available to entrants on relatively easy or favourable terms), it can become a self-fulfilling prophecy. And if incumbents retain a dominant market share, despite the entry of new firms and the extensive uptake of broadband by users, they have been able to maintain a strong influence over the pace at which networks are upgraded (to supply faster or more sophisticated broadband services) and also the technology which is used.

The extent and nature of broadband competition matters because it influences the degree of choice of supplier and service, prices and their evolution, and consequently the rate at which local and national markets have developed. It has become even more important as broadband markets have matured, access data rates have risen and, with that, pressures to upgrade existing networks or build new ones.

The dynamics of market growth and investment in broadband have therefore become a key policy issue. It is no longer the case that governments are satisfied with a healthy proportion of the population subscribing to basic broadband (and safeguards against a digital divide where some regions are poorly served). Instead they often wish to see investments in next generation broadband access. Consequently, ten years after full infrastructure liberalisation in the EU, the main policy question for fixed networks has moved from 'Which regulatory conditions best encourage the take-up of broadband?' to 'Which regulatory conditions facilitate investments in next generation access?' or 'Are market forces and competition sufficient to encourage the new investments?'

Despite the fact that several EU member states have for a long time been at the top of the global league tables in the growth and uptake of broadband (e.g., the Netherlands, Denmark and Sweden)[4], political concerns have been raised about the rate at which investments in upgraded broadband networks are being made in Europe,

relative to developments in Japan, or South Korea and even the USA. This concern has led to ambitious targets (for broadband availability, data rates and use) being set and calls for changes to the regulatory approach to try and stimulate investment.

To some extent this political concern is understandable given the way in which the EU's Digital Agenda[5] policy aims are linked to the broader EU 2020[6] objectives to improve the long-term growth performance (by raising total factor productivity and better exploiting resources). In that context, the European Union (EU) has set itself some fairly ambitious targets in a number of policy areas to improve economic performance and compete effectively with the rest of the world.[7]

The need for improved performance in Europe was already comprehensively set out in the Sapir report of 2003[8] and reflected the political objectives, at the time, of the Lisbon strategy.[9] More specific targets have continued to accumulate in the context of the EU's grand initiatives, of which the Innovation Union, Horizon 2020 and the Digital Agenda comprise key elements.

Headline targets have been set or reaffirmed for public and private investment in research and development and innovation, and for the supply and uptake of broadband technologies and services.[10] These targets reflect the recognition that growth in recent decades does not depend solely on investments in the traditional factors of labour

---

[4] See   www.oecd.org/sti/broadband/oecdbroadbandportal. htm

[5] *A Digital Agenda for Europe*, COM (2010) 245.

[6] *Europe 2020 – A strategy for smart, sustainable and inclusive growth*, COM (2010) 2020.

[7] Since 2008, the need to tackle various aspects of the financial crisis has largely overshadowed these long-term objectives, initially because of the need to aid or restructure a number of banks and to improve financial regulation, and subsequently because of the focus on fiscal consolidation and austerity programmes.

[8] *An Agenda for a Growing Europe*, report of July 2003, published in 2004.

[9] The aim of the Lisbon strategy was to make the EU 'the most competitive and dynamic knowledge-based economy in the world, capable of sustainable economic growth with more and better jobs and greater social cohesion', by 2010.

[10] The headline Digital Agenda targets for 2020 are that all Europeans have Internet access of above 30 Mbit/s and 50% or more of households subscribe to service above 100 Mbit/s.

and fixed and human capital. Instead a significant proportion of growth in advanced economies is driven by something else.[11] These additional (total factor) productivity improvements depend on intangible as well as tangible investments. Typically they involve investments in research and development and complimentary ICT investments in order to generate technological and non-technological innovations. Appropriate regulation and well-functioning product and labour markets also play an important role.[12]

Consequently, a better European growth performance depends, among other things, on investments in advanced communications technologies.[13] Yet the development and use of these technologies relies in turn on timely investments in networks including local broadband networks (fixed or mobile).

The inherent problem, however, is that setting targets for broadband data rates and use (rather than simply for availability) substitutes political wishes for market forces, and presents a problem for policy and regulation. Is regulation supposed to continue to try to mimic market forces, or should it be manipulated in order to try and achieve the political targets, and if so, how? Do the ambitious targets for broadband use imply that EU member states now have more latitude to pursue policies which they think will improve their broadband uptake performance or are they obliged to continue to follow the EU regulatory rules, albeit with additional constraints or requirements that go beyond addressing problems of market power?

The target-setting at EU level also complicates the relationship between EU regulation and its application by national regulatory authorities (NRAs). Are member states supposed to devote additional resources to try and accelerate their rate of broadband investment and uptake or is it sufficient to continue to assess and circumvent market power or commit to a regulatory stance that is designed to facilitate efficient investment and development?

Discussions with member states during the review of the Broadband State Aid Guidelines indicated that there was an expectation that public investments would be required to plug the gap between market development and the ambitious targets for availability and use that had been set (as market forces would be insufficient). This in turn implies a delicate balancing of instruments; between direct support for investment and the indirect influence of regulatory policy at local, national and EU levels.

Even at EU level, the rules of the game are relatively complicated. The formal legal requirements comprise both the body of EU regulatory legislation and practices (which have evolved over time) and also the application of EU competition policy – both Article 102 (abuse of dominance) and Article 107 (state aids). The EU also has financial instruments at its disposal because Structural Funds can be used to finance investments in broadband infrastructure in some regions of the European Union, subject to the EU competition policy guidelines.

The main three factors of influence at EU level therefore comprise:

(1) the aggregate targets for availability and use of broadband and any financial or other instruments that are used to support them,
(2) the regulatory rules of the game which involve addressing market power via access requirements, thereby affecting entry and investment incentives, and
(3) the application of EU competition policy, in particular the conditions imposed on public investments in broadband by the state aid guidelines.

But ultimately, it is the interaction of conditions at national and local level (within the context of these EU level factors), which determine investments in broadband and market developments.

Bearing in mind the substantial potential influence of EU-level rules, this chapter therefore seeks to provide a European Union context to the country

---

[11] This extra ingredient has come to be known as the 'knowledge economy': see for example EIB (2009).
[12] See Arnold, Nicoletti and Scarpetta (2011), McMorrow and Roeger (2009) and Haltiwanger (2011).
[13] A study published by the LSE (UK) in 2012 (sponsored by the customer management software company Convergys) claimed that a rise in broadband penetration of 10% can lead to an increase in per capita GDP of 0.9–1.5%.

chapters in this volume. That involves covering two separate but related aims. The first is the nature and impact of these three EU-level factors, which may influence the dynamics of broadband investments at national level and whether or not they facilitate or encourage investments in broadband. The second is the latitude that member states have to depart from these rules or to apply and combine them in a way that fully serves their national specificity and interest.

Section 3.2 briefly surveys broadband development in Europe and seeks to pick out the countries that appear to have been most successful in developing broadband capability and use. Section 3.3 examines some theoretical aspects concerning investments in network infrastructure. In particular, it considers investment incentives (for incumbents and potential entrants) against the backdrop of regulation.

Section 3.4 then seeks to draw some practical insights about the dynamics of investments (in the context of EU policy oversight) from examples where regulatory change has unleashed waves of new investment. Section 3.5 briefly summarises the results of empirical studies, which have sought to assess the impact of access regulation on broadband development. Section 3.6 takes a step back and considers the possible justifications for framing the rules of the game (for broadband investments) at EU level. Sections 3.7, 3.8 and 3.9 examine the three main EU-level influences in practice: i.e., targets for broadband, competition rules and the regulatory framework. Finally Section 3.10 specifically considers these influences in the context of the dynamics of investing in local fibre networks.

3.2 The development of broadband: the EU experience

Table 3.1 provides some indicators on the development or diffusion of broadband by individual EU member states between 2002 and 2010.

The data provide some insights on the growth or diffusion of broadband yet at the same time conceal many factors that are likely to be relevant in considering the dynamics of development. For example, a few member states (the Netherlands, Denmark and Sweden) appear to have maintained a leading role over the period. These three countries all have high per capita incomes, alternative infrastructures (such as cable) besides the established telephone network that can be exploited to provide broadband service, and regulators that have been active in trying to curb the market power of the incumbent.

In contrast, the table shows that Luxembourg appears to have converted an initial trailing role on broadband uptake into a relatively successful performance by 2010. What has changed along the way and does the transformation imply that high per capita income alone is insufficient to foster rapid broadband development?

Table 3.1 also indicates that Malta and Estonia appear to have fared much better than the other new EU member states. What lies behind the apparent success in these two countries and are there lessons that could be exploited elsewhere?

The key to Table 3.1 indicates that competitive supply of broadband depends on investments in alternative networks (such as cable or newly-built ones) or on service-based competition using inputs supplied by the incumbent. In recent years, a number of member states have witnessed the emergence of significant shares of the broadband market being provided by newly-built competing networks based on fibre, wireless local loop or wireless cellular technologies. This is the case in Denmark, Sweden, Estonia, Slovenia, Ireland, the Czech Republic, Hungary, Lithuania, Latvia, Slovakia, Poland, Bulgaria and Romania.

Interestingly, the technology choice for investments that have been made in such alternative networks appears to vary according to the maturity of the domestic broadband market. For instance, these alternative network investments are mainly fibre-based in Denmark, Sweden and Slovenia, fibre or wireless local loop in Estonia, mainly wireless local loop in the Czech Republic, Hungary and Slovakia, and predominantly using cellular technologies to deliver broadband in Lithuania, Latvia, Poland, Bulgaria and Romania where traditional fixed line broadband is least well-developed. Such trends indicate that it may be inappropriate to think in terms of a single

Table 3.1 EU broadband development by member state (subscribers/population), 2002–2006–2010[14]

2002				2006				2010			
MS	Subs. /pop.	Share (I) DSL	Share (I+E) Cable	MS	Subs. /pop.	Share (I) DSL	Share (E) Cable	MS	Subs. /pop.	Share (I) DSL	Share (E) Cable
BE	8.5%	50	40	NL	25.2%	45	38	NL	39%	42	38
DK	8.5%	54	31	DK	24.7%	45	16	DK	38%	43	9
SE	8.3%	43	21	FI	22.4%	53	8	LU	33%	65	17
NL	7.5%	30	66	SE	20.7%	38	18	SE	32%	34	20
AT	5.6%	32	60	BE	19.2%	48	38	DE	31%	46	10
FI	5.2%	65	20	UK	16.5%	25	31	FR	31%	44	4
DE	3.9%	93	1	FR	16.4%	45	6	UK	31%	28	21
ES	3.1%	56	25	LU	15.5%	74	9	BE	30%	47	44
FR	2.8%	60	15	AT	14.3%	40	40	FI	29%	52	7
PT	2.5%	17	80	EE	13.3%	46	28	MT	29%	48	46
UK	2.2%	22	55	DE	12.8%	60	0	EE	26%	41	21
IT	1.7%	65	0	MT	12.7%	31	41	SI	24%	39	24
LU	1.7%	88	5	IT	11.8%	71	0	AT	24%	53	29
IE	0.2%	36	54	ES	11.7%	53	21	CY	23%	76	7
GR	0%	n.a.	0	PT	11.6%	48	13	IE	23%	n.a.	17
				SI	9.8%	60	33	ES	23%	53	18
				LT	6.8%	44	21	IT	21%	55	0
				IE	6.7%	55	9	CZ	20%	33	22
				CZ	6.4%	42	21	HU	20%	33	37
				CY	6.3%	94	0	LT	20%	33	8
				HU	6.1%	50	27	PT	19%	43	40
				LV	5.7%	52	12	LV	19%	43	8
				PL	2.7%	64	23	GR	19%	52	0
				SK	2.6%	76	15	SK	16%	42	10
				GR	1.4%	69	0	PL	15%	35	27
								BG	14%	32	12
								RO	14%	28	15

Legend: Member states in descending order by percentage of subscriptions. DSL = digital subscriber line; I = Incumbent; E = Entrant.
Where there is no cable network, competitive supply depends on alternative or newly-built networks or on DSL services provided by entrants using regulated inputs from the incumbent telephone network.
Source: Adapted from European Commission data.

[14] The ratio of subscribers to population is a poor measure of broadband uptake, as explained in the text. A better measure is proportion of households subscribing, but usually requires measurement via comprehensive surveys. Moreover, it is not possible to translate historical data for the ratio of subscribers to population accurately to the better measure using information about average household size because broadband uptake is not uniform across households.

broadband development model for the EU. Instead, some countries are building on existing wire-based networks, while others seem likely to use wireless technologies extensively to supply broadband both to fixed premises and to users on the move, even if data-rates are more modest. In the former, rights of way and ease of building will be important, whereas in the latter access to frequency and licensing arrangements are likely to be crucial for investments.

Although Table 3.1 omits a range of indicators (quantitative and qualitative) that are likely to explain why broadband investments and broadband use have developed in the way that they have, it does seem possible to identify some of the features that foster rather than hinder broadband growth.

A cursory examination of the evolution of a simplistic ranking in broadband performance (based on subscriptions per population as shown in Table 3.1) shows that development has tended to be faster where the incumbent has a lower share of the market.

The implication appears to be that rivalry from a second infrastructure-based competitor, such as a cable network (or a new fibre network), boosts broadband uptake. Without that rivalry or competitive threat, some form of access regulation is needed to counter the market power of the dominant telecommunications network and assist entry and widen user choice. In addition, entry based on physical access (e.g., unbundled loops or shared access), appears to have provided a better foundation for broadband growth than entry based on virtual inputs such as bitstream or resale.[15]

But what characterizes a satisfactory level of broadband availability and use for a country at any given time? And which are the most important factors that will influence investment and the upgrading of networks to provide high bandwidth broadband.[16] Is there a way of systematically assessing the various factors that determine broadband development?

Some of the empirical studies that are summarised in Section 3.5 claim to have discovered the 'holy grail' concerning which factors help or hinder broadband development. Yet in seeking to draw on a broad sample of pooled time-series and cross-section data, many of these studies are handicapped by methodological drawbacks even where they attempt to deal systematically with interactions or endogenous effects between variables.

One key problem is that the studies commonly use 'broadband subscribers per 100 of the population' as the variable to be explained. In contrast, the diffusion of broadband and the assessment of market maturity are better measured by 'subscriptions per household'. In countries where household size is above average, subscriptions per population underestimate broadband uptake relative to countries with low household size. For example, in 2011 South Korea which had continually led the OECD rankings for broadband development slipped to fourth with respect to the former measure whereas it remained first on the basis of household subscriptions (with 98 per cent uptake).

Even correcting broadband subscriptions for the impact of household size fails to account for a number of other factors and measures that are a crucial part of the dynamics of the development of broadband over time. For example, a simple examination of the diffusion path of broadband for OECD countries between 2002 and 2012 shows that the initial leaders (S. Korea and Canada) have now been caught by many of the followers but it fails to recognise that the leading countries have moved on in terms of the broadband data rates and services offered and these vary widely within and between countries.

A number of measures illustrate these variations. They include access data rates and performance, technology (to the extent that this indicates the

---

[15] The former constitutes a more significant commitment to entry, as well as providing greater control over the retail product: see Cawley (2007).

[16] The OECD has in the past defined basic broadband as (inward) access data rates above 256 kbit/s but below 2 Mbit/s. In 2012, fast broadband was defined as between 2 and 24 Mbit/s, and superfast broadband in excess of 24 Mbit/s, but already in 2013 these data-rate dividing lines have been moved much higher as VDSL and fibre capabilities have improved and as DOCSIS 3.0 (over cable networks) has been deployed.

future potential for improving service or reducing cost), and also the range and choice of offerings that are available.

On the basis of the average data rates for broadband service, Japan was in the top spot in 2011 although it had slipped to sixteenth in the rankings based on subscribers per population. The technology used to supply broadband may also be important (to the extent that it indicates the future potential for data rates and quality of service delivery and the resource or cost efficiency of supplying broadband. On this basis Japan, South Korea, Slovakia and Sweden were leading the way in 2011 because they had the highest proportions of broadband supplied over fibre access.

Another relevant consideration could be the choice of offerings that are available, (including for example symmetric as well as asymmetric data rates)[17] bearing in mind that users may have widely differentiated needs. If for example it is the use of broadband by enterprises (rather than households) that is deemed to be important (and the key factor behind productivity improvements), then a different set of indicators needs to be used to illustrate development and needs.

The empirical analysis (referred to in Section 3.5) also begs the question of what exactly is being explained. If it is the state of broadband subscription or use relative to what might be expected from basic economic indicators, then Estonia and Slovenia (in Europe) punch above their weight relative to income per capita.

The implication is that there is a very wide range of factors (economic, demographic, topographical, historic and institutional) that combine to explain the evolution of broadband supply and demand. What then becomes interesting is trying to identify what made or what makes the difference for each of the countries or cases concerned. It is in this sense that case studies can provide valuable insights that are beyond the scope of the studies cited in Section 3.5; in particular, which combination of circumstances facilitated investment or which policy and institutional factors did most to

support the socio-economic ones and underpin broadband uptake. That is the value-added of the country studies in this book: their ability to identify the factors that made (or did not make) a difference.

The next three sections look at the possible lessons for broadband development that can be learnt respectively from theory, historical examples and empirical analysis.

3.3 Investment and innovation in broadband infrastructure and the impact of regulation

In recent decades, there has been a fundamental change in the regulation of the telecommunications sector. Regulation has shifted from a rate of return or 'cost-plus' approach of controlling the monopoly provider to various forms of incentive regulation[18], beginning with price-cap regulation (initially placed on retail services) and evolving, as entry barriers have been lifted, to regulating the price and non-price terms of access to the network of the incumbent or dominant market operator.

Despite the focus on these terms of access, the impact of regulation on investment nevertheless remains central for several reasons. Investment affects prices and quantities supplied in the long run, and delays in investment can have large welfare costs.[19] Secondly, the amount of investment in the sector is typically large relative to gross fixed capital formation in many other parts of the economy.[20] Thirdly, regulation can have a significant impact on investment[21] and changes in regulation have often led to major shifts in investment behaviour as illustrated in Section 3.4.

---

[17] Some user groups, including businesses, prefer symmetric broadband access service because of their requirements for sending as well as receiving data.

[18] The change from rate of return to incentive regulation has served to shift the risks associated with undertaking investments away from users and towards the owners of incumbent or regulated firms.

[19] See for example Waverman (2003) and Crandall and Jackson (2001), concerning the welfare associated with broadband deployment.

[20] Guthrie (2006) notes (Table 1) that the share of business investment in telecommunications is relatively higher than other infrastructure-based industries.

[21] Alesina et al. (2005).

Regulation influences the dynamics of broadband investments and innovation in a variety of ways. Entrants may depend on regulation to curb the market power of the incumbent and get a foothold (on the so-called 'ladder of investment'). The incumbent's plans for new investment or network upgrades may be dampened or encouraged by the prospect of regulation and the form that it takes. And an established entrant (such as a cable operator), even if not directly affected, may be concerned that extensive or excessive regulation will reduce its potential profits (and capacity to invest) by constraining prices or handing market share to other competitors.

This section considers investment and innovation incentives, with and without regulation, and some simple models are used to illustrate the relationship between competition and innovation, and the impact of regulation on investment behaviour. Schumpeter[22] emphasised the importance of dynamic efficiency and the value of innovation relative to price competition within a given market. The following stylised models illustrate the challenges for policymakers and regulators seeking to facilitate broadband investments and network upgrades.

The first model illustrates the sunk-cost effect, whereby an established firm has less incentive than an entrant to invest in a new technology. Imagine that the fixed costs of investing in old and new technologies are I(o) and I(n) respectively, and the present value of the respective operating costs are VC(o) and VC(n). Then (for a given level of demand for output, and ignoring any effects on price), a new entrant will choose to invest in the new technology rather than the old if: $I(n) + VC(n) < I(o) + VC(o)$. That could be the case for fibre-based networks because VC(n), (per unit of supply), is likely to be much lower than VC(o).

The established firm has already sunk its investment I(o), so this can be set to zero for the purposes of comparison of investment incentives. In addition, its accumulated experience in using the old or existing technology may mean that its true operating costs are a fraction of VC(o) and equal to $a*VC(o)$ where $a < 1$. It therefore faces a much tighter inequality than the entrant and is less likely to adopt the new technology.

The second model illustrates the replacement effect[23] (Arrow, 1962). It deals just with the incentive to innovate when an innovation opportunity is only available to an incumbent. Whereas an entrant could in principle invest in a new technology, take over the market and replace the incumbent monopolist, the monopolist can only replace itself. Imagine that the incumbent could develop an innovation that would cost I(t) per relevant time period but enable it to increase its monopoly profit from P(o) to P(n). It would do so if $P(n) - I(t) > P(o)$. Consider an alternative where a new firm could potentially invest to develop the innovation, enter the market, replace the incumbent and become the new monopolist. It would do so if $P(n) - I(t) > 0$, so again the incentive effect on the incumbent monopolist appears to be weaker.

An alternative way of portraying this asymmetric effect between incumbent and new entrant is to compare relative starting positions with either a state of market power or of competition. With market power, the incumbent can expend fixed cost F to invest in the new technology in order to lower costs and make new higher monopoly profit P(n) rather than P(o). In the second, an entrant or competing firm can invest to secure profit P(n) in place of an existing competitive market profit of zero. Provided the investment in the new technology (or temporary lower cost or superior position) secures the same level of profit P(n), the starting point with competition (or potential competition) would be more likely to induce innovation.

The two effects portrayed above work in the same direction and indicate the disincentive faced

---

[22] Baake et al. (2005) distinguish Schumpeter's earlier and later theories. In both, innovation creates competitive advantage. In the early theory, innovations propel the economy between competitive equilibria (and monopoly advantage is temporary). In the later theory, innovative leadership lays the foundation for competitive advantage in the next innovation stage, so the economy evolves to a system of dominant firms.

[23] It was Tirole (1988) who described the phenomenon as the replacement effect.

by the incumbent to innovate or invest if variable cost savings alone are insufficient to justify new investments or if investments cannibalise existing revenues. A practical example would be a reluctance to invest in advanced DSL technologies or to shift to an All-IP network for fear of undermining revenues from existing data services. Another pertinent example could involve delays in moving to an all optical or fibre access network.

A further (third) model can be used to illustrate the 'efficiency' effect whereby the incumbent has to assess the possibility of an entrant adopting the innovation, successfully entering and competing away some or all of its existing profit. It may compare a situation in which it innovates and either manages to retain its monopoly position and profit (or makes a lower duopoly profit), with the situation in which it does not innovate and either shares the market or is forced to exit altogether and earn nothing. In this situation, the incumbent may be induced to innovate to avoid the deterioration in profit from additional competition or in anticipation of the larger expected pay-off from retaining its leadership or dominant role.

In practice, all of the three effects or incentives categorised above may operate and it is not evident which will dominate. Aghion *et al.* (2005) find evidence of an inverted U-shaped relationship between competition and innovation for a number of sectors, so that innovation increases with competition and then tails off. A model involving incentives to break free from neck-and-neck competition (to preserve or increase profits) is developed to explain such a phenomenon.

Regulating to facilitate entry is already a fact of life in the EU for broadband. In that context, there has already been considerable debate about the nature of access regulation and how to determine appropriate access prices in a static context (for competition within existing markets).

The more fundamental issue concerns the impact of regulation and access charges in a dynamic context (i.e., the effect that regulation is likely to have on investment upgrades and innovation or competition for new markets). The granting of access (and the form and terms that it takes) can have an impact on the buy or build

decisions of entrants, on the timing of entry and on investment and innovation more generally[24].

An additional simple model serves to illustrate the buy or build choice[25]. Assume that a potential new supplier can enter the market by building its own (local access) infrastructure or by leasing (access) from the incumbent. If it builds its own network, it obtains a revenue or gross profit of P^F and incurs a cost of F. If it leases access, it obtains a gross profit of $P^S(r)$, which is a (decreasing) function of the leasing cost, r, and incurs a fixed fee of f.

In a static or one period setting, the entrant strictly prefers infrastructure based entry if

$$P^F - F > P^S(r) - f$$

If access terms improve via the lowering of the leasing cost or the fixed fee (f), then the balance would switch towards a preference for services based entry[26].

More importantly, regulation of access terms and prices affects the rate of return that infrastructure owners earn or expect to earn from their investments[27]. Therefore, the nature or expected

---

[24] The problem can be compared with the granting of intellectual property rights or patents. The granting of the right or reserve price is designed to provide the incentive to undertake the initial investment or innovation and the safeguard to make a return on it.

[25] In practice, there may be a range of alternatives to building infrastructure depending on the forms of access available, from reselling wholesale services, unbundled elements or indirect access, through to unbundled local loops. The relative prices of different types of access are likely to affect entry choices.

[26] It is this possibility for the entrant to decide between services or infrastructure-based entry, or to postpone a decision on building facilities (and buy access) that is said to confer an option value to the entrant. Setting a low price for access confers an option to wait and see and postpones the time at which the entrant would invest in its own facilities. This has led some to call for the option value (or at least a valuation of risk) to be included in the access charge, see Baumol (1999), Alleman et al. (2005).

[27] Returns on investments are uncertain, particularly where technological progress is rapid. Higher rates of technological progress increase the rate of economic depreciation and the required annual return from the asset. Technological progress is in turn endogenous and is stimulated by higher prices, including higher regulated access charges.

nature of *ex post* access regulation has a major impact on *ex ante* incentives to invest.

There has been limited analysis of access regulation, and the impact on investment, in a dynamic context. Much of the focus has been on designing optimal regulatory contracts (Laffont and Tirole, 1993; Armstrong and Sappington, 2004). In terms of how actual regulation affects investment, some insights are provided by the literature on investment timing or investment races (Gans and Williams, 1999; Gans, 2001). An alternative approach applies real option theory to the access-pricing problem (Dixit and Pindyck 1994).

Gans and King (2003) analyse the relevance of access holidays. The anticipation that access to future investments (if successful) will be regulated, lowers the *ex ante* expected rate of return, by truncating returns or profits in better states of the world. This means that some investments will not be undertaken, unless this risk is factored *ex ante* into the rate of return permitted by the regulator.

In this setting, the problem for the regulator is to make a clear *ex ante* commitment about the parts of the incumbent network to which access will be mandated (and on what terms), in order *ex post* to generate efficient entry and efficient levels of investment by both the incumbent and the entrant[28]. That usually involves complex judgements about the rates of return that will be permitted as well as the difficulty of credibly committing to a particular approach[29].

Guthrie (2006), in a survey of the literature on regulation and investment, examined the effect of regulated access charges on investment, where both services-based competition (SBC) and facilities-based competition (FBC) are feasible, so that various forms of downstream competition are

possible. The implications for the regulation of access pricing vary depending on whether there is a large cost difference between the two firms investing (the incumbent and an entrant), implying a waiting game, or whether there is a small cost difference, implying a pre-emption game.

In the waiting game, setting access prices in line with historical cost (rather than replacement cost) can accelerate investment, and greater dynamic efficiency can outweigh any loss of allocative efficiency. Therefore, setting access prices equal to long-run incremental cost may not be socially optimal.

In the pre-emptive setting, a higher access charge makes it more attractive to invest first and invest earlier. If this leads to investment occurring sooner than is socially optimal, then setting lower access charges can raise welfare.

The implication is that there is a complex relationship between optimal access charges, investment costs, nature of downstream competition (including the interaction between access charges and the timing of periods of SBC and FBC) and efficiency. Moreover, the relationship between optimal access pricing and costs varies depending on the setting and the nature of investments. Guthrie also points out that investing second gives the possibility to learn valuable information. This value from learning, and the (negative) effect on the leader's pay-off lowers the pre-emption incentive.

Regulatory decisions on access will therefore influence investment decisions and long-term market structures and competition in complex ways. One view[30] is that excessive access regulation (and particularly under-pricing of inputs) results in the incumbent losing both the capacity and the incentive to invest, whilst the entrant free-rides on those parts of the network that are made available and over-invests in parts of the network that are not. It is not easy to test such a view because the predicted outcome is not simply a reduction in investment levels but switches in the types of investment made and the firms making them.

---

[28] Basing access charges on incurred costs may be efficient in allocative terms, and productive efficiency (if it is an issue) can be addressed by imposing price-caps on input charges. The major problem therefore concerns dynamic efficiency.

[29] Access regulation that is based on cost recovery rules, whilst encouraging efficient utilisation of existing assets, risks discouraging investment. If firms anticipate (correctly) that the regulator will grant access at cost, once someone has invested, firms will wait for the investment to be undertaken by somebody else, and then seek access.

[30] Sidak and Spulber (1998) and Hausman and Sidak (1999) argue against local loop unbundling on this basis.

An alternative view[31] is that despite the difficulty of calculating appropriate access terms, regulation should mandate access to those parts of the network that are (the most) difficult to replicate over a given horizon. In this way, the entrant can combine its own inputs with access to the incumbent's network in complementary fashion. Over time, this permits the entrant to invest progressively in assets that are more difficult to replicate and thereby use the access inputs as stepping-stones or rungs of a ladder towards full facilities-based entry[32]. Testing this view implies establishing that the ratio of access inputs to own inputs declines over time.

Vogelsang (2010), in a survey that focuses on the theoretical work, summarises the dilemma for regulators in trying to facilitate efficient investment via the access rules and/or prices that they set. He notes that regulation can have ambivalent effects on investment. He proposes that 'intermediate' regulation (between the looser and tighter access rules and price standards that he describes) is likely to be most appropriate for inducing efficient investments and that genuine innovation should not be regulated although strict and verifiable checks are needed. At the same time, he notes the legal and institutional difficulty of regulators committing over a sufficiently long period.

3.4 Insights from earlier investment cycles in telecommunications

The country case studies in this book provide some important insights and lessons about the events and circumstances that trigger substantial commitments

to undertake infrastructure investments in order to supply broadband services.

Some additional examples are given in this section, either because they lie outside the scope of these case studies, or because they provide useful empirical background to the analysis of the influence of the EU-level rules on broadband investment that are discussed in this chapter.

The first illustration draws on the first two decades of investments in basic telephone networks in the USA.[33] After the Bell patents lapsed in 1894, (in the USA), there was a wave of investment in local access networks by independent operators seeking to compete with AT&T, which had been building a separate unconnected network. These investments were very localised but led to rapid increases in subscribers overall (about 12 per cent per year compared to average annual increases of 4–5 per cent before and after this period). The investments were motivated by the potential revenue streams of providing service and the value (and potential scale economies) of connecting together a significant body of customers. When these independent companies were taken over by AT&T (following the Kingsbury commitment to guarantee a universal service), the pace of investment and growth slowed.

The second example concerns the large investments that were made in long distance fibre networks following the lifting of restrictions on infrastructure competition in the European Union at the beginning of 1998 (Figure 3.1). The leased lines used by cross-border or pan-European companies to run their private voice and data networks were very expensive and well above underlying costs. Consequently, when restrictions on competing infrastructure were lifted many new and existing operators invested in long distance fibre-based trunk networks throughout Europe. Prices to third parties decreased by two or three orders of magnitude (in € per Mbit equivalent) in just a few years.

Many of the companies that invested subsequently went bankrupt because capacity rose sharply over a short period and prices fell very

---

[31] Cave and Vogelsang (2003). Armstrong (1999) argues in favour of local loop unbundling as a way of testing market demand and providing the ability to supply differentiated outputs to end-users.

[32] This approach is known as the 'ladder of investment' concept in a European context. It involves withdrawing mandatory access to inputs over time, as well as making them available in the first place on appropriate terms. Various strategies have been tried to counteract any disincentives to invest on the part of alternative access providers. In Canada it was announced that unbundled loops would only be available for 5 years. In the Netherlands, it was agreed in advance that the access charge for unbundled loops would gradually increase over a five year period.

[33] See Gabel (1994) for a more detailed account.

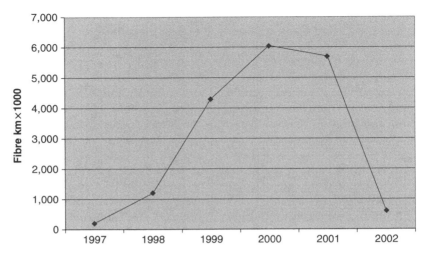

Figure 3.1 Investments in fibre, Europe, 1997–2002
Data source: Author based on data from Lemstra, 2006.

quickly.[34] But the capacity remained (and was transferred to new ownership) and these and subsequent investments served to provide the basis for Internet backbone networks in Europe, and avoid the cost and congestion of routing traffic via the USA.

The third example is closer to the topic treated in this book – that of investments in local broadband networks. It concerns the impact on entrants' investment behaviour of regulating access in the Netherlands, a country that has been at the forefront of the development of residential broadband subscriber markets. Tiscali, an Italian-based Internet and broadband services supplier (formed in 1998) sought to expand its market presence in the Netherlands by requesting access to wholesale bitstream services provided by the incumbent operator, KPN. The Dutch court rejected the request (in October 2003) and Tiscali instead decided to enter the market by leasing unbundled local loops (Figure 3.2), a form of access that was subject to regulatory oversight. Tiscali withdrew from the Dutch market in 2007 by selling its operations to KPN, but by then it had built a significant subscriber base.

One general lesson that can be drawn from these examples is that investment appears to flourish or take off in circumstances where the removal of entry barriers or market impediments triggers head-to-head rivalry to build a customer base or roll out services for which there is pent-up demand. Many of the examples of fast growth broadband markets outside the EU (e.g., South Korea, Canada and Iceland) appear to have been driven by fierce infrastructure-based competition.

More specifically, the first example illustrates how the potential advantage of being first to market, particularly in a greenfield context where there is value in connecting as many customers as possible, can drive investment. This has implications for member states where networks are not yet fully developed or where greenfield possibilities arise. It also shows that infrastructure investments take time; they are measured in decades and not years.

The second example shows that investment is spurred when there is pent-up demand, prices are above cost and entry restrictions are lifted. In the case of broadband, it indicates the potential investment incentives of both reducing entry or build costs where possible, and allowing investors to make profits (as well as losses).

The third example provides evidence that credible refusal of access (in this case by a court) can

---

[34] See Lemstra (2006).

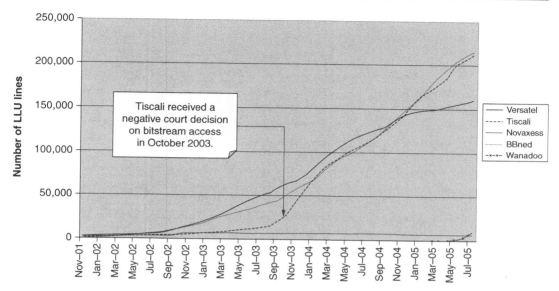

Figure 3.2 Unbundling and the impact of access regulation on entry, the Netherlands, 2001–2005
Data source: Author based on date from OPTA, the Dutch Regulatory Authority

spur an alternative entry strategy that involves less dependence on access to assets or inputs of the incumbent or a regulated firm. Conversely, easy access favours service-based entry, and hinders innovation. Either way, clear regulatory commitment is paramount.

3.5 Insights from empirical studies on the roll-out of broadband investments and the impact of access regulation

On balance, the empirical literature is inconclusive about whether access regulation stimulates or harms long-term competition and infrastructure investments, including the development of broadband.

The early empirical studies (focused mainly on the USA and on access regulation for telephone services, not broadband) were generally critical of the way access regulation had been applied in practice, and sceptical about the practical value of trying to achieve infrastructure competition via detailed access regulation. Generally, the USA evidence indicates that the ability to use unbundled access elements at low prices (prior to reversal of

the policy by the FCC) crowded out investments by incumbents and entrants.

In 2001, Cave, Rood, Majumdar, Valletti and Vogelsang performed one of the early studies in the European context to analyse the impact of access regulation and pricing on infrastructure competition[35]. It examined the interaction between access pricing and entry. The conclusion was that the way to promote infrastructure competition is to provide inexpensive access to assets that are not replicable, followed by a rising price trend applied successively to assets in descending order of replicability.

The notion that infrastructure competition can occur via step-wise investments in assets that are increasingly expensive or difficult to replicate is explored further by Cave (2004a, 2004b and 2005). In analysing the so-called 'ladder of investment' approach, it is stressed that it is important to determine terms of access appropriately[36], if and where access is mandated, and for

---

[35] A published version is available as Cave and Vogelsang (2003).
[36] Cave (2005) acknowledges that risk should be factored into access terms where appropriate, and recognising the

Table 3.2 Empirical studies of the impact of access regulation on facilities competition

Study	Results
Aron and Burnstein (2003)	Intra-platform competition has little effect on broadband growth, whereas inter-platform competition does.
Bacache, Bourreau and Gaudin (2011)	Entrants using unbundled local loops do not climb the ladder of investment and build their own infrastructure.
Briglauer, Ecker and Kugler (2011)	Claims that regulation has negatively affected NGA deployment.
Chang, Kosler and Majumdar (2003)	Some evidence in the USA that lower access prices have helped investment, but the opposite in Europe.
Crandall, Ingraham and Singer (2004)	Unbundling encourages entrants to delay facilities-based investments.
Crandall, Eisenach and Ingraham (2012)	The long-run effect of copper unbundling on household broadband penetration is negative.
Distaso, Lupo and Manenti (2004)	Inter-modal competition rather than competition on DSL-based entry drives broadband adoption.
Dotecon and Criterion Economics (2003)	Access regulation provides a substitute rather than a complement for investment (case studies in Europe and elsewhere).
Fabritz and Falk (2013)	Evidence that local deregulation increases investment in local broadband infrastructure by both incumbent and competitors.
Ford and Spiwak (2004)	Some evidence of unbundling supporting investment.
Hausman and Sidak (1999)	No evidence that unbundling supports stepping-stone investment or lowers telephony prices.
Hazlett and Bazelon (2005)	Mandatory UNE-P access associated with decreasing investment; end of line sharing has led to faster growth of DSL broadband.
Wallsten (2006)	Access regulation supporting telephone competition in USA (UNE-P) had a negative effect on broadband penetration.
Wallsten and Hausladen (2009)	Inverse relationship between unbundling and number of fibre broadband connections.
Waverman, Meschi, Reillier and Dasgupta (2007)	Lower unbundling prices deter development of alternative platforms or infrastructure.
Wood, Zarakas and Sappington (2004)	Entry choices of competing access operators in USA very sensitive to relative prices of unbundled elements (UNE-P) and unbundled loops (UNE-L).
Zarakas, Woroch, Wood, McFadden, Ilias and Liu (2005)	Higher prices of unbundled network elements tend to support more facilities-based competition, specifically inter-modal competition. Lower access prices encourage service-based (non-facilities) supply.

Source: Author.

regulators to credibly commit to the access policies that are chosen.

Table 3.2 summarises the results from a range of empirical studies that investigate whether and how

option value of mandatory access is one way to do this. See Dixit and Pindyck (1994) and Pindyck (2004 and 2005) for a consideration of investment and risk. Alleman et al. (2005) model optimal access prices in the face of sunk cost and uncertainty.

access regulation (and access pricing) influences investment and entry.

One pervasive difficulty, particularly with the empirical work analysing residential broadband uptake, is that the dependent variable is typically a periodic measure of aggregate broadband access (per 100 population), rather than the household decision on whether or not to subscribe to a given broadband service. It therefore is difficult to analyse the dynamics of household subscription decisions (with respect to socio-economic and institutional factors) relative to the long-term diffusion of broadband.

Chang, Kosler and Majumdar (2003) and Ford and Spiwak (2004) lean toward the view that lower access prices in the USA have helped investment or that the competition created by unbundling outweighs any disincentives to facilities-based entry. The former also finds evidence that higher access prices in Europe are associated with more investment.

In contrast Hazlett and Bazelon (2005) and others are critical of the 'stepping stones' or 'ladder' theory of investment. They examined the impact in the USA of the approach on the network unbundling element platform (UNE-P), which effectively ended in June 2005. They also look at the effect of the ending of line-sharing rules announced in February 2003. They found that the period of mandatory UNE-P access was associated with decreasing investments in competing access lines, (and by local incumbent operators, too). They also find accelerated growth of DSL broadband subscriptions following the end of mandatory line-sharing.

As comparable broadband data has become available in Europe, and access regulation has diminished in the USA, analysis has focused on whether and how access regulation affects broadband uptake and development.

Based on a number of country case studies, Dotecon and Criterion (2003) claim that there is strong evidence that platform competition drives broadband uptake and that there is little evidence in favour of access- or resale-based entry. They argue that inappropriate access policies (e.g., setting prices too low, or the risk of excessive access regulation) skews entry decisions in favour of access-based entry and away from infrastructure investments, despite the latter being feasible.

Distaso *et al.* (2004) examine the relationship between broadband uptake and the regulation of DSL inputs using data from fourteen EU countries. They tentatively suggest that inter-modal competition, rather than competition in DSL services, drives broadband adoption. Although competition between DSL suppliers can potentially promote diffusion, this effect seems to be almost completely overwhelmed by the negative indirect effect on inter-platform competition induced by promoting DSL entry via access regulation.

More recently, a number of studies have sought to assess the impact of (access) regulation (such as loop unbundling) not only on broadband growth but on the shift to next-generation access or upgraded broadband service. Some of the studies claim that systematic access regulation in Europe has slowed investment and innovation.

As indicated by the summary in Table 3.2, the empirical work is inconclusive about the impact of access regulation on long-term facilities-based competition. Vogelsang (2010) argues that much of the empirical work appears to be driven by partisan considerations as it focuses on regulation (or not) of the incumbent. On balance, there appears to be some support for the hypothesis that broadband develops more successfully in the presence of inter-modal or infrastructure-based competition and that access regulation that favours DSL-based entrants can blunt this impact.

In general, the empirical studies are broadly consistent with the theory (on investment incentives) described in Section 3.3 and also with the historical examples (concerning waves of investment) without bringing any clear insights on what should be done to best facilitate the roll-out of next-generation networks.

They do not provide enough evidence to suggest that the 'ladder of investment' theory is broken (as Ungerer 2013), but nor do they provide much evidence in its favour.

3.6 Possible justifications for setting the regulatory rules at EU level

So far, it has been argued that the rules of the game (in terms of entry possibilities, competitive conditions and regulatory rules) affect broadband investments, although the precise impact of access regulation is less clear. It has also been argued that other features, including historical and institutional factors, play an important role.

So, how important are the rules of the game that are framed at EU level? The three sections that follow this one examine different aspects of this EU-level influence – respectively the Digital

Agenda targets and related financial support, the role of EU competition policy (including the state aid guidelines) and the application at national level of the EU regulatory framework. This section seeks to assess what justifications there might be for framing so many of the rules at EU level.

The Digital Agenda for Europe has three broadband targets: basic broadband for all by 2013; secondly, all Europeans should have access to Internet of above 30 Mbit/s by 2020; and thirdly, also by 2020, 50 per cent or more of European households should have subscriptions above 100 Mbit/s. Targets concerning the availability of service seem reasonable enough but how do targets for subscription and use fit into the picture and what instruments are available for reaching such targets? After all, the EU also has regulatory and competition policy rules that seek to foster outcomes reached by competitive market conditions and the absence of illegal state aid or subsidy.

The wider or more general benefits of trying to accelerate broadband development across the EU depend on the links to general economic activity and potential incremental productivity increases that were mentioned in Section 3.2. It is conceivable that companies derive benefits from other enterprises having good broadband connections. It may also be the case that individuals derive benefits from other individuals having good service. Other agents and institutions are also part of the picture: government offices, research and educational establishments and the interaction between these and enterprises and individuals.

But why does not the pursuit of broadband development by individual member states suffice to satisfy such aims? Most countries have stated targets themselves and surely they know best when assessing their own priorities for progress or the likely success of using avenues such as government or educational broadband connectivity to stimulate uptake by households and enterprises.

One wider benefit (from a common EU approach) might be that the deployment and use of high performance broadband networks (in the longer term) hastens the point at which more costly traditional copper-based networks could be switched off. In addition, using fibre networks to distribute television programmes makes it easier

to recover the frequencies that have been used in the past by analogue terrestrial networks (to broadcast radio and TV). The transfer of some UHF and VHF frequencies for use by mobile communications networks could potentially be very valuable at EU level, where little progress has been made in creating integrated pan-European wireless networks for data and voice[37]. At the same time, member states have been reluctant to support or promote such EU-wide capability, so using it to justify the coordination of the rules for broadband seems a little far-fetched.

Table 3.3 seeks to summarise the various possible justifications for setting the rules at EU level and coordinating accordingly. It considers the possible benefits (and costs) that a common approach might produce on the supply side (e.g., EU-wide operations and branding), the demand side (common supplier for trans-border firms or users), market development (companies genuinely competing at EU level), and regulation (the synergies of a common approach or exchange of best practice).

Table 3.3 encapsulates some of the questions that EU policy and regulation has faced since the introduction of regulated competition – the link between liberalising and harmonising measures and how best to achieve the wider objectives of market development and innovation.

The balance between liberalization (to open markets and facilitate entry) and harmonisation (to maintain a level playing field for competition and exploit economies of scale and scope in a larger EU market) appeared to have been struck during the 2003 regulatory reform. The initial proposal for a two-tier hurdle for regulation of market power (to deal both with the dominance of the former monopoly incumbents and with the oligopolistic market influence of mobile companies) was dropped in favour of a single trigger based on competition law dominance on selected problem markets. That reform was intended simultaneously to address market power and deliver consistent

---

[37] Licensing remains a national preserve and companies that have networks and provide services in several member states have not consolidated their operations, in contrast to the USA where a few companies operate in all states.

Table 3.3 Possible benefits and synergies from a common EU approach

	Possible benefit	Drawback
Supply-side synergies	Entrants could supply broadband via a common business plan across national markets. The ability for suppliers to combine national markets could off-set scale disadvantages for entrants	Markets differ and a uniform approach irrespective of market conditions could distort investment decisions. Many leading broadband markets are small (e.g., Iceland, Denmark, Hong Kong). Scale aspects are more related to local density.
Demand-side synergies	Incumbents and others could supply across EU. EU businesses could use the same supplier across EU.	Does not require a common EU approach as it may emerge via competing wholesale suppliers. Large companies can develop their own cross-border networks.
Dynamic or long-term synergies	Efficiency benefit of more companies competing across a wider market. Co-ordinated re-farming and re-assignment of spectrum.	Forego potential benefit of regulatory competition and innovation. Actual economic benefits depend on broadband development rather than a uniform regulatory approach.
Regulatory synergies	Resource saving from a common regulatory plan and approach	National preferences and priorities on broadband vary. Less accountable to local needs.

Source: Author

regulation across the whole of the EU market. However, some problems persisted and became more acute (such as charges for mobile roaming and the development of EU-wide mobile Internet services) and concerns also surfaced regarding the incentives to invest in and upgrade broadband networks (see Section 3.10).

Instead of specifically addressing these substantive policy issues, the 2009 regulatory reform made some modest incremental changes to the regulatory framework. It did, however, reinforce the role of the EU regulator (BEREC) and reduce some of the discretion that national regulators had enjoyed when applying regulatory remedies. The changes probably brought more oversight to the regulation of market power but did not modify the fundamental approach, which remained based on competition law principles.

Consequently the Commission in 2013 proposed a further round of reforms, this time seeking more specifically to deliver a more integrated single market to tackle the perceived problems.

It appears that three relatively separate and different policy problems have been identified at EU level. One is the need to remove some of the barriers to the development of an EU-wide market in electronic services and deal with personal concerns about secure use of Internet. A second is to address the declining performance (internationally) of European mobile communications, including the need for a more integrated EU market. The third is the wish to accelerate progress towards the Digital Agenda targets for broadband. The first two objectives may well require more integrated or coordinated action at EU level but it is less evident that a more integrated EU market will help to deliver the third, unless there is a need for greater competition and deployment of wireless broadband, both locally and more widely.

Moreover, there are potential drawbacks from adopting a uniform approach. Firstly, national (or even local) conditions vary in respect of actual or potential competition from alternative infrastructure. Access regulation that is inappropriate for competitive conditions could discourage new infrastructure investments or conversely encourage wasteful duplication.

Secondly, given the difficulty of designing appropriate access regulation, there may be beneficial insights from seeing the outcome of differentiated intervention in adjacent markets, so that regulators in effect compete to find efficient approaches. That could be the case particularly for the transition to next-generation broadband networks. If it is unclear what drives new investments, there should be benefits from allowing local experimentation and sharing that experience.

3.7 The Digital Agenda targets for broadband and their link to EU policy instruments

Of the three targets for broadband announced in 2010 as part of the Digital Agenda for Europe, (see Section 3.5), it is the second and the third, in particular that will require significant investments and upgrading of existing networks. There appears to be an increasing acceptance that public funding (as well as market-driven private investment) will be needed to achieve the targets.[38]

If member states provide financial support for broadband investments, they are obliged to seek clearance from the Commission under state aid rules (Article 107). The Commission published its first formal guidelines on aid to broadband in 2009, and since then the number of (state aid) cases has risen significantly (see Section 3.8). The increasing (public) support for next generation broadband investments (in the context of the Digital Agenda targets) led the Commission to revisit its guidance in 2011 and new guidelines were adopted at the end of 2012.

In essence, the greater willingness of some member states or public authorities to finance some of the investments has pushed the state aid guidelines and the EU regulatory framework closer together and created a dilemma with respect to providing the incentives for the development of next generation broadband.

The EU regulatory framework (see Section 3.9) is based on the notion that appropriate remedies should be applied in the absence of effective competition in certain relevant markets. Such intervention aims to put incumbent and potential entrants on a more equal footing so that the ensuing competition improves user outcomes and drives

appropriate investment decisions over time. However, if regulated competition does not succeed in delivering sufficient investment to attain the broadband digital agenda targets, and supplementary public support is then granted (subject to state aid guidelines), such assistance is typically made subject to certain safeguards. Usually there are obligations for the designated investor and receiver of aid to comply with specified access obligations.

Yet if public support leads to a designated (and aided) monopoly infrastructure that is required to grant access to third parties, it is probably unreasonable to expect a second infrastructure (with similar capabilities) to be established. Why invest in new infrastructure if there is regulated access to newly established facilities?

The (ideal) prospective competitive model for driving efficient investment decisions (and the upgrading of broadband networks) has been based on the notion of 'two-plus' infrastructures, with the traditional telecommunications operator going head-to-head with an upgraded cable TV network, plus some additional provision via other technologies such as wireless, if and where the economics of density are favourable. However, that model seems unlikely to materialise if there is widespread funded support for investment upgrades subject to long-term access regulation, even if this competitive model could be viable in many countries or regions of the EU, albeit with remaining areas or 'pockets' being categorised by the designated monopoly infrastructure model.

The danger, therefore, is that the anticipated need for public support (and the detailed access regulation that goes with it) becomes a self-fulfilling prophecy even though the 'two plus' model might ultimately be viable for significant proportions of the population.[39] Conversely, it may be that a designated monopoly model with

---

[38] See section on the use of public funds in Papadias, Chirico and Gaal (2009).

[39] Interestingly, Liberty Global in 2012 published a study 'Re-thinking the Digital Agenda for Europe', (undertaken by WIK), which argues that cable will be a viable competitor to telecommunications networks in providing high performance broadband in the majority of EU member states. Analysis available from Liberty Global web-site: http://www.libertyglobal.com/PDF/public-policy/LGI-report-Re-thinking-the-Digital-Agenda-for-Europe.pdf

access is workable and appropriate for some regions, although it is not easy to reconcile with the philosophy behind the current EU regulatory framework which is supposed to facilitate competition and roll back regulation only when it emerges. Either way, uncertainty over the extent of future access regulation is not conducive to investment decisions, as shown in Section 3.3.

3.8 The role and influence of EU competition policy on broadband development

Two main strands of EU competition policy influence broadband investments and development.

The first impact is from action under Article 102 to prevent the abuse of dominance. The Commission has pursued several cases (usually following complaints by entrants) against price squeezes or other forms of anti-competitive behaviour.[40] A price squeeze can occur when there is insufficient margin between prices at the wholesale level (for access to inputs) and the retail level so that an efficient entrant cannot compete against the incumbent which is supplying both the input and also services to end-users.

The other strand of influence comes from the application of the state aid rules to public support for broadband investment. Between 2003 and 2006 the Commission issued twenty-three decisions on projects involving financial subsidies for broadband, most of them designed to improve coverage or service availability in rural areas. But from 2006 the number of cases steadily increased (59 during the three-year period 2010–2012), and there has also been a rise in the number of cases supporting next generation or fast broadband, including investments in urban regions.[41] In 2010, a total

amount of EUR 1.8 billion was authorised for state aid to broadband.

The increase in aid projects and cases led the Commission in 2009 to publish guidelines on the application of state aid rules to broadband networks.[42] The main aim was to provide guidance to public authorities about the design of effective and pro-competitive schemes for funding basic broadband and next-generation access (NGA) networks. The principal requirement is that aid must be used to remedy a market failure and to pursue cohesion objectives.

The guidelines distinguish (in notional terms) white, grey and black areas. White areas are those where broadband infrastructure does not exist or is unlikely to be developed in the near future (corresponding to a three-year horizon). Regions where only one broadband network operator is present are designated as grey areas and black areas are characterised by the presence of at least two or more broadband network providers. In black areas, it is considered that there should be no need for state intervention, whereas in grey areas, any possible support requires a detailed assessment, but may be allowed if it can be shown that existing infrastructure and services are insufficient to meet users' demands, and if there are no less-distortive measures available (including *ex ante* regulation).

A *sine qua non* condition for granting state aid is the obligation for the aid recipient to provide open access, regardless of the presence of significant market power (SMP); SMP in a relevant market is the trigger for imposing access obligations or remedies under the EU regulatory framework (see Section 3.9).

The 2009 guidelines also consider the possibility of granting state aid to assist the planned transition to NGA networks. The guidelines start from the premise that the distinction between white, grey and black areas is also relevant for assessing the compatibility of aid aiming to support the rapid development of NGA networks. A given area with no NGA broadband infrastructure is considered to

---

[40] See for example Commission decisions: 2003 Wanadoo France, 2003 Deutsche Telekom, 2007 Telefonica, 2009 Slovak Telecom and 2011 Telekomunikacja Polska (TP).

[41] A full list of Commission decisions on State aid to broadband is available at http://ec.europa.eu/competition/state_aid/legislation/specific_rules.html#broadband.

[42] Community Guidelines for the application of State aid rules in relation to the rapid deployment of broadband networks, OJ C 235, 30.9.2009, p. 7, revised in January 2013 by OJ C 25, 26.1.2013, p. 1.

be a 'white NGA area' but white NGA areas can also include areas where only one basic broadband infrastructure exists (i.e., grey areas for basic broadband).

The 2009 guidelines were reviewed in 2011 and 2012 and a revised version was adopted and published by the Commission in early 2013 (reference *supra*). The main change is that the 2013 guidelines give much more consideration to technological developments and the various ways in which advanced broadband services may be provided, so as to provide guidance on how public support for investment in ultra-fast networks in urban areas may be permitted without harming private investors or jeopardising pro-competitive outcomes.

3.9 The role and influence of the EU regulatory framework on broadband development

Since 2003, EU regulation operates by identifying and defining certain relevant markets and then applying regulatory remedies (such as mandatory access) if it is established that one or more undertakings has or have significant market power (SMP) in the market concerned.

National regulators are obliged to analyse these markets periodically, and apply regulatory remedies if they find SMP, in line with competition law dominance. In a bid to further enhance the consistency and coordination of the approach across all member states, the legislative reforms of 2009 introduced additional requirements, (respectively Article 7a and Article 7 of the revised Framework directive), concerning the regulatory remedies that are applied and the consultation of BEREC, the body of European Regulators.

In the case of broadband, the specific relevant markets to be examined are wholesale physical network infrastructure access and wholesale broadband access. Consequently, access remedies in the broadband area can be applied to both unbundled local loops (or other related facilities) and to virtual broadband inputs such as bitstream access (or other equivalent intermediate inputs to end-user services). Access requirements or remedies have

tended to evolve with market developments and with technical changes in network topology and the spread of fibre closer to end-users.

Two general types of problems have manifested themselves during the regulation of broadband and the mandating of access to the incumbent's network. The first is related to the assessment of market power and the setting of a range or mix of remedies to facilitate entry and competition. The second has been the design and evolution of regulation to best facilitate investment over time, and in particular the upgrading or replacement of local networks.

The main (initial) challenge for national regulatory authorities has been how they set the prices (and other terms) of the various forms of regulated access (their absolute and relative levels) so as to encourage the efficient development of broadband access in the medium term and investment in next generation networks in the longer term. Setting access prices for a number of inputs (e.g., unbundled loops, shared access and bitstream) runs the risk that regulation, rather than the market, will determine the pattern of entry and investment.

To some extent, the problem of regulating the terms (including prices) on which access inputs are made available depends on the view that national authorities take about the feasibility of certain forms of competition, including the ease (or difficulty) of replicating or substituting various network assets, over any given horizon. Even restricting mandated access to local loops (at regulated prices) has an impact on whether firms enter markets and the technologies that they choose.

The problem becomes more complex when applying regulatory remedies to other access inputs such as wholesale bitstream services. Then the regulator has to determine the location or locations in the network where an input is made available, as well as its price (or the way it is determined) relative to other available inputs. Costs will often depend on market uptake whilst end-user prices may be set initially so as to capture market share, so it may be difficult to establish a regulated benchmark for such an input.

Section 3.5 indicated that an important source of broadband competition has come from services offered by other infrastructures such as cable networks. Yet the market analysis approach of the EU regulatory framework focuses on market power at the wholesale or input level. Indeed, the Commission has often been reluctant to consider the indirect pricing constraint coming from cable-based services at the end-user or retail level.[43] This, and related aspects of the methodological approach in the EU framework, has often produced a tendency to over-regulate and require mandatory access to a range of regulated inputs.

But the biggest dilemma for the EU regulatory framework has been the potential impact of regulation on the incentives (for incumbents or entrants) to invest in next-generation access networks. In a bid to address the problem of the longer-term incentives to upgrade or invest in faster or better quality broadband access, the Commission sought to develop common regulatory recommendations specific to the development of NGA networks. This topic is briefly addressed in Section 3.10.

3.10 The dynamics of investing in broadband networks

Section 3.3 gave some insights into the relationship between access regulation and incentives to invest in new technologies or upgrade networks (see also Vogelsang, 2010).

An additional problem arises in the broadband area if and when network topology or technology changes. How should regulation be applied to create conditions for efficient investment in upgraded or next-generation networks as well as maintaining competition over current-generation networks and promoting incentives to build future-generation networks? For instance, the incentives to invest in next-generation networks could be muted if operators anticipate that they will be required to provide access to competitors on favourable terms.

The initial EU regulatory framework legislation provided only limited guidance on economic regulation in the face of market evolution or technological change and innovation. It refers to the

notion of 'emerging markets'. So far this notion has not been used in practice to conclude or argue that an innovation or a new form of access or service qualifies as an emerging market and is exempt from regulation. A related but weaker notion would be that an emerging market is one that constitutes a new market in the competition-policy sense. For example, extremely fast broadband (which could only be provided over local fibre access or its equivalent) might be deemed to qualify as an emerging market (separate from any currently defined broadband markets) and consequently would be free of regulation (at least for a given period).

The main feature of the EU framework in terms of economic regulation is that it is very flexible. Market areas can be added or dropped periodically and individual member states are able to define markets in a way that is appropriate to their national context, including geographical limits. They also have considerable discretion (despite the 2009 legislative revision) concerning the remedies that they apply following a finding of significant market power. Therein lies a major weakness. This very flexibility makes it difficult for a regulator to commit to a given regulatory stance for a sufficient time-scale (e.g., one that surpasses a market review period of about three years).

Given the uncertainty regarding the likely future regulation of advanced broadband services (including those based on digital subscriber loop technologies such as VDSL), the Commission in 2008 launched a series of consultations that culminated in the adoption (in 2010) of a recommendation on regulated access to NGA networks.[44]

The Commission refrained from using the notion of emerging markets to define and place some markets or infrastructure outside the Article 7 regulatory procedures and instead included the concept of a risk premium (incorporated in the allowable return to capital or used in the WACC calculation) to reward the risk associated with sinking investment into fibre and associated technologies.

---

[43] For a fuller explanation and analysis of direct and indirect pricing constraints, see section 4, chapter 9 of Cawley (2007).

[44] Commission Recommendation of 20 September 2010 on regulated access to NGA, (2010/572/EU).

In essence, the NGA recommendation draws on several principles in a bid to maintain investment incentives whilst imposing broadband access regulation whilst markets and network technologies evolve.

The main principle is that investment risk should be rewarded by means of a risk premium. The 'ladder of investment' principle is also maintained. One new principle is that for specific physical bottlenecks to competition, symmetrical access obligations (e.g., mutual access to ducts or rights of way) could complement asymmetrical obligations. The NGA recommendation also emphasised the value of NRAs usefully exploiting geographical market segmentation to differentiate remedies. And the fifth principle is that co-operative arrangements such as co-investment schemes to develop NGA networks are to be welcomed.

Despite the aim of the recommendation to improve regulatory certainty and promote efficient investments, it appears to have reinforced expectations of detailed ongoing access regulation with limited discretion to reward risky or innovative investments. In addition, it has led to a major debate on the appropriate level for the pricing of access to the legacy copper network of the incumbent.

ECTA (the European Competitive Telecommunications Association) has advocated lower access prices for current generation networks (the copper price). Otherwise, ECTA argues, incumbents will simply sweat existing assets and the incentive to move to next generation networks will be artificially low. In contrast ETNO (the European Telecommunications Network Operators' Association) has argued that higher copper prices will make fibre more attractive and will encourage customers to migrate to higher bandwidth services and investments to be made (see also Williamson *et al*, 2011).

The issue of appropriately regulating access to broadband inputs has consequently evolved into a three-fold problem: (a) fixing the price and terms of access to the legacy copper network, (b) considering the influence of these terms on the incentives for users (both final consumers and the intermediate users, who in turn supply services to end-users) to switch or migrate, and (c) deciding whether or not to regulate access to upgraded or next generation networks, and if so, on which terms.

In response to the debate about the pricing of unbundled copper loops and its impact on incentives to invest in fibre or upgrade network data rates, the Commission launched a further consultation in 2012 (building on the series of consultations for the NGA recommendation). It raised two questions in particular: Is there an argument for regulating access to the incumbent's local copper network on the basis of historic (rather than current or forward-looking) cost? and should there be a link between the pricing of access to the copper network and the development of fibre?

The consultation produced a range of very comprehensive and interesting responses and the Commission subsequently published a proposed recommendation on non-discrimination and cost-orientation obligations for key wholesale prices. Despite the sophisticated arguments and analysis that has accompanied the consultation process, the policy debate has focused on whether or not the regulated price of unbundled (copper) local loops should be harmonised in line with a EU benchmark. Such harmonisation could lead to regulated prices being raised or lowered (to the benchmark) depending on the member state concerned, with immediate consequences for the profitability of existing business operations.

Despite the ongoing consultations and recommendations, the dilemma of how to balance access regulation (based on the two relevant broadband markets) with incentives to invest (as described in Section 3.3) appears to remain unsolved and it seems to require an approach that goes beyond the analysis of competitive conditions on the two input markets that are currently the focus of the EU economic regulation.

3.11 Conclusions

This chapter has sought to examine the various influences of European Union legislation, regulation and policies on the development of broadband markets in member states and the investments that take place therein. It has also explored some of the insights that can be gleaned from theory, history and empirical work. The key EU-level influences are the Digital Agenda targets for broadband, the impact of competition policy including state aid rules, and the systematic application of the EU regulatory framework, which in turn is based on competition law principles.

The initial impression is that EU-level influence is extensive. In fact, the overt aim of the EU legislation is to foster a single market for electronic communications services and in particular the development of advanced broadband services, whilst avoiding anti-competitive distortions. In practice, member state markets have developed in very different ways, and the EU-level rules appear to have struggled to find the right balance between the application of a harmonised, coordinated approach and one which is conducive to facilitating efficient market development and investment in different regions.

Indeed, this chapter has pointed to an emerging conflict between the Digital Agenda targets and the regulatory framework. If regulated competition is insufficient to reach the targets and public subsidies are permitted in return for regulated access over lengthy periods of time, such action is likely to further diminish the incentives to build new infrastructure or upgrade existing networks. Consequently, the attempts to adapt the regulatory framework (via the NGA recommendation and/or modifying copper prices) in a bid to encourage new investment appear to be handicapped from the outset. Section 3.2 also indicated that it may be inappropriate to think in terms of a single broadband development model for the EU, given that in a significant number of member states, wireless technologies may be exploited for competing infrastructure investments.

From the material analysed in this chapter, several conclusions are pertinent.

The first is that the extensive empirical analysis that has occurred to date (even drawing on the rich variations in starting points, features and outcomes that are present in Europe) has not provided a clear answer about which factors most strongly influence and encourage broadband development. Much of the analysis has been partisan in trying to show whether access regulation supports or hinders broadband investment and development.

And in many cases the analysis has failed to properly identify and measure dependent or independent variables.

What is missing is a comprehensive analysis over time of the institutional as well as socio-economic and regulatory factors that have affected broadband roll-out and upgrades. For example, are there insights that help to address the dilemmas inherent in the stylised investment models of Section 3.3? It is suggested that the reader needs to turn to the case studies presented in this book to uncover some of those insights.

The second conclusion is that the EU-level rules are struggling to address the dilemma of how to safeguard strong investment incentives. The EU regulatory framework is extremely flexible. Relevant markets can be added or dropped periodically to adapt to technical and market changes. But that flexibility comes at a cost. So too does the narrow focus of market power analysis and the application of remedies to specified input markets. There is a tendency to resort to detailed access regulation – the identification of the input markets leads almost inevitably to remedies being applied there. Most importantly, it is virtually impossible for regulators to commit to a specified policy approach for a lengthy period of time because the framework requires them to continually review markets and apply regulatory remedies. Consequently, the fact that there is such a strong link in the regulatory framework between the oversight of market power and competition-law methods does mean that it is less well-adapted to deal with dynamic aspects including investment and innovation. And, as has been pointed out, the Digital Agenda targets appear to be strengthening the likelihood of a self-fulfilling prophecy of limited competition and detailed access remedies.

A third conclusion is that there does still seem to be sufficient latitude for member states and individual country regulators to work within the EU rules to encourage or facilitate broadband development and investment in ways that suit them. Despite the tendency for the Commission (in response to Article 7 notifications by NRAs concerning their regulatory proposals) to push for more regulation of the two wholesale markets, many member states have pursued their own regulatory agendas.

For example the UK has emphasised functional separation (in a bid to remove discriminatory practices and investment disincentives) and used geographic market segmentation to roll-back access regulation, France has been active in trying to remove or reduce physical impediments to entrants building new networks, whilst Germany has continued to explore the possibilities for using regulatory holidays to improve investment incentives. Other EU member states have their own blend of market and institutional factors affecting broadband development and for those insights the country chapters in this book are invaluable. Conversely, the amendments to the EU regulatory framework in 2009 gave both the Commission and BEREC stronger powers over remedies. However, it remains to be seen whether the increased involvement of BEREC will make it easier or not for member states to develop innovative solutions or differentiate remedies – as occurred, for example, with the geographic differentiation of the wholesale broadband access market, which was approved by the Commission for the UK and Portugal but rejected in several other cases[45].

The fourth conclusion concerns the relationship between the dynamics and trends in EU-level policy (and the recent emphasis on single market integration, rather than regulatory oversight per se), and the broader objectives behind broadband investment goals. Section 3.6, in examining the motives for establishing the regulatory rules at EU level and considering the evolution in regulation and policy, suggested that the return to emphasising single market integration (implying a more centralised policy approach even if implementation and oversight remains predominantly at national level) appears to be more relevant to achieving policy goals concerning the development of EU-wide electronic services (including safeguards for secure personal use) and European mobile communications than the objectives or targets for broadband deployment. It is likely that progress in all three policy areas would help to promote the more fundamental objectives of facilitating growth and innovation (including long-term productivity improvements) but again the first two policy objectives appear to be more crucial. Progress in the first two policy areas can also be expected to help broadband investments: the first by making broadband access more attractive to users; the second by facilitating better exploitation of wireless resources and promoting mobile Internet use across Europe. However, member states have so far been very reluctant to support the changes to spectrum allocation and assignment that would be required for a more pan-European approach to the provision of some mobile communications (and existing operators are more interested in consolidation in segmented national markets than on broader ones). In addition, the development of a genuine EU-wide market for electronic services can be expected to be difficult given the problems experienced in the past: for example, with cross-border broadcasting and (at a broader level) with many of the aims of the Services directive[46]. Consequently, a major impact on broadband investment or growth and innovation more generally is likely to be conditional on progress or changes in the other areas cited.

References

Aghion, P., Bloom, N., Blundell, R., Griffith R. and Howitt, P. (2005). Competition and innovation: an inverted U relationship? The Quarterly Journal of Economics, MIT Press, **120**(2): 701–728.

Alesina, A., Ardagan, S., Nicoletti, G. and Schiantarelli, F. (2005). Regulation and Investment, *Journal of the European Economic Association*, 3(4): 791–825.

Alleman, J., Rappoport, P. and Darby, L. (2005). Optimal pricing with sunk cost and uncertainty (mimeo), TPRC.

Armstrong, M. (1999). Arguments for local loop unbundling (mimeo).

---

[45] See Fabritz and Falck (2013) in conjunction with EC (2007) and EC (2008).

[46] Directive 2006/123/EC of the European Parliament and of the Council of 12 December 2006 on services in the internal market.

Armstrong, M. and Sappington, D. (2004). Regulation, competition and liberalisation (mimeo).

Arnold, J., Nicoletti, G. and Scarpetta, S. (2011). Regulation, resource allocation and productivity growth, *EIB Papers* **16**(1).

Aron, D. and Burnstein, D. (2003). Broadband Adoption in the United States: An Empirical Analysis (mimeo).

Arrow, K. (1962). Economic welfare and the allocation of resources for inventions. In Nelson, R.R. (ed.), The rate and direction of inventive activity: economic and social factors, Princeton University Press, Princeton, also reprinted in Lamberton, D.M., (ed.), 1997, The Economics of Communications and Information. UK: Edward Elgar.

Baake, P., Kamecke, U. and Wey, C. (2005). Efficient regulation of dynamic telecommunications markets and the new regulatory framework (mimeo).

Bacache, M., Bourreau, M. and Gaudinn, G. (2011). Dynamic Entry and investment in new infrastructures: empirical evidence from the telecoms industry. Telecom ParisTech working paper ESS-11-01.

Baumol, W. (1999). Option value analysis and telephone charges, in Alleman, J. and Noam, E. (eds.), *The new investment theory of real options and its implications for telecommunications economics*. Boston: Kluwer Academic.

Briglauer, W., Ecker, G. and Kugler, K. (2011). Regulation and investment in new generation access networks: recent evidence from the European Union Member States, Working Papers, Research Institute for Regulatory Economics, Vienna University.

Cave, M. (2004a). Remedies for broadband services. *Journal of Network Industries*, **5**(1), 23–49.

(2004b). Not regulating broadband wholesale access in the Netherlands, report for OPTA. March.

(2005). Encouraging infrastructure competition via the ladder of investment (mimeo).

Cave, M. and Vogelsang, I. (2003). How access pricing and entry interact, *Telecommunications Policy* **27**, 717–727.

Cave, Rood, Majumdar, Valletti and Vogelsang (2001) cited in Cave and Vogelsang (2003).

Cawley, R. (2007). The new EU Approach to sector regulation in the network infrastructure industries, PhD Thesis, Delft University of Technology.

Chang, H. Kosler, H. and Majumdar, S. (2003). Regulation and investment behaviour in the telecommunications sector. *Telecommunications Policy*, **27**, 677–700.

Crandall, R., Eisenach, J. and Ingraham, A. (2012). The long-run effects of copper unbundling and the implications for fiber (mimeo).

Crandall, R., Ingraham, A. and Singer, H. (2004). Do unbundling policies discourage CLEC facilities-based investment? *Topics in Economic Analysis and Policy* 4.

Crandall, R.W. and Jackson, C. L. (2001). The $500 Billion Opportunity: The Potential economic benefit of widespread diffusion of broadband Internet access,. *Criterion Economics*, July.

Di Mauro, L., and Inotai, A. (2004). Market analyses under the new regulatory framework for electronic communications: context and principles behind the Commission's first veto decision. *Competition Policy Newsletter*, No.2 Summer 52–55.

Distaso, W, Lupi, P. and Manenti, F. (2006). Platform competition and broadband uptake: theory and empirical evidence from the European Union, *Information Economics and Policy*, **18**(1).

Dixit, A. and Pindyck, R. (1994). *Investment under uncertainty*, Princeton University Press.

Dotecon and Criterion Economics (2003). Competition in broadband provision and its implications for regulatory policy, October.

Doyle, C. (2000). Local loop unbundling and regulatory risk. *Journal of Network Industries* 1, 33–54.

EC (2007). Comments pursuant to Article 7(3) of Directive 2002/21/EC: Wholesale broadband access in the UK (UK/2007/0733).

(2008). Comments pursuant to Article 7(3) of Directive 2002/21/EC: Wholesale broadband access in Portugal (PT/2008/0851).

Fabritz, N. and Falck, O. (2013). Investment in broadband infrastructure under local deregulation: evidence from the UK broadband market, CESifo working paper No. 4277.

Ford, G.S. and Spiwak, L.J. (2004). What is the effect of regulation on broadband investment, Phoenix Center Policy Paper, no 12–05.

Fudenberg, D. and Tirole, J. (2000). Pricing a network good to deter entry. *Journal of Industrial Economics* **XLVIII**(4).

Gabel, D.J. (1994). Competition in a Network Industry: The Telephone Industry, 1894–1910, *Journal of Economic History*, **54**(3).

Gans, J. (2001). Regulating private infrastructure investment: Optimal pricing for access to essential facilities, *Journal of Regulatory Economics*, **20**, 167–189.

Gans, J. and King, S. (2003). Access holidays for network investment, *Agenda* **10**(2), 163–178.

Gans, J. and Williams, P. (1999). Access regulation and the timing of infrastructure investment, *Economic Record*, **79**, 127–138.

Guthrie, G. (2006). Regulating infrastructure: the impact on risk and investment, *Journal of Economic Literature*, **44**, 925–972.

Haltiwanger, J. (2011). Firm dynamics and productivity growth, EIB Papers **16**(1).

Hausman, J. and Sidak, G. (1999). A consumer-welfare approach to the mandatory unbundling of telecommunications networks, *Yale Law Journal*, **109**, 420–505.

Hazlett, T. and Bazelon, C. (2005). Regulated unbundling of telecommunications networks: a stepping stone to facilities-based competition? (mimeo). TPRC 2005.

Laffont, J-J. and Tirole, J. (1993). *A theory of incentives in procurement and regulation*, Cambridge, MA, MIT Press.

Lemstra, W. (2006). The Internet bubble – the impact on the development path of the telecommunication sector, PhD Dissertation, Faculty of Technology, Policy and Management, TU Delft.

Liberty Global (2012). Re-thinking the Digital Agenda for Europe. www.libertyglobal.com/ PDF/public-policy/LGI-report-Re-thinking-the-Digital-Agenda-for-Europe.pdf

McMorrow, K. and Roeger, W. (2009). R&D capital and economic growth: the empirical evidence, EIB Papers **14**(1).

Papadias, L., Chirico, F. and Gaal. N. (2009). The new state aid broadband guidelines: not all black and white, *EC Competition Policy Newsletter*, Number **3**, 2009.

Pindyck, R. (2004). Mandatory unbundling and irreversible investment in telecom networks. NBER working paper no. 10287.

(2005). Pricing capital under mandatory unbundling and facilities sharing. NBER working paper no. 11225.

Sapir, A. (2004). An agenda for a growing Europe: making the EU economic system deliver, (The Sapir Report), Oxford University Press.

Sharkey, W. (1982), *The theory of natural monopoly*, Cambridge University Press.

Sidak, G. and Spulber, D. (1998). Givings, takings and fallacy of forward-looking costs, *New York University Law Review*, **5**, 1068–1164.

Spulber, D. and Sidak, J. G. (1997). Network access pricing and deregulation, July 1997.

Tirole, J. (1988). *The Theory of Industrial Organisation*, Cambridge, MA: MIT Press.

Ungerer, H. (2011). Back to the roots: the 1987 telecom green paper 25 years after – has European telecom liberalization fulfilled its promise for Europe in the Internet age? *Info* **16**(2): 14–24.

Valletti, T., and Estache, A. (1998). The theory of access pricing: an overview for infrastructure regulators. *World Bank*.

Valletti, T. (2003). The theory of access pricing and its linkages with investment incentives. *Telecommunications Policy*, **27**, 659–676.

Vogelsang, I. (2003). Price regulation of access to telecommunications networks. *Journal of Economic Literature*, **41**, 830–862.

Vogelsang, I (2010). Incentive regulation, investments and technological change, ifo working paper No. 2964.

Wallsten, S. (2006). Broadband and unbundling regulations in OECD countries, AEI Brookings Joint Centre for Regulatory Studies, working paper 06–16.

Wallsten, S. and Hausladen, S. (2009). Net neutrality, unbundling and their effects on international investment in next generation networks, *Review of Network Economics* **8**(1).

Waverman L. (2003). Regulatory incentives and deregulation in telecommunications, in C. Robinson (ed), *Competition and Regulation in Utility Markets*, E. Elgar, 138–159.

Waverman, L., Meschi, M., Reillier, B. and Dasgupta, K. (2007). *Access regulation and infrastructure investment in the telecommunications sector: an empirical investigation*, LECG working paper.

Williamson, B., Black, D. and Wilby, J. (2011). Costing Methodology and the Transition to Next Generation Access, a report for ETNO, March.

Wood, L., Zarakas, W.P. and Sappington, D. (2004). Wholesale pricing and local exchange competition, The Brattle Group.

Zarakas, W.P., Woroch, G., Wood, L., McFadden, D., Ilias, N. and Liu, P. (2005). Access pricing and investment in local exchange infrastructure, The Brattle Group.

PART 2

Case studies

The Netherlands

WOLTER LEMSTRA

4.1 Introduction

The dynamics of the broadband market in the Netherlands are a result of the interplay between private and public actors over a long period of time, which has led to a technological duopoly of operators exploiting the PSTN-telephony and the RTV-cable infrastructures. The infrastructure-based competition complemented by access-based competition has provided the country with a leading position in the broadband league tables, within Europe and globally[1] – a position that is now being challenged by a slower adoption of mobile broadband and by the investment challenges associated with the next technological transition, the introduction of Fiber-to-the-Home.

Both the public switched telephone network (PSTN) and the radio and television cable distribution network (RTV-cable) have reached a very high level of penetration, reaching nearly 100 per cent and 95 per cent of households, respectively. While narrowband access to the Internet started with dial-up connections using the PSTN, it has been the RTV-cable network that has led the development towards broadband, exploiting the inherently higher bandwidth of the coax cable, compared to the twisted copper pairs used in the telephone network.

The techno-duopoly has led to the extended exploitation of the existing infrastructures by the incumbent operators. Although deployment of fibre has occurred in the backbone, in metropolitan networks as well as in business parks, it did not reach private residences. Hence, municipalities eager to provide high quality communication services to their citizens and businesses have

declared 'market failure'. Together with housing corporations, they have taken initiatives for FttH deployment. This has led a new actor to appear in the broadband market, Reggefiber – a construction company building open passive FttH infrastructure for service operators to exploit; fundamentally changing the market dynamics. This prompted a strategic response by KPN, the incumbent PSTN operator, to take a minority share in Reggefiber.

In this summary of broadband market developments we can already recognize the interplay between the most important actors: the telecommunication (telecom) entrepreneurs, both incumbents and entrants, local government and housing corporations. In our quest for a deep understanding of the dynamics of broadband markets and our desire to make forward-looking statements with respect to the development of these markets, an appreciation of the historical development of the 'narrow band' markets is considered highly relevant, as it provides the fundamental infrastructure for the development of broadband markets.[2] Moreover, the historical account will provide us with an appreciation of the roles the various actors have played, insights into the development of market and industry dynamics and a deeper understanding of the social and political context of the industry, as well as any path dependencies. The periodization as introduced by Noam is applied (see Chapter 2 Research context and perspective, Section 2.4)

---

[1] See Chapter 1, Introduction providing the quantitative data at the beginning of the case study period and at the end of the case study period.

[2] Narrowband is defined in the context of this book as data rates below or equal to 144 kbit/s and broadband as data rates higher than 144 kbit/s; in other words narrowband includes dial-up Internet access using 56k modems and ISDN, broadband starts with the application of ADSL and DOCSIS 1.0. This definition is based on the 13th Implementation Report of the European Commission, Volume 2, p92: http://ec.europa.eu/information_society/policy/ecomm/library/communications_reports/annualreports/13th/index_en.htm.

This case study[3] is structured as follows: In Section 4.2 the development of the PSTN and the RTV-cable networks are captured, including the process of telecom reform, highlighting the role of entrepreneurs, municipalities and the central government in its development. In Section 4.3 the emergence of the Internet is covered. Section 4.4 follows with the development of broadband Internet access, including the role of ADSL and DOCSIS. In Section 4.5 the focus is on the first steps towards FttH, the early initiatives by the incumbent operator KPN and the role of the government. In Section 4.6 the role of municipalities in FttH development is discussed. In Section 4.7 follows a review of the implications of the transition to All-IP by KPN. Section 4.8 is dedicated to the emergence of Reggefiber. In Section 4.9 a review is provided of the broadband market today and the realization of the Digital Agenda targets. In Section 4.10 the salient items of this case study are identified as well as experiences that may be worth sharing.

Please note that, at various points in the case study, multiple perspectives are provided on developments in the same period: e.g., from the perspective of the entrepreneurs followed by the perspective of the government, or from the perspective of the telecommunications industry followed by the perspective of the radio and television sector. This means in the story line a return to the beginning of the particular period under review.

The interpretation of our case study findings in the broader context of European broadband market developments is the subject of Chapter 16 – the cross-case analysis.

4.2 Infrastructure developments as precursors to broadband

In this Section we capture those historical aspects of infrastructure developments that are relevant to explain the dynamics of broadband markets in the

Netherlands. Of particular interest are the changing roles of the key actors: the private firms, the municipalities and the national government.

4.2.1 Telephone 1.0 and policy 1.0

In the development of the telephone network in the Netherlands, private entrepreneurship played a leading role. For instance, the City of Amsterdam selected the Nederlandsche Bell Telephoon Maatschappij (NBTM) to build a telephone network under license from US-based International Bell Telephone Corporation (IBTC).[4] The network was placed into service in 1881. Private initiatives resulted in 43 local networks being created in the major cities. These private networks were operational for a significant period of time, between 10 and 34 years, for an average of 24.5 years. In 1896 upon the expiry of the NBTM license, the City of Amsterdam decided based on public interest considerations (quality and not-for profit objectives) to assume the exploitation of the local telephone network. The municipalities started to assume ownership and operational control with the transfer of the NBTM network in Amsterdam in 1896. This example was followed by seven transfers from private to municipal ownership and twenty new municipal network start-ups.[5] The municipal ownership lasted from 3 to 44 years, on average 21 years. From 1906 the state began to build and exploit new networks and to take over the private and municipal networks, essentially starting in 1916 and completed in 1927, with the exception of the municipal networks in the three largest cities: Amsterdam, Rotterdam and

---

[3] The critical review and suggestions for improvement of an earlier version of this chapter by Peter Anker, Paul Brand, Rob van Esch, Nico Van Eijk, Nicolai van Gorp, Frank van Iersel and Kees Neggers are highly appreciated.

[4] IBTC (International Bell Telephone Company, set up to exploit the Bell patents outside the USA) was selected based on having the lowest end-user tariffs (Hfl 118 per year), the highest revenues for the municipality (21.5% of gross proceeds) and the installation and exploitation of the network granted to a Dutch organisation, NBTM. (Hogesteeger, 1976; De Wit, 1998)

[5] Many of the local networks were small, outdated and suffering from underinvestment. This was an outcome of the license condition, which stated that the municipality would obtain the network at taxation value at the end of the licensing period or, alternatively, the licensee would have to dismantle the network.

the Hague which transitioned in 1940 under the Nazi occupation.

For the construction of the inter-local network only one licence was granted, to NBTM which subsequently operated the network as a monopoly. The inter-local network transitioned to the State in 1897 after just 10 years of operation. (Schuilenga, Tours, Visser and Bruggeman, 1981; De Wit, 1998)

4.2.2 Radio 1.0 and policy 1.0

The first experimental radio broadcasting service in the Netherlands was provided by a radio-amateur à Steringa Idzerda in The Hague in 1919. (De Boer, 1969; Blanken, 1992) In 1923 the Nederlandsche Seintoestellenfabriek (NSF) also started broadcasting services in Hilversum, using a license for manufacturing and testing. The content of the broadcasts was provided by the 'Hollandse Draad-looze Omroep', the precursor of the Dutch broadcasting membership-associations (AVRO, KRO, NCRV, VARA, VPRO, each inspired by a particular world view). Philips was a major sponsor of these broadcasts. In 1935 the Dutch government consolidated all broadcast transmitters under a new entity, NOZEMA, which undertook renewal of the transmitters in a new location – Lopik.[6] (Vogt, 1958; De Boer, 1969; Vles, 2008)

In 1924, the first wire-based radio transmission was started by Bauling on a commercial basis in the town of Koog aan de Zaan. For the subscribers the service was cheap compared to owning a radio set: only a headphone or loudspeaker was required, hence the service appealed to the working class. Radio distribution licenses were granted on a non-exclusive basis. The industry was led by entrepreneurs, essentially in a 'competition for the market'. A total of 800 private and municipally owned radio-distribution networks were built, with 35 networks in The Hague and 200 in Amsterdam of which only 9 served more than 1,000 subscribers.[7]

Some radio-distribution organisations operated as cooperatives, whereby volunteering members enabled lower tariffs. In some cities (e.g., The Hague) the telephone network was used for the distribution of the radio signals. Also 20 municipalities became radio-distribution operators exploiting a local monopoly position.

From 1931, these networks were directly linked to the radio stations by cable, thereby facilitating 'high quality' transmission.[8] Radio-distribution peaked with 51 per cent of total radio users by the end of 1932, a position unique in Europe. In 1940 under the Nazi regime, the radio-distribution systems were placed under the responsibility of the PTT. As upgrading towards TV distribution was not feasible, the decision to terminate radio-distribution service was taken in 1964, and the process was completed in 1975. (Schrijver, 1983; Arnbak, Van Cuilenburg and Dommering, 1991; Bordewijk, 2004)

4.2.3 Television 1.0 and policy 1.0

Television broadcasting on a regular basis was introduced in the Netherlands in 1951. Shortly thereafter, the use of equipment for the central reception and distribution of the signal (CAI) was introduced, primarily by housing corporations in high-rise buildings. These systems improved signal quality and reduced the need for individual antennas. The use of these systems was legally the prerogative of the PTT, which had the monopoly on distribution of broadcasting signals. However, during the 1950s and 1960s the practice was condoned for practical reasons. In 1963 the government proposed a central antenna system (CAS) to be built by the PTT. Casema, subsidiary of Nozema, jointly owned by PTT and the broadcasting organizations, was set up to provide the service. Pilot projects were conducted in The Hague. However, this initiative was rejected in parliament in 1975. In the same year, the monopoly position of the PTT was replaced by a concession system, which allowed the legalization of the CAI-systems.

---

[6] To avoid each broadcasting company having to install its own radio transmitter and for cost-saving reasons.

[7] By 1940, 800 radio-distribution networks, of which 20 were owned by the municipality, were serving 411,232 subscribers. (Arnbak, Van Cuilenburg and Dommering, 1991)

[8] During the evenings Radio Hilversum II, operating in the MW band, would be subject to interference from a radio station in Hungary.

Only one concession was made available per municipality and the municipality had a preferential position to exploit the concession or have the concession exploited by a third party.[9] Hence, cable networks became predominantly owned by the local governments. The exploitation of the networks was often delegated to the local or regional energy company or to private firms; also Casema was positioned to exploit these networks.[10] The future introduction of optical fibre to the home was recognized but considered largely incompatible with the cable systems and, based on a depreciation period of 10–15 years, it was not expected before the years 1990–2000. A research project DIVAC (digital subscriber access) was begun to explore the related challenges in 1982.[11] (Jelgersma and Titulaer, 1981; Schrijver, 1983; Davids, 1999; NLKabel, 2009)

4.2.4 Reflection on period 1.0

The important role of the municipalities in the development of the telephone and cable networks as described above should not come as a surprise, as municipalities have had an important role in infrastructure development in general. Consider, for instance, the development of the road system, the drinking water supply and the sewage system, as well as the local distribution networks for electricity and city gas (see for instance: Milward, 2005; Van der Woud, 2007; and also the Stadtwerke in Germany, Chapter 8). In their objective

---

[9] The municipalities discouraged the use of individual antennas and thereby stimulated the use of the CAI systems. The use of CAI systems was also financially attractive, as it generated income from the granting of rights-of-way. As the CAI systems were used for RTV only, there was no use for the business sector.

[10] In 1994, 56% of the licenses were still owned by the local government, 16% by a privatized local energy company and 6% by a regionally operating private company. The exploitation was handled in 34% of the cases by the privatized energy company, in 15% by the municipality, 15% by a regionally operating private company, and in 14% by a nationally operating private company. (VNG, 1994)

[11] The DIVAC project was aimed at obtaining technological experience and was carried out jointly by Philips, the PTT, and the Universities of Technology Delft and Eindhoven. (Arnbak, 1986)

of creating an attractive economic and social climate for business and citizens, good quality infrastructures play an important role. Moreover, competition between municipalities is to a large extent based on infrastructure supply: hence, their continued interest in telecom infrastructure, resulting in their current involvement in the roll-out of fibre.

4.2.5 Telecom 2.0 and policy 2.0

Perspective on the incumbent

The privatization of the incumbent operator PTT ran in parallel with the European Reform debate and was triggered by concerns voiced by the business sector in 1981. The emerging 'Information Society' was expected to require fundamental changes to allow the full benefits to be reaped. Subsequently, the Ministry of 'Verkeer en Waterstaat' (Public Works), responsible for the supervision of the PTT as one of its Departments, initiated the 'Swarttouw Committee' to investigate the (future) role of the PTT in the development of the ICTs and to identify the possible issues. The report was published in 1982. In the summer of 1984, the 'Steenbergen Committee' was installed to advise on the future position and structure of the PTT and on the required regulatory supervision. This Committee published its recommendations in 1985, which led to the decision to transform the PTT into a separate legal entity, initially with the state as the only shareholder, in 1986. The Committee also proposed the functional separation of the network and the licensed public service from those services being provided in competition; however, this suggestion was not adopted by the government. (Arnbak, 1986; Davids, 1999)

In June 1994, the privatisation process started with an initial public offering (IPO). The IPO covered 30 per cent of the shares. The company obtained the right to issue preferential shares as a way to fend off a potential hostile take-over.[12] Also the state, as remaining majority shareholder, could issue preferential shares to prevent a

---

[12] This instrument was used in 2013 to fend off the take-over attempt by Carlos Slim of América Móvil.

take-over by a candidate considered undesirable by the state. The state retained a so-called 'Golden Share', allowing it the right of veto on tariff increases, investment plans and merger plans.[13] These rights were deemed necessary to protect the public interest. Hence, in 1999 the state had to approve the acquisition by KPN of E-Plus, a mobile operator in Germany. This triggered discussion about the need to retain the 'Golden Share'. Partial state ownership and control was also said to have frustrated the intended merger between KPN and Telefónica. In 2003 the ownership by the state of the 'Golden Share' in KPN was challenged by the European Commission. At that time the State retained a 19 per cent share in KPN. Late in 2005, as the state's shares had fallen below 10 per cent, the Ministry of Finance announced its intention to relinquish the 'Golden Share'. In the fall of 2006 the state sold its remaining shares, completing an institutional change process that was triggered 25 years earlier in 1981. (NRC, 1994, 1999; Van Wijnbergen, 2000; Buddingh, 2003; NRC, 2003, 2005b, 2005a)

Perspective on the entrants

With the liberalization, new entrants emerged as subsidiaries of utility companies starting to exploit their internal communications infrastructures for external users, such as Enertel (energy) and Telfort (railways).[14] Operators of Dutch-origin as well as operators from abroad, such as Versatel and Tele2 respectively, entered the market based on carrier resale and later local loop unbundling. MFS, for example, entered the market to serve the business sector, in particular the financial sector.[15] Also joint ventures were established, such as KPNQwest – KPN the Dutch incumbent with Qwest from the USA – in pan-European fibre

networking. Other international and pan-European carriers that became active in the Netherlands targeting local operators and large multi-national corporations included AT&T, BT, COLT, Global Crossing, GTS, Interoute, Level3 and Worldcom/MCI. Moreover, KPN ventured abroad to invest in liberalizing incumbents (e.g., Eircom, Ireland, and SPT, Czech Republic), participated in new ventures (e.g., Utel in the Ukraine) and acquired new companies (e.g., E-Plus, the third largest mobile operator in Germany).

4.2.6 Cable 2.0 and policy 2.0

Already in 1981, the 'Swarttouw Committee' had recognized that the cable distribution networks could develop towards a broadband network by facilitating two-way communication. If these CATV networks were connected on a national scale, they could form a competitive threat for the PTT. As the telecom policy was based on a primary role for the PTT, the Committee suggested mitigating this threat by creating an integrated network (Davids, 1999). This position by the Committee was subject to both support and critique. The Scientific Council for Government Policy (WRR) concluded that cable networks were not necessarily to be integrated with the telephone network. The Ministry of Economic Affairs strongly opposed a monopoly of the PTT on all infrastructural networks.[16] The opposition resulted in the appointment of the 'Zegveld Committee' to investigate the issue. Their report, published in 1987, recommended that integration should take place as part of one future broadband fibre network for audio, image and data communication. In 1988, this option was included in an update of the Telecom Law. However, in 1992 it became clear that the cable operators, united in sector organisation VECAI, opposed the integration. In the same year the Parliament formally rejected the option. (Eenhoorn, 1994; Davids, 1999)

The EU-initiated Reform, which required the transposition of Directives into national legislation,

---

[13] Additional protection was provided through the corporate structure as a 'structuurvennootschap'. (Wessels, 1994)

[14] Based on an interim law enacted in 1996 and ahead of the EU regulations, the government granted two licenses for fixed telecommunications service provision on the basis of a beauty contest.

[15] Source: www.computable.nl/artikel/nieuws/205041/250449/mfs-communications-in-hoofdstad.html.

[16] Note that at that time PTT was still a department of the Ministry of Public Works.

changed the position of the cable operators vis-à-vis KPN. They were allowed to interconnect their networks, which was done mainly through optical fibre. The change in telecom policy brought an end to the concession system and, hence, municipally owned networks could be acquired by private entities.[17] By 2001, the result was that 29 cable operators were operating 647 cable networks, in a total of 504 municipalities, serving 6,159,972 subscribers. The consolidation process continued during the following decade around three firms: (1) UPC – owned by US-based Liberty Global, which acquired the cable network in Amsterdam (A2000[18]) in 1998; (2) Essent Kabelcom, a division of the energy company operating mainly in the north-eastern and south-eastern part of the country, combined with Multikabel (operating under the temporary name Zesko); and (3) Casema operating in the western and central part. The latter two merged to become Ziggo in 2008, leading to two major cable companies, Ziggo and UPC, essentially RTV monopolies in their own territories sharing the market, with at the second tier Caiway as the main player operating in the western and central part of the country. (Van Bockxmeer, Poel, Hulshof and Rutten, 2002; De Leeuw, 2009; NLKabel, 2009)

4.2.7 Reflections on the period 2.0

This period provides a nice illustration of the policy formation process in the Netherlands, with a strong emphasis on committees preparing policy advice based on broad stakeholder interactions, a pattern that we can observe again in the context of polices regarding broadband development.

The period has been relatively successful due to a central government advancing the liberalisation agenda: for example, market entry now requires only registration, not a license, and local governments facilitate entry by applying a 'liberal' application of the rights-of-way policy.

While the telecom reform resulted in new players entering the PSTN sector, thereby increasing competition, it led to consolidation of the local and regional RTV-cable monopolies into two major regional monopolies and a few smaller ones. This set the conditions for a techno-duopoly to emerge with the introduction of the Internet: on the one hand, between KPN, the dominant player in the PSTN, with access-based operators such as BBned and Tele2, and, on the other, the RTV-cable operators UPC and Ziggo.

4.3 Emergence of the internet in the Netherlands

As the Internet developed within the academic research institutes in the USA, the academic community in the Netherlands also played a leading role. But it was the (albeit closely related) Hack-tic community of self-declared 'techno-anarchists' that provided the first Internet access services outside the academic institutions.

In the following section, the leading role of SURFnet in the development of the Internet in the Netherlands is highlighted through an account of the institutional and technological developments.[19]

4.3.1 Leading networking role by academic community

Concerns regarding the impact of micro-electronic technologies on employment led to an investigation by the Rathenau Committee. This Committee emphasized the benefits of ICTs and advised the government to introduce a more aggressive policy on the use of ICTs in 1978. This led in 1984 to the publication of recommendations under the heading 'Informatica Stimuleringsplan', which included initiatives and funding to promote ICT usage in

---

[17] As a consequence KPN had to relinquish its shares in cable operator CASEMA.

[18] The municipal cable network of Amsterdam (KTA) was first acquired by United Philips Communications (UPC), a joint activity of Philips and US West, and the network was named A2000. The consortium became listed on the stock exchange and during the euphoric period in the late 1990s it was acquired by Liberty Global.

[19] Further information on the role of SURFnet can be found in 'ICT innovation as practiced by SURFnet' (Van Iersel and Neggers, 2010) and in the evaluation report of the government funding (Boekholt, Deuten, Nagle and Zuijdam, 2008).

higher education. The academic community responded and obtained governmental support for the development of a multi-year project plan, released in 1985 by the Samenwerkende Universitaire Rekenfaciliteiten (SURF) coordinating committee. In 1986 the government allocated NLG 300 million (approx. EUR 140 million) for the initial period 1987–1990 of implementation by the SURF Foundation. The data networking services to the universities and academic research centres were to be provided in cooperation with the incumbent telecom operator PTT (now KPN), for which they created a new legal entity SURFnet BV, with 51 per cent of the shares owned by the SURF Foundation and 49 per cent by the PTT.[20] The fourteen universities in the Netherlands agreed to obtain their data networking services from SURFnet for the next four years. (Verhoog, 2008)

On 25 April 1986 the management of the.nl domain name registration was granted to CWI. Piet Beertema became the Dutch equivalent of John Postel, until SIDN (Stichting Internet Domeinregistratie Nederland) as a foundation assumed this role in 1997. On 17 November 1988, EUnet, with its central node at CWI, received 'Internet connected status' with the NSFnet and the first connection from the Netherlands to the Internet was established by the academic research community of CWI in Amsterdam, using the first '.nl' country domain name: cwi.nl. Kees Neggers assumed chairmanship of RIPE-NCC, the Network Coordination Centre for European IP organisations.[21]

In 1987 SURFnet1 started to connect all fourteen universities using Datanet1, the packet-switched network based on the X.25 protocol operated by the PTT.[22] However, the ultimate aim was to develop one common network based on OSI-protocols that would meet the requirements of the user community. Hence, the deployment of SURFnet2, based on OSI and X.25, as of 1989.[23] In 1990 SURFnet2 was fully operational using 64 kbit/s links and also provided transport facilities based on the TCP/IP-protocol using a Cisco router, introduced following its popularity in the USA.[24] TCP/IP appeared to operate much better than expected and by the end of 1990 the decision was taken to focus on TCP/IP and to create a multi-protocol infrastructure SURFnet3, with 2 Mbit/s connections; the first step towards broadband access. By the time of its completion in 1992, TCP/IP had become the dominant protocol. In a parallel effort, SURFNet together with NORDUnet[25] created 'Ebone', the first European IP-backbone to become operational, in 1992. In the same year Erik Huizer became a member of the IETF and Kees Neggers was one of the founders of ISOC. (Verhoog, 2008)

As the Internet became more easily accessible (e.g., through the introduction of the Mosaic browser in 1993) SURFnet observed strong growing traffic volumes and decided to become the initial customer of KPN in the implementation of an ATM-based network under the name of SURFnet4 in 1994, initially providing up to 34 Mbit/s access connections and a 155 Mbit/s data rate in the backbone; to become an IP-based backbone network with data rates of 155 and 622 Mbit/s. (Verhoog, 2008)

In 1994 the plans for the Amsterdam Internet Exchange were announced. Through the AMS-IX Internet service providers (ISPs) exchange Internet traffic, a service initially managed by SURFnet. In 1997 twenty participants created the AMS-IX

---

[20] Note that at the time the PTT still had the monopoly on telecommunications infrastructure.

[21] Source: Kees Neggers and interview with Piet Beerta documented at www.netkwesties.nl/636/aartsvaders-nederlandse-internet.htm.

[22] Following a decision in 1976, Datanet 1 was officially inaugurated using ITT DPS 1500 equipment in 1982. The access data rates were 2400, 4800 and 9600 bit/s via the PSTN access lines and 48 kbit/s using leased lines. For a 2400 bit/s connection the monthly subscription fee was Hfl 400, plus 2.5 ct per call and per minute and 0.25 ct per data segment of 512 bits. Datanet 1 provided for

international connectivity, including Telenet and Tymnet in the USA. (Hamelberg, 1984)

[23] From the start of SURFnet the project funding by the government has been used to implement the new (innovative) network facilities, the institutes being connected have provided for the costs of operation. The use of open tendering in procurement of the network components and services became a matter of principle. (SURFnet, 2009)

[24] In 1999 SURFnet terminated the X.25 based services.

[25] NORDUnet combines the networks of the universities in Norway, Sweden, Finland, Denmark and Iceland since 1985.

Association to establish a Limited Liability Company (as a not-for-profit cooperative) to assume the exploitation and operational management of the exchange in 2002. In 2003, with 178 participants, AMS-IX became the largest Internet exchange worldwide. (Verhoog, 2008)

In 2000 the pilot phase of SURFnet5 started with 80 Gbit/s DWDM on glass fibre in the backbone and access connections of up to 20 Gbit/s. The network was completed by early 2002, connecting 170 institutes with approximately 500,000 users as of 2008. Even higher capacity needs were foreseen; hence, a hybrid network was developed providing IP-services next to optical network services as part of SURFnet6.[26] Following experiments started in 2002, a point-to-point network of optical light paths ([lambda] s) was implemented in 2004 with a node in the Netherlands called 'NetherLight' connecting to 'StarLight' in Chicago. The first 10 Gbit/s lightpath was delivered between the University of Groningen and SARA[27] in Amsterdam in support of the Lofar project in early 2006.[28] By the end of 2007, lightpath #220 was realized, the demand being much higher than anticipated, in particular for the Optical Private Network (OPN) feature. 'NetherLight', the node located at SARA in Amsterdam, became the European node in the GLORIAD network, a research network initiative to connect the USA, Russia and China through a global optical ring. (Verhoog, 2008; SURFnet, 2009)

In a parallel development, student housing complexes also were connected to SURFnet to provide students the same facilities as they enjoyed at the university campus. In 1990 ninety students of the University of Nijmegen were connected using the RTV-cable network and in Wageningen a pilot project was also set up. In 1998 the project 'Student Online' was aimed at connecting as many students and university staff as possible using the telephone network. In 1998–9 a thousand people were connected to SnelNet in Amsterdam, a collaboration between KPN, SURFnet and NOB Interactive Media providing 2 Mbit/s ADSL connections with a first trial of delay TV.[29] In 2000 further implementation pilot projects started with ADSL in Amsterdam, Delft and Twente, as well as the 'Fibre to the Dormitory' project which connected 2,600 student apartments in Delft with data rates of 10–100 Mbit/s. This project was followed by similar projects in the university cities of Groningen, Nijmegen, Enschede, Utrecht and Wageningen. Also in 2002, in the 'Freeband Impuls' project commissioned by the Ministry of Economic Affairs, SURFnet started trials to provide wireless access across multiple university sites for students and staff, leading to the now globally available eduroam service supporting users worldwide. (Verhoog, 2008) SURFnet continues to drive the technology agenda, for instance in cooperation with mobile providers in the integration of 4G and Wi-Fi as part of the GigaPort3 project.

4.3.2 Internet access for the business user

In the business community, data networking between IBM computers was facilitated by V-net, a host-to-host file transport network, using synchronous data link protocols (SDLC) developed from 1975 onward. By 1979 it included 285 nodes in Europe, Asia and North America serving some 1,400 computer systems. The early connections operated on dial-up telephone lines supporting data rates of 1200 to 2400 bit/s. (Van de Ven, 1984; Wikipedia, 2009d) In 1989, NLnet started to provide Internet access to enterprises, using dial-up connections. (Verhoog, 2008) This evolved into

---

[26] Funding of SURFnet6 has been obtained under the BSIK program, which involved a competition among contending projects and required a research dimension, which was at large provided by the University of Amsterdam. (SURFnet, 2009)

[27] SARA was founded in 1971 under the name Stichting Academisch Rekencentrum Amsterdam by the University of Amsterdam (UvA), Vrije Universiteit Amsterdam (VU) and the Stichting Mathematisch Centrum (now Centrum Wiskunde & Informatica). Initially SARA's work focused on data processing activities for the three founders.

[28] Lofar: Low Frequency Array, a novel software-based radio telescope. Using a large array of small omnidirectional antennas the signals are combined in software to create the image. (Astron, 2006)

[29] Source: www.computerwoorden.nl/direct–14656–Snelnet.htm.

dedicated Internet access and IP-networking services provided by specialized companies, such as BBned, Easynet, Eurofiber, Tele2, UNET and the local branches of global operators such as AT&T, BT Global Services, Colt and Verizon.

4.3.3 Internet access for the residential user

Anticipating growing demand for end-to-end digital services the PTTs under the auspices of the ITU agreed to create a new, fully digital, circuit-switched system called ISDN (Integrated Services Digital Network). The ISDN would build upon the already digital backbone network (IDN – Integrated Digital Network) and involve upgrading the access network to digital, providing narrowband access at 2×64 kbit/s (basic rate) to the residential user and 2 Mbit/s (primary rate) to the business user. The elaboration of the ISDN recommendations in the CCITT required three four-year study periods to be completed by1988. The development of the European standard by ETSI was completed in the early 1990s. Testing ISDN in practice started with a pilot project in Rotterdam in 1987.[30] Making the telephone switching systems ISDN-ready and having ISDN compatible terminals available led to a general introduction of the service in 1993. (Kaasschieter, 1985; Ekkelenkamp, Verstraaten and Wijbrands, 1992; Tanenbaum, 1996)

The same year the Mosaic browser was introduced to unlock the Internet for the wider public and the Hack-Tic[31] community established XS4ALL, the first dial-up Internet access provider open to the general public. (Hack-Tic, 1993)[32] In January 1994, in cooperation with De

Balie[33], followed the inauguration of FreeNet 'Digital Stad Amsterdam' aimed at bringing together citizens and policy makers in an online community (Meerman, 2004). VuurWerk Internet[34] started in 1996 as the first entity to provide web hosting and domain name registration services. (Wikipedia, 2010b)

While the notion of integrated services such as telephony, telefax, textfax, videotext, teletext, video and teleworking, based on circuit switching was not a huge success, ISDN did provide Internet access at 64 kbit/s at the price of a telephone call. By October 2000 17 per cent of internet access connections were using ISDN.[35] (CBS, 2001)

In 1996 CAI Westland[36], a cable network operator in the western part of the country, was the first cable operator to provide Internet access, using the DEMOS-1 system of DeltaKabel Telecom at a data rate of 115 kbit/s, using a flat rate. (Verbree, 1997; Wikipedia, 2010a)[37] Shortly thereafter, the major cable network providers became Internet access providers: UPC using the Chello brand name, Casema under the French Wanadoo brand, and Essent Kabelcom using the @Home brand.

The uptake of the Internet was directly related to the diffusion of PC to homes and businesses. Hence, the tax-break provided for the purchase of a 'home PC for business use' (PC privé project) should be mentioned as a factor that positively contributed to the adoption of the Internet.

---

[30] As ETSI-based equipment was not yet available, use was made of the German version of ISDN, which differed mainly in the modulation method applied on the copper loop.

[31] Hack-Tic was a magazine advertised as being aimed at 'techno-anarchists' that started to appear in 1989. (Hack-Tic, 2003)

[32] XS4ALL became a foundation to be transformed to a corporation XS4ALL Internet BV in 1996. In 1998 XS4ALL became a subsidiary of KPN Telecom (XS4ALL, 2010). Other early internet access providers include: EuroNet (acquired by Wanadoo), Demon, and WorldAccess (now Planet Internet, owned by KPN). Later ISPs included

WorldOnline (acquired by Tiscali in 2000), and Zonnet (Meerman, 2004).

[33] 'De Balie' is a platform being advertised as 'Playground for cultural progressives'.

[34] VuurWerk Internet was acquired by Versatel in 1999 (Wikipedia, 2010b).

[35] ISDN was attractive as it provided two communication channels, such that telephony and Internet access could be used simultaneously.

[36] CAI-Westland (CAIW) provides the services through a for-profit subsidiary, Kabelfoon. (Verbree, 1997)

[37] DeltaKabel had entered the cable networking market with a cable system product based on a license of the Dial-A-Program system of the British firm Rediffusion in 1974. (Schrijver, 1983; Dake and Boers, 1999)

4.3.4 Industry development and dynamics

The emergence of Internet access and service providers in the early 1990s was followed by consolidation in the late 1990s and early 2000s, driven by competition on margin and increasing needs for investment capital. The incumbent telecom operators were the main buyers, extending their ISP footprints and services portfolios. In many cases brand names were retained after an acquisition, representing a different service positioning and different market segments being targeted, including residential users and business users. In 1997 NLnet sold its commercialized Internet provision activities to UUNET, a subsidiary of WorldCom. The XS4ALL foundation was transformed into a corporation, XS4ALL Internet Ltd, in 1996 which in 1998 became a subsidiary of KPN Telecom. In 2006 XS4ALL acquired hcc!net and in 2007 Demon NL. In 1997 Planet Internet, owned by KPN, merged with WorldAccess, the ISP established by Videotex. IPS acquired WorldOnline and was subsequently taken over by Tiscali in 2000. (Meerman, 2004; XS4ALL, 2007; NLnet, 2010) In 2004 the Top-10 ISPs by size was composed of: XS4ALL, Demon, Planet, Bbeyond, BabyXL, VuurWerk, Tiscali, Lycos, PSINet and Wanadoo. (Meerman, 2004)

Internet service provision is tightly coupled to the underlying Internet access provision. For instance, cable network operators provide access only to their own ISP, while KPN provides access to multiple ISPs, both wholly owned subsidiaries and, through unbundling of its infrastructure, to independent ISPs.

4.3.5 Reflections on the emergence of the Internet

An important engine of Internet infrastructure development in the Netherlands has been the academic community through SURFnet. Supported by additional funding from the Ministry of Economic Affairs and the Ministry of Education, Culture and Science. SURFnet has pushed the operators, KPN and Telfort, and equipment providers, such as Cisco, Lucent Technologies and Nortel, into the deployment of leading-edge technologies; as well as opening up the market for dark fibre

connections. SURFnet was instrumental in the set-up of the AMS-IX, thereby creating a highly attractive up-to-date communications environment in the Netherlands. Via its ADSL and fibre to the dormitory projects, SURFnet has been instrumental in developing a market demand for broadband access at home.

More generally, the tax-break provided for the purchase of a 'PC at home for business use' (PC privé project) has also contributed positively to the adoption of the Internet.

4.4 Broadband developments

The telecom reform process and the emergence of the Internet have been largely independent processes running in parallel but reinforcing each other. The reform has positioned the incumbent telecom operator KPN and the incumbent cable operators for competition on access to the Internet. Real broadband developments are considered to have started in 2000 with the introduction of DOCSIS modems on the RTV-cable network and ADSL (asymmetrical digital subscriber line) on the PSTN.

4.4.1 Competition in internet access

In 1996 through a change in the Media Law, cable network operators were allowed to engage in competition. In 1997 also the provision of telecommunications services over cable networks was permitted. (MinOC&W, 2000) This allowed the cable sector to diversify its service portfolio to include Internet access and to provide voice/telephony service. This required significant investments to upgrade the cable network from one-way analogue RTV-signal distribution to two-way digital communications services provisioning. Given the broadband nature of the coaxial cable-distribution network, the cable sector took the lead in providing end-users with high data rate Internet access, up to 30 Mbit/s.[38] By the end of

---

[38] It should be noted that, depending on the network topology, the capacity is shared among a number of users.

1999 some 130,000 digital cable modems were in operation.[39]

In 2000 the first ADSL connections were provided by Demon using the network facilities of BabyXL Broadband (since 2002 part of Tiscali) and by XS4ALL, providing data rates of 512/ 64 kbit/s (downstream/upstream) and 1024/ 256 kbit/s. KPN started testing ADSL as part of the SnelNet project in 1998–9 and the roll-out started later in 2000. (MinV&W, 2000a; XS4ALL, 2001; Meerman, 2004)[40] In the following years ADSL gained significant market share.

In the 'competition *for* the market', data rates were increased step by step, resulting in a tit-for-tat competition between KPN, the wholesale-base operators BBned and Tele2, and the RTV-cable operators; only Essent Kabelcom with @Home followed a strategy of providing the highest data rate possible. (Van den Berg, 2004; Albrecht and Achterberg, 2008)

By March 2004 the cable operators collectively provided 1 million homes with Internet access, up from 250,000 in the year 2000. ADSL services were led by KPN with 913,000 subscribers, Wanadoo 350,000 (which includes cable access), Tiscali 140,000 and Zonnet 127,000. In 2004, 50 ISPs served a total of 4.5 million online households, approximately 65 per cent of total households. (Meerman, 2004)

By 2008, fixed broadband connections appeared to have reached a saturation level with approximately 5 million connections. The market share of ADSL was stabilizing, reaching 45 per cent (Kool, Arno, De Munck and Huveneers, 2008).

The competition in Internet access resulted in a top-two position in the penetration of broadband within Europe; whereby broadband was taken as downstream capacity equal to or higher than 144 kbit/s. (EC, 2008a) In terms of the broadband

performance index, again, the Netherlands assumed a top-two position, measured as a composite index of socio-economic context including the uptake of advance services, data rates, price, competition and coverage. (EC, 2008b)

With the market reaching apparent saturation, the 'competition *in* the market' increased in importance, and the 'race on speed' continued, with, for instance, UPC increasing the download data rate to 120 Mbit/s for its premium subscription offer in Amsterdam (NRC, 2008), and Ziggo announcing the upgrade from DOCSIS 2.0 to 3.0. (De Vries, 2009)[41]

4.4.2 Competition in voice

Competition between the CATV and PSTN networks started with Internet access. However, following the end of the PTT monopoly on telephony, the cable companies were allowed to provide voice services. Initially various techniques and standards were used, with very limited success. From 2004 onward the standard technique became Voice over IP (VoIP), supported by DOCSIS 1.1. The flat-fee-based offering was most attractive. In 2005 KPN responded with the introduction of VoIP based on ADSL, also on a flat-fee basis.

In 2004 Caiway started offering telephone service over the cable network. (Wikipedia, 2010a) In 2005 XS4ALL introduced VoIP, including a Webphone application as of July of 2006. (XS4ALL, 2007)

4.4.3 Competition in RTV-distribution

While the Internet protocol supports the distribution of video signals, the Internet is not ideally positioned for broadcasting TV signals in real-time. To facilitate infrastructure-based competition on the basis of Triple-play[42] offerings – television, telephony and internet combined – a consortium of KPN with broadcasting entities obtained a license

---

[39] In 2000 there was a debate as to whether the cable modems should be based on the DVB/RC (Euromodem) standard or the European version of the US DOCSIS (Data Over Cable Service Interface Specification) standard.
[40] The role of satellites in RTV-distribution remained small, estimated at some 325,000 receivers by the end of 1999, or approx. 5% of the RTV-access market. (MinOC&W, 2000; MinV&W, 2000a)

[41] The four-channel version of EuroDOCSIS 3.0 allows for a maximum data rate of 200 Mbit/s downstream and 108 Mbit/s upstream. (Wikipedia, 2009c)
[42] By mid 2008 the number of triple-play customers (RTV+Telephony+Internet) is approx 1.5 million. (OPTA, 2008e)

for nationwide terrestrial distribution of digital radio and television signals (DVB-T). The number of channels was limited to 23 TV-channels, plus 19 radio channels. In 2003, the service was launched under the name 'Digitenne' with country-wide coverage becoming possible after the shut-down of analogue TV broadcasting, the so-called Digital Dividend.[43] Meanwhile, KPN obtained 90 per cent of the shares and is now the sole provider of digital terrestrial TV broadcasting. The content is provided by the NPO (National Broadcasting Organisation) and by KPN. (KPN, 2009; Wikipedia, 2009b)

Also in 2003, KPN started to offer Video-on-Demand (VoD) via the Internet. From 2008, the company has added DVB services to handheld devices (DVB-H). Subsequently this services was terminated as TV-over-LTE is the more future-proof alternative.

From 2005, the major broadcasting stations also started to use the Internet as an alternative distribution channel, to offer delayed viewing of their programs (e.g., www.uitzendinggemist.nl).

OPTA, the Dutch National Regulatory Authority, concluded that, despite competition from Digitenne and satellite operators, the CATV operators in their respective service areas had significant market power, and, hence, regulation was deemed necessary (OPTA, 2009a). This new regulation replaced the 2006 ruling requiring access for RTV content providers to transfer programs using the RTV transmission service provided by the cable operators (OPTA, 2006a). By the end of 2009, the cable networks were scheduled to open-up for competition through wholesale access: that is, alternative service providers may access the CATV network for the transfer of RTV-signals. However, KPN was excluded from access to the cable networks, as cable operators are excluded from access to the

network of KPN. (Hijink, 2008) This decision was challenged in court and was rejected in August 2010; the court did not support the market analysis on the regional level. During 2011, proposals were submitted in Parliament in a renewed attempt to open-up the cable market. The new (national) market analysis by OPTA concluded that the market for digital television was sufficiently competitive and analogue television was going to be replaced by digital so there was no need for further regulation of the cable market. The regulator has retained this position for the regulatory period 2012–2014. (ACM, 2013e)

4.4.4 Reflections on broadband competition

Starting with a multitude of municipal cable operators in the 1970s the sector has been consolidating until very recently. In 2007 a major merger took place as the owners of Casema, the private equity firms Cinven and Warburg Pincus acquired Multikabel and Essent Kabelcom, to be merged into a new entity called Ziggo. The Dutch cable market is now served by two major players UPC and Ziggo, plus a few niche players.

With Ziggo owned by private equity firms, the endgame started with an IPO in March 2012. Through Barclay's Bank as issuing bank, Liberty Global, the parent company of UPC, acquired 12.7 per cent of the shares of Ziggo in March 2013. At that time rumours about a take-over of Ziggo by Liberty started to appear in the press. By July Liberty had extended its position to 28.5 per cent. In October 2013 Ziggo confirmed the receipt of a tentative take-over offer by Liberty, which they rejected as inadequate. Ziggo confirmed it was in discussion with Liberty Global in December 2013. Early in January 2014, Bloomberg reported that the take-over could be concluded shortly.[44]

KPN is the leading provider of ADSL under multiple brand names, in part acquired through consolidation (Het Net, Planet, XS4ALL).

---

[43] In 2006, a large part of the Digital Dividend has been assigned for the use by broadcasters, including Digitenne. To be able to assign the 800 MHz band for mobile communications in compliance with the EC rules, alternative frequencies have been assigned to Digitenne in the UHF band below 790 MHz. Source: www.frequentieland.nl/breedband/digitaal-dividend.htm.

[44] Sources: www.emerce.nl; www.netkwesties.nl; www.nieuws.nl; www.nu.nl; www.nrc.nl; www.telecompaper.com; www.z24.nl.

Moreover, through unbundling, other ADSL providers make use of the local loop owned by KPN (e.g., BBned/Tele2). The market is segmented as not all users require the highest possible data rates.

The market for broadband has become characterized by a techno-duopoly, consisting of KPN and its retail providers, providing broadband services on a national basis using the PSTN, and two major cable providers, Ziggo and UPC, each operating in a different part of the country, collectively providing close to national coverage, using the RTV network. There is strong competition in the market, based on price and data rates provided.

The question that can be raised is whether two competing firms are enough for a healthy development of the sector. (OPTA, 2006b) Clearly, the incumbent players are optimizing the utilization of their networks through an evolutionary approach. While fibre plays an important role in this evolution in the backbone and metropolitan networks, as well as in the feeder network to the street cabinets (FttC), the transition to FttH is apparently not (yet) attractive enough or considered not (yet) necessary from their business perspective. Third parties, in particular municipalities, were claiming 'market failure' and hence taking initiatives for the development of Fibre-to-the-Home – considered as the (more) future-proof trajectory.

This claim of 'market failure' has been investigated by the CPB, the Dutch bureau for economic policy analysis, following questions raised in Parliament. (Van Dijk et al., 2005) The core question was whether the then-current developments would be sufficient to match the increasing demand for broadband.[45] The investigation concluded that 'market failures in the Netherlands are limited to market power and, to some extent, to an increase in spill-over effects of knowledge. Current regulation by OPTA (the national regulatory agency) adequately deals with the issue of market power.'

The investigation suggested that 'the markets for broadband in the Netherlands function well in terms of competition (static efficiency) and innovation (dynamic efficiency). Hence, the best policy is to rely on market forces.'

The central government's policy remained focused on facilitation of, rather than intervention in, the development of broadband markets in general and the deployment of FttH in particular. But it did not prevent or block local governments from becoming involved, to a degree.

4.5 Developments towards FttH – telecom 3.0 and policy 3.0

For the first FttH deployment in the Netherlands we have to go back in time to 1991. In that year the first Fibre-to-the-Home (FttH) trial was carried out by the PTT in Amsterdam. The objective was to obtain operational experience, the principle technologies having been tried as part of national (COSNET) and European (RACE 1010) research programs. (Tromp, Nijhuis, Boomsma and Bakker, 1991; Van Bochove et al., 1991) The prevailing idea was to come to one national fibre infrastructure that would provide telephony, RTV-distribution and broadband-ISDN services. The roll-out was foreseen to start in 1993. The lack of willingness of the CATV operators to cooperate with KPN in one network roll-out, and the subsequent lack of support in Parliament brought this idea to an end.

However, in the new Telecom 2.0 – Policy 2.0 environment, the idea of a nationwide fibre network to the home re-appears. In 2003, KPN launched the 'Deltaplan Glas' initiative.[46] The plan was aimed at creating a fibre network covering 80 per cent of the homes by 2010, based on collaboration between the government and the industry at large. The plan argued a case of proven technology, the fibre access network being a natural monopoly, and competition to take place on

---

[45] These types of investigations and the interactions of member states with the European Commission led to guidelines by the EC on the use of state aid (EC, 2013).

[46] With an implied reference to the Deltawerken, a major initiative to improve the protection against the sea following the flooding in 1953.

the services level. The investments, estimated at EUR 8 billion, would be based on private and public contributions; the investments were considered to be of strategic importance for the nation. (KPN, 2003) The response from the cable sector was very similar to the initiative in 1993: 'Why would a cable company assist the competition, as they are experiencing the limits of ADSL?' (Crommelin, 2004)

Meanwhile, the penetration of fibre in the CATV networks had reached the street cabinets. The extension to the home remained a matter of economics and competition. As a result no FttH deployments were pursued by the operators. The apparent *status quo* or competitive hold-up appears to result from a high degree of uncertainty surrounding the business case for FttH, related to high investment costs, uncertainty in demand, lack of visibility with regard to 'killer applications' associated with a high willingness to pay, and the uncertainty regarding the regulation of FttH infrastructure in the future.

Notwithstanding, the deployment of fibre in the backbone network has been explosive during the euphoric period in the late 1990s, leading to what has been called a 'fibre glut'. During the same period many metropolitan fibre networks were rolled out, primarily connecting business users. (Lemstra, 2006) In 'green field' situations, the business case for FttH is much easier to make, so KPN has implemented Fibre-Only networks in two new city developments – in Amsterdam and in Utrecht. In a similar case Caiway, the cable operator, build an FttH network in the new housing area Woerdblok, in the city of Naaldwijk, providing HDTV, VoIP, and Internet access. (Wikipedia, 2010a)

4.5.1 Towards policy 3.0

In this section the role of the government in broadband development in general and FttH in particular is reviewed, starting with the Lisbon Agenda formulated in 2000. (EC, 2000).

In the translation of the Lisbon Agenda into national policy, the Dutch government emphasized access to a high quality broadband infrastructure,

whereby it assumed a technology-neutral position, driven by the opportunities these networks provide, rather than the technology or data rates being deployed. In short, the market should do the job. (MinEZ, 2004)

Nonetheless, the market can be assisted by providing information and reduced uncertainty. A number of investigations and reports by the Ministry of Public Works or the Ministry of Economic Affairs[47] were published around the year 2000, all aimed at broadband development: 'De Digitale Delta: e-Europa voorbij' (the translation of the eEurope Action Plan into national policy actions), 'Bouwstenennotitie breed-band' (Building blocks for broadband), 'Slim Graafwerk' (Clever trenching). Also in support of the municipalities wishing to contribute to the topic: 'Breedband Internet voor/door Gemeenten – Stedenlink' (Broadband Internet by and through municipalities) and the 'Gedogen mits. . .of een totaal andere weg' (Position paper on underground infrastructures and trenching rights) by the VNG (Cooperation platform of Dutch municipalities). (MinEZ, 1999; MinV&W, 2000b; Maclaine Pont and Van Till, 2001)[48]

In the report *De Digitale Delta* the Dutch government outlined its ICT-related policy objectives as follows:

(1) the availability of a first class, affordable, accessible and reliable telecommunications infrastructure;

(2) highly developed knowledge base and knowledge infrastructure and high degree of innovation based on close interaction between suppliers and users of ICT applications;

(3) professionals and citizens that have access to the latest electronic media and are capable of exploiting its opportunities;

---

[47] Until July 2002 the Ministry of Public Works was responsible for the post and telecommunications sector, when it was transferred to the Ministry of Economic Affairs.

[48] Along with these policy documents addressing infrastructure developments, complementary policy documents have been published on the use of these infrastructures, such as 'De digital economie' and 'Digitale implementatie Agenda. nl'. (CBS, 2001; MinEZ, 2011)

(4) laws and regulations that facilitate the development and application of ICT; and

(5) optimal use of ICTs in the governmental sector, which may serve as exemplar of ICT-usage. (MinEZ, 1999)

In 2000, the Ministry also took the initiative to create 'Kenniswijk' (Knowledge Quarter), a real-life environment to 'test the consumer market of the future', aimed at (1) breaking the perceived deadlock between infrastructure development and service development; (2) to improve the competitive position of the Netherlands; (3) to share the knowledge obtained through 'Stedenlink' (City link); and (4) to provide input for government policy. The all-fibre pilot project in the city of Nuenen, involving 7,500 households in an area representative of the Dutch population, was part of the 'Kenniswijk' project. (Kools and Serail, 2003)

By 2003–2004 the focus of the telecom policy was on assuring the proper functioning of markets and consumer protection, with an emphasis on continuity, safety, trust and quality. (MinEZ, 2003) Based on the 'Breedbandnota' , which recognized the various perspectives of market parties in relation to the roll-out of broadband, the policies can be summarized as shaping favourable preconditions for broadband development. (MinEZ, 2004)

4.6 Municipal FttH initiatives

As in the beginning of century the digital transmission capacity of copper lines was beefed-up through the use of modems, these were perceived as being limited in the data rates they could supply (ADSL up to 2 Mbit/s – and subject to the length of the copper line; cable modems up to 30 Mbit/s shared – 1.5 Mbit/s on average). The future-proof technology was considered to be optical fibre, of which the capacity runs into the Gigabit/s range. The transition towards such a future-proof infrastructure was readily recognized by municipalities, as it would facilitate the benefits they may be

able to obtain from the 'knowledge economy' and 'information society'.

4.6.1 The FttH case of Amsterdam

In 2001, the City Council of Amsterdam, observing ad-hoc plans being made for the deployment of fibre to the business and fibre to the home by private parties, placed the topic of fibre networking on the political agenda. The Council was concerned about a possible 'digital divide' emerging in the city, which was considered economically and socially undesirable. A second reason for involvement was the wish to channel the related digging activities to reduce the level of inconvenience to the public.

To address the issues properly, the City Council commissioned an investigation into: (1) the economic and social importance of FttH; (2) the expected capabilities of the existing infrastructure; (3) the expected demand for broadband by small firms and citizens; (4) whether the City should exert any influence on the developments; (5) if so, what goals should be pursued and what instruments should be used; and (6) what might be the financial implications. The resulting report *Amsterdam the Big Cherry?*, issued in 2002, concluded that the market will most probably not deliver an open infrastructure, nor fibre connections to every home and enterprise in Amsterdam, within the next 15 years. Hence, considering the economic and social importance, the local government may wish to take the initiative and guide the developments towards the creation of an open fibre infrastructure. (Weeder and Nijland, 2002) Based on the report, the City Council decided to investigate a more active involvement in the roll-out of a dense open-access fibre network. The next steps were investigated by a committee chaired by former Minister of Economic Affairs Andriessen. Meanwhile, the City Council decided to pursue fibre deployment in a new-built city area called Zeeburg. In 2003, the Andriessen report provided the necessary guidelines for the implementation of a city-wide FttH project, as a public-private partnership (PPP): the implementation of an open-access, passive network infrastructure, supporting service level competition. (Weeder, Nijland and Hotho, 2003) The recommendations were turned into an implementation plan 'Amsterdam: breedband in beweging' which was ready in 2004. (Weeder, Nijland and Konijn, 2004; Citynet, 2009)

By 2004, out of the top-30 cities[49] in the Netherlands 29 cities had (draft) plans for implementing fibre networks to connect governmental buildings, 23 had plans for Fibre-to-the-Business, and 15 had plans for Fibre-to-the-Home. (Linssen, 2005) One of the smaller but highly important initiatives was by the municipality of Appingedam. Early in 2004 it decided to commence the network roll-out, but had to interrupt the work within a few months, following a court decision in a case filed by the local CATV operator (Essent Kabelcom) against the city. The court decided that the initiative had to be presented to the European Commission for approval of (alleged) state support. The decision by the European Commission, issued in 2006, concluded that in this case financial support by the state was not allowed, given that the newly built network would represent unfair competition with the broadband networks of KPN and Essent. (Weeder, Nijland and Konijn, 2004; Schouten, 2006) Subsequently, Amsterdam and other municipalities filed their applications for EC approval, making sure their financial involvement was provided on the basis of the so-called 'market economy investor principle'.

In 2004, the municipality of Amsterdam started the European tendering process for construction of the network, resulting in the award to the combination of contractors BAM/DRAKA in 2005. In a negotiated arrangement, the exploitation of the fibre network on a wholesale basis was awarded to BBned to provide open, non-discriminatory access to retail operators. Subsequently, for the implementation of the fibre network, the city established a limited liability company Glasvezelnet Amsterdam (GNA) in 2006, in which the municipality participates for 1/3, the four housing corporations for 1/3, and investors for another 1/3; each party contributing EUR 6 million. (Citynet, 2009) This enabled the first phase of implementation,

40,000 connections, to start in 2006, subject to approval by the European Commission which was granted in December 2007. (NRC, 2007) It should be noted that UPC, the regional cable operator, has contested the fibre network plans of the municipality in the courts, at national and European level, albeit in vain.

Nonetheless, the debate on the involvement of municipalities in telecom infrastructure development in the Parliament resulted in tighter rules for participation of municipalities (and housing corporations) in telecommunication projects, becoming part of the 2006 revision of the Telecom Law. (Doorn, 2006; NU.nl, 2006) However, most of these restrictions were removed in the 2010 revision of the law, as part of an overall revision of laws and regulations to stimulate the growth of the economy following the crisis.[50]

4.6.2 The FttH case of Almere

Another municipality placing fibre high on the political agenda was Almere – near Amsterdam – a young and fast-growing city in the reclaimed Flevopolder. As a city with the ambition to leverage ICTs in all fields under its responsibility, including housing, employment, leisure and care, and inspired by the Stokab model in the City of Stockholm[51] and information from a fact-finding mission in the USA by the Ministry of Economic Affairs, it commissioned a study 'Almere op glas' in 2001. (Stratix, 2001) This study suggested an active role for the local government to implement an open-access 'First Mile' infrastructure in a new city development, Almere Poort. It proposed a demand-driven community-based network, whereby the municipality leverages its role given by the Telecom Law to coordinate infrastructure developments. The city would take the lead in creating the civil infrastructure as a public domain

---

[49] In 2009, the Netherlands had 441 municipalities.

[50] Source: Wet van 18 maart 2010, houdende regels met betrekking tot versnelde ontwikkeling en verwezenlijking van ruimtelijke en infrastructurele projecten (Crisis- en herstelwet). https://zoek.officielebekendmakingen.nl/stb-2010-135.html.

[51] See Chapter 7 for a detailed discussion of the Stokab model.

activity. A separate entity (net-co) acting on behalf of the users would be responsible for the implementation and exploitation of the network, subject to a tender. The end-user services were to be provided in competition. As such a maximum degree of unbundling would be achieved. By the city taking the lead in the realization of this network, the need for operators to create another fibre network in parallel would be pre-empted, but not excluded. By leveraging the use of the network by government institutions, including city offices and schools, effective demand aggregation and efficient roll-out of the network would allow prices for fibre to be similar to those of ADSL.

In the next phase three parallel developments became important. The City Council preferred as a first project connecting an existing city area that required an economic boost as it was suffering from a relatively high degree of unemployment. At the same time the City wanted to attract high-tech industry and institutions, such as the Institute for Information Engineering (linked to the Technical College in Amsterdam) and a division of SARA. These institutes require high data rate connectivity and thus connections with AMS-IX were established in 2001. This in turn made it attractive for BT and later Global Crossing, KPN and COLT also to set up facilities in Almere. Interactions with the existing operators showed that they were reluctant to participate in the pilot project due to conflicts of interest and a lack of willingness to assume risk. This combined result provided the momentum for the pilot phase of the project to be directed by the City, ultimately targeting 1,700 homes and 450 businesses in business parks, to be connected in 2003.[52] The project was subsidized with EUR 1 million by the Ministry of Economic Affairs. A special entity, the Almere Fibre Company Ltd (AFCo), was established for the implementation and maintenance of the civil works, with the City as the owner. In the subsequent tender process the newly established First Mile Venture (later to

acquire the ISP Unet and to assume this name) was selected as the infrastructure operator. (GemAlmere, 2004; Jansen, 2004; Halsema, 2012)[53]

The FttH part of the project was not successful because the willingness to pay was too low, resulting in a too low uptake but the FttB was successful and that became the focus of Unet's business. In 2006 the City followed up with a demand-aggregation project among local institutions, administrative buildings, schools, health centres, etc., leading to an FttInstitute project to connect 200 locations with fibre. The tender was won by Unet. This was followed by an FttB-project expanding the backbone to connect all business parks by fibre. The FttH initiative was rejuvenated by the idea of modelling it on the Amsterdam arrangements with 1/3 participation by the City, 1/3 by housing corporations and 1/3 by private investors. Initially KPN decided not to participate in the venture, but at the end of 2007 it joined the project with Reggefiber. Based on the evaluation of the pilot, the City made internal rearrangements such that implementation approvals could be obtained in 1–2 weeks rather than 13 weeks. This facilitated the connection of 60,000 homes within two years. XMS and Lybrand became new service providers, in addition to KPN and XS4ALL. By taking a leading role and being prepared to kick-start the project with pilot funding, the City of Almere assured that the private sector is actively deploying Fibre-to-the-Home in new and existing parts of the city. (GemAlmere, 2004; Jansen, 2004; Halsema, 2012)

4.6.3 Reflections on municipal initiatives

The involvement of so many municipalities in fibre initiatives, large and small, suggests that infrastructure supply is considered very important for economic development; the case of Almere is a clear example. The awareness of limited bandwidth available on copper and perception of fibre as future-proof explains their early involvement.

---

[52] The initial idea of co-ownership by the users was abandoned given that no party was willing to make the necessary arrangements. The targeted pilot service area was extended to be more representative of the population of Almere and to cover two business parks. (GemAlmere, 2004)

[53] Unet would link-up with Fastweb in Italy to share deployment experience. (GemAlmere, 2004)

While there were many initiatives, not too many have ultimately led to the actual deployment of municipally-led fibre. Issues around alleged state-aid, requiring upfront clearance, and the issues of funding and managing have been too cumbersome in many cases. Nonetheless, the push by municipalities has forced earlier deployments although in the end it have been commercial parties which became involved in the implementation and operations of municipal fibre networks, in part or in whole. See also Section 4.8 on Reggefiber and Chapter 7 for the municipal fibre deployments in Sweden.

4.7 The transition to All-IP

Another important development worth discussing is the transition of the PSTN from a circuit-switched network to a packet-switched network, becoming All-IP.

At the end of 2005, KPN announced plans to migrate its network to All-IP. The transition was considered necessary to remain competitive in broadband, to achieve cost reductions and to replace the network considered to have reached its end of life. Along with the upgrade of the core network to IP, the plan implied an upgrade of the feeder network to Fibre-to-the-Cabinet. With a shorter copper loop, broadband services using VDSL with data rates of up to 50 Mbit/s would become feasible.[54]

This plan was welcomed by the telecom regulator, OPTA, as a clear sign of investment in infrastructure; however, it impacted Policy 2.0, in particular with respect to unbundling, which hinges on access to the copper loop at the MDF in the central office. The KPN plan implied abolishing the MDFs in 1,361 exchange locations, to be replaced by approximately 200 'Metro Core' locations. The access to the copper loop remained possible at 28,000 street cabinets. Although sub-loop unbundling is part of Policy 2.0, the service was not taken up, as access at the exchange level is

financially much more attractive. The matter to be resolved is whether sufficiently attractive alternatives to MDF access were available to the alternative operators. (OPTA, 2006c)[55] Early in 2007, OPTA called upon all parties to come to an agreement on the phasing out of MDF-based access. This led to memorandums of understanding (MoUs) with the main parties: KPN and BBned, Orange and Tele2. However, reaching a final agreement was difficult. By February 2008, KPN submited an 'MDF migration agreement'. Recognizing that the All-IP project impacted many regulated market segments, OPTA decided to incorporate the impacts of All-IP in a general review of the markets, to be issued by the end of 2008. (OPTA, 2008a) After consultation with market parties, OPTA issued this new regulation with respect to the unbundling of the KPN access network to include sub-loop unbundling and an associated backhaul service (OPTA, 2008c).

4.8 The emergence of a new actor – Reggefiber

A new trajectory in broadband development started from an unexpected source, the civil engineering and construction industry.

The competition played out between KPN, UPC/Ziggo and BBNed/Tele2 had led to high broadband penetration and to increasing data rates. The competition led to FttC, but not to FttH deployment. And while KPN prepared its All-IP strategy in 2005, private equity firm Reggeborgh formed the optical fibre company Reggefiber, creating a new actor that reshaped the telecom scene.

Reggeborgh is the investment vehicle of Dick Wessels. Wessels had created the Wessels Group, active in building construction activities in the Netherlands and abroad. In 1990, the family-owned firm merged with the publicly listed IBB Kondor. In 1997 they in turn merged with Koninklijke Volker Stevin, which was the result of earlier mergers in the infrastructure construction industry.

---

[54] VDSL will replace ADSL, ADSL2, and ADSL2+, the latter providing a maximum download data rate of 24 Mbit/s which, depending on the length of the copper loop, will drop to a few Mbit/s. (Wikipedia, 2009a)

[55] In 4Q2007, out of the 3.5 million lines of KPN, approx. 650,000 are used by third parties. (OPTA, 2007)

The expertise of the Group in telecommunication obtained a boost when KPN transfered its infrastructure design, engineering and implementation subsidiary KPN Netwerkbouw which became the subsidiary VolkerWessels Telecom in 2002. (NMa, 2002; VolkerWessels, 2009)

The creation of Reggefiber resulted from an initiative by housing corporation Portaal, which planned to install fibre to the houses owned by Portaal. VolkerWessel Telecom had already been selected for the implementation. The need for investment capital led to Reggeborgh. From investment partner, Wessels became entrepreneur in fibre networking through the founding of Reggefiber. (Dekker, 2007)

In its business approach, Reggefiber took a long-term perspective on fibre deployment, applying a real estate model.[56] The objective was to reach a level of 2 million households by 2013, based on the principle of a passive infrastructure with open access. (Reggefiber, 2009)[57] Early projects included the cities of Deventer, Nuenen, and Hillegom. In 2006, Reggefiber became one of the investors in the Citynet project in Amsterdam. To link the various FttH projects, Reggeborgh acquired fibre backbone provider Eurofiber in 2006. (Dekker, 2007)[58] In 2007 KPN and Reggefiber announced their cooperation in providing FttH to 70,000 households in the city of Almere. (Almere Kennisstad, 2007)

The emergence of Reggefiber as a new player in the infrastructure arena changed the competition dynamics, as the initiatives by municipalities and housing corporations were not isolated any more but became linked. It appeared that Reggefiber was taking the 'first mover advantage', and was changing the rules of the game forcing the incumbent infrastructure players into services competition. Hence, the strategic move by KPN, to create

a joint venture with Reggefiber to provide FttH on a nationwide basis and to take a 41 per cent share (with an option to increase to a majority position) in the venture in May 2008, did not come as a surprise.

The participation of KPN in the joint venture with Reggefiber required approval by the competition authority NMa. Following an analysis in collaboration with OPTA, this approval was granted in December 2008. (NMa, 2008; OPTA, 2009c) A condition of the approval was that the fibre networks being deployed by the joint venture were to be open to other providers on a non-discriminatory basis.

Through the joint venture, KPN obtained influence on the exploitation of fibre networks in Amsterdam, Amersfoort, Deventer, Eindhoven, Nijmegen and a number of smaller towns, a total of 180,000 connections. (Olsthoorn, 2008) The appointment of Davids, former Senior Consultant, Corporate Strategy at KPN who had been involved in the development of KPN's vision of fibre networking, to become Director, Wholesale and Business Development at Reggefiber in February 2009 was a logical next step. (Reggefiber, 2009; Van Gool, 2009) Also in February 2009, Reggefiber increased its share in the Amsterdam fibre project to 70 per cent, while the municipality and the housing corporations reduced their share to a combined 30 per cent. (Dongen, 2009)

Influenced by these developments, OPTA issued a new wholesale regulation, including the unbundling of fibre at the Optical Distribution Frame. It based its analysis on the real-life case presented by Reggefiber. In the network architecture of Reggefiber the Area-PoPs serving approximately 2,500 homes are linked through a backhaul to a City-PoP serving approx. 20,000 homes (OPTA, 2008d, 2009b). Simultaneously and based on market consultation, OPTA issued a tariff regulation, based on a long-term horizon and aimed at large-scale build-out of FttH, using tariff caps at EUR 14.50 to EUR 17.50, depending on the capex level required (EUR 775-825 and EUR 975–1025 respectively). (OPTA, 2008b, 2009b).

Another 'third actor' on a separate trajectory in FttH deployment, the Amsterdam-based communications infrastructure fund CIF, started with the acquisition of cable assets owned by CaiWestland

---

[56] Its business model was to provide only the passive layer but, due to the absence of interested active operators at that time, it established its own active operator as a temporary measure.

[57] The number of households in the Netherlands is 7.2 million on a population of 16.5 million (CBS, 2009).

[58] In 2008 Eurofibre, Fastfibre and iConnext merge into Eurofibre. (Eurofiber, 2009)

(Caiway) to upgrade these to FttH and has since expanded through further acquisitions of smaller cable operators, mainly in the western and eastern parts of the country. Caiway is the service provider on these networks. Through CIF, FttH projects are being implemented in about 20 municipalities.[59] As of September 2012, FttH projects were being implemented in 210 municipalities, an increase of 70 municipalities since 2011. (Stratix, 2013)

To complete the landscape of FttH deployments, the end-user as 'third actor' should also be mentioned. A salient example are the residents in Hazenkamp, a suburb of the city Nijmegen, who established the Glazenkamp foundation to serve approximately 2,900 homes with FttH, with an uptake rate of 66 per cent.[60]

4.8.1 Policy 2.0 applied to telecom 3.0

As to be expected, the decisions by the NMa/OPTA were challenged in court, by cable providers UPC and Ziggo, alternative network providers BBned and Tele2, as well as ISPs Scarlet and Online, a subsidiary of T-Mobile (Emerce, 2009). Notwithstanding, the adaptation of the regulation by OPTA to accommodate the deployment of fibre to the cabinet and fibre to the home remained. The principle of open-access fibre networks, initiated by Reggefiber, became part of the regulation, as KPN became a shareholder in Reggefiber. The use of an actual fibre business case as starting point for setting the wholesale tariffs was novel. Therefore, we may conclude that so far Telecom 3.0 did not require a new policy but, rather, an extension of the existing Policy 2.0 to Policy 2.5.

4.9 The broadband market today

In this section the current outcome of these broadband developments is described and the prospect of achieving the Digital Agenda targets is assessed.

For a comparison with the outcome of the other country case studies please see Table 1.2 and 1.3 in Chapter 1 Introduction. The data is derived from reporting by the NRA – OPTA (now ACM)[61] – and from reports commissioned by the NRA. (OPTA, 2010; ACM, 2013a, 2013b, 2013c, 2013d; Telecompaper, 2013b) The number of households is derived from the National Statistics Office. (CBS, 2014)

4.9.1 Fixed broadband

Following a stabilization in broadband uptake around 2005, the increasing use of video on the Internet has driven the competition for higher data rates. ADSL2$^+$ is being replaced by VDSL and the capacity of VDSL is boosted through vectoring and bonding. While the maximum data rate on the copper twisted pair was 8/0.5 Mbit/s (download/upload) for ADSL and 24/1 Mbit/s for ADSL2, with the combination of FttC and VDSL data rates of 50/5 Mbit/s can be provided and with vectoring 80/8 Mbit/s becomes feasible. KPN started deployment of vectoring in September 2013. On the CATV network with the combination of FttC and DOCSIS-3 data rates in excess of 100 Mbit/s can be provided by reducing the number of users sharing the capacity, with further upgrades possible. (TNO, 2012)

By mid-2013 the total broadband connections stood at 6.7 million or 88% of households (total: 7.6 million).[62] DSL connections stood at 3.2 million or 48% and CATV connections at 3.0 million or 45%, while fibre accounted for 0.46 million or 7%. This implies a decrease 6.2 percentage points for DSL compared to 3Q2011 and an increase of 3 percentage points for CATV connections. The growth is small: over the last eight quarters the percentage of additions was 4.23% and exceeds the percentage of disconnects of 3.37% by only 0.9%.

---

[59] Source: www.cifinfrastructure.com and www.cif-glasvezel.nl/. CIR is managed by Bouwfonds REIM, as part of the Rabo Real Estate Group which is part of the Rabobank Group.
[60] Source: www.glazenkamp.nl.

[61] As of 1 January 2013 the consumer authority (CA), the sector specific authorities (OPTA and former DTe) and the competition authority (NMa) have been merged into one Authority Consumer and Market (ACM).
[62] Note that some of the broadband connections serve small and medium size enterprises, hence, the real penetration per household is lower than 90%.

Unbundling plays an important role with 3.2 million unbundled lines (44% of total) of which 78% is fully unbundled and 22% shared.

Broadband is increasingly subscribed to as part of a triple-play bundle, up from 39% to 56% over the period from mid-2011 to mid-2013. Broadband-only subscriptions dropped from 28% to 18%. The total number of bundled subscriptions reached 5.5 million by mid-2013, or approximately 75% of households.[63]

By mid-2013 broadband by download data rate provides the following picture:

- 1.1%   <2 Mbit/s;

- 30.7%   ≥ 2 Mbit/s – < 10 Mbit/s;

- 29.7%   ≥ 10 Mbit/s – < 30 Mbit/s;

- 33.2%   ≥ 30 Mbit/s – < 100 Mbit/s; and

- 5.4%   ≥ 100 Mbit/s.

Relative to the Digital Agenda targets for 2020, the target 100% of households having access to up to 30 Mbit/s is largely accomplished, with 7.4 million or 98% of homes connected to the cable network. With 2.5 million homes (33%) subscribed to up to 30 Mbit/s and 0.4 million (5%) over 30 up to 100 Mbit/s, achieving the subscription target of above 100 Mbit/s is still further away. Nonetheless, progress around 10% over the last two years in the category ≥ 30 Mbit/s – < 100 Mbit/s is promising. See Figure 4.1.

Moreover, the FttH deployment by Reggefiber is picking up pace. See Figure 4.2.[64] According to Stratix Consulting, the deployment of FttH in the Netherlands had reached the level of 1.9 million homes passed (25.1% of the total) and 626,000 homes subscribed (8.3%) by September 2013. This represents a conversion rate of around 30%. (Stratix, 2013).

Voice-over-Broadband reached 4.9 million connections, or 68% of total retail fixed telephony connections, with 9% ISDN and 23% PSTN (grand total: 7.2 million – 95% of households) by mid-2013. The average disconnect rate of 3.31% over the last eight quarters is slightly lower than the connect rate of 3.56%. Between end-2006 and the end-of 2012, fixed telephony revenues dropped by 30%.

RTV subscription revenues amounted to EUR 1.62 billion for 2012, this represents 7.4 million subscriptions. The share in revenue of non-cable operators has grown from 5% in 2006 to 24% in 2012 and, in terms of subscriptions, to 35%.

The importance of bundles increased to reach 50% for TV as part of triple-play and 9% for TV as part of dual-play with broadband by mid-2013. TV-only dropped from 57% to 40% between mid-2011 and mid-2013. Telephony as part of triple-play increased from 34% to 52% over the same period. Telephony-only dropped from 46% to 33%.

TV services are increasingly delivered as IPTV and hence the number of active connections on the cable network has dropped to 4.8 million or to 64% of the 7.4 million homes connected (98% of homes)[65] by mid-2013. Digital TV by technology stands at: 55% CATV; 16% DSL; 9% FttH/B; 9% terrestrial; and 11% satellite. (Telecompaper, 2013a)[66]

4.9.2 Mobile broadband

Although the main body of this case study has been dedicated to the development of fixed broadband, the current status of the mobile broadband market is included in this section to provide a complete market overview, in the light of the realization of the Digital Agenda for Europe. A short summary is provided on the development of the mobile market, with a focus on the number of players as an important parameter in determining mobile broadband dynamics. (MinEZ, 2010; Anker, 2013; TNO, 2013)

---

[63] The ACM reporting is based on company data provided by Atlantic, BBNed, BT, CAIW, COLT, Delta, Easynet, Esprit, KPN, Online, Pretium, Reggefiber, Scarlet, Tele2, T-Mobile, UPC, UPC business, Verizon, Vodafone and Ziggo.

[64] Figure from the report 'FTTH Monitor – 2013/Q3 Glasvezelontwikkelingen in Nederland', courtesy of Stratix Consulting.

[65] This includes connections to holiday homes, etc., which inflates the penetration level per home.

[66] Information from the report 'Dutch television market Q3 2013', courtesy of Telecompaper.

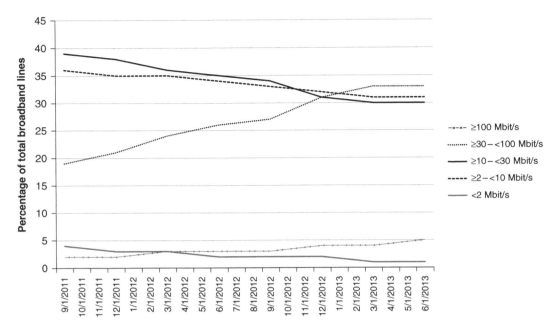

Figure 4.1 Broadband connections by data download rate as percentage of total, the Netherlands, 2011–2013
Data source: ACM, 2013a.

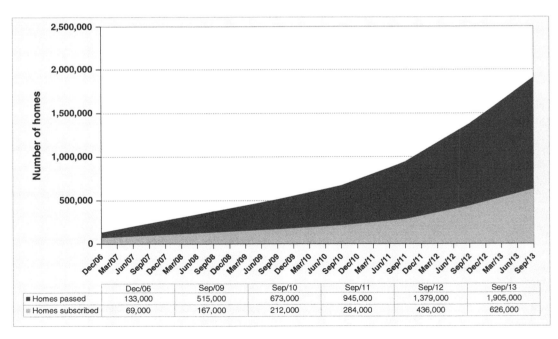

Figure 4.2 FttH deployment in the Netherlands, 2006–2013
Data source: Stratix Consulting, 2013.

Following the introduction of GSM by the PTT – now KPN – in 1994, the wireless cellular market became competitive in 1995, when Libertel – now Vodafone – won the beauty contest for a second GSM license.

In 1998, the auction of GSM-1800 MHz (called PCS at the time) introduced three more mobile players: Telfort – as a joint venture between the Dutch railways and BT; Dutchtone – backed by France Télécom and Deutsche Telekom (DT) and two major Dutch banks, Rabobank and ABNAMRO; and Ben – a collaboration between Belgacom and Tele Danmark. Shortly thereafter DT sold its interest in Dutchtone and BT acquired a 100 per cent interest in Telfort.

In 2000, the mobile broadband era started with the auction of five licenses for UMTS frequencies. All five operators plus Versatel participated. All existing operators managed to acquire UMTS licenses. Vodafone provided the first commercial service in 2004, with a data rate of 384 kbit/s. KPN followed in the same year. In 2006, T-Mobile launched its service including HSDPA, providing initial data rates of 1.8 Mbit/s, to be increased over time to 3.6 Mbit/s, 7.2 Mbit/s and later to 28.8 Mbit/s.

From 2000, a number of ownership changes followed but the number of operators stayed at five, each operating a network with (almost 100%) national coverage. In 2000, France Télécom acquired the UK-based Orange and rebranded its mobile telecommunications as Orange, hence Dutchtone became Orange. In 2001, BT divested its mobile activities to become mmO2 PLC with O2 as its brand name. Thus Telfort became O2. In 2002, O2 sold its Dutch interests to Greenfield Capital Partners, which re-introduced the Telfort brand. In 2003, T-Mobile had acquired all shares in Ben and the brand disappeared, to resurface again as a T-Mobile brand for SIM-only subscriptions in 2008.

From 2005 a consolidation wave started: Telfort was acquired by KPN, which retained the brand and returned the second license to the government. In 2007, Orange NL was acquired by T-Mobile and the Orange brand disappeared. Three main players resulted: KPN, Vodafone and T-Mobile.

In 2010 followed the auction of the 2.6 GHz band to expand mobile broadband capacity, with new entrants Tele2 and Ziggo4 – the consortium of the cable operators Ziggo and UPC. In 2012 followed the so-called multiband auction enabling 4G/LTE roll-out. It included the re-auctioning of GSM900 and GSM1800 spectrum, the new 'digital dividend' in the 800 MHz band and new, smaller blocks of spectrum in the 2.1 and 2.6 GHz bands; including the spectrum that Telfort had occupied. KPN, Vodafone, T-Mobile and Tele2 obtained licenses and thereby assured the continuation of their operations, while Ziggo4 did not obtain additional spectrum. KPN announced national coverage of LTE by the end of 1Q2014, T-Mobile aims at an 80^+ per cent coverage by the end of 2014, while Vodafone has launched 4G in a few major cities, but did not communicate any further targets. Tele2 and Ziggo4 combine the use of their new spectrum with existing MVNO arrangements with T-Mobile and Vodafone, respectively, to provide national coverage. Tele2 also entered into a passive network-sharing arrangement with T-Mobile. Ziggo and UPC also push Wi-Fi as part of their mobile broadband strategy. In January 2013, KPN announced its collaboration with FON, to extend its Wi-Fi strategy based on hotspots.[67]

The three main MNOs plus 52 MVNOs serve the Dutch market through 70 brands, generating EUR 5.8 billion in revenues in 2012. Data revenues (excluding SMS) have grown from just under 25%, reaching 35% by mid-2013. SIM-cards in the market reached 22.1 million in 3Q2012, with KPN (including its MVNOs) as the market leader with 47% of SIMs; Vodafone followed with 29% and T-Mobile with 24%. MVNOs accounted for 20.3% of total SIMs and 15% of revenues. ARPUs per operator ranged from EUR 21.70 to EUR 25.50. Broadband connections (combined and broadband-only) reached 52% and M2M an additional 5%. On 6 January 2014, the LTE coverage by KPN was 71% by population and 45.6% by area; Vodafone 30% and 12.5% respectively; and T-Mobile 21.7% and 6.5%, respectively, while Ziggo/UPC and

---

[67] Source: http://forum.kpn.com/t5/News-stream. For the FON approach to Wi-Fi see Chapter 5 in 'The Innovation Journey of Wi-Fi – The Road to Global Success' (Lemstra, Hayes and Groenewegen, 2010).

Tele2 had established only the minimums required by their coverage obligations.[68]

Since 2Q 2010, more calls are made on the mobile network than on the fixed network. The number of mobile calls over the period 2010–13 remained flat. As of 2H 2010 the number of SMSs started to fall, to stabilize at 50% in 2013, while the revenues dropped by close to 30%. The data volume doubled over the period 3Q 2011–2Q 2013 and the retail revenues by a factor of 2.3.

4.10 Case analysis

The case summary is provided with reference to the research questions formulated in Chapter 2 Research context and perspective.

Starting conditions

Fixed broadband developments in the Netherlands have benefitted from favourable starting conditions, which include almost 100 per cent connection of households to the PSTN and almost 95 per cent to the CATV network, allowing intense infrastructure-based competition to develop. The country enjoys a relatively high level of GDP per capita. Relatively favourable conditions for the deployment of fibre exist: the country has a high population density and is flat. However, little use can be made of ducts as most of the cables are buried directly.

Joining the European Union and the application of the regulatory framework

The Netherlands has been a founding member of the European Coal and Steel Community, the precursor of the EEC and the EU. Transposition of the EC Regulatory Framework has in general been timely. Nonetheless, the Dutch are not necessarily followers: municipal activities have pushed the clarification of state aid and provision of

---

[68] Based on company information collected by www.4Gdekking.nl and personal information from P. Brand, Stratix Consulting.

---

guidelines; more recently their net neutrality legislation was a first in Europe.

Role of the central government

In broadband development, the central government has been a facilitator: formulating a broadband agenda, sharing goals and information, attending to both demand and supply conditions. By creating a strong regulatory function a fairly level playing field was created. Market entry was facilitated, as no licenses were required, only registration. While the decisions of the NRA are challenged in court almost by default, there appears to be progress and no enduring contentious issues. With reference to the perception of government's role in Chapter 2 Research context and perspective, the Dutch government can be characterized as more regulatory than developmental, with the exception of stimulating innovation through the support of SURFnet. Policies have been fairly constant under changing cabinets, although the role of municipalities in fibre developments has been appreciated differently at different times.

Role of the academic community

While in most countries the academic community has played an important role at the time of the emergence of the Internet, with SURFnet its leading role has continued until today. The academic community, with financial support of the government, has been instrumental in pushing the technological frontier, resulting in the leading position of AMS-IX and the favourable infrastructural conditions for Internet firms to operate in and from the Netherlands.

Role of the local and regional government

Municipalities have played an important role in pushing the broadband agenda. First of all, they were instrumental in the development of the cable networks, which allowed infrastructure-based competition in broadband to develop. Subsequently, they enabled competition through the implementation of a 'liberal' right-of-way policy. More recently, they were important actors in driving the FttH agenda. This applies to the very large cities and to the smaller communities. Their influence was strongest in the early part of the decade as copper was perceived to be very limited and fibre as future-proof. It has resulted in much higher broadband awareness and an accelerated deployment by private parties. Also, provincial governments are increasingly active in stimulating or orchestrating broadband developments, in particular fibre deployments in so-called 'white areas'.

Recurring theme

The notion that high-quality broadband infrastructure is important to the country has led to recurring initiatives to invest in a 'national broadband network'. In the early days it was rejected by Parliament wishing to avoid too much power in the hands of the incumbent; more recently private actors preferred competition over collaboration.

Intensity and type of competition

In the early days of liberalisation and enabled by the Internet/telecom boom, many new entrants fuelled the competition: utility corporations turning into telecom operators, start-ups and entries from abroad. Consolidation followed the collapse of the telecom bubble and has become a constant factor: only a few alternative operators have survived serving the consumer market; a few more (mainly local operations of large telecom operators abroad) serve the business market. Competition is intense, infrastructure-based and access-based.[69] The

---

[69] In a parallel research effort, the quantitative analysis of broadband markets in the EU reveals that:

> Whilst access-based competition tends to take a smaller market share in the presence of cable, our analysis shows that the combination of infrastructure-based and access-based competition provides the best possible level of broadband performance. Drawing the conclusion that 'two is enough' for reaching optimal performance, i.e., infrastructure-based competition without access-based competition, is incorrect. This is indicated by the important role that the LLU wholesale price level has on broadband performance.
>
> (Lemstra, Van Gorp and Voogt, 2013).

nature of competition has evolved from price-based to become driven by providing higher data rates against relatively constant prices, with (waves of) special discounts to attract new customers.

Other actors

It has been 'third actors' – actors not directly involved in telecommunications provision, such as municipalities and housing corporations – that have stimulated broadband developments. A special and highly influential 'third actor' has been Reggefiber. Through the deployment of open-access fibre networks it has effectively broken the strategic 'waiting game' of PSTN and CATV incumbents with respect to fibre to the home deployments. And then there is another third actor: CIF (originally Rabo Bouwfonds – Communications Infrastructure Fund), the investment vehicle which has taken over several small CATV companies to convert their networks to FttH.

Achieving the Digital Agenda targets

The target of 100% of households having access to ≥ 30 Mbit/s is largely accomplished, with 95% of homes connected to the cable network which enables data rate of 100^+ Mbit/s. With 33% of homes subscribed to data rates of ≥ 30 Mbit/s and 5% to data rates of 100 Mbit/s or above, achievement of the 50% subscription target of above 100 Mbit/s is still further off. Nonetheless, progress around 10% in the category ≥ 30 Mbit/s – < 100 Mbit/s over the last two years is promising. Moreover, the roll-out of vectoring and bonding by KPN is planned to reach 70% of households by the end of 2014, facilitating data rates at or above 40 Mbit/s. Furthermore, FttH deployment is picking up pace. The deployment of FttH has reached the level of 25% of homes covered and 8% of homes subscribed by 2Q 2013. This represents a conversion ratio of around 30%. At the beginning of January 2014, the LTE coverage by KPN was 71% by population and 45.6% by area; Vodafone 30% and 12.5%; and T-Mobile 21.7% and 6.5%, respectively. Mobile broadband connections reached 10.2 million or 63% of the population.

Salient items in this country case

- The role of the academic community in pushing the technology frontier;
- The role of municipalities in FttH deployment;
- The role of housing corporations in providing demand bundling to kick-start fibre deployments;
- The emergence of a third actor 'breaking the waiting game' in terms of fibre to the home deployments;
- Early removal of regulatory uncertainty regarding fibre to the home, with open-access and wholesale price based on a real-life business case;
- Effective demand aggregation in towns and cities with a high degree of social cohesion.

Experiences that might benefit other member states in realizing the DAE targets

- The role of the academic community in pushing the technology frontier;
- The role of third parties in 'breaking the strategic waiting game'.

References

ACM (2013a). *Openbare rapportage breedband 2q2013*. Den Haag: Authoriteit Consument en Markt.

(2013b). *Openbare rapportage mobiel 2q2013*. Den Haag: Autoriteit Consument en Markt.

(2013c). *Openbare rapportage televisie 2q2013*. Den Haag: Autoriteit Consument en Markt.

(2013d). *Openbare rapportage vaste telefonie 2q2013*. Den Haag: Autoriteit Consument en Markt.

(2013e) Publicaties. Den Haag: Autoriteit Consument en Markt.

Albrecht, K. and E. Achterberg (2008). Breedbandmarkt ontwikkelingen 2003–2007/8. Houten, The Netherlands: Telecompaper.

Almere Kennisstad (2007). KPN and Reggefiber gaan krachten bundelen voor nieuw glasvezelnetwerk in Almere. Retrieved 2009-06-29, from www.almerekennisstad.nl/index.php?option=com_content&task=view&id.

Anker, P. (2013). Mobile communications in the Netherlands – Lessons from the past auctions. Canadian Spectrum Summit. Toronto: Ted Rogers School of Management, Ryerson University.

Arnbak, J. C. (1986). Development of transmission facilities for electronic media in the Netherlands. Eindhoven, the Netherlands: Eindhoven University of Technology.

Arnbak, J. C., J. J. Van Cuilenburg and E. J. Dommering (1991). *Openbare elektronische informatie voorziening*. Amsterdam: Otto Cramwinckel.

Astron (2006). LOFAR. Retrieved 2006-07-22, from www.lofar.org/p/geninfo.htm.

Blanken, I. J. (1992). *Geschiedenis van Philips Electronics N.V. Deel III*. Leiden, The Netherlands: Martinus Nijhoff.

Boekholt, P., J. Deuten, M. Nagle and F. Zuijdam (2008). Evaluatie ICES/KIS-2 – Tussen impuls en continuïteit. Amsterdam: Technopolis.

Bordewijk, P. (2004). *Goud in de grond – De geschiedenis van draadomroep en kabeltelevisie toegespits op Stadskabel Leiden*. Leiden, The Netherlands: Primavera Pers.

Buddingh, H. (2003). EU daagt staat om belang KPN, TPG. NRC-Handelsblad. Rottterdam.

CBS (2001). De digitale economie 2001. Heerlen: Centraal Bureau voor de Statistiek: p 186.

(2009). CBS Statline. Retrieved 2009-07-01, from http://statline.cbs.nl/StatWeb/.

(2014). StatLine. Heerlen/DenHaag: Centraal bureau voor de Statistiek.

Citynet (2009). Amsterdam en glas: geschiedenis Retrieved 2009-06-25, from www.citynet.nl/index.php?fuseaction=home.showPages.

Crommelin, D. (2004). Interview met Manuel Kohnstamm, MD Corporate Affairs UGC Europe. *Kabel & Breedband. 3*.

Dake, A. and J. Boers (1999). *De kabel: Kafka in de polder*. Amsterdam: Otto Cramwinckel.

Davids, M. (1999). *De weg naar zelfstandigheid – De voorgeschiedenis van de verzelfstandiging van de PTT in 1989*. Hilversum, The Netherlands: Verloren.

De Boer, P. A. (1969). *à Steringa Idzerda – de pionier van de radio-omroep*. Bussum: De Muiderkring.

De Leeuw, G. J. (2009). De kabelsector in cijfers. Delft: TUDelft.

De Vries, W. (2009). Ziggo zet nieuwe stap in uitrol docsis 3.0. Retrieved 2009-01-12, from www. tweakers.net.

De Wit, O. (1998). *Telefonie in Nederland 1877–1940* (Telephony in the Netherlands 1877–1940). Amsterdam: Otto Cramwinckel.

Dekker, V. (2007). Reggefiber bouwde jarenlang stilletjes aan nieuw telecomnet. Trouw. Amsterdam.

Dongen, K. (2009). Voortgang aanleg open glasvezelnet Amsterdam met Reggefiber/KPN. Retrieved 2009-07-01, from http://amsterdam.nl/ gemeente/college/maarten_van/redactionele/ voortgang_aanleg_open_glasvezelnet_ Amsterdam_met_ReggefiberKPN.

Doorn, J. (2006). Gemeenten mogen delnemen aan glasvezelprojecten. Retrieved 2009-07-03, from http://webwereld.nl/nieuws/41683/gemeenten-mogen-deelnemen-aan-glasvezelprojecten.html.

EC (2000). DOC/00/7: The Lisbon Council – An agenda of economic and social renewal for Europe. Brussels: European Commission.

(2008a). COCOM08-41 FINAL Broadband access in the EU: situation at 1 July 2008. Brussels: European Commission.

(2008b). SEC(2008)2507 Indexing broadband performance. Brussels: European Commision.

(2013). 2013/C 25/01 EU Guidelines for the application of State aid rules in relation to the rapid deployment of broadband networks. Brussels: European Commission.

Eenhoorn, H. B. (1994). De kabel: de weg naar een nieuw informatietijdperk. *I&I* **3**.

Ekkelenkamp, H., I. Verstraaten and R. Wijbrands (1992). *Het ISDN boek*. Amsterdam: Tutein Nothenius.

Emerce (2009). Breed verzet tegen KPN/Reggefiber. Retrieved 2009-06-29, from www.vnunet.nl/ avantgo/emerce/news.sp?id=2898907.

Eurofiber (2009). Organisatie. Retrieved 2009-07-01, from www.eurofiber.nl/organisatie.jsp.

GemAlmere (2004). Evaluatie van ervaringen in de Almere Fiber Pilot. Almere: Gemeente Almere.

Hack-Tic (1993). Power to the people. Retrieved 2010-11-02, from www.hacktic.nl/magazine/ 2252.htm.

(2003). Hack-Tic Magazine archive. Retrieved 2010-11-09, from www.hacktic.nl/index.html.

Halsema, F. (2012). Interview. Almere.

Hamelberg, P. J. C. (1984). Het Nederlandse datanet. *NGI Telematica*. Amsterdam: Nederlands Genootschap voor Informatica.

Hijink, M. (2008). Kabel gaat open voor concurrenten. *NRC Handelsblad*. Rotterdam.

Hogesteeger, G. (1976). De introductie van het fenomeen telefoon in Nederland. *Het PTT_Bedrijf XX*: 177–190.

Jansen, G. (2004). Almere fibre pilot. Breedband Congres, Amsterdam.

Jelgersma, P. and C. Titulaer (1981). *Kabeltelevisie; verleden, heden en toekomst*. Helmond: Uitgeverij Helmond.

Kaasschieter, J. J. (1985). CCITT standards on ISDN. *Trends in Telecommunications. 1*.

Kool, L., M. Arno, S. De Munck & S. Huveneers (2008). Marktrapportage Elektronische Communicatie, December 2008. Delft, The Netherlands: TNO Informatie- en Communicatietechnologie.

Kools, Q. H. and S. Serail (2003). Een onderzoek naar ICT in het dagelijks leven van bewoners in Kenniswijk anno 2003. Onderzoeksreeks. M. v. E. Zaken. The Hague: Ministerie van Economische Zaken, DGTP.

KPN (2003). Deltaplan Glas. The Hague, The Netherlands.

(2009). Digitenne. Retrieved 2009-06-25, from www.kpn.com/televosie/Digitenne/Digitenne-van-KPN/.

Lemstra, W. (2006). The Internet bubble and the impact on the development path of the telecommunication sector. (Dissertation.) Department of Technology, Policy and Management. Delft, The Netherlands: TUDelft. p 460.

Lemstra, W., V. Hayes and J. P. M. Groenewegen, Eds. (2010). *The innovation journey of Wi-Fi – The road to global success*. Cambridge, UK: Cambridge University Press.

Lemstra, W., A. van Gorp and B. Voogt (2013). Explaining broadband performance across the EU. Delft University of Technology Delft: p 63.

Linssen, F. (2005). De overheid in glasvezel – Een analytisch model voor glasvezel initiatieven. MSc thesis, Department Technology, Policy and Management. Delft, The Netherlands: TUDelft.

Maclaine Pont, P. and J. W. J. Van Till (2001). Breedband Internet voor/door gemeenten. Amsterdam: Stedenlink.

Meerman, K. (2004). ISPs en webhosters. Retrieved 2010-11-09, from www.emerce.nl/artikel_print. jsp?id=426847&rid-404797&site-247.

Milward, R. (2005). *Private and public enterprise in Europe – Energy, telecommunications and transport 1830–1990.* Cambridge, UK: Cambridge University Press.

MinEZ (1999). De digitale delta. The Hague: Ministry of Economic Affairs.

(2003). DGTP Policy agenda 2003–2004. the Hague: Ministry of Economic Affairs, DGTP.

(2004). De Breedbandnota – Een kwestie van tempo en betere benutting. Den Haag: Ministerie van Economische Zaken, Directoraat Generaal Telecommunicatie en Posterijen.

(2010). Consulatatiedocument mbt Strategische nota Mobiele communciatie. Den Haag: Ministerie van Economische Zaken: p 33.

(2011). Digitale implementatie agenda.nl. Den Haag: Ministerie van Economsiche Zaken, Landbouw en Innovatie.

MinOC&W (2000). Kabel en consument: Marktwerking en digitalisering. Den Haag: Ministerie van Onderwijs, Cultuur en Wetenschappen.

MinV&W (2000a). Netwerken in cijfers – Trendrapportage over ICT-Infrastructuren 2000. Den Haag: p 82.

(2000b). Netwerken in de delta – Eerste klas voorzieningen voor netwerkeconomie en informatiemaatschappij: Ministerie van Verkeer en Waterstaat p77.

NLKabel (2009). NLKabel geschiedenis. Retrieved 2009-05-10, from www.nlkabel.nl/nl/Home/Over-NLkabel/Geschiedenis.aspx.

NLnet (2010). A second start for the NLnet foudation: Some history. Retrieved 2010-11-10, from www.nlnet.nl/foundation/history/199804-usenix.html.

NMa (2002). Zaak 2987/Koninklijke Volker Wessels Stevin – KPN Netwerk Bouw.

(2008). NMa onder voorwaarden akkoord met joint venture KPN-Reggefiber. Retrieved 2009-06-29, from www.nmanet.nl/nderlands/home/Actueel/Nieuws_Persberichten.

NRC (1994). Staat ontvangt 6.9 mld; Aandeel KPN voor Hfl 49.75 naar de beurs. NRC-Handelsblad. Rotterdam.

(1999). Rol overheid in KPN ter discussie. NRC-Handelsblad. Rotterdam.

(2003). Financiën buigt niet in kwestie gouden aandeel. NRC-Handelsblad. Rotterdam.

(2005a). Staat casht met KPN. NRC-Handelsblad. Rotterdam.

(2005b). Staat doet afstand van vetorecht KPN. NRC-Handelsblad. Rotterdam.

(2007). Glasvezel in Adam toegestaan. NRC Handelsblad. Rotterdam.

(2008). UPC verhoogt snelheid internet. NRC Handelsblad. Rotterdam.

NU.nl (2006). Amsterdam: geen bemoeienis met glasvezelnetwerk.

Olsthoorn, P. (2008). Reggefiber glas al voor groot deel naar KPN. Retrieved 2009-01-12, from www.emerce.nl/artikel_print.jsp?id=2562285.

OPTA (2006a). De markten voor de doorgifte en verzorging van omroep transmissiediensten. The Hague: OPTA.

(2006b). Economic policy note, no. 6: Is two enough? The Hague: OPTA.

(2006c). KPN's Next Generation Network: All-IP. The Hague: OPTA.

(2007). Structurele monitoring breedband. The Hague: OPTA.

(2008a). All-IP stand van zaken. The Hague: OPTA.

(2008b). Consultatie Beleidsregels – Tariefregulering ontbundelde glastoegang: Nota van bevindingen. The Hague: OPTA.

(2008c). Markt analyse – Ontbundelde toegang op wholesale niveau. The Hague: OPTA.

(2008d). Marktanalyse – Ontbundelde toegang op wholesale niveau. The Hague: OPTA.

(2008e). Structurele monitoring multiplay. The Hague: OPTA.

(2009a). Marktanalyse Omroep. The Hague: OPTA.

(2009b). Tariefbesluit ontbundelde glastoegang (FttH) – Voorontwerp. The Hague: OPTA.

(2009c). Zienswijze van OPTA aan de NMa over KPN/Reggefiber. Retrieved 2009-06-29, from www.opta.nl/nl/actueel/alle-publicaties/publicatie/?id=2858.

(2010). OPTA jaarverslag 2010. The Hague: Onafhakelijke Post en Telecommunicatie Autoriteit.

Reggefiber (2009). Missie, visie en strategie. Retrieved 2009-06-29, from www.reggefiber.nl/missie-visie-en-strategie.html.

Schouten, E. (2006). Niemand kiest voor het Appingedam-model. *NRC Handelsblad.* Rotterdam.

Schrijver, F. J. (1983). De invoering van kabeltelevisie in Nederland. Voorstudies en achtergronden mediabeleid. W. R. v. h. Regeringsbeleid. Den Haag: WRR.

Schuilenga, J. H., J. D. Tours, J. G. Visser and J. Bruggeman, Eds. (1981). *Honderd jaar telefoon.*

Den Haag: Staatsbedrijf der Posterijen, Telegrafie en Telefonie.

Stratix (2001). Almere op glas. Schiphol: Stratix: p 77.

(2013). FTTH Monitor – 2013/Q3 Glasvezelontwikkelingen in Nederland. Hilversum, The Netherlands: Statix Consulting.

SURFnet (2009). Gigaport Next Generation Network: Lichtend voorbeeld van visie, durf en samenwerking. Utrecht, the Netherlands: SURFnet.

Tanenbaum, A. S. (1996). *Computer networks*. Upper Saddle River, NJ: Prentice-Hall.

Telecompaper (2013a). Dutch television market Q3 2013. Houten, The Netherlands: p 26.

(2013b). Monitor mobiele markt januari 2013 – report for OPTA. Houten, Netherlands: p 51.

TNO (2012). Evolution and prospects cable networks for broadband services. Delft: TNO.

(2013). Monitor draadloze technologie 2013. Delft, The Netherlands: TNO: p 35.

Tromp, H. R. C., H. T. Nijhuis, Y. Boomsma and J. Bakker (1991). Fibre-to-the-Home in The Netherlands. *Telecommunication access networks: Technology and service trends*. (Ed.) W. Lemstra. Amsterdam: Elsevier Science Publishers.

Van Bochove, A. C., M. O. Van Deventer, P. W. Hooijmans, M. T. Tomesen, P. P. G. Mols and G. D. Khoe (1991). Coherent transmission in the local loop. *Telecommunication access networks: Technology and service trends*. W. Lemstra. Amsterdam: Elsevier Science Publishers.

Van Bockxmeer, H. M., M. A. Poel, E. H. Hulshof and P. W. M. Rutten (2002). De Nederlandse kabelsector. Delft, The Netherlands: TNO.

Van de Ven, P. (1984). De opkomst van de computernetwerken. NRC Handelsblad. Rotterdam.

Van den Berg, R. (2004). Competition in Internet access in The Netherlands, 2000–2004. Delft: Delft University of Technology.

Van der Woud, A. (2007). *Een nieuwe wereld – Het ontstaan van het moderne Nederland* (A new world – The emergence of the modern Netherlands). Amsterdam: Prometheus – Bert Bakker.

Van Dijk, M., B. Minne, M. Mulder, J. Poort and H. Van der Wiel (2005). Do market failures hamper the perspectives of broadband? The Hague: CPB.

Van Gool, L. (2009). Jan davids, directie Reggefiber,: Bestaande kabeltelevisienetwerken verliezen de race. Retrieved 2009-06-29, from www.glasvezel.nu/nieuws/00897-20090319_jan-davids-dirctie-reggefiber.

Van Iersel, F. and K. Neggers (2010). ICT innovation as practicesed by SURFnet. The Hague: Ministry of Economic Affairs.

Van Wijnbergen, S. (2000). De WRR snapt niets van privatisering. *NRC-Handelsblad*. Rotterdam.

Verbree, A. (1997). De local loop voor bestaande en nieuwe diensten. Nationaal Overleg Telecommunciatie '97, Utrecht, the Netherlands: Euroforum.

Verhoog, J. (2008). SURFnet 1988–2008: Twintig jaar grensverleggend netwerken. Utrecht: Stichting SURFnet.

Vles, H. (2008). *Hallo Bandoeng – Nederlandse radiopioniers 1900–1945*. Zutphen, The Netherlands: Walburg Pers.

VNG (1994). Gemeentelijk beleid kabeltelevisienetten. Den Haag: Vereniging Nederlandse Gemeenten.

Vogt, W. (1958). *Spanne en spanning*. Hilversum: Philips Telecommunicatie Industrie.

VolkerWessels (2009). Historie. Retrieved 2009-06-29, from www.volkerwessels.com/bin/ibp.jsp?ibpDispWhat=zone&ibpPage=S3_geschiedenis.

Weeder, P. and M. H. J. Nijland (2002). Amsterdam, the big cherry? Amersfoort, The Netherlands: M&I/PARTNERS.

Weeder, P., M. H. J. Nijland and B. R. Hotho (2003). Amsterdam: slagkracht door glas – Advies Commissie Andriessen. Amersfoort, The Netherlands: M&I/PARTNERS.

Weeder, P., M. H. J. Nijland and J. Konijn (2004). Amsterdam: breedband in beweging. Amersfoort, The Netherlands: M&I/PARTNERS.

Wessels, P. (1994). Bescherming KPN smet op blazoen Staat en beurs. *NRC-Handelsblad*. Rotterdam.

Wikipedia (2009a). ADSL2. Retrieved 2009-07-01, from http://nl.wikipedia.org/w/index.php?title=ADSL2&printable=yes.

(2009b). Digitenne. Retrieved 2009-06-25, from http://nl.wikipedia.org/w/index.php?title=Digitenne&printable=yes.

(2009c). DOCSIS. Retrieved 2009-01-21, from htttp://en.wikipedia.org/w/index.php?title=DOCSIS&printable=yes.

(2009d). IBM VNET. Retrieved 2010-11-10, from http://en.wikipedia.org/w/index.php?title=IBM_VNET&printable=yes.

(2010a). Caiway. Retrieved 2010-06-21, from http://nl.wikipedia.org/w/index.php?title=Caiway.

(2010b). Geschiedenis van het internet in Nederland. Retrieved 2010-11-09, from http://nl.wikipedia.org/w/index.php?title=Geschiedenis_van_het_internet_in_Nederland.htm.

XS4ALL (2001). Bedrijfsportret: In bedrijf 1993 tot 2001. Retrieved 2010-11-09, from www.xs4all.nl/overxs4all/geschiedenis/vogelvlucht.php.

(2007). Bedrijfsportret 2007. Retrieved 2010-11-09, from www.xs4all.nl/overxs4all/geschiedenis/vogelvlucht.php.

(2010). Het begin van XS4ALL. Retrieved 2010-06-21, from www.xs4all.nl/overxs4all/geschiedenis/vogelvlucht.php.

Belgium: Flanders

MARLIES VAN DER WEE, SOFIE VERBRUGGE
AND REINHARD LAROY

Preamble: Flanders in Belgium

Belgium is a small but complex country, bounded by several states and for a small part by the North Sea. Its surface, only 30,500 km², covers a variety of landscapes, a coastal plain in the north-west, a plateau in the centre and the forested Ardennes uplands in the southern part of the country. Although small, the country is split into three different communities based on language and culture: the Dutch-speaking community in the north (about 60% of the population), the French-speaking (40%) in the south and a small area of German-speaking people (about 74,000 people) in the east of Belgium. Apart from this division, Belgium consists out of three regions: Flanders, Wallonia and the Brussels Capital Region located geographically between the former two (Belgium, 2011).

This complex geographical and cultural partition clearly has its political consequences. There are many different levels of political authority in Belgium. Next to the federal government, every community and region has its own council (legislative body) and government (executive body). Belgium is a monarchy with a King who is the Head of State, but who does not exercise any personal authority. The ministers of the federal government, communities and regions are fully responsible for signing new laws in their own field. For the telecommunications sector, the National Regulatory Authority, BIPT, is a federal institute, and responsible for all that concerns the telecommunications networks. On the other hand, the legal institutes for media (media regulator) fall under the responsibility of the communities, since these bodies regulate content and are therefore language-driven. Thirdly, there is the competition authority, which is federal but separate, a part of the Ministry of Economic Affairs.

With a total population of 10,951,665 (at 1 January 2011), Belgium is a densely populated state. The population density is considerably higher in the region of Flanders (about 460 people/km² in 2010) than in Wallonia (about 205 people/km² in 2010) (Eurostat, 2011).

The Belgian economy is mainly based on services, transport and trade (73% of the working population) (CIA, 2011). The share of industry (25% of the working population) keeps decreasing. The main industrial zones are currently located near the harbour cities of Antwerp, Bruges and Ghent. In Wallonia, the most important industrial sites are located along the two largest rivers: the Sambre and the Meuse. Agriculture is limited in Belgium (only 2% of the working population). Because of its central position in Europe, Belgium (especially its capital Brussels) is a very attractive location for central offices of international companies. This central position also requires Belgium to own a well-developed transportation infrastructure. There is an extensive network of highways, railways and waterways. Belgium has five international airports, among them the two large airports in Zaventem and Charleroi, and a number of international harbours, among which is the harbour of Antwerp, the second largest in Europe.

By the end of the 1980s, badly planned economic policies resulted in a public debt of 120% of the Gross Domestic Product (GDP). In the following period, the Belgian government made sure that every major decision fitted in the overall goal of reducing this major debt. By the end of 2006, the public debt was reduced to 100% and to 90% in 2008. Due to the financial crisis in recent years, this public debt has risen again to 99.7% in 2011 (CIA, 2011). All three major banks in Belgium suffered heavily from this crisis and the government was forced to intervene financially to prevent severe damage.

It is important to note that this paper focuses only on Flanders. As can be derived from this short introduction, the differences between Flanders and Wallonia are significant, both in the development of the telecom sector and in the emergence of different actors. The authors therefore chose to devote the remainder of this chapter to the development of telecommunications in the region of Flanders only. The focus will be on the development of fixed broadband, in particular infrastructure-based competition between the PSTN operator and the CATV-cable operator.

5.1 Introduction: the dual road of telephone and analogue television network development

Telecommunications started a long time ago but developed faster and faster as time went by, from communicating by means of carrier pigeons in the Middle Ages, over telegraph systems at the beginning of the 19th century to telephone networks deployed at the end of the 19th century, while cable networks for broadcast services emerged in the 1950s. This section provides a brief overview of the development of copper and coaxial cable networks, since, in Flanders, they are now both used to offer broadband connectivity.

5.1.1 The development of the copper network

Introduction to communication services in Belgium (1879–1930)

The first telephone line was installed by the Belgian telegraph service at the Parliament in 1879. The first telephone call between two cities (Brussels and Antwerp) took place in 1884 and the first international conversation (with France) in 1886. The first commercial exploitation was set up by a subsidiary of the International Bell Telephone Company (IBTC) (Dienst Pers en Informatie, 1982). This subsidiary, the N.V. Bell Telephone Manufacturing Company, was founded

in 1882 with the aim of introducing public telephony in Europe (Vanden Berghen, 2012). In 1886, the Belgian state granted Bell the installation of the first local telephone network in Ostend.

The networks owned by Bell worked fine in the densely populated cities, but did not succeed in connecting people in the rural areas. Additionally, the private ownership of the various local networks made it difficult to interconnect them. In 1893, the Belgian state bought back the concessions and thereby regained control of the various local networks. In 1896, the Belgian state decided to establish a public company that received total control of the telephone sector. The company started by taking over the remaining private networks; the final goal was to provide telephone service throughout the entire country. By 1913, the major part of Belgium had access to telephones, principally through public booths installed in most railway stations and post offices (Wikipedia, 2011).

Monopolistic situation: RTT (1930–1991)

With the outbreak of the First World War, the Belgian authorities had to deal with great financial trouble and could no longer support the public telephone company. This led to an abrupt suspension of telecommunication services in Belgium. In order to avoid losing facilities due to lack of financial means in the future, a new company was founded under the name of RTT (Regie Telegraaf en Telefonie) in 1930, which inherited a subscriber base of about 225,000 customers. This public company still owned the monopoly over the whole telephone network, but was set up as an autonomous institution, no longer depending on the funding provided by the authorities. Competition was out of the question, as all threats of entry and substitute products were locked out by law, which determined that the RTT not only had the monopoly of owning and exploiting the copper network but also the sole rights to offering services and equipment. Its independence soon appeared to be primarily theoretical, as the economic crisis of the 1930s caused the RTT to become involved in the industrial and employment policy of the state. To reduce the high unemployment rate, the RTT was forced to create jobs through the expansion and total automation of the Belgian telephone network. In the period from 1930 to the beginning of the Second World War, the RTT succeeded in increasing its customer base by almost one third, reaching a subscriber base of more than 300,000 customers.

During World War II, the Belgian telephone network experienced serious damage and parts of its lines were destroyed. The RTT lost more than 70,000 subscribers. To support the fast developing economy, that characterized the period after the Second World War, the state decided to intervene financially to give a boost to the telecommunication sector. The growing number of subscribers (from 350,000 in 1946 to 522,000 in 1951 and 1,049,000 in 1965) stimulated the RTT to invest heavily in its network. As a consequence, the Belgian telephone network became one of the most developed and most progressive at the time[1].

But this boom had its negative side. At the end of the 1960s, the saturation of the market put a stop to the increasing revenue trend, and losses started to accumulate. Then, in 1973, the civil engineer Paul Demaegt, an RTT employee, revealed that Germain Baudrain, the administrative director of RTT at the time, no longer put up the construction and decoration of RTT-buildings out to public tender, but awarded it to private enterprises in which the director himself owned shares. This led to an augmentation of the RTT's losses. Although the telecom network remained well maintained, questions about the RTT's efficiency arose. Customers (especially business subscribers) started to realize that the prices they were paying were too high for the quality of service they received. This awareness also arose in other countries, was a major cause for regulatory intervention and provided the justification for serious restructuring of the sector during the 1980s and 1990s.

---

[1] In 1965, Belgium counted 9,428,100 inhabitants. Assuming three people per household, almost one-third of all Belgian households were directly connected to the network.

Towards the liberalization of the Belgian market (1991–1998)

The first legislation concerning the use of the telephone was published in 1896, with the monopolization of the network and the foundation of the first public company. The first real Telecommunications Law appeared in 1930, together with the formation of the RTT. This law remained relatively unchanged for about sixty years, as nothing fundamentally changed concerning the monopolistic situation of the RTT.

The major cause of change resulted from the publishing of the Green Paper on the development of the common market for telecommunication services and equipment (European Commission, 1987). This paper aimed at initiating discussions in Europe concerning the development of a common market for telecommunications. Also, the decreasing satisfaction of Belgian customers made the authorities realize that change was needed. On 21 March 1991, the proposals from the Green Paper were incorporated in Belgian law (Belgium, 1991), which led to the foundation of two institutions: Belgacom, an autonomous telecommunications operator with a monopoly in the copper telephone network and the BIPT (Belgian Institute for Postal Services & Telecommunications), a regulatory authority.

- *Belgian Institute for Postal services and Telecommunications (BIPT)*

    The BIPT is the Belgian National Regulatory Authority, positioned as an independent institution. The role of the Ministry of Telecommunications is limited to selecting and assigning (by means of a Royal Decree) the executive board members every six years. BIPT funds itself using revenues from the management of licenses and numbering. Its main responsibilities include (BIPT, 2011):

    – correct application of the laws concerning telecommunications (radio, television, telephone and Internet services) and postal services;
    – oversight of the transition of the necessary European directives into Belgian law (although this obligation is to be shifted to the Directorate-General (DG) Telecom of the Ministry of Economic Affairs);

– management of scarce resources, i.e., the radio frequency spectrum and the numbering space;
– mediation when differences between telecom operators occur;
– granting of licenses to new entrants.

To prevent conflicts of interest between the telecom operators and the BIPT, the latter is forbidden to practise commercial activities.

At the same time, another institution was founded next to the BIPT: the Office of the Ombudsman for Telecommunications (Ombudsdienst Telecommunicatie, 2011). This organization serves as a mediator between customers and telecom operators. It is a completely different institution, independent of the operators, authorities and regulators. Whenever a customer has a complaint concerning an operator, if this customer cannot come to an agreement with the operator, he or she can turn to the Ombudsman for intervention.

Every year, the organization submits a report on the major complaints. This report can be seen as a representation of the Belgian customer's demands and complaints, which can be used to further improve the existing infrastructures and services.

- *Belgacom*

    The Law of 1991 aimed to transform the Belgian market in order to make it more receptive to competition. Belgacom was created as a successor of the RTT and still owned the entire Belgian telephone network. The main difference between the RTT and Belgacom concerned the degree of monopoly. The RTT had the monopoly of exploiting the whole telephone network, while Belgacom only inherited the monopoly on 'public telecommunications'. The Law of 1991 defined public telecommunications as (Belgium, 1991):
    – construction, maintenance, modernization and operation of public telecommunications infrastructure;
    – exploitation of the reserved services (including telephone and telegraph service, provisioning of fixed links) for third parties;
    – construction, maintenance and operation of the publicly accessible establishments located on the public domain and intended for telecommunications.

In 1994, the Bangemann Report from the European Commission provided the official recognition for the complete liberalization of the European telecommunications market. As a response to this report, the government decided to privatize Belgacom in that same year by selling 50% -1 of its shares to the ADSB Consortium, consisting of Ameritech, Tele Danmark and Singapore Telecom, plus three Belgian financial institutions: Sofina, Dexia and KBC. The other 50% + 1 share stayed in the possession of the Belgian authorities, the state thus remaining the major shareholder. The state believed this privatization to be necessary to counter competition from international rivals, because of the attractive position of Belgacom as the only telecom operator in a country in the centre of Europe, but also to be able to face the competition to emerge from the domestic CATV operators, as the European directives authorized the 'commercial exploitation of non-reserved services on alternative infrastructures'. Next to reducing the threat of entry, the Belgian state used the proceeds from this privatization to reduce the huge public debt the country had to deal with at that time.

1994 was also the year of the foundation of the first Belgian mobile network: Proximus. This network and the old analogue Mob2 system were transferred later that year to a separate subsidiary, Belgacom Mobile. Belgacom owned 75% of shares; the other 25% was in the hands of US-based Air Touch which was acquired by Vodafone in 1999. Today, Belgacom again owns 100% of the shares. As mentioned in the introduction to this chapter, we will not explore the development of the mobile market in further detail. Only the facts that are important in relation to the actors in the fixed broadband market and the services offered will be addressed.

Belgacom entered the Internet market in 1996 with the acquisition of 25% of the shares of Skynet, a company providing Internet services that was founded in 1995. Before 1995, it was principally the academic world that made use of the Internet through the research network, BELNET, that could be used free of charge by the Belgian universities thanks to funding from the federal government. Belgacom acquired the remaining 75% of Skynet shares two years later. The subsidiary Belgacom Skynet was officially born, and customers could gain access to narrowband Internet using dial-up.

5.1.2 The development of the cable network

Introduction to cable services in Belgium

The distribution of television channels by cable networks originated in the United States of America in 1947. Belgium was the first country on the European mainland that established cable distribution networks in the early 1950s. The first cable lines were installed in large apartment buildings where the residents invested jointly in one antenna and distributed the signals using cable. Soon, some of those networks were combined into inter-municipal networks, sometimes with the participation of a private firm. The initiator was NV Coditel, which set up a cable network in Saint-Servais (close to Namur, in the Walloon region) in 1960. Liège, Verviers and Visé were connected to the network in the following years. The regions of Brussels and Flanders followed the lead of Coditel with the foundation of similar companies in their regions. The number of subscribers grew rapidly: more than 50% of Belgian viewers had subscribed by 1976 and about 88% in 1985 (De Bens, 1986). There are several reasons for this boost. First of all, cabling was promising in both densely populated and rural areas. Urban areas with lots of inhabitants gave the cable companies the advantages of economies of scale, while the poor antenna-reception in the rural areas formed a good incentive for the roll-out of a more reliable cable network. Another important motive included the linguistic duality in Belgium. The Dutch-speaking part was interested in receiving foreign TV-channels from the Netherlands and, analogously, the French-speaking part wanted to watch French TV-shows and movies. Last but not least, cable networks also served an aesthetic purpose: once homes were connected to the cable network, the jungle of antennas could be removed.

Because of the large difference in content between the Flemish and Walloon television services, the authorities decided to put the regulations and legislations for cable networks – and television in general – under the responsibility of the communities (media regulators). It is important to note that although the cable operators were autonomous companies, a formal approval from the RTT was necessary for the establishment and exploitation of any cable network, irrespective of size. By 1996, thirty-eight cable companies with a total subscription base of 95% of households made Belgium the world's leading country for cable coverage. Despite the large number of cable companies, competition wasn't present at the time, as every cable company operated only in its own geographical region.

The demand for more programs and channels caused serious expansion campaigns during the 1980s and 1990s, each time increasing the available bandwidth per user and thereby enhancing the quantity and quality of the services offered. Starting in the 1990s, local companies merged in order to be able to keep up with the required investments and to improve the services. Only a couple of big companies remained, mainly based on geographical coverage. After a series of important mergers, driven by both public and private actors, only one cable company remained in Flanders: Telenet. The interactions leading to the current shape and status of the cable company were important for the market structure and development of broadband in Flanders; hence, they are the case's focus in the next section.

5.1.3 Case focus: the Flemish initiatives leading to the founding and survival of Telenet

In Flanders, the project 'Multimedia in Vlaanderen' (Van Batselaer et al., 1997) was aimed at developing an information society in Flanders[2]. This project was presented by the Flemish government in April 1996 and based on domestic studies as well as conclusions from European and international studies. The objectives of this

---

[2] Such a government-driven project cannot be identified in the Walloon region of Belgium.

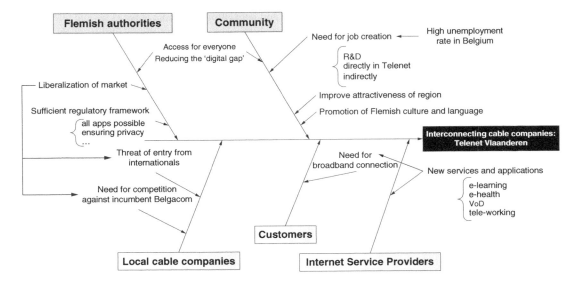

Figure 5.1 Impact diagram representing the important causes for theTelenet Vlaanderen project

project were multi-fold (Van den Brande, 1996), see also Figure 5.1:

- conversion of the Flemish cable infrastructure into an interactive broadband network offering broadcast, telecommunication and multimedia services;
- creation of a stable regulatory institution and legislation based on competition;
- promotion of research and development in the sector of information technology;
- assignment of an exemplary role to the Flemish government in the set-up of pilot projects;
- creation of additional jobs.

The objective of this project was to create new applications and to lay the foundation of an information society in Flanders, as well as to create a united cable company as a competitor to Belgacom in Flanders. The policy plan of 1996 gave some examples of future applications, some of which are now commonly used: e-learning, e-working, e-shopping, e-administration, video-on-demand, e-health and many more.

The major consequence of the project was the foundation of Telenet Vlaanderen, set up to interconnect and potentially unite the independent Flemish cable companies to achieve an interactive broadband network offering broadcast and

telecommunications, as well as multimedia services to all citizens. This foundation provided a good fit within the project 'Telenet in Vlaanderen', the major sub-project of 'Multimedia in Vlaanderen'.

The reasons for this project were twofold. On the one hand, the infrastructure was insufficiently used, although Flanders possessed one of the densest cable networks in the world. The legal restrictions imposed upon the cable networks (every action in the cable sector must be approved by the RTT) limited the application possibilities. At the time, there were many small cable companies, each covering their own region with their own infrastructure but lacking interconnection between the different regions and infrastructures. On the other hand, with the liberalization of the telecom market of January 1998 (authorized by the European Commission) on the horizon, a need arose for competition with the incumbent Belgacom and other possible international entrants.

A thorough feasibility study performed by the GIMV (Gewestelijke InvesteringsMaatschappij voor Vlaanderen, a European venture capitalist with public funds and experience in private equity (GIMV, 1998)), estimated the investment costs at BEF50 billion (about EUR 1.25 billion). A starting capital of BEF17 billion (about EUR 420,000) was provided by a consortium of four large partners in the Telenet Holding: MediaOne (25%), the Flemish inter-municipal corporations (35%), GIMV (20%) and a financial consortium with representatives of the Flemish media and several financial groups (20%). A major part of this total investment was invested in rolling out an extensive fibre backbone of about 635 km in order to connect the individual networks of the various cable companies, which was completed in July 1997. Through the use of switching centres and by making the amplifiers in the coaxial network bi-directional, two-way traffic became possible, thereby enabling many additional applications, as such creating a playing field for innovation.

As a consequence of the 'Multimedia in Vlaanderen' project, a set of new enterprises arose from the merger of the former local cable companies. Apart from the foundation of Telenet itself, 1996 was characterized by the creation of UPC Belgium (United Pan-Europe Communications Belgium), founded as a joint venture of Philips and UIH (United International Holding), with US-based Liberty Global and UPC Broadband as major stakeholders. Its network took over the existing networks in seven communes of Brussels (Etterbeek, Ganshoren, Jette, Koekelberg, Schaerbeek, Berchem-Holy-Agathe and Forest) and three communes of Flanders (Heverlee, Kessel-Lo and Leeuwen). Another cable company, Interkabel Vlaanderen, resulted from the merger of three local 'intercommunales': Interelectra (province of Limburg and the Antwerp city of Laakdal), PBE (region of Hageland in the province of Vlaams-Brabant), WVEM (regions of Diskmuide en Wevelgem in the province of West-Vlaanderen, region Halle-Vilvoorde in the province of Vlaams-Brabant and the cities of Beerse and Vosselaar in the province of Antwerp) and Integan (region of Antwerp and city of Essen). Interkabel Vlaanderen offered broadband services, cable television and INDI, a digital television platform.

Although the business plan for Telenet was ambitious, the first Internet access offer, branded Pandora (launched in August 1997), was too expensive (about EUR 50 per month), leading to a delay of the expected boom in uptake and very high debts. Furthermore, Telenet (Pandora) only

received revenues from offering additional services; the network revenues stayed with the network owners (privately owned and geographically divided 'intercommunales'). In 2002, the newly appointed CEO, Duco Sickinghe, changed the strategy of the company. By buying into the intercommunales (UPC Belgium in 2006[3], Interkabel Vlaanderen in 2008[4]) in return for a share in the larger Telenet, he could refinance the entire operation, using the ensured revenues from the network (cable TV revenues previously destined for the intercommunales) as collateral. Through the takeover of about 850,000 customers of UPC and Interkabel, Telenet acquired the fourth and final important part of the Flemish cable network. This strategic move prevented Belgacom from entering the cable infrastructure business, and therefore made Telenet a full competitor on the infrastructure level using its HFC (Hybrid Fibre Coaxial) architecture.

Apart from the strategy change, the Belgian NRA, BIPT, had an important influence on the business case for Telenet: that is, an interconnection agreement signed with Belgacom on the application of asymmetric regulation on termination fees to the advantage of Telenet meant a large extra income for Telenet, and saved the company to some extent (as without this measure, Telenet

---

[3] In November 2006 UPC Belgium was taken over by Telenet with, as major advantage for Telenet, the expansion of its geographical region to Brussels and an increase of its subscribers by about 42,000. Starting from 9 July 2007, Telenet offered all its services to the former customers of UPC Belgium.

[4] In November 2007 the press reported that Interkabel Vlaanderen and Telenet had concluded a policy agreement on the takeover of distribution of analogue and digital television (INDI) from Interkabel by Telenet. The other large telecom operator in Belgium, Belgacom, reacted by instituting legal proceedings, stating that the auction should be a public one. On 10 June 2008 Belgacom made an offer of EUR 420 million, but this wasn't sufficient to persuade Interkabel, which decided to accept a final offer of EUR 427 million from Telenet on 28 June 2008 (Van Leemputten, 28/06/2008; Telenet, 1/10/2008). It is important to note here the role of the competition authority, which watched the development closely: given the complementarity of the coverage of Telenet and Interkabel, there was no problem about the takeover, but this would have been a concern if Belgacom had won the bid.

might have gone bankrupt). Some even considered this asymmetric regulation as an indirect subsidy from Belgacom to Telenet, justified in the context of creating a level playing field in telecoms in Flanders. Although this justification may be subject to discussion, it led to the current duopoly situation where Belgacom and Telenet compete for broadband customers.

5.2 Case description: From narrowband to broadband in Flanders – a duopoly market

Although the European telecom reform aimed at introducing more competition by allowing new entrants to compete on the copper network of the incumbent, it largely resulted in a competitive duopoly between the incumbent operator Belgacom and the cable operator Telenet. This section will describe the evolution and the most important events in the development of broadband (Internet), while focusing on the tit-for-tat competition between copper and cable. A summary of the most important events for both operators is given in Figure 5.2 and Figure 5.4, respectively. Although this paper focuses on the development of fixed broadband markets, we also include a timeline for mobile communications because all operators

offer quadruple play services (including television, Internet and fixed and mobile telephony).

5.2.1 Belgacom in a competitive setting

Starting 1 January 1998, the Belgian telecom market was completely liberalized, whereby Belgacom was obliged to open up its network to new entrants. Local Loop Unbundling (LLU) was legislated in October 2000, allowing access to the network of the incumbent from 1 January 2001 onwards. Belgacom first issued a Reference Unbundling Offer (RUO) in December 2000, which was reviewed and rejected by the BIPT several times. The publication of the documents was found inadequate and the standard contracts contained a number of clauses that formed a serious obstruction to new entrants (as stated in the review of Belgacom's Reference LLU Offer, 12-03-2001 (BIPT, 12/03/2001; 14/03/2001). The final BRUO-proposal (Belgacom's RUO) was approved by the BIPT in March 2001 and included rental possibilities on three levels: full LLU, line sharing and sub-loop unbundling. Bitstream access was granted a few months later through a separate reference offer. The Belgian market became not only officially but also practically open to OLOs (Other Licensed Operators).

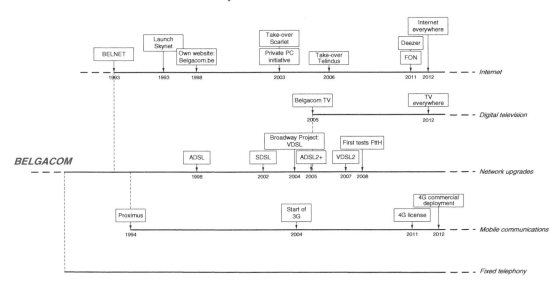

Figure 5.2 Timeline presenting the most important events in the history of Belgacom

Because of this newly introduced competition, Belgacom had to improve its applications and services in order to maintain its strong position on the telecom market. Figure 5.2 provides an overview of the most important events that characterized Belgacom's history. In the following paragraphs we will discuss these events.

Broadband Internet: network upgrades

In order to stay competitive, a prime requirement is to have a competitive network. After emergence of the public Internet and dial-up use in 1995, the real story of commercial broadband Internet using the PSTN network of Belgacom begins in 1998, with the execution of a pilot project for the testing of ADSL (asymmetric digital subscriber line), 'the high-data rate access roads to the information highway'. The project included 1,000 customers in several large Belgian cities (Antwerp, Brussels, Leuven, Liège, Mechelen, Ghent and Charleroi). Belgacom predicted that, by using this new technology, transferring information at data rates up to 8 Mbit/s (download) and 600 kbit/s (upload) per user would become everyday reality in the near future.

Because of the success of the pilot project (80% of the test public approved of the possibilities of the service and agreed to recommend it), Belgacom Skynet was one of the first operators (world-wide) to introduce ADSL commercially in April 1999. Soon, ADSL covered 30 to 35% of Belgacom's telephone customers. The intention was to achieve coverage of 70% by the end of 2000. This objective was exceeded when in November 2000, ADSL services were available to 75% of Belgian population. By the end of 2002, the coverage was almost complete when 98% of the inhabitants had access to ADSL services (Belgacom, 15/01/2003), making Belgium the leader in Europe. In 2010, DSL coverage had reached 99.85% of the Belgian population. In terms of uptake, Belgacom had 517,000 subscribers by the end of 2002, an increase of 290,000 since the end of 2001. This number doubled again in the next two years, reaching the milestone of 1 million in 2004 (Belgacom, 25/02/2004). By June 2011, Belgacom had 1,835,000 subscribers.

Not only did technical measures give rise to network upgrades and expansion of uptake; at the end of 2008, the acquisition of Scarlet, a Dutch telecom company specialized in low-cost Internet offers, increased the market share of Belgacom by 5%. Both the BIPT and the OLOs reacted quite negatively to this acquisition; however, IBPT approved the acquisition on the condition that Scarlet's backbone was sold. Not only did this take-over increase Belgacom's market share but it also allowed Belgacom to offer a low-cost brand (although Scarlet is fully owned by Belgacom, the name is retained) (De Tijd, 09/09/2008).

In 2002, Belgacom launched SDSL (Symmetric DSL), which provides a fast Internet connection with the same maximum available data rates in both directions (up and down). SDSL was primarily developed for business customers. The need for higher data rates made Belgacom explore the opportunities of fibre deployment within the scope of the Broadway project that was launched in 2004. This project aimed at upgrading the network to a combined copper and fibre network. The goal was to connect the central offices to the street cabinets using optical fibre (the so-called Fibre-to-the-Cabinet, FttC) and to roll out a VDSL platform between the street cabinets and the end users. The VDSL technology was introduced commercially on 2 November 2004 and by investing EUR 103 million in 2006, VDSL coverage of 45% was reached by the end of that year. This VDSL technology offered data rates up to 8 Mbit/s download and 400 kbit/s upload by the beginning of 2005. Because the equipment vendor Alcatel Lucent no longer supported the particular VDSL technology (incompatible with ADSL and too much spectral noise) and because the need for higher data rates was urgent due to the introduction of digital television, Belgacom implemented ADSL2+ in 2005 as a temporary solution until the new VDSL2 standard would be ready at the end of 2007. By 2009, a total investment of about EUR 500 million had led to the deployment of 14,000 km of fibre, connecting 17,000 ROPs (Remote Optical Platforms) representing a FttC coverage of about 70%. Thanks to the early investments in the Broadway project and the high ranking of the VDSL2-coverage (second place in Europe in 2009),

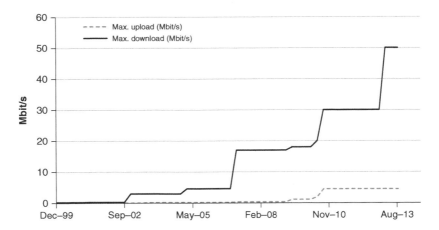

Figure 5.3 Evolution of the data rates offered by Belgacom, Dec. 1999–Aug. 2013 (for residential customers)
Data sources: Belgacom, 10/09/2003, 3/05/2004, 11/01/2005, 09/01/2008, 17/11/2008, 28/05/2010, 27/08/2010.

Belgacom received the 2009 Innovations Award from Global Telecommunications Business (Belgacom, 29/10/2004; 09/09/2009).

Because of the increasing demand for higher bandwidths and in order to stay competitive vis-à-vis the cable operator Telenet, Belgacom decided to invest further in applications using optical fibre. The first tests concerning Fibre-to-the-Home (FttH), bringing the optical fibre into the living room of the customer, were executed in Rochefort in 2008 and extended to Sint-Truiden and La Louvière in 2009 (Belgacom, 09/09/2009) but no commercial deployment was envisaged yet.

On the one hand, Belgacom was deploying VDSL2 to all its customers, having reached a national coverage of 78.9% at the end of 2011, aiming for 85% by the end of 2013. On the other hand, Belgacom recognized the limitations of VDSL2, and therefore already communicated their 'Get to fast, faster' strategy (Belgacom, 27/09/2011). In a partnership with Alcatel-Lucent, Belgacom aims at maximizing the VDSL2 throughput by using the new state-of-the-art vectoring technology. VDSL2 vectoring is a noise-cancelling technology that will allow the use of VDSL2 at its theoretical data rates, which will allow rates of 100 Mbit/s and beyond to be transmitted on copper cables. Belgacom opted for this upgrade because it will bring high data rate broadband to the end-consumer in a fast and cost effective way. Tests of VDSL2 vectoring started at the end of 2012.

Apart from vectoring, other technological upgrades on VDSL are possible to boost bandwidth capabilities. In VDSL bonding, two physical twisted pairs to each customer are used instead of one, which almost doubles the data rate. However, as there are few spare copper pairs in Belgium, it is unlikely that this upgrade can be implemented for every customer. Phantoming adds a third – virtual – twisted pair, which would bring data rates up to 200 Mbit/s to each individual household[5]. Combining all options (bonding, phantoming and vectoring) would allow the DSL network to offer data rates of about 300 Mbit/s (Alcatel-Lucent, 2010, 2011).

The graph in Figure 5.3 provides an overview of the most important changes concerning the available data rates for residential users.

Broadband Internet: applications and services

Next to the gradual upgrading of its network and the extensions towards mobile services and digital television offerings, Belgacom also extended its services over the years into different fields.

[5] However, there is a lot of skepticism around the phantoming concept, as there are no successful field test results available yet.

In 1998, for example, Belgacom launched its own website www.belgacom.be. The main purpose of this site was to clearly communicate (new) applications and services and their prices to (potential) customers. The faster ADSL connections provided a passage to the development of new applications. In 2003, Skynet's Internet access activities were transferred to Belgacom to optimize service provisioning. Since then, Skynet is appointed to develop the new activities of the Belgacom Group, such as the further expansion of the portal site Skynet.be, broadband video, 50 years of television, vrtnieuws.net and Big Brother, legal downloading of music with the Skynet Music Club, the publishing of personal blogs, etc.

Within the concept of providing 'ICT for everyone', Belgacom participated in a number of governmental projects. In 2003, for instance, Belgacom was one of the partners in the Private PC initiative. The objective of this project was to boost PC penetration through new legislation that provided tax benefits for companies that equip their employees with a home computer and Internet connection, (Belgacom, 16/05/2003). At the beginning of 2004, Belgacom launched 'Teleworking Plug and Work'. The application is a hardware solution that can be plugged into the ADSL Ethernet modem, making it possible for the teleworker to access corporate data over the Internet in a secure manner (Belgacom, 09/01/2004).

Another important acquisition involved Telindus, a company founded in 1969 which offered ICT services and solutions to the corporate and public sector. Its headquarters were located in Heverlee (close to Leuven). By taking over several foreign companies, it had grown into an international company with establishments in Thailand and China. Telindus was taken over by Belgacom at the beginning of 2006, after a hostile bidding war with France Télécom, among others. Telindus became a subsidiary of Belgacom and kept operating under its own name. After reviewing Telindus's position in each country where it operated, Belgacom decided to retain only the operations in six countries: Belgium, the Netherlands, France, Luxembourg, Great Britain and Spain (Broens, 30/09/2008).

In 2011, Belgacom signed an agreement with the Spanish company FON, which represents the world's largest Wi-Fi community: over 4 million customers share their wireless access points with other users, and this on a worldwide scale (Belgacom, 14/11/2011). The principle of this sharing lies in setting up two access points using the client's Wi-Fi modem: one (main) access point for private use, one (lower-capacity) access point for other customers of the FON community. The service is free for all customers of Belgacom; they only have to subscribe online to give 'visitors' access to their own modems, and to receive the username and password with which to use the connectivity provided by other FON users. In this way, Belgacom's customers have free access to all FON enabled Wi-Fi connection points, both inside Belgium and abroad.

In 2011, by concluding a contract with Deezer, a music streaming company, Belgacom was the first operator in Belgium able to offer free and unlimited access to over 13 million songs. The service is offered for free to anyone owning a Generation Pack subscription, or for EUR 4.99 per month for other Belgacom customers (Belgacom, 08/12/2011).

Finally, Belgacom introduced 'Internet Everywhere' in 2012, allowing its customers to opt for a single subscription to be connected everywhere, through the fixed network or using Wi-Fi at home, through the Wi-Fi FON spots or the 3G Proximus network (Belgacom, 28/03/2012).

Mobile communications and digital television

Along with exploiting the network for the use of fixed telephony and Internet, Belgacom started conducting trials for the offering of digital television in November 2004. Belgacom TV was introduced commercially in June of 2005. Using both the earlier VDSL and the ADSL2+ technology deployed thereafter, Belgacom TV was accessible to 79.5% of Belgian households at the end of that year. In June 2009, Belgacom TV had 589,000 subscribers, around 12% of households.

In May 2005, Belgacom acquired the rights to broadcast the Belgian Jupiler Football League (Belgacom, 09/05/2005) thereby setting a hard deadline for the launch of their new digital television services. Only some important matches would be broadcast using the public broadcast channels

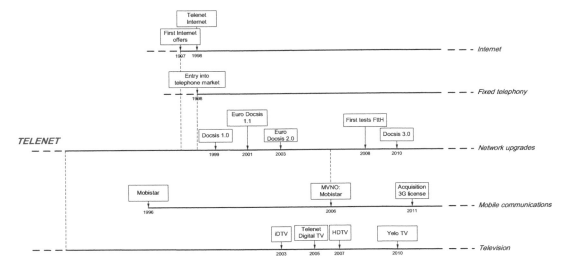

Figure 5.4 Timeline showing the most important events in the history of Telenet

(VRT and RTBF); all additional material would be distributed exclusively on Belgacom's digital television platform. The monopoly rights gave Belgacom an important strategic advantage over Telenet. Because those rights are not exclusive anymore, Belgacom launched 'Belgacom 11+', a new channel exclusive to Belgacom subscribers, broadcasting UEFA, Spanish and Portuguese soccer league matches (Belgacom, 02/07/2012).

Belgacom entered the mobile market in 1994 under the Proximus brand (see also Section 5.1.1). Although Belgacom had offered 3G services under the same Proximus brand for some time, the acquisition of a license for operation in the 1.8 GHz and the 2.6 GHz bands (acquired for EUR 20.22 million in November 2011) allowed Belgacom to be the first Belgian operator to offer 4G services. 4G was introduced commercially in 8 Belgian cities in November 2012, and extended to 17 cities by March 2013. Nowadays, Belgacom is a quadruple-play operator offering broadband Internet fixed telephony, mobile telephony, digital television and Internet access through 3G and 4G.

This multi-medium platform comprising fixed broadband, worldwide Wi-Fi access through FON and the mobile network of Proximus is used by Belgacom not only in its packaged offers (see 'Internet everywhere' as described above) but also in its services. In July 2011, Belgacom launched its

field test of 'TV everywhere', allowing its clients to watch TV on all their devices using the nearest available Internet source (fixed, Wi-Fi, 3G/4G) (Belgacom, 20/08/2013). After a trial period of about one year, Belgacom officially launched the service in September 2008. It is now offered for free to customers subscribed to a 'maxi pack', and for EUR 4.95 per month to other customers.

5.2.2 Telenet: an infrastructure-based competitor with similar offers

Starting in 1998, a duopoly of Belgacom and Telenet now dominates the telecommunications market in Flanders. Both companies upgraded their networks and services gradually, in order to counter the competitive pressure. This paragraph focuses on the evolution of Telenet, the Flemish cable operator. Comparison to the corresponding services offered by Belgacom is made where possible. An overview of the applications and services offered by Telenet, as well as a summary of the most important upgrades is shown in Figure 5.4.

Broadband Internet: network upgrades

Figure 5.5 shows the evolution of the data rates offered by Telenet. To provide its services, Telenet uses a HFC network, which consists of fibre

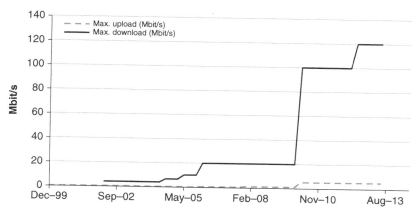

Figure 5.5 Evolution of the data rates offered by Telenet, Dec. 1999-Aug. 2013 (for residential customers)
Data sources: Telenet, 14/12/2005, 20/06/2007, 21/05/2008, 08/02/2010, 7/06/2012.

backbones and coaxial access in the areas served. To provide broadband access, Telenet uses the DOCSIS (Data over Cable Service Interface Specification) technology. The first version of this technology (DOCSIS 1.0) was developed in 1997 by CableLabs for the US market. To match the European cable frequency spectrum, the standard was adapted and the Euro-DOCSIS technology was born. The first upgrade (DOCSIS 1.1) was launched in 2001. Now, Telenet uses the European version of DOCSIS 3.0, which allows them to offer a download data rate of 100 Mbit/s and more (Boonefaes, 2005–2006; CableLabs, 2011).

Over the years, Telenet launched various new products, each time increasing the data rates. The first telecom product was launched in 1998 under its 'Home', 'Do' and 'Young' packages. Telenet Internet XL came to the market in September 2000, providing a downstream rate of 1 Mbit/s and an upstream rate of 256 kbit/s, thereby doubling their previous offer. In 2002, Telenet Internet XL offered download data rates up to 4 Mbit/s, while Euro-DOCSIS 2.0, introduced in 2003 as part of Telenet ExpressNet, enabled an upgrade to 10 Mbit/s. Download data rates increased to 20 Mbit/s in the fall of 2005. In 2010 followed the introduction of DOCSIS 3.0 with a download rate of 100 Mbit/s and an upload of 4 Mbit/s.

In March 2010, Telenet launched 'Digital Wave 2015', a project aimed at improving the existing network over the next five years, with an investment of about EUR 30 million every year. Through

the roll-out of an extensive fibre network, Telenet wants to promote the transformation of Flanders into a digital and networked economy. Along with the transformation of the network itself, Telenet aims to develop a number of new applications, such as remote medical services, call centre video assistance over the Internet, 3D television, video on demand, mobile television, new file-sharing and synchronization and e-government (Telenet, 3/03/2010). Telenet keeps upgrading its network by gradually reducing the size of the service areas (SAs). An SA is the part of the network that connects the end-customers to the first local collection point through the use of coaxial cables. From the collection point onward only fibre cables are used.

Since the available data rates offered by Telenet nowadays are much higher than those of Belgacom, the motivation to upgrade towards FttH is weaker. Telenet, however, did intend to keep up the current level of investment in their network, within the scope of the Digital Wave 2015 project. They are currently expanding their DOCSIS 3.0 technology (using channel bonding to increase data rates to over 100 Mbit/s) to all customers, and keep on increasing the available bandwidth by reducing the size of their service areas. These projects allowed Telenet to increase the data rates again in June 2012, to a maximum download rate of 120 Mbit/s and upload of 5 Mbit/s for residential customers (Telenet, 7/06/2012). Plans for deploying FttH have not been announced so far.

Broadband Internet: Applications and public service

In March 2003, Telenet launched XboxLive, an online-gaming service from Microsoft, for its high-speed cable Internet customers. Telenet also took over the activities of Hypertrust in February 2006. Hypertrust, founded in May 2000, was the first European organization that offered secure communication and storage services on the Internet under the slogan 'Your content in action' (Finance.nl, 22/07/2003). Telenet also entered the advertising business in July 2008, with the founding of a new Media Sales House, in cooperation with 'Concentra en Var' – the advertising department of the VRT (the Flemish public broadcast channel). The objective of this new independent entity was the acquisition of advertising and the development of a centralized advertising platform with extended segmentation possibilities (Telenet, 2/07/2008).

Telenet also offers mobile Internet to its customers through Wi-Fi hotspots. The first 120 hotspots were set up in 2003. In May 2006, Telenet reached an agreement with Signpost to launch 'Student Hotspot' (Telenet, 31/05/2006). The objective of this product is to provide all students and academics with access to all Telenet hotspots (in public locations like airports, restaurants, railway stations etc.) in Belgium and Luxembourg for rather low tariffs (EUR 7.95 per month). Telenet further adopted the principle of Wi-Fi–sharing under their Wi-Free brand (Telenet, 14/12/2011). They have several services using this principle. Their hotspot network allows Telenet subscribers to freely access these hotspots, which are Wi-Fi access points in public locations. In Belgium and Luxembourg, 1200 of those locations already exist. In 2011, Telenet extended the offer to 'Home spots', in which customers share part of their own bandwidth with other customers (the principle is basically the same as used by Belgacom). When finished (if all customers' modems are updated), this gives Telenet subscribers access to over 0.5 million extra Wi-Fi access points by the end of summer 2012 (Telenet, 27/02/2012). A recent article confirms the realization of this target: in January 2013, Telenet customers had access to about 700,000 Wi-Fi homespots and about 1200 hotspots (Vief, 29/01/2013).

Mobile communications and digital television

A first test project for interactive digital television (iDTV) was started by Telenet in 2003, in cooperation with Interkabel (which in the meantime has been acquired by Telenet) and some Flemish broadcasters. In 2005, hardly three months after Belgacom's TV launch, Telenet introduced Telenet Digital TV, including extra services such as an electronic programme guide, request for missed shows and Prime, a set of movie channels. Prime is the former Canal+ Vlaanderen which Telenet took over in 2003. In December 2007, Telenet was the first to introduce digital TV in high definition (HD). To lower entry barriers, customers of Telenet can obtain the HD digicorder on a rental basis.

Following the launch of the Yelo app in 2010 (making it possible to watch TV on your smartphone or tablet), Telenet launched 'Yelo TV' in the fall of 2012 and commercialized it beginning 2013. Yelo TV allows Telenet's customers to watch their favourite content (live or recorded) on any screen in the house (TV screen, tablet, smartphone, laptop, etc.).

Telenet didn't limit its services to the fixed market for long. On 13 February 2006, Telenet signed a partnership agreement with Mobistar, one of the most important Belgian providers of mobile telephony. Telenet thus became an MVNO (Mobile Virtual Network Operator) and created the possibility of quadruple play (broadband Internet fixed telephone line, digital television and mobile phone). The first bundled offers (one bill for all requested services) were sold in August of that same year. With the contracting of Alcatel-Lucent for the deployment of mobile network elements on 16 July 2009, Telenet became the first European cable operator that is also a full MVNO[6]. On 27 June 2011, Telenet, together with Tecteo (the Walloon cable operator), acquired a license to operate in the 3G-spectrum band (Telenet, 27/06/2011). This acquisition of the radio spectrum license improved Telenet's position on the mobile market, as well as on the

---

[6] A full MVNO (Mobile Virtual Network Operator) owns all necessary end-equipment to provide mobile connectivity, and only leases the use of antennas and spectrum from a 'real' mobile operator. This allows more flexibility in terms of product offerings and ranges than the light MVNO.

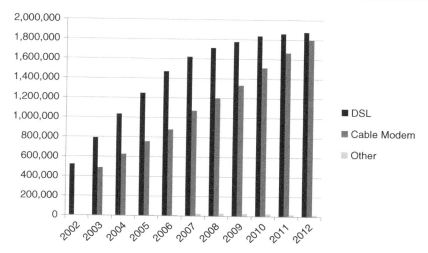

Figure 5.6 Broadband subscriptions, Belgium, 2002–2012
Data source: Point-Topic, 2013.

telecommunications market in general, as this 'mobile extension' gave Telenet the opportunity to offer more competitive services and prices. Although Telenet ran tests for 4G (Telenet, 17/06/2010), they did not participate in the 4G auction. Instead Telenet concluded a contract renewal with Mobistar as full MVNO; the agreement between Telenet and Mobistar was prolonged until 2017, which also implies that the 3G license was never used. In May 2012 BIPT argued that the 3G-license should be used within a term of seven months to avoid losing the license (Blyaert, 15/05/2012). In June 2013 BIPT imposed an administrative penalty of EUR 5000 on Telenet (and the Walloon cable operator Tecteo) for not using the 3G-license. They were given a 6-month period to comply (BIPT, 2013b).

5.3 Case analysis: Does the duopoly setting with tit-for-tat competition suffice to realize the Digital Agenda targets?

For a very long period, telephone service provision in Belgium has been characterized by a monopoly regime and it was the imminent threat of competition, supported by the pressure from Europe, that prompted the Flemish government to start a project through which the telecom market structure in Flanders would radically change. Telenet was

founded and became the key competitor for the incumbent Belgacom in the Flemish fixed broadband market (Figure 5.6) and, as such, stimulated competition, innovation and price reduction. By describing concrete examples and events, this section will analyse the dynamics of the Flemish broadband market and provide insights into the road to reach Europe's Digital Agenda targets.

5.3.1 Marketing strategies: focus on own strengths

From the previous section it is clear that, although there are some smaller niche players present, the fixed broadband market in Flanders is dominated by Belgacom and Telenet, each having a close-to-100% coverage with their networks (DSL and DOCSIS, respectively). However, since the available data rates on those networks differ significantly (maximum download data rates for residential users are 30 Mbit/s for Belgacom versus 120 Mbit/s for Telenet), both players market their offers using different key services and promotions.

Since mid-2012 Telenet focuses its marketing strategy on data rates and simplicity, for both the fixed and mobile markets. In July 2012, Telenet launched King and Kong, two straightforward tariff schemes for its mobile customers. Both are bundles including voice, SMS and mobile data for a fixed amount per month. To attract or convince fixed Telenet customers, discounts are given. In June 2013 Telenet launched a similar offer for its fixed services: Whop and Whoppa bundles including digital television, VoIP telephony and fixed and Wi-Fi Internet through their Wi-Free hotspots. Their advertising emphasizes the high data rates reached (Whoppa: 'for whom fast isn't fast enough') and the inclusion of all services into one simple and transparent bundle.

Belgacom, as a quadruple-play operator, goes one step further in bundling its services. Because Proximus is a subsidiary of Belgacom, they are able to offer both mobile and fixed Internet in one package: the 'Generation pack'. Various options exist, for different download limits, voice and SMS usages, etc. Telenet could follow the same strategy by making use of its full MVNO contract but has not taken this path so far.

Another field of competition is the broadcasting of football matches. Although Belgacom long had the monopoly on the Jupiler Pro League Football (the main football competition in Belgium), this right is not exclusive anymore. Both Telenet and Belgacom now try to attract customers with their football channels, Telenet even promising 2,222 live goals on its Sporting Telenet channel for the upcoming season, or a refund of all subscription fees.

5.3.2 Regulatory setting: unbundling obligation and the new telecom law

Unbundling obligation

1998 was the year of the liberalization of the European telecom market. The incumbent Belgacom was obliged to open up its network to new entrants. Belgacom remained owner of the network but had to provide network access to other operators. The consequence of this liberalization was the rise of many new OLOs (Other Licensed Operators) in the following years (e.g., British Telecom, MCI, Colt, Versatel, Coditel, Tele2, Dommel, EDPnet, Mobistar, Eleven, Scarlet). This fragmentation of the market in the field of the copper network stood in great contrast to the intense concentration of the market in the cable network. This is an important observation: while Belgacom was obliged to open up its network, the cable companies were asked to form a united cable network.

However, the fragmentation of the market remained limited, as the new entrants had to combine the significant investments attached to the start-up of a new company with the need to offer low prices to attract customers. New entrants had to offer cheaper and/or better products than the incumbent, because they had to overcome customer loyalty for the existing brands. More firms in the market made the competitors play each other off by using aggressive pricing to attract more customers. This on-going price pressure made it hard for the new entrants to survive, forcing some to end their activities (e.g., Eleven) or to sell their activities to another operator (e.g., Versatel, Tele2, Scarlet).

Other operators managed to develop a customer base of significant size. An excellent example here is the operator Schedom, which provides a cheap Internet connection for urban subscribers under the brand name Dommel. Its success is implicit in the selection of the market segment. By focusing only on urban, densely populated areas (including many students and gamers), Schedom can keep its line prices low (Dommel, 2011). Other operators, like Scarlet, were taken over by Belgacom, although Scarlet remains an autonomous subsidiary (Scarlet, 2011).

The impact of the unbundling obligation remained marginal until the BIPT lowered LLU prices in 2006.[7] The scale of the alternative operators was by then large enough to climb further on the ladder of investment and to invest in unbundling. These investments were stopped in 2008 when the economic crisis hit and when Belgacom announced that it intended to close down 10% of its MDFs (Main Distribution Frames) as a consequence of the move to an all-IP infrastructure and VDSL deployments in the sub-loop. Because the planned closure impacted 40% of the unbundled lines, the BIPT intervened

---

[7] BIPT decision of 29 November 2006 on blocks and tie cable tariffs.

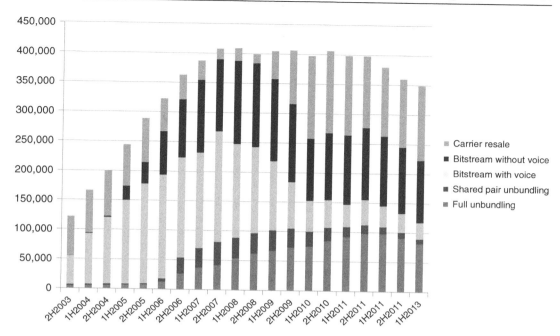

Legend:
- Carrier resale
- Bitstream without voice
- Bitstream with voice
- Shared pair unbundling
- Full unbundling

Figure 5.7 The use of wholesale access, Belgium, 2H 2003 – 1H 2013
Data source: BIPT, 2013a.

with additional obligations[8] to guarantee a fair return on investments for the alternative operators, but the investments in unbundling never recovered. See also Figure 5.7. Carrier resale has gained in volume due to take-overs (Scarlet by Belgacom, LLU network Base by Mobistar) and to the move from ADSL2+ to VDSL2 (no subloop unbundling).

Although Telenet long enjoyed a monopoly on the cable network and services, the CRC (Conference of Media Regulators) and the Belgian NRA (BIPT) published a proposal for opening up the cable network in 2010. This proposal was transformed into a formal decision on 1 July 2011, in which the authorities regulated Telenet and the other cable operators and created an obligation to provide wholesale access to analogue television and broadband Internet services, as well as opening up the digital television platform. Telenet responded stating that regulating analogue TV is not useful because of the declining number of

subscribers and that regulating digital TV is not necessary, as in that market there is enough competition from different platforms (cable, IPTV, satellite, DTT and Internet TV). They furthermore argued that regulating the most important competitor to the SMP incumbent would definitely not enhance the infrastructure-based competition the European Commission favours (Telenet, 18/07/2011, 21/06/2011, 21/12/2010, 26/05/2011). Notwithstanding the arguments Telenet put forward, they were all rejected by the regulators. The regulators and operators are now defining the implementation of the decisions; a final decision from the Court is expected for end 2013 (Belgacom, 2013a). The CRC has already approved the qualitative elements of the decision, calling for Telenet to provide the access within a six-month period after the official request (either through impress payment or signed letter of intent) of the alternative operator (CRC, 2013). However, a final outcome of the court case is not expected before mid-2014 (Telenet, 2013).

Concerning the current LLU and bitstream access regulation of Belgacom's network, the

[8] Decision of 12 November 2008 concerning the addendum NGN/NGA complementing the market analysis of 10 January 2008.

BIPT is also re-evaluating its models for calculating the price caps, following the European guideline to stabilize the prices for copper lines between EUR 8 and EUR 10 per month, as such increasing the flexibility for the deployment of fibre-based networks. As mentioned above, these caps were set in 2010, and remained unchanged until 2012.

The new telecom law (2012)

In July 2012, a new telecom law was voted in Parliament, focusing on transparency, competition promotion and (universal) service obligation. The law requires customer protection by obliging the operator to be transparent in their communication with their clients and by allowing customers to change operators for free. Every contract can be modified or terminated by the client after a period of six months, without needing to specify a (legal) reason. Finally, the law includes a quality of service obligation, whereby the BIPT can enforce a minimum quality level when certain requirements are not being met. With this law, the Belgian telecom market should comply with, if not exceed, the requirements set by the European Commission.

The effect of the telecom law became visible quickly after it was put into force at the beginning of October 2012. The number of ported mobile numbers rose from 71,000 in September to 160,000 in October of that same year (see Figure 5.8). Although the effect slowed down later in the year (136,000 in November, 151,000 in December), it remains significant and demonstrates the impact of telecom regulation in Belgium. This strong increase in ported mobile numbers can be fully attributed to the new telecom law, but certainly also finds a cause in the launch of the competitive King and Kong subscriptions by Telenet, strategically positioned two months before the implementation of the telecom law.

The effect on the fixed market was lower, but still significant, with a net increase of about 9,000 ported numbers (an average of 29,038 ported numbers per month before versus an average of 38,131 after the implementation date).

VDSL vectoring or VDSL unbundling?

A final regulatory intervention worth mentioning is the recent withdrawal of the VDSL sub-loop unbundling requirement by the BIPT (CRC, 2011). For VDSL vectoring to function properly (i.e., to effectively cancel out cross-talk) the copper lines connected to the DSLAMs should be handled as one bundle, which would imply the bundle is controlled by the same operator.[9] Moreover, the business case for sub-loop unbundling is less attractive as the aggregation point moves lower into the network; hence, it does not attract many OLOs, BIPT has decided to withdraw this obligation in order to stimulate the commercial deployment of VDSL vectoring, thereby ensuring the competitiveness of Belgacom's DSL with Telenet's DOCSIS network. Because of the withdrawal of sub-loop unbundling, in the same decision the BIPT enhanced the obligation to provide bitstream by adding multicast functionality and allowing more differentiation possibilities for active access at local and regional level.[10]

5.3.3 External influences: blocking of 4G by Apple

Besides the regulatory influences, there are some other external influences affecting the telecom market in Flanders and Belgium, including the competitive interplay between the market parties. One salient example of this kind of influence is the impact of Apple blocking 4G access on iPhones. Although the recently launched iPhone 5 supports 4G functionality, it has not been activated in Belgium. Belgacom communicated the following: '4G functionality is currently not activated on these devices making it impossible to use the Proximus 4G network. Apple will decide when 4G will be available for their devices on our network. This also applies to the 4G network of other operators.' (Belgacom, 2013b).

---

[9] In recent publications it is argued that vectoring could work effectively in an unbundled environment.
[10] This enhanced form of bitstream is also called Virtual Unbundled Local Access (VULA).

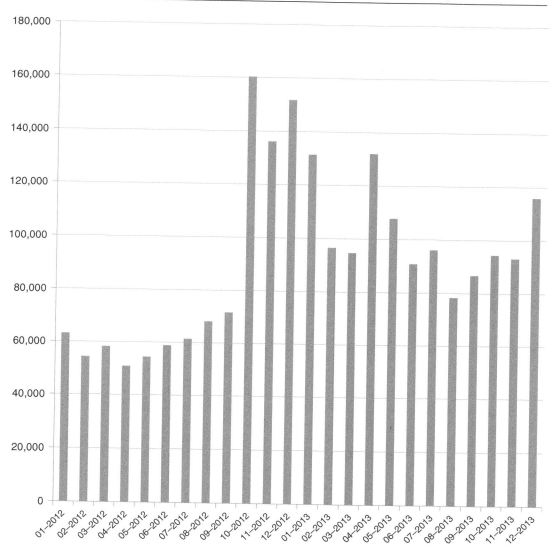

Figure 5.8 Ported mobile numbers per month, Belgium, 2012–2013
Data source: BIPT, 2013a.

In January 2013 Apple updated the iOS operating system, allowing iPads to surf on the 4G-network but ignored the iPhone. Proximus, the mobile brand of Belgacom, was not aware, nor notified of Apple's plan and believes it to be a pure commercial decision (Stevens, 2013). Mobistar, on the other hand, is listed as a provider allowed to offer 4G on the iPhone, but they have no 4G network operational yet.

5.4 Realizing the Digital Agenda targets

Concerning the 100% coverage goal of 30 Mbit/s or more, set out by the Digital Agenda for Europe, 98% was reached by the end of 2011: 85% of households via VDSL, 95.5% via the DOCSIS 3.0 technology. Belgium is the leader when it comes to the uptake of high data rate broadband. At the end of 2012, the penetration of fixed broadband

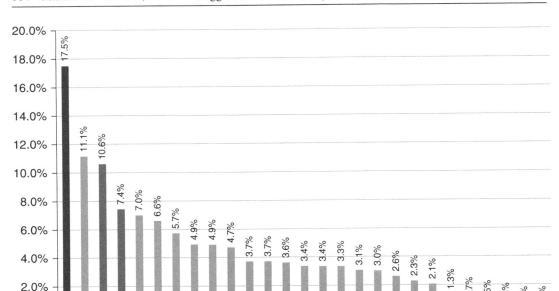

Figure 5.9 Penetration of fixed broadband ≥30 Mbit/s in Europe, 2012 (in percentage of households)
Source: BIPT, 2012.

amounted to 17.5% of households (Figure 5.9), The second goal, reaching 50% uptake of high-data rate broadband (>=100 Mbit/s) by 2020 is, however, further away: an uptake of 3.4% was reached by the end of 2012.

Forecasts, however, are optimistic for Belgium. According to Akama, Belgium ranks tenth globally with observed average data rates of 6.1 Mbit/s and ranks sixth on observed peak data rates of 26.7 Mbit/s (Akamai, 2012). Analysys Mason communicated that Belgium is one of six countries that should reach the 50% uptake goal of high-data rate broadband by 2020 (Figure 5.10). Furthermore, although total revenues in the telecom market decreased in 2012, the percentage of revenues re-invested increased to 17.4%.

However, the road to reach these targets differs strongly from other countries sharing the same goals. Belgacom communicated its VDSL vectoring strategy to achieve the goals set out in the Digital Agenda to the European Commission (European Commission, 2011), while FttH is more common in other countries. In Belgium, FttH

coverage remains small: 0.2% at the end of 2011. Therefore, Belgacom commented that the Commission should assure 'technological neutrality when considering investments in broadband infrastructure in view of reaching the Digital Agenda'. They stated that there is too much focus on FttH, while the developments by Alcatel-Lucent clearly indicate that the targets can also be reached with gradual upgrades of VDSL.

Whereas Belgacom reaches data rates of 30 Mbit/s and more, Telenet is far ahead, offering data rates up to 120 Mbit/s using their DOCSIS 3.0 technology, which is available to 95.5% of households.

Although neither operator opts for a revolutionary FttH deployment, the opportunities and possibilities for such a rollout are still being examined by the NRA (Laroy, 2009). This examination includes thorough cost analyses, assessing the relative weight of the trenching costs versus the service provisioning and operational costs, investigating opportunities of synergetic rollout with other utility network owners, as well as assessing the impact of

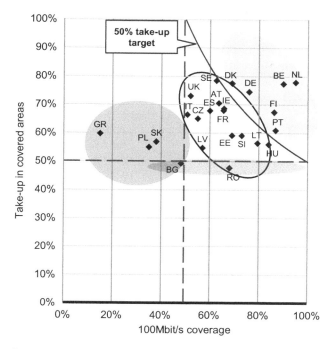

Figure 5.10 Forecast likelihood of reaching 100 Mbit/s by 2020, EU *Source:* Yardley, 2012.

public-private partnerships involving the local municipalities following examples such as the Netherlands. The Belgian NRA proposes to harmonize and standardize the right of way, to stimulate sharing of infrastructure (e.g. empty ducts), to investigate the opportunities of decreasing the price for the last mile (e.g. by allowing aerial deployment or micro-trenching), etc.

5.5 Conclusions and reflections

The status of broadband coverage and uptake in Belgium is at the top of the league in Europe. The country has reached the 2013 goals of the Digital Agenda already. Six of the fifteen ICT goals set in the Digital Agenda for Europe for 2015 were already met in mid-2013 (FOD Economie, 25/06/2013). Positive points are the percentage of broadband connections (58% of the fixed connections have data rates over 30 Mbit/s, 12% are ultrafast broadband with data rates greater than 100 Mbit/s, and widespread computer (98%)

and Internet (97%) use. However, there is still room for improvement: the prices for multiple-play offers, as well as for smartphone use (voice, SMS and data), were significantly higher than the European average in 2012 and, although enterprises want to hire ICT experts, they experience difficulties in filling the vacancies.

Although the duopoly between incumbent DSL and DOCSIS operators has brought relatively fast broadband to Flemish consumers, the dominant market position of both players and the lack of more competition keep prices high for end-users. These dominant players rule the price settings and pace of network upgrades, as the barrier to market entry appears to be too high. This phenomenon is especially visible in the fixed market, where the infrastructure assets are important. In the mobile market, competition is fiercer; entry is largely controlled by radio spectrum regulation and through license auctions. Supported by the new telecom law of 2012 (see Section 5.3.2), competition has increased and prices have been significantly reduced over the last year.

Considering the Digital Agenda goals set out by Europe, Belgium is well on the way to reaching them, as multiple sources confirm. However, these goals will most probably be reached without much FttH deployment. Although Belgium holds a leading position in Europe, it is still far behind in comparison to Asian countries such as Korea and Japan. The question then rises as to how important FttH deployment is in the realization of the Digital Agenda for 2020. While its deployment may not be as urgent, will it be inevitable at some point in the future?

Another concern lies with the uptake: although both prominent market players are at the forefront, each with its own technology, the uptake of the high-end subscriptions remains rather low. Should the NRA intervene more to reduce consumer prices, or focus more on raising awareness about the opportunities and possible new applications high-data rate broadband will entail?

References

Akamai (2012) The Akamai State of the Internet Report. from www.akamai.com/stateoftheinternet/.

Alcatel-Lucent. (2010). Alcatel-Lucent Bell Labs achieves industry first: 300 Megabits per second over just two traditional DSL lines. Press release Paris, April 21, 2010. Available at www.alcatel-lucent.com/press/2010/002043.

(2011). Innovations in Broadband Access: Phantom Mode. from www.alcatel-lucent.com/features/phantom/.

Analysys Mason. (2012). Policy orientations to reach the European Digital Agenda. Expert report for Telecom Itali and Telefonica.

Belgacom. (15/01/2003). Press Release: Now 98% of Belgium's population can be connected to ADSL – End of 2002: 517,000 customers connected to Belgacom's ultra-fast Internet. www.belgacom.com/group/en/jsp/dynamic/pressreleaselist.jsp.

(16/05/2003). Press release: e-Home: the Private PC initiative from Belgacom, Hewlett-Packard, Intel and Microsoft. www.belgacom.com/group/en/jsp/dynamic/pressreleaselist.jsp.

(10/09/2003). Press release: New ADSL Go services for gamers and multiple PC users. www.belgacom.com/group/en/jsp/dynamic/pressreleaselist.jsp.

(09/01/2004). Press release: Belgacom has developed Teleworking Plug&Work for the increasing number of teleworkers. www.belgacom.com/group/en/jsp/dynamic/pressreleaselist.jsp

(25/02/2004). Press release: Belgacom has 1,000,000 active surfers! www.belgacom.com/group/en/jsp/dynamic/pressreleaselist.jsp

(3/05/2004). Press release: Belgacom boosts its ADSL offer, for both residential and business customers: Increase in upstream speed for traditional packages and low-cost entry-level offer from 1 June. www.belgacom.com/group/en/jsp/dynamic/pressreleaselist.jsp.

(29/10/2004). Press release: Belgacom launches Belgacom VDSL, the fastest internet solution in Belgium. www.belgacom.com/group/en/jsp/dynamic/pressreleaselist.jsp.

(11/01/2005). Press release: Belgacom improves and expands ADSL offering. www.belgacom.com/group/en/jsp/dynamic/pressreleaselist.jsp.

(09/05/2005). Press release: The Professional Football League awards Belgian football broadcasting rights to Belgacom. www.belgacom.com/group/en/jsp/dynamic/pressreleaselist.jsp.

(09/01/2008). Press release: Belgacom offers its ADSL customers more. www.belgacom.com/group/en/jsp/dynamic/pressreleaselist.jsp.

(17/11/2008). Press release: Stopt Belgacom met ADSL? 10 jaar ADSL: gisteren, vandaag en morgen. www.belgacom.com/group/en/jsp/dynamic/pressreleaselist.jsp

(09/09/2009). Press release: Netwerk van Belgacom bij wereldtop, De toekomst wordt verder voorbereid met proefprojecten. www.belgacom.com/group/en/jsp/dynamic/pressreleaselist.jsp.

(28/05/2010). Press release: Belgacom again sets the tone and boosts the Internet still further.

(27/08/2010). Press release: Belgacom boosts the Internet even more, for the third time this year.

(27/09/2011). Press Release: Belgacom and Alcatel-Lucent pave the way for next generation broadband in Europe. www.belgacom.com/be-en/newsdetail/ND_20110927_alcatel_lucent.page

(14/11/2011). Press release: Belgacom and Fon set up the largest wireless Internet network in

Belgium. www.belgacom.com/group/eu-en/
newsdetail/ND_20111114_bgc_reseau_wifi.
page?

(08/12/2011). Press release: Muziekdienst Deezer
onbeperkt en gratis in Belgacom Generation
packs. www.belgacom.com/be-nl/newsdetail/
ND_20111208_deezer_lancement.page.

(28/03/2012). Press release: Belgacom vindt
internet opnieuw uit. www.belgacom.com/be-nl/
newsdetail/ND_20120328_internet_everywhere.
page.

(02/07/2012). Press release: Belgacom stelt haar
nieuw voetbalaanbod voor en lanceert
'Belgacom 11+', een nieuwe zender naast
'Belgacom 11'. www.belgacom.com/be-nl/
newsdetail/ND_20120702_foot.page.

(20/08/2013). Press release: TV Overal = tv-
kijken, waar men zich ook bevindt. www.
belgacom.com/be-nl/newsdetail/
ND_20120820_tv_everywhere.page.

(2013a). Belgacom Annual report 2012. www.
belgacom.com/be-en/subhome/
SH_Annual_report.page.

(2013b). I have an iPhone5 /iPad Mini/iPad4 and
I can't surf on 4G, but the device supports the
functionality – Belgacom support website. from
http://support.en.belgacom.be/app/answers/
detail/a_id/15908/~/i-have-an-iphone5-%
2Fipad-mini%2Fipad4-and-i-cant-surf-on-4g,-
but-the-device.

Belgium. (1991). Wet van 21 maart 1991 betreffende
de hervorming van sommige economische
overheidsbedrijven.

(2011). Informatie en diensten van de overheid.
www.belgium.be

Belgium, Cable. (2011). Historiek en evolutie van de
Kabel. from www.cablebelgium.be/documents/
de-kabel-in-belgie/historiek.xml

BIPT. (12/03/2001). Advies van het BIPT betreffende
het referentieaanbod van Belgacom voor de
ontbundelde toegang tot het aansluitnetwerk.
www.bipt.be.

(14/03/2001). Advies van het BIPT van 13 maart
2001 betreffende de Belgacom-tarieven voor de
ontbundelde toegang tot the aansluitnetwerk.
www.bipt.be.

(2011). Belgian Institute for Postal Services and
Telecommunications. www.bipt.be

(2012). Economische situatie van de telecomsector
2012.

(2013a). Belgian Institute for Postal Services and
Telecommunications. www.bipt.be/.

(2013b). BIPT Council decision of 28 June 2013
imposing an administrative penalty upon
Telenet-Tecteo Bidco for non-compliance with
Article 4 §1 of the Royal Decree of 18 January
2001 laying down the specifications and the
procedure for granting licences for third-
generation mobile telecommunications systems
and imposing a deadline to put an end to the
non-compliance with it. Brussels: BIPT.

Blyaert, Luc. (15/05/2012). Telenet en VOO dreigen
licentie te verliezen. http://datanews.knack.be/
ict/nieuws/telenet-en-voo-dreigen-3g-licentie-te-
verliezen/article-4000095980947.htm#.

Boonefaes, Elie. (2005–2006). Evolutie van vaste
toegangsnetwerken in België. De weg naar Fiber
to the Home. University of Ghent, Ghent.

Broens, B. (30/09/2008). Belgacom plooit Telindus
terug tot zes landen, De Tijd. www.nieuwsblad.
be/Article/Detail.aspx?
ArticleID=DMF30092008_011.

CableLabs. (2011). Revolutionizing Cable
Technology. www.cablelabs.com.

CIA. (2011). The World Factbook.

CRC. (2011). Decision of the Conference of
Regulators of the electronic communications
sector (CRC) of 1 July 2011 regarding the
analysis of the broadband markets. Brussels:
Conference of Media Regulators.

(2013). Decision of the Conference of Regulators
of the electronic communications sector (CRC)
of 3 September 2013 regarding Telenet's
wholesale offer. Brussels: Conference of Media
Regulators.

De Bens, Els. (1986). Cable Penetration and
Competition among Belgian and Foreign station.
European Journal of Communication, 1,
477–492.

Dienst Pers en Informatie, Bell Mfg Co N.V. (Ed.).
(1982). Bell Telephone Manufacturing
Company. Antwerp: Imperama N.V.

Dommel. (2011). Nooit meer kiezen tussen goed en
goedkoop. from www.dommel.com

Europe, Digital Agenda for. (2011). Visualization of
Digital Agenda Scoreboard indicators. from
http://scoreboard.lod2.eu/index.php

European Commission. (1987). Green Paper on the
development of the common market for
telecommunications services and equipment.
Brussels: Commission of the European
Communities.

(2011). Belgacom reaction to the Commission
consultation regarding costing methodologies

for key wholesale access prices in electronic communications. Brussels: European Commission.

Eurostat. (2011). Your key to European statistics (main tables on population data).

Finance.nl. (22/07/2003). HyperTrust haalt 1,3 miljoen euro kapitaal op en mikt op Nederland. http://finance.nl/content/view/4928

FOD Economie. (25/06/2013). De FOD Economie publiceert zijn Barometer van de informatiemaatschappij 2013. http://statbel.fgov.be/

FOD Economie. (2013). Statistics Belgium http://statbel.fgov.be/

GIMV. (1998). Gewestelijke InvesteringsMaatschappij voor Vlaanderen. www.gimv.com

Laroy, R. (2009). Raadpleging van de raad van het BIPT met betrekking to de adviesnota van het BIPT aan minister V. Van Quickenborne over mogelijke beleidsmaatregelen die bijdragen tot het stuimuleren van fiber to the home. In BIPT (Ed.). Brussels.

OECD. (2012). Key ICT Indicators. www.oecd.org/document/23/0,3746,en_2649_37441_33987543_1_1_1_37441,00.html

Point-Topic. (2011a). Belgium Broadband Overview. http://point-topic.com/content/operatorSource/profiles2/belgium-broadband-overview.htm.

(2011b). World Broadband Statistics: advanced report. http://clientgbs.point-topic.com/report/.

(2013). Country profiles. http://subscribers.point-topic.com/profiles?isLicensed=true.

Scarlet. (2011). Internet, Téléphone, TV. www.scarlet.be.

Stevens, A. (2013, 29/01/2013). iPhone 5 nog steeds niet op Belgische 4G, de Standaard.

Telecommunicatie, Ombudsdienst. (2011). Ombudsdienst voor telecommunicatie. www.ombudsmantelecom.be.

Telenet. (1/10/2008). Press release: Formele afronding akkoord Vlaamse Openbare Kabelmaatschappijen, Interkabel en Telenet. http://telenet.be/1758/0/1/nl/over_telenet/over_ons.htm.

(2/07/2008). Press release: Concentra en Var, de reclameregie van de VRT. http://telenet.be/1758/0/1/nl/over_telenet/over_ons.htm.

(3/03/2010). Press release: Telenet bouwt mee aan de digitale snelweg van morgen en lanceert:

'Digital Wave 2015'. http://telenet.be/1758/0/1/nl/over_telenet/over_ons.htm

(7/06/2012). Press release: Telenet helemaal klaar voor digitale evolutie. http://hugin.info/136600/R/1618000/516395.pdf.

(08/02/2010). Press release: Telenet onthult nieuwe generatie internet. http://telenet.be/1758/0/1/nl/over_telenet/over_ons.htm.

(14/12/2005). Press release: Telenet verdubbelt internetsnelheid in januari. http://telenet.be/1758/0/1/nl/over_telenet/over_ons.htm.

(14/12/2011). Press release: Na de Hotspot, nu de 'Homespot'. Een half miljoen extra gratis WiFi-locaties. http://hugin.info/136600/R/1571280/488724.pdf.

(17/06/2010). Press release: Telenet internet aan 120 km per uur op de autosnelweg in Mechelen. De toekomst van supersnel mobiel internetten met 4G. http://corporate.telenet.be/pers_media/persberichten.

(18/07/2011). Press release: Telenet to appeal CRC's final decision to regulate the Belgian broadcasting market. http://hugin.info/136600/R/1531778/466276.pdf

(20/06/2007). Press release: Telenet lanceert BasicNet. http://telenet.be/1758/0/1/nl/over_telenet/over_ons.htm

(21/05/2008). Press release: Telenet past volumes ExpressNet en TurboNet aan. http://telenet.be/1758/0/1/nl/over_telenet/over_ons.htm

(21/06/2011). Press Release: European Commission has serious concerns about proposed cable regulation. http://hugin.info/136600/R/1524938/460641.pdf.

(21/12/2010). Press Release: Telenet reacts to preliminary proposal to regulate certain services over cable. http://hugin.info/136600/R/1474405/410680.pdf.

(26/05/2011). Press Release: Telenet still considers the amended regulation proposal to be inadequate. http://hugin.info/136600/R/1519228/455755.pdf.

(27/02/2012). Press release: Telenet rolt zijn homespots verder uit. http://hugin.info/136600/R/1589209/498991.pdf.

(27/06/2011). Press Release: Telenet to acquire valuable 3G- and 2G-spectrum, strengthening its challenger position in mobile. http://corporate.telenet.be/en/pers_media/persberichten.

(31/05/2006). Press release: Telenet en Signpost lanceren hotspotformule voor hoger onderwijs.

http://telenet.be/1758/0/1/nl/over_telenet/
over_ons.htm.
(2013). Telenet – first nine months 2013. Investor
and analyst presentation.

Tijd, De. (09/09/2008, 16/02/2008). Belgacom koopt
concurrent, *De Tijd*.

United Nations. (2013). Statistics Division.
http://unstats.un.org/unsd/default.htm.

Van Batselaer, B., Lobet-Maris, C., Pierson, J.
(1997). Development of Multimedia in Belgium.

Van den Brande, Luc. (1996). Beleidsbrief:
Multimedia in Vlaanderen – Vlaanderen,
sterregio op de informatiesnelweg.

Van Leemputten, Pieterjan. (28/06/2008).
Definitief akkoord tussen Telenet en Interkabel:

Mechels kabelbedrijf biedt meer dan Belgacom:
ZDNet.

Vanden Berghen, F. (2012). Het internet uit de 19e
eeuw. Over de opkomst van de allereerste vorm
van de elektronische telecommunicatie in België
en Europa: de telegrafie.

Vief. (29/01/2013). Buitenshuis surfen: Vind hier
gratis hotspots en homespots. www.vief.be/
vrije-tijd/buitenshuis-surfen-vind-hier-je-gratis-
hotspots-en-homespots.html.

Wikipedia. (2011). Belgacom. http://nl.wikipedia.org/
wiki/Belgacom.

Yardley, M. (2012) Building the European Digital
Infrastructure. Workshop presentation, Analysys
Mason.

CHAPTER 6

Denmark

ANDERS HENTEN AND MORTEN FALCH

6.1 Introduction to the case study

Inspired, on the one hand, by what is often termed old or traditional institutional economics with Thorstein Veblen (1973, first published in 1899) and John R. Commons (1934) as important early contributors and, on the other hand, by a political economy framework putting emphasis on the interplay and interdependence between political, economic, and technological developments (Melody, 2007), this contribution examines the actors and factors that influence broadband developments in Denmark – with an emphasis on the telecom operators and the political-administrative institutions.

As not all important aspects of the developments can be included in the analysis, the focus is on the critical incidents and the major actors and factors affecting developments. Such an approach presupposes that the development of broadband is not always a continuous trajectory but includes turning points, where new actors and factors affecting developments enter the 'game' or where important changes in the relationships between technology, market, and policy take place.

At some moments, technology factors may be the most important in driving broadband developments. At others, it will be political and regulatory or economic and market actors and factors that are the primary drivers. In the 1980s and the first part of the 1990s, broadband was, first and foremost, a technology issue with research and development initiatives of technology providers and public institutions in connection with, for instance, the European RACE research program.[1] It was also a

policy issue in the sense that national states attempted to promote broadband developments by pushing and funding initiatives like the Danish hybrid network or in France the large Plan Cable[2]. When telecoms were fully liberalized in Denmark in 1996, it was a rather 'academic' issue, at first, in the new regulatory structure whether broadband should be included in the universal service provision. It was only when ADSL reached the European markets that broadband regulation became a hot issue. From then on, the drivers of fixed broadband developments were primarily market initiatives of the operators and regulations enacted by policy-makers and implemented by regulators. In the present situation, policy initiatives such as the broadband goals of the EU and Danish national goals are important drivers of broadband developments. And, in the mobile area, 3G and LTE have allowed for the development of mobile broadband connectivity.

An ongoing issue in the policy debates on broadband developments is concerned with infrastructure and service competition (Henten and Skouby, 2005). Although infrastructure competition became an element in Danish broadband policies with the strategy of 'many pipes to the home' being promoted from 1999, emphasis in the Danish broadband policies has been on service competition. 'Many pipes to the home' has, to a large extent, been an advocacy for deploying many different broadband technologies more than an advocacy for promoting infrastructure competition. The PSTN incumbent TDC has, for instance, been allowed to maintain its cable operation in contrast to many other countries, where incumbents had to

---

[1] RACE: Research and Development in Advanced Communications Technologies for Europe. The program was active in the mid-1980s, aimed at the introduction of broadband telecommunications systems and services.

[2] Plan Cable: See, for instance, Raymond Kuhn: *The media in France*. London: Routledge (1995).

divest their cable interests or have been prevented from entering the cable market.

The ladder of investment theory expounded by Martin Cave (2006) has been an important guide in Danish telecom policy and regulation. When ADSL reached the market in Denmark, the Danish authorities were quick to implement a relatively strict policy for interconnection and infrastructure access. Interconnection and access prices were regulated to become among the lowest in Europe. However, in accordance with the ladder of investment theory, LRAIC (Long Run Average Incremental Cost) prices were later set in such a manner that interconnection and access prices would increase, which presumably would lead telecom operators to consider competing on the basis of investments in new infrastructures instead of using the network of the incumbent.

Against this background we will explore the development of the telecommunications market and aim to explain its performance.

6.1.1 Historical framing and overview of developments

In contrast to most other monopoly telecom markets, prior to liberalization there was not *one* national operator in Denmark. The Danish telecom market was indeed a monopoly market, but the monopolies were regional. In the late phase of the monopoly era, there were four regional operators, and it could be claimed that there was a kind of yardstick competition between these operators. In combination with a relatively high GDP per capita, this contributed to a well-developed penetration of fixed-line telephony in Denmark compared to most other countries.

In 1990, a holding company named Tele Danmark was formed in order to unite the regional operators and in 1995 the regional structure was entirely abandoned. Before the establishment of Tele Danmark, the fixed-line penetration rate had reached approximately 57 per 100 inhabitants, and when fixed-line telecommunications was liberalized in Denmark in 1996, the penetration rate had increased to approximately 62 per 100. Up until 2001, the penetration rate of fixed-line telephony kept on increasing, reaching its peak at

approx. 72 per 100 – and has decreased ever since, being no more than around 25 per 100 in 2012; these figures include ISDN. PSTN-based telephony actually started decreasing even before 2000. Regarding broadband, the point is that the fixed-line telephony access infrastructure in Denmark is very well developed, which is important for the strength of DSL.

Tele Danmark (to be renamed TDC in 2000) was established with the explicit purpose of strengthening the Danish position in what was seen as a soon-to-be international telecom market. The liberalization trends, developing in the early to mid-1980s and receiving a strong platform at the European level with the 1987 Green Paper (CEC, 1987), were to a large extent seen – maybe not as a threat but at least as a serious challenge by the majority of politicians and the telecom administrations in Denmark. It was thus not the liberalization of the Danish telecom market which was the primary goal of Danish telecom policies at the beginning of the 1990s but, rather, the defense and strengthening of a Danish 'national champion'. Hence, in the European context, Denmark was not among the front runners with respect to telecom liberalization at the beginning of the 1990s. However, this changed in the mid-1990s, as it became clear to the Danish government that liberalization would eventually be the result of international developments. In 1995, the Danish government issued a policy strategy document entitled *Bedst og billigst hennem reel konkurrence* ('Best and cheapest by way of real competition') (Forskningsministeriet, 1995), which inaugurated a swift change in Danish telecom policies. First, value-added fixed-line services were liberalized, and in 1996, eighteen months before the EU's 1998 deadline, the provision of fixed-line infrastructure and fixed-line telephony services were also liberalized.

Ahead of this development, customer premises equipment (CPE) had been liberalized in 1990, and two companies had been licensed in 1991 to operate 2G mobile networks in the 900 MHz band. One of these was the Danish incumbent Tele Danmark and the other was a new Danish company called Sonofon, which was later taken over by the Norwegian incumbent Telenor. In 1997 licenses for GSM 1800 were awarded, which resulted in four mobile network providers operating GSM networks (900 and 1800 MHz): Tele Danmark, Sonofon, Telia (the Swedish incumbent), and Mobilix (later Orange). Further in the process, in 2001, a new mobile infrastructure provider, 3 (Hutchison Whampoa), entered Denmark in connection with the 3G licenses. Upon Telia taking over Orange in 2004, there are four mobile infrastructure providers (TDC, Telia, Telenor, and 3) in Denmark at present, of which two of them (Telia and Telenor) have started sharing their mobile infrastructures. All four operators offer 3G as well as LTE ('4G'), allowing for mobile broadband.

In 1997, the Danish state sold its shares in Tele Danmark, resulting in the American operator Ameritech (later SBC, following the merger between Ameritech and SBC) becoming the dominant shareholder in Tele Danmark. This came as a real surprise to the Danish public, as hitherto the main thrust in the international liberalization of telecommunications had been the creation of a strong Danish operator; and what would then be the result of a US company taking over? In reality, it did not result in any major changes and was, to a large extent, an expression of different confluent developments:

(1) the Danish telecom market had quickly become one of the most liberal markets in Europe;
(2) the Danish market was one of the most advanced telecom markets, technologically;
(3) the Danish market being advanced with respect to penetration, it was seen as a kind of test market; and
(4) last but not least, Ameritech paid a vast sum of money for the Tele Danmark shares, which alleviated the financial situation of the Danish state.

The Ministry of Finance was the main driver behind this development.

With the Danish state selling its shares in Tele Danmark, the incumbent operator became totally privatized. The state did not even maintain a 'golden share' or any other special right of intervention. And further down the trajectory, the vast majority of shares in the company were sold to a group of private equity funds. This also created a degree of unrest: it was one thing to sell the company to another telecom company with strategic interests in the telecom field but quite another to sell the company to equity funds without any special interest in telecom and whose primary raison d'être is to extract as much money as possible from their acquisitions.

As in most other European countries, until the mid-1990s the Internet was used almost only in universities – and only by a small minority at those universities. Tele Danmark gave priority to trials and marketing of videotex solutions, and it was not until 1995 that the final attempt with videotex was given up in Denmark and Tele Danmark started focusing on the Internet. ADSL was introduced in Denmark in 1999. The first to offer ADSL was a small Danish company, Cybercity (later to be bought by Telenor), and Tele Danmark followed quickly thereafter. Cable modems were also introduced in Denmark in 1999, first by Stofa (which at that time had been taken over by Telia) and shortly thereafter by Tele Danmark. The uptake especially of ADSL but also of cable modems grew very quickly, and broadband penetration in Denmark has for many years been among the highest in the OECD countries. DSL and cable modem solutions constitute the mainstay of fixed broadband access in Denmark.

In addition to DSL and cable modem solutions, fibre in the access networks also started to develop. However, fibre penetration is not near the level attained in either Japan or Korea, and also Sweden and Norway are somewhat ahead of Denmark. But fibre has started growing, mainly promoted by energy companies. In the past few years, TDC has also given more attention to the fibre access market by acquiring the fibre operation of DONG, the largest energy provider in Denmark, in 2009 and the broadband access company ComX in 2013. The energy companies have been the promoters of fibre in the access networks. One of the energy companies also offered a WiMAX solution for a number of years but had to close it down in 2012 because of lack of profit and future development possibilities. In 2012, another energy company, Syd Energi (SE), made a bold move and bought Stofa, making SE the second largest cable modem access provider in Denmark after TDC.

The result is that the broadband access market in Denmark is based on DSL and cable solutions as well as fibre access – in addition to the very fast-growing mobile access market. TDC is the dominant player in the DSL market. The cable access market has two main players, TDC and Stofa, with TDC being the dominant one. In the fibre area, the energy companies with their cooperation in the company Waoo! are the largest players, followed by TDC. And in the mobile market, the dominant players are the four mobile infrastructure providers: TDC, Telia, Telenor, and 3, with TDC being the largest one. In addition to these players, there are a large number of service providers of various kinds. In Denmark, companies do not need a license to operate in the telecom field, except for mobile infrastructure providers. New service-based companies are being established constantly and can grow to a considerable size in terms of subscriptions, especially in the mobile area. However, almost as quickly as these companies grow in the market, they are taken over by the main infrastructure providers. The business models of some of the newcomers actually aim at being taken over by the larger players.

As can be seen from this brief overview of operators, the Danish incumbent TDC is present on all platforms. In most other European countries with cable TV networks, the incumbent telecom operators can have no cable operations – in the interests of promoting infrastructure competition. In Denmark, however, this has not happened, and the result is that TDC is the all-dominant player in the Danish broadband market.

In this contribution, this issue is further discussed, as are the possible implications of equity funds having owned the incumbent operator TDC. Furthermore, the implications of the use of different kinds of infrastructures are examined. Moreover, the paper aims to shed light on the importance of the interplay between service development and infrastructure development. For the period leading up to the introduction of broadband via ADSL in Denmark in 1999, the most important developments seem to be

the establishment of a national incumbent in 1991, the full and relatively early liberalization of all telecommunications in 1996, and the great emphasis that has been put on service developments from the policy side.

6.1.2 Structure of the chapter

First, development in the policy framework is described in Section 6.2. This is followed by an introduction to the key actors in the telecom area in Section 6.3. In Section 6.4, investments are examined. In Section 6.5, the coverage issue is addressed. Section 6.6 analyses how competition has evolved, and Sections 6.7 and 6.8 look at how the market has performed from a demand side perspective. Section 6.7 thereby looks at the uptake of broadband, while Section 6.8 goes into other aspects of the EU Digital Agenda targets regarding the use of services by private citizens as well as private companies. Finally, the main actors in the development of broadband – operators, political and administrative institutions – are discussed in Section 6.9, and conclusions and reflections are put forward in Sections 6.10 and 6.11.

6.2 Telecommunications policy and regulation

Traditionally there has been a broad political consensus around the general information and communication technology policies and the more specific telecom-related policies in Denmark. There have been no major differences in these policy areas between the liberal and right-wing parties, on the one hand, and the social-democratic or left-wing parties, on the other. Lately, however, policy discussions regarding the financing of future investments in broadband infrastructures have erupted.

Hitherto, the general policy trend has been not to intervene on the supply side by way of public investments but to focus on policy initiatives on the demand side in terms of public use of communication infrastructures and public services requiring Internet access. This implies public support for the development of service and application areas related to public sector functions and institutions. The policy is thus demand and service oriented, and very little public money has been going into building or extending broadband infrastructures. Two of the more recent exceptions have been the public research and education network and a few municipalities using public money for local broadband initiatives. Generally, following the liberalization in the mid-1990s, broadband infrastructure construction has, been left to private enterprises, and political influence has been exercised through the setting of a regulatory framework and through policy initiatives mainly on the demand side.

The phases of telecom policy and regulation in Denmark are clearly related to the phases of the telecom policies of the EU – but now and then Denmark has been a laggard and now and then it has been ahead. The first phase of the liberalization process started in the mid-1980s and ended in the mid-1990s with the introduction of a fully liberalized telecom market in 1996. This can be seen as the phase with a gradual, and at times reluctant, adaptation to the new competitive market situation. The second phase was inaugurated by the policy decision to fully liberalize the Danish telecom market in 1996 and ended in 1999 with a political agreement in Parliament constituting the undisputed policy foundation for Danish telecom policies for many years. This can be seen as the phase where the policy foundation was consolidated and where the focus was almost entirely on promoting service based competition in the fixed broadband area. This was followed by a third phase with continuous adjustments to market developments on the basis of a policy platform promoting competition and with a greater emphasis on infrastructure competition. This third phase, however, seems to be reaching its end at present. At a broader international scale and in Denmark, too, there is an increasing focus on building new infrastructures and less focus on creating competition. This signals a new turn in telecom policies, which has only begun to materialize in the Danish context.

In addition to an elaboration on these different phases, with a focus on telecom regulatory policies, a sub-section on ICT demand-side policies is included. While there are clearly separate phases in the regulatory policies, the broader ICT policies are very consistent over the whole period, starting with the '*Informationssamfundet år 2000*' (The information society year 2000) (Forskningsministeriet, 1994) from 1994. The emphasis always has been on stimulating demand for services and applications and on developing public services and applications, whereas public economic support for the development of the infrastructure has not received any priority.

6.2.1 The first phase – reluctant liberalization and focus on industrial policy

The first phase began in the 1980s resulting in the liberalization of customer premises equipment (CPE) in 1990 and the licensing of two competing mobile operators in 1991. Telephone subscribers had already begun to buy their own phones in super markets and attach them to the network in the 1980s, and at that time mobile telephony was not seen as a central revenue generator for telecom operators. In this early phase, and in the beginning of the 1990s, the Danish government was reluctant to infringe upon the powers and privileges of the incumbent (formed by merging the former regional monopoly operators and a state-owned international operator in 1990), and the liberalization process was mainly driven by the requirements from the European Commission.

In addition to the reluctant adaptation to the new upcoming liberalization, there was also a recognition that other types of communications were on their way, requiring more bandwidth than existing kinds of communications. An initiative to invest in broadband facilities was taken in this phase – in 1985, when it was decided to build a so-called hybrid network. This network had a dual purpose: (1) to provide private households, connected to a cable TV network, with TV and radio channels; and (2) to provide private companies and public institutions with high-speed data channels (mainly for the purpose of two-way video-transmission). Four out of twelve fibres in the system were dedicated to radio and TV broadcast. Another four fibres were allocated for the high-speed network, and the remaining four fibres were reserved for future use. The project was initiated as a public investment but was foreseen to be self-financing within six to seven years. In the first planning phase, an estimate by the Ministry of Public Works was that the total investment would be approximately DKK 4 billion (equalling approx. DKK 8.5 billion in 2013) including telecom company investments and investments by cable antenna communities (Østergaard, 1986). The real investments were only a fragment of this, so the 'grand' project was never realized to the originally anticipated extent.

The idea with this shared infrastructure was to pave the way for a fully integrated broadband network by sharing the costs with cable TV subscribers. In addition, the project was seen as a support for Danish industry. In the initial phase, the network was based on the Danish DOCAT (Digital Optical Community Antenna Trunk) standard, and the large Danish producer of cables, NKT, lobbied strongly for the project. Thus, the hybrid network would create more demand for Danish-produced telecom equipment and, at the same time, provide Danish industry with access to new advanced communication services.

However, the number of companies using the hybrid network as a communication facility remained extremely low and in reality the network became a cable-TV network. In 1995, the network was closed down as a separate network and integrated into the Tele Danmark (later TDC) networks. Today, the most important remaining impact of this hybrid network is that it allowed Tele Danmark to engage in the provision of cable TV services – a market they were denied by regulation until then.

Another important initiative in this period was the formation of Tele Danmark. Up to 1990, the Danish telecom market was served by four regional operators, all with dominant public ownership. Long distance and international communication was under the auspices of the department for Post and Telecom. The reason for this merger was to prevent the emerging competition among the regional operators and to create one strong Danish player in the international telecom market.

While the hybrid network and the creation of Tele Danmark both strengthened the government-controlled monopoly, a more liberal approach was taken in the area of mobile communications. Two operators were licensed to operate mobile networks in Denmark in 1991. The incumbent received a license, and the other was assigned to a new company named Sonofon, which was later taken over by Telenor. Sonofon was established as a joint venture between the Danish telecom company Great Northern Telegraph Company and the American Bell South. The reason for the mobile exception to the rule was that mobile, at that point of time, was not considered an essential part of the telecom area, as fixed line telephony constituted the cornerstone of the telecom business. Furthermore, the initiative could strengthen the Danish position before the expected liberalization of the telecom markets.

6.2.2 Second phase – promotion of real competition

While Denmark in the late 1980s and the first part of the 1990s 'dragged its feet' with respect to reforming its telecom market, the government, led by the social democrats at that time, saw 'the writing on the wall' with information society plans and suggestions for reforming the telecom area coming out of the US and from the European Commission. The decision was made to take a proactive stance on the potential of information and communication technologies and to reform the telecom market. This was in a sense an innovation of the Danish policies in the area – a radical innovation – which was subsequently followed by a continuous stream of incremental additions.

This fundamental change started with the creation of new ministry of Research and Telecommunication and the publication of '*Informationssamfundet år 2000*' (Forskningsministeriet, 1994). The report aimed at presenting a vision/project for how 'modern information technology will bind together public institutions and businesses and constitute a proposition to the citizens' (Forskningsministeriet, 1994). One year later, the

Ministry of Research issued a report entitled '*Bedst og billigst gennem reel konkurrence*' ('Best and cheapest by way of real competition') (Forsknings-ministeriet, 1995), which came to function as a kind of blueprint for the process of liberalizing the Danish telecom market.

In spite of various qualifications made since then, this overall policy strategy is still valid. Competition on the Danish market was to be promoted through an early liberalization combined with a rather strict competition regulation. The idea was that Denmark should be among the first countries in Europe to liberalize its telecom market and, thereby, attract foreign telecom investments.

Therefore, the Danish parliament made a decision aiming to complete the liberalization process for services and infrastructure eighteen months ahead of the 1998 target set for liberalization of the European telecom markets. Since then and until recently, it has been a priority to stimulate competition and Danish telecom legislation has been ahead of the requirements set by European framework regulations in most areas.

In this period, France Telecom chose Denmark as the destination for their first major foreign investment in Europe. They established a new mobile operator, Mobilix, and contributed to making the Danish mobile market one of the most innovative and competitive in the world.

Whereas there was infrastructure competition in the mobile area, the emphasis was on service based competition in the fixed network market, and a key issue was to ensure open access and low interconnection charges in order to enable new entrants to compete with the incumbent operator, Tele Danmark. The Interconnection Act was passed, stipulating *inter alia* that operators with a significant share of the market (that is to say more than 25%) were to grant interconnection to other operators at cost-based prices and on terms that were objective, transparent, and non-discriminatory.

Another initiative taken in order to promote competition was the unbundling of the local loop. This was introduced in 1998, when Mobilix wanted to introduce ADSL before this service was available from Tele Danmark.

The pricing principles for unbundling introduced in 1996 were based on historical costs. The principle was to allow the inclusion of the total extra costs related to the provision of the service plus a reasonable margin. However, if the dominant operator (the incumbent carrier) had a market share of more than 80%, only 30% of the operating costs should be included. This implied that the incumbent operator should bear a part of the costs until the new entrants had obtained a reasonable market share. In this way, the incumbent was required to subsidize its competitors until some of them had established themselves on the Danish market. This approach was compatible with the investment ladder strategy later described by Martin Cave (2006).

To ensure low interconnection rates, the historical cost approach was supplemented by a best-practice clause in 1998, enabling the national telecom regulator to reduce interconnection charges to the international level for best practice even if Tele Danmark was able to document that the actual costs were higher. The definition of best practice was subsequently changed after several debates between the telecom agency, Tele Danmark and the new entrants. 'Best practice' came to be defined as the average of the interconnection rates in the three countries with the lowest interconnection rates. It was also possible for the regulatory agency to reduce rates if they were lower in just one country. However, in this case, corrections for country-specific conditions should be made in advance. By definition, the best practice clause kept the Danish interconnection rates among the lowest in Europe and the charges were reduced to one-third within five years (Falch, 2002).

Stimulating competition was not the only policy created to facilitate infrastructure development. In order to ensure coverage in rural as well urban areas, a universal service obligation was adopted in 1996 and Tele Danmark, as the incumbent operator, was appointed as the universal operator in all markets. However, Denmark went further than demanded by the EU legislation, as Tele Danmark had an obligation to provide ISDN and leased lines in addition to provision of ordinary phone services.

Table 6.1 Average total cost per fully unbundled loop (€ per month), Denmark and EU, 2002, 2009 and 2011

	2002	2009	2011
Denmark	12.10	11.34	10.44
EU average	22.60	9.760	9.70

Data sources: EU: Telecommunications Regulatory Package – VIII Implementation report – Annex I – Corrigendum March 2003; Telecommunications Regulatory Package – XII Implementation report – Annex I, 2010.

6.2.3 The third phase – technology-neutral regulation

In 1997 the EU issued a Green Paper on the convergence of communication technologies (CEC, 1997). The markets were increasingly developing from vertical to horizontal structures, and different infrastructures were starting to deliver essentially the same services. One of the implications was a greater emphasis on promoting different infrastructures in order to create 'real' – meaning infrastructure-based – competition instead of just service competition. In Denmark, this found an expression in the political aim of 'several pipes to the home' announced in a political framework agreement signed in September 1999. The government added to the 'best and cheapest' policy the goal of promoting public access to the network society. Fostering competition was seen as the principal means to achieve this goal, through initiatives aimed at stimulating the creation of competing access routes for consumers.

This policy has been termed by the government as technology-neutral and market-oriented. Such a characterization is obviously self-congratulatory to some extent, as the overall policy and regulatory framework favors some kinds of infrastructure developments over others and specifically favours certain technology developments in the wireless broadband area. However, the characterization is correct in the sense that public money is not allocated for the development of specific types of network infrastructures.

Following the political agreement of September 1999, much of the existing legislation for the telecom sector was consolidated into the Act on Competitive Conditions and Consumer Interests in the Telecommunications Market in July 2000. By the adoption of the new legislation, it was decided that interconnection rates in the future should be based on LRAIC (long run average incremental costs). The regulatory agency, Telestyrelsen, therefore initiated the construction of a cost model for the Danish telecom networks, building on the LRAIC concept. Interconnection charges, set on basis of the LRAIC model, took effect from 1 January 2003. Ordinary interconnect charges were reduced by 17–36%, but the LRAIC price calculated for raw copper was 24% above the current price at the time (Falch, 2002). Therefore, it was decided to implement this price increase on raw copper over a period of seven years. As a result, interconnection charges have increased from among the lowest in Europe to a little above the EU average. See Table 6.1.

It can be argued that the LRAIC approach for calculating the interconnection rates is objective and scientific. Still, there is plenty of room for discretion in the price-setting. In Denmark, the LRAIC model was elaborated in collaboration with TDC as well as a group of new entrants. The new-entrant group was dominated by mobile operators and their primary interest was to ensure low rates for fixed termination of mobile calls. Furthermore, an increase in prices for raw copper was in accordance with the 'several pipes to the home' strategy, as it would presumably promote infrastructure investments by alternative operators. It would, therefore, be in line with an investment ladder strategy, as increasing interconnection charges were supposed to incentivize new operators to invest in new infrastructure instead of relying on old infrastructure owned by the incumbent.

At present, the price regulation of wholesale broadband services has become less strict than at the turn of the century. However, the regulation in other areas regarding open access is broader in its scope than in most other European countries. The telecom legislation does not distinguish between different types of fixed communication networks. This implies that the same regulation applies to copper wire, coaxial cable, and optical fibre networks and an SMP operator can be required to open any network regardless of the technical platform used.

The inclusion of cable and optical networks is relatively new. In December 2009 the regulatory agency required TDC to open their cable network, enabling other operators to use this infrastructure for the provision of broadband services. The implementation of this, however, has caused problems. An LRAIC model has been developed, but no competing service providers are currently able to offer broadband on TDC's cable network because of the technical frequency allocation of the network.

Since June 2011 TDC has also been required by the regulator to open its fibre-based broadband access network to other operators and service providers. This applies not only to the current subscribers of TDC, but also to homes passed. Potential broadband subscribers can demand to be connected to TDCs optical network if the network passes their home in a distance of less than 30 m. The costs of connection, which are estimated to be around EUR 2,000, must be paid by TDC – even if the customer wants to subscribe to a competing operator.

One can argue that the Danish telecom regulation is in line with the technology-neutral principle recommended by the European Commission. However, the Commission does not recommend including fibre and cable networks in the definition of the market for broadband access (market 5). Denmark is, indeed, not the only country that applies a definition that deviates from the EU recommendation on this point. Cable access is included in market 5 in eleven other EU countries (Valcke *et al.*, 2011). However, Denmark is the only country, where this has been followed by a request to an operator to provide open access to cable as well as to fibre networks. The best explanation for this state of affairs is that TDC has a stake in, if not dominates, all fixed infrastructures.

6.2.4 A fourth phase of regulation?

Lately, the contours of a new phase seem to be appearing internationally. This phase puts less emphasis on stimulating competition and more emphasis on infrastructure construction. The reason is that it has turned out to be difficult to stimulate infrastructure competition if it did not already exists on the basis of a legacy cable network, and that the companies investing in new infrastructures (fully or partly optical networks) complain that there is no incentive to invest if competitors can obtain access to the new networks on equal terms. TDC has also argued along these lines.

In 2010, a new policy initiative was presented in Denmark. This initiative was launched against the background of the general international surge of broadband plans in connection with the financial and economic crisis starting in 2008. In Denmark, a High Speed Committee was established to examine whether initiatives were needed to support broadband development. The results of the deliberations of the committee illustrate the general political priorities in Danish ICT and broadband policies with a focus on the demand side. There were no suggestions for using public money for broadband development.

However, the irony of the matter was that, even though this was fully in line with longstanding Danish ICT and broadband policies, the minister responsible for the ICT area at that point apparently felt that something more had to be done. Therefore, a policy statement was issued saying that by 2020 '100 Mbit/s or more for all households and enterprises' would need to be available. There was no economic backing for this goal. It was merely an expression of intent for the market players to realize. The only tangible political measure to implement broadband was concerned with requirements regarding coverage by operators in connection with license auctions for mobile broadband frequencies. In addition, the minister announced a constant 'political attention' to broadband development – which is rather intangible but nevertheless puts pressure on operators to make available higher broadband data rates to everyone.

In 2011 a new government came into office. One of their first initiatives was to dissolve the national IT and telecom regulator, the IT and Telecom Agency. This move might not be as drastic as it seems at first glance, as most of the activities have been continued in other departments, but public attention on ICT as a specific policy area was reduced. In their recently published plan for broadband and mobile infrastructures (Erhvervsstyrelsen, 2013), the policy initiatives are in line with the initiatives suggested by the High Speed Committee but with slightly more active participation by the public sector. For the first time, the government will be engaged in direct economic support to public infrastructure developments. It granted EUR 6 million to a specific region (Bornholm), and encouraged public-private partnerships in other regions. Even though the amount is very small, it marks a change from the former policy. And more initiatives are demanded by various actors, including fibre operators, Telia and Telenor, organizations of business and residential users, and municipalities. In an address in October 2013 to the minister of Business and Growth, these organizations asked for re-opening of the political agreement from 1999. Their precise aims were not clear but appear to demand a new approach to Danish ICT policies.

6.2.5 Demand-stimulating policies

While regulatory policies have undergone continuous incremental changes since the early liberalization, the policy on the demand side has remained basically unchanged since 'The information society year 2000' report of 1994. It is based on the understanding that infrastructure and service development initiatives are mutually interdependent. However, the Danish policy has, until now, been to intervene in this interdependent relationship by way of promoting the service side.

This includes the promotion of G2G e-government: i.e., the use of ICTs internally in public administrations and between public administrations in different areas and at different levels. But, more importantly for broadband development, it also includes the promotion of electronic communications between public

administrations and citizens and businesses. An example of such initiatives is that public administrations no longer accept paper based invoices from companies with which they do business. Also, all-electronic tax reporting between the tax authorities and citizens and companies has become the norm as of 2012, although other means of communicating with the authorities remain possible for people who do not use the Internet, such as the elderly. Also from 2012, all students applying to higher educational institutions must do this electronically. Another example is the cooperation of a public-private-partnership between the state and financial institutions regarding identity management in electronic communications: the same identity management system is used in electronic communications between citizens and public administrations and for electronic banking. The implications of such initiatives are that there is increased pressure on citizens and companies to communicate electronically and, therefore, to use broadband connections.

A characteristic example in this context was the broadband policy initiative presented by the High Speed Committee in 2010 (Højhastighedskomiteen, 2010). Seven areas of policy initiatives were given priority. The first two were digitalization of the public sector, and using the public sector as a platform for innovation. This was followed by suggestions regarding the development of cloud computing and information and IT competency and by initiatives regarding the environment, climate and green IT, as well as research and development in the IT area. This policy input is perfectly in line with policy initiatives since the mid-1990s.

6.3 Operators on the Danish market

6.3.1 TDC – the incumbent operator

The incumbent operator – first named Tele Danmark and later TDC – was created by a political initiative in 1990 as a holding company owning the four regional monopolies and one international operator that existed at that time.

A large share of the total stock, resulting in a controlling interest, was later sold to a foreign company, Ameritech, which later merged with another American operator, SBC. In 2006, a group of private equity (PE) companies took over 87.9% of the TDC stock – a share that has been reduced gradually, with a final PE exit in September 2013.

As the incumbent operator, TDC is by far the largest supplier of physical broadband infrastructure. TDC is the only provider of a copper based infrastructure covering close to 100 per cent of all households. TDC also possesses the largest cable network, covering more than half of all households (homes passed). And, since 2003 they have laid down fibre tubes whenever a new building has been constructed, and they now own an extensive fibre network of 45,000 km.

TDC follows a strategy where gradually copper-based facilities are replaced by optical fibre and the DSLAMs are moved closer to the customer. In this way, it becomes possible to provide DSL services at higher data rates without providing a full FttH solution. Through the use of vectoring technology, TDC will be able to provide 100 Mbit/s and eventually up to 250 Mbit/s using the existing copper cables. TDC expects that the market share of copper-based solutions will decrease, although copper will still have a role to play in 2020.

TDC provides FttH as well. In 2009, TDC acquired DONG Energy's 7,000 km fibre network with 15,000 end users in the capital region. In 2013 TDC bought the broadband provider ComX, also in the capital region. With these networks, TDC now has a fibre network, which covers more than 200,000 households (homes passed), and this number is expected to increase to 500,000 in 2020, or approximately 20 per cent of total households.

The role and impact of PE ownership has been subject to extensive discussion (Nyrup, 2007). While the data rates offered to consumers have not developed as fast as predicted (ITST, 2011), it is not obvious that the PE take-over changed the course of development significantly. For telecom users in Denmark, the most significant implication is that TDC has continued the course which was laid in the Ameritech/SBC period: i.e., to be a second mover with respect to new network solutions on the Danish market and not to use the Danish market as a test bed for wider international initiatives.

On the other hand, PE ownership has had severe consequences for the international presence of TDC, as the PE owners sold off most of the international operations and turned TDC into a company operating primarily in the Danish market. During the past decade, the two other large incumbent Nordic operators, TeliaSonera and Telenor, have become sizeable international players, while TDC has shrunk to become basically a national player.

6.3.2 The largest competitors

Next to TDC, the three largest competitors on the Danish market are the two other Nordic incumbents, TeliaSonera (under the brand name of Telia in the Danish market), Telenor, and the operator 3. Telia and Telenor are operating in fixed as well as mobile markets. However, both companies focus on mobile communications, as it has been difficult to penetrate the fixed market, while 3 is a mobile-only company.

Telenor Denmark, with a turnover of EUR 765 million in 2012, is the second largest provider of broadband and telephony in Denmark. Telenor entered the Danish market in 2000 through the acquisition of a majority share of Sonofon. In the Danish market, Telenor is first of all a mobile operator, but has also achieved a position as major provider of broadband services through the acquisition of Cybercity in 2005. Cybercity was established in 1995 and had for a short while, up to 2000, a higher DSL market share than TDC, on the then relatively small DSL market using unbundling of TDC's network. In 2012, Telenor had around 175,000 DSL customers and a market share of approximately 15 per cent. However, the company does not own a copper infrastructure and depends on TDC's access network for the provision of DSL services.

Telia Denmark is part of the Swedish/Finnish incumbent telecom operator TeliaSonera and the third largest telecom operator on the Danish market with a turnover of around EUR 683 million in

2012 when they had approximately 75,000 DSL customers (6.3% market share). Until 2010, they had their own cable infrastructure, as they owned the Danish cable operator Stofa. Telia was the first operator to introduce LTE services on the Danish market in late 2010 and their strategy is to market mobile broadband as an alternative to fixed broadband. The selling of their cable business in 2010 can be seen as part of this strategy.

In 2013, Telia and Telenor started offering mobile broadband jointly, using infrastructure sharing. The purpose is obviously cost savings, but it also indicates the severe competitive pressure for competitors to TDC in any technology area on the Danish market.

The operator 3 (Hutchison-Whampoa) entered the Danish market in 2003 in connection with the launch of 3G in Denmark. 3 was the first on the Danish market with 3G and the company was the largest 3G provider and promoter for a long time, while the other providers held back their 3G operation because of lack of services requiring 3G capacity. 3, however, was forced to enter the 3G market as soon as possible as they, unlike their MNO competitors, did not hold a 2G license as a fallback. The market share of 3 fell when the other MNOs started launching 3G, and 3 held approximately 10 per cent of the mobile market in 2012.

6.3.3 Syd Energi and other energy companies

In addition to DONG Energy, which sold its network facilities to TDC, other energy companies have invested in fibre networks since 2000, and their networks pass around 700,000 households (approx. 25 per cent of total households). Approximately 200,000 customers are connected or are about to be connected. Since the economic downturn started in 2008, the energy companies have scaled down their investment activities and are focusing instead on obtaining more customers to be connected to the existing infrastructure.

The most important player among the energy companies is SE (Syd Energi). SE is the energy provider in South Jutland. This region is one of the least densely populated regions in Denmark but,

due to SE, it is also the region with the best coverage of optical fibre.

In February 2013, the Competition Authority approved the acquisition of Stofa by SE. In the cable access market, Stofa is the second-largest provider of broadband via cable after TDC. In 2011, 414,000 customers were connected to the Stofa network, approximately 20 per cent of the CATV market. Out of these, 151,000 were supplied with broadband. Stofa was formerly owned by Telia but was acquired by the Swedish private equity firm Ratos in 2010. Their infrastructure covers major cities especially in Jutland and Funen. There is little overlap with TDCs cable network and hence the direct competition between the two is limited.

In September 2010, the energy companies formed Waoo! in order to promote broadband services via their fibre infrastructure. With 155,000 customers (4.5 per cent of households), Waoo! is the most important provider of broadband via fibre.

6.3.4 Other infrastructure providers

Another player in the Danish market is COLT Telecom. They operate their own fibre network in Copenhagen and provide wholesale and retail services to business customers. GlobalConnect is yet another company and has been on the market since 1998. They provide dark fibre on a wholesale basis.

Fixed wireless infrastructures do not play a significant role in the Danish broadband market. Two licenses have been issued, one to TDC and another to Skyline which provided approximately 40,000 fixed wireless connections in 2010, but went bankrupt in June 2012.

In the early phase of broadband development, an interesting phenomenon that contributed to market expansion was the emergence of a few local community-based alternative network providers. These operators were established in order to serve a market need in primarily rural areas, where services provided by the major operators were either inadequate or very expensive. By far the largest example of such a network provider is Djursland. net. Djursland.net took off in year 2000, when the development of a wireless broadband network covering a population of 82,000 began.

This network was once one of the largest alternative broadband operators in Europe. The organization was dissolved in 2009, but the network facilities are still in operation. At present, this type of alternative networks is less important, as coverage by competing solutions has improved. Moreover, some of these networks have been taken over by Dansk Bredbånd, which later was bought by Waoo!, the broadband company owned by a cooperation of local energy companies. However, the alternative networks have played a role in establishing early coverage in rural areas.

6.3.5 Other service providers

There are many providers of retail broadband service on the Danish market – in the DSL field as well as the mobile area (as MVNOs). The development pattern, which has been seen repeatedly, is that service providers open with cheaper and more attractive pricing for users than the existing operators. They grow to a considerable size, running with an increasing deficit, but with a quickly developing number of subscribers. Finally, they are bought up by one of the large network operators, interested in both acquiring the subscriber base and preventing these operators from being taken over by one of their competitors.

6.4 Telecommunications investments

The level of public telecom investments in Denmark is high compared to other OECD countries, both with regard to telecom investments per capita and telecom investments per access line. Within the EU, considering the average over the period 2009–2011, Denmark ranked as number one in investment per access path and number two, after Luxembourg, in investment per capita (OECD, 2013).

The investments have followed the same trend as in other OECD countries with a rapid growth in telecom investments in the 1990s and a peak just before the burst of the telecom bubble in 2001. The growth in this period can be attributed mainly to

two related factors. First, that the rapid growth in mobile communications necessitated major expansions of mobile network facilities. Second, the liberalization implied investment in alternative networks by the new entrants.

Another peak in telecom investments can be observed in 2008 before the start of the current financial crisis. Denmark has experienced more fluctuations in investment levels than other OECD countries have. In 2002–2008 the growth was higher and the subsequent decline was also steeper. Danish telecom investments continued to fall in 2010 and 2011, while telecom investments within the EU experienced a growth of 3 per cent from 2009 to 2010. In spite of this recent decline, the Danish investment rate is still well above average.

While the investments made by TDC have remained fairly stable, the investments made by new entrants have fluctuated strongly. See Figure 6.1. As TDC was taken over by a private equity group in February 2006, there was a concern that this would have a negative impact on telecom investments. However, this is not confirmed by the investment figures. Up to 2008, there was a high growth in investments made by other operators, while the investments made by TDC remained stable. On the other hand, TDC's investments have been stable also after 2008, while the other operators reduced their investments.

This could indicate a higher dependence on economic downturns and upturns by the other operators. Another reason may be the entry of energy companies into the telecom market. Energy companies have invested heavily in fibre since 2000. However, until now, these investments have not been very successful in terms of generating new revenue, and the energy companies have lost DKK 5,300 million (EUR 700 million) on these activities (Ingeniøren, 11 May 2012).

6.5 Broadband developments and coverage

From the beginning, DSL has been the most important technology applied to offer widespread access to broadband services. ADSL was introduced as a service in mid-1999. Coverage

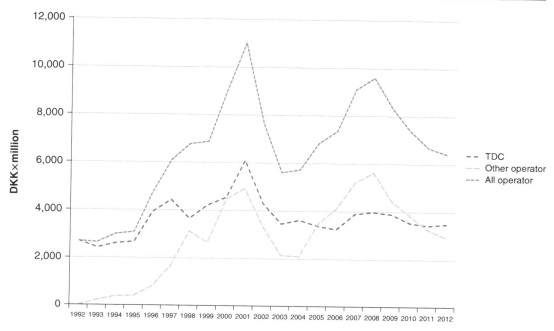

Figure 6.1 Public telecom investments, Denmark, 1992–2012
Data sources: TDC annual reports; Danish Business Bureau: Economic key figures 2007–2011; National
IT & Telecom Agency: Annual telecom statistics 1992–2006.

developed rapidly to include the majority of the
population and already by 2003 reached 90
per cent. Cable as an infrastructure for broadband
services was introduced later in 1999. Also in this
case, coverage developed rapidly. In 2003, most of
the cable infrastructure was upgraded to provide
broadband services. Cable coverage, however,
is limited by the fact that the cable networks only
cover parts of the population: 63 per cent of the
households are covered by broadband via cable.
Coverage of wireless services has developed even
faster due to lower investment costs and a higher
level of competition.

As a result, at least two different access technologies (DSL and mobile) are available for the
vast majority of the population. DSL covers 99 per
cent of the population; 3G has a similar level of
coverage, but the data rates are much lower;
LTE was introduced in the Danish market in
December 2010 and is available in all urban areas.
Cable is also widely available, while fibre coverage
is much lower.

It follows that, with the exception of fibre, all
access technologies have succeeded in gaining a
high level of coverage within a few years of their
introduction. This is partly a result of competition
in the different segments of the broadband market
and partly an outcome of a deliberate policy,
with universal coverage of broadband services
having been a policy goal for more than a decade.
Furthermore, it is partly due to the socio-economic
environment.

In contrast to Sweden and Finland, the Danish
telecom regulation does not provide for a universal service obligation for broadband, but the
mere formulation of universal coverage of broadband services as a policy goal has put pressure,
especially on TDC, to provide extensive coverage
of broadband services.

In addition, Denmark is a high-income country,
where households rapidly take up new technologies. Furthermore, the Danish geography implies
that the investments needed for coverage of the
majority of the population are affordable for most

network technologies – at least in comparison with those required in other Scandinavian countries.

The coverage of fibre connections has developed at a slower pace than the coverage of any other access technology. This is primarily due to the high costs related to the implementation of FttH, but it is also a result of the expansion strategy chosen by TDC. TDC replaces their copper based network with fibre based network facilities in a way that the optical part of the network and the DSLAMs move gradually closer to the end customer. It is, therefore, the alternative providers, mainly energy companies, that provide the major share of the full fibre access connections.

6.6 Intensity of competition

Despite the good coverage of several infrastructures, there is still a long way to go before one can conclude that the broadband market is a market with real facility-based competition. TDC has high market shares in all available platforms and it has a dominating position in almost all geographical areas. However, as LTE becomes a real alternative to fixed broadband access, this will challenge TDC's dominant position, as all of the four mobile network operators are able to provide a fully integrated broadband infrastructure using this technology, although Telia and Telenor are cooperating in the joint TT platform.

The retail market for broadband is dominated by the same operators as the market for physical broadband infrastructures, notwithstanding the efforts made to separate the two markets through the requirements for open access. Table 6.2 shows that wholesale broadband access – excluding

Table 6.2 Wholesale broadband access, excluding bitstream, Denmark, 2008–2010

% of lines	Copper	Fibre	Cable	Total
2008	6.5	9.7	0	5.4
2009	8.2	9.4	0	6.4
2010	7.8	7.9	0	6.0

Data source: IT & Telestyrelsen: Engrosmarkedet for fysisk netværksinfrastrukturadgang (marked 4). 30 September 2011.

bitstream access – constitutes only a small share of the total. This indicates that bitstream-based competition has only to a small extent developed into competition on the higher rungs of the 'ladder of investment'. See also Figure 6.2.

Early developments in the Danish broadband market clearly illustrate the strategic advantage related to ownership of physical infrastructure. DSL was in Denmark first introduced by Cybercity. TDC was not very eager to introduce this service, as they wanted to protect their market for services charged per minute, such as ISDN. At the turn of the century, the DSL market was shared among three operators, each having a 30–40% market share. In 2000, TDC initiated an aggressive promotion of their services with substantial reductions in prices and, in two years' time, TDC's market share increased from 30% to 79%. TDC was accused of predatory pricing but when the case was resolved in 2003 it was too late for the two new entrants to regain their former position.

From 2006 to 2009, new entrants on the DSL market climbed up the investment ladder, increasing their use of full unbundling compared to the use of bitstream access. Thus full unbundling of the local loop increased from 62% to 68%, while bitstream access decreased from 31% to 23% of total wholesale. However, this development was reversed in 2009–2012. The share of bitstream access has increased to 30%. This development deviates from the general trend within the EU. In the EU, the number for full unbundling tripled from 2007–2010 and increased to more than 70% in 2012. See Figure 6.2.

It is likely that the share of full unbundling will decrease further as a result of future upgrades of the infrastructure. As TDC moves the DSLAMs closer to the customers in order to be able to provide more capacity to each subscriber, the business case for new entrants to use raw copper becomes less attractive. New entrants will need to make substantial investments in additional equipment and, when the number of potential customers decreases to 100–150 customers per DSLAM in total for all operators, the payback time will be ten years or more. New entrants may, therefore, either climb down the ladder again or make use of other technologies for provision of last-mile connectivity.

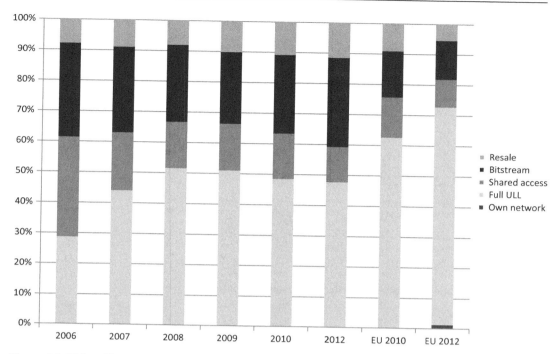

Figure 6.2 Unbundling by type, Denmark 2006–2012 and EU 2010–2012
Data sources: Bredbåndsredegørelsen 2010, National IT and Telecom Agency, Denmark and EU
Commission: Broadband access in the EU: situation at 1 July 2010, COCOM10–29, DG INFSO/C4, Brussels,
21 November 2010, European Commission: Electronic Communications Market Indicators, Brussels 2012.

By 2012 TDC had a market share of 74% for DSL and 66% of the market for broadband via cable, compared to the European average for cable of 3.1%. TDC has been able to maintain a high market share partly because they have acquired some of the most successful of the new independent actors on the broadband market. This includes Fullrate and A+. Both companies provided DSL services using the TDC infrastructures and both were acquired by TDC in 2010. The only providers with a significant market share in DSL at present are Telia and Telenor.

As a result of these developments, for all fixed platforms combined, the level of competition in Denmark is well below the European average. TDC's market share in fixed broadband connections was 61% in 2012, while the average market share for incumbent operators was 42.6%. See also Table 6.3. Only the incumbents in Cyprus and Luxembourg had a higher market share than TDC. Moreover, the TDC market share has remained fairly constant since 2005. The main reason is that TDC is the dominant provider on two out of three fixed broadband platforms. The Danish market thus differs from the rest of Europe, as Denmark is the only country where the incumbent dominates cable as well as DSL services.

6.7 Demand for broadband services

In 2012 the penetration of fixed broadband was 39.6 per 100 inhabitants. This is a slight increase compared to 2010, when the penetration was 38.2. In 2012, 85% of private households had access to fixed broadband compared to 44% in 2005. This makes Denmark one of the countries with the highest broadband penetration in the world. On the other hand, it seems that the market for fixed broadband has reached saturation, partly due to substitution of mobile solutions. See Table 6.4.

Table 6.3 Incumbent market shares – DSL and fixed broadband total, Denmark and EU, 2003–2012

%	Year	Denmark	EU average
DSL access	2003	82.1	77.9
	2008	67.5	55.9
	2010	73.0	55.0
	2012	74.0	54.0
Broadband total	2003	67.9	58.7
	2008	59.0	45.6
	2010	63.1	44.0
	2012	61.0	42.6

Data sources: Telecom statistics – first half of 2003 National IT and Telecom Agency, Denmark, EU Commission: Broadband access in the EU: situation at 1 July 2008 COCOM08–41 FINAL DG INFSO/B3 Brussels, 28 November 2008 and statistics. EU Commission: Broadband access in the EU: situation at 1 July 2010, COCOM10–29, DG INFSO/C4, Brussels, 21st November 2010, EU Commission: Broadband lines in the EU: situation at 1 July 2012, DG CNECT/F4 Brussels, 18/02/2013.

Table 6.4: Broadband penetration by technology, Denmark, 2002–2012

(Million)	2002	2005	2010	2012	2012 Share of fixed broadband connection
DSL	307,000	837,000	1,243,000	1,192,000	57%
Cable	134,000	462,000	559,000	609,000	29%
Fibre	18,000	117,000	171,000	272,000	13%
FWA, including WiMAX	1,500	4,800	49,000	12,000	1%
Fixed broadband total	460,500	1,420,800	2,022,000	2,085,000	100%
Mobile broadband subscriptions	-	-	3,441,000	5,427,000	-

Data sources: Erhvervsstyrelsen: Tele statistics various years.

The penetration is, to a large extent, uniform across regions, but the uptake is slightly above average in the capital region and slightly below average in Southern Jutland. These minor differences seem to be due to differences in demography (age profile) rather than differences in availability of broadband access.

The increase in demand for higher bandwidth is primarily driven by download and streaming of video and music, and the data rate has increased rapidly within the past two years. In 2008, less than 20% of the connections had download rates of 10 Mbit/s or more. In 2012 more than half of the connections were at that level.

The demand for dual-play (telephony and Internet access) and especially triple-play (telephony, Internet access, and television) has also increased

rapidly within the last few years. The number of triple-play connections grew from 23,000 in 2008 to more than 353,000 in mid-2013.

For the Danish business users, 99% of companies with at least 10 employees had Internet access in 2013; 63% had access via DSL; 57% had mobile broadband access; 54% had another (than DSL) fixed access connection. Note that the uptake figures add up to more than 100%, as companies use different broadband connections at the same time.

6.8 Realizing the Digital Agenda targets

In 2006, Denmark had a broadband household coverage of 40% with at least 2 Mbit/s. This had grown to close to 100% by 2010 (IT &

Telestyrelsen 2010a). See Table 6.5. By 2012, 97% of the population had access to broadband at 10 Mbit/s. The Danish policy ambition is that all citizens should have access to 100 Mbit/s downstream by 2020. In 2012, 65% of the population had that opportunity. See Table 6.6.

In addition to the coverage and penetration of broadband, information on the use of services and applications is also important to assess broadband developments. There is an interrelationship between the coverage and penetration of broadband and the supply and demand for electronic services. This case study argues that public policy in Denmark was intended to stimulate both supply and demand for electronic services, thus also stimulating broadband development. It is therefore relevant to look at public uses of electronic services.

In an overview for 2012 on electronic interaction by citizens with public authorities, provided by Eurostat for the Digital Agenda Scoreboard 2013, Denmark was the leading country among EU countries with 92% of citizens interacting electronically with public authorities, while the EU average stood at 62%.

A comparison with other Nordic countries and with the EU27 average indicates that Denmark is in the forefront with respect to information retrieval, as well as with sending information to public institutions. In terms of download of forms, Denmark is at the same level as other Nordic countries, while the level is twice as high as the EU27 average. See Table 6.7.

When looking at the electronic interaction between businesses and public authorities, Denmark also scores higher than the EU average. In this context, however, Finland is in the lead on all accounts among Nordic countries (information retrieval, download of forms, sending forms, etc.).

Table 6.5 Broadband coverage, Denmark, 2001–2012

Access Technology	% of population covered			
	2001	2005	2010	2012
DSL	64	98	99	99
Cable	14	60	61	63
Fibre	0	9	31	41
3G	0	90	99	No data
FWA, including WiMAX	90	90	76	No data
LTE*	-	-	-	65
Total		**>98**	**100**	**100**

* LTE was introduced in December 2010.
Data sources: ITST, Bredbåndsredegørelsen, 2010; Erhvervsstyrelsen: Bredbåndskortlægning 2012; European Commission, Digital Agenda Scoreboard 2013.

Table 6.6 Estimated coverage by downstream and upstream data rate (% of households), Denmark, 2009–2012

% Households	2009	2010	2011	2012
100 Mbit/s downstream	-	25	38	65
50 Mbit/s downstream	-	68	74	77
30 Mbit/s downstream	-	74	80	83
10 Mbit/s downstream	77	92	96	97
2 Mbit/s downstream	98	99	99.9	99.9
100 Mbit/s upstream	-	24	30	32
50 Mbit/s upstream	-	29	34	38
30 Mbit/s upstream	-	30	35	39
10 Mbit/s upstream	-	45	56	79
2 Mbit/s upstream	-	90	97	97

Data source: Erhvervsstyrelsen: Bredbåndskortlægning 2012.

Table 6.7 Electronic contacts with public institutions, percentage of population (age 16–74), Nordic countries and EU, 2012

	Denmark	Finland	Norway	Sweden	EU27
Information retrieval (% of population)	80	61	73	74	39
Download of forms etc. (% of population)	53	55	54	48	27
Sending information to public institutions (% of population)	69	45	51	45	22

Data source: Danmarks Statistik: IT-anvendelse i befolkningen – EU sammenligninger, 2012.

Table 6.8: Share of companies using electronic invoices, Denmark, 2007–2011

%	2007	2009	2011
Denmark	37	38	54
Finland	27	24	63
Norway	29	32	32
Sweden	18	25	28
EU-27	18	23	21

Source: European Commission, Digital Agenda Scoreboard (accessed May 2013)

Electronic invoicing is a case in point. The Danish government decided that by 2008, public institutions would accept only electronic invoices. This would increase efficiency in the handling of invoices between private and public institutions, but would presumably also be an incentive for private companies to take up electronic invoicing between one another. As it turns out, the use of electronic invoicing among Danish companies clearly has been subject to a considerable growth. However, the increase in Finland has been even higher. See Table 6.8.

This illustrates the importance of electronic communications with public authorities for theuptake of broadband in Denmark. In general terms, there is a mutual correlation between broadband extension and the use of electronic services. Increased uptake of broadband will lead to growing use of electronic applications and services and vice versa. The high penetration of broadband in Denmark is closely correlated with the pervasive use of electronic services. This provides policy intervention with different handles on development

of broadband – either via supporting broadband development directly or via support for electronic services, or both. In Denmark, support for electronic services has hitherto been chosen.

6.9 Case analysis

The most important actors in the development of broadband, since the introduction of ADSL in Denmark in 1999, have been the operators in the different access technology fields and the national political-administrative institutions, including the telecom regulator. Potentially there could have been other actors such as large content providers, equipment providers, or local political-administrative entities. However, there are no large national content providers, nor any large equipment manufacturers, in Denmark and the municipalities have not played a significant role in the development of broadband. In specific cases, local authorities have taken initiatives to promote broadband in their local areas but they have not been major institutions in broadband development.

6.9.1 Operators

In the DSL field, the national incumbent, TDC and its affiliates, is by far the largest provider. TDC owns the copper access infrastructure in Denmark and has almost three-quarters of the DSL market. In the cable area, TDC is also the largest broadband provider with approximately two-thirds of that market. The other major cable provider is Stofa, which is now owned by Syd Energi (SE), one of the energy companies that hitherto have concentrated mainly on fibre access. The mobile broadband market is more evenly distributed between the four mobile infrastructure providers (TDC, Telia, Telenor, and 3) and their affiliates. The fibre access market is dominated by the energy companies, with TDC trailing behind, seeking to follow the fibre market in order to expand its fibre activities when needed.

With respect to broadband, in none of the four access technology areas (DSL, cable modem, mobile, fibre) has the incumbent TDC been the first-mover. Cybercity (later taken over by Telenor) was the first-mover in the DSL area; Stofa was the first cable modem provider; 3 was first in 3G-based mobile broadband; and the energy companies are the leaders in the fibre market. All the while, TDC has, maintained a strategy of being a follower and moving quickly into the dominant role in a particular market segment when challenged by the first-mover – with fibre being an exception at present. In contrast to other European countries, the incumbent operator has been permitted to be present in all four broadband market segments.

In addition to the four main technology areas, there have been two interesting broadband initiatives involving other technology solutions. One is a self-organized grass-roots initiative in Djursland (the 'nose' of the Jutland peninsula) where activists built a local broadband access network based on Wi-Fi to serve the rural areas of Djursland.[3] This initiative was started in 2000, when the broadband offers of the traditional Internet Service Providers were lacking or considered insufficient. The Wi-Fi network still exists (in 2013) and serves approximately one third of broadband connections in Djursland, which has a population of approximately 80,000 inhabitants. But it has remained a relatively isolated initiative and has not had any broader influence on Danish broadband developments.

The other initiative is concerned with WiMAX

technology. In 2005, two licenses for providing WiMAX were awarded – one of the licenses to TDC. However, TDC announced right away that they did not intend to use the license but had acquired it in order to prepared: i.e., to see whether this market would develop. The other license led to actual deployment of WiMAX by a succession of companies with Skyline, owned by an energy company, as the last one. Skyline went broke in 2012 and had to abandon approx. 40,000 customers in rural and semi-rural areas in Jutland. Some of them have complained that they subsequently lacked sufficient broadband connectivity.

An important dynamic regarding broadband pricing relates to retail providers having entered the market offering a better deal to customers and acquiring a sizeable market share. After a while, when a sufficiently large number of subscribers have shifted to the new service provider, the company is taken over by one of the large market players, primarily TDC, Telia, or Telenor. These players actually have a mutual understanding that this is an untenable situation, undermining the profitability of the markets, but it has been difficult to act accordingly when new service providers have attracted a large number of customers and are up for sale. The business model for such service providers is to attract as many customers as possible, running with a deficit, and then to be bought up by one of the large network operators. This business model is especially prevalent in the mobile area (entrant MVNOs).

In the fixed network area, the incumbent TDC is very dominant. The affiliates of other Nordic incumbent operators, Telia and Telenor, have tried to break into the Danish fixed broadband market. This applies especially to Telia with its former ownership of the cable company Stofa. However, they have not really succeeded and have lately retreated to prioritize the mobile area, where they have joined forces with Telenor in the joint operation named TT. By mid-2013, TT offered the best LTE network in Denmark, and Telia and Telenor put all their strengths and ambitions in Denmark into mobile broadband.

In public debates on the fixed network markets, the main dividing line in Danish telecommunications has been between the Danish incumbent TDC on

---

[3] See for the deployment of Wi-Fi in under-served areas the chapter contributed by Melody in Lemstra, Hayes and Groenewegen *The Innovation Journey of Wi-Fi – The Road to Global Success* (2010).

one side and all the other operators on the other. This includes the incumbents from other Nordic countries that have generally required better conditions for service providers on the Danish market – conditions they would often not grant to competing service providers in their home markets.

The only fixed network area where TDC is really being challenged is in fibre access. In the energy industry, Denmark has a number of local and regional companies. As these companies have rights of way and often dig up the ground in order to reach energy customers, they also started to offer fibre access a decade ago.

Hitherto TDC has not given much priority to fibre access. Their strategy has been to deploy fibre ever closer to the end-users but to use copper for the last stretch as part of their VDSL strategy. One result is that the energy companies dominate the fibre access market, and another is that the highest bandwidths offered in Denmark are generally in the provincial regions in Southern and Mid-Jutland (on the peninsula), where the energy companies have been most active in fibre deployment. In most other European countries, fibre is mainly offered in densely populated urban areas.

In order to contain this situation, TDC in 2009 bought the largest fibre operation in Denmark. This fibre operation had been running with huge deficits and DONG Energy had, therefore, tried for some time to sell it. Eventually, TDC bought it, but has not used this acquisition to boost their fibre operation or sought to attract new end-users to their fibre acquisition. Apparently their strategy is to wait with fibre-to-the-home and push fibre ever closer to the end-users as part of their VDSL roll-out.

The energy companies offering fibre joined forces in 2010, creating the joint marketing company Waoo!. In 2012, a new development took place when one of the energy companies, SE, acquired the cable company Stofa and thereafter left Waoo!. This suddenly made SE a far larger broadband provider than the other energy companies. How this will influence the strategic actions of the energy companies in the coming years is difficult to say. During the past few years, there has been a virtual political and market struggle between TDC, on the one hand, and the energy

companies on the other. The energy companies have been seeking to present themselves as the companies that will deliver 'true' high-speed broadband to households and companies, while TDC argues that they upgrade their broadband networks when the actual demand is there.

In 2006, private equity funds took over ownership of TDC. The equity funds acquired 87.9% of the TDC shares but could not get hold of another 2.1% to reach 90%, which according to Danish law would permit them to force the remaining shareholders to sell their shares. Nevertheless, the equity funds totally dominated TDC, which raised some concern although not from the political authorities, nor the regulator. The concern was that equity funds are focused on short-term profitability rather than on long-term investments in the business they are entering. What has happened was that the international operations of TDC have been sold off.[4] While TDC as well as Telia and Telenor had started internationalizing when the telecom markets were liberalized around the world, TDC has become a company focusing primarily on the Danish market and to some extent the Nordic market, while Telia and especially Telenor are international players.

The question is then whether the ownership of TDC by the equity funds has undermined the development of telecommunications in Denmark, by causing a lack of investments in infrastructure and new services. This, however, does not seem to be the case – although the counter-factual development cannot be produced. The overall result has been that TDC has focused primarily on the Danish market, but not that the Danish market has been starved of investments. Through the periods of different kinds of ownership, TDC has maintained a relatively conservative and reactive market strategy – following other market players and responding once they have gained momentum and become a possible threat.

---

[4] For an analysis of private equity in telecommunications see Lemstra and Groenewegen (2009). *Markets and public values – The potential effects of Private Equity Leveraged Buyouts on the safeguarding of public values in the telecommunications sector*. Delft, The Netherlands: TUDelft.

6.9.2 Political-administrative institutions

In all countries, the national political-administrative institutions including the telecom regulator play an important role for the development of broadband. In the case of Denmark, there are at least two issues which are important to address.

One is the great emphasis that the policy system has put on the development of services and applications to be delivered on broadband, including the role of state institutions in promoting the uptake of broadband-based services and applications. Until very recently there has been a general agreement in the political system that no national public money should go into general telecom infrastructure investments. The focus has been on how to push and develop the use of the infrastructural resources, while the infrastructural investments have been left entirely in the hands of the operators.

The other issue is the development of the regulatory institutions. Because of the historical structure with regional operators in Denmark partly privately owned, there were actually separate telecommunication regulatory institutions in Denmark through major parts of the 20th century. However, with the then-upcoming liberalization in mind, a new independent regulator was created in 1990. This regulator was very active in the 1990s, especially in the period following the full liberalization in 1996 and in the first years following the year 2000. Nevertheless, the regulatory institution lost momentum thereafter in connection with the lack of political attention and initiatives from the policy side. With the coming to power of a new center-left government in 2011, the regulator was split up into different parts, and the traditional telecommunication regulatory assignments were transferred to the Danish Business Authority under the Ministry of Business and Growth.

There has been an overall agreement in the Danish political system concerning telecom and ICT policies, and there have been no significant policy shifts with changing governments. This applies to the whole period since the liberalization in the mid-1990s. However, lately there have been some disturbances in the Danish telecom policy arena. These disturbances relate to the expansion of broadband networks.

A political goal was set that all households and companies in Denmark must have access to at least 100 Mbit/s downstream by 2020. By the end of 2012, 65% of households and companies already had access to 100 Mbit/s or more. However, the difficulty is reaching the remaining households.

What the results of the political process will be is difficult to predict, but there are signs of unrest in the policy environment that have not been observed since the policy agreement regarding telecommunications in the parliament in 1999. And it is the broadband issue which is causing this unrest. In 2009, the government established a High Speed Committee, which in 2010 presented its deliberations and suggestions. The suggestions by the committee centred on the promotion of services and applications but, shortly after the presentation of the High Speed Committee report, the government issued its policy goal of 100 Mbit/s for all. At first, this did not create much alarm but as the implementation deadline comes closer, the political debate has started to focus on how this policy goal will be met.

So far, the policy focus has been on advancing services and applications. The various governments and their administrations have time and again issued reports and taken steps to promote the use of broadband-based services. This has entailed initiatives, such as promoting the internal use of broadband-based services in governmental institutions and also requiring those who wish to communicate with public institutions to use electronic means. In 2012, a small number of public services (central and municipal) started the transition to full digital provision. For the coming years, a wide range of public services will be transitioned to digital provision. These administrative goals are well in line with the original Danish policy approach in the area.

6.9.3 Expectations based on theory

In the introduction we addressed the 'ladder of investment' concept (Cave, 2006) and posed the question whether the market has responded as intended to the application of LRAIC-based access pricing. The crude answer is 'no' or 'maybe to some extent'. If climbing the 'ladder' from resale to full unbundling is considered, there has been no such development in Denmark since 2008. If new infrastructures are considered, the answer is 'maybe'. New operators obviously have not built alternative PSTN infrastructures, as TDC has such a network with full national coverage. Telia tried with the cable operation of Stofa to become an alternative infrastructure provider but it sold Stofa to a private equity firm, later to be bought by the electricity company SE. Today, the strategic focus of Telia as well as Telenor in the Danish market is on mobile broadband. As for the electricity companies, which have become the primary drivers of fibre in the access networks, they never considered offering broadband with service provision via the PSTN of TDC. The overall conclusion, therefore, must be that actual infrastructure and service competition is driven much more by strategic moves by operators than by a theory of gradual growth towards infrastructure provision. The increasing interconnection and access prices must be inputs to the strategic considerations by alternative operators. However, it is not clear that this has been the main driver.

In the Danish market, there is a more even distribution of the different access technologies than in most other European broadband markets. Nevertheless, DSL plays the central role. An important reason is the national coverage of the PSTN for many years. DSL is, therefore, a natural technology trajectory. This indicates that path dependency (David, 2007) is an important element in broadband developments.

Another central issue is the relationship between competition and innovation (Aghion et al., 2002). The Danish case clearly illustrates a positive correlation between competition and innovation in infrastructure developments. The Danish incumbent has been a 'second mover' regarding new infrastructures. TDC was neither the first on the Danish market to launch ADSL nor the first to offer cable access. The same applies to fibre and mobile broadband. How these access technologies would have developed without competition is impossible to say, but it is clear that alternative access offers have put pressure on TDC to advance their operations in the different technology areas.

Last but not least, the question regarding the interrelationships between service and application provision and infrastructure provision deserves mentioning. The question is what comes first: the demand and provision for services and applications or the demand and provision for infrastructure. This is, of course, a chicken and egg discussion. However, the important point is that Danish broadband policies have given priority to stimulating service and application developments. The extent to which this differs from other countries can be discussed. However, the political priorities in Denmark have been clear since the new policy direction was announced in 1994–1995 – with one interesting exception being the sudden policy priority of reaching 100 Mbit/s downstream coverage by 2020, which was clearly inspired by broadband initiatives taken in a number of other countries following the financial and economic crisis starting in 2008.

6.10 Conclusions

The major conclusions to be drawn from the Danish case study are the following:

- Denmark was for a number of years the leader among OECD countries with respect to broadband penetration – however not in terms of low prices or data rates. At present, Denmark is not number one anymore, but remains among the leading countries. Fixed broadband penetration has found a saturation level close to 40% in relation to the number of inhabitants. The reason is that households will have only one fixed broadband connection, while the number of mobile broadband connections has grown to more than one per person and will grow further with the use of mobile machine-to-machine connections.
- When discussing the reasons for the relatively high broadband penetration in Denmark, one should consider the relatively high level of GDP per capita. However, this is not the only reason. One also needs to pay attention to the full national coverage and high quality of the PSTN in Denmark, which facilitated the development of ADSL and now VDSL. Moreover, the

proactive role of the regulator in the first years after the introduction of DSL has been an important contributing factor. Furthermore, there has been pressure on businesses and residential users from the political-administrative institutions to adopt broadband by way of promoting electronic communications with citizens and businesses.

- The fast uptake of broadband, resulting in a high level of penetration, to a large extent has been driven by service-level competition. Unlike in other countries, the Danish incumbent operator TDC has been allowed to deploy all kinds of broadband infrastructures, including cable. This means that infrastructure-based competition has been constrained for many years. However, in recent years infrastructure competition has become stronger with the development, first and foremost, of mobile broadband, but also due to fibre access provided by the telecom operations of the energy companies.
- The fact that TDC has permission to deliver broadband on all infrastructure platforms has implied that competition on the Danish broadband market is weaker than in the EU on average. While the market share of TDC has been relatively constant during the past decade at around 60% of the fixed broadband market, the average market share of incumbents in the EU has fallen from approximately 60% to approximately 40%.
- While many different companies have competed with TDC in the broadband market, among them the other Nordic incumbents, these operators are focusing on alternative infrastructures, primarily mobile and fibre. Telia and Telenor are concentrating their effort on mobile broadband, while the energy companies are concentrating on fibre. Mobile broadband is developing very fast, whereas fibre is developing at a much slower pace.
- An important question concerning Danish telecom development has been whether the takeover of TDC by private equity has slowed down progress of the Danish telecom market, as private equity firms do not necessarily have a keen interest in extending and improving the telecom system, given their short-term money-making mission. However, in the Danish case this is not clear. In the period of private-equity

dominance of TDC, the company followed basically the same 'second mover' strategy as it did before private equity stepped in. The consequences in the international markets have been much clearer, TDC has almost disappeared, in contrast to an ongoing presence of its Nordic 'sister' companies Telia and Telenor.

6.11 Reflections on possible future developments

While Danish telecom policies have been very constant since the political agreement in 1999, there is a certain degree of political uncertainty at the moment. For the first time in years, disagreement with the 1999 political foundation has been voiced by industry representatives and political decision-makers. Taken together with the international shift from the promotion of competition to the promotion of infrastructure investments this seems to signal a change in telecom policies.

A more fundamental change will come with the further development of mobile broadband. While fibre has been seen as the 'future proof' broadband technology, mobile broadband is developing quickly in terms of higher data rates. This can change the broadband market in a fundamental way, as infrastructure competition is much stronger in the mobile field than in the fixed field.

Additional factors of change are related to the development of Over-The-Top (OTT) applications. This development reflects the increasing influence of the IT sector in converging ICT fields and will lead to changing business models and changing investment patterns in telecommunications. Moreover, content-oriented networking seems to complement transport-oriented networking.

Taken together, these new developments will strongly influence broadband developments in the coming years. Even though TDC seems to sit in a stable position, with strong market dominance in the Danish fixed broadband market, the reality very well may be that it is sitting on a volcano in terms of the policy framework, mobile and fibre developments, and increasing role of the IT sector in the convergence of information technologies, telecommunications and media.

References

Aghion, P., Bloom, N., Blundell, R., Griffith, R. and Howitt, P. (2002). Competition and innovation: An inverted relationship. NBER WP, no. 9269. NBER Program.

Cave, M. (2006). Encouraging infrastructure competition via the ladder of investment. *Telecommunications Policy*, **30**(3–4), pp. 223–237.

CEC (1987). Green Paper on the development of the common market for telecommunications services and equipment, COM(87) 290 final.

(2007). Impact assessment on the proposal to amend the European regulatory framework. Working document – SEC (2007) 1472. Brussels: European Commission.

Commons, J.R. (1934). *Institutional Economic: Its Role in Political Economy*. New York: Macmillan.

Danmarks Statistik (2011). IT-anvendelse i den offentlige sektor – 2011. København: DS.

(2013a). IT-anvendelse i befolkningen – EU sammenligninger, 2012. København: DS.

(2013b). It-anvendelse i virksomheder. København: DS.

David, P. (2007). Path dependence: A foundational concept for historical science, *Cliometrica* no. **1**, pp. 91–114.

Economist Intelligence Unit (2010). Digital Economy Rankings 2010. London: The Economist.

Erhvervsstyrelsen (2012), Bredbåndskortlægning 2012. København: Erhvervsstyrelsen.

(2013), Bedre bredbånd og mobildækning i hele Danmark. København: Erhvervsstyrelsen.

Tele statistics various years. København: Erhvervsstyrelsen.

European Commission: Telecommunications Regulatory Package – VIII Implementation report – Annex I – Corrigendum March 2003.

(2010a). A Digital Agenda for Europe. COM (2010) 245 final/2. Brussels, 26.8.2010.

(2010b). Broadband access in the EU: situation at 1 July 2010, COCOM10–29, DG INFSO/C4, Brussels, 21st November 2010.

(2010c). Telecommunications Regulatory Package – XII Implementation report – Annex I.

(2012). Electronic Communications Market Indicators. Brussels.

(2013a). Digital Agenda Scoreboard. http://ec.europa.eu/digital-agenda/en/scoreboard.

(2013b) Broadband lines in the EU: situation at 1 July 2012, DG CNECT/F4 Brussels, 18/02/2013

Falch, M. (2002). TELRIC – the way towards competition? A European point of view. *Review of Network Economics*, **1**(2), 6.

Falch, M. and Henten, A. (2009). Achieving Universal Access to Broadband. *Informatica Economica*, **13**(2), pp. 166–174.

(2010). Public Private Partnerships as a Tool for Stimulating Investments in Broadband. *Telecommunications Policy*, **34**(9), pp. 496–504.

Forskningsministeriet (1994). Informationssamfundet år 2000. København: Forskningsministeriet.

(1995). Bedst og billigst gennem reel konkurrence. København: Forskningsministeriet.

Henten, A. and Skouby, K.E. (2005). Regulation of local loop access: Infrastructure versus service competition in fixed line access: The case of Denmark. CMI Working papers no. 105. Lyngby: CTI.

Højhastighedskomiteen (2010). Danmark som højhastighedssamfund. København: ITST. Ingeniøren, 11 May 2012.

IT & Telestyrelsen (2010a), Bredbåndsredegørelsen. København: ITST.

(2010b). IT og telepolitisk redegørelse 2010. København: ITST.

(2010c). Analyse af engrosreguleringen på bredbåndsmarkedet. København: ITST.

(2010d). Det digitale samfund 2010. København: ITST.

(2011). Engrosmarkedet for fysisk netværksinfrastrukturadgang (marked 4). København: ITST.

(2012). Det digitale samfund 2012. København: ITST.

Kuhn, R. (1995). *The media in France*. London: Routledge.

Lemstra, W. and Groenewegen, J. P. M. (2009). Markets and public values – The potential effects of Private Equity Leveraged Buyouts on the safeguarding of public values in the telecommunications sector. Delft, The Netherlands: TUDelft.

Lemstra, W., Hayes, V. and Groenewegen, J. P. M. (2010). *The innovation journey of Wi-Fi – The road to global success*. Cambridge, UK: Cambridge University Press.

Melody, W.H. (2007). Markets and Policies in New Knowledge Economies, in Robin Mansell et al (eds.): *The Oxford Handbook of Information and Communication Technologies*, Oxford University Press, pp. 55–74.

NITA (2010). Ambitious New Broadband Goal for Denmark, 15 June 2010. Copenhagen: National IT and Telecom Agency.

OECD (2013). OECD Broadband Portal. www.oecd.org/document/54/0,3343, en_2649_34225_38690102_1_1_1_1,00.html

(2012). OECD Communications Outlook 2011. Paris: OECD Publishing.

(2013). OECD Communications Outlook 2031. Paris: OECD Publishing.

Prehn, O. (1986). Hybridnettet er på vej – stadigvæk. Status over etableringen af et dansk hydbridnet. *MedieKultur – Journal of Media and Communication Research*, **2**(2).

Rasmussen, P.N. (eds.) (2007). I grådighedens tid. København: Informations Forlag.

Socialdemokraterne (2013). Internet og mobiletelefoni til alle. Socialdemokraterne.

Valcke, P., Hou, L. and Stevens, D. (2011). Open Internet access to CATV networks: Experiences from the EU. 22nd European ITS conference, Budapest, 18–21 September 2011.

Veblen, T. (1973). *The theory of the leisure class*. Boston: Houghton Mifflin. (First published in 1899).

World Economic Forum (2011). The Global Information Technology Report 2010–2011. Geneva: World Economic Forum.

Østergaard, B.S. (1986). Politik og økonomi bag beslutningen om et dansk hybridnet. *Politica*, **18**(4).

Sweden

MARCO FORZATI AND CRISTER MATTSSON

7.1 Introduction to the case study

Swedish broadband development is based on a long tradition of advancements in telecommunications. At the beginning of 1900 Stockholm was already one of the most telephone-dense cities in the world. Ericsson, in cooperation with the Swedish national telephone operator Televerket (today Telia), drove the development of Swedish telecom during much of the twentieth century.

Today the city of Stockholm, the home of Kista Science City and Stokab, is the pre-eminent example of advancements in the ICTs. Kista Science City is a high-tech suburb with more than 1,000 ICT enterprises with 24,000 employees, 6,800 university students and 1,100 researchers. Stokab is an operator-neutral fibre network that today is used by 100 operators and 700 enterprises. With its 1.25 million kilometres of fibre, Stokab's network makes Stockholm the most densely fibred city in Europe, and facilitated the deployment of the first LTE/4G mobile network in the world. The socio-economic benefits of Stokab's open fibre network have recently been analysed in a study by Forzati and Mattsson, showing that the socio-economic return is almost three times the investment in 2013. See Figure 7.1.

In this country case study we first provide background information on the historical developments in Section 7.2. This is followed in Section 7.3 by a discussion of broadband policy and regulation. In Section 7.4 we discuss the development of municipal and regional FttH networks, which is the focus of this case study. In Section 7.5 we go one level deeper and discus four rural FttH network developments. In Section 7.6 we capture the Stokab developments and discuss the socio-economic benefits. In Section 7.7 we conclude with the state-of-affairs of broadband developments in

Sweden as of 2013 and reflect on the realization of the Digital Agenda for Europe.

7.2 History of telephone and narrowband networks in Sweden

The history of modern telecommunications in Sweden can be formally traced back to the founding of the *Kongliga Elektriska Telegraf-Werket* in 1853 when the first electric telegraph line was established between Stockholm and Uppsala. This was the government agency for telegraph and postal services. From 1871 the company was known as Kongliga Telegrafverket. The first telephone network in Sweden opened in 1880, as a result of an initiative by former Telegrafverket employees. As telecommunication technology changed, Telegrafverket expanded to include telephone services but entered the early telephone industry in Sweden as a latecomer. The first telephone services in Sweden were provided by small local organizations. Through securing a national monopoly on long distance telephone lines, Telegrafverket was able over time to control and take over the local networks. The national network, branded Rikstelefon, was supplied with telephones produced by LM Ericsson.

Telegrafverket effectively monopolised the market with its purchase of the telephone company Stockholms Allmänna in 1918. When it was renamed Televerket in 1953, the parent company and its subsidiaries had a de facto national monopoly.

Until 1980 only Televerket/Ericsson telephones were allowed on the Swedish telephone network. In 1993 the telecom market was deregulated. Televerket was transformed into a corporation, Telia AB. Telia has since merged with the Finnish Sonera, and is now known as TeliaSonera.

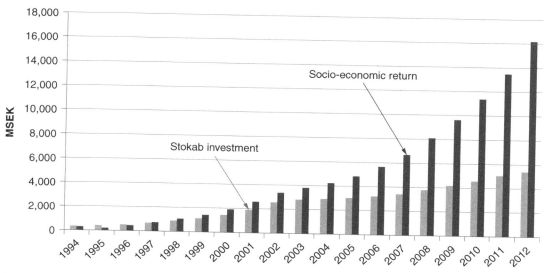

Figure 7.1 Investment and socio-economic return of Stokab, Sweden, 1994–2012
Source: Forzati and Mattson, 2013.

7.3 Swedish broadband policy and regulation

7.3.1 Swedish broadband policy

The current broadband evolution started in 1999–2000 with a government bill that was aimed to support national and local initiatives and investments. The headline was 'Trust to IT, Access to IT and IT competence'. The trust included security and technology. Access implied broadband provision with national, regional and local network support, including SMEs and schools. The financial support included SEK 2.5 billion (or roughly EUR 280 million) to a national operator-neutral backbone, SEK 3.2 billion (in the form of tax breaks) to municipalities to develop access and SEK 2.6 billion to regional networks and to create local infrastructure plans.

This was an important political declaration that ICT and broadband are important for society, and all local politicians and authorities started to discuss and plan broadband deployments. However, after the so-called IT bubble burst, these activities cooled down somewhat.

The current Minister for Information Technology and Energy has restarted a program to speed up broadband development: she launched a Swedish Digital Agenda and formed a broadband commission (Bredbandsforum) together with the regulator (PTS) and the industry to promote broadband development. Bredbandsforum has started several programmes; for example, fibre to the farms, which is a broadband cooperative model.

The Swedish Government's broadband policy is documented in an official publication, *Regeringskansliet* (2009). There one can read that the overall objective is for Sweden to have world-class broadband. A high use of IT and the Internet is good for Sweden in terms of growth, competitiveness and innovation. It contributes to the development of a sustainable society, and also helps to meet the challenges of increased globalization, climate change and an ageing population in a sparsely populated country. A prerequisite for meeting the challenges set out in the Digital Agenda is access to high-speed broadband across the country. Swedish targets are: 40% of households and businesses should have access to at least 100 Mbit/s by 2015 and 90% in 2020. It is important that Swedish businesses and households in all parts of the country can take advantage of the opportunities offered by powerful broadband access. Then traditional work practices can change, new services and business models can evolve and new behaviours can emerge.

The central tenet is that electronic communications and broadband access should be provided by the market. The government should not control the market, nor the development of technology. Their task is to create good conditions for the market and remove barriers in the development of broadband by ensuring there is relevant regulation in place.

7.3.2 Regulation

Municipal planning responsibilities are clarified in the Planning and Building Act as reinforcing the connection to the infrastructure for electronic communications. The government has also initiated a so-called Broadband Council for collaboration and dialogue on the deployment of broadband. Furthermore, the Swedish NRA – the Post and Telecom Authority (PTS) – is assigned the task of investigating how radio-frequency bands for electronic communications can be used to improve accessibility in areas which lack broadband access, or with low-capacity and low-quality broadband. The universal service obligation is revised to reflect a minimum level of functional Internet access.

While FttB/FttH networks have been deployed massively in Sweden for over a decade, regulation impacting fibre access networks (be it directly or indirectly) has started to appear only recently.

In May 2010 the PTS passed decisions regulating the wholesale market for (physical) network infrastructure access (including LLU and shared access) as well as the wholesale market for broadband access. The Decision on the market for physical network infrastructure access (LLU) includes both copper and fibre lines. In addition to the provisioning of fibre access, it also requires the incumbent to deploy new fibre infrastructure in existing ducts if requested by an operator who is willing to pay the cost of the investment. However, this decision has been appealed in some parts and a court ruling on this issue is still pending. Concerns have been expressed that the reference offer of the incumbent does not correspond to the Decision of the NRA, as it does not allow the purchase of access to fibre between the incumbent's Metropolitan Point of Presence and the network termination

points connecting buildings, so-called 'Fibre to the Building', FttB[1].

In August 2009, the government introduced an amendment to the competition law (which came into force on 1 January 2010) aimed at preventing the state, municipalities or regional governments from engaging in commercial activities in a way that is harmful to competition. The new legal provisions came as a response to the numerous complaints received by the national competition authority (NCA) regarding the problems encountered by private operators when competing with public ones. Certain operators still consider that some housing companies owned by the municipalities are trying to eliminate competition by allowing only one electronic communications provider to offer services in their blocks of flats.

In 2009 the PTS was assigned the task of studying open networks and services, and reached the following conclusions:

1. Openness creates the prerequisites for innovation and competitiveness but must be balanced against other interests worthy of protection, such as incentives to invest and network security.
2. Openness is promoted by securing non-discrimination and effective competition.
3. Openness is of great significance and it is therefore important that suppliers in their marketing activities and in applicable terms and conditions provide clear and specific information with respect to lock-in periods and restrictions relating to Internet access and access to services.

The report that concluded the study states that one essential challenge to openness today is *restrictions in access to passive infrastructure* (e.g., dark fibre). A second major challenge can be traced back to insufficient consumer mobility due to long lock-in periods, high transition costs and other *lock-in effects*[2]. One challenge which affects several levels

---

[1] On 10 February 2011, PTS issued an injunction ordering the incumbent to provide access to FttB, in accordance with the decisions and to adjust the reference offer accordingly. On 25 February 2011 the incumbent appealed the injunction at the administrative court.

[2] A third challenge – less immediately relevant to FttX – is based on an increasing demand for mobility leading to a

in the value chain relates to openness when managing electronic communications over the Internet, *network neutrality*. The report suggests several measures aimed at securing openness, measures which take all interests worthy of protection into consideration – especially incentives to invest and network security. PTS suggests stronger principles for equal treatment when building new infrastructure, increased access to existing infrastructure, mandated information to consumers regarding possible pitfalls, the importance of openness and, finally, increased transparency regarding the existence of potential limitations of Internet traffic such as prioritization of traffic and blocking of services.

Somewhat controversially, PTS has recently decided to introduce price regulation for TeliaSonera, recognizing its position of significant market power (SMP). The price regulation is based on four broad and complex models. These models calculate the cost (or would-be cost) for Telia to install fibre throughout the entire country to every household and business. A price per connection is then calculated and, because Telia currently only has x % of the broadband market, the price that Telia can charge is x% (currently roughly 50%) of the calculated price per connection. While this regulation only applies to TeliaSonera, this puts a de facto price regulation on the whole market that is below the actual price of dark fibre. If another actor – a municipality network, for instance – charges the actual deployment cost, it risks losing customers to TeliaSonera. If it tries to compete with TeliaSonera to retain customers and applies TeliaSonera's regulated price, it risks be taken to court for illegal state aid for setting a price below production costs (which the PTS model effectively requires). This in turn leads to a re-evaluation of municipal networks, which can affect municipal finances and thus provide fewer opportunities for fibre investment.

It is interesting that, against a certain widespread understanding in Sweden, the position of the Swedish regulator (PTS) is that staying on the passive level is no guarantee that the market is

not distorted. For instance, if a service is currently provided by other actors on commercial terms and on a competitive basis, installing a fibre infrastructure which allows others to come onto the market at potentially lower prices is per se distorting the market. Naturally, that would not apply if the fibre network is responding to a need which the market (with the current infrastructure) cannot provide. This can be seen as an academic question. In any case, PTS's mantra is that the market should take care of NGA deployment.

7.3.3 Regulatory trends

The price regulation of TeliaSonera's fibre access introduced by PTS has generated a lively and somewhat bitter debate. It is believed that the price regulation represents a de-facto price standard which is going to make any fibre investment uneconomical and even politically unattractive (due to the risk of incurring state aid allegations). This position is widely held in the market and there is a significant degree of uncertainty on the future of this contested regulation, especially after a report commissioned by the Swedish Association of Local Authorities and Regions (SKL) (Deloitte, 2011). The report's goal was to examine the impact of the price regulation and its results pointed to several risks; it concludes that there is no justification for claims a regulated charge for dark fibre will benefit end-users through lower prices and better choices.

SKL points out that many municipalities have invested heavily in fibre networks to assure access to modern broadband for their inhabitants. Municipalities have built up those networks because private investors were not taking such initiatives. Now those public investments are at risk of being frozen completely. SKL is discussing a scenario in which the market will develop towards a single, dominant player: i.e., a return to the monopoly of twenty years ago. TeliaSonera is backing the requests that this regulation be phased out, or the calculation model modified, claiming that claim this regulation and the specific model used are based on past circumstances no longer present and that, as the market has changed dramatically, so should the regulatory agenda.

shortage of spectrum enabling wireless communications with high area coverage, which limits the ability to access the Internet from any location.

Given this controversy, it can be expected that these rules are going to be amended, if not repealed altogether.

7.3.4 Government support and state-aid issues

The government bill '99/00' identified those areas where the market was too weak for a commercial roll-out. Hence, any such region or municipality could apply for financial support to deploy broadband networks. All municipalities received money to develop a local ICT infrastructure plan. This plan, which must include the connection of public buildings, such as schools, hospitals, etc., is the basis on which to apply for additional government funding for the actual network deployment. A crucial prerequisite to qualify for funding is that the network must be operator-neutral. This was widely viewed as being compliant with EU state aid rules in the sense that intervention was made in situations of market failure and acted upon to support the telecom market with a fibre infrastructure for all, rather than to compete with market actors. This was confirmed, as no claims of illegal state-aid were filed against the municipal initiatives.

7.4 Swedish municipal and regional FttH networks

Because much of the broadband development in Sweden has taken place on the initiative of municipalities and at the regional level, we dedicate this chapter to these developments and provide the background to and an overview of the municipal development. Moreover, we present four different FttH-case studies.

Sweden has 290 municipalities (*kommuner*). The population size of these municipalities varies from 2,500 (*Bjurholms kommun*, in Västerbotten in the North) to around 800,000 (*Stockholms kommun*, covering the city centre and some suburbs of Stockholm)[3]. Around 175 municipalities in

Sweden (out of 290) have deployed fibre networks in the past ten to fifteen years. Some of these municipal networks have recently formed regional associations to interconnect the various networks and to facilitate access to the providers of end-user services, as well as to provide access to wholesale market actors. To date, all 175 networks are still active and most of them are turning a positive (65%) or a balanced (10%) result. Some of them were started as private investments while some others have been sold to private businesses; currently 7 per cent of the municipal networks are privately owned.

7.4.1 Drivers for FttH deployments and broadband strategies

As is the case elsewhere, there is an underlying belief accompanying these fibre access network projects in Sweden: a political conviction that increased broadband penetration leads to social, environmental and economic benefits. Broadband infrastructure, primarily fibre, is increasingly seen as the fourth utility, and it is considered the task of the public administration to make sure that this utility is put in place one way or another. This, combined with the lack of commercial operators willing to invest in broadband, provides the major driver for the regional and municipal deployments described in this study. All the cases analysed concern predominantly rural areas, meaning that the population density is very low. This implies on the one hand that the investment costs are high and, on the other hand and more importantly, the potential revenues per deployment are significantly lower. This breaks not only the traditional FttH business case on the basis of traditional triple-play, already not a very strong case in very dense areas, but also the upgrading of central offices with DSL to connect only a few end-users. This is typically the case in the areas analysed in this study.

This is also a familiar situation in other European regions in which, due to the topography of the area, the access to broadband services was scarce

---

[3] The municipalities have municipal governments, and are further divided into parishes. The parish division is traditionally used by the Church of Sweden but also serves as a measure for Swedish censuses and elections.

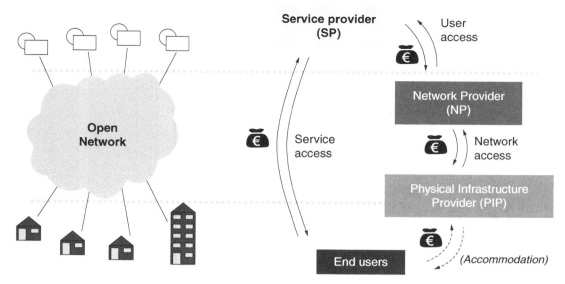

Figure 7.2 The open network model and typical open access value chain
Source: Adapted from Forzati et al. (2010).

and many areas were not being equipped with ADSL, which prompted the local governments to intervene[4]

However, once the infrastructure is deployed and activated, it is important to get the end-users on-board to use the network. According to the experiences from the projects analysed here, an important driver for service uptake has been the availability of high-speed Internet service. However, a second wave of subscriptions is now anticipated to be driven by TV-services (especially HD) which can be provided cheaper, with higher quality and flexibility of use and with broader choice.

A very important driver to generate interest and support in the deployment phase and high uptake in the operations phase is the presence of local fibre champions and a positive ICT culture. This is of course linked to historic factors (e.g., Hudiksvall had LM Ericsson and the Fiber Optic Valley, which helps to explain why it was so much ahead of the neighbouring municipality, Nordanstig), but the lack of such a catalyst can be compensated to a

great extent by visionary politicians and by running extensive and continuous information campaigns among the population.

7.4.2 The open access business models

The dominant business model among Swedish municipal fibre network operations is an open access network model. The four cases described in this chapter reflect different flavours of such a model; therefore this section describes the model and reviews experiences obtained in Sweden.

The open network model, in which services are provided on a fair and non-discriminatory basis to the network users based on a shared infrastructure, is enabled by conceptually separating the roles of service provision and network provision. See Figure 7.2. Due to the different technical and economic characteristics of the different layers of the network, different roles and actors can be identified. A fibre access network broadly consists of a *passive infrastructure* (including right-of-way acquisition, trenching, cable duct construction, fibre cable installation and connections to home and office premises), and *active equipment* (transponders,

---

[4] See also the case studies on Spain, Poland and France in this book.

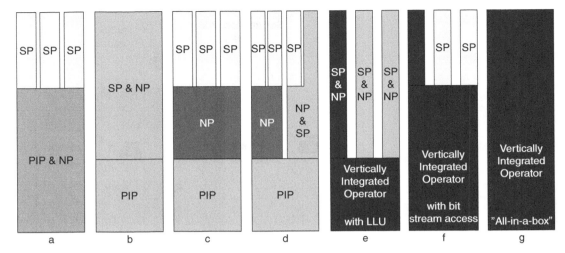

Figure 7.3 Access network business models
Source: Adapted from Forzati et al. (2010).

routers and switches, control and management servers). The passive infrastructure is typically characterized by high CAPEX, low OPEX, low economies of scale (individual connections to homes and offices), and is highly local, hard to duplicate and hence subject to regulation. The active equipment is characterized by lower CAPEX, higher OPEX, higher economies of scale, and is subject to less regulation if provided in competition. These factors allow a further role separation between a physical infrastructure provider (PIP), which owns and maintains the passive infrastructure (typically real estate companies, municipalities or utilities), and the network provider (NP) which operates (and typically owns) the active equipment (incumbent operators, new independent operators or specialized broadband companies).

Depending on which roles different market actors assume, the network will be open at different levels and different business models will arise, as illustrated in Figure 7.3. A single actor may act both as PIP and NP (7.3, a), in which case the network is open at the service level. If the roles of NP and PIP are separate (b, c and d), then openness at the passive infrastructure level is achieved. Generally, one PIP operates the passive infrastructure, while one or several NPs can be allowed to operate the active infrastructure, typically over a fixed period of time, at the end of which

the contract may or may not be renewed (in which case a new NP is designated and active equipment may need to be replaced). Most often, economies of scale make it impractical to have a truly multi-NP network (although larger networks may assign the operation of different geographical parts of the network to a different NP). Independently of the specific model, however, the NP should offer different service providers (SPs) access to the network on non-discriminatory conditions. The end users typically purchase services directly from the service providers. The NP receives revenue from the SP and pays a (one-time) connection fee to the PIP for network access.

If the NP also acts as SP (b) the network cannot be described as really open according to the definitions applied, but it is still more open than the conventional vertically integrated FttH model in (g), which most incumbent operators follow today. In case of local loop unbundling (LLU, Figure 7.3e), a vertically integrated operator is still present, but there can be multiple actors working as combined NP and SP. In case of bitstream access the vertically integrated operator assumes the role of NP, but there can be multiple SPs offering their services using wholesale bitstream access.

Note that some of the roles shown in Figure 7.3 can be divided into several others and that the delineation between the various roles is not always as clear as the figure suggests. However, the figure provides a fair idea of which types of business models with respect to open access are used in Sweden today. Although the degree of 'openness' will vary depending on the type of actor and the layer in the network that is considered.

The first optical access networks in Sweden were built around the turn of the twenty-first century by Bredbandsbolaget, TeliaSonera and a number of municipalities. While Bredbandsbolaget and TeliaSonera are vertically integrated operators, owning the whole value chain from fibre infrastructure to services, for the municipality networks the situation was different. In most cases a municipal company both owned and operated the network (PIP + NP). Although situations with only external SPs existed, in many cases, the municipalities also acted as SPs, sometimes in competition with other SPs. This became a default as it had been difficult to attract external SPs for several reasons:

(1) limited number of subscribers;
(2) connection procedures (both technical and administrative) varying from network to network, thereby hindering economies of scale for the SPs;
(3) a small number of SPs, much fewer than today;
(4) lack of business actors taking the role of NP and handling the contacts with the SPs, etc.

The market has matured considerably during the past ten years. The process of connecting SPs is now much simpler, technology has improved, there are network providers handling SPs as wholesale clients, the number of SP is now much higher, etc. Also, many municipalities have come to the conclusion that they should focus more on providing infrastructure to their citizens, rather than competing with commercial companies in the services market.

Although the market is not yet fully mature, in general municipal network operations have moved downwards in the value chain – increasingly closer to just owning the fibre infrastructure (pure PIP role) – while network operation (NP role) and service delivery (SP role) are left to other players (other municipal utilities, independent operators, or even large telcos such as TeliaSonera). Despite the clearer roles, many smaller municipal networks

struggle economically, due to a reduced revenue share in a marketplace with many competing players. This has led to a consolidation process where municipal networks either have been acquired by competitors or have started to collaborate closely. This consolidation process is still ongoing.

7.4.3 Services and uptake rate

Services present on Swedish FttH networks are predominantly voice (both stand-alone IP and over-the-top), Internet and TV, which make up the classic triple-play. Different data rates for Internet service are generally offered, from 1 Mbit/s to 1 Gbit/s. The most commonly offered and commonly subscribed services are 10 Mbit/s and 100 Mbit/s, for which the retail prices range between EUR 10 and EUR 30[5]. Telephony is generally quite cheap but it is not a driver of uptake. Internet service is provided almost exclusively over an Ethernet point-to-point solution; thus, there are two alternative configurations regarding the customer-premise equipment (CPE):

- For FttH, a CPE consisting of an O/E (optical/electrical) converter and an integrated switch (sometimes a router) which functions as a service separator using VLAN (virtual local area network) tags;
- For an FttP + in-building LAN, if only Internet-based services are provided, a simple O/E converter and a switch are placed in the basement of a multi-dwelling unit: CAT 5 or CAT 6 copper cables are then drawn to each apartment; hence, end-users do not need any special CPE and can connect the Ethernet CAT 5/6 cable to their computer or home Wi-Fi router; otherwise, a solution similar to the FttH case is followed.

TV over the FttH connections are usually provided using a VLAN, and the service is then separated at the CPE. TV packages usually include must-carry channels (around eight national and regional

---

[5] For the reader's convenience, all monetary values are expressed in euros (€), at a nominal long-term exchange rate of EUR 1=SEK 9. Temporary fluctuations of up to 10% may occur.

channels), plus bundles of four to six channels for a cost of EUR 5 to EUR 10 per bundle. Both traditional proprietary TV platforms are present (with a cost of roughly EUR 15 for the basic package) and now there is also the so-called open-TVplatform, using a Sweden-wide standard open platform, which allows the end-user to change TV-provider without having to change the set-top box. Prices for basic packages with the latter are as low as EUR 3.50 per month.

Other services such as video-on-demand, home-security (video-surveillance), cloud services (back-up, remote hard drive, antivirus, etc.) are starting to appear, although these are for the moment few in number and the added value compared to equivalent over-the-top services (e.g., running over the Internet connection) is not always clear. Several e-health pilot projects have been run but, for the time being, the big breakthrough is still to come (although SMEs like Open Care are very active). When it comes to e-government services, these are for the time being limited to over-the-top, web-based basic services also available elsewhere, but arguably of better quality through FttH.

A service that is potentially of interest is teleworking, including teleworking centres. While teleworking is an increasingly popular phenomenon in Sweden, and one which is greatly encouraged by fibre networks, teleworking centres never really picked up. One reason for this may be the generally very good home connections, enabling distance working without the extra cost for office space.

The uptake of services in the Swedish municipal networks varies. As an indication, the average uptake on the networks operated by Zitius (currently active in ten municipalities) is roughly 35 per cent. The trend appears to be similar to the uptake of cable-TV, and that is generally gradual. As further reference, the Deutsche Telekom led research project OASE[6] works on different scenarios: a *'conservative'* one in which a 60% uptake is reached in 20 years (in areas with high ADSL density and relying on a traditional triple-play-driven, vertically integrated business model) and

an *'aggressive'* scenario in which the same uptake is reached in 8.5 years. Interestingly, even this is conservative in some cases: some rural, single-dwelling-unit areas in Hudiksvall and Säffle have uptake rates of 80% or more only a few years after deployment. Queues of households wishing to be connected to fibre (for an entry fee of EUR 1500) are now the case in Hudiksvall.

7.4.4 Observed socio-economic benefits

One of the first effects that was observed in FttH municipal networks in Sweden is a saving of 30% to 50% of the total municipal data and telecommunication costs (see also Forzati et al. 2012). This is partly due to increased efficiency (reduced equipment, energy consumption, and footprint per unit of transmitted information) and partly due to the fact that the high-capacity fibre network allows for more competition between service providers and thus lower prices.

In 1996, the city of Stockholm started purchasing telephony services from the open market, which was unique for public organizations in Europe at that time. The city had recently connected its operational sites and offices with its own fibre network. This allowed it to procure its telephony in full competition and to drive down costs. The city's external telephony cost was between EUR 15 and EUR 20 million. The competition made available on its fibre-optic network resulted in a savings of 30%. However, this is a conservative estimate, and savings have probably grown larger over time, says Per-Olof Gustavsson, who at that time was active in the City of Stockholm's city council office. In Jönköping, where the fibre connection has been less extensive, the savings figure was around 10 to 15 per cent.

Similar savings have been observed at regional administrations as well. The Stockholm Regional Council (*Stockholms läns landsting*) reduced its data and telecommunications costs by 50%, equivalent to roughly EUR 8 million, thanks to the fibre network. In Norrbotten, a fibre network has been installed linking 5 hospitals, 33 clinics and 34 dental clinics, which reduced communication costs also by 50% while providing fifty times faster communication. Service providers have been

---

[6] Source: www.ict-oase.eu.

able to create solutions for digitized medical records, transmission of digital radiography, digital recipes, video-conferencing and IP telephony.

Another interesting fact is that the Swedish tenants' association (*Hyresgästföreningen*) has agreed with property owners' associations and housing companies to an increase in the rent of around EUR 5 per month. This can be considered a conservative evaluation of the perceived added value of fibre connection for the end-user because it makes available high-quality services at lower prices, especially entertainment and communications, the ability to work remotely and more free choice of work and housing, improved individual health, reduced need for hospitalization, simpler and more transparent interaction with public services, etc.

Indirect effects that were observed included the reduction in migration to larger cities (a problem among rural municipalities in Sweden) and improved employment, due to the availability of an ICT infrastructure that prevents businesses from moving to the cities, creates new business opportunities and allows people to stay in or move to rural areas with higher quality of life, thanks to a healthy local business environment and the possibilities offered by distance working. See for details the four cases described in Section 7.5.

7.4.5 Successes, challenges and future directions

Fibre deployments in Sweden have been successful in general when it comes to public support and end-user uptake. In some cases, requests for fibre connections exceed the roll-out capacity and queues have been forming. This success has been visible especially in rural areas where alternatives for Internet connections are lacking, and where bottom-up approaches (e.g., in terms of co-operatives to build village networks) are often used to gather support for centrally driven initiatives. Sometimes the municipality only needs to connect the existing village networks and build out the metropolitan section of the network.

In the urban areas it is often more challenging to gather significant uptake, especially among privately-owned multi-dwelling units (MDUs).

Publicly owned MDUs are usually inclined to sign up, thanks to the involvement of the housing organizations, which see fibre not only as an infrastructure upgrade but also as a tool to simplify the provision of traditional services (the fibre network they connect to is usually an open network, therefore leaving the choice of Internet and TV providers to the tenants, which is seen as highly desirable) and more advanced services, such as estate management tools (remote surveillance, etc.).

Among the challenges being faced by municipal fibre network owners is that of attracting service providers, especially in the smaller and more remote municipalities. This has been to some degree solved by forming regional networks, which are a type of federation of small municipality networks[7]. These regional networks provide the scale, visibility and 'single-interface' towards the service-provider market, and have proven to be very successful in bringing service providers to all member municipalities. Another positive effect is that they have made it possible for small networks to rent out dark fibre to the wholesale market (this currently accounts for 30% to 70% of municipal network revenues).

The financial situation is generally quite positive, with municipal network companies showing positive results after ten years (with less than 25% of them currently showing negative results)[8], although different business models and different situations have led to different outcomes, also depending on how depreciation and one-time connection fees are accounted. In general, companies that only invest in passive infrastructure (PIP role), and contract out the network management (NP role) tend to have a leaner organization, an easier business case (similar to a municipal utility), and a better medium- to long-term financial situation. For these fully functionally-separated networks,

---

[7] Some examples are Skånet, Norrsken (both analysed in this chapter), Norrlänk, Västlänk, AC-Net and IT Norrbotten; in some cases (e.g., Norrsken) there have also been discussions of forming a big common and open net, although for the time being all member networks remain independent and sometimes apply different business models.

[8] Source: *Svenska Stadsnätsföreningens, Marknadsrapport 2012*, Stockholm, 2012.

negotiation on price in the NP contract is a delicate balancing act, although market prices are now starting to appear. Some companies, still vertically integrated, tend to be in a relatively good financial situation, although in most cases their fibre deployment is limited to the nodes for xDSL backhauling (FttN). Extending fibre to the premises (FttH/FttB) will require extensive investments, which will significantly affect the cost-revenue balance. Another delicate factor is the accounting, in particular the choice of the depreciation period for the investment and the distribution of the revenue from the one-off connection fees: fine tuning these parameters can in some cases make or break the business case.

A practical and important limitation of FttH in general is its reliance on power at the end-users' premises, which makes it challenging to deploy critical services on fibre connections (such as nurse alarms for elderly and reduced mobility citizens). There are several solutions being investigated and tested but none is sufficiently reliable yet, so the issue remains for the time being.

Turning to future directions and trends, the most important one is probably a general move down the value chain. Encouraged by the SSNf (Swedish Association of Urban Networks) and SKL (Swedish Association of Municipalities and Regions), many municipal networks are migrating from vertical integration towards a layered model, in which the municipal network company only owns and operates the passive infrastructure. The rationale for this is that passive infrastructure is a familiar business for municipalities and their utilities[9], while active equipment is better left to the market[10]. While in general this is seen as the right way to go, and there are no more municipalities

choosing to build a new fibre network and operate the active layer themselves, some challenges remain with this layered model, which should be mentioned:

- Some municipalities have moved away from the integrated PIP/NP model but are currently stuck in a hybrid model (whereby some connectivity services are still offered), which risks removing traditional revenue streams while leaving important residual overhead and running costs (see the Hudiksvall case).

- The contracting-out of the NP role implies that specialized local technical staff is not needed anymore: while this reduces the costs significantly and brings about more specialized competence overall, it has the drawback of increasing the potential response time in fault-management (see also the Säffle case).

- The open access business model has been a success in bringing freedom of choice and low prices, but also poses some challenges in the management of the responsibility areas (fault management and first-line support) between the service providers and the network provider (running the actual network connectivity). A standard for open network interfaces would probably help make things run smoother[11].

Among other trends and future directions, we note that redundancy (generally in the form of rings) is recognised more and more as a critical feature of the network, in order to attract businesses and public sector actors. Also, a progressive defragmentation of the municipal networks is taking place, partly thanks to the emergence and success of regional federations mentioned above and partly to a consolidation process whereby some municipal networks are either acquired or effectively merged into larger neighbouring networks, thanks to contracting out the NP role. Among the effects seen are a reduction of resource duplication, increased professionalism and general synergetic effects. However, to do that on a regional basis

---

[9] Installing and operating the passive fibre plant is a typical infrastructure management activity involving right-of-way, trenching, cable-duct-laying and local-office premises; it is typically characterized by high CAPEX, low OPEX and low economies of scale; it is highly local, hard to duplicate and inherently subject to regulation.

[10] In contrast, active equipment (transponders, routers and switches, control and management servers) is characterized by high OPEX and economies of scale; it needs to be upgraded more frequently, and requires extensive and up-to-date technical competence.

[11] The recently initiated Open Network Forum (www.opennetworkforum.org) is looking at the possibility of starting to standardize and currently is generating interest in the Swedish FttH business.

(e.g., by centralizing the tens or hundreds of technicians scattered in various municipal networks) would provide a great resource for all, although that is seen as too big a challenge at present.

7.5 Four rural FttH cases

There are 175 municipalities in Sweden that have deployed fibre networks in the past ten to fifteen years. In this section we analyse two such examples:

- Hudiksvall, a municipality covering a large but sparsely populated area in northern Sweden, with a long history of investment in FttH and ICT in general; and with a hybrid open-access business model;
- Säffle, a municipality in central Sweden which deployed an FttH network relatively recently, following a strictly open-access business model, and with the involvement of a major telecom operator (the incumbent TeliaSonera) with the exclusive role of network provider (and, at the start of the project, excluded from selling services).

The two deployments tell different stories and can therefore be useful in providing a more complete picture of local government-backed FttH deployments in rural regions. Säffle's deployment stems from necessity (the lack of broadband alternatives), whereas Hudiksvall's experience is born out of opportunity (the presence of Ericsson and the leveraging of competence and resources).

We also review two regional networks[12], which are in effect federations of municipal networks at a regional (or super-regional) level:

- Skånet, a regional passive network deployed through a public-private partnership (PPP) between the Skåne Regional Council in southern Sweden, sixteen municipalities and a major telecom operator, Tele2;
- Norrsken, a layer 2 network owned by municipalities, municipal networks and the region of Gävleborg in central-northern Sweden. The

network allows the provision of services to/from any municipality in the consortium, as well as Stockholm.

In the following, we present an analysis of the four cases in detail.

7.5.1 Hudiksvall

The Hudiksvall municipality (*Hudiksvalls kommun*) is situated in Gävleborg County, on the coast of central northern Sweden, some 300 km north of Stockholm, 130 km north of Gävle (population: roughly 100,000) and 84 km south of Sundsvall (population: roughly 50,000), to which it is connected by the E4 highway and the East Coast Railway (*Ostkustbanan*). The municipal seat is in the town of Hudiksvall.

The town of Hudiksvall is located on the coast, and the municipal territory extends along the coast as well as for several tens of kilometres inland. The territory is largely rural but includes several towns and villages. Roughly 40% of the population lives in the main town, so the fibre deployment is of several very different characters: urban in town, 'sub-urban' in the villages, and sparsely rural in the largest part of the territory.

The largest employers are the municipality and the county council, with around 38% of the workforce. Although in decline during the twentieth century, the forest industry represents half of the industrial activity; the largest private employer is the Holmen paper product company, with about 10% of the workforce. The electronics industry has become an important sector (19% of the workforce) and is dominated by Ericsson Network Technologies, making optical and copper cables for telecommunication systems. This, together with efforts by the municipality and the leveraging of European structural funds, has led in more recent times to the development of fibre research and speciality production[13].

---

[12] See Section 7.4.5 for more considerations in the formation of regional networks.

[13] The forest industry has for centuries played an important role in the Hudiksvall economy. Wood production activity at the beginning of the century prompted technology innovations and generated manufacturing competence and know-how: e.g., in hydraulics and mechanics. Ericsson Network

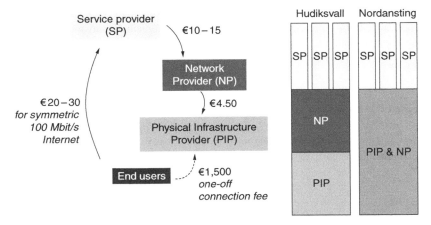

Figure 7.4 The business model for the Fiberstaden fibre network, Sweden
Source: Authors.

Broadband strategy, Fiberstaden and the fibre initiative

Hudiksvall started installing fibre in 2002. Since 2006 the fibre initiative has been managed by Fiberstaden, founded by the municipality of Hudiksvall, whose vision is 'to build tomorrow's infrastructure, based on fibre connections'. Fiberstaden runs fibre network operations and manages the IT operations for Hudiksvall as well as its neighbouring municipality to the north, Nordanstig (population 10,000).

The project started in 2006 to connect central offices in Hudiksvall (Nordastig joined the initiative in 2008) to provide the backhaul for the ADSL lines. In the Hudiksvall and Nordasting area, a typical local central office connects around 100 to 150 customers, up to 700 in the largest central office. Today, in some villages (30 km from town) 25% to 50% of households are connected to fibre. Among those connected, uptake of Internet service is almost 100%.

Technologies was established here to take advantage of such an ecosystem for its production of cables and network elements. Cable production was initially copper-based; when Ericsson started producing optical fibres, it was natural to locate production here. In the late 1990s the Fibre Optic Valley hub was established to encourage manufacturing, research, development and education in fibre optics. Many of Ericsson's production activities have since moved to lower-cost locations but several local companies have been started by former Ericsson employees.

Fiberstaden's mission looks a little different in the two municipalities: in both it does the operation and support of the IT environment for the public administration. However, in Nordanstig Fiberstaden has responsibility for the operation and expansion of the network and they are also one of the five Internet service providers available on the network, whereas in Hudiksvall, after having contracted out the NP role, they are only responsible for the development of the passive network.

Business model

Fiberstaden operates a hybrid between a vertical integration and an open access business model. (See also Figure 7.4.) The role of the NP is currently given to Zitius in Hudiksvall, but Fiberstaden still sells wholesale connectivity services. In Nordanstig, Fiberstaden acts as an integrated PIP+NP. In both cases, the networks are owned by municipalities directly, not by Fiberstaden. In Hudiksvall, Zitius offers a broad range of services, through a portal called *bredbandsväljaren.se* ('the broadband chooser'), where all services carried over the network (currently offered by twenty SPs) can be ordered in one place. However, once a service is purchased, the end-user pays directly to the service providers and all communication takes place directly between SP and end-user. The service providers are attracted to this model thanks to the nationwide presence of Zitius (so an SP only needs a point of presence in Stockholm to serve a large number of end-users across the whole country).

Ten service providers have switches in Hudiksvall and five SPs have switches in Nordansting. Fiberstaden also offers point-to-point transmission capacity to companies and, increasingly, dark fibre (e.g., to Tele2 to connect 4G masts; TTC; Norrsken; and Telia). Currently, 30% of Fiberstaden's revenue comes from dark fibre and wholesale connectivity services.

As part of the retail business model, the media converter at the customer's premises is owned by Fiberstaden. Fiberstaden receives EUR 4.50 per month per active customer from the NP Zitius. Troubleshooting is taken care of by Fiberstaden; Zitius has no local staff.

In theory, the end-user has no need to know about the existence of the NP and indeed the bredbandsväljaren.se portal is accessible directly from the municipality's website and from the websites of the individual SPs. At the municipal website the PIP is presented as a municipal service, just like water, electricity or sewage. Zitius is not even mentioned in bredbandsväljaren.se, despite its being managed by the company. However, challenges remain, notably in fault management, as a clear demarcation of responsibilities is missing, leading to end-users being sent back and forth between SP, NP, and PIP when faults occur.

The price to connect a single home to the property border is EUR 1,500 (the actual cost is estimated to be roughly double), while property owners take responsibility for the digging across the property.

Public and commercial services present on the network

Wholesale capacity services, both dark fibre, and bitstream point-to-point (10 Mbit/s, 100 Mbit/s, or other data rates as required) are offered over the network by the municipality PIP, Fiberstaden. These are typically services targeted to companies.

Several end-user services are offered at the moment by different SPs over the network operated by the NP Zitius. Typical services are traditional triple-play: telephony, TV and Internet

access. There are also other IT services being offered like cloud and web hosting for small companies.

When it comes to public services, Hudiksvall *kommun* (the municipality) has an information-rich and well organized website, www.hudiksvall.se, which represents the major information interface with the citizens. The website is also an important tool for communication with and feedback from the citizens. Inköp Gävleborg, the public procurement and contracting authority for Hudiskvall and eight other municipalities in the region, has a website (www.inkopgavleborg.se/) which is the major information, application and transparency tool for public procurement in the region. All public procurement is announced there and all current and past contracts are easily available. The library service is also regional, and it has an online search and reservation system (www.helgebiblioteken.se/). A reservation can be made online for any book in any of the forty-seven libraries, to be collected at any library. An e-lending service (e-books, audio, music, and database search) is also available.

Examples of the socio-economic impact of fibre

Hudiksvall started installing fibre in 2002. Since then, the number of firms in the Hudiksvall municipality has increased by 6% to 14% per year between 2004 and 2009. Representatives of Hudiksvall's municipality say that fibre has a positive impact on the municipality's overall business climate. Moreover, there are examples of companies moving from Hudiksvall town towards more rural areas of the municipality thanks to cheaper rent.

Hudiksvall previously had, like many rural northern municipalities, a negative population growth, but since the installation of its fibre-optic network, the municipality stopped losing residents. In December 2002 its population had fallen to 37,048 (down 4% since 1994). The decline halted in 2002 when a significant number of households were connected by fibre. See Figure 7.5. This suggests that the effect of fibre investment may have a fairly rapid impact on population trends, although other factors may also have contributed. Similarly, thanks to fibre, in Nordanstig one can

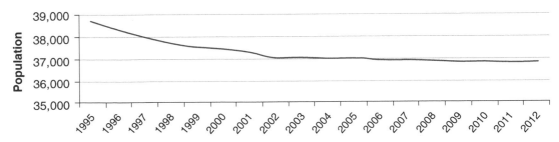

Figure 7.5 Population evolution in Hudiksvall, Sweden, 1995–2012
Data source: Statistics Sweden (SCB).

now see people returning to the municipality after having left years ago.

There are many examples of the effects of fibre on individuals in the local communities: for instance, in the village of Lindefallet, between Hudiksvall and Söderhamn, where 98% of the residents are connected to fibre. Several people decided not to move, thanks to fibre. Peter Engstrom, 34 years old, and Linn Sjoberg, 30 years old, chose to build a house in Lindefallet because of fibre, which is seen as a prerequisite for living close to the forests and nature without feeling completely isolated. Peter and Heather Nilsson moved from California to raise their four children in a safe environment, and journalist Marie Sandberg and author Georg Johansson moved there from Brussels. Several local companies have managed to assert themselves in an increasingly competitive environment thanks to fibre, and even farms are connected to fibre.

Since fibre was deployed in 2004, the population increased by 7.5% in a village that has neither a school, nor a health clinic, nor an industrial area. The investment in fibre, in combination with active associations, makes Lindefallet a lively village and thus a village that people want move to and to invest in.

Successes, challenges and future directions

On the bright side, many people want to have fibre and are queuing up to be connected. Moreover fibre is offering a broader range of TV channels at lower prices than cable-TV, where this exists. TV services over fibre have just started to be offered but Fiberstaden's CEO Bia Larsson is convinced it will be the driving force for people to migrate to fibre. IP telephony and Skype are also very popular drivers. Moreover, service packaging is also very important.

The present operational difficulties seem to be caused by the hybrid business model currently in place. Originally, Fiberstaden also assumed the NP role, which led the company into trouble with unsatisfied customers (due to lack of proper competence and an adequate organization to support it). Following the recommendation by the National association of Municipalities and regions (SKL) to the municipalities to give up the NP role, Fiberstaden decided to outsource the active network management to network provider Zitius (at the time owned by Ericsson). However, it retained this role in the less mature network of Nordanstig. According to the CEO, this did not really make things better. A possible explanation may be that this process was only executed in part: Fiberstaden still sells connectivity services (they only gave up the retail sector) so they still have active equipment to take care of, with all the work and competence needs involved. This should be compared to the experiences of Säffle, where the municipal company only takes care of the passive infrastructure and is very satisfied with that set-up.

The loss of direct revenues from end-users, and a badly negotiated price with Zitius, led to a deteriorated financial situation. Fiberstaden began in 2006 with EUR 100,000 gross profit, last year they had a EUR 300,000 loss.

The fact that Zitius has no local staff is seen as problematic. Hudiksvall now plans to negotiate the new NP contract together with the municipality of Söderhamn to strengthen their negotiation position. Another point of difference raised by Mrs. Larsson is that in Soderhamn the municipality does not own the network directly but through the equivalent of Fiberstaden, which is considered a better model.

Finally, Mrs. Larsson strongly believes that redundancy needs to be implemented (rings, but not the last node) as it will be required by businesses and the public sector.

7.5.2 Säffle

The Säffle municipality (*Säffle kommun*) is in Värmland County in west central Sweden. Its seat is located in the town of Säffle. The municipality covers a peninsula in Lake Vänern (*Värmlandsnäs*), and includes a large freshwater archipelago.

In the town of Säffle, the economy is largely based on industry. Säffle has continued to grow as the wood pulp industry has expanded in Sweden. The pulp mill in Säffle has been a major driver of the local economy. In the remainder of the municipality farming is important. The Värmlandsnäs peninsula is very significant to the economy through pork production. The area supplies more than 200,000 people with pork. The archipelago off the peninsula (which also has old rune stones and other ancient monuments) is a tourist attraction.

The territory is largely rural with smaller localities of few hundred inhabitants each. Two-thirds of the population are concentrated in the main town, so fibre deployment is of three very different types: urban in town, covering the largest portion of the population, 'sub-urban' in the villages, and rural in the largest part of the territory.

In its broadband strategy, the Säffle municipality declared that every household should have access to a high-speed network. Due to the lack of commercial operators ready to invest in broadband in the municipality, it decided to start a fibre deployment project through a municipality-owned company called Säkom. All investments have been made on commercial terms and have received financing partly by EU structural funds and partly through commercial loans.

Broadband strategy, Säkom and the fibre initiative

The work started in rural areas because that was where broadband was lagging. Säkom has built a 930 km long fibre-optic network that connects 92% of households and businesses in rural Säffle, connecting from 30 to 50 more households each year. The project in rural areas is now complete[14] and Säkom began implementation to the urban areas of Säffle with 1,227 apartments which will shortly replace cable-TV with TV-over-fibre. All types of property (apartment buildings, villas and other properties) are offered a connection to the Säffle fibre network.

Business model

Säkom operates a 'pure' open access business model (variant (c) in Figure 7.3; see also Figure 7.6). The NP role was taken by Telia by agreement in autumn 2009. This was later amended and Telia is now allowed to offer services. Säkom is a small organization, which the CEO likes to define as a group of 'qualified purchasers'. Säkom needs to be financially independent in the long term, but does not need to generate profits.

The separation of the PIP and NP role makes it viable for operators to join and provide connectivity and service provision, because long-term investment for the infrastructure deployment, which typically has a horizon of five to ten years, is no longer part of their business case. On the other hand, the municipality is in a position to accept a longer-term return on investment and assume the capital investment in infrastructure, while avoiding responsibility for technical issues in which it does not have enough competence. Moreover, the NP contract was awarded to a national operator which can rely on significant economies of scale, bringing down the operating cost of the network.

---

[14] Only 200 out of 2,500 rural households are not connected because they decided not to participate in the project; however, they have the opportunity to be connected whenever they wish in the future.

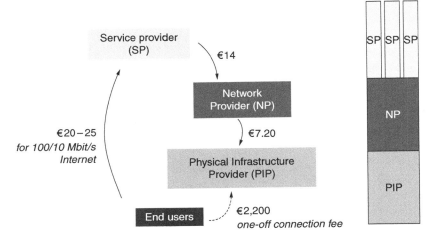

Figure 7.6 The business model for the Säffle fibre network, Sweden
Source: Authors.

At the same time, the business case for service providers is enhanced by the existence of infrastructure and connectivity, so they can focus on efficient service provisioning (with cost reduction coming from know-how and economies of scale due to their national or sometimes international scale), customer care, marketing and product development. Efficient service provisioning is especially important for Internet service (increasingly seen as a commodity), where price and reliability are the major selling points, whereas the TV product offering is an important differentiating factor.

Telia was awarded the NP contract with the obligation to provide and connect at least three ISPs, two TV providers, and two providers of prioritized IP telephony (today there are five ISPs, three TV and two priority IP-telephony providers). Telia was not allowed to sell services initially. It was argued that if Telia had been allowed to sell services in the beginning, other SPs would have found it hard to establish a viable position. However, this decision was not very popular with the citizens. Once other SPs had the time to become established and Telia was not considered dominant anymore, this ban was removed.

As part of the business model, the media converter is provided and maintained free of charge by the NP (Telia) and, when buying services other than just Internet, the service separator is also provided and maintained by Telia. First-line

support is taken care of by the service providers, although end-users frequently call Säkom (PIP), which nonetheless thinks that this first-line burden is manageable. With time, communication between PIP and NP has improved considerably. Telia as NP has concluded service contracts with outside firms for installation and maintenance (in Säffle and nearby Karlstad).

There are two types of service-level agreements (SLAs) in place: restoring services within twenty-four hours, if fewer than twenty-four users are affected, and restoring services within six hours, if twenty-four users or more are affected. The SLA was invoked when the TV service started to have problems last autumn; these then escalated, and on New Year's Eve one TV service (from SP Server-ado) was down until 3 January. The NP Telia offered three months of free TV as compensation.

The digging cost is EUR 4.50/m on average (varying between EUR 2/m to EUR 11/m in the rural area, and around EUR 35/m in town), which increases to around EUR 8/m to EUR 10/m if connection costs are included. Housing cooperatives and housing companies have to pay EUR 2,200 to connect to the fibre network, while the in-building network is their own responsibility. An agreement was reached whereby housing companies pay EUR 11 per month per apartment and the tenant pays EUR 2 per month to Säkom for 15 years.

In addition to the retail sector, Säkom is offering dark fibre rental to business users and large organizations. Among the current clients are 'Net for Mobility' (dark fibre rental for ten years), the municipality and the Swedish Church. Businesses that have expressed an interest in dark fibre include the ICA food chain, TDC, and others. Capacity is not really limited, as ninety-six fibres are installed in the backbone network and twenty-four fibres to the nodes.

Currently a price per-kilometre is charged, but other models like price per connection, and prices for specific fibre spans are being considered; some are more popular than others. Large firms are currently connected to the copper network and they are generally bound by long-term contracts. When these run out, they are likely to migrate to fibre.

Public and commercial services present over the network

The services currently offered over the network are the following:

- Internet service (five providers present), at price of EUR 20–30 for symmetrical 10 Mbit/s, and EUR 25–35 for 100 Mbit/s downstream and 10 Mbit/s upstream. Symmetrical 100 Mbit/s is also offered, but at rather high price (above EUR 50).
- TV is provided by three SPs: Alltele, Telia and the open platform Severado: the base package is offered free of charge (the national broadcaster's four must-carry channels, plus three other channels); other channel packages can be bought on the Telia or Severado portals. A service separator is needed and provided free of charge by the NP. In the case of Telia, a set-top box is available on loan, while for Severado the open set-top box must be purchased at EUR 150. A degree of complexity (service separator, set-top box, Internet, NP, SP, etc.) means the solution can sometimes be perceived as challenging by end-users.
- Priority IP-telephony is offered by two providers (Alltele and Telia): the cheaper one is EUR 4 per month for a basic plan, or EUR 15 for a flat plan.

Examples of socio-economic impact of fibre

One positive effect that can be observed already is the creation of a new industry segment related to the fibre network installation in the municipality: fibre installers (now building other networks) and maintenance activities which are local, on contract from the NP and SPs.

An effect of the housing companies having provided fibre to their dwelling units is that more young people are moving in and that there are no empty apartments anymore.

Another welcome effect is that businesses can now expand within the municipality and do not threaten to move. Interestingly, also, some companies were able to move from central Säffle to the more rural area in order to save on rents.

Successes, challenges and future directions

Säkom was started in 2007 and is still in the red but the ambition is to reach break-even in 2016. Information provision to the population is seen as very important to generate support for the deployment and for increased uptake.

While housing companies are now 100% connected via FttH (and of these, after six months, 100% have subscribed to IP-TV and around 15% to Internet), private property owners often do not see a real motivation to connect. They see the cost of around EUR 400 to EUR 500 per apartment but they do not really see the concrete benefits.

A problem that is not resolved yet is that power goes down every now and then in the countryside, which results in service problems because the nurse alarms for elderly and reduced-mobility citizens (*trigghetslarm*) need to be active at all times. Providing e-health services over fibre has to take these practical problems into account.

Säkom is satisfied with Telia as network provider. However, there is an issue with interworking with other SPs using different equipment, and it is indeed the case that the network equipment works better with Telia's services. (This shows in a neat way why NP and SP roles should be taken up by independent entities in order to guarantee fair and non-discriminatory conditions for all SPs.) According to Säkom's CEO, Sabine Zimmerl-Berg, it would be good to have a standard for open networks but she thinks it is going to be hard to achieve.

7.5.3 Norrsken (central-northern Sweden)

The central-northern regions (*län* in Swedish) of Dalarna, Gävleborg, Västernorrland, Jämtland and Västerbotten represent mostly rural regions with middle incomes and a low population density (generally below ten per square kiometre on average).

The territory is largely rural, generally characterized by medium-size towns along the coast (from 10,000 to 80,000 inhabitants) in which by far the larger portion of the population is concentrated, as well as a large number of smaller localities of a few hundred to a few thousand inhabitants each, inland, at very large distances from each other and generally surrounded by farmland.

About Norrsken and the fibre initiative

There are several municipal networks in the region, which are similar to Säffle in terms of deployment. The Norrsken initiative was originally started to satisfy an interest in renting a dark fibre between Gävle and Stockholm to provide access to service providers from the capital up to the Gävleborg region. Therefore discussion began with other regions and municipalities. Some municipal networks had the same problem: e.g., Härnosand missed a great opportunity for a large business to be established in 2001 because there was no good broadband access (the speed requested was 155 Mbit/s). So they pooled fibre connections and started a company called Norrsken.

Today the Norrsken network, which federates several municipal networks into a regional network, comprises 15,000 km of fibre cable, and covers thirty-four municipalities in nine counties and provides more than 120,000 households and 8,000 businesses with the same opportunities for telecommunications as provided in major cities. The network is also directly connected by fibre with Stokab (the city of Stockholm's extensive fibre network), which represents a great advantage because pretty much all service providers operating

in Sweden can use the connectivity offered by Norrsken to seamlessly transport their services to any municipal network in the Norrsken 'federation'.

Norrsken is a seven-employee holding company owned by the local governments and the utilities[15]. This centralized activity is intended to optimize resources, streamline operations and ensure quality in order to develop and provide competitiveness for customers in the regions in which they operate. The municipalities are responsible for deploying their own local fibre networks. Norrsken also offers connectivity services over those fibres on a rental basis. In the beginning SDH-based transmission was deployed, which in retrospect was an error. And indeed, when Norrsken transferred to wavelength division multiplexing (WDM), the business deals started to be signed.

Business model

Norrsken AB is a healthy operating company (150 employees, over EUR 60 million turnover, showing positive net income since 2004, rated AAA by Scandinavian rating agency Soliditet) and offering connectivity solutions at fibre, wavelength and Layer 2 levels (with standard Ethernet interfaces) to transport Internet, TV/video, voice/audio, as well as internal corporate communications. Besides public administrations and service providers, the 8,000-strong customer base includes real estate, private businesses, retail chains, hotels, etc.

A big role for Norrsken is to act as a common business interface for service providers. This facilitates creating the critical mass of services offered over the network, which makes it attractive for end-users to connect. Interestingly, the same type of role separation seen in the single-municipality networks has now been adopted by this regional backbone provider. Norrsken AB is responsible for

[15] Besides the Gävleborg region, all the twenty-one Norrsken members are municipal networks or entities running them (municipalities and public utility companies), with the exception of Dalarenergi, which is now privately owned (by power utility Fortum) but still works pretty much like a public utility, and the Kramfors network which was sold to operator Alltele.

the product offerings and customer relations, while the actual network operation is contracted out to an external network provider, currently Fiberdata AB.

Different municipalities connected to the Norrsken network apply different business models, even in different areas within a municipality. For instance, in the city of Gävle, *Gavlenet* the fibre network owned by the municipal utility company, uses a vertically integrated model with bitstream access for services other than Internet (type f in Figure 7.3), while *Gavlegårdarna*, which connects municipal housing units, follows a model of type c, with Zitius as NP.

According to Norrsken's CEO, Björn Jonsson, municipal infrastructure operators that also work as network providers find it hard to attract service providers. The few remaining vertically integrated networks generally offer good retail Internet prices, but they are often limited to fibre to the node (with DSL on the last mile). More investment will therefore be needed in the future, which may put pressure on their financial situation in the medium term.

Public and commercial services present on the network

The regional network supports the public and commercial services to the extent they are provided across the municipal boundaries.

Examples of socio-economic impact of regional fibre networking

Norrsken's most important success is probably that it enables the presence of competitive service providers in northern municipal networks, especially in remote regions. This facilitates the creation of a critical mass of services offered on the network, which makes it attractive for end-users to connect.

This has important implications for the provision of public administration (PA) services as well: unless there is a large base (high uptake rate) of connected and digitally competent citizens (regular users of commercial services over FttH connections), the launch and adoption of advanced PA services (from e-health to e-government) will be very challenging. This applies within a

municipality but also for services provided on a regional basis.

Another effect is that it is creating a market for dark fibre and connectivity services in central and northern Sweden, increasing competition and thus lowering prices.

Successes, challenges and future directions

While in the beginning it was not easy to assert and properly communicate the role of Norrsken (which some municipalities tended to see as a competitor), today Norrsken is seen as a great success, appreciated by all consortium members. There was even a discussion about forming a big common open network but that never happened, mainly due to the different business models in different municipalities. According to the CEO of Norrsken, one challenge is to obtain more contracts from the public sector (in which politics is often a barrier).

The presence of Norrsken as a federation also provides the potential opportunity to pool the more than one hundred technicians scattered through various municipal networks. This would avoid duplications, create specialized competences and generate synergies in general. This remains a big challenge, especially considering the political-level agreement needed to enable this.

7.5.4 Skånet

Skåne is the southernmost region (*län*) in Sweden, and includes thirty-three municipalities (*kommuner*), the largest being Malmö (301,000 inhabitants), Helsingborg (130,000), Lund (111,000 inhabitants) and Kristianstad (80,000 inhabitants).

Around 130 km long from north to south, Scania covers less than 3% of Sweden's total area, but the population of approximately 1,230,000 represents 13% of Sweden's total. Skåne is mainly a hilly territory; with moderate population density (110 inhabitants/km^2), it is among the most densely populated regions in Sweden. Skåne is a relatively wealthy region, with intensive farming as well as a thriving high-tech and academic metropole.

Historically, Skåne has had a good penetration of broadband connections provided by DSL.

A higher regional goal now applies: 100 Mbit/s to almost everyone in Skåne by 2020, meaning fibre to the home.

SkåNet and the BAS fibre initiative

The fibre project in Skåne was started in 2002 when the thirty-three municipalities in the region received EUR 22 million in state funds for broadband development. It was decided to put the money in a common fund and use the money to complete fibre deployment in the seventeen municipalities that did not have municipal fibre networks, as well as to expand the networks in the sixteen municipalities that already did have fibre.

SkåNet was then set up in 2003 by Region Skåne and the Skåne Association of Municipalities to coordinate the planning, implementation and development of an open IT infrastructure in Skåne. SkåNet also has an important role in the development of Skåne's broadband strategy, to generate statistics and to support documentation on the developments. Skånet, which is a neutral player without commercial interests, is responsible for ensuring that contracts and their terms are respected. SkåNet monitors that the network is open and competitively neutral, and therefore plays an important role as guarantor that everyone operates under equal conditions.

The network, which today goes under the name BAS (Broadband for all in Skåne), consists of 2,000 kilometres of fibre cable and connects more than 300 switching centres in towns and villages where customers can always choose from at least two service providers.

The BAS network has been implemented through a PPP agreement (public-private partnership) with Tele2, as a result of a public tender, and is based on a combination of new construction and the existing routes within the Tele2 and municipal networks. About 70 per cent of the network is owned by Tele2 and 30 per cent by the sixteen municipal networks. The idea is that every municipal network, as well as the Tele2 network, should function as ingress for the entire BAS network, which increases the number of connections on the market.

Business model

In order to finance the cost of the deployment of the network (close to EUR 100 million) a PPP approach was followed. Under such a scheme, the municipalities and the municipal networks would provide the government grants (EUR 22 million), while a private contractor would provide a direct investment to top up the capital required. To make the deal worthwhile for the private investor, the agreement included a substantial eight-year contract to deliver services to the public sector in the region (roughly EUR 8 million per year for the public health care system and roughly EUR 2 million per year for regional administration). Moreover, having a unified network would increase the revenue prospects from dark fibre leases. Today, there are about thirty-five customers who rent dark fiber, mostly operators but also banks and large companies. Dark fibre leasing to mobile operators for LTE backhaul generates approx. EUR 10 million annually.

The winning bidder for the network deployment and management was Tele2. The contract mandates open access and regulates the price: dark fibre access must be granted to any other operator, and the lease price for dark fibre is set to EUR 0.50 per metre per year (about five times lower than the market price at the time the contract was signed), which has become the de-facto price in Skåne and in line with prices in Stockholm, for example. Tele2's operation contract has just been extended by another five years.

In order to achieve price transparency and predictability, the price is published openly on SkåNet's website and the pricing model is well known by market actors. An operator who wants to lease dark fibre on a particular route can calculate what the cost will be. Volume discounts are available, but these also are equal for all on pre-defined volumes and are published. There is now a discussion of introducing more specific pricing for different links in order to reflect the differences in commercial value of different sections of the network.

Regarding the specific municipal networks in Skåne, most of them follow the business model variation (c) in Figure 7.3, and OpenNet (which was recently purchased by Telenor's Open Universe) is a successful NP in the region (with NP contracts throughout the whole of Sweden).

Public and commercial services present over the network

It is mainly traditional triple-play services which are offered in the municipalities of Skåne, like the ones described in the other cases. Similar types of web-based PA services present elsewhere are offered by most Skåne municipalities.

All the communications between health care centres in the region today run over the BAS network. There are plans to start pilot projects, together with the University of Lund, to offer e-health services to the households as well.

Unlike Norrsken, on the BAS network no wavelength or bitstream access services are provided to businesses and operators: only dark fibre leases. Nationwide connectivity is provided through collaboration with four other regional and national network operators, both public and private. via the consortium called Easy Fibre.

Examples of socio-economic impact of fibre

As for Norrsken, the main benefit of Skånet, according to its CEO, Christer Lannestam, is the availability of an infrastructure for the future. But another important factor is the political dialogue it has generated. It is crucial to create interest, awareness and engagement regarding the question of broadband as a social infrastructure.

Successes, challenges and future directions

Skånet has been a great success: today more citizens in the region are connected with fibre than would have been the case without BAS, and all municipalities have been included.

There are now pilot projects running to accelerate deployment and uptake: for instance, one in Helsingborg (with 20,000 single-unit houses), whereby areas with 100 houses are offered 1 Gbit/s for EUR 75 and free connection as long as 50% of households sign up. The first area has

just passed 54% and will start deployment soon; meanwhile more end-users are signing up.

Skånet has also initiated collaboration with Lund University on the development and testing of new e-health services.

In the two rural FttH projects and the two regional fibre networking projects the benefits of FttH by municipalities have been focused mainly on direct benefits to the municipalities and anecdotal accounts of benefits experienced by end-users. For one longstanding example of municipal deployment of fibre, Stokab, a first study has been deployed to assess the wider socio-economic benefits. The following section is dedicated to this study.

7.6 Stokab: Stockholm's fibre network and its socio-economic benefits

For almost twenty years, the City of Stockholm, via the fully owned company Stokab, has invested strategically in the development of an open, operator-neutral fibre network for everyone. A recent study (Forzati and Mattsson, 2013) shows that these investments have achieved the desired effects on the city's ICT development and the establishment of ICT-related activities, but also that they have generated significant economic benefits for society, enterprises and citizens.

The socio-economic return on Stokab's investment in fibre infrastructure to date is estimated in this study to be over SEK 16 billion, or EUR 1.8 billion. This result is based on a few effects that are quantifiable. It is expected that the actual return on investments is much larger.

7.6.1 The Stokab model

Stokab owns and is responsible for the passive fibre network, while market players operate and deliver services over the network. Stockholm's basic idea is that IT infrastructure should be available to the whole society – public sector, telecom operators, and other businesses alike. Therefore Stokab's network is designed to facilitate competition: the fibre network is open to everyone on equal terms.

The aim of the network's deployment is to create an ICT infrastructure that allows competition by giving telecom operators and other companies and organizations access to the infrastructure. This vision differs from the prevailing opinion in the rest of Europe, where fibre and broadband networks are often considered as networks for telecom operators. Stokab, however, has inspired several municipal and regional fibre networks throughout Europe and beyond, whereby the open access network model is becoming increasingly better appreciated. Stockholm is often cited as a world-class ICT city.

Aside from passive fibre lines, Stokab provides physical space in nodes equipped with power, cooling, etc. Stokab's fibre network connects almost all multi-dwelling units and commercial properties in the Stockholm municipality: about 90 per cent of households and almost 100 per cent of enterprises have the possibility of signing up for a fibre-based connection.

An extensive backbone network connects industrial areas, all major healthcare facilities and urban centres in the region. The fibre network is available in all parts of the municipality and as an extensive interconnecting network throughout the region. With its 1.25 million kilometres of fibre (in 5,000 km of cables), Stockholm is one of the world's most developed cities in terms of fibre.

Since the company's inception in 1994, the passive network structure and the business model have been designed to enable all stakeholders to define their own network structures. The lease of the network can expand as well as shrink based on a player's need.

In 2012, Stokab had over 100 telecom operators and more than 700 companies and organizations as customers. These can lease fibre directly from Stokab to deliver services in competition. Virtually all telecom operators in Sweden have facilities in Stokab network nodes. National and international fibre connections reach Stokab nodes so that all operators can gain access to links throughout Sweden and the rest of the world, through virtually any operator.

7.6.2 Socio-economic return on investment

Stokab had great importance for Stockholm's businesses and IT-development. Without Stokab's fibre network, science parks like Kista, north of town, would probably not have developed into what is today's success: Kista Science City, for instance, has more than 1,000 ICT companies and around 24,000 employees, as well as 6,800 university students and 1,100 researchers within the field of ICT. It is an attractive environment for ICT companies and developers so it is not surprising that all major IT and telecom companies, as well as universities and research institutes like Swedish ICT, have offices in Kista.

The fibre network has also facilitated innovations and new enterprises such as Spotify and Skype. Media companies have also been able to produce television in a whole new way.

For the past twenty years, Stokab has invested an average of more than SEK 250 million per year, to total of SEK5.4 billion up to 2012. This investment has been possible thanks to the profits generated by Stokab. Break-even was reached in 2001 and the accumulated profit has now passed 1 billion SEK. Until now the profit level has been low compared with the investment level due to the heavy upfront investments required in the initial phase. From the year 2005, the returns have increased steadily, enabling further major investments. It is worth mentioning that the fibre network was built without public funding and was instead financed through loans and revenues.

Through this extensive open fibre network provided by a neutral player, telecom operators can lease and design their own fibre networks without having to make costly investments or having to pay expensive leasing fees to a competitor. Today, to lease fibre in Stockholm costs less (sometimes much less) than half as much as in other capitals around the world. This translates into lower costs, not only for operators but also for all enterprises that have a need for fast and reliable communications. Lower lease prices propagate down the value chain and stimulate entrepreneurship and new service developments.

The fibre network also delivers a wide range of indirect effects to society. It enables, for example,

the more effective use of cloud services, videoconferencing, healthcare, distance education, and other
bandwidth-hungry services like HD-TV, video on
demand and other streaming media. Moreover,
innovation power is unleashed when both small
businesses and households have access to the same
broadband connectivity that previously was only
available to large companies.

As the telecom operators compete on equal
terms, competition is fierce in Stockholm, which
leads to lower prices for broadband compared to
cities where competition is weaker. Savings due to
lower broadband costs for companies are estimated
at approximately SEK 75 million per year if compared to the capital city of Denmark, Copenhagen.
The difference becomes even more significant
when other, more expensive, European cities are
used as the benchmark.

Stockholm's city housing companies have had
a major role in the development of broadband.
Early on they adopted a broadband policy to
connect their properties to Stokab's network and
to install fibre all the way to each apartment.
They are also installing home networks inside
the apartments with outlets in every room.
Through collaboration models, they have inspired
other property owners of multi-dwelling units to
join Stokab's network. The housing companies'
accumulated investment now amounts to nearly
SEK 2 billion.

Building a property network also has other
merits beyond the mere delivery of broadband
services to the tenants. Since the property owners
connect all parts of the property, the communications network can also be used for managing,
monitoring and measuring the facilities. By connecting multi-dwelling units with fibre, property
owners have been able to use control and automation services more effectively (electronic locks,
surveillance, etc.), while at the same time being
able to raise the rent as the fibre connection has
given tenants an added value. Until now, fibre
connectivity has led to an increase in use value
for the tenants and a higher property value for
municipal housing companies in Stockholm
(nearly 100,000 apartments) of SEK 1.85 billion,
as well as increased rental revenues of over
SEK 30 million per year. These effects cover the

housing companies' investments almost in full and
are expected to grow in the coming years.

Generally, when building a 4G/LTE network,
70–80% of the total cost derives from deployment
of fibre infrastructure. In principle, each base station needs to be connected to fibre to sustain the
high 4G/LTE capacity. Leasing the required fibre
connections, instead of investing in a private backhaul network, can significantly reduce the deployment cost for 4G/LTE. The world's first 4G/LTE
network was installed in Stockholm. Net4Mobility
(jointly owned by operators Telenor and Tele2)
states that 4G/LTE would not have been launched
in Stockholm if the necessary fibre had not been
available to lease from Stokab. Today, four 4G/
LTE-networks with extensive coverage are operating in Stockholm.

As Stockholm City and Stockholm County have
been able to connect their premises with fibre, it
has become possible to purchase data and telecommunications services on an open market. This has
generated a cost saving for the municipality and for
the county of about SEK 2 billion over the years
1996–2012.

Stokab procures its deployment, operations,
materials, planning, etc., from the private market.
The procurement process and the large investments
made over the years have generated a direct economic activity that is estimated to be over
SEK 5 billion in revenues for the supplier industry.

Several studies show that high-capacity broadband leads to growth and the creation of jobs
beyond the direct economic activity generated in
the supplier industry: e.g., through the development and use of advanced services and products,
as well as higher ICT competence, which in turn
leads to increased productivity and entrepreneurship. According to Acreo's econometric model, the
'job value' which the fibre network has created in
Stockholm is estimated at about SEK 7.7 billion.

7.7 State of the telecommunications market in Sweden at the end of 2012

Returning from a focus on FttH to broadband
developments in general, this final section provides
an overview of the state of affairs for Sweden

based on the most recent reporting by the national regulator PTS.

According to PTS (2013), the total revenue of the electronic communications retail market in 2012 amounted to SEK 53 billion, or EUR 6 billion. Compared to 2011, this is a small decrease, mainly due to the revenue from fixed-line telephony services decreasing by 12 per cent. The revenue from mobile telephony and data services continues to increase overall, but not as fast as in previous years. The revenue from mobile voice and data increased by 21 per cent in 2012, amounting to SEK 7 billion.

The number of subscribers who have used services on the 4G network (LTE) was approximately 240,000 at the end of 2012, an increase by 210,000 subscribers over the previous year.

Mobile networks were used to send and receive 176,000 terabytes of data in 2012, which is an increase of 75 per cent compared to 2011. The number of text messages (SMS) decreased by approximately 6 per cent in 2012, while the number of multimedia messages (MMS) increased by 15 per cent. The number of outgoing call minutes from the mobile network increased by 5 per cent in 2012 and amounted to 24 million minutes. At the same time, outgoing traffic minutes from the fixed-line network decreased by 14 per cent in 2012, meaning that the number of outgoing traffic minutes decreased by a total of 3 per cent.

The number of fibre-optic broadband subscriptions increased by 16 per cent, or by 143,000 subscriptions, in 2012, and at the end of the year there were over a million such subscriptions. The number of subscriptions to both xDSL broadband and cable-TV decreased in 2012. Nonetheless, the total number of fixed broadband subscriptions increased by 1 per cent.

The demand for high data rates continues to increase, and the number of subscriptions to broadband services with data transfer rates of 100 Mbit/s or higher was 755,000 at the end of 2012. This corresponds to a quarter of all fixed-line broadband subscriptions. PTS has asked, for the first time, for data regarding subscriptions with a data transfer rate of over 1 Gbit/s, and at the end of 2012 there were approximately 1,000 of these connections.

TV subscriptions via fibre-optic and fibre-optic LAN were the distribution channels for traditional TV services which continued to increase the most. The number of TV subscriptions via fibre-optic and fibre-optic LAN increased by 103,000, or 41 per cent, thus amounting to 354,000 on the final day of December 2012.

The Digital Agenda targets set for 2020 are well within reach. Approximately 70% of all broadband lines have data rates of 30 Mbit/s or more at the end of 2012. Coverage of 100 Mbit/s is provided through cable network connections at approximately 600,000 at the end of 2012 and fibre connections at approximately 1 million, covering around 37% of households. By the end of 2013, the uptake of broadband of 100 Mbit/s or more stood at 975,000 connections or approximately 22% of households, while LTE stood at 1.5 million (PTS, 2014).

References

Acreo Swedish ICT (2013). Socio-economic return of Stokab investment. Retrieved from www.acreo.se/sites/default/files/pub/acreo.se/EXPERTISE/broadband/socio-economic_return_of_stokab_investment_twocolumns_notjustify.pdf.

Analysis Mason. (2008). The costs of deploying fibre-based next-generation broadband infrastructure. London: Final report for the Broadband Stakeholder Group. Retrieved from www.broadbanduk.org/component/option,com_docman/task,doc_view/gid,1036/Itemid,63/.

(2009). Competitive models in GPON. London: Ofcom. Retrieved from www.ofcom.org.uk/research/technology/research/emer_tech/sbt/Analysys_Mason_GPON_Final_R1.pdf.

De-Antonio, J., Feijóo, C., Gómez-Barroso, J., Rojo, D., and Marín, A. (2006). A European perspective on the deployment of next generation networks. *The Journal of the Communications Network*, **5**(2) (April–June), 47–55.

Deloitte (2011) Konsekvensutredning avseende regleringen av Marknad 4, October 2011. Retrieved from www.ssnf.org/Documents/Rapporter%20o%20Remisser/Rapporter/

Konsekvensutredning%20av%20regleringen%
20av%20Marknad%204%20Slutversion%
20111102.pdf.

European Commission (2009a). Recommendation on
regulated access to Next Generation Access
networks. Retrieved from http://europa.eu/rapid/
press-release_IP-08-1370_en.pdf.

(2009b). State aid: Commission adopts Guidelines
for broadband networks Retrieved from http://ec.
europa.eu/information_society/newsroom/cf/
dae/itemdetail.cfm?type=251&typeName=
News Article&item_id=5250.

(2009c). Progress report on the single European
electronic communications market 2008 (14th
report). Retrieved from http://ec.europa.eu/
information_society/policy/ecomm/doc/
implementation_enforcement/annualreports/
14threport/commen.pdf.

(2010a). Commission Recomendation of
20 September 2010 on regulated access to Next
Generation Access Networks (NGA).

(2010b). European Digital Competitiveness
report 2010. Volume 2, SEC(2010) 627
(Country profiles, Commission staff working
document).

(2012). EU Guidelines for the application of state
aid rules in relation to the rapid deployment of
broadband networks, draft 2012. Retrieved from
http://ec.europa.eu/competition/consultations/
2012_broadband_guidelines/en.pdf.

EUROSTAT (2010), Urban-rural typology. Eurostat
regional yearbook, Statistics Explained.
Retrieved March 2010, from http://epp.eurostat.
ec.europa.eu/statistics_explained/index.php/
Urban-rural_typology.

Felten, B. (2012), Successful FttH Service Strategies.
Study for the FttH Council Europe, study for the
FttH Council Europe, July 2012.

Forzati, M. (2012). Socio-economic effects of FttH/
FTTx in Sweden. (invited) Proceedings of the
International Conference on Transparent Optical
Networks (ICTON), Warwick, 2012.

Forzati, M., Larsen, C. P., and Mattsson C. (2010).
Open access networks, the Swedish experience.
(invited) Proceedings of the International
Conference on Transparent Optical Networks
(ICTON) 2010. Munich, Germany, paper We.
A4.5.

Forzati, M. and Mattsson, C. (2013). Twenty years of
open fibre network in Stockholm: a socio-
economic study. (invited) Proceedings of the
International Conference on Transparent

Optical Networks (ICTON), Cartagena, Spain,
23–27.

Forzati, M., Mattsson, C., and Aal E-Raza S. (2012).
Early effects of FttH/FttX on employment and
population evolution, an analysis of the
2007–2010 time period in Sweden. Proceedings
of the 11th Conference of Telecommunication,
Media and Internet Techno-Economics (CTTE),
Athens, 2012.

GSA (2011). Evolution to LTE Report.
Sawbridgeworth: Global Mobile Suppliers
Association. Retrieved from www.gsacom.com/
downloads/pdf/.

IDATE (2008). Broadband coverage in Europe.
Final Report. Montpellier: DG INFSO,
European Commission. Retrieved from http://ec.
europa.eu/information_society/eeurope/i2010/
docs/benchmarking/broadband_coverage_2008.
pdf.

Lightwave (2012). MTG acquires Swedish FttH open
access communications operator. *Lightwave
Magazine*, 30 July 2012.

Netsize (2009). The Netsize guide. Mobile society &
me: when worlds combine. Cologne

(2010). The Netsize guide. Mobile rennaisance.
Cologne.

Noam, E. (2010). Regulation 3.0 for telecom 3.0.
Telecommunications Policy, **34**(1–2), 4–10.

OASE (2012). EU FP7 project ICT-OASE,
Deliverable D6.3, (December 2012), www.ict-
oase.eu.

OECD (2010a). Average advertised broadband
download speed, by country, kbit/s, October 2009.
Paris: OECD Broadband Portal. Retrieved from
www.oecd.org/dataoecd/10/53/39575086.xls.

(2010b). Indicators of broadband coverage. Paris:
OECD. Retrieved from www.oecd.org/sti/
telecom.

Patton, F. (2012). La banda larga in Italia: il caso
Provincia Autonoma di Trento, Trentino
Network report, 2012.

Pereira, J. P. R. (2007). A cost model for broadband
access networks: FTTx versus WiMAX. Paper
presented at the Access Networks & Workshops,
2007. AccessNets '07. Second International
Conference.

PTS (2013). Svensk Telemarknad 2012, Post- och
telestyrelsen rapport PTS-ER 2013:15.

(2014). Svensk Telemarknad 2013, Post- och
telestyrelsen rapport PTS-ER 2014:18.

Ramos, S. (2005). Contribución al estudio,
caracterización y desarrollo del sector europeo

de comunicaciones móviles e Internet móvil. Unpublished PhD Dissertation, Universidad Politécnica de Madrid.

Ramos, S., Arcos, M., and Armuña, C. (2009). The role of public administrations in developing the electronic communications infrastructures in Spain. *Info*, **11**(6), 69–81.

Regeringskansliet (2009): Swedish Government's Regeringskansliet, Bredbandsstrategi för Sverige, (N2009/8317/ITP). Retrieved on 16 January 2013 from www.regeringen.se/bredband.

Rupp, K., and Selberherr, S. (2010). The economic limit to Moore's Law. *Proceedings of the IEEE*, **98**(3), 351–353.

Sherif, M. H., and Maeda, Y. (2010). Standards for broadband access and beyond. *IEEE Communications Magazine*, **48**(10), 136–138.

Siciliani, P. (2010). Access regulation on NGA – A financial, market-led solution to bridge the gap between US and European diverging regulatory approaches. *Telecommunications Policy*, **34** (5–6), 287–298.

Sigurdsson, H. M., Thorsteinsson, S. E., and Stidsen, T. K. (2004). Cost optimization methods in the design of next generation networks. *IEEE Communications Magazine*, **42**(9), 118–122.

Svenska Stadsnätsföreningen (2012), Marknadsrapport 2012. Stockholm, 2012.

TeliaSonera (2012) Samråd avseende kalkylmodellen för det fasta nätet – Förslag till reviderade riktlinjer för kalkylmodellens utformning, 15 May 2012.

Germany

JUAN RENDON SCHNEIR AND OLGA BATURA

8.1 Introduction to the case study

The deployment of broadband infrastructure in Germany is perceived by members of the private and public sectors as an important element that will help Germany to strengthen its leading economic position in Europe and in the world. In this chapter we describe the evolution of the broadband market in Germany and analyse the role played by the public and private sectors in the expansion of fixed and mobile penetration in the country. We study the broadband developments from 1996 up to and including 2013, consider the achievement of the European Commission Digital Agenda targets for 2020 and assess the effectiveness of the policy measures applied in recent years.

This chapter is divided into the following sections: The public policies related to broadband deployment are described in Section 8.2. Section 8.3 describes the evolution of the broadband market. In Section 8.4 the level of achievement of the Digital Agenda targets is presented, whereas Section 8.5 discusses the lessons that can be learnt from the dynamics of the broadband market in Germany. Finally, the conclusions are presented in Section 8.6.

8.2 Public policies

8.2.1 Public policies related to broadband deployment

According to German constitutional law (Grundgesetz (GG), 2012), exclusive legislative competence in the field of telecommunications lies with the federal level (Art. 73 (1) Nr. 7 GG). Telecommunications are thereby understood as a technical process of signal transmission with the possibility

of reproduction at the place of destination, including the provisioning of technical infrastructure and equipment at the beginning and the end of the transmission line (Nettesheim, 2009).

Moreover, the federal level has an obligation to provide for blanket coverage of the state territory with basic telecommunications services of adequate quality (Art. 87f (1) GG) – universal service. In doing so, the state assumes responsibility as a guarantor of subsistence and will provide for a legal and regulatory framework allowing for a market supply of necessary infrastructure and services (Nettesheim, 2009).

Content-related issues of transmitted signals, broadcasting and media law remain the domain of the sixteen German federal states (*Bundesländer* or *Länder* for short). This does not mean, however, that the *Länder* are prohibited from any activity that contributes to telecommunications infrastructure development. On the contrary, as long as they comply with competition law and state aid rules, the *Länder* and municipalities may take measures that complement and enhance telecommunications provision above the minimum level (Kühling and Neumann, 2012).

8.2.2 Definition of broadband in Germany

There is no legal definition of broadband in the German telecommunications law (*Telekommunikationsgesetz*, TKG). The analysis of various policy documents of the German government leads to the conclusion that broadband is a connection whose transmission rate clearly exceeds that of the Integrated Services Digital Network (ISDN): i.e., 144 kbit/s. Until 2009, for statistical purposes, the minimum transmission rate of 384 kbit/s downstream was used (Breitbandatlas 2009-02), but the current broadband strategy of the federal government introduced a more appropriate and up-to-date notion of '1 Mbit/s broadband', defined as a minimum of 1 Mbit/s downstream and 128 kbit/s upstream, which is considered a basic level provision (Breitbandatlas 2009–02; BMWi, 2009).

8.2.3 The first phase: market liberalization framework and the beginning of broadband promotion

The German telecommunications law adopted in 1996 did not contain provisions directly dealing with the development of the broadband infrastructure nor mentioned the promotion and support for application of innovative and new technologies (TKG, 1996). Its objective was to promote competition and universal coverage with telecommunications services through sector-specific regulation (Art. 1). The only provisions of relevance for the development of infrastructure as an alternative to the copper lines of the Public Switched Telephone Network (PSTN) of the incumbent were those implementing the European Directive 90/387/EEC of 28 June 1990 (European Communities, 1990), on the establishment of the internal market for telecommunications services through the implementation of Open Network Provision (ONP). According to these provisions, a dominant provider of public telecommunications services and infrastructure had to ensure access to and interconnection with its network for its competitors and users under non-discriminatory conditions (TKG, 1996, Art. 33 and 35). Also, sharing of public conduits or ducts was foreseen in the case where the laying of new telecommunications cables was impossible or required disproportionally high expenses (Art. 51).

The initial roll-out of the broadband networks was complicated by the heterogeneity of ownership of various parts of the public telecommunications network. While the backbone telecommunications network belonged to the incumbent Deutsche Telekom, the ownership of the local loop was not uniform. The local access networks were owned (named in the order of diminishing ownership) by Deutsche Telekom, Deutsche Bank, Bosch Telecom and a number of small and very small network operators (Möschel, 2001). Due to this particularity, coordination of investments was

necessary both for the backbone infrastructure and the local loop.

Following the European Commission Directive 96/19/EEC, amending Directive 90/388/EEC with regard to the implementation of full competition in telecommunications markets, the German telecommunications market was fully liberalized on 01.01.1998. Subsequently, Germany unbundled the copper local loop, in compliance with Regulation (EC) No 2887/2000 of the European Parliament and of the Council on Unbundled Access to the Local Loop (European Communities, 2000) and Commission's Recommendation on Unbundled Access to the Local Loop (European Commission, 2000), thus enabling the competitive provision of a full range of electronic communications services, which includes broadband multimedia and high-speed internet.

Similarly to the European Union (EU) broadband policy (Cava-Ferreruela and Alabau-Muñoz, 2005), the development of broadband infrastructure in Germany has been considered a policy measure aimed at the realization of the information society and, therefore, was promoted in subordination to the respective initiatives. This approach of 'embedded broadband promotion' was adopted in one of the first, but still relevant, policy measures of the federal government: the 'Initiative D21'. Initiative D21 is a partnership between the political actors at the federal, regional (*Länder*) and local levels on the one hand, and interested economic partners from all industry sectors on the other. Projects supported through Initiative D21 should be non-profit and practice oriented and contribute to overall societal development and economic growth.

Simultaneously, the German government led the adoption of broadband technologies creating (additional) demand and applying innovative applications and services. In 1999 an eGovernment initiative for local governance – MEDIA@-KOMM – started with the aim to develop and apply multimedia in towns and communities (DIW, 2004). Within the initiative BundOnline 2005, launched in 2000, a modernization of the federal administration was carried out, whereby all governmental services suitable for such provision were transformed into online services (BMI, 2006). The measures appeared to be a success such that follow-up projects were launched. MEDIA@KOMM-Transfer was carried out in 2004–2007 for the promotion of regional and local eGovernment and relevant international cooperation. The ongoing MEDIA@KOMM-Innovation project aims to support the development of regional and local eGovernment networks and provides for the exchange of experience and best practices, as well as for harmonization and standardization of eGovernment solutions.

In March 2002, the Federal Government and the members of the Initiative D21 founded the *Deutsche Breitbandinitiative*, which is an open platform for dialogue amongst industry, science institutes and the government in order to enable networking and experience and knowledge transfer and to strengthen contacts between the decisive actors. It does not have its own budget, but serves as a cross-sectional project active in all the fields where broadband solutions are possible but not yet implemented (DIW, 2004). In June 2003, the *Deutsche Breitbandinitiative* adopted an action plan which was to complement the infrastructure development by supporting the creation of broadband services, applications and content, stimulating demand, enhancing security and raising users' awareness (BMWi & BMBF, 2003). The promotion of an investment-friendly climate was intended to attract private investors, who were to assume the main financial burden of the broadband roll-out.

8.2.4 The second phase: greater consideration of information society requirements

The eEurope 2005 Action Plan for the development of the information society (European Commission, 2002), which focused in part on broadband as a necessary infrastructure to provide high-speed connectivity – and thus stimulate and enable use of advanced applications and services by public and private parties – required all member states to adopt national broadband plans. The German action programme *Informationsgesellschaft Deutschland 2006* was adopted in December 2003 and continued the line of embedded broadband promotion (BMWi and BMBF,

2003). To realize the information society, the development of an appropriate infrastructure was deemed indispensable and telecommunications and broadband were identified as the very first spheres of activity of the German ICT policy. The action programme had the objective of making broadband the dominant access technology by 2005 and of reaching a broadband penetration level of over 50% by 2010 (BMWi and BMBF, 2003).

The responsibility for implementation was divided between the Federal Ministry of Education and Research, which deals with technological development, and the Federal Ministry of Economics and Technology, which is in charge of promoting the application of technologies (DIW, 2004). The federal action programme largely embraced the key steps proposed by the *Deutsche Breitbandinitiative*, notably the central role of private investments in broadband development. It renounced subsidies as distorting competition, making an exception only for financing from the EU structural funds – the European Regional Development Fund and the European Agricultural Fund for Rural Development. Furthermore, the action programme followed the strategy of stimulating the supply by promoting the demand. Internet usage and eGovernment initiatives were to be promoted as part of this programme. In this context, the programme DeutschlandOnline of 2003 became an umbrella project for federal, regional and local levels of governance (Thome, 2006).

The new version of the German telecommunications law of 2004, implementing the revised EU framework, aimed at improving the general investment climate for infrastructure projects. Yet, the promotion of broadband and next-generation networks was not singled out as a priority. Rather, the promotion of efficient investments in infrastructure and the support of innovations were listed among the objectives of the law (TKG, 2004, Art. 2). Accordingly, a number of provisions were designed to secure the planning and investments for the undertakings. Article 21 of the TKG, which deals with the imposition of access obligations on dominant infrastructure providers, stated explicitly that, when considering this regulatory measure, the *Bundesnetzagentur* (BNetzA), the German telecommunications regulator, had to take into account the initial investments of the infrastructure's owner as well as the necessity to create incentives for further investments in infrastructure in order to promote competition in the infrastructure market. Where access obligations were imposed on a dominant provider, the Bundesnetzagentur had also to regulate its interconnection prices (TKG, 2004, Art. 30(1)). When fixing the price, the regulator had to take into account infrastructure- or service-specific risks connected to the capital invested (Art. 31(4)). All adopted regulatory measures were part of the ex-ante sector-specific regulation, meaning that the intensity of the regulation depended on the existence of effective competition within the market at hand and of significant market power of the network provider in question (Christmann, Ensslin and Wachs, 2005).

The subsequent action programme of the federal government *iD2010 – Informationsgesellschaft Deutschland 2010*, was adopted in 2006 in line with the EU i2010 strategy 'A European Information Society for growth and development' (European Commission, 2005) and continued the promotion of information-society-oriented broadband development (BMWi, 2006) applying the two-prong strategy: the supply should be improved and the demand created. By that time, the supply had increased rapidly and the federal government announced that a new realistic objective was household penetration of 98 per cent by 2008, irrespective of the type of network. The creation of an interactive broadband atlas would permit a better assessment of broadband coverage and demonstrate broadband access potential for the users, industry and policy-makers. Further studies of broadband development and dialogue within the *Deutsche Breitbandinitiative* were to pursue the same objective. On the demand side of the market, a steady growth was predicted, such that a 50% level of uptake by German households was expected well before 2010. It could be enhanced by further innovation related to services and content and be supported by creating the appropriate conditions for it: the digitalization of information channels and the convergence of the media.

In 2007, the so-called 'regulatory holiday' provision was introduced as Article 9a of the TKG, intended to directly promote broadband development. Accordingly, new markets were not to be regulated unless there were sufficient grounds to assume that lack of regulation would hinder development of sustainable competition in the market in question in the long term. The regulatory holiday provision exempted Deutsche Telekom from having to grant competitors access to its new VDSL network. The new market definition encompassed those markets for services or products that differed substantially from services and products already available and did not merely replace them (TKG, 2004, Art. 3 Nr. 12a), thus embracing both various broadband and new generation technologies and services (BMWi, 2009).

The European Commission raised objections against this provision, claiming violations of Articles 6 to 8(1) and (2), 15(3) and 16 of Directive 2002/21/EC of the European Parliament and of the Council of 7 March 2002 on a common regulatory framework for electronic communications networks and services (European Communities, 2002b) and violation of Article 8(4) of Directive 2002/19/EC of the European Parliament and of the Council of 7 March 2002 on access to, and interconnection of, electronic communications networks and associated facilities (European Communities, 2002a), as well as a violation of Article 17(2) of Directive 2002/22/EC of the European Parliament and of the Council of 7 March 2002 on universal service and users' rights relating to electronic communications networks and services (European Communities, 2002c). The Court of Justice of the European Union upheld the Commission's claim, finding that the amendment to the TKG meant an undue legislative interference into regulatory competences of the national regulatory authority that seriously restricted regulatory discretion of the Bundesnetzagentur regarding the market definition and market analysis (CJEU, 2009). As a consequence, Art. 9a had to be removed in the new version of TKG in 2012.

8.2.5 The third phase: intensified and targeted policy of broadband promotion

After almost ten years of subordination of broadband development to the needs of the information society, the so-called broadband strategy of the federal government adopted in 2009 'broke ranks' in terms of its approach: it deals exclusively with broadband development, leaving other information society topics outside its scope (BMWi, 2009). Another novelty is the differentiation between the broadband data rates (1 Mbit/s, 2 Mbit/s and 50 Mbit/s). The federal government set two objectives, which correspond to the measures to strengthen the German economy declared in the second recovery package approved in January 2009 (*Pakt für Beschäftigung und Stabilität in Deutschland zur Sicherheit der Arbeitsplätze, Stärkung der Wachstumskräfte und Modernisierung des Landes,* – Bundestag, 2009):

1. to close the gaps ('white areas') in broadband coverage and to ensure an ubiquitous availability of 1 Mbit/s broadband by the end of 2010 and
2. to provide a 50 Mbit/s broadband access to 75 per cent of all households by 2014. This will constitute a basis for further fast deployment of high-data rate connections for the whole territory.

To realize the objectives of the German broadband strategy, several measures were proposed, to be kept updated and adjusted depending on the progress of the strategy's implementation:

For example, the existing infrastructure and facilities will be shared in order to avoid duplication of infrastructure.

A broadband atlas and a database on all relevant building sites and projects will be developed.

Furthermore, demand-oriented empty ducts will be laid and construction of telecommunications infrastructure will be undertaken in cooperation and coordination with other utility sectors (for instance, water supply).

The described measures will be carried out in close cooperation with the *Länder* and the local authorities and this teamwork will be strengthened through the establishment of working groups within the Federal Ministry for Economics and Technology, consisting of representatives of the *Länder* and the federal government.

In this context, financing through the so-called 'joint tasks' has been improved. Already in 2008,

the financing of broadband infrastructure roll-out became possible for rural areas, where broadband development was not commercially profitable, within the Joint Task for the Improvement of Agrarian Structures and Coast Protection (GAK) of the Federal Ministry for Food, Agriculture and Consumer Protection. The *Länder* can propose their own measures to be included in the GAK framework at the federal level, containing principles and general requirements for integrated rural development. When approved, the framework plan is to be implemented at the *Länder* level (GAK-Gesetz, Art. 7-9). This plan expired at the end of 2013 and foresaw in Part B financial support for rural areas that lack or are short of sufficient broadband provision and can prove business and household demand (GAK-Rahmenplan, 2011). The respective local authorities or associations could apply for financing through subsidies, grants or loans from the federal government. With these means they can complement private and communal investments in projects for infrastructure roll-out and accompanying activities (planning, consulting, informational events, etc). In the new framework the laying of empty ducts has been rendered eligible for financing and the federal subsidy ceiling has been increased from 60% to 90% with the remainder provided by the *Land*. The limit of the subsidy per project was also raised up to EUR 500,000.

The laying of empty ducts is perceived to be a decisive measure for the development of high-speed communications networks. For its promotion, a special umbrella framework has been created at the federal level that provides general conditions for subsidies at the local level and eliminates the necessity to notify the Commission (*Bundesrahmenregelung Leerrohre*, 2011) of every single community measure. It was approved by the Commission in July 2010 and provides EUR 600 million over the period of five years (until 2015) for development of passive infrastructure in 'white' and 'grey' areas.

Additionally, since mid-2009 structurally weak areas, especially in eastern Germany, can rely on financing through the Joint Task for the Improvement of Regional Economic Structure (GRW) of the Federal Ministry of Economics and

Technology for the development of a high-quality broadband network that provides a minimum service of 2 Mbit/s. Similar to GAK, a coordination framework defining eligibility for financing areas and measures was adopted to be implemented by the *Länder* (GRW-Gesetz, Art. 4-6). The conditions for a subsidy require a higher data rate (at least 2 Mbit/s) and evidence of an inadequate cost-performance ratio in comparison to adjacent urban areas (GRW-Koordinationsrahmen, Attachment 4, Number 3.2.4.).

It appears that the available funds have been actively used. The EUR 10 million provided annually by the federal state under the GAK was overdrawn in 2011 and 2012 (EUR 19.2 million and EUR 14.7 million, respectively) which became possible due to the remaining sums from the early years of the fund and thanks to excess payments from the *Länder*. Due to this success, the fund, originally to end in 2013, will continue its operation until 2018 (Goldmedia, 2013). Funding via GRW has had a more modest success (2012 with EUR 2.9 Million was the peak year) because GRW financial means are committed not to broadband development but to development of structurally weak regions in general and are used for various projects (Goldmedia, 2013).

Under the second recovery package, which expired at the end of 2010, additional financing was available for the cases not falling under the Joint Tasks (Börnsen, 2009). The attractive features of this mechanism were the absence of the subsidy limit per project and the possibility to apply for regional projects not being carried out by local authorities.

One more source of financing has been established directly for undertakings: according to the Law on Future Investments (*Zukunftsinvestitionsgesetz* – ZuInvPG, 2009) the *Länder* can provide local authorities with finances which they in their turn can make available to undertakings developing or operating broadband networks. The *Länder* have the competence to decide whether and under what conditions financing provided by the Law on Future Investments will be used. For instance, undertakings may apply for guarantees by the federal government and/or *Länder* that assume a default risk of up to 90 per cent.

Besides the joint financing, some *Länder* (Bavaria, North Rhine-Westphalia, Rhineland-Palatinate, Schleswig-Holstein and Thuringia) have their own financing programmes that offer cheap long-term loans allowing 10 to 20 years return on investment (Goldmedia, 2013). It will also be noted that the aforementioned EU structural funds – European Regional Development Fund (founded in 1999) and European Agricultural Fund for Rural Development (founded in 2005) – present an additional funding possibility which is, yet, of a secondary character in relation to the national financing opportunities (BMWi and BMELV, 2009).

The latest amendments to the German telecommunications law of 2012 follow the line of the governmental strategy to strengthen the promotion of broadband development and declare the 'acceleration of development of heavy-duty public telecommunications networks of next generation' as one of the major objectives of telecommunications regulation (TKG, 2012, Art. 2(2) Nr. 5). Having dropped the 'regulatory holiday' provision, TKG 2012 relies strongly on enhancing security of planning and investment for undertakings, thus further developing the approach launched in TKG 2004, as well as on facilitating risk sharing and cooperation among investors (Körber, 2011).

Over time, the regulatory framework has stabilized and become more precise, thus enhancing security of planning and investment. The law aims at objective, transparent, non-discriminatory and proportional regulatory principles underpinning the work of the *Bundesnetzagentur*, which will be substantiated by maintaining the same regulatory concept over longer appropriate periods of time, to increase predictability of regulation, and by considering investors' risks in case of access obligations, by allowing for risk-sharing agreements between undertakings, by prohibiting discrimination and promoting competition, as well as by recognizing the complementary and transitional character of regulatory measures in relation to competition (TKG, 2012, Art. 2(3)).

A more straightforward measure to improve the investment climate is the possible adoption by the *Bundesnetzagentur* of periodic administrative rulings (*Verwaltungsvorschrift*) describing the general regulatory requirements. To assess efficient investments and innovation regarding new and enhanced infrastructure, a methodology for risk determination, criteria for establishment of access conditions and prices for risk-sharing models, and examples of risk-sharing models will be considered by the regulator (TKG, 2012, Art. 15a(2)). On the basis of such administrative rulings and upon request of any provider of a public telecommunications network contemplating development of new-generation networks, the *Bundesnetzagentur* is to provide region-specific information about expected changes in the regulatory framework or measures (TKG, 2012, Art. 15a(4)). To further improve consistency and predictability of regulation, as well as the security of planning and investment for undertakings, the *Bundesnetzagentur* has the potential to expand market regulation periods from three to a maximum of six years, provided the European Commission has no objections to such prolongation (TKG, 2012, Art. 14(2)).

Next to the already mentioned provisions of Article 15a(2) facilitating risks sharing, the regulatory measures on the basis of Articles 30 and 32 of the TKG create additional incentives for this practice. When regulating the prices charged by dominant network providers for access (both services and facilities), the *Bundesnetzagentur* will consider initial investments and allow for an appropriate return (risk premium) upon the invested capital, as well as take in utmost account special risks and risk-sharing agreements between undertakings regarding next-generation networks (TKG, 2012, Art. 30(3) and 32(3) Nr. 3).

In addition to sharing investment risks, TKG 2012 seeks to promote actual infrastructure sharing between undertakings. Previous legislation dealt with only one aspect of these issues, namely with cooperation when laying ducts and wires. According to Art. 21(2), the *Bundesnetzagentur*, acting upon a request or ex officio, may impose on a dominant provider of public telecommunications networks, among other obligations, the requirement to ensure open access to certain network elements or facilities, including unbundled broadband access. At the same time, a number of obligations are to be imposed on a dominant provider under Art. 21(3), including access to passive network elements and open access to technical interfaces, protocols and other key technologies necessary for services or interoperability of services, as well as collocation and other types of sharing of buildings, ducts, poles and other facilities.

In order to achieve the targeted data rate of 50 Mbit/s and more, and to prevent signal degradation, it is necessary to at least partially upgrade the copper wire between the distribution frame in the local exchange and the subscriber terminal with fibre. To do this, the new Art. 77a (TKG 2012) guarantees access to the relevant network infrastructure on the premises in two ways: either by collocation of wires of competing providers in the same conduits or by sharing the existing wires if duplication of the infrastructure is economically inefficient or technologically impossible (Kind and Schramm, 2012). The *Bundesnetzagentur*'s order to co-locate or share the wires and conduits in question can be addressed not only to network providers but also to other owners of (passive) infrastructure who do not operate the networks. Moreover, the imposition of the obligation does not depend on the market power of the addressee but has the objective of achieving synergy effects in relation to the network infrastructure (TKG, 2012, Art. 77a(1); Kind and Schramm, 2012). The *Bundesnetzagentur* can create an inventory of all facilities that can be used for telecommunications purposes (for instance, ducts, poles, antennas, etc.) and can request the relevant information from telecommunications providers and other legal entities in possession of such facilities (TKG, 2012, Art. 77a(3)).

In order to further minimize the costs of the development of new broadband networks, TKG 2012 allows the collocation of telecommunications infrastructure with other facilities (water, gas pipes, power lines). Upon a written request from an interested provider of public telecommunications networks, undertakings and legal persons in possession of facilities that can be used for the development and laying of next-generation networks are obliged to make an offer to share such facilities (TKG, 2012, Art. 77b(1)). Additionally, Art. 77c-77e provide for sharing of roads, waterways and railway infrastructure belonging to the federal government.

The investment climate for broadband development is further improved by initial regulation of the deployment of innovative laying techniques. Commonly, telecommunications infrastructure will be laid in compliance with the standards set by the German Institute for Standardization (*Deutsches Institut für Normung*, DIN) in the General Technical Instruction for the usage of roads for cables and telecommunications lines (*Allgemeine Technische Bestimmungen für die Benutzung von Straßen durch Leitungen und Telekommunikationslinien*, ATB-BeStra) which prescribes, for instance, a certain depth and width of trenches for the wires. Art. 68(2) of TKG 2012 provides for an exhaustive list of requirements to be fulfilled for a request to be approved by the carrier of public easement allowing the requesting provider to lay fibre infrastructure with the help of micro- or mini-trenching techniques in deviation from the aforementioned DIN standards.

An important measure to promote innovative broadband technologies is the decision of the *Bundesnetzagentur* of Summer 2013 to slightly ease the incumbent's obligation to provide access to the sub-loop segment of the network. Now Deutsche Telekom may refuse access to the sub-loop if it is necessary to enable implementation of vectoring at the street cabinet (by Deutsche Telekom itself or another company). All competitors will still be able to interconnect at the cabinet using optical fibre and implement vectoring if they offer an appropriate bitstream product under open access arrangements.

8.2.6 Broadband-related radio frequency spectrum measures

Like other national policies in the radio spectrum field, German policy is subject to the limitations imposed by decisions about radio frequency allocation and uses adopted at the international (International Telecommunications Union, ITU) and regional (European Conference of Postal and Telecommunications Administrations (CEPT)) and EU institution levels (*Bundesnetzagentur*, 2013a; TKG-Kommentar, 2013). Implementing the international allocation of spectrum frequencies, the federal government adopted a national frequencies

regulation that allocates certain frequency bands for certain uses. On its basis, the *Bundesnetzagentur* draws up a detailed spectrum frequency plan which is then used to assign frequencies to individual operators (TKG 2012, Art. 52 ff.). Furthermore, physical characteristics of spectrum frequencies impose further constraints on their use for broadband provision. Due to this, measures in the field of spectrum frequencies are dubbed 'supporting policy' ('*Unterstützende Frequenzpolitik*'), meaning that they will be used in order to close the gaps in the provision of broadband in rural areas and in order to improve mobile use of ICT (BMWi, 2012).

Arguably, the relevance of radio spectrum for high data rate transmission has become apparent with the development of the Universal Mobile Telecommunications System (UMTS) standard and its commercial deployment. In contrast to the second-generation standard (Global System for Mobile Telecommunications, GSM), in addition to voice UMTS would allow transmission of data and video at a much higher rate of up to 2 Mbit/s, with all participants constantly sending data packets on the same frequency band. This led both operators and policy-makers to believe that in the near future UMTS would replace not only GSM but also parts of the landlines used for Internet provision (Petzel, 2006). These and other factors played a decisive role in the auction for UMTS licences in summer 2000, total proceeds of which were an exceptionally high sum of about EUR 50 billion paid by six winners. The licences included an obligation to deploy an own UMTS network by 2003 and to reach a theoretical supply rate of 25% of population by the end of 2003 and 50% by the end of 2005 (Petzel, 2006). The auction was strongly criticized by its participants, scholars and other observers and the 'UMTS euphoria' soon died away as the winners struggled – and ultimately failed – to fulfil their licence obligations (Virnich, 2003; Petzel, 2006).

Radio frequency spectrum policy has come to play an increasingly important role again during the third phase of broadband policy development due to the launch of the commercial use of the Long-Term Evolution (LTE) standard. It has been recognised that mobile and wireless solutions in general are instrumental in closing the gaps in the provision of basic broadband to rural and remote areas. Their effective application depends, however, on the availability of spectrum and its efficient use.

In May 2010, promptly following the requirements of the EU law (European Commission, 2010a) and in compliance with the broadband strategy, Germany auctioned the 800 MHz frequencies for mobile operators. Herewith, Germany was the first EU member state to make use of the Digital Dividend. As a result of the auction, in autumn 2010 new licences were issued for more than 11,000 locations to use LTE base stations. The licence conditions obliged the operators to provide mobile broadband in a particular priority order, starting with towns and communities short of infrastructure of less than 5,000 residents (*Bundesnetzagentur*, 2013a; Goldmedia, 2013).

Germany intends to stay at the forefront of the exploitation of the radio spectrum for broadband development. Thus, in the context of the discussions in the ITU about reallocation of frequencies of 700 MHz spectrum (Digital Dividend II), the federal government launched a discussion process, established a Mobile Media 2020 Forum and developed an ICT strategy in order to identify the demand for frequencies and their possible use (BMWi, 2010; 2012). In this context, in 2013 the *Bundesnetzagentur* launched public consultations on the basis of the discussion paper on the process of assignment of 700 MHz and 1.5 GHz frequencies as well as the 900 MHz- and 1800 MHz frequencies, of which the rights of use expire in 2016 (*Bundesnetzagentur*, 2013b). Besides, the regulatory authority drafted scenarios of possible future allocation of these frequencies and started a formal procedure for demand assessment for the time after 2017 (*Bundesnetzagentur*, 2011; 2012).

8.3. Progress in the broadband market

The broadband market in Germany was initially driven by the existing fixed-network infrastructure. This infrastructure was essentially based on copper and cable access networks. At a later stage the deployment of high-capacity transmission wireless networks enabled the provisioning of ubiquitous

wireless access to the Internet. As is explained in this section, the incumbent and alternative operators played a key role in the development of the broadband market.

8.3.1 Background about the incumbent operator

The incumbent operator, Deutsche Telekom, belonged originally to the *Deutsche Bundespost*, a public institution created in 1947 which was in charge of postal and telecommunications services in the later Federal Republic of Germany. Before that time, the *Deutsche Bundespost* was called the *Reichspost*. In 1989 the *Deutsche Bundespost* was divided into three public companies: *Deutsche Bundespost Postdienst* for the postal service, *Deutsche Bundespost Postbank* for the postal banks and *Deutsche Bundespost Telekom* for the communications service. The *Deutsche Bundespost Telekom* became the Deutsche Telekom AG in 1995 and was subsequently privatized in 1996. Currently, the German federal government has a direct ownership of 15% of the shares of Deutsche Telekom and owns further 17% indirectly through the Kreditanstalt für Wiederaufbau (KfW) bank.

Traditionally Deutsche Telekom has been the company that invested in telecommunications assets. But, when comparing the investment made in fixed, mobile and cable networks which provide broadband, telephony and video services, the alternative operators combined have invested more than Deutsche Telekom in every year of the period 2002–2013. For the period considered, the alternative operators have contributed 53.7% of the total investment, whereas Deutsche Telekom has provided 46.3% (Dialog Consult-VATM, 2013).

8.3.2 Differences between the new and old Bundesländer

After the reunification of Germany in 1990, the government made important efforts such that the PSTN infrastructure in the new *Bundesländer* and in the old *Bundesländer* would become similar. But there are still differences between the regions as regards broadband infrastructure. For low-capacity broadband services, which have a data rate up to 1 Mbit/s and which are available through fixed and wireless networks such as Digital Subscriber Line (xDSL), Wireless Local Area Network (WLAN), LTE, UMTS, cable, Fibre to the X (FttX) and Worldwide Interoperability for Microwave Access (WiMAX), all the *Bundesländer* had a broadband household coverage of more than 98.5% in 2013 (Breitbandatlas, 2013).

However, for broadband services of more than 50 Mbit/s which can be provided through xDSL, Fttx, cable and WLAN networks, there are differences. In 2013, ten of the old *Bundesländer* had a household broadband coverage of 50 to 95%, whereas only one old *Bundesland* had a coverage of 10 to 50%. The five new *Bundesländer* had a broadband availability of 10 to 50% (Breitbandatlas, 2013).

8.3.3 Fixed broadband market

Fixed broadband penetration

In 2012, the fixed broadband penetration of Germany was 34.2% (see Table 1.3 in Chapter 1 Introduction). In terms of fixed broadband penetration the situation in Germany, as compared to other OECD countries, has changed over time. Until 2006 Germany was behind the average of OECD countries in terms of fixed broadband penetration, but since 2006 the fixed broadband penetration of Germany is better than that of the average of OECD countries (OECD, 2013).

Competition in the fixed broadband market

The predominant network in the fixed broadband market in Germany is the copper wire-based access network. Figure 8.1 depicts the different types of fixed access used for the period 2002–2013. The figure reflects the xDSL, coaxial cable and fibre-based networks. Other types of access networks, such as power-line- and satellite-based networks, were not included due to the limited number of broadband lines deployed.

In 2002 the only type of fixed broadband deployed was through copper lines. In 2013, 80% of broadband lines were based on xDSL. The average annual increase between 2002 and 2009

was 38%. The incumbent operator is the provider of the majority of xDSL lines, including the wholesale lines used by the alternative operators.

In recent years the cable networks have been playing an increasingly important role. For the period 2007–2013 the average annual increase of cable access lines was 35%. With only 0.3 million homes connected with Fibre to the Home/Building (FttH/B) networks, the fibre-based access networks represented only 1% of the broadband lines in 2013.

At the beginning of 2007, the xDSL lines amounted to around 95% of the fixed broadband access lines. There were six major DSL providers in Germany: Deutsche Telekom with 48.2%, United Internet with 14.9%; HanseNet (which later became Telefonica) with 13.3%; Arcor (which later became Vodafone) with 13.1%; Freenet (later 1&1) with 7.4%; and Versatel with 3.2% market share (DSLWEB, 2007).

In 2013, the total number of all types of fixed broadband lines was 28.3 million. Deutsche Telekom had still the majority of broadband access lines with a 43.8% market share, followed by 1&1 with 12.0%, Vodafone with 10.6%, UnityMedia Kabel BW with 8.5%, Telefonica with 8.1% and Kabel Deutschland with 7.1%. EWE Gruppe, Versatel, NetCologne and M-Net had less than 3% market share each (Dialog Consult-VATM, 2013).

Cable operators play an increasingly important role in broadband provisioning: in 2006 only 3.4% of the broadband lines were provided by cable operators, whereas in 2013 this has increased to 18.9% of the lines.

The reuse of the copper lines

Deutsche Telekom owns and operates the majority of xDSL lines. In 2013, Deutsche Telekom provided 54.1% of the DSL lines in retail mode, whereas 7.9% of the lines were sold in resale mode. Another 38% of the xDSL lines were provided on a wholesale basis to be managed by alternative operators. It has to be taken into account that the majority of the lines managed by alternative operators use the unbundled copper lines of Deutsche Telekom.

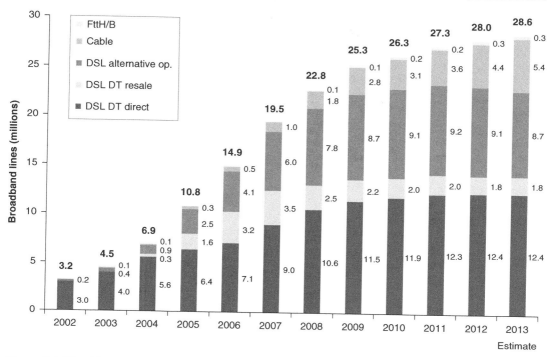

Figure 8.1 Fixed broadband connections by technology, Germany 2002–2013
Data sources: Based on Bundesnetzagentur (2013c); Dialog Consult-VATM, 2013.

The transmission capacity of the copper-based access lines has improved over time. The ADSL lines employed in 1999 provided a downlink data rate of 0.7 Mbit/s. The downlink data rate of the xDSL lines in 2002 and 2004 were 1.5 and 3 Mbit/s, respectively. ADSL2$^+$ lines provided a data rate of 16 Mbit/s at the beginning of 2006. Between 2006 and 2012 over 22 million lines were switched to ADSL2$^+$ in more than a thousand cities in Germany. VDSL2 lines deployed since 2006 provide a download speed of up to 50 Mbit/s. As of 2012, 11.6 million households in fifty cities were covered with VDSL2.

Operators in Germany have been considering the possibility of improving the capacity of access lines by using techniques such as vectoring and bonding, which can enable a data rate of 100 Mbit/s for certain segment lengths. To achieve these rates, fibre to the street cabinet (Fibre to the Cabinet, FttC) or to the distribution point (Fibre to the Distribution Point, FttDP) is to be deployed.

With these broadband capacities it is possible for xDSL lines to compete on data rates with fibre and cable networks. If operators deploy vectoring and G.fast, which provides up to 1 Gbit/s over 100 m, then the lifespan of copper lines will be extended further. In 2012 Deutsche Telekom announced that it was going to use xDSL lines with vectoring to provide downstream transmission rates of up to 100 Mbit/s, and in the summer of 2013 a regulatory basis was established for this deployment.

The importance of cable networks

The German *Bundespost* constructed the RTV-cable network at the beginning of the 1980s. This cable network was separated from Deutsche Telekom in 1998 and transferred to Kabel Deutschland GmbH (KDG), which was fully owned by Deutsche Telekom. The network managed by KDG was divided into nine regions in order to prepare it for sale to potential investors. The operator Ish, which was owned by Liberty Global, acquired the cable network in Nordrhein-Westfalen in 2002, whereas iesy, also owned by Liberty Global, acquired the network in Hessen. Kabel BW bought the network in Baden-Württemberg. The other six networks were sold to Kabel Deutschland Gruppe in 2003. The operators ish and iesy merged in 2007 and created the cable operator UnityMedia. Kabel Deutschland operates networks in the other *Bundesländer*, with the exception of Nordrhein-Westfalen, Hessen and Baden-Württemberg. In 2011 Liberty Global, which owns Unity Media, bought Kabel BW.

Figure 8.1 shows than since 2007 the growth of CATV-based broadband lines exceeds that of PSTN-based access lines. By deploying the Data Over Cable Service Interface Specification (DOCSIS) 3.0, the transmission capacity of cable networks has increased significantly, achieving 100 Mbit/s and more.

In comparison with fibre-based operators, cable network operators are in a better position in terms of coverage. In 2011, around 48% of the households were passed by cable and only 2% by FttH/B networks. In 2013 cable operators had 5.4 million broadband subscribers. The most important cable operators in 2011 were Kabel Deutschland, UnityMedia, Kabel BW, TeleColumbus and Primacom (WIK, 2012). Cable operators provide video, broadband and telephony services. As of 2011, 13.7% of the customers base of the cable operators had a broadband subscription, whereas 72.6% had only a TV subscription (Dialog Consult-VATM, 2011).

Limited FttH/B roll-out

In Germany, there is little deployment of FttH/B networks. As of 2012 there were 0.8 million households passed and 0.3 million households connected to FttH/B networks (Dialog Consult-VATM, 2012). Plausible reasons for this lack of massive FttH/B deployment are: the competition from cable operators, the volume of investment needed to deploy the passive infrastructure of fibre-based networks, the current massive use of copper-based xDSL lines and the possibility of upgrading them for continued use into the future.

So far Deutsche Telekom has not made a massive investment in FttH/B networks. Deutsche Telekom makes investments in FttH/B networks where it sees a clear positive business case. For example, it has deployed fibre-based networks to connect apartment buildings or in urban areas where there is a significant number of potential subscribers that are likely to sign a contract with the incumbent operator. Many of the current FttH/B networks deployed in Germany have been built by city carriers and municipal public utilities companies (*Stadtwerke*). In several cases, these companies already owned the passive infrastructure and they needed only to deploy the fibre, which meant a strong reduction of the total cost.

8.3.4 Mobile broadband market

Mobile operators

In January 2013 there were 33.6 million subscribers, which had access to mobile broadband networks. This represents a penetration of 41.1%. Since 2008 the number of mobile broadband subscribers – initially only through UMTS and later through LTE networks – has grown steadily over the years: in 2008 it was 13.6 million; in 2009 it was 19.0; in 2010 it was 21.2; in 2011 it was 28.6; and by January 2013 it had reached 33.6 million (*Bundesnetzagentur*, 2013c).

The operators that own physical infrastructure to provide wireless services in Germany are Telekom Deutschland (which belongs to the Deutsche Telekom group), Vodafone, E-Plus and Telefónica O2. As of 2013, the total number of SIM cards activated, which are used to provide telephony and broadband services, was 114.1 million. Telekom Deutschland, Vodafone, E-Plus and Telefónica O2 had market shares of 32.9%, 28.0%, 22.0% and 17.1%, respectively, measured on the basis of the SIM cards provided (Dialog Consult-VATM, 2013).

Evolution of wireless networks

A succession of wireless broadband networks has been introduced in the German market over the last years. The first wireless broadband networks were

Table 8.1: Monthly volume of data per user and annual increase, Germany, 2008–2013

	2008	2009	2010	2011	2012	2013 Estimate
Fixed network	9 GB 36%	10 GB 7%	11 GB 8%	12 GB 9%	13 GB 10%	15 GB 15%
Mobile network	22 MB 340%	62 MB 181%	117 MB 88%	170 MB 45%	227 MB 33%	261 MB 14%

Data source: Based on Dialog Consult-VATM, 2013.

based on GPRS (General Packet Radio Service) and HSCSD (High Speed Circuit Switched Data), which were denoted as 2.5G (Generation) networks. In theory it was possible to achieve 115 kbit/s with GPRS and 57.6 kbit/s using HSCSD.

It took some time to deploy 3G UMTS networks after the auction of the licenses for the spectrum was concluded. The auction took place in 2000, while Vodafone was the first mobile operator to start using this network in 2004. One of the reasons for this delay was the lack of appropriate mobile handsets. With UMTS it became possible, in theory, to achieve 384 kbit/s for downstream transmission.

In 2006 the UMTS-based system High Speed Packet Access (HSPA) was able to provide, in theory, downstream and upstream data rate of 1.8 Mbit/s and 384 kbit/s, respectively. In 2007 the High Speed Downlink Packet Access (HSDPA) and High Speed Uplink Packet Access (HSUPA) networks were able to provide downlink rates of up to 7.2 Mbit/s and 3.6 Mbit/s, respectively. HSPA$^+$ networks, denoted as HSPA Evolution, are able to provide up to 28 Mbit/s on the downlink and 11 Mbit/s on the uplink. HSPA$^+$ networks are also called 3.5G networks.

The first broadband services based on the 4G LTE network were announced by Vodafone and Telekom Deutschland for a few villages and communities in Germany at the end of 2010. Telekom Deutschland, Vodafone and Telefonica O2 started providing services using the LTE networks in rural areas first, as was agreed in the conditions for the auction of the spectrum. In theory, the downstream transmission capacity could be up to 100 Mbit/s. In practice, with very good transmission conditions and a very reduced number of users generating traffic in the same cell, it is possible to reach around 50 Mbit/s. An improvement of LTE is

LTE-Advanced which, again in theory and under optimal conditions, could provide up to 1 Gbit/s on the downlink; in practice carrier aggregation could provide up to 225 Mbit/s. First small-scale tests were reported by Vodafone and Telefonica in November 2013.

8.3.5 Fixed versus mobile broadband

As a result of the deployment of the 3G and 4G LTE wireless networks, and the increasing use of smartphones, the usage of mobile broadband services has grown. As an illustration, Table 8.1 shows the development of the monthly volume of data on fixed and mobile access lines and the corresponding percentage of increase. While the volume of data transmitted through the fixed networks is much higher than that transmitted using the mobile network (15 GB vs. 261 MB in 2013), the growth in mobile data use is much higher.

It remains to be seen to what degree the deployment of LTE networks, which provide higher data rates, will continue motivating users to replace their fixed broadband access lines with mobile broadband access.

8.4 Realizing the Digital Agenda targets

The objectives of the German broadband strategy were set in anticipation of the European strategy for smart, sustainable and inclusive growth, known as Europe 2020, and at first glance appear to be far more ambitious. However, they do not correspond fully with the benchmarks of the Digital Agenda as they address the supply side exclusively. The EU Flagship Initiative 'A Digital Agenda for Europe' aims at broadband access for all citizens by 2013, access for all to 30 Mbit/s or above by 2020, with 50% or more of European households subscribing to Internet connections above 100 Mbit/s (European Commission, 2010b). By contrast, the German broadband strategy envisages ubiquitous coverage with 1 Mbit/s broadband by the end of 2010 and 50 Mbit/s broadband access to 75% of all households by 2014. In 2012, due to the progress of implementation, these objectives were adjusted to include a universal availability of 50 Mbit/s by 2018.

As of mid-2013, 58.4% of all the households in Germany had the possibility of gaining access to a fixed or wireless broadband network with a minimum capacity of 50 Mbit/s, 77.2% to a capacity of 16 Mbit/s and 99.8% to 1 Mbit/s. Regarding access through fixed broadband networks, 58.2%, 85.7% and 95.5% of households were passed by networks with a minimum capacity of 50 Mbit/s, 16 Mbit/s and 1 Mbit/s, respectively (*Breitbandatlas*, 2013). In 2012 Next Generation Access networks that support a downstream capacity of at least 30 Mbit/s covered 66.2% of households (European Commission, 2013). In January 2013, the fixed broadband penetration rate was 34.2%. The penetration rate of high-speed connections of at least 30 Mbit/s was 12%, whereas the penetration rate of very fast connections of at least 100 Mbit/s was 1.2% (European Commission, 2013).

With regard to mobile networks, in 2012 access to HSPA 3G networks was available to 90.4% of the population, whereas 4G LTE networks were available to 51.7%. As of mid-2013, the broadband wireless networks with capacities of 16 Mbit/s, 6 Mbit/s and 1 Mbit/s were available to 4.6%, 48.9% and 95.8% of the households, respectively (*Breitbandatlas*, 2013). The broadband mobile penetration rate was 41.1% as of January 2013 (European Commission, 2013).

8.5 Case analysis

8.5.1 Operators

The fixed broadband market is characterized by an extensive use of xDSL lines, dominated by the incumbent operator Deutsche Telekom. Alternative operators have been relying on the regulated unbundled lines of Deutsche Telekom for competition. Infrastructure-based competition is provided by cable operators who own their own access networks. By using DOCSIS 3.0 cable operators are able to provide a high-speed broadband service and they have been able to realize the highest growth rate in fixed broadband lines in recent years.

In the wireless broadband market four operators own physical wireless access infrastructure and the competition between them is quite strong.

8.5.2 Main features of policy developments

Cooperation between the federal, regional and local levels of government has proven to be the central element of the policy measures aimed at broadband development in Germany. Coordinated efforts were first made to boost the demand side in the early years of broadband deployment, while the supply side was expected to be driven more or less by market forces alone, once the competition had been introduced and some general anti-competitive regulatory safeguards related to the market power of the incumbent had been adopted. However, over recent years governmental efforts have become increasingly concentrated on support of the supply side and range from incentive measures to promote and facilitate investment (risk and infrastructure sharing, consideration of investment for price-setting measures, etc.) to the provision of financial support in various forms. Market failures in rural areas have required an even more direct public involvement in the form of infrastructure and services provision by *Stadtwerke* (communal enterprises) and laying of empty ducts by municipalities for their subsequent rental to the broadband providers. At the same time, demand-promoting measures have retreated to the background, so that currently German policy can be called a bit one-sided.

These developments indicate a possible (re)turn of German telecommunications policy towards industrialism, at least with regards to fixed broadband development.

Throughout most of the period considered, Germany has been a close follower of the policies developed by the European Commission in

Brussels. However, realizing the growing importance of broadband for Germany's competitiveness and its status as a European and global economic power has resulted in attempts to anticipate – and even determine to a degree – the EU's information society policies and broadband policy in particular. For instance, Germany was hard on the Commission's heels auctioning the first Digital Dividend and nowadays it is preparing most thoroughly for the second round.

Against this background, one should consider the fast growing importance of the radio spectrum policy as part of the broadband developments during recent years. So far, the policy measures in this field are very different from the measures for the promotion of fixed broadband: the federal government is mostly concerned with the provision of the scarce resource of radio frequencies.

8.5.3 Expectations based on theory

Taking the theory of the ladder of investment as a way to analyse the level of competition achieved by the different operators in the fixed network market, the following points can be observed:

- Alternative operators have not had the motivation to deploy their own fixed broadband access infrastructure. The conditions to use the copper lines of the incumbent operator were quite clear and attractive, and hence they have been using the local loop of Deutsche Telekom to provide broadband services. This has brought competition to the services market.
- Introduction of new broadband technologies (vectoring), extending the life of copper wire is likely to cement this situation and further postpone the emergence of infrastructure-based competition from alternative operators.
- Cable operators are using the access networks that were initially deployed to provide TV services. By employing DOCSIS 3.0, they are able to provide a high-speed broadband access service. Cable networks are not regulated: that is, they are not subject to any access or price regulation. Increasing infrastructure-based competition has been the result.

- There is limited deployment of FttH/B networks. Neither the incumbent operator nor the alternative operators have identified an attractive business case to make the necessary investment in large-scale roll-out of fibre-based networks.

8.5.4 Lessons learned

The following lessons can be derived from the case analysis made:

- Our analysis shows that even though German telecommunications policy and regulation are technologically neutral, they impact the deployment of xDSL-, cable- and fibre-based networks in different ways. While policy measures seem to respond beneficially to the needs of xDSL and cable providers, fibre providers – both the incumbent and alternative operators – lack motivation and resources to roll out infrastructure.
- The policy and legal framework has failed to provide sufficient measures for alternative operators to enter into infrastructure-based competition with the incumbent. However, the latest (2012) amendments to the German Telecommunications Law are intended to address this issue; their full effect is yet to be seen.
- Setting high data rate targets as part of the broadband strategy – i.e., pushing beyond the capabilities of xDSL networks – could be instrumental in promotion of fibre and cable development. However, the recent development in vectoring and bonding technologies will extend the life of the copper lines. It may move the alternative operators down the 'ladder of investment', as unbundling becomes more complicated and potentially less attractive, driving alternative operators to procure bitstream-like access instead. With this development, effective infrastructure-based competition becomes more unlikely in the near future.
- With about half of all households being covered by cable networks, infrastructure-based competition nevertheless is likely to grow as users demand increasingly higher data rates.

- The market strength of the incumbent operator remains significant and, thus, justifies continued asymmetrical regulation.
- Mobile broadband networks play an increasingly important role due to the higher data rates they can provide, but at the moment they are predominantly used to ensure basic broadband coverage (1 Mbit/s) and to close the gaps in fixed broadband provision. Fixed access networks continue to provide much higher data rates. Moreover, mobile networks are becoming increasingly dependent on fibre-based fixed backhaul networks.

Technology is another important driver of the broadband development in Germany as the case of the mobile broadband suggests. Commercial use of the LTE standard combined with the prompt auctioning of the required radio spectrum has allowed the closing of the gaps in basic broadband provision and achievement of ubiquitous coverage. Further technological developments in this area are likely to enhance the significance of mobile and wireless broadband beyond the subsistence provision, and current radio spectrum policy consultations are providing the pathway for its deployment.

8.6 Conclusions

In this chapter we have analysed the development of the broadband market in Germany and the results in terms of broadband penetration and competition that have been achieved so far.

The results show that in the fixed broadband market alternative operators have been competing strongly with the incumbent operator by using the regulated copper-based access network of Deutsche Telekom. On the other hand, cable operators have upgraded their networks with DOCSIS 3.0 and have been using their networks to compete head-on with other fixed broadband operators. In the wireless broadband market there are four different operators who are competing intensely to serve end-users.

Policy and regulatory measures have played central roles in these developments, enabling and facilitating access to infrastructure and resources and promoting an investment-friendly climate. However, one-sided incentives and demand-stimulating measures seem to encounter their limits as the market does not react to them according to expectations, especially in failing to supply high-speed broadband to the rural areas. The government is becoming more intensively involved in the supply-side, de-emphasizing demand-oriented activities. Implications of this policy shift may be felt more strongly in the near future, when the announced objectives beyond the basic broadband coverage are to be realized.

References

Börnsen, A. (2009). Breitband? Sofort! . . . Aber wie? Technik und Strategien für die Umsetzung vor Ort. Kurzstudie im Auftrag der Friedrich-Ebert-Stiftung. Berlin: Stabsabt. der Friedrich-Ebert-Stiftung.

Breitbandatlas (2009-02). Part 2: Methodik und weitere Ergebnisse.

  (2013). Bericht zum Breitbandatlas Mitte 2013 im Auftrag des Bundesministeriums für Wirtschaft und Technologie (BMWi). Teil 1: Ergebnisse. Mid-2013.

Bundesministerium des Innern (BMI) (2006). BundOnline 2005: Abschlussbericht – Status und Ausblick.

Bundesministerium für Wirtschaft und Technologie (BMWi) and Bundesministerium für Bildung und Forschung (BMBF) (2003). Informationsgesellschaft Deutschland 2006: Aktionsprogramm der Bundesregierung.

Bundesministerium für Wirtschaft und Technologie (BMWi) and Bundesministerium für Ernährung, Landwirtschaft und Verbraucherschutz (BMELV) (2009). Möglichkeiten der Breitbandförderung: Ein Leitfaden.

Bundesministerium für Wirtschaft und Technologie (BMWi) (2006). iD2010 – Informationsgesellschaft Deutschland 2010: Aktionsprogramm der Bundesregierung.

  (2009). Breitbandstrategie der Bundesregierung.

  (2010). IKT-Strategie der Bundesregierung 'Deutschland Digital 2015'.

  (2011). Rahmenregelung der Bundesregierung zur Bereitstellung von Leerrohren

(Kabelschutzrohren) durch die öffentliche Hand zur Herstellung einer flächendeckenden Breitbandversorgung (BRLR).

(2012). Mobile Informationsgesellschaft der Zukunft. Diskussionspapier 'Mobile Media 2020'.

Bundesnetzagentur (2011). Ermittlung des Frequenzbedarfs in den Bereichen von 880-915 MHz sowie von 1725–1785 MHz und von 1820–1880 MHz für den drahtlosen Netzzugang zum Angebot von Telekommunikationsdiensten ab dem 1. Januar 2017.

(2012). Szenarien zur künftigen Bereitstellung von Frequenzen in den Bereichen von 900 MHz und 1800 MHz und in den weiteren Frequenzbereichen. (Szenarienpapier Projekt 2016).

(2013a). Strategische Aspekte zur Verfügbarkeit von Frequenzen für den Breitbandausbau in Deutschland.

(2013b). Konsultationsentwurf zur Anordnung und Wahl des Verfahrens zur Vergabe von Frequenzen in den Bereichen 700 MHz, 900 MHz, 1800 MHz sowie im Bereich 1452–1492 MHz für den drahtlosen Netzzugang.

(2013c). Jahresbericht 2012.

Bundesrahmenregelung Leerrohre (2011). Rahmenregelung der Bundesregierung zur Bereitstellung von Leerrohren (Kabelschutzrohren) durch die öffentliche Hand zur Herstellung einer flächendeckenden Breitbandversorgung. Retreived from www.zukunft-breitband.de/SharedDocs/DE/Anlage/ZukunftBreitband/rahmenregelung-der-bundesregierung-zur-bereitstellung-von-leerrohren-angepasst.pdf?__blob=publicationFile

Bundestag (2009). Pakt für Beschäftigung und Stabilität in Deutschland zur Sicherheit der Arbeitsplätze, Stärkung der Wachstumskräfte und Modernisierung des Landes. Retrieved from: http://archiv.bundesregierung.de/Content/DE/Artikel/2009/01/2009-01-22-infos-konjunkturpaket-cvd.html

Cava-Ferreruela, I. and Alabau-Muñoz, A. (2005). Evolution of the European Broadband Policy: Analysis and Perspective. Retrieved from http://userpage.fu-berlin.de/~jmueller/its/conf/porto05/papers/Cava%20Ferreruela.pdf.

Christmann, S., Enßlin, H. and Wachs, F.-C. (2005). Der Markt für Breitbandkabel in der digitalen Übergangsphase – Ordnungspolitische

Herausforderungen für die deutsche Medienpolitik. *MultiMedia und Recht*, 291–294.

CJEU (2009). Judgment of Court of Justice of the European Union of 3 December 2009, European Commission v Federal Republic of Germany, case C-424/07, ECR [2009] I-11431.

Deutsches Institut für Wirtschaftsforschung (DIW) (2004). Rahmenbedingungen für eine Breitbandoffensive in Deutschland.

Dialog Consult-VATM (2011). 13. Telekommunikationsmarktanalyse Deutschland 2011.

(2012). 14. Telekommunikationsmarktanalyse Deutschland 2012.

(2013). 15. Telekommunikationsmarktanalyse Deutschland 2013.

DSLWEB (2007). DSLWEB Marktreport Q1 2007. Retrieved from: www.dslweb.de/.

European Commission (2000). Commission's Recommendation on Unbundled Access to the Local Loop enabling the competitive provision of a full range of electronic communications services including broadband multimedia and high-speed internet, 2000/417/EC.

(2002). Communication from the Commission to the Council, the European Parliament, the Economic and Social Committee and the Committee of the Regions. eEurope 2005: An information society for all, COM(2002) 263 final.

(2005). Communication from the Commission to the Council, the European Parliament, the Economic and Social Committee and the Committee of the Regions. i2010 – A European Information Society for growth and employment, COM(2005) 229 final.

(2010a). Commission Decision 2010/267 of 6 May 2010 on harmonised technical conditions of use in the 790–862 MHz frequency band for terrestrial systems capable of providing electronic communications services in the European Union, OJ L 117/95 of 11.05.2010.

(2010b). Communication from the Commission. Europe 2020 – A European strategy for smart, sustainable and inclusive growth, COM(2010) 2020 final.

European Commission (2013). Commission Staff Working Document. Digital Agenda Scoreboard 2013, SWD (2013) 217 final.

European Communities (1990). European Directive 90/387/EEC of 28 June 1990 on the establishment of the internal market for telecommunications services through the implementation of open network provision (ONP), OJ L 192/1 of 24.07.1990.

(2000). Regulation (EC) No 2887/2000 of the European Parliament and of the Council on Unbundled Access to the Local Loop, OJ L 336/4 of 30.12.2000.

(2002a). Directive 2002/19/EC of the European Parliament and of the Council of 7 March 2002 on access to, and interconnection of, electronic communications networks and associated facilities, OJ L 108/7 of 24.04.2002.

(2002b). Directive 2002/21/EC of the European Parliament and of the Council of 7 March 2002 on a common regulatory framework for electronic communications networks and services, OJ L 108/33 of 24.04.2002.

(2002c). Directive 2002/22/EC of the European Parliament and of the Council of 7 March 2002 on universal service and users' rights relating to electronic communications networks and services, OJ L 108/51 of 24.04.2002.

GAK-Rahmenplan (2011): Grundsätze der Förderung der integrierten ländlichen Entwicklung, Teil II, Teil B 'Breitbandversorgung ländlicher Räume'.

Gesetz über die Gemeinschaftsaufgabe 'Verbesserung der regionalen Wirtschaftsstruktur' (GRW-Gesetz) of 6 October 1969 (BGBl. I S. 1861), last amended by Article 8 of the law of 7 September 2007 (BGBl. I S. 2246).

Gesetz über Gemeinschaftsaufgabe 'Verbesserung der Agrarstruktur und des Küstenschutzes' (GAK-Gesetz) of 3 September 1969, as amended by publication of 21 July 1988 (BGBl. I S. 1055), last amended by Article 9 of the law of 9 December 2010 (BGBl. I S. 1934).

Gesetz zur Umsetzung von Zukunftsinvestitionen der Kommunen und Länder (Zukunftsinvestitionsgesetz) of 2 March 2009, BGBl. I S. 416, 428.

Goldmedia (2013). Dritter Monitoringbericht zur Breitbandstrategie der Bundesregierung. Studien im Auftrag des Bundesministeriums für Wirtschaft und Technologie.

Grundgesetz für die Bundesrepublik Deutschland (GG). Basic Law for the Federal Republic of Germany in the revised version published in the Federal Law Gazette Part III, classification

number 100-1, as last amended by the Act of 11 July 2012.

Kind, B. and Schramm, M. (2012). Infrastrukturrecht nach dem neuen TKG 2012. *N6R*, **3**–4, 140–148.

Kommentar zum Telekommunikationsgesetz (TKG-Kommentar) (2013), 3rd edition, A. Berndt and F.J. Säcker (eds.), Frankfurt/Main: Deutscher Fachverlag.

Koordinierungsrahmen der Gemeinschaftsaufgabe 'Verbesserung der regionalen Wirtschaftsstruktur' ab 2009 (GRW-Koordinationsrahmen).

Körber, T. (2011). TKG-Novelle 2011: Breitbandausbau im Spannungsfeld von Europäisierung, Regionalisierung und Netzneutralität. *MultiMedia und Recht*, **4**, 215–221.

Kühling, J. and Neumann, K.-H. (2012). Ökonomische und rechtliche Rahmenbedingungen zum Ausbau und zur Finanzierung von Breitband-Hochleistungsinfrastrukturen in dünn besiedelten Gebieten. In R. Inderst, J. Kühling, K.-H. Neumann und M. Peitz (Eds.), *Der Ausbau neuer Netze in der Telekommunikation*, Baden-Baden: Nomos, 165–226.

Möschel, W. (2001). Die Öffnung der Breitbandkabelnetze für den Wettbewerb – Die Sicht der Monopolkommission. *MultiMedia und Recht-Beilage*, 13–19.

Nettesheim, M. (2009). Die Wirtschaftsverfassung des Telekommunikationssektors: Der grundsetzliche Rahmen. In F.J. Säcker (Ed.), *Berliner Kommentar zum Telekommunikationsgesetz*, Frankfurt/Main: Verlag Recht und Wirtschaft GmbH, 183–207.

OECD (2013). Broadband Portal. Historical time series. Fixed and Wireless Broadband Penetration. June 2013. Retrieved from: www.oecd.org/internet/broadband/oecdbroadbandportal.htm.

Petzel, R. (2006). Das Versteigerungsverfahren nach dem Telekommunikationsgesetz: Rechtsfragen an die Herkunft und Entwicklung der Nutzungsrechtsvergabe am Funkfrequenzspektrum als Regulierungsfolgerecht, Hamburg: Kovač.

Telekommunikationsgesetz (TKG) of 25 July 1996, BGBl. I S. 1120, Retrieved from www.gesetze-im-internet.de/bundesrecht/tkg/gesamt.pdf.

new revised version of 22 June 2004 BGBl. I S. 1190.

new revised version of 9 May 2012 BGBl. I Nr. 19.

Thome, R. (2006). Von BundOnline 2005 zu DeutschlandOnline. *Wirtschaftsinformatik,* **48**, 301–303.

Virnich, M. (2003). Universal Mobile Telecommunications System – Eine aktuelle Bestandsaufnahme. Retrieved from: www. milieuziektes.nl/Rapporten/. Virnich_UMTS_AktuelleBestandsaufnahme.pdf.

WIK (2012). Analyse der Kabelbranche und ihrer Migrationsstrategien auf dem Weg in die NGA-Welt. *WIK Diskussionsbeitrag Nr.* 365. February 2012.

United Kingdom

CHAPTER 9

RICHARD CADMAN

9.1 Introduction to the case study

Like other OECD[1] and EU countries, the UK now has a mature broadband market with penetration above 80% of households[2]. This places the UK ninth in the OECD and sixth in the EU league tables of broadband adoption. Today, the average headline access data rate is around 9.4 Mbit/s, however, the two principal network operators, BT and Virgin Media, have upgraded their networks to offer access data rates of up to 100 Mbit/s in the more densely populated areas of the country. The UK government had the objective of all households having access to at least 2 Mbit/s by 2012, which might be considered unambitious.

Where the UK differs from other countries is that it was the first country to adopt 'equivalence of input' (EOI) and 'functional separation' of the incumbent operator, BT, to enhance competition in the broadband market. The functional separation of BT came about as a result of a set of Undertakings[3] signed between BT and the regulator, Ofcom, in 2005, following the Telecoms Strategic Review (TSR). The purpose of EOI and functional separation was to deter BT, which was the dominant provider of unbundled local loops and wholesale broadband access, from discriminating against its retail competitors. At the time of the TSR discrimination, in particular non-price discrimination, was considered a major roadblock to the development of a dynamic broadband market. Such behaviour

by the dominant firm may be hard to detect by entrants and regulators, and it may have been the expectation, rather than the experience, of discrimination that concerned rival operators. Nevertheless, Ofcom stated in its second TSR document that competing operators who rely on BT for access 'have experienced twenty years of:

- *Slow product development;*
- *Inferior quality wholesale products;*
- *Poor transactional process; and*
- *A general lack of transparency.*'[4]

Since the adoption of the Undertakings in the UK, other countries, notably Sweden, New Zealand and Australia, have also adopted versions of functional separation, while Italy introduced a form of functional separation in 2002 (see Chapter 10). In 2009 the European Union adopted a revised Framework Directive in which functional separation was included as an exceptional remedy that national regulatory authorities (NRAs) could impose on firms with significant market power (SMP) if all other remedies had not corrected competition problems[5].

This case study, therefore, concentrates on Ofcom's Telecoms Strategic Review and the resulting Undertakings. Section 9.2 describes the state of the broadband market prior to the adoption of the Undertakings in 2005. Section 9.3 examines the TSR, setting out the background to the review; summarising the responses from some of the players

---

[1] Organisation for Economic Co-operation and Development (OECD).
[2] Source: Ofcom, 'Telecommunications Market Data Update, Q2 2013.
[3] Ofcom *Final statements on the Strategic Review of Telecommunications, and undertakings in lieu of a reference under the Enterprise Act 2002,* 22 September 2005.

[4] Ofcom *Strategic Review of Telecommunications: Phase 2 Consultation Document,* (para. 1.19).
[5] Directive 2002/19/EC of the European Parliament and of the Council of 7 March 2002 on access to, and interconnection of, electronic communications networks and associated facilities (Access Directive) as amended by Directive 2009/140/EC, Article 13a.

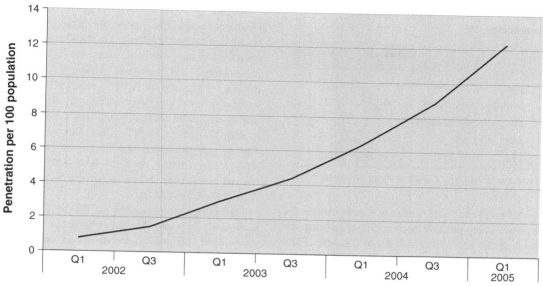

Figure 9.1 Broadband penetration, UK, 2002–2005
Data source: ECTA Broadband Scorecard.

in the market; and finally describing the key remedies of equivalence of input (EOI) and 'functional separation' defined in the Undertakings. Section 9.4 describes the market today and shows how both the retail and wholesale broadband markets have evolved since the Undertakings. Section 9.5 presents the case conclusions.

9.2 The broadband market before 2005

Broadband was first made commercially available in the United Kingdom in April 1999 by the two cable operators, NTL and Telewest[6], although BT did not launch a commercial DSL service until July 2000. BT was relatively late in launching commercial DSL compared with its counterparts in other European countries.

By the first quarter of 2005 (just before the implementation of the Undertakings), penetration had reached 7.25 million lines, 31% of households. The rate of growth was beginning to accelerate, as can be seen in Figure 9.1.

Table 9.1 shows the launch date of cable and DSL in the five largest EU member states together with the penetration level by June 2005, by which time the UK had the second-highest level of penetration in this group of countries.

At the time, the market was dominated by ISPs who resold BT's bitstream products. These firms accounted for 46% of all broadband customers. BT and the two cable companies had 1.8 million and 2.1 million customers respectively. The share of the market taken by LLU was very small: just 39,500 customers. The average data rate of broadband access was a little over 1 Mbit/s[7].

At the retail level, the market was relatively competitive. No firm had a market share greater than around 24%, which compared well with countries such as France and Germany, where France Telecom and Deutsche Telekom had retail market shares closer to 50%. However, at the wholesale level there was a very different picture. As most retailers relied on BT's infrastructure to provide services, BT had a wholesale market share of around 70%.

[6] These two companies have since merged to form Virgin Media.

[7] Source: Ofcom, author's calculation.

Table 9.1 Broadband launch dates and penetration, UK

	Launch DSL	Launch Cable	Penetration June 2005
France	November 1999	1997	32%
Germany	August 1999	2001	23%
Italy	December 1999	-	28%
Spain	1999	2000	22%
UK	July 2000	April 1999	31%

Data source: OECD, ECTA Broadband Scorecard.

Although the retail market was competitive, the overwhelming reliance of competitors on bitstream products for access meant that they had little if any opportunity to differentiate their products from BT's. In essence BT set all the parameters of service quality from access data rate to repair times and there was no ability for its rivals to provide a higher quality services. Therefore, BT's competitors could only compete by charging a lower price, and so needed to have lower retail costs.

Further, BT's dominant position in the wholesale market and its presence in the retail market led to the potential to discriminate against its downstream rivals, although no such discrimination was ever proven. Discrimination can take either price or non-price forms. Price discrimination refers to the charging of a different price for an essential input to internal and external customers, without any cost-based justification. External customers are usually charged the higher price and so are unable to compete with the vertically integrated firm. Non-price discrimination refers to providing lower quality of service to external customers compared with the integrated firm's own retail business. Longer installation times, longer repair times and slower product development are all examples of non-price discrimination. This behaviour is designed to advantage the integrated firm and harm its rivals[8].

Starting in April 2003, Ofcom's predecessor, Oftel, conducted an *ex ante* review of the wholesale broadband access (WBA) market. This review, conducted under the Communications Act 2003, which implemented the European Union's Common Regulatory Framework (CRF)[9], found BT to have significant market power (SMP) in the WBA market and Oftel therefore imposed a number of *ex ante* obligations on BT in the relevant market. The obligations that a national regulatory authority (NRA) may impose on firms with SMP on the relevant market are set out in Articles 9–15 of the Access Directive (AD).

Two obligations imposed on BT by Oftel are particularly important for the purposes of this case study. First, BT was under an obligation of 'No undue discrimination'. How the Communications Act 2003 and Oftel interpreted this obligation is central to understanding the actions that Ofcom took as a result of the TSR.

Article 10AD describes the obligation of non-discrimination and consists of two paragraphs:

1. *A national regulatory authority may, in accordance with the provisions of Article 8, impose obligations of non-discrimination, in relation to interconnection and/or access.*
2. *Obligations of non-discrimination shall ensure, in particular, that the [SMP] operator applies equivalent conditions in equivalent circumstances to other undertakings providing equivalent services, and provides services and information to others under the same conditions and of the same quality as it provides for its own services, or those of its subsidiaries or partners.*

The CRF was transposed into UK law by the Communications Act 2003, which entered into force on July 23rd 2003. The non-discrimination obligation is set out in Section 87(6)(a) which allows the regulator to impose *'a condition*

---

[8] There has been substantial academic analysis on the incentives of vertically integrated firms with upstream market to harm their rivals in downstream markets. For a good discussion in the context of the UK telecoms sector, see M. Cave, L. Correa and P. Crocioni (2006), Regulating for non-price discrimination: The case of UK fixed telecoms, in *Competition and Regulation in Network Industries* 2006 (3).

[9] The CRF is a set of five Directives designed to establish a consistent regulatory process across the EU based on the principles of competition law, although with market investigations, or 'reviews' conducted *ex ante*.

requiring the dominant provider not to discriminate unduly against particular persons, or against a particular description of persons, in relation to matters connected with network access to the relevant network or with the availability of the relevant facilities.'

In neither the EU Directive nor the UK law is discrimination banned outright. Article 10AD requires only that the operator 'applies equivalent conditions in equivalent circumstances' whilst UK law proscribes the dominant provider from 'unduly discriminating'.

In a document discussing how it intended to impose access obligations under the new regulations, the then-regulator, Oftel, gave guidance as to its interpretation of non-discrimination.[10] Perhaps the most significant section is 3.8, which reads:

> Non-discrimination' does not necessarily mean that there should be no differences in treatment between undertakings, rather that any differences should be objectively justifiable, for example by:
>
> a) differences in underlying costs, or
> b) no material adverse effect of competition.

In section 3.11 Oftel says that it would find differences in underlying costs to be a valid justification for making different products available on different terms to different parties.

The implication of the above is that BT could legitimately treat external customers differently from its own downstream business if such different treatment was objectively justifiable. Such a difference in treatment would not technically be discriminatory, although it may feel that way to a competing operator.

In 2005 Ofcom, which replaced Oftel as the regulator in 2004, set out guidelines for how it would investigate potential cases of discrimination on competition grounds[11]. It described undue discrimination as 'when an SMP provider does not

reflect relevant differences between (or does not reflect relevant similarities in) the circumstances of customers in the transaction conditions it offers, and where such behaviour could harm competition' (page 7). Ofcom then provides the example of the SMP operator providing different levels of reliability to customers in similar circumstances at the same price 'and this was capable of harming competition between the two customers'. 'Customers' here includes the downstream division of the vertically integrated SMP provider that competes with an external customer.

Material harm to competition is therefore a critical element of the meaning of discrimination as defined in UK law.

Although BT was never found to have behaved in such a manner, nevertheless and as we shall discuss later, the problem of discrimination became central to Ofcom's Telecoms Strategic Review and led directly to the obligation in the Undertakings of 'equivalence of input'.

The second relevant obligation imposed on BT was accounting separation, which is described in Article 11 AD:

> A national regulatory authority may, in accordance with the provisions of Article 8, impose obligations for accounting separation in relation to specified activities related to interconnection and/or access.
>
> In particular, a national regulatory authority may require a vertically integrated company to make transparent its wholesale prices and its internal transfer prices inter alia to ensure compliance where there is a requirement for non-discrimination under Article 10 or, where necessary, to prevent unfair cross-subsidy.

The need for accounting separation was described by the Director General of Oftel in his 2003 consultation on financial reporting in which he states:

> Financial reporting is an essential part of regulation. As an economic regulator, the Director frequently requires high quality financial information from regulated companies. This is because certain obligations placed on regulated companies require rigorous and effective monitoring in order to ensure compliance and, in the case of

---

[10] Oftel (2002) *Imposing Access Obligations under the new EU Directives*, sections 3.4–3.11.

[11] Ofcom (2005) *Undue discrimination by SMP providers: How Ofcom will investigate potential contraventions on competition grounds of Requirements not to unduly discriminate imposed on SMP providers.*

non-compliance, allow the Director to take appropriate action.[12]

One of the specific reasons given for the need for cost accounting is that the SMP operator can demonstrate its compliance with the non-discrimination obligation (para. 2.3). This view is supported by the European Regulators Group (ERG):

> *Accounting separation should ensure that a vertically integrated company makes transparent its wholesale prices and its internal transfer prices especially where there is a requirement for non-discrimination.*[13]

The ERG makes it clear that the accounting separation obligation exists to counter price discrimination, where an SMP operator charges a higher price externally than it does internally. It is also an instrument to make transparent any inappropriate cross-subsidy, for example between a product subject to competition and a monopoly product allowing the dominant firm to appear to be reducing its costs, and therefore prices, in competitive markets whilst raising them in monopoly markets. Cave and Martin describe the central benefit of accounting separation:

> Separate accounting with identical interconnection and internal transfer prices provides the regulator ex post with information about the profitability of wholesale services, and enables him or her to detect abuse of monopoly power in the bottleneck facility by observing and comparing rates of return earned on 'wholesale' and 'retail' activity.[14]

Accounting separation has three problems. First, if an upstream monopolist faces different costs to serve its internal and external customers then it may legitimately charge different prices. Secondly, the regulated firm has an incentive to assign costs strategically by over-allocating costs to monopoly parts of the business and reducing costs in the competitive areas. Finally, accounting separation provides no transparency for non-price discrimination. The upstream monopolist still has the incentive to harm its rivals and detection is still difficult.

It is this third problem which was of most concern to competitive operators, and eventually to Ofcom. Whilst accounting separation could make transparent, and therefore deter, price discrimination, it was of no use in preventing non-price discrimination.

9.3 The Telecoms Strategic Review

9.3.1 The market before the review

The UK first introduced competition in the telecoms market in 1984 with the licensing of Mercury Communications as the sole competitor to BT in domestic markets. In return Mercury entered into commitments to develop a domestic trunk network, but relied on BT for local access, except in some business districts. It used the Cable & Wireless international network for overseas calls. In 1985, Oftel determined interconnection prices between the two firms that were initially favourable to Mercury, as a method of supporting entry.

In 1991, following the UK government's review of the duopoly, this period of 'managed competition'' drew to an end as other firms were permitted to enter the market. The end of the duopoly allowed cable companies, until then permitted to offer telephony only in partnership with Mercury or BT, to enter the market providing infrastructure-based competition to BT, which was Oftel's preferred form of competition.

A further policy designed to support infrastructure competition was differential access prices for service-based and infrastructure-based competitors. The former had to buy inputs from BT at discounted retail prices, whilst the latter could buy at lower wholesale rates that were the same as BT charged internally[15].

---

[12] Oftel (2003) *Financial Reporting Obligations in SMP Markets: A consultation on accounting separation and cost accounting*, para. 2.1.

[13] European Regulators Group (2003) *ERG Common Position on the approach to Appropriate remedies in the new regulatory framework*, page 49.

[14] M. Cave and I. Martin (1994), The costs and benefits of accounting separation *Telecommunications Policy* 18 (1), 12–20.

[15] For a more detailed analysis of competition before the TSR, see Cave and Williamson (1996) Entry, Competition

By the time of the review, the UK telecoms market was more competitive than most other markets at the retail level. BT had a market share of around 25% in the retail broadband market, 82% of exchange lines and 60% of fixed traffic[16]. BT's strength in the calls market came from 'other calls' (including calls to free dial-up internet access), which accounted for 47% of all minutes and in which BT had a 70% market share. By contrast, BT had only a 34% share of international call minutes, although such calls were only a small part of the market (just 2.3%).

9.3.2 The review

As early as 2002 some players in the telecoms market began to lobby for a strategic review of telecoms regulation and the break-up of BT[17]. Those who argued for a review believed that the market was being held back by the vertically integrated nature of BT and that separation would increase dynamic competition in retail markets. They argued that investment by competitors was being held back because they expected BT to use its integrated structure to sabotage any product development by rivals, thus preventing investors from earning a reasonable return on any investment. It was not necessary for BT actually to have harmed its rivals for them to change their behaviour; all that was required was an expectation of discrimination to deter investment. Although there is little hard evidence to support the claim that investment was being held back, the very low uptake of LLU can be seen as backing up the claim. In July 2004, there were just 13,000 LLU lines out of a total of 4.4 million broadband access lines.

Ofcom launched the TSR in April 2004 with a first phase consultation document[18] in which it set out the purpose of the TSR as to:

assess the options for enhancing value and choice in the UK telecommunications sector. It will have a particular focus on assessing the prospects for maintaining and developing effective competition in the UK telecoms markets, while also considering investment and innovation (para. 3.2).

Ofcom set out its analysis of the sector looking both at the level of competition at the time and towards the future with an analysis of technology trends. Stakeholders were asked 'five fundamental questions' and sixteen more detailed questions. The five fundamental questions were:

Question 1: In relation to the interests of citizen-consumers, what are the key attributes of a well-functioning telecoms market?

Question 2: Where can effective and sustainable competition be achieved in the UK telecoms market?

Question 3: Is there scope for a significant reduction in regulation, or is the market power of incumbents too entrenched?

Question 4: How can Ofcom incentivise efficient and timely investment in next generation networks?

Question 5: At varying times since 1984, the case has been made for structural or operational separation of BT, or the delivery of full functional equivalence. Are these still relevant questions?

In the Phase 1 consultation document, Ofcom found a mixed picture of benefits to UK consumers. It found, for example, that whilst there was plenty of competition in the fixed voice market, most of this was based on service provision and that BT still provided most access infrastructure, despite Oftel's policy of infrastructure competition. Similarly, BT dominated the broadband access market at wholesale level, although the retail market was competitive[19]. Ofcom's overall conclusion, therefore, was that the 20 years of competition prior to the TSR resulted in only partial benefits for UK consumers in both residential and business markets.

Responses were received from over eighty interested parties, including fixed and mobile operators,

---

and Regulation in UK Telecommunications, *Oxford Review of Economic Policy,* 12 (4), 100–121.

[16] Source: Ofcom *Telecoms Market Data Tables, Q2 2005.*

[17] Notably Cable & Wireless, for whom the author worked as a consultant on a project related to the separation of BT.

[18] Ofcom (2004) *Strategic Review of Telecommunications: Phase 1 Consultation Document.*

[19] Ibid, page 22.

consumer representative organizations, independent experts and individuals with no affiliation. Although the responses were wide ranging, a central theme to emerge was the problem of discrimination and the ineffectiveness of the legal/regulatory regime to prevent such behaviour. Some operators went further and argued that both Article 10AD and the UK law allowed dominant operators to discriminate by not providing equivalent products in equivalent circumstances.

In its response to the TSR, Cable & Wireless, then the UK's second-largest fixed line operator and which had absorbed Mercury Communications in 1997, stated:

> By far the biggest issue for this review is the problem of discrimination as regulating to prevent discrimination remains the key unsolved problem of regulation. Although there are existing regulatory rules and structures to deal with the problem of discrimination, in practice they have been ineffective in preventing BT from favouring its own operations.
>
> The examples of such discrimination are endless. In the world of broadband, BT was allowed to create an LLU[20] product which was prohibitively expensive, not industrialised and not fit-for-purpose, which meant that it was entirely unsuitable for mass-market take-up. The result is that there is currently virtually no competition in broadband based on LLU. In the world of narrowband voice, there is a similar story to tell. The basic monopoly access network building blocks to narrowband competition, such as call origination, carrier pre-selection and wholesale line rental have all been made available to BT's competitors on sub-standard terms, such that the cost base of competitors, and the maximum functionality they can offer to customers, are compromised. Again, the result is that BT has been permitted to retain an artificially high market share in narrowband voice to the detriment of innovation and of end-users.[21]

Energis, another competitor to BT which has subsequently been acquired by Cable & Wireless,

discussed the problem of 'undue discrimination'. It stated:

> Oftel's approach to equivalence (in common with many regulators in telecommunications around the world) took as its starting point a formal requirement for equal treatment (or non-discrimination) and then engaged in a series of compromises based on equivalence of outcome to produce the detail of regulatory decisions.
>
> The essence of this approach can be seen in the debate over the use of the term 'undue' discrimination. This approach embedded the concept of 'due' discrimination in the regulatory regime, allowing differences between the systems that BT used to supply itself, and competitors, where there were 'objectively justifiable' differences. The problem with that approach is that it assumed that Oftel would be effectively empowered to distinguish between 'due' and 'undue' discrimination. While in many cases this approach seems to have worked, in other markets, that hasn't been the case.[22]

Energis was established in 1992 by the national electricity transportation network, National Grid. It used National Grid's network to develop a fibre-optic trunk network which formed the basis of its offering to business customers. Energis, through its subsidiary PlanetOnline, worked with the electronics retailer Dixons to create Freeserve, an Internet service provider (ISP) providing free dial-up Internet access based on an 0800 number. At its peak in 2000, Energis had a stock market valuation of £10 billion, however in July 2002 it was placed into receivership and was acquired by Cable & Wireless in 2005 for a little under £600 million.

The essence of these responses was that preventing discrimination was not enough when the obligation of 'no undue discrimination' allowed justifiably different treatment by the dominant firm of its own downstream business and that of its competitors and allowed different treatment when there was no material effect on competition.

Cable & Wireless's example of LLU provides a good example. LLU allows competitive operators to rent the copper local loop that runs between

---

[20] Local Loop Unbundling.
[21] Cable & Wireless *Response to the Ofcom 'Strategic Review of Telecommunications Phase 1 consultation document'*.

[22] Energis *Response to the Ofcom 'Strategic Review of Telecommunications Phase 1' consultation document*.

the local exchange and the customer premises. The LLU customer needs to install its own equipment in the local exchange to allow broadband signals to be sent over the local loop. It can then sell that service to consumers. BT, like other incumbent operators in their own countries, does not use LLU to provide broadband access themselves. So BT's retail division was buying a different product from its competitors[23].

There was a similar concern with narrowband or traditional voice access products. The externally supplied product is known as wholesale line rental (WLR) and allows a downstream competitor to rent from BT a local exchange line conditioned for voice services. BT itself did not use WLR to provide voice services at the time of the TSR.

Referring back to the legal definitions of discrimination, BT could well argue that differences between internal and external cost and terms were justified and that therefore they were not discriminating under the definition of 'undue discrimination'.

However, such a defence was unnecessary as no discrimination cases were successfully brought against BT: indeed Ofcom did not find explicit evidence of discrimination during its review. What became clear, however, was that competing communications providers (CPs) lacked confidence in a system that allowed BT to duly discriminate as evidenced by the paragraphs from the Cable & Wireless and Energis responses quoted above. The expectation of different treatment was enough to change the behaviour of downstream competitors.

On 18 November 2004, Ofcom issued its Phase 2 consultation document.[24] This reviewed the comments received from the first phase and put forward specific proposals for future regulation of the electronic communications market.

Central to Ofcom's analysis in Phase 2 was the concept of 'enduring economic bottlenecks'

(para. 1.17) which it described as those areas of the network where 'effective, infrastructure based competition is unlikely to emerge in the medium term'. In possibly the most damning paragraph in the Phase 2 consultation, Ofcom said that competing operators who rely on BT for access '*have experienced twenty years of*:

- *Slow product development;*
- *Inferior quality wholesale products;*
- *Poor transactional process; and*
- *A general lack of transparency.*' (para. 1.19)

Ofcom concluded that the 'no undue discrimination' remedy by itself had proved inadequate to address the competition problems caused by economic bottlenecks and that a stronger remedy was needed. It partially laid the blame at the door of its predecessor, Oftel.

Oftel's approach might be characterized as accepting certain differences of outcome which arise from the existence of asymmetrical inputs for BT's downstream businesses and those of third parties, provided these were not material or deliberately or perversely created by BT to impede competition. Oftel worked to ensure that wholesale products specifically designed by BT under regulatory pressure were as close to being fit-for-purpose as possible. But clearly this approach has not resolved the continuing problems of lack of equality of access in a number of areas. Firstly, BT faces weak incentives to comply and, as a result, the achievement of fit-for-purpose products which BT itself has no interest in using or selling has required a high degree of regulatory intervention. Secondly, the process permits differences between the treatment of BT's wholesale customers and its own retail activities which, while relatively insignificant in isolation, constitute significant disadvantages when taken in combination. (para. 6.11)

In the last sentence of this quote, Ofcom discusses what has been referred to as 'cumulative materiality'. This is the idea that it is possible for there to be many minor differences between an internal and an external wholesale product which, when each difference is taken alone, appear unimportant but which when they have a cumulative impact can result in a significant disadvantage for the external customer.

---

[23] Ofcom also agreed with this statement by C&W. In the Phase 2 consultation document it said 'We believe that similar stories could be told about carrier pre-selection, wholesale line rental, partial private circuits and indirect access in their early days' (para. 6.3).

[24] Ofcom *Strategic Review of Telecommunications: Phase 2 Consultation Document*.

9.3.3 Equivalence of input

Ofcom's principal proposal arising from the TSR was to strengthen the non-discrimination remedy by requiring what it termed 'real equality of access' which would prevent BT having justifiable reasons for providing different services internally and externally. This would require 'equivalence' at the product level and clear behavioural changes by BT.

At the product level, Ofcom stated that equality of access implies BT's wholesale customers should have access to:

- the same or a similar set of regulated wholesale products as BT's own retail activities;
- at the same prices as BT's own retail activities; and
- using the same or similar transactional processes as BT's own retail activities. (para. 1.36)

Ofcom termed these characteristics of equality of access 'equivalence of input'. One purpose of the proposal was to strengthen the incentives for BT to provide fit-for-purpose wholesale products without intrusive regulation.

Ofcom also stated that it was important that there is equivalence throughout the product development process and product life cycle. It implied that BT's wholesale customers have the same ability as BT's retail activities to introduce changes or have problems addressed.

The final stage of the TR was the issuing by Ofcom of a 'Statement' including a set of undertakings by BT in lieu of a reference under the Enterprise Act 2002[25]. Paragraph 2 (Definitions and Interpretation) of Annex A sets out what is meant by Equivalence of Input

'Equivalence of Inputs' or 'EOI' means that BT provides, in respect of a particular product or service, the same product or service to all Communications Providers (including BT) on the same timescales, terms and conditions (including price and service levels) by means of the same systems and processes, and includes the provision to all Communications Providers (including BT) of the same Commercial Information about such products, services, systems and processes. In

particular, it includes the use by BT of such systems and processes in the same way as other Communications Providers and with the same degree of reliability and performance as experienced by other Communications Providers. (page 61)

Since the signing of the original Undertakings a number of amendments have been introduced and brought together in a consolidated version. In this consolidated version 'same' is helpfully defined as meaning 'exactly the same'.

Whereas the non-discrimination requirement left room for some degree of ambiguity, the definition of EOI makes it clear that BT must provide exactly the same products internally and externally under the same conditions, etc.

The list of products to which EOI was applied is set out in paragraph 3.1 of the Undertakings. These are:

a) Wholesale Analogue Line Rental
b) Wholesale ISDN2 Line Rental   } WLR
c) Wholesale ISDN30 Line Rental
d) Wholesale Extension Service   (WES)
e) Shared Metallic Path Facility   (SMPF)
f) Metallic Path Facility   (MPF)
g) IPStream
h) Backhaul Extension Service   (BES)

These products existed at the time of the TSR and were offered by BT in the wholesale market. Thus it can be argued that they had to be reverse engineered to be offered under EOI terms.

However, the Undertakings also commit BT to providing certain (at the time) future services on an EOI basis (para. 3.1). These are listed as:

a) Wholesale Extension Service Access Product;
b) Wholesale Extension Service Backhaul Product;
c) Wholesale End-to-End Ethernet Service;
d) IP based Bitstream Network Access products that are the successors to IPStream or DataStream; and
e) A successor product to Wholesale Line Rental if:
  i) such a product is provided using BT's NGN, based on Multi-Service Access Node (MSAN) access; and

---

[25] Ofcom (2005) 'Statement' (see note 3).

ii) BT is determined by Ofcom to have SMP in a Network Access market or markets which includes that product.

Looking further to what was in 2005 the future, the Undertakings place certain obligations on BT regarding the provision of next-generation networks (NGN). Section 11 of the Undertakings makes it clear that BT will provide network access to its NGN on an EOI basis.

The Undertakings seek to ensure that BT designs-inequivalence of inputs into future products. Thus whilst there may have been a cost associated in ensuring that 'old' products were made fit for EOI, new products should not incur the same costs.

Ofcom also introduced the concept of 'equivalence of outcome' which was a weaker form of equivalence, more akin to non-discrimination, and was applied to products that at the time were expected to become redundant as they were overtaken by new services such as those listed above.

The difference between the *ex post* remedy of non-discrimination applied *ex ante* and the design of the specific *ex ante* remedy is central to an understanding of the Undertakings and their impact on the UK telecommunications market.

EOI was and remains a radical change from the 'no undue discrimination' requirement placed on BT in markets where it has SMP. Under the non-discrimination approach, BT did not have to design-in to existing products and processes the equality of treatment of internal and external customers. Each could use a different product and process and differences between the two could be justified, allowing BT to charge different prices or to impose other non-price terms.

BT, or indeed any other incumbent firm, could legitimately argue that its network was built for use by a single integrated firm and was not designed for access by other networks. It was designed to carry calls from the calling party to the receiving party (end-to-end calling) and not to pick up calls or deliver calls to other (national) networks. Therefore, BT could argue that it faced lower costs to deliver a call end-to-end on its own network than to carry calls to or from an interconnected network. Likewise it could argue that it could provide different order-processing systems internally and externally.

Therefore, under the definition of non-discrimination adopted by Ofcom, its treatment of internal and external customers differently was objectively justifiable and therefore not unduly discriminatory. Nevertheless, industry participants and Ofcom determined that the competition policy principle of non-discrimination was not sufficient to stimulate effective and sustainable competition downstream of the economic bottleneck and so a stronger, specifically *ex ante* remedy was required to overcome the incentive to discriminate.

That remedy, equivalence of input (EOI), requires equal treatment to be designed into products. BT's commitment in the Undertakings is to provide the 'same' product, timescales and information with the same degree of reliability. BT is also expected to respond to requests for new services from wholesale customers using the same process: i.e., it should not distinguish between a request from BT Retail and external customers.

There has been no legal testing of equivalence but it would seem unlikely from the unequivocal wording of the Undertakings that BT could claim external customers were not in an 'analogous situation' to their internal customers.

Equivalence can therefore be regarded as a specifically *ex ante* approach to redress incentives for discrimination, whereas the 'no undue discrimination' obligation was an *ex post* remedy applied *ex ante*.

9.3.4 Functional separation

In the Undertakings, BT also agreed to a change its organization form and incentives for managers. The new organization form became known as 'functional separation' though the term itself is not used in the Undertakings. BT made a significant number of commitments, the three most important and relevant of which were to establish:

- *a separate Access Services business unit with a separate brand name:* One of the first deliverables from BT was the establishment of Openreach, a new business unit separated from the rest of BT with responsibility for providing the majority of the input equivalent wholesale products. Although not explicit within the

Undertakings, it was a perceived aim of BT, through establishing Openreach, to develop a different culture which treated all of its customers in an equivalent manner. The introduction of Openreach ensured that there was a 'clean' interface with all the operators competing in the downstream markets and greater transparency for monitoring compliance with the Undertakings;

- *a Code of Practice for employees:* it was obviously essential that the detailed set of commitments made in the Undertakings was understood clearly by the employees affected and so a simple code of practice was needed, backed up by training and support services for employees;
- *an Equality of Access Board (EAB):* this body provided an independent means to monitor the implementation and administration of the Undertakings, to ensure that BT remains compliant with its commitments. Although it is a body internal to BT, its independence comes from the fact that three of its five directors are required to be independent of BT.

The purpose of these organisational changes was to remove the incentive to discriminate and so to facilitate the implementation of equivalence of input. Openreach managers have a set of incentives that are not connected to the overall performance of BT, but only to the performance of Openreach. In theory at least, this should encourage managers only to consider their own division, rather than the effect of their decisions on the profitability of other divisions or the business overall.

9.3.5 Parallel actions

The signing and implementation of the Undertakings were not the only actions taken by Ofcom to attempt to stimulate the take up of LLU and therefore change the competitive dynamics in the UK market. Two other actions were important: Ofcom's review of the wholesale local access market (WLAM) and the setting up of the Office of Telecoms Adjudication (OTA).

In May 2004, Ofcom began its market review of the WLAM in line with its obligations under the CRF. The review defined the market on technologically neutral grounds such that both copper local loops and the cable access networks fell in the same market definition. Ofcom found BT to have SMP in the relevant market and so imposed a number of *ex ante* remedies designed to ensure access to local loops by third parties on fair and reasonable terms.

For the purposes of this case study, the most important obligation placed on BT was that of cost orientation. Condition FA3 of the formal Notification required that BT provide network access for a price that was 'reasonably derived from the costs of provision based on a forward looking long run incremental cost (LRIC) approach and allowing an appropriate mark up for the recovery of common costs including an appropriate return on capital employed.'

To establish the appropriate cost oriented price, Ofcom also investigated BT's weighted average cost of capital (WACC) calculating a separate WACC for BT's low-risk local access network business and the rest of the company, and the value of BT's copper network. Both these consultations provided Ofcom with evidence that allowed it to reduce the price of both fully- and partly- unbundled local loops.

Table 9.2 shows the development of the price of fully- and partially-unbundled loops from 2002–2009[26]. The data show a sharp decline in the monthly rental average cost of the first year between 2003 and 2005 with some fluctuation of charges since then but at prices between one-half and two-thirds of the 2005 price.

The substantial reduction in the price of unbundled local loops would clearly have a significant impact on the economics of unbundling for competitive operators and may well have been at least as important as the functional separation of BT in encouraging investment by competitors.

The second parallel development was the establishment of the Office of Telecom Adjudicator (OTA) in 2005, now superseded by OTA2.

---

[26] Data source: European Commission Implementation Reports 2003–2009. These prices are shown in euro in the Implementation Report. Prices have been converted to Sterling and then back to euro using the average exchange rate for the period.

Table 9.2 Cost of LLU, UK, 2002–2009

	Euro	
	Full	Partial
2002	24.27	21.50
2003	24.27	21.50
2004	15.44	6.28
2005	10.48	3.12
2006	12.77	2.12
2007	12.77	3.06
2008	10.25	3.04
2009	11.06	3.16

Data sources: European Commission, Implementation Reports 2003–2009.

The principal purpose of the OTA was to ensure that the processes for LLU and other 'current generation' access products (for example, wholesale line rental) were industrialised and 'fit for purpose'. It was technically independent of both Ofcom and the industry although its accommodation was provided by Ofcom and its members were representatives of BT and its competitors.

The original OTA was established to 'facilitate swift implementation of the processes necessary to enable competitors to gain access to BT's local loop on an equivalent basis to that enjoyed by BT's own businesses. The Telecommunications Adjudicator will also be able to bring all parties together to find a prompt mediated resolution of working-level implementation disputes.'

OTA2 has a slightly different objective: 'OTA2 will facilitate the swift implementation of processes where necessary to enable a wider range of Communications Providers and End Users to benefit from clear and focused improvements, in particular where multi-lateral engagement is necessary.'

The OTA2 website sets out a six point 'vision':

- the OTA2 will champion end user issues;
- Communications Providers will benefit from a competitive telecommunications infrastructure based on Openreach products that has no operational barriers to success;
- there will be implementation (as quickly as is reasonably possible) of new product

functionality, features and services relating to In-scope Products that will be seamlessly introduced;
- migrations between broadband and narrowband products of both BT and other Communications Providers will be seamless, timely and with minimal interruption to service for end users;
- dips in operational quality performance of In-scope Products provided by Openreach will be unusual and will be proactively managed by Openreach to ensure the least impact on Communications Providers and end users; and
- participation by Communications Providers in the OTA2 Scheme will be widespread and representative.

Although OTA2 mentions end users in its objectives, the scheme participants are all drawn from the supply side of the market with no user representatives. The main scheme participants are the larger communications providers: BT, Openreach, BSkyB, Cable & Wireless, Everything Everywhere, Exponential-e, Global Crossing, O2, Scottish and Southern, Talk-Talk Group and Virgin Media. Smaller communications providers are represented through the Federation of Communications Services.

Equivalence of inputs and functional separation, reduced LLU prices and the OTA can be seen as a three-pronged strategy to encourage the development of LLU as the principal wholesale product for broadband access. It may not be possible to separate the effectiveness of any one part of the strategy and of course it may be that the three together were critical to ensure increased adoption of LLU. In the next section of this case study we examine the UK broadband market today, at both the retail and wholesale levels.

9.4 The broadband market today

9.4.1 The retail market

Broadband penetration has increased substantially since July 2005 and now stands at 22.1 million lines or 83.7% of households[27]. This level of

---

[27] Source: Ofcom, *Telecommunications Market Data Update, Q2 2013.*

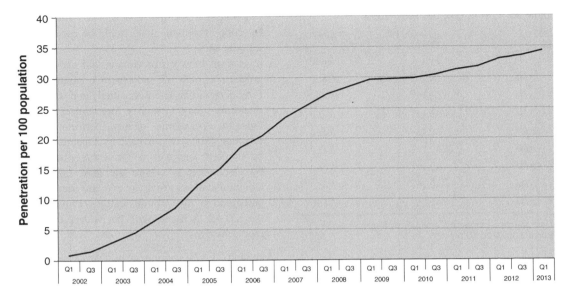

Figure 9.2 Broadband Penetration, UK, 2002–2013
Data sources: ECTA; Ofcom.

household penetration places the UK ninth in the OECD countries and 6th in the EU, behind Sweden, the Netherlands, Denmark, Finland and Luxembourg. South Korea, Iceland and Norway also have higher levels of household penetration than the UK.

Figure 9.2 below extends Figure 9.1 to cover the period 2002–2013. A comparison of the rate of growth of broadband lines in the UK before and after the Undertakings shows no significant difference: diffusion of broadband continues to show the classic 'S' shaped growth. There appears to be a slowdown in the growth of broadband in the wake of the 2008 financial crisis, with growth resuming in late 2010.

The retail broadband market has also seen substantial consolidation amongst suppliers. The four largest suppliers (BT, Sky, TalkTalk and Virgin Media) now have a combined market share in excess of 90%. At the time of the Undertakings, neither Sky nor TalkTalk was a significant player in the retail market, so both have entered the market on the back of an improved climate for LLU.

Sky's market growth has been largely organic, benefiting from its strong position in the Pay-TV market to cross sell broadband to its existing customer base. TalkTalk Group, by contrast, has been acquisitive, acquiring the UK customer bases of AOL and Tiscali.

Table 9.3 shows various acquisitions that have taken place in the market over the period 2006–2009.

Ofcom explains the spate of mergers and acquisitions in the sector by the increased need for scale as a result of the increase in the uptake of LLU. For each unbundled exchange, the unit costs fall with each additional subscriber, meaning that scale is important for an ISP operator to be profitable, compared with using wholesale bitstream products from BT.

Whilst consumers' choice of supplier may have diminished since 2006, consumers have benefited from an increase in the average connection speeds available.

Figure 9.3 shows the average actual broadband data rates for the period 2009–2013, which has grown steadily from 4 Mbit/s in 2009 to over 14 Mbit/s in 2013. Between 2012 and 2013 there was an exceptionally large increase in actual access data rates as more customers signed up to 'superfast' broadband products based on fibre to the cabinet or DOCSIS3.

Table 9.3 Selected ISP mergers, UK, 2006–2013

Date	Target	Acquirer
June 2006	Be Unlimited	O2
July 2006	Toucan	Pipex
July 2006	Bulldog (retail customer base)	Pipex
August 2006	Video Networks	Tiscali
October 2006	AOL UK	Carphone Warehouse
July 2007	Pipex	Tiscali
July 2009	Tiscali	Carphone Warehouse
February 2013	Virgin Media	Liberty Global
March 2013	O2 (Domestic broadband)[28]	Sky

Data source: Ofcom Communications Market Report 2013.

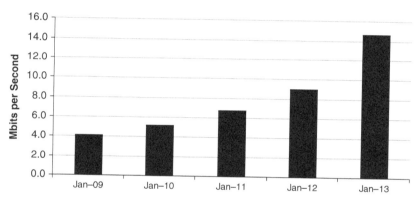

Figure 9.3 Average broadband connection data rates, UK, 2009–2013
Data source: Ofcom.

This increase in average connection data rates has largely been driven by the upgrade of DSL lines from ADSL to ADSL2$^+$ and by the upgrade of the Virgin Media cable network to DOCSIS3.

Table 9.4 below shows a selection of super-fast broadband implementations and trials as identified by Ofcom in July 2009.

Since July 2009, there have been a number of further announcements, in particular by BT and Virgin Media.

In October 2010, Virgin Media announced plans to upgrade to 100 Mbit/s from December 2010 with the entire network being upgraded by mid-2012[29]. In March 2011, Virgin Media announced that its 100 Mbit/s service had passed one million homes and was on track to meet the 2012 deadline. In November 2013, Virgin Media announced plans to increase the access data rate to over 150 Mbit/s to all of the 12.5 million homes its network passes in 2014[30].

BT has responded to Virgin Media's various upgrades, and arguably to political pressure, by launching Fibre to the Home (FttH) and Fibre to the Cabinet (FttC) products, which it retails under

[28] Note: Sky acquired only O2's domestic UK broadband business and not the mobile network.

[29] Virgin Media press release 27 October 2010.
[30] Virgin Media Press Release 11 November 2013.

Table 9.4 Selected super-fast broadband implementations and trials, UK, July 2009

Company	Deployment type	Max. download data rate	Technology	Where	Scale	When
Virgin Media	Commercial	50 Mbit/s	DOCSIS 3.0 cable	Virgin Media cable footprint	12.6 mln homes by summer 2009	Roll-out started Q4 2008
Fibrecity (H2O Networks)	Commercial	100 Mbit/s	FttH	Bournemouth and Dundee	c.88,000 homes on completion	Rollout started Q1 2009
Titanic Quarter (Redstone plc)	Commercial	100 Mbit/s	FttH	Belfast	5,000+ homes on completion	First tenants in H2 2009
BT	Commercial	Burst to 100 Mbit/s	FttH	Ebbsfleet valley	10,000 homes on completion	Serving <100 homes
Virgin Media	Trial	200 Mbit/s	DOCSIS3.0 cable	Ashford, Kent	c.100 homes	May 2009 for six months
BT	Pilot	40 Mbit/s	FttC	Muswell Hill and Whitchurch	c.15,000 homes	Deployed in July 2009

Data source: Ofcom Communications Market Report 2009.

the brand 'Infinity'. This fibre based service provides access data rates of up to 40 Mbit/s. Infinity was first trialled in exchanges in London, Cheshire and Glasgow and in January 2014 was available in around 1,900 local exchange areas covering over 75% of UK homes[31].

In January 2013, according to the EC Broadband Scorecard, 14.5% of broadband lines provided data rates of 30 Mbit/s up to 99 Mbit/s, while 0.9% provided data rates of 100 Mbit/s or above.

9.4.2 Broadband services

With the growth in the average access data rate has come a change in how the Internet is used. One of the most important applications that demands high bandwidth is 'catch-up TV', through services such as BBC i-player, and the equivalent from the other TV channels, which has enjoyed particularly strong growth. In March 2013, there were 272 million requests for TV and radio programmes on BBC i-Player, up from 78 million in 2009[32]. Equivalent data on ITV Player were not available.

BT has also entered the TV market offering IPTV over its FttC/H network. In 2013 BT secured the rights to show Champions League football matches live with a bid of over £800 million putting it squarely in competition with Sky's and Virgin Media's TV offerings. In fact, over 2013 there has been a noticeable shift in the locus of competition in broadband markets from Internet access to TV, with products such as 'Sky plus' and Virgin Media's TiVo becoming increasingly popular.

9.4.3 The wholesale market

Whilst there have been many changes in the retail market, it is perhaps the wholesale market that has seen most change since the Undertakings were signed.

In 2006, 2010 and 2013, Ofcom conducted market reviews of the wholesale broadband access

---

[31] Source: SamKnows. Website www.samknows.com checked 24 January 2014.

[32] Source: BBC i-player Monthly Performance Pack, March 2013.

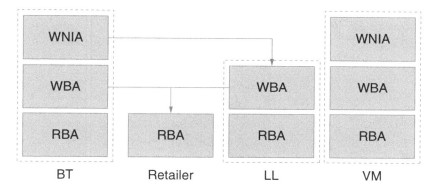

Figure 9.4 Broadband market structure, UK, 2013

Legend: WNIA: Wholesale Network Infrastructure Access (Market 4 in the EC 2007 Recommendation); WBA: Wholesale Broadband Access (Market 5); RBA: Retail Broadband Access (not included in the 2007 Recommendation); VM: Virgin Media (the cable operator).

(WBA) market . This market lies at the intermediate level between the wholesale local access market (WLAM) and the retail broadband market (RBM). Whereas BT and Virgin Media self-supply the whole broadband value chain, most other ISPs operate only in the WBAM or retail market. LLU operators enter at the WBA level, buying unbundled local loops as their input, while retail ISPs enter at the retail level, buy bitstream access either from BT or an LLU provider that operates in the WBA market, as illustrated in Figure 9.4. It should though be noted that most LLU operators also buy bitstream access from BT in areas where it is uneconomic for them to place their own equipment in exchanges and purchase unbundled loops.

When Ofcom's predecessor, Oftel, first reviewed the WBAM in 2003, it was only able to identify one national market[33] and Oftel found BT to have SMP in that market. By the time Ofcom reviewed the market again in 2006 and 2010, it found there to be three geographic markets based on the number of LLU operators plus Virgin Media present in

exchange area. According to the 2010 market definition the three markets are defined as:

- Market 1: exchanges where only BT is present (11.7% of premises);
- Market 2: exchanges where two Principal Operators (POs) are present or forecast and exchanges where three POs are present or forecast but where BTs share is greater than or equal to 50 per cent (10.0% of premises); and
- Market 3: exchanges where four or more POs are present or forecast and exchanges where three POs are present or forecast but where BTs share is less than 50 per cent (77.6% of premises).

In the final statement Ofcom found BT to have SMP in Markets one and two, but no firm was found to have SMP in Market 3. This means that in exchange areas covering more than three quarters of all premises, BT is no longer dominant. Although the market definitions and size of the markets was somewhat different in the 2006 WBAM review, the finding of SMP was the same.

By 2013, the market had developed yet further and Ofcom found only two markets:

- Market A: exchange areas where there are no more than two Principal Operators (POs) present or forecast to be present, which accounts for 9.6% of UK premises.

---

[33] For historic reasons the city of Kingston upon Hull in northeast England has never been part of the BT network. Therefore Oftel in fact found two geographic markets, 'the Hull area' and the rest of the UK. For the purposes of this case study, however, we shall ignore the Hull area.

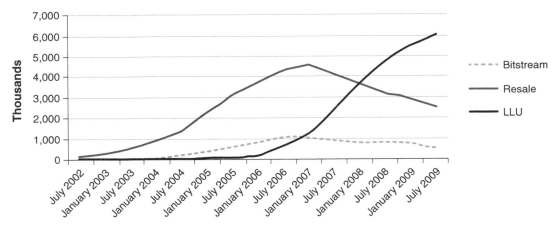

Figure 9.5 Wholesale copper access methods, UK, 2002–2009
Data *source:* Based on ECTA Broadband Scorecard.

- Market B: exchange areas where there are three or more POs present or forecast to be present, which accounts for 89.7% of UK premises[34].

This finding is a major change from the 2003 market review. Ofcom found that effectively competitive markets were operating below the retail level and thus the retail market in some 90% of the UK was not dependent on regulation at the wholesale level, albeit it is dependent on regulation at the LLU level.

This change in the market structure, and thus the finding of SMP, has come about because ISPs have substituted LLU for bitstream or wholesale access. TalkTalk Group now has over 2,700 exchanges enabled, covering some 24 million homes within 5 km from the exchange, 97% of all households. Sky has enabled over 2,300 exchanges covering 23.3 million homes within 5 km[35].

Figure 9.5 shows the number of wholesale copper access lines, i.e., those not offered by BT, by type: resale, bitstream and LLU. Resale lines peaked in January 2007 as LLU began to take an increasing share of the market. Until January 2006 almost no customers accessed broadband via LLU, but by January 2008 LLU was the most popular single method of wholesale copper access and by July 2010 two-thirds of wholesale copper access lines were via LLU. In July 2010 some 29% of all retail access lines were via LLU, whilst bitstream and resale combined reached around 22%.

Over the same period, cable's share of the market has declined from 59% to 20%. In part, this decline is due to BT extending its broadband availability to around 99% of homes whilst cable still only reaches about 55% of homes: BT's larger physical reach ensures that twisted copper wire has been able to gain a larger market share.

What we have seen in the UK therefore is a dramatic change in the nature of competition from one based on a mix of cable and the reselling of BT's bitstream products, to one where LLU has a significant and growing market share with unbundled loops largely replacing bitstream.

This change in the wholesale market is important as LLU allows ISPs considerably more control over their own products. Whilst care should always be taken over simple correlations, especially over time, Figure 9.6 shows a strong correlation between LLU as a share of all competitive copper access lines and the weighted average access data rate enjoyed by users. However, it should be noted

---

[34] Source: Ofcom, *Review of wholesale broadband access markets* 1 August 2013. The Hull area accounts for the remaining 1.3% of households.
[35] Source: www.samknows.com.

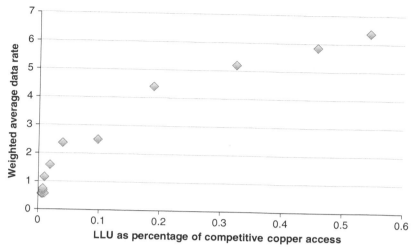

9.6 Relationship between LLU and average access data rate, UK, 2002–2008
Data source: Ofcom.

that the greatest percentage increase in access data rates happen when LLU had only a very low market share (less than 10%).

9.5 Conclusions

During the decade 2000–2010, the UK broadband market has experienced substantial changes. Cable broadband was launched in 1999 and a DSL version with a wholesale variant was not available until 2000. The few customers who took up broadband could only get access data rates of 512 kbit/s. Today, over 80% of households have a fixed broadband connection and the market is still growing, although the rate of growth has slowed. Access data rates of up to 100 Mbit/s are available to all households passed by the Virgin Media network and rates of at least 40 Mbit/s to around 85% of households passed by the BT FttH/C network.

Until 2005 the broadband market was relatively undynamic: other than Virgin Media, BT's rivals relied on BT's wholesale bitstream products which meant that they could not differentiate the service quality they offered customers. Local loop unbundling (LLU) had hardly been taken up in 2005, with just a few tens of thousands of lines

unbundled. However, access via bitstream meant that barriers to entry were low and so the retail market was fragmented compared with many other countries which had a retail market dominated by the incumbent operator.

The market today is very different. LLU is now prevalent throughout the country and the level of competition in the WBA market is such that Ofcom has been able to find exchange areas covering some 90% of the population free from a firm with significant market power. This change has largely come about because Ofcom forced through three key regulatory changes in 2005: EOI and the functional separation of BT; reduced LLU prices and the creation of the OTA with a brief to make LLU work.

Since that time we can see a 'virtuous circle' evolving as LLU-based ISPs installed more advanced DSLAMs, based on ADSL2$^+$ and ADSL Max, allowing them to offer access data rates of up to 24 Mbit/s. Both BT and Virgin Media have responded to this competitive pressure by investing in FttC/H and DOCSIS3.0 respectively, allowing them to offer 'super-fast' broadband. As higher data access rates have become available, Internet usage has changed to take advantage of this higher bandwidth, with catch-up TV being a particularly popular application.

The rate of diffusion of broadband amongst UK consumers appears to have been hardly affected by the regulatory changes of 2005. However, there have been a number of fundamental changes in the structure of the market and the quality of services available to consumers since 2005.

The regulatory reforms introduced by Ofcom in 2005 can be said to mark the watershed between the relatively undynamic early days of broadband and the more dynamic second half of the decade. What cannot be concluded with any degree of certainty is the effect any individual reform had or whether it was the package of the three reforms together that helped change the market. The much-heralded reform of EOI and functional separation may have been necessary but there is insufficient evidence to know whether it would have been sufficient in the absence of lower prices and the OTA. What can be concluded with certainty, however, is that UK consumers today enjoy the advantages of a highly competitive market, much higher data access rates and a lower price per Mbit/s than their predecessors did in 2000 or indeed 2005.

Italy

DAVIDE GALLINO, CLAUDIO LEPORELLI AND ALBERTO NUCCIARELLI

10.1 Introduction to the case study

This section highlights the latest developments of the Italian telecommunications market. The main body of this chapter is focused on the development of broadband, covering fixed and mobile networks. Section 10.2 briefly recalls, for an understanding of the starting conditions, the historical developments including the early days of liberalization. Section 10.3 illustrates the correlation of television and broadband. Section 10.4 moves on in the analysis to investigate the development of the broadband sector, the role of unbundling, and the investments levels. Section 10.5 discusses, the model of functional separation and equivalence of Telecom Italia (TI). Section 10.6 covers current developments with FttX and LTE, and Section 10.7 reviews the achievement of the Digital Agenda targets. Section 10.8 provides the case analysis and Section 10.9 provides the conclusions.

The growing Italian broadband market is still typified by the 'original sin': that is, the lack of a cable-TV operator[1] and the inherent competitive pressure that might come with it. Absent CATV, the broadband market chiefly relied on local loop unbundling and bitstream access and has moved, to a certain extent, towards a complementarity between landlines and mobile networks. In 2013, the number of fixed lines decreased, down 2.3% year over year (YoY), from 21.8 to 21.3 million. At the same time the number of broadband lines increased: + 2% YoY from 13.6 to 13.9 million lines, as the average connection data rate grew: +23% YoY. Further increases were noted in the number of IPv4 addresses: +12% YoY.[2]

With regard to mobile broadband, more than 32 million SIMs were used for mobile data traffic (+20% YoY, 2Q 2013). Mobile broadband also contributed to foster overall connectivity, since 4.8% of citizens had access to broadband only over wireless networks. Some 8.8% of the Italian citizens using fixed networks were below the 'digital divide' in 2013: 3.8% had no DSL; 3.2% of broadband connections had data rates under 2 Mbit/s; 2% had 'nominal' or inconsistent coverage due to the length of the lines and other factors affecting performance. The resulting total was a (fixed and mobile) broadband divide figure of 4%.[3]

While the performance of fixed and mobile networks remains substantially different so far, fixed/mobile substitutability is a trend bound to become more important when 3.5G and 4G broadband access services can perform at a similar level to the alternative DSL broadband services, or can compensate for the lack of broadband service in low-density areas.

It is difficult to quantify how broadband is being used in micro-businesses (3 to 19 people), which represent the bulk of the Italian economy, due to overlap with residential broadband usage within families and their closer circles. However, data published by the National Institute of Statistics (ISTAT) in December 2013 showed that about 67% had a company website, about 44% sold goods using e-commerce in 2013 and 96.8% of SMEs with at least ten employees used a broadband connection to the Internet in 2013.[4] With regard to households, in 2013, 60.7% had a broadband connection to access the Internet, with some differences between north and south.

---

[1] See Section 10.3 for details.
[2] Sources: AGCOM, 2Q 2013 and, for capacity and IP addresses, *Akamai's Second Quarter, 2013 State of the Internet Report*.

[3] All data in this paragraph sourced by AGCOM, 2Q 2013.
[4] Source: ISTAT, the National Institute of Statistics.

Of the population above six years of age, 54.8% used the Internet and 33.5% used the Internet almost daily in 2013[5]. It is fair to say, looking at this data, that 2013 marked a huge step up in broadband consumption, for both households and companies.'

Historically, the lack of CATV, together with a strong presence of commercial free-to-air television, has led to durable monopolistic conditions. Those were alleviated by the deregulation imposed by the European legislation (which in Italy essentially started in 1995 with the introduction of 'closed user groups,' to be followed by public voice telephony from 1 January 1998) and implemented by the Ministry of Communications and AGCOM, Europe's first integrated regulator for telecom and media, which started operations in March 1998. The privatization of Telecom Italia (in 1997) also significantly conditioned the early days of telecommunications liberalization in Italy.

The liberalization subsequently focused on wholesale-based competition by creating favourable conditions for the uptake of local loop unbundling (LLU). Linked – again –to television, as the Competition Authority (AGCM) would only allow TI to enter the free-to-air television market in exchange for favourable access conditions to its own civil infrastructure – to the advantage of altnets (alternative network operators) – in 2001.

Regulatory-based access to the civil infrastructure, coupled with an entrepreneurial vision, led to the first attempt in Europe by an alternative operator – E.Biscom/Fastweb – to build a nationwide network based on FttH in 1999. This attempt only partially succeeded, although Fastweb does manage to this day to serve roughly 15% of its customer base (1.9 million in 2Q 2013)[6] with various fibre-based solutions (FttH/FttCurb). Fastweb has also deployed an FttX infrastructure with roughly 2 million homes passed and is now developing its FttCab presence. In addition to this, Metroweb, an infrastructure-only provider, provides FttH access to roughly 0.3 million homes passed in Milan and other cities in northern Italy.

With regard to the overall infrastructural development, the upgrade of the national network is ultimately based on the provision of broadband and ultra-fast broadband (in excess of 30 Mbit/s) in all major cities, using mainly VDSL2$^+$ as a technology and mobile broadband using 3.5G and 4G with important overlaps in coverage. The industrial plan of TI for the period 2014–2016 foresees coverage of 50% of the population based on FttCab and 80% based on LTE.

Lastly, in terms of reinforcing competition in the fixed voice and broadband markets, the importance of the Italian model of equivalence of access should not be underestimated in understanding the actual operating conditions for alternative network operators.

10.2 From the historical network to the early days of liberalization

10.2.1 Telecom 1.0: the history of the Italian telecommunications sector (1853–1995)

In 1853, the Italian government established a government-granted monopoly on long-distance transmissions (i.e., telegraphy service) sanctioning a strong public presence in the telecom sector, with the main consequence that all relationships between the state, the licensee and the customers had to be regulated by laws. A law of 1892 enforced public presence by stating that, on licence expiry, all installations should return to public ownership, without any compensation fee. The main effect of such a normative prescription was to reduce the propensity to invest and, as a consequence, to restrain the increase of users, especially in the smaller cities. However, because of the deployment of the first long-distance networks, from 1904 to 1907 the overall number of customers increased, though remaining far below that of similar European countries.

In 1923, a Royal Decree (R.D. n.339) initially reserved to the state the right of installation and operation of telephone networks for both private and public use. However, in 1925 existing concessions were consolidated and awarded to five

[5] Source: *Le tecnologie ICT nelle Imprese e Cittadini e nuove tecnologie*, ISTAT 19 December 2013.
[6] Source: AGCOM.

private companies (Stipel, Telve, Timo, Teti and Set) for regional telephony and R.D. 884/1925 entitled the state agency ASST (*Azienda di Stato per i Servizi Telefonici*) to coordinate and interconnect them for interregional and international calls. Moreover, other private companies, Italcable, financed by Italian migrants to Argentina, and Italo Radio, were entitled to provide intercontinental telegraph and telephone services from 1921 to 1941, the year that they merged.

The basic rationale of such a governance model for the Italian telecommunications system stemmed from the necessity to avoid a high concentration of services in the hands of a single (private and/or foreign) licensee, while reaching the economic policy objective of using private funds to finance investments, a necessity given the heavy public debts accumulated during World War I.

The radical shift towards the full public control of the telecommunications sector began in the late 1920s and was scaled up in 1933 with the foundation of IRI (*Istituto per la Ricostruzione Industriale*; i.e., the Institute for Industrial Reconstruction, a state-owned conglomerate aimed at counterbalancing the effects of the global depression on the Italian economy) and STET (*Societa' Torinese per l'Esercizio Telefonico*), its sector holding for telephony. STET acquired control of Stipel, Telve, and Timo – i.e., the telecommunications assets of SIP (*Società Idroelettrica Piemontese*) – through the emission of state guaranteed bonds, which could be converted into shares.

STET became public in 1936 and by the end of the conversion process more than the 40% of the equity was in private hands. In 1958 STET also acquired the control of the remaining private licensees (SET and TETI). In 1964, following the nationalization of electric utilities in ENEL, through the enforcement of D.P.R. n.1594/1964, the five regional licensees merged with SIP. Note that the regional electric utilities were also controlled by IRI. Hence the nationalization indemnities obtained by SIP could be used to finance the diffusion and modernization of the telephone services. The merged company was renamed *Società Italiana per l'Esercizio Telefonico* (SIP) and became the nationwide licensee

responsible for almost all telecommunications within and among the 210 newly-established districts. It was controlled by STET but also retained the private shareholders of the previous SIP, who were attracted by the profitability of the telephone business.

In the same year, STET also acquired the control of Italcable and Telespazio (responsible for satellite communications). As a result, STET was entitled to technically and managerially address all the licensees in the telecommunications sector, while the state agency ASST, still in charge of national long-distance and international services, lost much of its strategic role.

Moreover, especially in the 1980s, STET pursued a strategy of vertical integration and expansion in the adjacent industries of the emerging ICT ecosystem: IT services, telecom manufacturing, infrastructure building, research and development, data services, publishing and advertising. The attempt to enter the cable-TV business failed, because of both technical and regulatory problems, and the venture was transformed into a satellite Pay-TV platform.

The redesign of the governance structure of the whole sector spurred a new growth period in terms of users and installations. From 1964 and for almost ten years, a steady growth in the rate of user uptake was recorded, also as a consequence of substantial investments to update the network, the introduction of new tariff policies for both local and long-distance calls, the abrogation of additional fees for residents outside the cities and, last but not least, the low risks associated with a monopolized structure of the sector. In those times, major attention was also given to cost control, reduction of the financial leverage and the use of depreciation for self-financing.

During and after the oil crisis of the 1970s, the sector suffered due to the tariff freeze imposed by the government to try to keep inflation under control.

In contrast, during the 1980s SIP enjoyed a close relation with the government, which provided funds channelled through IRI to increase equity, allowed the increase of tariffs and the decrease of licence fees; and allowed the flow of subsidies from international and long distance traffic to the operation of local networks. SIP also received financial support from the Italian bank CDP (*Cassa Depositi e Prestiti*, which finances public infrastructures using postal savings) and the EIB (European Investment Bank). This enabled the company to sustain heavy capital expenditures in network capacity expansion and modernization, and helped to reduce the gap in infrastructure quality between northern and southern Italy.

The first half of the 1990s saw further important steps in the growth of SIP, such as the activation of the first large-scale mobile network and of the first digital access network – ISDN.

In 1994, the consolidation of the mixed public-private monopoly of telecommunications services controlled by IRI was completed: STET, SIP, Italcable, Telespazio, Iritel (formerly ASST) and SIRM (maritime services) were all merged to form TI.

10.2.2 From monopoly to competition: the early days (1995–1998) and beyond

The public-private telecom monopoly has fostered the development of a telecommunications system with users' interests protected in terms of availability of services and the level of tariffs (within the usual pre-liberalization context of tariff unbalance and publicly-financed universal service obligations). High fixed costs for network deployment and economies of scale justified the monopoly of the access network at a micro-economic level. However, the creation of a European telecom regulatory framework and the ambitious ideas exposed in the Green Paper (1987), substantiated in 1990 by the 'twin Directive set' (Competition in telecommunications and Open Network Provision), eventually led to the liberalization of the Italian market, with sizeable effects on competition. At the same time, the privatization of TI became a core issue at both national and European levels, as it contributed to pay off IRI's debts in other industries and prepare for Italy's adoption of the euro, from 1 Jan 1999 starting with non-physical payments.

A long-term reform process was initiated with State Law n.58/1992 transforming the state agency ASST into IRI-owned Iritel in order to separate ownership and management from regulation. The

reform of the governance system was more precisely defined in 1995 and 1997 by the establishment of the regulatory authorities for public utility services (State Law 481/1995) and the actual setting up of the *Autorità per le Garanzie nelle Comunicazioni* (AGCOM, the telecommunications and media regulator, Law 249/1997), which began its operations in March 1998 (more on the creation of AGCOM in Section 10.2.4). The new corporate model required major organizational changes such as adopting a divisional structure to make the different lines of business more independent and their individual performances more visible. Moreover, key legislative initiatives targeted the abolition of exclusive and special rights previously assigned to the incumbent. Crucially, D.P.R. 22/12/1994 introduced non-exclusivity for the incumbent in the provision of mobile communication based on GSM technology[7]. Moreover, State Law n.103/1995 – finally transposing EC Directive 90/388 – allowed any European service provider to offer (existing or potential) data services and closed user groups to business customers. Overall, the full transposition of European Directives was quite slow, mostly due to lobbying and delaying actions from established industry groups.

Among the most important steps, was the enactment of D.L. n.546/1996, converted into State Law n.650/1996, which allowed the government to more easily implement the EU directives; State Law 55/1997 and D.P.R. 318/1997 provided the core elements of access and interconnection as well as universal service.

Full liberalization was completed with the (emotional, one could say) award of the first authorization for public voice telephony service in February 1998 to Infostrada (today owned by Wind), quickly followed by a large platoon of network and service operators. The most notable were Fastweb, Wind, BT-Albacom and Tiscali. Vodafone entered the fixed broadband business at a later stage, although today it has a substantial customer base, almost as large as Fastweb. Wind,

---

[7] The TACS service started in 1990. While Telecom Italia was created via the incorporation of four different companies in July 1994, TIM – Telecom Italia Mobile – was established in 1995; at the same time as GSM was launched in Italy.

currently the most important competitor to TI in terms of fixed broadband market share, was born in 1997 as a spin-off of the national electricity incumbent (ENEL). France Telecom and Deutsche Telekom were part of the initial set of key shareholders. However, they soon exited the venture and sold their shares to ENEL. In 2005, ENEL then sold Wind to Wind Telecom S.p.A. (formerly Weather Investments) owned by the Egyptian group that also owned Orascom Telecom. In 2011, Wind became part of the Vimpelcom group, following a merger between the Russian company, with the participation of Telenor, and the Egyptian Orascom Telecom. Wind started off as an integrated fixed and mobile operator and incorporated Infostrada, but was able to exploit this integration only to a certain extent. Today, Wind is a major mobile operator.

10.2.3 The early days of Internet access in Italy

Internet access 'in Italy' (i.e., by means of a permanent physical node) started as early as 1986 in Pisa. Italy was tied for third European country to get on the Net, following the UK and Norway and at the same time as the Netherlands.[8] Generalized access to the Internet was essentially launched as a scientific project – at a cost equivalent to about EUR 2.5 billion – in 1988 to unify the various scientific institutions and their large computers in Italy by means of a single network, GARR (*Gruppo Armonizzazione Reti della Ricerca* – from the ministerial committee which gave its name to the network).

The first commercial ISPs for residential users appeared several years later, in 1992–1993, building on their experience with bulletin board systems (BBS). In 1994 I.net became the first ISP for business customers, joined a little later by IT.NET.

I.NET and IT.NET used links provided by Unisource and Pipex, respectively. However, the carrier network, the landing points of the marine cables and all the core connections that made

narrowband traffic possible were almost entirely provided by TI; without TI little would have happened in this regard.

However, as noted in other countries, the incumbent was essentially taken offguard with respect to the 'early adoption of the Internet' when considered as a mass-market for businesses (which TI only entered in 1996) and residential customers (with TI's first offer in 1998, under the brand name of TOL – Telecom Italia Online).

With regard to the residential market, the uptake of Internet access (with very slow and expensive connections, especially if long distance calls were required) was a bottom-up affair, more from the edge than from the core. Especially between 1992–1996, Internet access was mainly propagated by former BBS (bulletin board system) managers turned into service providers. Names like Agorà, MC Link, Video On Line and I.net, amongst others, are early examples of more professional services, all active since 1992–1993. Agorà, based in Rome, was particularly significant as it was born out of necessity, for the Radical party (a small political party, which became an important civil liberties movement in the 1970s) to connect with its many affiliates throughout Europe using the Internet as a means to avoid costly phone calls and faxes. Video On Line (started in 1993) was the first mass-oriented provider and it built on its connection with the research center CRS4, at that time directed by the Nobel prize laureate Carlo Rubbia, also a former director of CERN (where the Web was born). See Figure 10.1 for a screenshot of its home page. Video On Line is (self) credited with hosting Europe's first online version of a daily newspaper (*L'Unione Sarda*) in March 1994.

Tiscali, which was established January 1998, was considered an heir to Video On Line, as they both originated from Sardinia and as it fostered the mass-market adoption of access to the Internet, being the 'ideal type' of a bold, fast competitor, without ever making a profit in more than 10 years of its operations.

Tiscali's key strategic move consisted in pioneering the 'reverse' (indirect) interconnection mechanism. From March 1999 onward, Tiscali

---

[8] Other local networks had temporary connections, also via satellite, already in 1982.

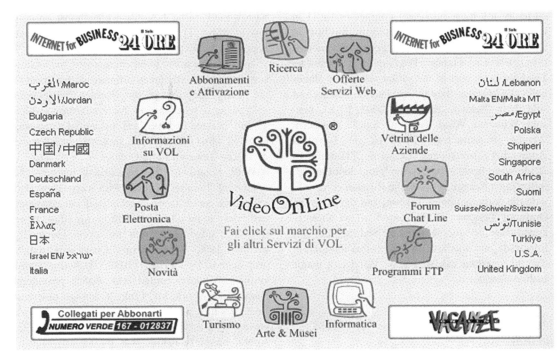

Figure 10.1 Video Online home page, Italy, 1996
Source: Video Online, 1996.

offered a subscription-free Internet service whereby the customers only had to pay for the time they were online. Tiscali then derived its income from the 'indirect interconnection' option, whereby the interconnected operator (TI in this case) pays to a carrier (Tiscali) an interconnection charge for bringing traffic to its network. In other words, TI offered an interconnection service to the third-party operator Tiscali. At the time, giving up paid subscriptions was a bold move, which allowed Tiscali to gain an important share of the market. This made Tiscali's IPO in October 1999 a real success: at the apex of the dotcom bubble, Tiscali exceeded Fiat's market valuation. Tiscali used these financial resources to expand its ISP operations in several advanced European countries. But in subsequent years economic and financial problems forced it to sell all its ventures outside Italy.

Another extremely successful IPO was at the origin of E-Biscom in March 2000. This venture was the result of an agreement with AEM (the energy utility of Milan) to create an infrastructure

company (Metroweb) and a telecoms operator (Fastweb). E. Biscom had participations of 33% and 70%, respectively. E.Biscom was incorporated into Fastweb in 2004.

10.2.4 AGCOM, the first integrated regulator in Europe

AGCOM (*Autorità per le Garanzie nelle Comunicazioni*) was created as a single, or 'integrated/convergent' regulator in July 1997 with the task of applying European legislation in telecoms and media. However, operations only started in March 1998, with the formal appointment of the first board. It was essentially modeled after the experience of the Canadian regulator (CRTC) and the Federal Communications Commission (FCC) in the US. For the first time in Europe, a regulator would be responsible for jointly regulating media and telecommunications. Others, like OFCOM in the UK, followed suit only several years later. AGCOM superseded the Media

Authority[9] and inherited most of its competences from the Ministry of Communications (now part of MISE, the Ministry for economic development), although some job-sharing with the latter continues to this day, especially with regard to the issuance of authorizations, spectrum management and broadband policies. Overall e-policy making, including today's 'Digital Agenda for Italy' initiative, is managed by the Prime Minister's office, together with MISE. In 1998, creating an integrated regulator was ambitious. However, while a number of telecom/media subjects are discussed jointly by AGCOM's board, the management of single regulatory issues remains largely divided between the regulators' offices and treated without too much emphasis on 'convergence'.

On the other hand, being 'convergent' has often put AGCOM at the forefront of regulatory and market developments, sometimes resulting in innovative thinking. Nevertheless, critics have pointed out that, especially with regard to audio-visual matters, the governance of the regulator exposed the regulator to political influence, with a President appointed by the Prime Minister and a board of four Commissioners nominated by the Parliament.

In the end, if regulatory performance should be judged by metrics, it is uncontestable that Italian consumers benefit from low retail prices (including mobile pricing, notwithstanding termination rates which for a number of years remained within the higher bracket of EU members), and ease of choice (one mobile number out of four in Italy is ported). Today, TI has roughly 14 million direct access lines (63% of the access market) while a further 7.2 million lines of its network are managed by altnets. In addition, 0.5 million lines (NGA/FWA) are owned by alternative network operators.[10]

10.2.5 The privatization of TI

A few key points of the privatization of TI are relevant for our discussion on the Italian broadband market.

The privatization model chosen for TI is the subject of several, mostly critical, analyses. They all underline that the original model (a public company with a large set of shareholders) failed to be properly implemented (or, was the problem inherent in the model of choice?) and that, eventually, controlling shareholders emerged and charged the company with high financial leverage. The debt still hampers investment, and has radically down-shifted the position of the company in the international markets. It is difficult to disentangle the complementary effects of privatization, liberalization, pro-competitive regulation, financial bubble and global difficulties of telecom operators in engaging with the Internet world. However, there is no doubt that under these circumstances the privatized company was unable to pursue the same bold growth strategy and to secure to the shareholders the same handsome financial performance as the previous mixed-capital venture.

Essentially, the private TI went through four distinct changes of controlling groups. Firstly, in 1997, the Treasury granted the control of the company to a small nucleus of investors including Ifil (the Agnelli family), Mediobanca and other recently privatized banks, bank foundations[11] and building companies, with the private placement of less than 10% of voting rights. Moreover the Treasury placed most of its other shares through a public offering: about 1.5 million small investors acquired 32% of the equity. The weakness of these initial core investors led to what has been labeled as the largest hostile takeover in European history in 1999: Olivetti bought 51% of the equity through a public offering. The investment, worth more than EUR 30 billion, was financed with debt but also by selling to Mannesmann the control of Infostrada (subsequently acquired by Wind), and that of Omnitel, the second Italian mobile operator, eventually acquired by Vodafone.

The operation, as much as the original privatization, was marked by heavy-handed intervention from political parties leading to a leveraged buy-out which made no economic sense and allowed a

---

[9] *Garante per l'Editoria.*
[10] Source: AGCOM, 2Q 2013.

[11] Bank foundations are a type of not-for-profit organization with a particular fiscal structure.

few key investors to take control of TI through a long chain of Chinese boxes that ended in Bell, a Luxembourg-based holding company.

In 2001, the third change of the controlling group did not require a public offering. Olimpia, an ad-hoc vehicle created by the Pirelli and Benetton groups, banks and some of the Bell shareholders, acquired 23% of Olivetti's equity from Bell, paying twice the market value; EUR 7 billion in cash was sufficient to acquire the control of TI, a company which at the time had a market capitalization of EUR 55 billion.

A lot of divestments, consolidations (between Olivetti and TI) and the buyback of the floating capital of TIM were executed only to help the controlling group to pay its debts. But eventually Olimpia had to give up and a new vehicle, Telco, took control of TI with 23% of equity in 2007. Telefónica of Spain owns more than 40% of Telco and has negotiated a further increase of its holdings, *de-facto* becoming the controlling shareholder of TI. These leveraged buy-outs (LBOs) resulted in a huge debt that peaked at EUR 40 billion in 2005.[12] After years of painstakingly repaying, the debt is 'down' to EUR 28.2 billion as of 31 December 2012.[13] However, for many years investments have been severely constrained in order to assist Bell, Olimpia and now Telco to maintain their control.

10.3 Television, Internet, and mobile broadband

10.3.1 Broadband development: the importance of television in shaping competition and regulation in Italy

No serious discussion on the evolution of broadband in Italy can take place, in our view, if the role of television is not carefully considered. As we pointed out in the introduction, the 'original sin' of Italian broadband is the lack of competitive pressure stemming from the absence of CATV. Television competition also affected access

conditions following regulation introduced by the Competition Authority.

The early liberalization of the free-to-air (FTA) television market, also allowing foreign broadcasters to transmit from Italian territory, was coupled with legislation (DPR 29 Marzo 1973, n. 156) that briskly halted CATV in its infancy. Part of that legislation was later on declared unconstitutional and amended in 1975. However, by then FTA TV was already established as the (cheaper) means of choice for local broadcasters, essentially making the deployment of a nationwide CATV uneconomical.

As around 1995 it became conceivable to use a CATV infrastructure to compete with emerging pay-TV satellite services and as a broadband vehicle, TI chose to invest heavily in the so called Socrate Plan, aimed at deploying a fibre+coaxial cable network in all major Italian cities[14]. This move was criticized as a market pre-emption by the dominant player in infrastructure, as it took place on the verge of full liberalization from 1 January 1998. However, the passive infrastructure was only partially deployed as TI's broadband investments were shifted towards ADSL. The pay-TV company of the TI group (Stream, created in 1997) migrated to satellite and was eventually sold to Newscorp in 2003.

The business model of Fastweb, a joint venture of the Milan municipal utility AEM and e.Biscom, a new entrant that went public in 2000 just before the explosion of the dotcom bubble, also was centred on the convergence between broadband and television. The first investments in Milan benefited from synergies with AEM's existing and new electricity infrastructures. Further expansions in

---

[12] Source: TI's Financial reports 2006.
[13] Source: TI's Financial reports 1Q 2013.

[14] The ambitious broadcasting/broadband network platform project Socrate was to deploy fibre-optic and coaxial cables in the 19 biggest Italian cities, with the target to reach about 10 million people by 2002. The network was meant to have a data rate of 1.5 Mbit/s download and 64 kbit/s upload, providing cable TV programmes and interactive services, and increase the company value within the scenario of the upcoming liberalized market. Right after the privatization had started in 1997, however, the Socrate project slowed down due to changes in Telecom's governance structure and the deployment of xDSL systems over copper networks to enable fast Internet connections to both residential and business customers.

other cities benefited from a landmark decision[15] of AGCM (the Competition Authority) which, as a compensation for allowing TI to enter the analogue terrestrial FTA television market, forced the company to provide non-discriminatory access to all of its civil infrastructure from 1 April 2001. Many kilometres of ducts (3000–6000), all located in premium areas and initially constructed for the Socrate network, were thus reused.

Fastweb – having incorporated E.Biscom and now a part of Swisscom – today has roughly 290,000 live customers served over FttB (Fibre to the Building) and has passed more than 2 million residential or business units. Nonetheless, the overwhelming majority of its customers are now served via DSL technology. In fact, the price range of FttB services initially offered by Fastweb met with relatively limited response; it was not competitive with cheaper ADSL services and triple-play was offered at prices between EUR 50–80 per month. Moreover, at the time Youtube did not exist nor did thousands of other services available today, which probably would have convinced more customers to sign up.

Both TI and Fastweb have for many years, but with limited success, attempted to distribute video content on their networks through proprietary IPTV services, the lack of control on premium content being the main difficulty, even if Newscorp/SKY had been required by the European Commission to sell its premium content on the wholesale market to distributors on different platforms.

The pay-TV sector now sees SKY and the digital terrestrial television (DTT) group Mediaset (controlled by the Berlusconi family) as the main competing actors. Many other small scale local broadcaster adopt a *real estate* business model: i.e., they exploit regulations that might remunerate them when spectrum will be assigned using market mechanisms (probably) to mobile operators, or lease it to operators that need it to enrich their terrestrial offerings. Both attitudes are *de-facto* incentivized by the low administrative price of the spectrum.

At present, the major broadcasters have a mixed attitude with respect to the broadband network. On one hand, they strenuously defend their proprietary platforms against the risk of substitution and the old linear television model against the new video services offered by over the top operators (OTT) via the web. On the other hand, they increasingly use the broadband network as a complement, notably through catch-up TV, and using proprietary set-top-boxes connected to broadband as buffers and storage to realize quasi-on-demand video offerings.

As we will see in the following section, to further increase fixed broadband penetration and make the development of NGA infrastructures economically viable, a big jump ahead in the demand for video services through the broadband network is probably necessary in a country like Italy, characterized by low PC use at home and high diffusion of mobile services.

10.3.2 The evolution of fixed broadband in a mobile nation with low PC penetration

In the 2003–2004 period following strict enforcement of LLU regulations, Italy had the highest relative growth rate of broadband access lines in Europe.[16] In the same period ADSL lines increased from 9.2 to 14.6% of the total European DSL market. By 2005 Italy was relatively well placed in comparison with other EU member states, although cable really made a difference in countries with competing CATV infrastructure such as the Netherlands and the UK.[17] The LLU price reduction continued between 2005 and 2008, fostering the take-up of broadband. However, starting with 2009, a number of price hikes were enacted. This did not reverse the trend of increasing market shares for altnets but, coupled with the outburst of the economic crisis, made the competitive scenario significantly more challenging.

---

[15] AGCM, *Provvedimento* n. 9142 (C4158) Seat Pagine Gialle/Cecchi Gori Communications, Aug. 2000.

[16] In terms of absolute variation, always with reference to the 2003–2004 period, the highest increases were recorded in France and in the United Kingdom, immediately before Italy. Source. AGCOM's annual report, 2005.
[17] Source: SEC(2006)193, Annex to the Implementation Report, EC.

Table 10.1 Fixed access lines, incumbent and altnets, Italy, 2011–2013

Million lines	2Q 2011	3Q 2011	4Q 2011	1Q 2012	2Q 2012	3Q 2012	4Q 2012	1Q 2013	2Q 2013
Telecom Italia fixed access lines	14.99	14.86	14.68	14.48	14.30	14.16	14.00	13.78	13.55
Altnets access lines	7.35	7.31	7.42	7.50	7.53	7.51	7.66	7.76	7.78
Total	22.34	22.16	22.11	21.98	21.83	21.67	21.66	21.53	21.33

Data source: AGCOM 2013.

Table 10.2 Altnets' access lines by technology, Italy, 2011–2013

Million lines	2Q 2011	3Q 2011	4Q 2011	1Q 2012	2Q 2012	3Q 2012	4Q 2012	1Q 2013	2Q 2013
LLU (voice, voice+data)	4.94	4.92	5.02	5.09	5.15	5.18	5.26	5.35	5.38
Wholesale Line Rental	1.02	0.98	0.96	0.93	0.87	0.83	0.80	0.77	0.74
Naked DSL	1.05	1.06	1.09	1.08	1.08	1.06	1.11	1.12	1.11
Fibre	0.29	0.27	0.28	0.28	0.28	0.28	0.29	0.29	0.29
WiMAX	0.06	0.07	0.09	0.11	0.14	0.17	0.19	0.23	0.25
Total	7.35	7.31	7.42	7.50	7.53	7.51	7.66	7.76	7.78

Data source: AGCOM 2013.

In recent years, broadband penetration has continued to grow, despite the on-going recession in the country. Demographics and digital literacy have certainly played an important role in broadband take-up. Similarly to other countries, the absolute number of fixed lines is decreasing constantly, while the percentage of broadband lines (in proportion to total lines) and the market share of altnets are increasing. See Table 10.1 and 10.2.

The detailed, internationally harmonized annual survey of the Italian statistical office (ISTAT) on *Aspects of daily life* shows that the take-up of broadband is still low, although strongly increased in comparison to the previous year: 60.7% of Italian households had a broadband connection at home in 2013. The share of households that had a personal computer at home was 62.8%.

In other words, most of those that appreciate the Internet have adopted a broadband connection but Italy is characterized by a sharp divide in terms of computer literacy, education, age, income, social and employment conditions and regional development; that excludes a surprisingly large part of the population, typically the older and the less educated, from the benefits of the Information Society.

No single factor taken alone is sufficient to explain the divide but many of them are correlated and have a synergistic effect on exclusion. However, low income very often acts as the main barrier for households in which children could promote the adoption. In contrast, the lack of technological skills and of cultural interests are the main barrier for older people.

As Internet adoption continues to grow, albeit at a slow pace, those main factors become even more relevant to characterize the excluded household. See also Table 10.3 and 10.4.

The infrastructural divide does not play a major role in explaining exclusion. However, if broadband services are not available or the quality and speed of the connection is low, further barriers could become evident. With respect to the scope of actually used services and applications: it is doubtful that a demand for ultra-fast broadband connections could reach the critical mass for economic feasibility if consumers don't become regular users of video content services. Note, in particular, that current 3G broadband contracts limit the monthly traffic to 1–2 GB and are therefore unsuitable for regular use of high-quality streaming or near-video-on-demand

Table 10.3 Broadband and PC penetration by household type, Italy, December 2013

Percentage of households with a broadband connection at home and of household owning a PC (within brackets)			
Households with at least one child < 18yrs	85.7 (87.8%)	Households composed of individuals of 65 and over	12.7% (14.8%)
Households living in Northern and Central Italy	63.3% (65.4%)	Southern Italy and major islands	57.2% (55%)

Data source: Istat, Aspects of daily life (*Cittadini e nuove tecnologie*, December 2013).s

Table 10.4 Mobile subscriptions, Italy, 2004–2013

	2004	2006	2008	2010	2011	2012	2013 (Q2)	Penetration (Q2–2013)
Million SIMs	63,153	80,416	90,341	90,605	92,393	92,724	92,683	154%

Data source: AGCOM 2013.

services on connected TV sets. On the contrary, these services could be attractive for elderly people that don't use the Internet but have fixed lines and spend a lot of time watching television.

Another factor that needs to be taken into account when evaluating the broadband evolution in Italy is the traditional divide between desktop penetration and mobile adoption, which in recent years further increased due to the strong take-up of smartphones and tablets and the reduction of active landlines. Traditionally, Italy ranked in the lower echelons of comparable countries in Europe in PC penetration, which is in part a result of lower education and digital literacy rate and an unfavourable demography. However, with 92.7 million SIM cards for a population of 60 million, out of which 34.2 million are SIMs which generate IP traffic (8.6 million are for data-only cards)[18], Italy is certainly a strongly mobile-oriented country.

The mobile trend was set in 1995, with the massive adoption of pre-paid subscription and SIM cards based on top-up recharge. From the same year, post-paid subscriptions were, and continue to be, penalized by a 'luxury' tax. Prepaid subscriptions were first offered by TIM, the mobile brand of TI, as a successful reaction when Omnitel entered the market as the second Italian mobile network operator (MNO).

The relevance of mobile has to be factored in with regard to all future broadband plans. While mobility is key everywhere in the world, particularly in Italy the fourth generation of mobile – with its significant comparative performance advantage over third generation – will almost certainly play a dominant role in broadband penetration overall. This assumption is consistent with the interest shown by MNOs at the time of the auction for LTE frequencies in September 2011, which generated close to EUR 4 billion of revenues for the Italian Treasury.

LTE-based commercial offers are now available from TIM and Vodafone, while Wind is currently deploying its 4G network starting with the most population-dense areas[19]. The current 4G coverage is above 40% of population.[20] Mobile traffic in Italy in 3Q 2012 was up 32% year-over-year.[21]

10.4 Broadband, unbundling and the investment challenge

10.4.1 LLU regulation as a means to foster national infrastructure deployment

In the 'ladder of investment' concept, popularized amongst others by M. Cave (of Warwick University, UK), Local Loop Unbundling (LLU) occupies an important place. While not akin to competition by providing a fully alternative infrastructure, LLU

---

[18] Source: AGCOM, data at 2Q 2013.

[19] H3G withdrew early in the auction for 800 MHz frequencies but purchased rights of use in the upper bands.
[20] Source: TIM October 2013.   [21] Source: AGCOM.

is nevertheless relevant in terms of investments from alternative network operators, although largely based on renting the incumbents' loops.

In Italy, LLU played an important role in creating a level playing field. Its enactment in Italian legislation preceded the European requirements: in 1999, AGCOM started technical analysis, provided guidelines and designed monitoring. TI published its first reference offer in 2000. However, for some years implementation was difficult because of cumbersome procedures and economic conditions that made it hard for altnets to replicate the incumbent's retail offers.

During those years AGCOM was developing, its landmark approach to non-discrimination in fixed telephony (Del. 152/02/CONS), first applied to interconnection costs as the base of replicability of the incumbents' offers. Subsequently, non-discrimination coupled with regulatory accounting were used (Del. 3/03/CIR) to determine that the 'LLU reference offer' for 2003 had to be improved. The incumbent's retail access offers were not replicable by an efficient OLO using LLU, lacking an adequate cost model and considering possible inefficiencies of the access network, while discounting future cost reductions led to the decision to set lower LLU monthly fees, these being reduced to the best European benchmark, the Danish one at EUR 8.30/month[22].

To incentivize the growth of the broadband market and to implement the second EU policy framework (including directives 2002/19/CE, 2002/20/CE and 2002/21/CE), some complementary actions were taken: (1) quicker implementation of the 2002 regulatory framework in a single Code (namely, *Codice delle comunicazioni elettroniche*, D.Lgs 259/2003), and (2) the launch of a national program for broadband development in southern Italy (Law 80/2005)[23] to reduce the digital divide in the south[24].

Meanwhile, the Competition Authority (AGCM) was investigating the non-replicable TI offers to business customers (Case A351, initiated 5 June 2003), which ended with the State Council judgment 1271/2006 of 10 March 2006, resulting in a fine of EUR 115 million imposed on TI). In an attempt to improve its position in the antitrust case, TI agreed to keep the price of LLU stable until December 2006; it was at EUR 8.30/month at the end of 2004. In fact, in subsequent years the monthly fee was further reduced, applying a network cap (until December 2007) and using historical cost data for civil works costs.

In Italy, LLU regulation was thus championed as a means to foster infrastructure deployment. It was expected that lowering prices for renting loops and easing collocation at the central office level would allow for the emergence of stronger competitors, who would be capable of further investments and innovation when building on a sufficiently large customer base, similar to E.Biscom/Fastweb at the turn of the millennium.

However, since 2010, AGCOM reversed the path followed until that moment, allowing for increasing prices for LLU: EUR 8.70/month from 1 May 2010, EUR 9.02/month from 1 January 2011 and EUR 9.28/month from 1 January 2012.

The price increases for unbundling and other wholesale services were made conditional on the verification by AGCOM of the attainment by TI of certain parameters measuring quality improvement and modernization of TI's access network. In 2013, however, changes in the cost model and other considerations related to the cost of capital have led to a generalized reduction in the price of regulated wholesale services, including services provided over next-generation access networks. This decision generated a confrontation with the European Commission, which however ended with AGCOM sticking to the reductions and

---

[22] See Leporelli and Reverberi (2004a and 2004b) for an analysis of the replicability conditions.
[23] Since 2001 AGCOM has mandated unbundling of the local loop (LLU) and the wholesale offers; retail offers were regulated at the time but this is no longer the case.
[24] Although several areas in the north, especially Alpine valleys are still underserved. Ciapanna and Sabbatini

(2008) analysed the development of Italian telecom regulation framework by highlighting the main changes in the Italian law system. They also illustrated the main interventions at national and regional level and explained how the legislation and regulatory environment evolved across the years 1995–2009.

setting up an additional obligation for TI to grant access at the cabinet level.

Overall, notwithstanding a certain continuity in investments in fixed networks, it can be said that in the last five years the development of networks did not occur at the same pace as in some other European countries. For some, this is the consequence of a continuing 'muddling-through' of investment strategies in the fixed networks, which was already visible between 2005 and 2008 (Caio, 2009). For others the explanation is to be found in the weak demand, which for different segments of the population is related to lack of skills or interest or to income problems, and to a minor degree to the lack of advanced applications.

During these years, on one hand, the telecom incumbent focused on convergence and the provision of integrated services, accessible independently of the customers' devices. On the other hand, Fastweb tried to follow the growing demand for higher data rates by offering higher speed over existing lines and IPTV in major Italian cities,[25] rather than developing further portions of the network. Furthermore, as broadly discussed within the ISBUL project,[26] measures on the demand side favoured customers willing to use new broadband services on the base of the existing broadband networks. In fact, incentives were allocated to carriers; as a consequence, they were able to reach final customers only indirectly and did not promote the competition among carriers that favoured broadband diffusion in areas where LLU was deployed. This probably made it possible for some subscribers to pay less for low data rates but did not lead to a better performance or significantly widen the customer base.

Other initiatives, taken at the legislative and policy level, were aimed at fostering the take-up

of broadband services.[27] Specifically, in 2003 the central government initiated a long-term project to bring broadband networks to southern Italian regions to reduce the digital divide. The project was managed by the CIPE[28], coordinated by Sviluppo Italia[29] through Infratel S.p.A.[30] and operated by the latter. Since 2005 the project has been managed through Law 80/2005 – in accordance with regional authorities, carriers and utilities.[31] It aimed to deploy about 1,800 km of fibre – to modernize the primary backhaul network down to central offices and allow for minimal broadband services – in 265 municipalities in southern regions with a budget of up to EUR 230 million.

The digital divide for broadband was reduced to approximately 4% of the population by 2013. Furthermore, the establishment in 2010 of a special committee at ministerial level[32] and a *Memorandum of understanding* among the central government, the regulator, TI and Fastweb fostered the development of a country-wide broadband program to streamline the deployment of fibre networks and to reduce the digital divide in the regions, including the sharing of information and investment plans.

Today, there is still a substantial gap in terms of broadband penetration between Italy and comparable EU member states. The combined effect of private firms' strategies and public policies has led to at least three main effects: (1) the creation of a infrastructural gap between Italy and European

---

[25] Source: ITU, 2005.

[26] Source: ISBUL, 2010. The ISBUL (*Infrastrutture e Servizi a Banda Larga e Ultra Larga*) project was a research initiative initiated in 2009 by the AGCOM to unravel the main determinants of the Italian broadband sector. With a total funding of about EUR 700,000, the project was led by the University of Rome 'La Sapienza' and put together academics from different universities, doing research on broadband economics (www.progettoisbul.net).

[27] See for example the D.Lgs 198/2002.

[28] CIPE (*Comitato Interministeriale per la Programmazione Economica*) is a committee made up of representatives of different ministries with specific competences in the allocation and management of funds to be spent for public investment projects. CIPE Decision n.83/2003 regulated the programme.

[29] Sviluppo Italia S.p.A. was established in 1999 to attract foreign investments and foster the industrial development of southern Italy. In 2007 it was renamed into Invitalia S.p.A. (*Agenzia nazionale per l'attrazione degli investimenti e lo sviluppo d'impresa*).

[30] Infratel S.p.A. (*Infrastrutture e Telecomunicazioni per l'Italia*) is an in-house company of the Ministry of Economic Development and it is responsible for carrying out the Broadband Program.

[31] Source: ISBUL, 2010.

[32] Comitato interministeriale per la banda larga.

forerunners (e.g., Denmark, the Netherlands, Sweden); (2) a substantial stagnation of demand evolution; and (3) the lack of a strong stimulus for the digitalization of public and business activities, with a negative effect on the creation of start-ups, level of investments by service providers and so forth.

10.4.2 Regional broadband development: different models, one target?

The difficulties in implementing a national Digital Agenda are in part related to the Italian institutional framework that assigns concurrent or exclusive authority over many public policies to regions. Moreover, cumbersome procedures and inefficient decisional processes have caused, in many cases, an insufficient and delayed use of the European regional development and cohesion funds. As a consequence, infrastructure deployment initiatives at the regional level are marked by significant differences and their success strongly depends on market, governance and geographical factors (see also Nucciarelli et al., 2013)[33]. A number of regions, provinces, and other local bodies initiated investment in broadband infrastructures in the first years of this century, with the aim of connecting administrative offices and other public service buildings. In contrast, the central government had developed a centralized procurement mechanism for telecommunications services based on public tendering. The Lepida network, conceived in 2002 and owned by Region Emilia-Romagna, is probably the most ambitious project of this kind. It is managed since 2007 by Lepida S.p.A. an in-house service provider owned by the region (and other public bodies, such as provinces,

municipalities and universities, each with a single share). The network has been deployed by sharing ducts with the optical network of regional multiservice utilities, which also managed the construction process. The fibre network has a geographic component (2,600 km of ducts connecting 372 points of presence), a metropolitan component (several optical MANs with 448 km of ducts connecting 721 buildings), and a fixed wireless component. From 2011, Lepida also stipulates a 15-year IRU (indefeasible right of use) with public service operators in order to use its surplus dark fibre to resolve the digital divide in underserved areas. Moreover, it sells backhaul capacity to small local ISPs and WISPs.

It is envisaged that, using Lepida, ultra-fast connectivity could be made available to the industrial clusters that characterize the region: Emilia Romagna is home to Ferrari and to a myriad of advanced mechanical and machine tools firms.

The first examples of regional support for investments by public service operators, based on the so called 'Scottish model', are the Sardinia and Tuscany state aid regimes, aimed at bridging the digital divide in rural areas, which were approved in 2006. The Sardinia tender specified that the aid, EUR 6.1 million provided by regional and state resources, had to be used to upgrade the central offices of TI in order to offer ADSL services in unserved towns. In Tuscany the four provincial tenders were technologically neutral and required a download data rate of at least 640 kbit/s to be provided. Three of them were attributed to small regional wireless operators, the fourth to TI. A number of subsequent regional projects followed these models.

More recently two of the richest and most developed regions in the north, Lombardia and Trentino (*Provincia Autonoma di Trento* – an autonomous entity), have developed plans for both bridging the digital divide and deploying ultra-fast broadband. Note that Milan, the capital city of Lombardia, is already well-endowed in terms of modern infrastructure (passive fibre infrastructure owned by Metroweb and used by Fastweb and now by TI) for FttB/FttH residential services. Therefore it was excluded from the regional plan. In the other densely populated areas of the region,

---

[33] Nucciarelli et al. (2010; 2013) analysed regional projects (e.g., Progetto Banda Ultra Larga Lombardia, Trentino Network, Lepida Emilia Romagna, Terrecablate Siena) variously developed in the last decade to elaborate on the role and function of public-private interplay and to investigate the main threats to local broadband initiatives. The analysis organized the findings into four main categories (i.e., project targets, governance mechanisms, network structure, and provision of services) according to the conceptual framework illustrated in Nucciarelli et al. (2010).

the economic feasibility of the initial project (based on a mixture of point-to-point and G-PON FttH architectures) requires the switch-off of the copper access network.

In both cases, the digital divide component of the plan has passed the state-aid scrutiny, while the ultra-fast component is still in discussion: in Lombardia the regional administration did not succeed in obtaining the agreement of TI and the major OLOs; in Trentino the OLOs have opposed the agreement reached between TI and the regional agency.[34]

In 2010, the *Provincia di Trento* had initially obtained clearance from the State Aid – Competition Directorate in Brussels for its plan of 'widespread' ultra-fast broadband to small cities and villages, which are nevertheless supported by a very strong, all-year-round tourism industry in the area (the Dolomites) and the willingness to retain and develop several clusters of advanced 'green economy' industries. The plan envisaged, on one hand, the deployment of a backbone fibre network, which the public-owned company Trentino Network has deployed and, on the other hand, the roll-out of a fibre-based access network.

The aim of the plan was to create an ultra-fast broadband network to cover 100% of the population and of business enterprises by 2018, by creating a company with both public and private capital dedicated to covering 60% of provincial users (areas of medium profitability) while the low profitability areas were to be covered directly by the public company Trentino Network.

By 2012 almost 800 km of fibre were deployed in the backhaul and primary access network to connect 92 nodes. The access network is now integrated by HIPERLANs and, xDSL based broadband offered on a commercial basis by TI.

However, in 2012 DG Competition (EC) opened an investigation of the project since it felt that it should have been examined under the state aid procedure: at the time of writing the investigation is not finished but it is highly likely that changed market conditions, together with the delay

generated by the investigation, will put an end to the ultra-broadband segment of the project.

A further interesting regional plan comes from another region of Mezzogiorno, where the Region of Sardinia aims to create a passive optical fibre infrastructure over a period of four to five years, according to a project-financing model. The project involves the construction of cable ducts and, at the same time, exploiting the civil works for creation of a methane pipeline. In this way, the region intends to make access to ultra-fast broadband available to citizens, by including the new fibre-optic access infrastructure in the works for the gas pipeline and making it available to the telecommunications operators.

10.4.3 National framework schemes for broadband and ultra-fast broadband

The European Digital Agenda requires that member states develop national plans for broadband in order to attain the common European goals in terms of reach, data rates and adoption (broadband at 30 Mbit/s for all, 50% of households with 100 Mbit/s connections) by 2020. The Ministry for economic development (MISE) has been entitled by Law 69/2009 to coordinate specific initiatives for the local development of broadband, while overall coordination for the Digital Agenda is retained by the Prime Minister's office.

MISE has proposed three state-aid framework regimes that have passed the scrutiny of the European Commission. The first regime, N 646/2009, aims to use resources from the European Agricultural Fund for Rural Development. It envisages the concession to public service operators of fibre backhaul deployed through public tenders and financial support to end-users for the acquisition of customer premises equipment (such as antennas or modems) which are required to use wireless or satellite technologies in the most remote areas. The second regime, SA.33807 (2011/N) and the third, SA.34199 (2012/N) are framework schemes for deployment of broadband and ultra-fast broadband, respectively.

To ease the administrative burden, a single, country-wide state aid scheme can be used to cover 'under one umbrella' the different regional or local

---

[34] For a list of European Commission's decision on the compatibility of State Aid regulation with Italian regional projects see Nucciarelli et al. (2013).

projects that will originate from the availability of funding instruments, mostly at local level. However, in case local authorities intend to deviate from the framework, they will be required to notify the European Commission of the amendments separately. Moreover, Infratel – the in-house company of the ministry – provides a one-stop shop for the technical aspects of the projects and assists local authorities in the tender process.

The underlying logic is to facilitate the achievements of the infrastructural targets of the European Digital Agenda focusing on the 'white' areas: that is, those with market failure or low-density areas. Public money is to be assigned to a network operator and associated civil works contractors for the deployment of next-generation networks. Public money typically covers 70% of the total cost. Access must be granted by the network operator on a non-discriminatory basis, with rigid clawback schemes ensuring a fair, but not excessive, return on the private capital invested. Existing infrastructures can be transferred to the project as part of the bid. This 'gap funding' approach is used also in the ultra-fast broadband scheme.

In addition, a 'Direct Intervention' and a public-private partnership (PPP) approach are considered. In the case of direct intervention, the passive infrastructure will be owned by the public body that promoted the project, a concessionaire will be selected by a tender procedure to be in charge of the provision of wholesale services, and several service providers (but not the concessionaire) will provide the retail services. In the PPP model, the private partner will be chosen through an open tender procedure. The private partner has to develop a detailed business plan, including technical and financial aspects. The partnership will own and operate the infrastructure, providing non-discriminatory access to the retail service providers.

10.5 The Italian model of functional separation: from equivalence of output to equivalence of input

The case study on Italy seems particularly interesting in the light of the discussion on functional separation.[35] Starting from 2009, AGCOM has accepted Undertakings (or Commitments) offered by TI, based on the principle of equivalence of output (EoO). This solution, which is still in place in 2013, is finally evolving towards equivalence of input (EoI).

AGCOM has for a long time applied, and continues to apply, the two key concepts of non-discrimination and equivalence of access within the framework of the European legislation in the telecommunications sector. From this framework, following a detailed market definition and analysis, obligations are imposed on operators identified as having significant market power, However, non-discrimination between the incumbent's downstream arm and the altnets competing in downstream markets has been pursued using additional tools. With regard to wholesale service delivery and network provisions, the Undertakings have contributed, based on an EoO model, to address a number of issues, ultimately improving consumers' choice and competition at large.

In the European regulatory framework, there are two types of equivalence:

Equivalence of Inputs (EoI): the downstream access product retailed by the incumbent uses exactly the same physical upstream inputs as the downstream product supplied to its competitors, e.g., same tie-cables, same electronic equipment, same exchange space, etc. The (wholesale) product development process is therefore exactly equivalent in its provision in terms of functionality and price.

Equivalence of Outputs (EoO): the access products offered by the incumbent operator to

---

[35] Separation aims to reduce the vertical integration of companies. To reach this aim, different forms of separation have been adopted ranging from less (accounting) to more (ownership) intrusive ones. Functional (or operational) separation consists of the gradual splitting up of a vertically integrated company along the lines of its operational practices. This form of separation can be implemented in various degrees (e.g., creation of a wholesale division, business separation) and lead to the legal separation of business units (see also Cave, 2006). Literature has investigated the potential impact of separation on investment incentives (Tropina et al., 2010), its possible disadvantages (CEPS, 2008), and other European experiences (Whalley and Curven, 2008; Cadman, 2010; Teppayayon and Bohlin, 2010).

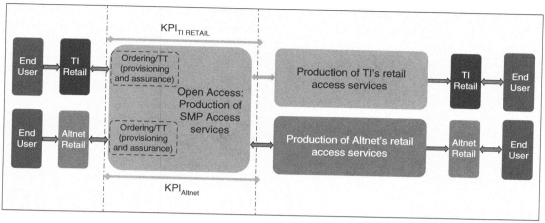

Figure 10.2 The equivalence of output model, Italy
Source: Telecom Italia.

alternative operators are comparable to the products it provides to its retail division in terms of functionality and price, but they may be provided by different systems and processes.[36]

In pursuing non-discrimination, AGCOM started well ahead of time and imposed a first set of rules to ensure equivalence of access in 2002. Those rules, including margin squeeze tests, were updated periodically (most recently in January 2010). In addition, starting from 2008, as a result of accepting TI's undertakings (effective from 1 January 2009), monitoring and implementing EoO became an iterative process. See Figure 10.2 for the EoO model. Such processes imply close monitoring, facilitating technical solutions and implementing detailed business support and operational support systems. The current model has a relatively long history.

July 2000

In July 2000, twenty-six alternative network operators wrote a joint letter to AGCOM to protest against the discriminatory practices, which, according to them, were used by TI, the incumbent operator. TI was accused of delaying (business/technical) operations, squeezing the margins

of alternative operators, discriminating these operators to the advantage of the downstream divisions of TI operating in the same markets and using technical and economical discrimination as an anti-competitive weapon.

May 2002

Following a year-long investigation, including a detailed procedure and the opinion of the national Competition Authority, a landmark decision (152/02/Cons) was adopted by AGCOM in May 2002. That decision focused on ensuring equivalence of access and non-discrimination ('*parità di trattamento interna-esterna*'). The decision imposed on TI (as SMP operator) included the adoption of margin squeeze tests, accounting separation and a cost accounting methodology. Functional separation between the IT-systems of the wholesale and retail divisions of TI was also imposed, together with publishing service level agreements (SLAs) to ensure technical non-discrimination.

The decision has been amended over the years (most recently in 2011, with a complete redesign of the margin squeeze tests), but its key principles (economical and technical non-discrimination, equivalence of access) remain central and fundamental to a number of AGCOM's decisions, including market analysis and related remedies

---

[36] BEREC guidance on functional separation – BoR (10) 44, 7–8.

for insufficient competition imposed by obligations in line with the EU legislative framework.

2006–2008

During this period, the issue of a possible separation of TI's access network was at the core of the institutional debate, both from a general policy and from a regulatory point of view.

Law 248 of August 4, 2006, taking inspiration from the EU 'modernization' Regulation[37] provided AGCOM with the powers to evaluate and accept commitments offered by operators within the limits of AGCOM's competences and within the task of promoting competition in the provision of electronic communication networks, services and associated facilities and, eventually, to make them binding (Article 14 bis)[38].

That summer, a lively political discussion started on the possibility and the merits of imposing a structural separation of TI's access network activities. The key reasoning was that, due to the two successive LBOs which had created a huge debt to be repaid by TI to its shareholders (mainly to the most important Italian banks), selling the access network of TI and creating a 'newco' could create value and shelter the company from an hostile takeover. Also, a key part of the 'Rovati plan' (from the name of one of the PM advisors) was the divestiture of the mobile arm of TI, TI Mobile (TIM), a proposal that ran directly against the strategic decisions of part of TI's top management at the time. The animated public discussion finally led, ten days after the publication of the plan (6 Sept 2006), to the resignation of the former CEO of TI, M. Tronchetti Provera, to mark his opposition to a board decision that supported the divestiture.

However, in the following months, with a new CEO (F. Bernabé) TI repeatedly opposed any kind of structural separation plan, arguing that the access network is an irreplaceable asset whose expropriation would represent a major and totally disproportionate remedy. Bernabé also explained that a functional separation would jeopardize the investments and put at risk the solvency of TI and its capability of addressing its leverage.[39]

Based on market analysis performed by AGCOM under the EU regulatory framework, TI was confirmed as dominant in all fixed network markets; in particular, the national wholesale market was typified by a single fixed access network, not economically replicable and competition in all fixed national retail markets relied on wholesale products offered by TI.

On the basis of such market analysis findings (and also under the threat of several on-going proceeding for sanctioning TI's regulatory infringements), TI proposed a number of undertakings to AGCOM, aiming at introducing a model of functional separation for the provision of wholesale access services.

2008–2009

At the end of a long and thorough scrutiny process (based on several interactions with TI to improve the Undertakings and a subsequent public consultation), a detailed set of new undertakings (Impegni[40]), aimed at improving the competitive scenario in Italy and concretely addressing a number of technical and practical issues in TI's working relation with the alternative network operators, was finally accepted by AGCOM in late 2008. It became binding from 1 January 2009.

As a matter of fact, the Undertakings were prompted by two different families of problems: practices which were already sanctioned by the regulator with heavy fines imposed on TI, and regulatory/discrimination issues to be addressed by a number of mostly technical and process-design implementations. The two key incentives for TI in proposing the Undertakings were: freezing, and ultimately avoiding, the potentially heavy sanctions for violation of fair business practices and avoiding scrutiny by the Competition

---

[37] EC Regulation n.1/2003.

[38] Functional separation as a regulatory remedy is now possible in the 'new' regulatory framework (2009 Review).

[39] See for instance Public hearing, Lower House, Italian Parliament, 30 Sept 2008 (*Resoconto della IX Commissione permanente (Trasporti, poste e telecomunicazioni)* 30 settembre 2008).

[40] Decision 718/08/Cons.

Authority if abusive discrimination could be proved by the alternative operators.

This led to the creation of one large set of undertakings articulated over sixteen groups of actions.

2009– 2010

Following notification to the European Commission of the proposed remedies on wholesale broadband access and wholesale local loop markets, and the detailed comments of the Commission, some of the Undertakings became formal regulatory remedies based on the market analysis proceeding under Article 7 of the Framework Directive. Indeed, the Commission, while endorsing the non-discriminatory approach underlying the Commitments, formally pointed out in a comment letter[41] that voluntary undertakings cannot replace regulatory obligations and clarified that NRAs should notify them of any voluntary undertakings by SMP operators as long as they constitute, directly relate or are ancillary to remedies.[42]

2011–2012

Work continued on a regular basis to implement all of the Undertakings; at the end of 2011, some Undertakings were considered fully implemented and TI was discharged from potentially heavy sanctions. Monitoring of some key commitments remains in force to ensure the smooth implementation and compliance.

In 2014, the Commitments will be reassessed in the transition to an equivalence of input model, taking into account the publication of the EC Recommendation on non-discrimination[43] and the technological evolution of the network and fibre to the cabinet procedures.

---

[41] See Press Release IP/09/1613, containing links to relevant material.

[42] Interactions between NRAs and the European Commission in case of voluntary separation are now dictated by the new art.13b of the Access Directive.

[43] Commission recommendation on consistent non-discrimination obligations and costing methodologies to promote competition and enhance the broadband investment environment – C(2013) 5761.

10.6 Current developments: FttX and LTE as complementary systems?

10.6.1 Extending the life cycle of copper using fibre

In the period 2009–2013, TI has steadily deployed fiber in its own access network. Primary and secondary network coverage now reach into 0.8 million households; coupled with Fastweb's 2 million homes passed, this provides for coverage of around 14% of households. However, TI is also laying down copper and the installment of fibre is primarily aimed at deploying a state-of-the-art VDSL-2 network. TI thus intends to extend the life cycle of copper. In addition to the NGA rules adopted by AGCOM in January 2012 (which can be summarized by unbundling of fibre 'when technically possible' and an obligation to provide alternative end-to-end services), and in April 2013 (bitstream/VULA over FttH and FttCab, NGAN Access), three sub-proceedings, now contained in the forthcoming market analysis, should further enhance regulatory certainty for future choices:

1. Evaluate the regulatory impact of enhanced VDSL and VDSL2 technologies on TI's sub-loop unbundling (SLU) obligations. These include VDSL 'vectoring' (aimed at eliminating interference or 'crosstalk' between copper pairs in a cable), 'bonding' (combining several copper pairs to realize a higher data rate), and of the 'phantom mode' concept (providing a third communication channel, using a 'virtual pair' in addition to the physical pair).

2. Update the BU-LRIC (bottom-up long range incremental costs) model for regulated NGA access products, and provide the definition of areas where there is no infrastructure competition in order to implement geographically differentiated price regulation for virtual unbundled access (VULA) and wholesale broadband access (WBA) at parent node level.

3. Evaluation of the conditions for imposing 'symmetric obligations' to provide access to physical infrastructure of which duplication would be economically inefficient or physically impossible.

10.6.2 Mobile broadband deployment

The complementary tier of development to look into is certainly represented by mobile broadband and implementation of LTE (long-term evolution, the fourth generation of mobile telephony). Following an auction in September 2011, four operators are now at work to deploy the new networks (TIM and Vodafone already launched commercial offers in 2012) with different coverage and performance strategies, reflecting differences in the assigned spectrum right of use).

The outcome of these strategies will certainly mark a deep impact on the deployment of next generation access networks, especially in a country like Italy with such a strong mobile foothold.

Already, in several parts of the country the actual difference in terms of data rates between mobile and fixed network is not a major challenge for LTE to bridge. LTE will test the resiliency of fixed networks as we know them.

Throughout the country, mobile networks are being modernized by massive deployment of fibre to connect thousands of base stations and ensure backhaul quality, as well as by incentivizing users to offload mobile traffic to Wi-Fi hotspots connected to the fixed network.

In Italy the 4G coverage requirements – unlike Germany's, in this case – did not request the operators to start from rural zones. However, today the pattern of 3G usage already shows that mobile broadband is used often for lack of fixed broadband in semi-dense zones or very low-density areas.

10.7 Achieving the Digital Agenda for Europe targets: Italy's positioning

For a long time, Italy had no formally established Digital Agenda, although it actively participated in the discussion at the European level which led to the definition of the Digital Agenda for Europe. However, in the period 2006–2012 several initiatives were implemented, mainly focusing on reducing the digital divide in southern Italy but with regional plans also addressing the north. In addition, as already pointed out in this chapter, other regional plans in economically important regions, such as Lombardia,

Trentino – Alto Adige and Emilia Romagna, started to address next-generation networks, which, with regard to the national footprint, are largely deployed in competition by TI and Fastweb.

The Italian Digital Agenda (ADI) was established in the form of a High Level Steering Committee, a pivotal entity coordinating several public entities[44]. Another decree (18 October 2012, n° 179 'Further urgent measures for the growth of the country' – cd Growth measure 2.0) established a formal planning process for implementing the ADI. The actions foreseen in the European Digital Agenda are attributed to six working groups: infrastructure, e-commerce, e-government, digital competences, research and innovation, and smart communities. Items of immediate relevance for broadband services include: digital identity, open data, digital education, digital health, digital divide, electronic payments and digital justice.

At the time of writing, the most updated document benchmarking the achievement of the targets of the Digital Agenda for Europe is the *Digital Agenda Scoreboard 2013*.[45]

With 13.7 million broadband lines, Italy assumes the fourth position in the EU28 in terms of total lines. In terms of penetration it assumes a position between Slovakia and Portugal with 22.5% against the EU average of 28.8%. In terms of data rates: 83.7% of broadband lines have a data rate at or above 2 Mbit/s; 14.2% are at or above 10 Mbit/s; and only 0.1% is at or above 30 Mbit/s.

In November 2013, the Italian government created a group to monitor the adequacy of investments and efforts to reach the targets of the European Digital Agenda. In January 2014 the group delivered a report which shed a more optimistic light on the take up of faster broadband networks, together with some important caveats.[46]

---

[44] The Minister for Economic Development, The Minister for Public Administration and simplification, the Minister for territorial cohesion, the Minister of Education, Universities and Research and the Ministry of Economy and Finance.

[45] Brussels, 12.06.2013, SWD(2013) 217 final Commission Staff Working Document.

[46] The English version of the report (slides) is available at www.slideshare.net/Palazzo_Chigi/achieving-the-objectives-of-the-digital-agenda-for-europe-dae-in-italy-prospects-and-challenges.

10.8 Case analysis

This section takes a deeper look into the current and prospective situation of broadband and ultra-fast broadband in Italy. The bottom line is that, while the existing situation in terms of future-proof infrastructure and innovative services is not entirely encouraging, there are also some positive signs of development.

As mentioned, the role of demographics, with a markedly ageing curve, and unfavourable geography, with many small cities scattered over predominantly hilly or mountainous terrain, are negative factors in broadband development, especially when coupled with the absence of cable-TV. In addition, the impact of two consecutive leveraged buy-outs on the ability of TI to invest in infrastructure has been huge, and might finally result in Telefonica taking full control of the company.

In this complex environment, with regard to prices and overall quality of service, AGCOM played an important role in fostering competition by focussing early on local loop unbundling and by trying to develop a sound 'equivalence of output' model. Also, it was probably beneficial for the system to have an integrated regulator able to deal with convergent markets, such as telecom and media, as a single entity.

In the last five years or so, the impact of broadband networks on economic growth is broadly acknowledged (see e.g., Czernich, 2011), the increasing demand for higher data rates, and the EC's strategy supporting the development of broadband infrastructures (i.e., the Digital Agenda for Europe) raised new challenges within the Italian telecom system. The 'Caio report' showed that until mid-2009 about 13% of Italian households suffered from the digital divide by being excluded from any kind of Internet connection or being connected at a data rate below 640 kbit/s (Caio, 2009).

However, as argued by Tonetti (2011), the development of broadband infrastructures has received a new impulse from 2008 on. At the EU level, the European Economic Recovery Plan (Communication COM(2008) 800 Final) along with the Community Guidelines on State Aid rules

(Communication 2009/C 235/04), encouraged a new wave of investments in the Italian market, based on the introduction of a series of laws to streamline and simplify the procedures to initiate broadband projects in peripheral areas, at both local and national level (see Laws 133/2008 and 69/2009). Infrastructure development was considered subject to project financing rules and strictly linked to the necessity that technical and organizational structure of projects contribute to a network system open to competition, in line with national and EU laws. However, public and private funding aimed at: (1) technological improvement of public and private communications networks; (2) the provision of advanced information and communication services to the country as a whole; and (3) the reduction of the socio-economic gap among the regions, have been announced several times, but budgets were never or only fractionally allocated and spent. In 2013, after multiple changes in the destination of the funds, a decision was finally taken to allocate a number of appropriations as planned.

On the regulatory level, AGCOM has tried to create a more balanced playing field by enforcing the principle of equivalence of access and non-discrimination (already in 2002, with the decision 152/02/CONS) and subsequently to foster the development of next-generation access networks (NGN) with the implementation of equivalence in access to new NGN infrastructures (Deliberation 731/09/CONS) (see also Bourreau et al. 2009, Avenali et. al. 2010a, 2010b). In fact, AGCOM imposed on TI the obligation to provide access to ducts, as well as to dark fibre, to alternative operators intending to deploy fibre networks. Moreover, in line with the European Commission's Recommendation on regulated access to next-generation access networks (C (2010)6223 – 2010/572/EU) and the accompanying document (SEC(2010) 1037 final) and the related Communication C(2010)472, AGCOM incentivized co-investments, although it did not impose any obligation for the unbundling of new fibre networks. This decision may be reconsidered when commercial products for managing different wavelengths become available on the market. Nonetheless, TI has been forced to provide to alternative network operators end-to-end NGAN services and bitstream/VULA (virtual unbundled local access) services as of 2013.

Nowadays, the deployment of NGA is widely considered an innovation with potential positive economic growth especially at a time of wide economic-financial crisis. Moreover, a wide debate has developed in recent years about the different degrees of public involvement in the investment strategies for NGA, at both national and municipal (or regional) level. As illustrated by Nucciarelli et al., (2010) local governments can take the lead or at least stimulate broadband initiatives, for instance by promoting public Wi-Fi networks in specific spots, as for instance the Province of Rome[47] did. This is also possible because of flexible and alternative models for public-private partnerships. Sharing stakeholders' competences and allowing public actors to create the basis for provision of a public service is a prerequisite to exploit efficiencies in management and operations carried into the projects by private investors. In a nutshell, public-private partnerships can be considered as an alternative method to provide access to a variety of infrastructure resources and, by their own nature, they force a look at the long-term implications of broadband initiatives, also in terms of policy strategies.

This is one of the rationales behind the on-going debate at the central government level about the implementation of a package of stimuli for GDP growth in the upcoming years. The intention to foster the deployment of broadband infrastructures confirms at least two main factors in investment trends, not only at the Italian level but also at the EU28 one. The first factor deals with raising the importance of public commitment. Large (but also local) projects cannot be made operational without public funding as it helps to remove barriers to private investments, especially in grey and black areas, as the Commission observed in its 2009 Guidelines. Moreover, public funding could play a key role in the deployment of NGA especially

where high costs make outlays for municipal (or regional) Fibre-to-the-Home networks unfeasible and unmanageable for private operators. However, the sustainability of an Italian Internet model does not only rely on the degree of sustainability of investments. In fact, as also argued by Caio and Sideri (2011)[48], there also exists a digital divide different from the geographical one. About 40% of Italian families do not own a personal computer, which has a significant impact on the digital divide of people in terms of computer and Internet skills. The degree of digital literacy also impacts on demand growth and its qualitative evolution. On a more positive note, the massive take-up of smartphones, and increasingly of tablets, compensates for the initial lag in PC penetration. Recent data continue to show that the percentage of microcompanies that are still not using the Net or, in some cases, do not own a computer, is extraordinary – up to 20% in some regions. This is more a cultural divide than a digital divide based on the lack of high-speed broadband.

10.9 Conclusions

The development of monopolistic markets is always closely linked to the investment strategies implemented by the single player. Infrastructure and services development as well as R&D activities and the evolution of demand themselves closely depend upon the actions taken in the market by the monopolistic player.

The Italian telecom sector – as in all countries where a state-controlled carrier operated with legal monopoly status – has evolved over decades, following the highs and lows of TI which for many years has been responsible for the innovation of the telecom and related sectors. After market liberalization occurred, the market opened to competition leading to a gradual reduction of prices for end customers, but also to the fragmentation of the investment actions taken to update infrastructures using emerging technologies and demand expectations.

---

[47] In Italy, a province is an administrative territory, roughly equivalent to a county in the UK, with similar heterogeneity in terms of population and size.

[48] See also Caio (2009).

The development of the broadband sector followed a path of initial high growth due to the action of the incumbent TI and successive slow-down as a consequence of the lack of leadership by TI in the ICT (Information and Communication Technology) ecosystem. Multiple investors (both public and private) stepped into the market and service providers proliferated to intercept the added value created by integrated communication solutions and interoperable systems and technologies.

The broadband sector currently suffers the lack of platform competition, as no cable infrastructure exists. Competition between xDSL and fibre exists since the early stages of the broadband development and has been characterized by a preliminary deployment of fibre connections (i.e., Fastweb and the Socrate project) but then became depressed by fragmented initiatives in support of demand.

These initiatives were not aimed at stimulating new demand for higher data rates nor to target the specific barriers to adoption of specific demand segments (household income, digital literacy, insufficient quality of e-government), as analysed in Dolente et al. (2010) and Leporelli (2010) but rather at decreasing the prices to be paid by the generality of final customers (even those with greater willingness to pay and/or located in high-cost areas) to the benefit of low-quality xDSL connections. Accordingly, repetitive, inefficient and indirect demand support to the generality of customers, along with the lack of stimuli for an infrastructural upgrade, targeted both to the areas in which NGA infrastructure (FttC in most cases) will be sustainable and to improve the average quality of basic broadband connectivity available to actual users, has led to a gradual decrease of innovation, which has resulted in stand-alone and regional initiatives by both the incumbent and its competitors. Thereafter, demand did not develop due both to a substantial lack of infrastructures (largely not being developed because of demand uncertainties) and to a low degree of digital literacy and willingness to pay of low income or elderly households.

To resolve the current stagnation in investments and in leadership, two main points should be considered:

– the reduction of the digital divide among the population, aiming at increasing the digital skills of the younger generation as well as the elderly with programmes to be tailored to their specific needs (avoiding 'digital crusades' with untargeted funding); and
– the creation of a legislative and policy framework within which public and private stakeholders can develop investment strategies and schedule operations for the medium-to long-run.

References

Avenali, A., Matteucci, G., and Reverberi, P. (2010a). Dynamic access pricing and investment in alternative infrastructures. *International Journal of Industrial Organization*, **28**(2), 167–175.

(2010b) How does vertical industry structure affect investment in infrastructure quality? Department of Computer and System Sciences Antonio Ruberti Technical Reports 2.8.

Bourreau, M., Hombert, J., Pouyet, J., and Schutz, N. (2009). Upstream competition between vertically integrated firms. *Ecole Polytechnique*, Cahier de recherche 54.

Cadman, R. (2010). Means not ends: Deterring discrimination through equivalence and functional separation. *Telecommunications Policy*, **34**(7), 366–374.

Caio, F. (2009). Portare l'Italia verso la leadership europea nella banda larga. Considerazioni sulle opzioni di politica industriale. Caio report for the Italian Ministry of economic development, March 2009.

Caio, F., and Sideri, M. (2011). Banda stretta. Milano: Rizzoli.

Cave, M. (2006). Six degrees of separation: operational separation as a remedy in European telecommunications regulation. *Communications and Strategies*, **64**, 89–103.

CEPS – Center for European Policy Studies (2008). Achieving the internal market for e-communications.Retrieved from http://shop. ceps.eu/BookDetail.php?item_id=1676.

Ciapanna, E., and Sabbatini, D. (2008). Broadband in Italy: An Overview (October 14, 2008). Bank of Italy Occasional Paper No. 34.

Available at http://dx.doi.org/10.2139/
ssrn.1357453.

Czernich, N. (2011). The emergence of broadband
internet and consequences for economic and
social development München: Ifo-Inst. für
Wirtschaftsforschung.

Dolente, C., Galea, J. J., and Leporelli, C. (2010).
Next generation access and digital divide:
opposite sides of the same coin? Paper
presented at the 21th ITS European Regional
Conference, Copenhagen, Denmark,
September 2010.

EC (1987). COM(87)2 290: Green paper on
the development of the common market
for telecommunications services and equipment.
Brussels: European Commission.

Leporelli, C., and Reverberi, P. (2004a). Praticabilità
dell''unbundling': aspetti regolamentari e tutela
della concorrenza. *Mercato concorrenza
regole*, **6**(1), 127–156.

(2004b). Pro-competitive regulation of local
loop unbundling. Paper presented at the
15th ITS European Regional Conference,
Berlin, Germany, September 4–7, 2004.
Available at www.researchgate.net/profile/
Claudio_Leporelli/publications/

Leporelli C. (2010). I temi chiave del progetto
ISBUL: un punto di vista su problemi emersi,
risultati ottenuti, proposte maturate. Paper
available at www.progettoisbul.net.

Nucciarelli, A., Sadowski B., and Achard, P. (2010).
Emerging models of public–private interplay for
European broadband access: Evidence from the
Netherlands and Italy. *Telecommunications
Policy* **34**, 513–527

Nucciarelli, A., Castaldo A., Conte E., and
Sadowski B. (2013). Unlocking the potential of
Italian broadband: Case studies and policy
lessons. *Telecommunications Policy*, **37**(10),
955–969.

Teppayayon, O., and Bohlin, E. (2010). Functional
separation in Swedish broadband market: Next
step of improving competition.
Telecommunications Policy, **34**(7), 375–383.

Tonetti, A. (2011). La nuova disciplina per lo
sviluppo della banda larga: vera
semplificazione? *Mercato concorrenza regole*,
1, 117.

Tropina, T., Whalley, J., and Curven, P. (2010).
Functional separation within the European
Union: debates and challenges. *Telematics and
Informatics*, **27**(3), 231–241.

Video Online, 1996.

Whalley, J., and Curven, P. (2008). Is functional
separation BT-style the answer?
Communications and Strategies, **71**, 145–161.

France

AUDREY LORIDAN-BAUDRIER

11.1 Introduction to the case study

This case study aims to provide deep insights into the dynamics of French broadband markets, which in turn could provide valuable inputs into the policy and regulatory debate on how to stimulate broadband development leading to the realization of the Digital Agenda for Europe with a 2020 target.

The past few years have seen major transformations in the French broadband industry and in French regulatory governance more generally. On the industry side, major changes have been necessary to the strategies of actors to adapt core networks to support the new fixed and mobile access interfaces. On the regulatory side, changes in the French broadband markets have been evolutionary. They are characterized by a complex interplay between public and private actors.

The industry currently faces two major issues:

- The first major challenge is the development of ultra-fast broadband networks, fixed and mobile. It requires balancing the objectives of competition, investment and planning, and therefore consideration of ways, from a regulatory perspective, that ensure the deployment of open networks to be used in the long-term;
- The second issue concerns the relations between the different actors in the value chain (suppliers, operators, service providers, content producers, consumers or users) whose strategies raise complex issues including that of the 'neutrality' of the Internet and more generally of electronic communications networks.

The French case study aims at identifying and analysing the challenges and dynamics of the trajectories of fixed and mobile broadband markets through a set of key indicators and an economic analysis of the competitive and regulatory developments of the industry.

The goal is to discuss these trends and their consequences for the industry trajectory in order to provide a comprehensive analysis of French broadband markets based on up-to-date information.

This study is expected to address in particular the role of regulation and competition in the uptake and developments of next-generation fixed and/or mobile broadband networks. It includes in particular the following key highlights:

- Identifiying of new market patterns;
- Analysing of firms' strategies;
- Analysing the role of public actors as key players in broadband markets;
- Showing the regulatory approaches and explaining how they impact investment and competition within the markets;
- Providing an understanding of the attitude of incumbent players regarding the open access initiatives and the regulator's measures to promote partnership and shared infrastructure.

The French case study investigates the following research question: How does broadband market regulation affect competition and industry structure? To answer this question, background data on telecom metrics has been used.

The material presented here is intended: (1) to consolidate and disseminate the latest developments in French broadband markets; (2) to share experiences and lessons learned from the deployments of the broadband technologies; and (3) to analyse the broadband markets in a comprehensive and detailed manner so it can be useful for comparative studies in this area.

The French case study consists of the following sections. In this section, we sketch the case by introducing the main trends and stakes in matters of economic and social benefits and market competition. In Section 11.2, we put into perspective the historical development milestones that led from narrowband to broadband. In Section 11.3, we depict the major stakeholders from the public and private spheres in order to better understand their interactions. In Section 11.4, we distinguish the main kinds of next-generation access technologies and consider Orange's civil engineering infrastructure features. These elements are essential to understand the main stakes in broadband deployment considered in Section 11.5. In Section 11.6 we review broadband regulation mechanisms and infrastructure sharing. In Sections 11.7 and 11.8, we discuss successively the market risks and dynamics and investment strategies before analysing the impact of broadband regulation mechanisms. Section 11.9 addresses the achievement of the Digital Agenda targets. In Section 11.10 the current market dynamics are discussed and in Section 11.11 the case analysis is provided and some remarks about lessons learned, possible generalizations and recommendations conclude the case.

11.2 Main trends and major stakes

11.2.1 Digital economy benefits

The digital economy represents about EUR 115 billion or 6% of GDP in France and nearly 300,000 direct and indirect jobs[1]. It is one of the most dynamic sectors, providing high added-value products and services. In particular the Internet is the cause of one quarter of growth in France between 2000 and 2008 (COE-Rexecode, 2011). The investment corresponding to the digital infrastructure and equipment (core networks, backbone networks, terminals) can be estimated to be at least EUR 50 billion in this decade (IDATE, 2010).

[1] Outsourced jobs (related to purchases or investments): call centers, fibre installers, service companies in computer engineering: 150,000; direct employment of the five main operators (Orange, SFR, Bouygues Telecom, Iliad Telecom and OMEA): 126,000; Other direct employment. All other listed companies under the NAF Code 6420 Telecommunications: other operators, manufacturers, etc.: 34,000.

In France, the revenues from the digital economy are estimated at EUR 97 billion or 5% of GDP. In this number, electronic communications services represent a turnover in the final market of nearly EUR 45.1 billion or 2.3% of GDP. The electronic communications operators invest around EUR 6.5 billion per year and accounted for 128,810 direct jobs in 2012. This sector is of vital importance to the development of fast and ultra-fast broadband Internet, fixed and mobile services.

Broadband market growth in France is mainly driven by digital subscriber line (DSL) offers. It results in access-based competition that seeks to promote local loop unbundling (LLU). The widespread availability of LLU has helped to increase both competition and innovation, providing operators with direct access to the copper pairs. Sector-specific regulation has helped operators to move up the ladder of investment by maintaining economic leeway between wholesale offers for accessing the local copper loop and the regional counterpart, bitstream. In addition, the Fibre-to-the-Home (FttH) networks are expanding quickly and have been deployed across more than 9,900 km of roadway, although these roll-outs are currently concentrated in the country's most densely populated cities.

In 1Q 2013 the fixed broadband market included over 30.9 million households covered, nearly 24.22 million subscribers to high-speed broadband Internet and 1.705 million subscribers to ultra-fast Internet, all operators and all technologies combined, including:

- 22,100,000 ADSL subscribers;
- 365,000 Fibre-to-the-Home (FttH) or Fibre-to-the-Building (FttB) subscribers;
- 675,000 other subscribers at data rates greater than or equal to 100 Mbit/s;
- 665,000 other subscribers at data rates between 30 and 100 Mbit/s;
- 385,000 other subscribers with cable, Wi-Fi, satellite or radio-based local loop.

11.2.2 Market boosters

Because of consumers' growing demand for content and higher data rate access, the market is moving to ultra-fast broadband solutions with the deployment of new optical fibre in the local loop. Ultra-fast broadband already makes it possible to achieve relatively high symmetrical bitrates. It helps to stimulate the development of enhanced services, particularly in the broadcasting area, including the simultaneous reception of several high definition channels.

The mobile market has had strong growth with the explosion of data traffic made possible through the deployment of 3G networks (introduced in 2010), availability of terminals adapted to new uses and the establishment of offers more attractive to consumers. Indeed, the continuous improvement of mobile networks and the availability of end-user terminals with better performance pushed the offer for data-oriented services with data rates similar to fixed access networks in a mobile environment. Today, mobile service offerings can largely meet the end-user demand in terms of traffic. The following drivers are boosting the mobile broadband traffic:

- The market shares of smartphones, tablets and dongles are experiencing significant growth;
- Video-sharing platforms based on user generated content are succeeding;
- Internet browsing and access to emails lead the growth of broadband subscriptions;
- Social networking and microblogging are essential mobile applications; almost 45% of French Internet users visited a social network in 2013 (CREDOC, 2013).

11.2.3 New competition challenges

A key question is whether the entry in 2010 of a fourth mobile operator – Free Mobile – increased competition to benefit consumers. Prices in France are indeed above the European average and tend to favour large consumers. To what extent can the new entrant destabilize the mobile market? Because the incumbents are strong, the new entrant, given its size, probably would be the first to disappear in case of a price war. France Télécom and Free willingly signed a 2G roaming agreement, which has been extended to 3G roaming. Indeed, Free Mobile has been recently granted national

roaming rights on the 3G network of France Télécom[2] as a means of completing the footprint of its own 3G network, i.e., to complement its own network coverage obligation of 25% of the population. Will this agreement help spur a new momentum in the French mobile market? Has the French mobile market still significant growth potential? These are a few questions that we aim to answer in this chapter.

The issue of deployment of open networks is arising even more acutely in the case of ultra-fast fixed Internet. Indeed, the deployment of these new networks must not lead to a weakening of competition and even less to a remonopolization of the local loop. It is essential in this context to ensure that the final part of optical fibre networks into homes and businesses, which forms a potential bottleneck, is open and technologically neutral, while preserving incentives for investment and infrastructure competition. This requires regulation to set some *ex-ante* rules to provide certainty and visibility to the actors.

11.2.4 Economic model renewal

Successful long-term deployment of broadband networks raises the crucial question of the underlying economic models based on the interplay between contents and networks: the deployment of ultra-fast Internet makes possible the explosion of new uses. Conversely the existence of attractive content stimulates the appetite of consumers for ultra-fast services and supports the deployment of networks. In this context, the question is about sharing value and financing networks between the various links in the value chain. Where operators occupy by nature an important role in the deployment of next generation networks and the marketing of next generation services, the French case study intends to show that local authorities have a key role to play in the successful deployment of FttH, in particular in rural areas, as

---

[2] Since February 2012 and the passage of fixed-line telephony under the Orange brand, all solutions marketed by France Telecom uses this brand, which on July 1, 2013 became the new name of the group.

confirmed by 78% of mayors in the rural areas, who consider the availability of fixed broadband a priority for their town.

11.3 Historical developments: from narrowband to broadband

11.3.1 Key milestones of the French telecommunications industry

The history of French telecommunications is largely that of political intervention in scientific progress. Political control over telegraphic services was pursued as early as 1837. The French king, Louis-Philippe, perhaps saw this as a logical extension of the control of the press, which Charles X had initiated as part of the July Ordinances of 1830. State monopoly of telegraphic services, for military and political reasons, was finally established in 1851. The French Post Office gradually absorbed the telegraph service, one minister becoming responsible for post and telegraph service in early 1879.

Between 1890 and 1915 the number of phones in France more than doubled every five years, rising from 15,400 to 357,500. However, the distribution of phones in proportion to the population was modest. One of the main reasons for this slow growth was the method of financing networks. The cities that wished to acquire a telecommunication system had to provide the administration with the initial financing. The administration later reimbursed the locality in proportion to the receipts from subscribers to the new network. Unequal distribution of phone networks across the country and lack of inter-regional connections resulted from this approach.

Between the two World Wars the French Government policy ensured that the telephone service was geared more closely to the needs of the commercial and industrial sectors, and that modern services were provided to all at the same price across the country. The setting of more, and better quality, lines was also begun, using underground cables. Arteries of lines radiating from Paris to many regional telephone exchanges were constructed between 1924 and 1938. Finally, the replacement of manual by automatic exchanges was gradually achieved, using the rotary system.

Paris, its suburbs and eventually the main provincial centres saw their exchanges automated from the 1930s. In the countryside, however, the problem of modernizing 25,000 exchanges, half of which supported less than five subscribers, had to be approached differently and a semi-automatic system resulted. Nevertheless, France still had one of the lowest ratios of phones to people in 1938 with 3.79 per cent whereas the United States had 15.27 per cent, Sweden 12.47 per cent, and the United Kingdom 6.74 per cent. Most French phones were used for business purposes and in the home the phone barely penetrated below the upper middle classes. Most phones were to be found in urban areas of northern France; elsewhere, only the exclusive resorts, such as Biarritz, Nice, and Cannes, were well-equipped.

French telephone, telegraph, and radio communications services suffered greatly from World War II. The cable network suffered similarly, with equipment and buildings destroyed or badly damaged. In the several post-war economic plans, no priority was given to the telecommunications sector and between 1947 and 1966 only 0.2 per cent of the country's gross national product was spent on telecommunications. However, the creation of the *Centre National d'Etudes des Télécommunications* (CNET), now Orange Labs, in 1944 was all-important in encouraging further experimentation. From the mid-1940s new technical advances were made as a result of this official collaboration with the French telecommunications and electronics industry. The first coaxial links connected Paris to Toulouse in 1947 and coaxial cable gradually replaced the old paired wire. Shortly thereafter NATO financing ensured the development of transatlantic coaxial connections.

In the mid-1960s digital switching experiments had begun in France and by 1970 fibre-optic cable began to be used to support signal transmission. This research was paralleled by work at CNET into the problems of fully electronic, i.e., digital, connections. The national operator had an under-equipped infrastructure due to delayed technological development, which represented around two per cent of

France's gross national product. However, at that time the system began to be modernized as part of a long-term digitalization strategy.

11.3.2 Towards the modern era

By 1986 France had 25 million main lines which supported the connection of 96 per cent of French homes, as well as the development of many innovative products and services, such as the Teletel videotex system. From 1983 Teletel began to replace paper phone directories and its Minitel terminals were purchased in substantial quantities to create a largely captive market. In 1989 the Teletel system boasted a total of 85 million connection hours through 5 million terminals. The connection of Teletel to Transpac, the French national packet-switching network, implied that subscribers throughout the country could use other services, regardless of distance. National and international business connections combining voice and text distribution via the 'Numeris' ISDN system became possible, although full utilization would have to wait until the mid-1990s.

Such successes can be attributed to a consistent and monopolistic government policy and efficient investment in telecommunications equipment. By the 1990s, France's hundred per cent digital phone system was among the most modern in the world. Yet, events in the telecommunications world would soon overtake the company and its monopoly. The burdens of bureaucracy soon left the company struggling to catch up with the rest of the worldwide industry, already undergoing a process of deregulation and privatization that would transform the nature of the telecommunications business. Eyeing the success of other recently denationalized telephone providers, particularly the British system, and the telecom activities of the BPO, now renamed British Telecom, the French Government adopted a new name, France Télécom, giving it at least the appearance of keeping up with modern industry trends.

Demands for full deregulation of the European telecommunications industry resulted from the Commission of the European Communities (CEC) Green Paper in 1987. In part, the inability of monopoly organizations to cope with rapid technological change, and also the need for competition essential to support an economy driven more by information than production has contributed to these moves.

The French law passed on 2 July 1990 on the organization of public posts and telecommunications services transformed *Direction Générale des Télécommunications* into a public-service carrier with corporate legal status under the name France Télécom. This legal reform substantially changed the contractual relations between France's national operator and its partners. From 1 January 1991, these relations became governed by the French concept of 'private law'. Thus, from that time France Télécom gained budgetary, managerial, and organizational independence, like most of its European competitors. Yet the company remained under the guardianship and tight control of the Ministry of Posts and Telecommunications. The company's monopoly status remained intact.

France Télécom faced the loss of portions of its monopoly after 1993, under the terms of the European Community's Open Network Provision of 1989 which guaranteed to all value-added network (VAN) service providers equal access to their countries' telecommunications infrastructure. The supply of terminal equipment, such as telefax machines and telephone handsets, and VANs' services such as home banking, then became open to competition, although strictly licensed. Competition in the provision of computer data transfer was also allowed, provided that private firms did not undercut France Télécom.

In the late 1980s and early 1990s the French telecommunications industry tried to achieve the international scope necessary to compete in new markets such as car telephones and radio-telephone paging equipment. France Télécom emerged as one of the world's top four public telecommunications carriers.

During the late 1990s, France Télécom found itself rushing to catch up with many of the major developments in the telecommunications industry. In particular, the company was very late to the Internet table, a lateness blamed on the company's complacency with its Minitel 'cash cow'. But the Minitel service, which had not seen any significant technological advancement since its introduction in 1983, quickly paled in comparison to the Internet, and particularly with the rise of the World Wide Web. In May 1996 France Télécom finally introduced its own Internet service provider, dubbed Wanadoo. The company also joined the growing wave of mergers and partnerships sweeping the telecommunications industry, announcing its intention to form a partnership with Deutsche Telekom and Sprint Communications, called Global One.

In 1997 the company joined another joint-venture partnership, Infostrada, formed by Olivetti Corporation and Bell Atlantic, which brought the company into Italy's recently deregulated telecommunications industry. During the 1990s, France Télécom began entering international markets including Argentina, Mexico, Indonesia, Senegal and Vietnam. In recognition of its own growing international nature, the company removed the *accent aigu* from the spelling of its name, becoming France Telecom in 1993.

In the meantime, France Telecom, or at least its management, eyed with some envy the developments of the European telecommunications industry, as country after country denationalized their telephone carriers and ended their government monopolies, a process culminating in Deutsche Telekom's deregulation in 1996. An initial attempt to end French government control of the company and bring the company to the stock market was brutally rebuffed by France Telecom's own employees, 75 per cent of whom participated in a strike protesting the move which would end their civil servant status. The next attempt to denationalize the company had to wait until 1995, and again was quashed by an employee strike. But several months later the French government passed a new law transforming the company into a *Société Anonyme*. This event took place on 1 January 1997. It resulted in a public company in name if not yet in fact. The date for the company's entry on the Paris Bourse was set for June 1997 for a sale of shares worth from FFR 25 billion (EUR 3.8 billion) to FFR 40 billion (EUR 6 billion), the largest public offering ever in France.

France's government, led by the right wing, seemed prepared to allow France Telecom to leap into the new telecommunications era. However, the national election of May 1997 brought the Socialist Party to power, vowing to stop, or at least to postpone, the public offering. Although placed on hold, France Telecom's public offering (which would result in the French government's share being reduced to some 55 per cent) seemed inevitable and likely to occur before the European Union's 1 January 1998 deadline.

11.3.3 From France Telecom to Orange

The *Direction générale des Télécommunications* became France Telecom on 1 January 1988. France Telecom provided fixed telephony services and was also moving towards mobile services and the provision of Internet access. Between 2000 and 2003, the purchase of Orange (UK) gave a new dimension to the company, which became the leading ISP despite a fierce price war.

In September 2004, the French state sold some of its shares so that it would not be the majority shareholder any more. Hence France Telecom became a private company – 115 years after its nationalization the phone became private again in France. A number of important corporate events followed.

On 27 July 2005 France Telecom announced the takeover of 80% of the mobile phone operator Amena, which had 24% of the market in Spain, for EUR 6.4 billion of which EUR 3 billion corresponded to a capital increase.

By 2005 France Telecom was the second-largest ADSL operator worldwide, after China Telecom and before SBC Communications, and the first European ADSL operator, according to the company Dataxis France.

Since 1 June 2006 France Telecom has been commercializing all its products and services outside France under a single brand: Orange.

In June 2007 the French state sold another 5% of its France Telecom shares. As a result the public shareholding (French state and ERAP) represented 27%. At the same time, France Telecom sold Orange Netherlands and bought out the Spanish Internet service provider Ya and the Austrian mobile phone operator One.

On 21 September 2010 France Telecom contributed up to 40% of the capital of Meditelecom (with the Méditel brand), the second mobile phone operator in Morocco. When the operation was set up, Meditelecom had 10 million customers. The agreement planned that France Telecom would increase its share to 49% of the capital by 2015.

In February 2012, the fixed-line telephony services came under the Orange brand. Since then all solutions marketed by France Telecom have been using this brand. On 1 July 2013 Orange became the new name of the group.

11.3.4 Decisive reforms and liberalization policies

The transformation of France Telecom from a monopoly provider of public services into a provider of services to consumers in a competitive market took place gradually and with some difficulty. Since 1998 the telecommunications market in France has been fully competitive in accordance with the EU directives. However, as the cost of installing infrastructure is very high, the competition has chosen to build its own backbone cable and optical fibre network and has not chosen to build its own access infrastructure. Therefore, the opening of the market was essentially based on the provision of France Telecom's infrastructure to its competitors. In other words, France Telecom was instructed to allow competitors to use its network, providing them with access to the telecommunications market and allowing them to propose access offers based on its facilities (using France Telecom's wholesale offers, unbundling, etc.).

The constraint imposed on France Telecom was essentially legislative and regulatory. The system was and is still based on the imposition of rules by the French government and the European Union. Economic frameworks have been put in place by the government to apply the appropriate regulation (e.g., validation of interconnection rates, validation of wholesale tariffs). A strict enforcement of the rules by the French regulator (ARCEP) and the Competition Authority (especially by denunciation of competitors) has been put in place. As a result, France Telecom has been repeatedly condemned to heavy fines for obstructing free competition.

11.4 Major stakeholders in broadband development

11.4.1 The French government and the regulator

The parliament, the government and the regulator have worked to facilitate the access to ultra-fast broadband by the population and businesses.

The law for the modernization of the economy of 4 August 2008 required the pooling of FttH networks and the access to fibre for new buildings. It creates a 'right to fibre' based on the same principle as the 'right to the antenna'. The law on the fight against the digital divide (Pintat Act) of 17 December 2009 aimed to prevent the emergence of a new digital divide. It defined the digital territorial coverage master plan and created the digital development fund for territories (FANT) to finance the deployment in areas not covered by private initiative. Moreover, the government set goals for the deployment of very high data rates on the whole territory – 70% of the population to be covered in 2020 and 100% by 2025 – and made this a priority of the program of investments for the future.

To achieve these objectives, the government introduced a national 'high-speed' plan in June 2010 to concomitantly stimulate investment by operators beyond the densest areas and to support digital development projects driven by local authorities. Furthermore, the state has mobilized EUR 900 million in subsidies for future investments through the National Fund for the Digital Society (FSN) to support public initiative networks (PINs) that are complementary to deployments based on private initiative.

To take into account the expectations of local authorities, expressed through their associations, the government has made the following decisions[3]:

- Regional advisory committees for regional digital development (CCRANT) involving local authorities and operators have been put in place in areas under the authority of the *Préfet*, which guarantees the coherence of projects and good

---

[3] See www.investissement-avenir.gouvernement.fr; www.caissedesdepots.fr; www.territoires.gouv.fr.

coverage of all territories. Their purpose shall be to promote the quality of the dialogue between the private and public operators and ensure the proper implementation of commitments;

- The maximum co-financing ceilings were raised from EUR 350 to EUR 433 per outlet in order to better take into account the situation of the most rural areas. In addition, the maximum amount of this intervention is doubled for the connection of businesses located in areas of activities intended to be labelled 'high-speed activity area' and tripled for priority education and health buildings;
- The rates of assistance applicable for the overseas departments were increased to take into account their specificity. In addition overseas communities not currently connected to the Internet by submarine cable could file a grant application specifically for this purpose.

The funded 'high-speed' national program was published on 1 July 2010 and had three components:

- *To stimulate investment of network operators outside densely populated areas.* Non-subsidized but long-maturity loans may be granted to high-speed network operators, active outside the very densely populated areas. They will enhance the investment capacity of operators or of delegated public initiative networks. This component amounts to EUR 1 billion and was opened in summer 2011;
- *To support digital development projects of local authorities.* Funding will be provided to support the projects of local authorities that are complementary to the deployments based on private initiative. This financial support is mainly intended for the deployment of fibre networks to the subscriber. In addition, the public initiative projects may contain the deployment of alternative technologies to improve the quality of broadband access (wireline network modernization, deployment of wireless networks or satellite equipment). This component amounts to EUR 900 million and was also opened in summer 2011;
- *To ensure coverage of areas which are the most difficult to access.* Research and development

work dedicated to satellite technologies have been funded to continue covering sparsely populated areas. This is a component of the digital national fund with EUR 100 million, of which EUR 40 million was allocated in 2011 to prepare the next generation of satellites dedicated to provide access to high-speed internet.

As the incumbents are the major players regarding FttH, their strategies are being monitored closely by ARCEP, the French regulator, in deciding to define strong measures if and when necessary. ARCEP was created in 1997 as an independent administrative authority responsible for (among other tasks):

- defining the conditions of access to lines and therefore today's FttH deployment and sharing of new FttH networks;
- determining the specific obligations to be imposed on operators identified as having significant market power (SMP). It is important today in facilitating broadband deployment, whereby obligations are imposed on Orange regarding access to civil engineering infrastructure or access to the sub-loop of its copper access network.

Moreover, ARCEP leads the GRACO group which was set-up for the exchange of information between ARCEP, local authorities and operators[4].

11.4.2 Public and private stakeholders

The telecommunications market was opened to competition in January 1998 and since July 2003 operators are no longer subject to authorization. Each operator has the ability to define its investment projects without being subject to roll-out or coverage obligations. Only operators that use radio frequencies may be subject to such obligations; this applies to mobile operators and network operators using terrestrial radio fixed access.

Among the operators that deploy networks a distinction can be made between:

---

[4] See www.arcep.fr/collectivités.

- operators active in the retail market, including the major national operators (i.e., Bouygues Telecom, Free, Numericable, Orange, SFR) which have already begun the deployment of high data rate networks, mainly in large cities; and
- wholesale-only operators, usually led by a local authority, deploying wireless networks to offer wholesale services to operators in the retail market (e.g., Altitude infrastructure, Axione, Covage, SFR Communities, Tutor).

Among the suppliers of Internet access are the large national operators, but also local and specialized operators. End-users can generally benefit from different competing service offers on the same access network.

11.4.3 Local authorities

The deployment of new networks is a major industrial and financial project that involves both private operators and public authorities at various levels, including local authorities that are key stakeholders in the digital development of their territory. They can often play a major role in the deployment of ultra-fast Internet.

Since 2004, the French legislative framework has allowed communities to act as operators in the electronic communications sector. This has never been the case before. From that moment they have been able to reinforce their action in relation to regional digital development in the field of high and very-high data rate networks.[5] Local

authorities can play a decisive role in furthering regional development by enabling the broadband roll-out by operators through measures that encourage them to share their resources. They can also provide local information on underground infrastructure, help coordinate civil engineering works, install ducts for future use, authorise less costly civil engineering infrastructure and wiring on building facades, and encourage the pre-installation of fibre in new buildings and in buildings undergoing major renovations.

Many communities have begun thinking about the deployment on their territory of new ultra-fast networks. According to the law on the fight against the digital divide, this thinking is to be reflected in the development of master plans. Twenty projects of ultra-fast public initiative networks have already been built or are being defined. Some of them are conducted on a departmental or regional scale and deal with more than 100,000 lines.

Local authorities are involved at several stages (ARCEP 2011a). First of all, they develop, usually at the departmental level, the digital territorial development master plan (SDTAN) under article 24 of the Law on the fight against the digital divide of 17 December 2009. These indicative documents are essential. They provide an inventory of existing networks and of digital coverage. Moreover, they identify projects in progress or being planned. They also present the vision of the territory in matters of digital coverage and include action scenarios on how to achieve the vision, according to a strategy to promote consistency between private investment and public intervention. Subsequently, local authorities are consulted by the operators while they are deploying their networks. Finally, local authorities may decide to take a public initiative for network deployment, such as the law allows in accordance with the regulatory framework. These networks enable FttH deployment beyond the territories that would be covered by private operators. They also allow meeting the expectations of the population in the territories that will not benefit in the short term from fibre deployments, through the implementation of alternative solutions providing higher data rates.

---

[5] The law introduced in the General Code of Territorial Communities (CGCT) in article L.1425–1 defining the conditions for communities to intervene in the area of the electronic communications sector. Communities can be an operator: that is to say, establish and operate networks. Except in case of failure of private initiative, their activity is limited to the wholesale market and does not directly address end customers. The involvement of communities should respect the principles of equality and free competition in the electronic communications market. The network deployed at the initiative of a community does not enjoy a legal monopoly: that is to say, established by an Act or regulation. Private operators are thus likely, in some jurisdictions, to deploy networks in competition with those built at the initiative of local authorities. The converse is also possible under some conditions.

Local authorities' financial contribution to FttH roll-outs in more sparsely populated areas could be decisive and depend on:

- the European Commission guidelines on state aid;
- the role of the *Caisse des Dépôts* in helping local authorities to finance fibre deployment projects;
- the possibility of public-private partnerships with minority public funding in order to deploy fibre.

Local authorities can also help operators in their fibre roll-outs:

- by providing field studies identifying the best configurations and available infrastructure;
- by making available civil engineering ducts or overhead infrastructure for fibre deployment and space to host the concentration points;
- by installing additional ducts during road work;
- by authorizing the installation of cables on the facade of buildings;
- by permitting use of light engineering, installation of street cabinets, etc.

Upgrading the copper network is an alternative to full fibre deployment, which may be a solution for less densely populated areas in order to pave the way for FttH in the future. And, the demand for broadband upgrades is growing, which is becoming a major concern for a rising number of local authorities. Upgrading broadband through 'classic' sub-loop unbundling can lead to a real improvement in access rates for customers. However, there are high risks in such a roll-out for alternative operators, as sub-loop unbundling could be a way for the incumbent to regain market share.

While local authorities and public utilities are at the forefront of deployment and management of FttH infrastructure and networks, the implementation of the business models of FttH, especially the ones triggered by public entities, may encounter quite some hurdles and could diverge from local authorities as simple passive infrastructure providers to info-structure providers with active services provisioning.

Communities can benefit from state support within the framework of the national high-speed programme, particularly when their initiatives have a coherent strategy as defined in a SDTAN. To ensure consistency between the various initiatives in the territory, it is essential that local and regional operators align their strategies and, conversely, that operators provide transparency of their deployment projects.

Some communities have already initiated the operational phase of their projects, including the selection of private partners, the construction, and the technical and commercial operations. Many more are in the design phase. Hence, a sharp increase in public procurement procedures is expected between 2014 and 2016.

There is a high diversity in arrangements being used: including public service concessions, the farming-out of works contracts, market-based contracting (for design, construction, operation, and maintenance), and partnership contracts, among others. This will provide for different learning trajectories in the roll-out of broadband outside the major cities.

Although the implementation of high data rate broadband, including fibre to the premises, appears as inevitable, there are significant technical, economic, legal and financial risks that local authorities are facing and need to manage. They therefore tend to use private providers to help them manage these risks.[6]

11.5 Next-generation access technologies and network renewal

Before distinguishing and discussing the main kinds of next-generation access technologies, which are crucial for cost-effective broadband 'last-mile' access solutions, we are going to consider Orange's civil engineering infrastructure, which is essential for alternative operators to be able to supply end-users with ultra-fast broadband services.

---

[6] Source: Club collectivités territoriales de la Mission Ecoter, *Colloque Comment maîtriser les risqué dans les montages très haut debit*, 8 novembre 2013, Paris.

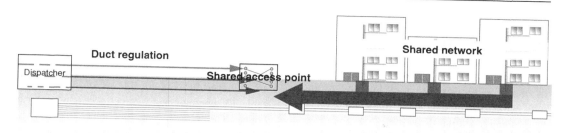

Figure 11.1 Network elements subject to regulation, France
Source: ARCEP, 2009.

11.5.1 Orange's civil infrastructure

Orange's network is historically structured as a hierarchy with, at the lowest level, close to 13,000 main distribution nodes or subscriber connections points called NRAs (*nœud de raccordement d'abonné* (subscriber connection node) – the main distribution frame (MDF)) which terminate several hundred to tens of thousands of telephone lines (on average 2,500 lines), and approximately 126,000 sub-distributors (SR) of varying sizes comprising an average of 250 lines.

The civil engineering infrastructure, including the ducts, pipes, etc., provides the canal for the cables with the wires connecting the NRAs and SRs with the homes and businesses. The point in the network where the subscriber's wires can be accessed by the alternative operator is important, as the level of aggregation that is provided determines the cost of providing services. The point of access also determines which part of the network is replicated and which part is shared.

For the deployment of FttH the availability of empty ducts and pipes as well as poles is important. Orange has a considerable civil engineering infrastructure that supports the telephone network, including:

- 350,000 km of civil engineering underground pipes (sheaths), and
- about 13 million posts and millions of supports on utility poles, usually managed by ERDF, the energy grid operator.

However, some of the cables of the telephone network are buried directly in the ground. In that case, it is not possible to rely on existing civil engineering infrastructure to facilitate the deployment of a new fibre network.

In cases of FttH, one or more fibres can be deployed from the access point to the home, or into an apartment building or business premises. If one fibre is used, the final part of the connection becomes shared; that is, multiple operators must have access to the fibre for end-users to be able to choose among operators. Figure 11.1 reflects the elements of the network infrastructure, highlighting the access point.

On the one hand, multi-fibre roll-out has several advantages:

- operators can be independent, having their own network from end to end, whereas sharing a fibre involves complex interactions;
- operators can implement their own technology and differentiate their service offering on that basis;
- consumers can have the choice of several offers from different ISPs, and churn costs should be low.

On the other hand, the constraint created for the building operator seems reasonable, at least when the shared access point is located near or inside the building:

- limited cost difference between a single and a multi-fibre roll-out;
- OPEX is likely to be lower for a multi-fibre roll-out, which is particularly significant as the infrastructure will be used for several decades.

11.5.2 DSL technologies

The telephone network of Orange covers the entire territory; hence, the use of xDSL technologies (including ADSL) on this network allows 98.5% of homes to be provided with broadband, albeit with variations in data rates (depending on line length) and territorial disparities.

To provide xDSL on access lines connected to an NRA, an operator can install a device for injecting a high-speed signal, the DSLAM. The data rate that can be offered varies from 20 Mbit/s for customers close to the NRA to 512 kbps for customers with longer lines. On very long lines, broadband cannot be provided due to too much attenuation of the signal.

Since 2007, Orange has installed a DSLAM in all sites with NRAs, which provides 98.5% of the population with access to xDSL broadband. Alternative operators (Bouygues Telecom, Free, SFR, etc.) have co-located DSLAMs in about 5,600 NRAs, which allows them to use unbundled access to offer broadband to over 83% of the population.

To increase the data rate on Orange's access network the equipment generating and receiving the xDSL signals (DSLAM or equivalent) needs to be positioned closer to the subscribers, for example by positioning it near the sub-distributor in a street cabinet. By connecting the DSLAM through fibre to the nearest switching centre, the copper lines are shortened and the fibre is moved closer to the homes. The increase in data rate should allow more than 95% of the concerned subscribers to receive xDSL access at a rate greater than 10 Mbit/s. The impact of the increasing data rate is even stronger when the homes are clustered around the sub-distributor, for example in a village.

By the end of March 2011, xDSL subscriptions offered by operators such as Orange, SFR, Free and Bouygues Telecom accounted for almost 93% of Internet access (excluding low-speed and mobile). Data rates provided by xDSL technologies range from 512 kbit/s to about 20 Mbit/s. The deployment of VDSL technology will further increase the available rates on some parts of the network, increasing the rates to around 50 Mbit/s.

11.5.3 Cable networks

In the 1980s and 1990s, coaxial cable networks were deployed for the distribution of broadcasting services, mainly in cities. Most of these networks are managed by Numericable which is the largest cable-TV operator and Internet access provider in France. The company was founded in July 2007 by the merger of two cable companies, Noos and NC Numericable.[7] The company has 1,300 employees, nearly 8 million connectable outlets enabling broadband access and 1 million subscribers. Since the end of 2010, Numericable has been updating and replacing existing equipment with new generation equipment that supports the Euro Docsis 3.0 specification.

The deployment of optical fibre close to the connected home (FttLA for 'Fiber to the Last Amplifier') can improve performance and provide access to an ultra-high data rate. To date, Numericable has completed the modernization of nearly 4 million outlets on which a download rate of around 100 Mbit/s (shared by several users) is provided. The upload rate is in turn much lower, of about 5 Mbit/s per subscriber.

11.5.4 Radio local loop networks

Radio systems for terrestrial fixed access (Wi-Fi, WiMAX, etc.) have been deployed mainly in areas poorly covered by xDSL networks. The data rates provided by WiMAX and Wi-Fi are strongly dependent on the backhaul capacity, the number of base stations and the number of users per base station. They can range from a few to tens of Mbit/s. These networks are usually managed by local operators or by specialized ones. Thanks largely to the intervention of local authorities tens of thousands of households and businesses are now connected to broadband through terrestrial wireless networks for fixed access.

Developments of WiMAX and Wi-Fi standards and the introduction of new technologies (including LTE) will provide for higher data rates in the medium term. To take full advantage of the performance of these new technologies, it will be

---

[7] See www.numericable.fr.

necessary that the base stations are connected to the core network through an optical fibre link.

11.5.5 Satellite networks

Existing satellite networks allow broadband access to the Internet with theoretical data rates up to 2 Mbit/s. This access technology has some inherent limitations (latency, data quotas) inconsistent with highly interactive uses (e.g., network games) or with extensive use of connection (e.g., video). Satellite access is mainly used in areas which are not served by terrestrial networks. The recent launch of satellites based on newer technologies (e.g., Ka-Sat) will allow download rates of around 10 Mbit/s per subscriber to be offered.

11.5.6 Mobile networks

In 2008, the government issued a plan *France Numérique 2012* with a view to providing guidance to the administration and to set targets regarding the digital economy. This plan aimed at supporting the economy with the following priorities:

- to enable any citizen to access networks and digital services;
- to develop the production and offers of digital contents;
- to increase and diversify the digital usages and services in enterprises, administrations and personal environments; and
- to modernize the governance of the digital economy.

Specific actions referring to radio frequency spectrum for mobile communication were included in the plan as follows:

- to start the request for applications for the use of available frequencies in the 2.1 and 2.6 GHz bands based on three objectives: to promote competition, derive the best value from spectrum and ensure the best possible coverage of the territory;
- to allocate the sub-band 790–862 MHz, released by the analogue TV switch-off, to cover the territory with fixed and mobile high data-rate networks.

Subsequently the remaining spectrum at 2 GHz (with the exception of the 2010–2025 MHz band for which no authorisation has been delivered yet) was granted to Free Mobile, enabling a new mobile operator to enter the French market in 2010.

In June 2011, the spectrum at 2.6 GHz (only the paired bands: 2x70 MHz) was assigned through a single-round combinatorial auction for a total of EUR 936 million to the existing operators Orange, SFR, Bouygues Telecom and Free Mobile. In December 2011 the spectrum at 800 MHz was granted through a single-round combinatorial auction for a total of EUR 3.5 billion to three operators, Orange, SFR and Bouygues Telecom.

Both the 2.6 GHz and 800 MHz assignment procedures included a scheme[8] that was designed to encourage carriers to open their networks fully to mobile virtual network operators (full MVNOs). Among the priorities set for the assignment of licences were coverage obligations aimed at regional digital development (99.6% of the population and the priority roads to be covered within 15 years), and increasing the intensity of competition with the presence of at least four operators in the 2.6 GHz band.

The migration from 3G to 4G is to be carried out over a period of several years, as was the case with the transition from 2G to 3G. In early 2011, 3G networks covered more than 95% of the population. In 2013 they achieved similar coverage to that of 2G networks; that is, more than 99.8% of the population.

Meanwhile, mobile operators look for strategies and solutions that will enhance their existing 3G networks while addressing their 4G deployment obligations. In the coming years 4G will significantly increase the performance of mobile networks. LTE technology allows shared theoretical data rates of several tens of Mbit/s or even 100 Mbit/s, which could correspond under operational conditions to actual rates of several Mbit/s or even tens of Mbit/s.

---

[8] The call for applications invited candidates to make commitments to improve competition in the wholesale market and increase the commercial autonomy of MVNOs on the retail market. It also invited them to offer MVNOs greater technical autonomy and better economic conditions.

11.5.7 Fixed-mobile complementarity

Mobile technologies also allow for fixed use: as such, they are a substitute for fixed networks. However, the new 4G mobile networks to be deployed will present, as it is the case today for 3G/3G$^+$ networks, different operational characteristics compared to fixed networks, either in terms of pattern of use, quality of service or data volume. Therefore they are not a full substitute for fixed and ultra-fast broadband networks. The deployment of high and very-high data rate mobile networks is to be integrated into an overall consideration of the national plan. Indeed the transition from high to very-high data rate mobile requires connecting radio transmitters with fibre and therefore the deployment of fibre closer to the premises.

Whatever the technologies, including terrestrial and satellite solutions, access to broadband and ultra-fast Internet will need to be implemented in a complementary manner. This complementarity will allow meeting the immediate needs of rural areas as well as isolated areas without compromising the long-term objective of ultra-fast broadband access for all. This is particularly relevant where the investments in the increase of data rates can be reused as part of the investment in the transition to FttH. To realize this complementarity effective local planning is necessary. Thanks to local planning, it will be possible to identify detailed local needs and priorities and determine the adequate technology. Master plans are one of the best tools for this type of technology planning.

11.6 Main stakes in broadband deployment

11.6.1 Socio-economic stakes

The deployment of ultra-fast networks is an important factor in the development of innovative services for the benefit of individuals and businesses. These economic and social stakes are a factor in the attractiveness and long-term development of the territories.

On the one hand, FttH networks are expected to unleash their economic potential and societal benefits by opening up the first/last mile bandwidth bottleneck, thereby strengthening the information society while avoiding a digital divide. FttH networks hold great promise to enable the support of a wide range of new and emerging services and applications, such as quadruple-play, video on demand, videoconferencing, peer-to-peer audio/video filesharing, multichannel high-definition television (HDTV), multimedia/multiparty online gaming, telemedicine, telecommuting and surveillance.

On the other hand, wireless technologies have seen tremendous success over the years and they have become increasingly popular due to their fast deployment and their ability to provide flexible and ubiquitous Internet access. In particular, next-generation fixed wireless broadband networks (e.g., deployed as wireless mesh networks, WMNs) are currently motivated by several applications including broadband home networking, neighbourhood networking and enterprise networking.

The following figures reflect the use by consumers of the new broadband services (CREDOC, 2013):

- 71% of people are connected to the Internet at home for leisure, work, study, communication with relatives, shopping, etc.;
- 25% of people use the Internet for work or training;
- 43% of people use the Internet for administrative declarations or tax returns.

However, the quality of Internet access varies depending on location:

- Approximately 13% of households cannot have a download rate of 2 Mbit/s or higher. Below this threshold the quality of access is inadequate for some services;
- Approximately one out of four households cannot receive television services via their connection to the Internet. Moreover, one out of two cannot benefit from high definition television.

According to IDATE, France certainly ranks behind South Korea, Japan or the United States but is at the forefront of European countries, including the Scandinavian countries, in the coverage of FttH/FttB. The delay is not due to the percentage of households covered by high data rate networks, but to actual subscriptions. Indeed, only about 10% of eligible households actually subscribed. The reason for this is the high quality of ADSL and the lack of promotional offers by broadband operators until 2011. The first campaign began only in 2012.

11.6.2 Industrial stakes

The deployment of FttH networks is a major industrial project that requires the mobilization of technical resources and expertise.

In France, optical fibre does not represent a new technology. Indeed, it has been deployed over the last twenty years at the national level, in the so-called transport networks. To facilitate broadband, it has been deployed subsequently in the networks connecting telephone exchanges (the collection networks), first by Orange and later by alternative operators, as well as by local authorities, along with the unbundling of Orange's local networks. New fibre local loops have been deployed to subscribers (residential and business premises) such that residents and businesses have access to the most innovative digital services.

FttH network deployment is a major industrial project because this deployment requires the large-scale mobilization of technical resources and expertise for production of optical fibre and network installation. The optical fibre service to all buildings requires the deployment of a network of over one million kilometres of fibre. This project can be compared to the deployment of the telephone network in the 1970s and 1980s, which had required more than 15 years.

11.6.3 Financial stakes

The financial burden of FttH deployment can be estimated nationally at about EUR 25 billion. This cost is highly dependent on population density, dispersion of housing and the availability of civil engineering infrastructures. Hence, this cost can be around EUR 400 per line in an urban area, while it can exceed EUR 2000 in rural areas where housing is scattered. The cost of deployment is not proportional to the population covered. That is, the cost of

FttH coverage of 80% of the population and businesses represents about half of the total FttH deployment cost.

While a major part of investments is likely to be carried out by private operators, public funding is also needed. Public financing could help make high data rate networks economically feasible where the costs would otherwise be prohibitive. According to the current regulatory policy, such public funding should be targeted to alleviate barriers to private investment. The requirements on public funding will depend on the income that may be derived from the exploitation of new FttH networks, which in turn depends on user demand for very high data rates and new services.

The deployment of fibre to the sub-distributor should generally represent the largest part of the costs of the implementation of higher data rates. This cost is highly dependent on the length of the fibre and civil engineering infrastructure. In 80% of cases, the implementation cost is between EUR 30,000 and EUR 50,000 per sub-distributor. According to the obligations imposed by ARCEP, an access offer must be made available by Orange at a price reflecting the costs, including costs associated with hosting alternative operators according to cost orientation policy (ARCEP (2011b)).

The total cost is up to EUR 100,000 per sub-distributor. This amount depends heavily on the cost of deploying fibre to sub-distributors, which often fits into a larger project. This cost is generally borne by the local community backing the deployment, which then retains ownership of the facilities.

However, many investment proposals, in particular those involving infrastructure sharing by private sector operators or resulting from public-private co-operation, are perceived by potential investors as high risk transactions and therefore more likely to fail in attracting private financing. This may be because they have a longer payback period or simply because the promoters are too small and inexperienced to attract the interest of large financial institutions. Difficult liquidity conditions and uncertain economic prospects also limit the willingness to accept risk by private investors and, in effect, raise the financing costs.

Local and regional authorities are increasingly exploring alternative financing arrangements, including public-private partnerships (PPP) for financing broadband infrastructure. These solutions aim to optimize synergies from combining public and private sector financial resources as well as their respective competencies in regulation and in risk-based investments.

11.7 Broadband regulation mechanisms

The broadband regulation is based on the use of a large degree of sharing and providing incentives to investment. In this respect the regulation of Orange's civil engineering infrastructure is essential for the deployment of an optical fibre local loop such that alternative operators also can supply end-users with ultra-fast broadband services.

11.7.1 Regulating access to Orange's civil infrastructure

Accessing buildings is currently the major obstacle to FttH roll-outs for all operators. As a result, the French Government proposed legislative measures that outline the principle of sharing the terminal section of optical fibre networks and endowed the regulator ARCEP with regulatory powers in that area, notably for setting the technical and pricing terms for a system of infrastructure sharing. This stage of the roll-out requires property (co)owners to sign an agreement with a carrier who will need to perform work inside the (potentially co-owned) property. This choice of 'building operator' should in no way impede each of the building occupants' freedom to choose their actual service provider.

In FttH projects civil engineering is the main cost factor (50% to 80% of the total roll-out cost); hence, access to existing civil engineering infrastructure is important to reduce the total costs. In accordance with the market analysis decision of 25 July 2008 (markets 4 and 5), Orange must provide access to its civil engineering infrastructure under transparent, non-discriminatory and cost-oriented conditions. Pursuant to the decision of ARCEP in July 2008, Orange is obliged to provide access to its ducts to other operators

deploying FttH networks. The offer by Orange for that purpose is regulated by ARCEP, including its price. The offer must:

- provide efficient sharing of available space between different operators;
- promote the independence of operators involved in deploying such infrastructure;
- be offered at a price reflecting the costs incurred by Orange (cost orientation) and incorporating a smooth transition of subscribers to FttH;
- be independent of the length of the lines on the pooled portion of the networks, so as not to penalize deployment in rural areas.

Pursuant to a decision of ARCEP on 14 June 2011, Orange must also provide access to its poles and distribution points to other operators deploying FttH networks. This infrastructure will therefore be leveraged, especially in rural areas, where it is expected to reduce deployment costs. All operators need to be able to access this essential infrastructure to invest in ultra-fast broadband.

11.7.2 Infrastructure sharing: contractual and financial mechanisms

In addition, the Law on Modernising the Economy (4 August 2008) sets out specific rules for providing access to the last mile of ultra-fast broadband networks. This law states that the building operator must sign an agreement with the owner of the building. The agreement specifies the terms and conditions that apply to the deployment, maintenance and management of the fibre network in the building. The deployment of the fibre inside the building is financed entirely by the operator (at no cost to the owner). Once the agreement is signed, the building operator has six months to deploy the network (except for the last mile which involves agreements with other operators). The terms governing sharing between operators are not stipulated in this agreement, but rather in the agreements between operators.

To allow other operators to offer their services in homes that may be connected to the shared network, the operator who deployed this part of the network must offer them a passive access at the point of sharing. Such access must allow operators to control the entire technical chain by installing their own equipment at the sharing point.

Access can be done in several ways:

- co-financing offer: The operator participates in the financing of the shared network prior to its deployment by purchasing a usage right for the long term;
- access offer: After the deployment of the network, the operator buys a long term usage right;
- offer comprising access to the leased line (on the model of the local loop unbundling).

Investment offers or access offers allow an operator to have a long-term usage right on all or part of the fibre of the shared network. It also allows sharing of financial risk between the different operators who will then use the shared network to provide ultra-fast services.

These offers must be offered to other operators irrespective of whether the project is being carried out by a private operator or a local authority as part of a network of public initiative. When the project is supported by a local authority, co-financing should enable the mobilization of a maximum of private capital and encourage the effective use of the network by the major national operators.

In municipalities that constitute the 'very dense areas', co-financing amounts to a split of the total cost of the shared network between different operators. On the remainder of the territory, given the high cost of network deployment and the various investment capacities of the operators, co-financing will be gradual. It may well result in the acquisition of a permanent usage right on a limited number of lines deployed in a single project.

In principle, the co-financing of FttH networks shared by several operators should encourage investment while ensuring sustainable competition in the retail market. It secures the project for the operator that deploys the network by guaranteeing 'customers' from the initial project onward.

11.8 Mitigation of market risks

The deployment of a new local loop that runs to subscribers' homes also means significant market risks that should be mitigated as much as possible.

We can distinguish here two main kinds of risk. The first one is the risk of creating a local monopoly in each building. The second one is about the inconsistency in fibre deployments due to the complex interplay amongst the various stakeholders.

11.8.1 Risk of local monopoly

To mitigate the risk of local monopoly, operators are required by regulation to share the terminating sections of their optical fibre network. In other words, the first operator to install fibre in a building should provide other operators access to it under conditions that enable effective competition, allowing them to market a competitive offer to the residents.

For this purpose, the regulatory framework for FttH deployment outside dense areas has been detailed since the beginning of 2011. As a result, Orange must henceforth offer a range of 'shared connection points' (SCPs). The related SCP service offer can be used by an operator made responsible for network deployment by a local authority as part of a public initiative.

Orange published its wholesale offer to access its fibre networks (FttH) outside dense areas in July 2011. In accordance with the principles set by the regulator ARCEP, the offer allows the pooling of networks in non-dense areas, giving end-users the choice of any service provider.

To meet this requirement and allow the full development of the new injection point near the sub-distributor, Orange signed an agreement with Free (Iliad Group) on deployments to be done in 2011 and 2012. Orange is to spend EUR 2 billion by 2015 to provide the optical fibre in 3,600 municipalities with coverage of 10 million households in 2015 and 15 million households in 2020, nearly 60% of French households.

11.8.2 Risk of deployment inconsistency

Spontaneous and unplanned deployments by multiple operators might lead to inconsistencies such as coverage holes (a few unserved homes between two pooling areas corresponding to two distinct pooling points), over-coverage (a few houses covered by two pooling areas under the responsibility of two different operators) or additional costs (if an operator deploys a FttH network for an entire neighbourhood with the exception of one street). That is why deployments should be made taking into account the views of all public and private actors involved in roll-out projects. This implies some complementarity between public and private projects and some coherence of the various projects of public initiative networks. Only strategic planning at a sufficiently large geographic scale can provide this overall consistency.

11.9 NGA investment strategies

The need for investment, both to maintain and upgrade existing networks and to build up the new fixed and mobile networks. can be estimated at around EUR 6 billion per year during the following 15 years[9].

The country's leading carriers have announced ultra-fast broadband deployment plans and the first roll-outs have already begun in Paris and several other major cities. DSL market players have opted to deploy new optical fibre local loops to the home. These new fibre networks open up new opportunities for LLU operators wanting to invest in their own local loop and so migrate from a strategy based on leasing to one based on investment. Cable operators are also working to upgrade their coaxial networks by pulling fibre to the premises.

To mobilize all investment capabilities to support the widespread deployment of FttH in the territory, it is desirable that the public and private initiatives be complementary and well-articulated. This particular issue requires, firstly, specifying deployment costs, secondly, describing the respective features of both types of investment.

---

[9] Source: *Déploiement des réseaux très haut débit sur l'ensemble du territoire national: rapport d'étude technologies et coûts de déploiement, mécanismes de soutien possibles*. Etude réalisée pour le compte de la DATAR par les cabinets Tactis et Seban & Associés, janvier 2010.

11.9.1 Sharing deployment costs

The investments required of an operator to roll out an FttH network correspond essentially to the cost of building a new local loop that extends to the subscriber premises. Civil engineering is by far the largest cost item when constructing a new local loop. If an operator were forced to undertake its own civil engineering and to open trenches across the city, deployment costs would run into the tens of billions of euros across France. Pioneer roll-outs are thus taking place in cities where existing infrastructure can be reused: the incumbent carrier is deploying optical fibre in the ducts inherited from the former monopoly, while alternative operators are installing fibre in the underground sewer networks (e.g., in Paris) and in city-owned ducts (e.g., in Montpellier).

Finally the overall capital cost of deployment of fibre for all is estimated at EUR 25 billion. This cost is expected to be borne primarily by the private sector. However, public investment will be essential because the low population density of much of the French territory makes deployment costs unaffordable for the operators.

11.9.2 Private initiative

Private operators deploy FttH networks in the areas where it is economically viable. Given the deployment costs and expected revenues, they focus mainly on deployments in urban areas. Already, as part of the national 'high-speed' programme, private operators have announced their intention to cover nearly 57% of households, corresponding to about 3,400 cities located in over 200 large urban areas throughout the territory, by 2020.

Private initiatives are encouraged by the regulatory framework which allows:

– mutual investments between private investors (operators) where the deployment of multiple networks would not be economically feasible (about 85% of the population and more than 95% of the territory);
– the deployment of competing networks, if the operators wish, where competition is economically feasible (about 15% of the population and less than 5% of the territory).

11.9.3 Public initiative

In mid-2010, 215 projects of the public initiative networks (PINs) type were identified, including 111 covering more than 60,000 inhabitants. Different types of communities are the source of PINs: regions, departments, joint associations and cities. They are usually set-up in partnership with a private operator, under different legal constructs: direct control, public service concession (concession or lease) or public private partnerships (PPP).

The public initiative networks deployed to date have mainly resulted in:

- unbundling of nearly 40% of telephone lines, primarily through the deployment of fibre collect networks (ARCEP);
- connecting by fibre nearly 4,400 business zones (AVICCA);
- improving the broadband coverage of areas not eligible for ADSL (called 'white areas').

Local authorities may start FttH deployment projects throughout the territory to the extent that they comply with legislative frameworks (Article L.1425–1 of the General Code of the Local Authorities). However, in view of the EU rules, public initiatives should not contain state aid in the territories that would be subject to private projects. Hence, a public initiative is legally more constrained for the territories that would be subject to private projects.

11.10 Realizing the Digital Agenda targets

11.10.1 Territory coverage: DSL deployment

On 30 June 2011 the wholesale broadband DSL market was nearly 11.2 million lines, of which more than 8.3 million were fully unbundled. Local loop unbundling, in particular full LLU, drives market growth. In the retail broadband market, these DSL access lines are marketed by alternative operators to residential users and to enterprises.

Thanks to local authorities' projects, backhaul networks were developed in more sparsely populated areas. Around half of the EUR 2.1 billion invested came from public financing. As a result 1,420 new exchanges have been unbundled for use by alternative operators serving 4.6 million households.

11.10.2 Territorial coverage: fibre deployment

By cutting the link between the location of people or activities and urban areas, which over time have gradually concentrated much of the population, production and services, broadband deployment gives a chance to the most rural areas, which constitute the bulk of the territory. In contrast, areas that will not have access to ultra-fast broadband at affordable costs may experience an inevitable decline.

However, France is slow to complete its coverage of mobile and broadband Internet. It is slow in deploying networks with very high data rates that will succeed standard broadband networks. This is especially true in the rural areas, as the marginal cost of a subscriber is much higher than in urban areas, which discourages private operators to invest (SENAT, 2011). In this context, cheaper radio-based technologies could still be a useful supplement to fibre in less dense areas.

Moreover, FttB started off well with over 250,000 subscribers, including those connected to the network of Numericable, but the FttH proposition does not seem to convince potential subscribers. While 900,000 homes are connected, only 10% of them have subscribed. With high quality and inexpensive ADSL available in very dense areas where fibre has been deployed first, consumers still do not recognize a need to move from the old copper pair to fibre.

The framework for the deployment of fibre provides for a high level of sharing of networks (90%) over almost the whole territory (95% of the surface and 80% of the population). In the remaining dense areas, sharing is imposed only for the final part of the network (access to the buildings), whereby the operators have the choice to share or not the other parts of the network.

Since 2009, the main operators are engaged in fibre deployments on the 'horizontal' part; that is to say, located on the public domain rather than entering the building. On the one hand, there is FttH deployed by Orange, SFR and Free, and, on the other hand, fibre being deployed by Numericable to replace the portion of the coaxial cables located on public property, the so-called fibre to the amplifier (FttA), with the terminal portion remaining as coaxial cable. Fibre deployments are taking place in about forty cities.

FttH networks are currently deployed mainly in large cities. They allow subscribers at this stage to benefit from a symmetrical rate of about 100 Mbit/s; that is, in both the downlink and the uplink. There are 148 municipalities (representing 20 urban areas) constituting the 'dense areas' characterized by a high proportion of collective buildings.

The number of houses covered by FttH has evolved significantly since 2010. Approximately 2.4 million homes have access to ultra-fast FttH offers: this means that their occupants can subscribe to commercial offers of at least one Internet access provider using this technology. In addition, fibre has been deployed to the foot of buildings representing 3 million dwelling units, the latter being described as 'ready-to-be-connected'. The number of homes covered is up about 33% compared to 30 June 2010. Moreover, about 4.2 million homes are eligible for ultra-fast optical fibre offers based on coaxial cable, of which just over 1.2 million are outside the very dense areas.

11.11 Market dynamics

The retail broadband market is dynamic and competitive thanks to innovative offers and productive efficiency. Business models have been defined by the market based on infrastructure-based competition.

On the demand side the household penetration rate is about 75%, thanks to:

- the boom of IP telephony accounting for more than 50% of traffic;
- the IPTV boom with more than 7 million users.

As to theoretical data rates, over 50% of the population have access to more than 10 Mbit/s and 75% to more than 4 Mbit/s.

More generally, the ultra-fast broadband market is characterized by the following three main trends: (1) the decline in fixed voice lines due to the growth in broadband and mobile minutes; (2) customers becoming more demanding of increasing data rates; and (3) competition moving from pure price competition to service- and segment-specific offers.

11.11.1 Decline in fixed voice and growth in broadband and mobile services

Mobile networks were originally developed to provide a mobile communication service. They are now used less and less for voice. There has been a decrease in the average consumption of voice per mobile user since 2007, from approximately 157 minutes per user per month to 140 minutes in 2010. This is particularly due to the widespread use of unlimited voice offerings over fixed broadband lines and the increased popularity of instant messaging. This trend is reflected in the decline in revenues of narrowband services in recent years.

11.11.2 Growing demand for bandwidth

The number of mobile users has been increasing steadily since the early 2000s. With the mobile penetration rate being defined as the ratio of the number of active SIM cards to the size of the French population, the penetration is more than 108%, with 73.7 million users in 1Q 2013.

Among the users of mobile services, it is necessary to identify two types of use:

- historical use, corresponding to interpersonal communications services such as voice and SMS;
- new use, corresponding to the transmission of data services and media at large (Internet, MMS, e-mail, but also streaming, mobile TV, etc.) via sophisticated terminals[10] that is made possible by the development of 3G networks.

---

[10] According to the UMTS Forum, one phone out of two sold in France will be a smartphone in 2014. In addition, Cisco expects that, within the mobile fleet, one phone out of three in 2014 is a smartphone, an increase greater than 100% over 2009.

Indeed in the installed base there is a strong growth of terminals providing access to mobile data services (Internet and multimedia). In the first quarter of 2011, three-quarters of handset sales were multimedia-capable, half of which was composed of smartphones.[11]

As the number of mobile phone users is growing moderately, the number of mobile users exclusively focused on use of data continues to increase in turn, representing a more and more important share in the overall number of mobile users. Thus, early in 2011, nearly one SIM card out of ten is a non-voice SIM card.

11.11.3 Price competition issues and mobile market sustainability

Despite the sector's concentration, competition is still going strong. Since 2008, the three main operators have had a more than 90% market share, while Orange alone is just under 50%. Even if the growing market turns into a churn market, purchase rates vary widely because of new players (Free Mobile, Bouygues, Darty) and a greater diversity of offerings (quadruple-play, etc.). Moreover, nowadays there are thirty-nine mobile virtual network operators (MVNO) and three trademark license agreements.

The retail market is characterized by volume growth and a downward trend in prices resulting in lower revenues: -2.2% in 2011.[12] Accelerating smartphone adoption is driving data revenue growth. Mobile network operators' revenues and EBITDA margins are more and more under pressure, while data services are growing quickly. Voice and SMS still represent the lion's share of revenues. Regulatory pressure is exercised on termination rates and international roaming.

The existing mobile tariff structure is highly leveraged on voice and SMS revenues, while operators are competing on 'all you can eat' data downloads at unsustainable costs. It is not possible to monetize demand for heavy data entertainment content because consumers value content, not

gigabytes per month. The current solution tends to restrict mobile broadband use rather than embrace growing demand. This is actually a dilemma for mobile network operators (MNOs) because 85% of their revenues come from voice and 70% of their costs come from data. For example, the average usage is more than 400 MB/month/user for Orange.

MVNOs can be distinguished in four categories, each having its own specific marketing strategy. The first category can be called 'ethnic MVNO'; operators in this category target a specific nationality or origin, specific border residents or tourists. This category differs in offering aggressive rates for international calls. With this position, an 'ethnic MVNO' obtains higher revenue per user than the average by handling a higher proportion of international calls.

The second category is designated as 'low-cost MVNO', whereby operators offer more aggressive pricing by focusing on tightly controlling customer acquisition and operating costs. Various strategies are used to achieve the lower costs: customer acquisition via Internet, dematerialization of administrative support (invoicing, payment processing) and use of voice servers.

The third category is called 'brand operator'; this type of operator targets a specific population group based on a well-known brand name. Here we find the media (radio, television), the retail stores, banks, etc. Additional value-added services may be offered to attract the target population and to improve the revenue per subscriber: e.g., downloading music, variety show results, SMS votes or vouchers as a lump sum. Their targets are specific demographic niches: e.g., to attract young people, as applied by Breizh Mobile, Universal Music Mobile, Virgin Mobile, MTV, NRJ Mobile. However there are also major retail distributors, such as Mobile Leclerc, Carrefour Mobile, Auchan Mobile, banks and major service providers.

The issue of mobile tariffs is becoming more prevalent in public opinion. Indeed, three-quarters of people believe that individuals who have very low incomes should be eligible for a lower social tariff in order to connect to the Internet at home. The idea of a social tariff is defended by all population groups: youth, seniors, managers,

[11] Source: GroupM / SFR Régie, *3rd Observatory of Mobile Internet, April 2011.*
[12] Source: *12th DigiWorld Yearbook.*

workers, employees, high income users, middle class, low-income users, non-Internet users (CRE-DOC, 2013).

However, mobile tariffs are still relatively high in France. Mobile operators try to get consumers involved in binding offers over 12 or 24 months and intend to make consumers pay 15 eurocents per minute on average. On the tariff issue, Free has shaken-up the retail market by proposing non-binding offerings only, to address the demand of users to call 'without counting' as in the fixed telephony market.

In September 2011 Orange launched a 'low cost' brand called 'Sosh' to try to compete with Free. The Sosh brand has lower rates than those typically charged by Orange. It is distributed via the Internet and has a subscription model with no commitment. Sosh targets the 'digital natives' who are using their smartphones more for data than for voice.

The new brand of Orange can be compared to 'B&You', launched by Bouygues Telecom in early July 2011[13], and to that of SFR which was unveiled in June 2011. The SFR offer called 'Car-rées' is without commitment and without handset subsidy. As for Free, it offers an unlimited mobile package for Freebox subscribers and another one for the non-Freebox subscribers.

The Free offering is a promotional offer only, reserved for a few millions of people. The issue is about the sustainability of the mobile market.

11.11.4 Regulation of the value chain

Successful long-term deployment of broadband networks raises the question of the underlying economic model. Indeed, the deployment of ultra-fast broadband makes possible the explosion of new uses. Conversely, the existence of attractive content stimulates the appetite of consumers for ultra-fast services and supports the deployment of networks. In this context, the question naturally arises of sharing the value and of financing networks between the various links in the value chain.

---

[13] This offer without commitment and without mobile terminal is designed for independent users with a developed technological culture and using the Internet freely.

Actors seek to position themselves in the value chain based on extending their traditional role as suppliers developing service platforms; service providers are developing operating systems for mobile devices; and, finally, some telecom operators are investing in content. These strategies are reflected in particular through policies of exclusivity, which are not reprehensible in themselves but which raise competition issues. The Competition Authority has, by its opinion of 7 July 2009, set out the framework and limitations of these exclusive mechanisms (Competition Authority, 2011).

Beyond issues related to strategies implemented by the actors, there is the more general topic of relations between the various links in the chain, including between 'content' and 'containers'. This problem then joined the issue of neutrality of the Internet, and more generally of network neutrality.

11.12 Case analysis

If the French situation in matters of broadband can be taken as an example, the penetration of ultra-fast broadband seems still to be insufficient. In fact, the dynamics and quality of the existing broadband networks seem to hinder the development of ultra-fast broadband in France. The challenge is now to incite financially and organize more clearly the deployment of optical fibre local loop.

The coverage of France by ultra-fast broadband networks will not only result from the strength of market players, but will be achieved through a combination of several actions:

– First, at the strategic level: the parliament intervened in laying down the principles and objectives for the fight against the Digital Divide; then, the government and the regulator determined the scope of the regulation and, finally, local authorities, usually the 'départements' have completed the development of regional planning networks. Local authorities, as well as the various state bodies and policy makers, have taken responsibility as planners;

– Second, at the operational level, are the initiatives of the private operators and local authorities as operators;

– Third, at the tactical level: The government has provided for regulation to reduce the costs and increase the funding to close the digital divide.

Neutrality and flexibility of the regulation mechanisms are aimed at balancing the investment and financing on the more-or-less centralized deployments, regardless of the political choices made.

11.12.1 Lessons learned

Next to the impulse from public authorities and utilities, the regulatory policy is essential and has a major impact on the features of the French broadband market, even if embedded within the European regulatory framework.

An infrastructure-based competition must gain a significant geographic footprint in areas where dynamic competition is possible. The regulatory framework has to be clear and provide incentives to invest in those zones. The first roll-outs have helped to measure consumers' willingness to pay for new services and enabled the industrialization of the roll-out processes.

At the same time, roll-outs in less densely populated areas must be prepared by promoting shared investment, the deployment of networks open to all operators and local authority involvement when private investment is insufficient.

At the European level and across member states, public authorities could build or finance sector-specific infrastructure in line with the *State aid Broadband Guidelines*, allowing fair and non-discriminatory access to broadband operators, thereby triggering the take-off of competitive service provision in areas that would otherwise be uneconomic to serve.

11.12.2 Possible generalizations

Local authorities should also consider using fibre core networks that have been or are being constructed to link up public entities (schools, libraries, clinics) in order to bring ultra-fast connections to unserved communities.

In order to speed up the use of state aid for broadband, member states should notify the EC of their national framework schemes and thereby avoid multiple notifications of individual projects.

As actions are undertaken predominantly at local level, it is necessary to develop and improve mechanisms to enable local actors to obtain relevant information to reduce investment costs.

11.12.3 Some recommendations

Could the results achieved in the French context be transposed to other countries, and under what conditions?

The regulator should enable operators to invest in ultra-fast broadband under equal conditions, which means:

– access to existing infrastructure, especially civil engineering which is the largest cost item;
– sharing new investments, especially in the last mile.

Sharing the last mile allows:

– operators to limit overall roll-out costs;
– only a single installation in buildings, instead of multiple ones by different operators;
– the prevention of local monopolies;
– building residents to have a choice of ISPs for their ultra-fast services.

To define the rules for ultra-fast broadband regulations, different aspects have to be tackled with the stakeholders:

– relations between property owners and network operators (using a sample agreement);
– technical aspects (definition of the engineering rules for infrastructure sharing, based on the principle of technological neutrality);
– assessing the cost of the different solutions;
– establishing pricing principles.

To support PPPs, it would be necessary to mobilize the know-how as well as to channel existing and future technical assistance funds to project preparation and to structuring complex multi-party financial transactions in a rapidly changing environment.

To match the needs of investment projects in terms of flexibility, maturity and risk, it would be necessary to set up concrete proposals for financing instruments to complement existing means of financing broadband infrastructure. Such instruments could be of debt, guarantee or equity type or a combination thereof. These instruments should also be designed to serve as conduits for funds earmarked by local and regional authorities and by private sector investors for financing the roll out of broadband infrastructure.

To unlock the financing for the higher-risk infrastructure projects, such instruments would require dedicated financial resources. To illustrate the potential impact, a financial contribution is likely to attract other funds from public or private sectors which could underpin gross investment depending on the financing needs and the risk profiles of the underlying projects.

References

ARCEP (Autorité de régulation des Communications électroniques et des Postes) (2009). Toward FTTH, presentation by Joëlle Toledano, ARCEP Commissioner at DigiWorld Summit, Montpellier, November 18.

(2011a). La montée vers le très haut débit sur l'ensemble du territoire. Guide sur le déploiement de la fibre optique à l'usage des élus et des collectivités territoriales, juillet.

(2011b). Rapport public au Parlement sur les coûts de la boucle locale cuivre de France Télécom et leur évolution dans le cadre de la transition du cuivre vers la fibre, décembre.

(2013a). Observatoire des marchés des communications électroniques, Services fixes haut et très haut débit (Marché de gros), Services mobiles. Résultats trimestriels en 2010, 2011, 2012, 2013.

(2013b). Recommandation de l'ARCEP sur l'identification des lignes en fibre optique jusqu'à l'abonné (FttH), avril.

ACUF (2010). Association des communautés urbaines de France. Le déploiement du très haut débit: quels enjeux pour les métropoles françaises?

Autorité de la Concurrence (2011). Rapport annuel. Direction de l'information légale et administrative, Paris, 2012. ISBN : 978-2-11-008929-8.

AVICCA, Divers rapports. Association des Villes et Collectivités pour les Communications électroniques et l'Audiovisuel, www.avicca.org.

COE-Rexecode (2011). L'économie numérique et la croissance. *Document de travail N°24, mai.*

CREDOC (2013). La diffusion des technologies de l'information et de la communication dans la société française. Rapport n°297. Etude réalisée à la demande du Conseil Général de l'économie, de l'Industrie, de l'énergie et des Technologies et de l'Autorité de Régulation des Communications électroniques et des Postes. Novembre.

DATAR (2010). Déploiement des réseaux très haut débit sur l'ensemble du territoire national: rapport d'étude technologies et coûts de déploiement, mécanismes de soutien possibles. Etude réalisée pour le compte de la DATAR par les cabinets Tactis et Seban & Associés, janvier.

European Commission (2010). Communication from the Commission to the European parliament, the Council, the European economic and social Committee and the Committee of the regions. European Broadband: investing in digitally driven growth. COM(2010) 472.

Grémont E. (2005). Restructuration de l'Europe des Télécoms (1997–2005). Observatoire politico-économique des structures du Capitalisme (OpesC), décembre.

IDATE (2010). DigiWorld Yearbook. Montpellier, France: IDATE.

Little, Arthur D. (2011). L'économie des télécoms en France, Etude pour la Fédération Française des Télécoms.

SENAT (2011). Rapport d'information n°730, 6 juillet.

Shami, A., Maier, M., and Assi, C. (2009). *Broadband Access Networks: Technologies and Deployments*, Springer.

Spain

CLAUDIO FEIJÓO, JOSÉ-LUIS GÓMEZ-BARROSO, RAFAEL
COOMONTE AND SERGIO RAMOS

12.1 Introduction to the case study

As in other EU countries, the dynamics of the
broadband market in Spain have broadly followed
the three main stages of the electronic communications regulatory framework set out by the EU[1]:
initial liberalization, first stages of competition
and introduction of next-generation networks
(Gómez-Barroso and Feijóo, 2010). Broadband
had a merely token presence in the residential
market before the first stage of liberalization,
which took place in Spain during 1999 and 2000.
From 1999 to around 2004, the market was
dominated by ADSL technology – provided by
the incumbent Telefónica and a number of ISPs
that used bitstream access regulation. Cable
modem technology was also relevant, but only
in those places where cable operators were
already present in the market[2]. The overall broadband penetration (subscriptions per 100 inhabitants) was just 5% in 2003, a slow and relatively
delayed departure point compared with other EU
countries. From 2004 to the present, service-based
competition has significantly increased with the
adoption of local loop unbundling regulation
and new measures to ease bitstream access,
still with ADSL as the dominant technology.
In contrast, facilities-based competition has
stagnated mainly due to the financial difficulties

of cable operators that have almost completely
stopped the deployment of new infrastructures
since around 2006. However, with modest investments in upgrading existing networks, a relevant
proportion of cable broadband connections
already comply with the DOCSIS 3.0 standard,
and this has fuelled competition in the next-
generation access networks (NGAN) domain, at
least in those zones where cable operators are
present. As a consequence, NGAN based on fibre
(FttX) technologies have been deployed slowly
from 2010 in Spain, led by the incumbent operator. On the wireless side, 4G mobile technologies
(LTE) started their deployment in mid-2013 in
some of the main cities through mobile operators
Vodafone and Orange, a move supported by the
huge success of 3G mobile technologies and
devices in Spain.

As a summary of the current situation in
the fixed broadband market, the latest data available (April 2013[3]) from CMT, the National Regulatory Authority, display an overall fixed
broadband penetration of 25.5% (11,763,025 fixed
broadband subscriptions), showing a 1.1% growth
year-on-year. The breakdown of the number of
broadband lines displays 79.1% of xDSL lines
(network coverage: 99% of the population),
17.4% cable modem lines (60.2% coverage) and
3.5% fibre-to-the-home (FttH) (12% coverage).
In the mobile domain, 3G and beyond network
coverage reaches up to 83% of the population with
22.42 million broadband mobile accesses (54% of
all mobile accesses in Spain).

This case study on Spain, therefore, examines in
detail the industry structure and dynamics that
have led to the current situation in broadband and

---

[1] Given the monopolistic situation in fixed telephony in
Spain before 1996 – when plans for a second national
operator were launched – it would have been extremely
difficult to introduce competition in such a short period
without the interjection of the EC. In general, at the national
level the action taken has been rather reactive than proactive
in terms of the impact of regulation on telecommunications
markets.
[2] About 45% of total premises at the end of this period,
according to data from CMT.

[3] Data accessed in July 2013.

its distinguishing features. The main hypothesis of the case rests on the influence of the economic, political, social and cultural context in the development of broadband markets, therefore creating unique paths for each country or region. To this end, the case investigates the competitive dynamics through empirical research, paying special attention to the investments in infrastructure upgrades, the regulatory and competitive decisions during the process, the use of structural funds and public aid, and the peculiarities of market demand. Of special interest in the case study are the evolution of the limitations (population, coverage, technologies) of broadband market forces, the role of public administrations (national, regional, local) in the development of broadband and their practical approaches to 'market failures' (regional differences are examined throughout the case), the role of wireless technologies and spectrum management, and a view on the deployment of next-generation networks.

With this logic in mind, the case study is structured into seven main sections. This introductory section is followed by some background on the origins of Internet access (narrowband) in Spain– Section 12.2. From there, a detailed account of the evolution of fixed broadband markets and regulation is presented in Sections 12.3 through 12.6. Section 12.7 is devoted to mobile broadband. The interplay between national and local/regional administrations is discussed in Section 12.8. The evaluation of the achievements of the Digital Agenda is captured in Section 12.9. A summary of the main conclusions of the case analysis and some reflections on the future of broadband close the chapter in Sections 12.10 and 12.11.

12.2 The origins of Internet access and broadband markets in Spain: the pre-liberalization days

The development of the Internet in Spain began in the 1980s in the context of scientific and technological research. Early developments were conducted in experimental projects, mostly at the Technical University of Madrid jointly with other universities outside Spain. It was also at that time

when the first connections between major universities and research centres in the country were made as a first step towards the creation of RedIris[4] in 1988, a public research network especially designed to support the increasing needs of the Spanish R&D community.

The first commercial provider of Internet services appeared in 1991: Goya Servicios Telemáticos, a university spin-off. Three years later, the market started to show an increasing commercial interest in the Internet and some early competition arose: Spritel, which had been providing an email service via RedIris, acquired its own connections and started to offer services, and Servicom appeared shortly thereafter. However, the turning point in Internet development took place in 1995[5] following the entry into the Spanish market of the Internet transit services of large telephone (Telefónica, BT and Sprint) and computer (IBM, ICL-Fujitsu) companies. As a direct consequence, more than twenty new suppliers appeared in the market (Sarenet, Cinet, Intercom, Abaforum, Asertel, Off-Campus, etc.). Within this scenario, international operators facilitated high-capacity lines (usually 64 kbit/s) so Spanish Internet providers could receive calls from access customers. Sprint, BT Telecom and France Telecom were the first networks to be fully operative. Later, Telefónica Data Transmission (Telefónica Data) began to provide services to ISPs, offering a cheaper alternative to overcome the main obstacle to the growth of the commercial Internet in Spain: the high cost of international connectivity. With this objective, Telefónica launched

---

[4] RedIris is the public ISP offering connectivity and advanced services to universities, research centres and other parts of the public administration in Spain. It is the Spanish partner in the European Geant network. RedIris administratively is part of Red.es, the Spanish public agency for the development of the information society, in turn belonging to the Ministry of Industry, Energy and Commerce.

[5] At that time, Spain was still lagging far behind other countries in Internet development given the high cost of connectivity fees. Thus, a user, in addition to the supplier's invoice, had to pay the cost of the call to the closest node, which for most meant the payment of international charges. This prevented mass adoption and it was the main reason why in 1995 Spain only had 30,000 Internet users.

InfoVía[6] in 1995, a service that would greatly boost the development of the Internet in Spain (and also in Latin America, where Telefónica has shares in many incumbent telcos), conceived both as an independent (private) network similar to the Internet but 'in Spanish' and as an alternative access to the Internet at the price of a local call. As a direct consequence of the release of InfoVía, there were more than 400 ISPs in the market in 1997. Consolidation also began in 1997; for example, EUnet acquired Goya Servicios Telemáticos, which was acquired two years later by KPNQwest.

The second element of interest prior to the full liberalization of telecommunication markets was the decision of the Spanish government to create a second national operator, Retevisión, to crowd the market as much as possible since there were considerable fears of the consequences of other countries' incumbents entering the national market. This second operator obtained the most widespread alternative networks not commercially available at that moment: the audiovisual distribution system for terrestrial television. Interestingly, this was a broadband transport network as it was prepared to carry several television channels across the Spanish territory. Thus, in early 1998, coinciding with the entry of Retevisión in the fixed telephony market, the growing interest of operators (Telefónica, Retevisión and BT) to integrate Internet access into their portfolios increased the number of main ISP acquisitions. Thus, Retevisión acquired Servicom and RedesTB, BT took control of Arrakis, CTV and Jet Internet became part of Uni2 (a France Télécom brand), and Telefónica launched Terra. In September 1998 Retevisión launched its own Internet access platform, Iddeo, to compete with Telefónica's InfoVía service.

The next step in the evolution of Internet access took place with the advent of telecommunications liberalization in December 1998, when the market was opened to competition and the Spanish NRA set the end of the InfoVía service provision as 1 December of that year to avoid the monopolistic behaviour of the incumbent operator[7].

Flat rates were introduced by Retevisión in July 2000 and followed by Telefónica in November of that year. With this new business strategy, Retevisión caused considerable disruption to the business model of connectivity provision and subsequent ruin for many ISPs used to simply charging a per-minute telephone tariff. Therefore, although the number of users had grown tremendously since the launch of InfoVía, the introduction of a flat rate at an affordable price meant a new surge in the use of the Internet. Thus, the number of users increased by three million in just one year, reaching seven million in total by 2001.

12.3 Development of fixed broadband in Spain: general guidelines

As mentioned in the previous section, on 1 December 1998 the Spanish telecommunications market was opened to the introduction of full competition. At that time, Internet access represented 0.3% of the sector's overall turnover. It consisted of traditional telephone line access and until 1999 no commercial high-data-rate (broadband) access service was offered.

Indeed, it was in 1999 when two events marked the start of the commercial broadband offer in Spain. On one hand, a decree was passed forcing the former monopoly (Telefónica) to provide indirect access to its clients' subscriber loops. On the other hand, cable operators, who had won

---

[6] At the national level, InfoVía seemed to have greater features than the direct access to the Internet at the time for three main reasons: access to the Internet and its services through more than 100 providers competing on this network, costs through InfoVía were much lower than the cost of direct access to the Internet provider (since only a local call was required) and access quality seemed to be better as InfoVía was specifically designed and sized by Telefónica.

[7] Telefónica reacted by launching InfoVía Plus with the objective of solving the bandwidth problems due to the significant increase in Internet users. However, the loss of monopolistic status and introduction of competition accelerated a pace of change that clashed with the traditional management scheme of InfoVía, which had practically disappeared two years later.

their (regional) licenses through tenders awarded in 1998, started their commercial operations.

The next year, the regulator continued its work to promote the broadband market with two new actions. In March 2000 public tenders awarded licenses to operate wireless fixed access (WLL, wireless local loop) systems in the 3.4–3.6 GHz and 24.5–26.5 GHz frequencies. Furthermore, during the last days of the year, the access regulation was modified to define fully-unbundled subscriber loop access. With these two new actions, the basic framework for the development of broadband was defined in a stable manner.

The market developed quickly and during 2002 the first million broadband accesses were reached. However, it must be noted that until the first months of 2004, there continued to be fewer broadband users than switched Internet users. Between 2002 and 2006, the growth curve was steep. Growth slowed from that moment on and in 2010 the market started to show the first signs of maturity with modest growth rates.

The 9.8 million broadband lines operating in 2009 represented a penetration of 20.7 lines per 100 inhabitants, a value below that of the EU average at the time (24.8). Three years later, in 2012, there were 11.5 million broadband lines and penetration was 24.9 lines per 100 inhabitants, still below the EU average of 26. Considering the number of households instead of inhabitants, penetration rose to 51% (as compared to 56% in the EU) in 2009 and reached 66.9% in 2012, again below the EU average of 72.5%. The geographical distribution of access is notoriously uneven and thus, for example, in 2012 penetration in the Madrid municipality was 32.9% and it was 38.7% in Barcelona, well above the national and European averages. Penetration in municipalities with more than 100,000 and fewer than 500,000 inhabitants was 27.2%, still above the average, while municipalities of 1,000 to 5,000 inhabitants had a meagre 17.9% penetration and municipalities of fewer than 1,000 inhabitants a 12.6% penetration.

Despite the early awarding of licenses for fixed wireless access and the subsequent introduction of other technological options, the indisputably predominant access technologies were – and still are – xDSL and cable networks. Together they represented 96% of the total number of broadband lines in December 2012.

Cable access (HFC) represented 20% of the market at the end of 2009 and 18.7% in 2012. During recent years, cable has slowly lost some share to xDSL accesses (the cable share represented 25.2% in 2003 and 21.6% in 2006), and now to FttH. However, HFC is the main component of the installed base of NGAN. Of the 12.8 million lines installed, 9.6 million belong to cable (2.4 million active) and the remaining 3.2 million to FttH.

The remaining 4% of broadband lines (460,000 lines) is composed of FttH with 337,000 lines (2.9% of the total number of lines, double the number for the preceding year) and mostly wireless fixed access (123,000 lines). As a summary, Figure 12.1 depicts the evolution in broadband lines by technology.

Another main trend in the evolution of broadband is the increase in lines with higher data rates. Technological evolution in the shape of the update of HFC to DOCSIS 3.0, usage of VDSL instead of ADSL and emergence of FttH were mostly responsible for this trend. In particular, at the end of 2012, 63% of broadband lines enjoyed data rates higher than 10 Mbit/s compared with 54% a year before. Moving the threshold to 30 Mbit/s, namely into the NGAN domain, 10% of broadband lines had at least this data rate, a growth of 64% compared with the year before. Of these, 60% corresponded to DOCSIS 3.0, 27% to FttH and 13% to VDSL.

Another trend that has progressively defined itself over time is the bundling of broadband with other services. In 2005 three out of every four broadband clients also purchased one or more additional services. By the end of 2007 this percentage exceeded 90% and in 2009 it represented 95.6% (75.1% purchased broadband with voice calls, 1.6% with television and 19.0% with both voice calls and television). In 2012, an additional trend emerged, from triple-play to quadruple- or quintuple-play (adding mobile voice and data), with 10% of total broadband lines being packaged in this manner.

Lastly, it is necessary to note that broadband is not a cheap service in Spain. The average expense

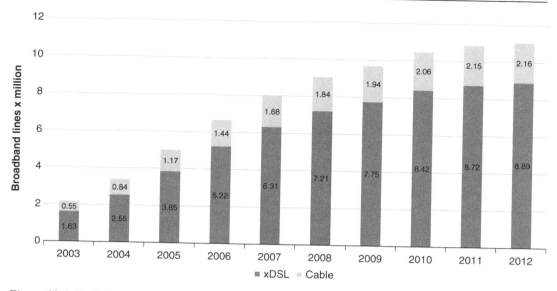

Figure 12.1 Evolution in broadband lines by technology, Spain, 2003–2012
Data source: CMT, 2013.

per household for a bundle including broadband and voice calls was EUR 42.80[8] in 2009 (per month, line fee included). This price has dropped continually in recent years and in 2012 it was EUR 36.10 for the same bundle with broadband data rates of 10–15 Mbit/s. In the case of data rates higher than 30 Mbit/s, the average effective price was EUR 41.10 in 2012.

12.4 Analysis by technologies: xDSL and FttH

The Decree of March 26th, 1999[9] heralded the start of the commercial introduction of ADSL. Its declared purpose was to force the incumbent operator (Telefónica) to provide other operators with indirect access to subscriber loops in order to include ADSL. This access was to be offered in three modalities with a maximum binary flow

of 256 kbit/s, 512 kbit/s or 2 Mbit/s in the operator-to-user direction. This Decree was valid for only eighteen months given that the Royal Decree 3456/2000[10] abolished it completely by establishing fully-unbundled subscriber loop access. The second temporary provision established that the conditions for the commercial offer of wholesale loop access resulting from the abolished Decree would be maintained (except for the price) for at least two years.

Initially heavy-handed intervention was the norm and deployment requirements were established. The 1999 Decree established in its first additional provision a national ADSL coverage plan. For each of the 109 districts defined, a single indirect access point to the subscriber loop was established; this is where the flows of information from local switches located in that area were to be concentrated. These switches were in charge of progressively providing the usage of ADSL

[8] As a reference, the legal minimum wage in Spain in 2013 was EUR 645.30 per month.
[9] Order of March 26, 1999, which establishes conditions for provision of indirect access to the local loop of the fixed public telephone network (BOE 10/4/1999).

[10] Royal Decree 3456/2000, of December 22, adopting the Regulation that establishes the conditions for local loop access to the incumbent's fixed public telephone network (BOE 23/12/2000).

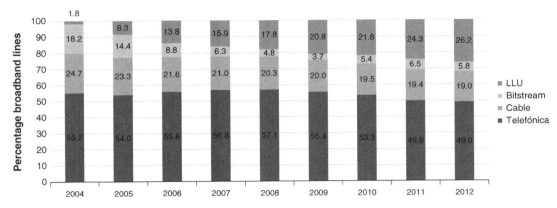

Figure 12.2 Evolution of broadband lines by type of access, Spain, 2004–2012
Data sources: CMT, 2010; CMT, 2013.

technology. However, the Royal Decree on local loop unbundling (LLU) terminated all ADSL deployment requirements, as it moved the possibility of installing a DSL-switch (DSLAM) in the local telephony office.

The implementation of ADSL proved to be a fast commercial success, particularly from the summer of 2001 onward, when Telefónica was authorised to provide the service directly. It is important to remember that previously only ISPs using the network of Telefónica were allowed to provide these services. From 2000 to 2004, in spite of the regulation on local loop unbundling, it was bitstream access which created competition in the xDSL market. It was only from 2005 on that LLU started to have some importance as a means of alternative xDSL operators reaching the end user. The slow uptake was caused by the conflicts raised by the incumbent regarding the practical implementation of local loop unbundling. In addition, a reduction in fully unbundled loop wholesale prices in 2006 helped in the following years to emphasise the trend of changing the wholesale access modality. However, the introduction at the end of 2009 of a new wholesale access modality, obviating the need to purchase a telephone service with Telefónica, allowed operators to market new offers, and wholesale access requests grew again. As shown in the summary depicted in Figure 12.2, the incumbent operator kept a relatively constant

market share from 2004 until about 2010. During this period, the 'ladder of investment' theory held for the first rungs, translating indirect access into local loop unbundling. However, the situation changed from 2010 to 2012, when there was a well-discussed decline in the incumbent's market share for the first time.

Recently, there have been new developments in this part of the broadband market. First, a new regulation was put in place during 2012 ('New Ethernet Broadband Service') to allow indirect access without replicating the quality of service (QoS) offered by the incumbent, thereby introducing greater flexibility into alternative operators' market offers. It is still too soon to draw conclusions about future prospects.

Second, VDSL, FttC/B and FttH have been available in the market since 2009, but mostly from the incumbent operator. In this sense, the last rungs in the ladder of investment concept remain unfulfilled. Regulation for FttH remains light with provisions mainly for duct sharing and network sharing inside buildings – a domain where Spain has been cited as the EU reference. Lately, during 2013, operators have announced co-investments in fibre deployment: on one side, Telefónica and Jazztel (the main alternative fixed operator) and, on the other, Vodafone and Orange.

In fact, uncertainties about the deployment of fibre-based NGNs together with their role as basic infrastructures of the Information Society knowledge economy have prompted a growing number of studies, reports and papers from the industry, regulation authorities and academia about the circumstances of their deployment. The Spanish NRA issued a report on prospective of fibre deployment in Spain (CMT, 2009) to be used as the basis for a fibre-based NGN regulatory framework. The report assumes the usual hypothesis of these studies: sharing public works and infrastructures (trenching and ducts, as well as in buildings) where possible and deployment carried out progressively as demand for FttH services increases. The main conclusion of the report is that the deployment of FttH networks will be carried out gradually, starting in areas where deployment costs are lower and estimated income is higher, with an advantage for operators who arrive first in terms of their investment recovery periods. It is expected that by 2023 (a 15-year period since the investments in fibre optics were supposed to begin in 2008), between 43% and 46% of Spanish households will have FttH Internet access supplied either by Telefónica or by other operators. At the end of 2012, 18.4% of households were passed by fibre. Main cities, such as Madrid and Barcelona, were expected to sustain two to three alternative fibre optic networks in addition to Telefónica's. However, according to the report, there may not be sufficient demand to incentivize the presence of any alternatives to Telefónica in less populated areas. In such cases, owing to the lack of attraction in terms of investment, actions from public authorities would be desirable[11]. Alternative operators would have practically no presence in smaller municipalities (those with fewer than 1,000

inhabitants) and, if they were present, they would take more than 15 years to recover their investments. Municipalities with populations between 1,000 and one million inhabitants could have FttH network access provided by an alternative operator in competition with the incumbent within 15 years. In municipalities with more than 50,000 inhabitants, alternative operators that deploy fibre optic networks would be able to recover their investments within 9 to 12 years at most. The investment recovery period for municipalities between 5,000 and 50,000 inhabitants would be between 13 and 15 years.

12.5 Analysis by technologies: hybrid fibre-coaxial cable

In Spain, cable television had not been developed and no specific regulating framework was in force prior to 1990. Therefore, when, later than in other EU countries, the first initiatives for deploying cable networks appeared in the early 1990s, their regulation encountered a legal vacuum. Initially, the government prosecuted these initial installations; the jurisprudence backed this approach until 1994, when the Constitutional Court found this situation to be unacceptable. Although its repercussions were modest[12], it was blatantly obvious that the legal vacuum needed to be filled.

The government's answer was the Cable Telecommunications Act finally published in December 1995[13]. This Act regulated the cable *telecommunications* service but not the cable *television* service. At that time, the European Commission had not yet abolished the restrictions on provision of soon-to-be-liberalized telecommunication services over cable television networks.

The 42/1995 Act organised the cable telecommunications service into unspecified territorial districts, with a scope that could swing from part of a

---

[11] All the figures mentioned above are the most conservative estimations from the report; they look at deployment across the whole country, namely from non-niche operators with deployment plans for the country as a whole, and the estimates take into consideration the low uptake for premium services (with added-value services that are only supported by fibre optic). Cable operators have not been taken into consideration in the feasibility analysis despite being the obvious form of competition for fibre optic services and alternative network being present. Furthermore, the study assumes that all alternative operators deploy their FttH networks by purchasing ducts and infrastructure from Telefónica.

[12] The scope of each of these networks was modest since many of them were simple 'community VCRs' that did not go beyond the scope of a resident's associations. However, it was not as modest as regards the number of households involved, which in 1993 reached 1,600,000.

[13] Law 42/1995, December 22, for cable telecommunications (BOE 23/12/1995).

municipal area to groups of several municipalities, always with a minimum of 50,000 and a maximum of two million inhabitants. Following the setting up (and subsequent extension) process, the Spanish map was divided into 43 districts, 14 of which did not exceed the territory of a municipal area and the rest including several municipalities with geographic extensions of extremely different nature. The regulations allowed two operators to provide services in each district: Telefónica Cable (a new branch of the incumbent) by default and the winner of a public tender. The first tenders were awarded at the end of August 1997, but it was in 1998 when most authorizations were awarded and concession agreements signed. Generally, new operators started their roll-out and service implementation in 1999. Telefónica Cable, on the other hand, needed to comply with an 18-month moratorium, later increased to 24 months, before starting to provide services. This moratorium became eternal since Telefónica, despite having stated in the media that it maintained its interest in the cable business, focused its strategy on developing ADSL and never used the cable license as such.

One of the criteria used for awarding the license responded to the coverage predictions of the district and the periods required fulfilling them. The twelve initial cable operators included in the schedules submitted to the tenders a series of commitments for network deployment that would be not only universal but also very fast. Fairly soon, it was obvious that such expectations would not be met. The economic situation of the ICT industry, the deployment of ADSL by Telefónica[14] and factors such as the occasional slowness of local governments in awarding the civil works licenses soon changed the scenario. After some hard bargaining[15], in October 2002 the government 'adapted' the obligations and commitments of cable operators in order for them to approach their

investment decisions 'in a more rational way and better adapted to the conditions of their market'.

Despite these considerable initial problems, broadband market dynamism allowed for the number of cable modem lines to grow strongly up to 2006. However, since that year, the growth has been much more modest and, in fact, cable is now losing market share as shown in Figure 12.2. During this time, a series of mergers and purchases have led to a single operator (Ono) holding 75% of cable access lines and a 14.8% share of the broadband market, leaving out some regional operators mostly in the north of Spain (R in Galicia, TeleCable in Asturias and Euskaltel in the Basque country). Ono also holds most of the assets of the former 'second national operator' Retevisión.

Cable has pioneered two main developments in broadband markets in Spain, later to be followed by the incumbent operator. First, by 2009 approximately 45% of cable users had already purchased triple-play (as opposed to 15% of Telefónica's broadband clients and 5% in the case of the remaining operators at that time). Second, cable launched higher data rates early. Again by 2009, 15.9% of cable subscribers already enjoyed throughputs of 10 to 20 Mbit/s and 1.4% above 20 Mbit/s. Later in 2011 and 2012, they launched DOCSIS 3.0, advertising data rates of at least 50 Mbit/s, a key trigger of the subsequent FttH deployment. As mentioned before, in 2012 cable technologies in Spain accounted for 60% of NGAN subscribers and 62% of installed access lines.

12.6 Analysis by technologies: fixed wireless access

The tenders for awarding six so-called 'loop via radio' licenses (WLL), three in the frequency band between 3.4 and 3.6 GHz and another three in the 24.5 to 26.5 GHz band, were published in October 1999[16] and awarded five months later.

---

[14] By the end of 2001, cable reached 17.9% of households, while 82.1% of the switched telephone networks were prepared to use ADSL.

[15] Which included cable operators' peculiar request for Telefónica's investment into cable at the same conditions applicable to them.

[16] Order of October 7, 1999 approving the contract documents for the award of three C2 type individual licenses for the establishment and operation of fixed public radio access networks in the 3.4 to 3.6 GHz band (BOE 9/10/1999). Idem for the 26 GHz band (same BOE).

The tender-winning consortiums were made up of companies with experience in the sector, as well as many others who intended to take positions in the telecommunications market that was then considered to be more than promising. In addition to the six awardees, the second and third telephony operators, which in 1998 had already received authorization to operate in the higher band (Uni2) or in both (Retevisión), were awarded licenses by default. The geographic scope of the licenses covered the whole national territory.

As was the case with the cable tenders, the winners published projects that were much more ambitious than the minimum required by the call for tenders. For example, one of the consortiums that won a license in the 26 GHz band promised to cover 'at least' all the Spanish cities with over 50,000 inhabitants in less than four years. In reality, the situation never matched the forecast in the companies' plans. In the case of WLL, it can be said that it was never even remotely close. In 2002 all operators combined had just 818 clients and the residential sector provided no income whatsoever. Continuing with the parallels with cable, the Ministry for Science and Technology decided to relax the commitments of WLL technology operators ('to allow them to optimise their deployments and design them according to demand criteria'). Here as well, a merger process occurred, leaving only a few surviving companies.

The replacement of the TRAC system (*Telefonía Rural de Acceso Celular*, cellular access rural telephony, launched originally to complete the universal service obligations on voice telephony) seemed to be able to lend some strength to WLL operators. It provided services to 260,000 clients located in remote rural areas. The replacement of TRAC became unavoidable to meet the provisions of the 2002 universal service Directive, since the existing TRAC did not provide *functional* access to the Internet. It was suggested that WLL technology was the most suitable to replace TRAC lines, but the operator ultimately required to carry out the replacement (Telefónica) did not hold a license to use this technology. Nonetheless, Telefónica did call for tenders to select interested operators. The award process was delayed and it did not end until late 2008. Ultimately, the replacement process was carried out using a mix of technological options (with GPRS as the main ingredient) among which WLL (in the shape of LMDS) was included although with no significant role.

Lacking other external stimuli, the fixed wireless access offer is only present today in a handful of cities. During 2009–2011, it seemed that WiMAX, as the next-generation technology in WLL, could become at least a niche solution for those areas lacking a proper wired broadband connection, such as suburban or spread out residential areas. As of 2012, WLL lines amounted to just 120,000, suggesting that it is not (and never has been) an alternative to the traditional loop or to cable in Spain.

12.7 Analysis by technologies: mobile broadband

It stands without question that the deployment of new generations of mobile communications technologies, 3G and beyond, has changed substantially the scenario of broadband access. In practice, mobile technologies have become a platform able to complement – but also increasingly to compete with – traditional fixed broadband access.

From about 2000, Spanish mobile operators have been well aware of the opportunities involved in mobile broadband services. In fact, the Spanish government was the second EU member state after Finland to attempt to launch UMTS 3G technology: the process for granting four licenses for the new technology was initiated on 10 November 1999. The government opted for a beauty contest (with a fee per license of EUR 129.2 million), which resulted on 10 March 2000 in the three existing operators at the time – Telefónica, Airtel (now Vodafone) and Amena (now Orange) – receiving 3G licenses and a fourth new license for Xfera (now Yoigo). As specified in its offer, Xfera scheduled the beginning of its operations for 1 August 2000 with a total investment of about EUR 7,800 million in a brand new mobile network. However, the unavailability of suitable terminals for 3G technology and the financial difficulties derived from the dotcom bubble

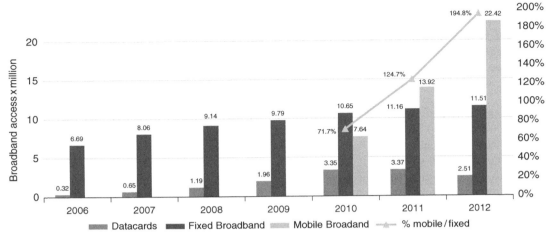

Figure 12.3 Mobile broadband access related to total broadband, Spain, 2006–2012
Data sources: CMT, 2010; CMT, 2013.

delayed *sine die* the launch of its services (as well as two new licenses that were considered for the DCS-1800 band).

Owing to these difficulties in early UMTS deployment, the 'leap to the next generation' took place through smaller steps using several intermediate extensions of the existing 2G technologies, generically called 2.5G. Telefónica started its WAP service in March 2000, its *e-moción* platform for content and applications three months later and launched WAP over GPRS during January 2001. In June 2001 Amena opened a similar service for business customers and in November made it available to all users. In December 2001 Vodafone (which took control of Airtel in early 2001) followed. The MMS (Multimedia Messaging System) appeared in the market in 2002. Officially, the launch of UMTS services had been delayed by the government from 1 August 2001 to 1 June 2002. In practice, there was no commercial offering until February 2004 and, even then, it was only addressed to laptop computers (using PCMCIA cards) since no other terminals were available. In July 2005 Amena was sold to France Telecom, changing its name to Orange in October 2006. In December 2006 Yoigo began its activities after the majority of Xfera shares were sold to TeliaSonera.

During 2007 the new 3.5G technology was launched (HSDPA, later followed by HSUPA to configure the full HDPA standard), improving the available data rates, mainly for urban users. Also during 2007, commercial offers for mobile data access were already generally available. At the end of 2008, ten operators (the four network mobile operators and six additional mobile virtual network operators) were offering flat monthly fees (always with a data cap) for mobile Internet access. At this point, the number of mobile broadband subscribers (datacards for laptops and mobile devices with a monthly subscription to mobile Internet) was 11.5% of the total number of broadband subscribers (Figure 12.3), reaching 16.7% by the end of 2009.

In fact, based on data from the XIV Implementation Report (EC, 2009), Spain led the penetration of mobile broadband with regard to the total number of mobile subscribers with 25.9%. In April 2013, mobile broadband penetration was 54%, still in the top three of EU countries. Finally, 4G mobile technologies (LTE) started their deployment in mid-2013 in some of the main cities through Vodafone and Orange.

From a regulatory perspective, the model in place has supported the cycle of investment – the renewal of technology. In fact, it can be said

(Ramos, 2005) that the competitive scenario of mobile communications in Spain – and in most European countries – has been characterized by a 'light-handed' approach where the basic instrument has been the introduction of new operators using the transition between technology generations. Therefore, the level of competition has increased one step at a time as new licenses have been granted: from two operators with analogue 1G (Telefónica and Vodafone), three operators when 2G was installed (Orange), to a fourth mobile network operator with the introduction of 3G (Yoigo). The result so far is Telefónica with four licenses (TACS, GSM-900, DCS-1800, IMT-2000), Vodafone with three (GSM-900, DCS-1800, IMT-2000), Orange with two (DCS-1800, IMT-2000) and Yoigo with just one (IMT-2000). In addition, Telefónica and Orange have obtained licenses to operate in the GSM-900 extended frequency band in exchange for a promise to complete coverage in underserved areas. The difficulties in the re-farming of spectrum in Spain in the presence of these asymmetries in the licensing process should not come as a surprise. Thus, the mobile regulatory model in Spain has been directed to promote facilities-based competition and, as a consequence, the vertical integration ('silo model') of infrastructures and services.

Within this model, the necessary conditions have been set for operators to bet on continuous investment in networks and infrastructures, a must for mobile technologies where the lifecycle of assets is much shorter than in fixed technologies. The result has been a 'virtuous circle' of investments and innovation where prices for consumers have decreased following a soft glide path that has favoured the recovery of investments and innovations in next-generation technology. This level of investment has affected the coverage of mobile communications in terms of both population and territory. In particular, mobile broadband coverage was already at 85% of the population in 2007 (IDATE, 2008) and beyond 90% in early 2010. Coverage of the territory is among the highest of the 'large' countries in Europe (only the UK does slightly better) and it is above the average of EU15 (at 83%) and well above the average of EU27 (at 77%) despite the comparatively low density of population and its dispersion in Spain.

However, in the case of LTE, the mobile industry's virtuous cycle of investment, innovation and adoption of services has been broken, being replaced by a cycle that runs in the opposite direction. Now the innovation and adoption of services require investments from mobile operators although these will not necessarily lead to an increase in operators' revenues. Moreover, both forces will remain strong during the period considered, fuelled by pre-existing utility and the established habits of mobile broadband consumers. Therefore, the pressure on operators to make the required investments and increase available data rates will only increase.

As a final summary of the mobile markets in Spain, Figure 12.4 displays the evolution of total revenues for mobile network operators. It is interesting to note the positive evolution of the fourth mobile network operator and mobile virtual network operators, proving that the market still had margins for higher levels of competition, at least in the short run. In addition, the total size of the market has been shrinking since 2009 due to the economic crisis, increasing levels of competition and the substitution of services (SMS by instant messaging, voice calls by flat data rates).

12.8 The public perspective on the deployment of broadband infrastructure: efforts towards universal broadband

As shown in the previous sections, the euphoria with which enormous investments in new networks were planned was soon buried under the reality of their slow progress. Outside metropolitan areas, the actual basis for extending fixed broadband infrastructures geographically has been (and continues to be) the improvement of the initial infrastructure and not the deployment of new networks. Since in Spain, as stated above, no cable networks have been deployed in the past beyond urban areas, the result is that in any area with a low population density the evolution of broadband geographic coverage has depended almost exclusively on ADSL. The adaptation of exchanges

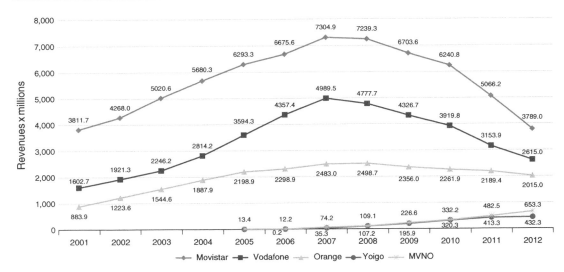

Figure 12.4 Total revenues in the mobile market by operator, Spain, 2001–2012
Data source: CMT (2002–2013).

to provide ADSL was initially very fast but slowed as the most potentially profitable areas were covered, leaving a map of areas (basically rural ones) that the European Commission would call 'white areas', namely those without broadband connectivity.

Public administrations were aware of the delay with which broadband would reach rural areas, even if the most optimistic plans were met. In fact, since relatively early – January 2001 – there have been calls to extend broadband coverage into rural areas: during the presentation of the master guidelines of the first Spanish programme (Info XXI) for promoting the information society[17], one of the ten strategic objectives included was the extension of broadband access networks to cities with fewer than 50,000 inhabitants. Those municipalities

joining the so-called 'Rural Internet' programme were promised the installation of a 'public broadband access point' based on satellite technology. In addition to the connection, the equipment for the community space and expenses generated during three years would be financed.

The lack of correspondence between the objectives of this 'first-generation' development plan for the information society, the resources actually available and the objectives achieved resulted in the creation of the so-called 'Soto Commission'[18] to review what the main lines of action should be to promote the information society in Spain. As a result, a new plan, 'España.es', was passed in July 2003. The programme provided three 'horizontal' guidelines: strengthening the offer of content and services to promote demand, improving accessibility, particularly by establishing public access points, and communication efforts addressed to the society. It already included a specific plan for extending broadband into rural areas, but it was not started within the lifespan of the overarching

---

[17] The 'Info XXI: la Sociedad de la Inform@ción para todos, 2000–2003' programme was passed over a year earlier, on 23 December 1999, almost at the same time as the first document of the *e*Europe initiative. Its spirit was in line with the European programme that stated that political support was required for developing broadband, particularly in cases where market dynamics would not be enough to achieve an adequate deployment of these infrastructures along with a package of offers that would be attractive to users.

[18] Special Commission for the Study of the Information Society, chaired by Mr Juan Soto-Serrano, president of HP Spain at the time.

plan because of the complexity of arrangements with both EU structural funding and regional governments.

In any case, again this plan only partially fulfilled its main goals on information society development and a new plan was sought. In 2005, while the European Commission was designing a European framework strategy for the following five-year period – the i2010 initiative – the Spanish government prepared a new convergence plan to re-attempt to speed up the transformation of the country into an information society. The convergence referred to the distance as regards the other European countries, but also aimed to correct domestic inequalities. The new Avanza plan[19] boasted the 'National Programme for the extension of broadband access in rural zones' (PEBA). The activities for the start of the programme were based on the cooperation of regional governments and local municipalities, although only those regional governments interested in coordinating their actions with those of the Ministry participated in the programme in practice.[20]

The PEBA programme managed a high degree of objective achievement. It was formulated using public-private cooperation models, where beneficiary operators invested EUR 85 million, while the central administration added EUR 8 million in subsidies and EUR 17 million in refundable credits. The tenders, based on the technological neutrality principle and on competition between operators, required that users receive at least 256 kbit/s in the most unfavourable cases and that a service be offered with a maximum monthly fee at a 'reasonable' price. When the programme concluded in 2008, broadband coverage had reached 98% of the population. Obviously, wireless technologies were already present in

the market when the projects were developed and in addition to ADSL, WiMAX, satellite and 3G/HSDPA were also used.

It is also worth highlighting that by 2010 almost every regional government had its own development plan, usually including specific strategies for broadband development[21]. Further, a considerable number of municipalities had launched their own strategies and plans (Ramos, Arcos, and Armuña, 2009). These were largely based on structural funding that has lately vanished.[22]

These strategies ranged from complementary plans to those of PEBA previously discussed to the launch of public operators aimed at bridging the gaps in provision by commercial operators. Typically, regional initiatives were based on public ownership with public network management, such as Asturias, or with private management, such as Catalunya and Consell Insular de Menorca. The Asturcon network was the first public FttH network in Spain. The management of the network is public and customers can choose among four private operators. This network has been deployed with European structural funding for industrial restructuring. The case of Xarxa Oberta in Catalunya uses the concession model. The regional government is the owner but a private operator manages the network.

Two main policy objectives emerge in these regional and local initiatives: territorial balance and social equity. A number of the broadband network deployment projects with public participation aim to provide services that are broadly available in other parts of the country but that are not available in a specific 'white area', in order to reduce the eventual disadvantages suffered by the businesses and consumers of the area. Other projects aim at the early development of advanced electronic communications infrastructures and services (such as the deployment of NGAN or municipal wireless networks) as a means to create potential

---

[19] 'Plan 2006–2010 para el desarrollo de la Sociedad de la Información y de Convergencia con Europa y entre Comunidades Autónomas y Ciudades Autónomas'.

[20] This means that other communities maintained their own independent programmes, that broadband extension initiatives have not been exclusively initiated by the central government and that there exists a series of regional (and even local) plans seeking the same goal.

[21] www.bandaancha.es/EstrategiaBandaAncha/Paginas/IniciativasAutonomicas.aspx.

[22] See the analysis of FEDEA at www.crisis09.es/redes/aapp.html.

competitive advantages in their region, thus increasing the economic development of that geographical area.

Obviously, these strategies were not always aligned with national plans or market rules, creating frequent discussion or even intervention from regulatory bodies[23]. Moreover, there was little data about potential demand or the sustainability of business models in this first wave of initiatives. In addition, and according to Spanish regulations, any electronic communications action provided by public administrations must guarantee compliance with the provisions of the LGTel[24] and compliance and enforcement of the principles set forth in it, particularly maintaining effective competition in telecommunications markets. In addition to this general principle, the CMT states that the provision of electronic communications services by public administrations must be financed by the revenues generated from commercial exploitation, it not being allowed to compensate for losses using public funds (the private investor principle). Further, structural separation is required between the public body providing the services and those bodies in charge of passing rights of way for network deployment. In addition, the benefits of public intervention compared with its costs must be proven. As a consequence of these rules, it seems that the deployment of open access infrastructures ('neutral operator') and management by an independent entity is (almost) the only possible solution, while the provision of final customer services seems to be a much more difficult case to prove. However, and as a final summary, it can be said that regional plans have succeeded in contributing to the extension of broadband availability in white areas. Therefore, in parallel with the growing importance of the information society concept

over the past decade and a half, a transition has been made from public administrations' main regulatory role to considering the diverse – and practical – public intervention patterns that ensure the deployment of broadband infrastructures and services and increase of data rates (Feijóo and Milne, 2008).

12.9 Achieving the Digital Agenda targets

From 2009–2010, public strategies for the universal provision of broadband in Spain forked in two separate directions. On one side was the continuation of information society development to achieve ultra-fast broadband for the majority of the population; on the other was the extension of universal service obligations to include a minimum broadband data rate for the whole population, particularly in those areas with a lack of appropriate infrastructures.

The continuation of the Avanza Plan – Avanza2 – set out rather ambitious objectives: 70% of the population with broadband availability at 50 Mbit/s or higher and 60% of the population with broadband availability at 100 Mbit/s or higher by 2015. No specifications on quality of service (QoS) or distribution of data rates between upstream and downstream were available. There were also no indications of how and why market competition was going to achieve these levels of broadband availability. Thus, as of 2013, achieving these targets with a serious QoS looks relatively improbable.

The latest information society development plan in Spain – fifth generation – called the *Digital Agenda for Spain* points in the same direction, considerably reducing the objectives of the previous plan and aiming at full coverage for households with at least 30 Mbit/s by 2020, with 50% of households having adopted data rates higher than 100 Mbit/s by 2020; these are the same targets as in the Digital Agenda for Europe (DAE). Again no specifications on QoS were available and, therefore, it is unclear, for instance, whether 4G mobile communications availability alone would be considered enough to meet this goal. This part of the Digital Agenda for Spain is developed through a National Strategy of

[23] In local government projects, the main purpose at the time was providing free Wi-Fi Internet access to citizens. This was a main source of conflict among local municipalities and the CMT, as the regulator did not allow this form of service provision (for free) on a permanent basis, but only for limited periods or limited services.

[24] Telecommunications Regulatory Framework in Spain i.e., 'General Law on Telecommunications'.

Ultrafast Networks[25] published in June 2013 that strangely contains specific objectives only for 2015, although the general objectives are set for 2020. It expects availability of 100 Mbit/s connections for 50% of the population by 2015 and considers the departure point of 2012 with 46% availability of HFC and 9% of FttH. Interestingly, then, cable is counted as able to provide 100 Mbit/s and, as new deployments of cable operators are improbable, meeting that goal depends either on the fibre deployments of the incumbent operator or in enhancements in the provided DOCSIS standard. The second objective is achieving 25% NGN penetration – above 30 Mbit/s – by 2015, although again the potential contribution of mobile communications is unclear and remains unspecified. The third objective consists of achieving a 70% (75% in other texts) penetration rate for 4G by 2015. According to the plan, the main tools to achieve these goals lie in reforms to the regulatory framework to decrease deployment costs, the use of public funding in white and grey areas, coordination of the various administrations involved in network deployment, allocation of the available spectrum and diverse measures to encourage demand. However, most of the secondary regulations required to implement these tools remain unpublished at the time of writing.

Regarding universal service obligations, after several previous attempts, in January 2012 operators started to provide broadband of at least 1 Mbit/s, thereby in practice including a modest degree of broadband among the objectives of universal service. In the most remote rural locations, the technologies used to comply with this regulation are mobile communications, fixed wireless access and satellite. Some regional governments had already declared this type of broadband to be a universal service (Andalucía famously) as early as 2009. The Digital Agenda for Spain also mentions achieving at least 30 Mbit/s in municipalities of fewer than 5,000 inhabitants by means of wireless technologies. No QoS is mentioned at the time of writing.

As a summary from the perspective of the DAE, all of its main actions are included in the new Digital Agenda for Spain. Regarding their status, the inclusion of basic broadband connections at 1 Mbit/s in the universal service obligations has already been achieved; see above. Legal and institutional support for NGN deployments was already foreseen in Plan Avanza 2 (Action 46 of DAE). In fact, financial support targets have been put in place in the Spanish version of DAE, although with budgets according to current financial constraints in Spain and using structural funding where possible. On the regulatory side, a new version of the General Law for Telecommunications is under parliamentary discussion as of October 2013, its main aim being to foster the deployment of NGA networks. Some measures (e.g., setting at 6 months the maximum delay to grant rights of way to operators) have already been approved in Royal Decree-Law 13/2012, transposing the revised Directives approved in 2009. However, in practice this is seldom achieved and competences scattered across levels of administrations are still a main bottleneck in telecom infrastructure deployment. Also, coverage maps are developed annually, as they are a critical tool for the design and implementation of potential broadband aid schemes. Along the same lines, the Spanish NRA has issued detailed regulation for sharing of civil works and ducts. In this regard Spain had since the early 2000s a pioneering regulation for access to in-building infrastructures that has been updated to cope with technological developments. Ongoing revision of the Telecommunications Law will include provisions fostering the reuse of available infrastructures (Action 47 of DAE). In addition, the digital dividend spectrum auction took place in 2011, although television spectrum has still to be fully re-farmed at the time of writing to allow its use for next generation mobile communications. The 900 MHz, 1800 MHz and 2.5–2.69 GHz frequency bands are available and authorised for third- and fourth-generation mobile services use, with the 3.4–3.6 GHz frequency band under way. Spain also implemented the transfer or leasing of right of use in the harmonised bands although detailed regulation is still pending (Action 49 of DAE). As a general note on the DAE achievements, Spanish performance is better in those actions that are linked to legal or direct administrative action in one specific level of administration. However, when multiple stakeholders are required or multiple jurisdictions are involved, its performance tends to be weaker.

25 www.agendadigital.gob.es/planes-actuaciones/Paginas/plan-telecomunicaciones-redes.aspx.

12.10 Case analysis

The dynamics of the broadband market in Spain have followed the stages of the electronic communications regulatory framework set out by the EU. However, within this broad picture, Spain has a number of distinct features described in detail in previous sections but impossible to understand without first acknowledging some of its distinct geographical, social and economic features.

From the geographical perspective, Spain is one of the most mountainous countries in Europe, only behind Switzerland and Austria[26]. This fact has caused many difficulties for the extension of every type of infrastructure and, obviously, the broadband telecommunications case has been no different. As a main instance, universal service for voice telephony was only completed in the 1980s with the use of wireless solutions (the previously-mentioned TRAC system) – in reality, the deployment of 1G analogue mobile telephony. When Internet access was included as a universal service in the early 2000s, this system for rural areas had to be upgraded, again using wireless technology, because of the difficulties of rolling out wired solutions. As another main instance of the influence of geography, during 2004 a plan for broadband extension in rural areas (the previously-mentioned PEBA) was started using regional funding to update local exchanges to be prepared to provide DSL services.

Related in part to geographical factors, the distribution of the Spanish population is highly heterogeneous. The twenty-nine municipalities with populations over 200,000 inhabitants represent 29.7% of the total population, but only 1.71% of the total surface area. At the same time, municipalities that fall within the definition of rural, i.e., population density lower than 300 inhabitants/km^2 (EUROSTAT, 2010), account for 7,401 municipalities of the total 8,112, encompassing 33.6% of the total population and 94.8% of the territory. This simple fact, as well as the previously mentioned geographical barriers, explains rather convincingly

why many infrastructures easily reach about 60% of the population in Spain and why it is considerably more costly to reach the remaining 40%. Cable deployment is a good example of this case.

Another decisive element is the irregular distribution of wealth across regions in Spain. For example, the autonomous region of Madrid, with 13.7% of the total Spanish population and 18% of Spain's GDP, takes up just 1.59% of the total surface, while Navarra, a region with a similar surface (2.05% of the total) has just 1.35% of the total population and its contribution to total GDP is a meagre 1.7%. Broadband deployment is obviously affected by this heterogeneity: while the average penetration of broadband in households in Spain is 66.9%[27], Madrid, the region with the highest penetration (77. 3%) is 10 points above the average while Extremadura – the poorest region – has a penetration of 10 points below it, at 57.9%. Table 12.1 and Table 12.2 summarise the regional differences in Spain, showing that the averages are not a good indicator of the real situation.

These factors, in combination with the market structure, have resulted in a peculiar combination of below-average adoption[28] and an above-average level of availability of broadband connectivity (but based on legacy technologies, basically DSL) in comparison with similar countries[29].

In fact, the structure of the market, and the competition within it, is distinctive for Spain. Telefónica, the national incumbent operator, retained a market share in broadband higher than the average of comparable cases[30]. Cable in Spain (composed of Ono

---

[26] Mountain areas in Europe: Analysis of mountain areas in EU Member States, acceding and other European countries. European Commission. January 2004.

[27] ONTSI report 'La Sociedad en Red 2012'.

[28] According to CMT data from April 2013, broadband penetration in Spain (number of broadband subscriptions per 100 inhabitants) was 25.5% compared with an average of 26% in OECD countries at June 2012 (OECD Broadband Portal), and an average of 28.8% in the EU (Digital Agenda Scoreboard at December 2012).

[29] According to OECD data from 2009, Internet access through DSL technologies was available in Spain for 99% of the population, while the OECD average remained at 92%. Using Digital Agenda Scoreboard data from 2010, Internet access through broadband technologies was available in Spain for 99% of the population, while the EU average remained at 95.3%.

[30] In January 2013, the incumbent operator had a market share of 48.8%, above the 42.3% average in the EU (Digital Agenda Scoreboard).

Table 12.1 Demographic and economic data, Spain

Zone	Population (inhabitants)	Percentage of total population	Surface (km²)	Percentage of total surface	Population density (inh/km2)	GDP per capita (2008)(€)	Rate to the national GDP level	Total GDP (2008)(€)	Contribution to Spain's GDP
Andalucía	8,302,923	17.76%	87,597.71	17.31%	94.78	18,507	77.00%	148,710,898	13.60%
Aragón	1,345,473	2.88%	47,720.25	9.43%	28.2	26,323	109.00%	34,088,269	3.10%
Asturias (Principado de)	1,085,289	2.32%	10,603.57	2.10%	102.3	22,559	93.90%	23,752,804	2.20%
Baleares (Islas)	1,095,426	2.34%	4,991.66	0.99%	219.45	25,967	108.00%	27,334,601	2.50%
Canarias	2,103,992	4.50%	7,446.95	1.47%	282.53	21,105	87.90%	43,248,707	3.90%
Cantabria	589,235	1.26%	5,321.34	1.05%	110.73	24,508	102.00%	14,027,720	1.30%
Castilla y León	2,563,521	5.48%	94,225.96	18.62%	27.21	23,361	97.30%	58,067,761	5.30%
Castilla-La Mancha	2,081,313	4.45%	79,461.97	15.71%	26.19	18,471	76.90%	36,448,165	3.30%
Cataluña	7,475,420	15.99%	32,113.41	6.35%	232.78	28,095	117.00%	202,805,851	18.60%
Comunidad Valenciana	5,094,675	10.90%	23,254.52	4.60%	219.08	21,468	89.40%	105,554,211	9.70%
Extremadura	1,102,410	2.36%	41,581.98	8.22%	26.51	16,820	70.10%	18,033,734	1.70%
Galicia	2,796,089	5.98%	29,574.38	5.85%	94.54	20,619	85.80%	56,290,249	5.20%
Madrid (Comunidad de)	6,386,932	13.66%	8,027.69	1.59%	795.61	31,110	129.00%	193,477,917	18.00%
Murcia (Región de)	1,446,520	3.09%	11,313.11	2.24%	127.86	19,692	82.00%	27,943,667	2.60%
Navarra (Comunidad Foral de)	630,578	1.35%	10,390.36	2.05%	60.69	30,614	127.00%	18,544,139	1.70%
País Vasco	2,172,175	4.65%	7,235.13	1.43%	300.23	32,133	133.00%	68,281,522	6.20%
Rioja (La)	321,702	0.69%	5,045.25	1.00%	63.76	25,895	107.00%	8,033,559	0.70%
Ceuta	78,674	0.17%	19.48	0.00%	4039.37	22,320	92.90%	1,611,846	0.20%
Melilla	73,460	0.16%	13.41	0.00%	5476.62	21,493	89.50%	1,494,776	0.10%
Spain	46,745,807	100%	505,938.13	100%	92.39	24,020	100%	1,088,502,000	100%

Data source: INE, 2010.

Table 12.2 Regional evolution of broadband penetration (subscriptions per 100 households), Spain, 2004–2012

Zone	2004	2005	2006	2007	2008	2009	2010	2011	2012
Spain	14.7	21.1	29.3	39.2	44.6	51.3	57.4	61.9	66.7
Andalucía	11.5	17.1	24.2	35.0	38.9	46.3	52.9	56.2	63.1
Aragón	15.3	20.1	29.7	39.9	45.2	50.8	58.3	62.7	67.8
Asturias (Principado de)	15.8	25.5	32.3	38.9	47.7	51.2	58.0	62.4	67.1
Baleares (Islas)	22.0	25.5	34.0	44.8	49.9	58.2	64.3	66.5	71.5
Canarias	16.1	23.8	35.0	42.5	45.4	52.9	56.6	60.5	64.6
Cantabria	15.0	20.7	32.0	41.9	49.4	55.2	56.9	65.7	68.0
Castilla y León	9.7	16.7	23.8	32.5	34.8	41.1	47.1	54.2	62.4
Castilla-La Mancha	8.6	13.1	20.7	28.3	36.3	43.8	51.9	57.5	61.6
Cataluña	19.4	26.9	36.6	46.0	52.5	60.5	67.2	69.3	70.6
Comunidad Valenciana	14.8	19.3	24.3	36.7	42.5	46.9	52.1	59.6	60.0
Extremadura	7.2	10.8	16.3	23.2	35.3	39.4	45.9	52.2	57.9
Galicia	9.0	13.8	19.4	25.7	31.8	38.3	46.5	51.6	62.3
Madrid (Comunidad de)	19.9	28.1	39.6	51.7	57.9	62.6	65.9	71.4	77.3
Murcia (Región de)	12.7	16.8	25.8	31.5	35.8	44.4	51.2	59.3	63.8
Navarra (Comunidad Foral de)	10.8	17.2	26.6	40.1	44.0	52.4	58.8	63.1	68.2
País Vasco	14.7	23.2	29.5	40.0	43.7	55.2	63.2	64.9	71.4
Rioja (La)	10.3	17.9	26.2	37.4	45.1	48.0	54.6	58.1	64.5
Ceuta	23.1	32.7	37.2	46.2	46.0	45.6	61.2	65.0	70.2
Melilla	12.6	21.2	39.2	47.7	45.9	50.8	65.8	59.3	64.8

Data source: INE, 2013; CMT, 2013.

as the main operator and other smaller regional operators) has only been deployed since the mid-1990s and it remains limited, fundamentally to urban areas with relatively high population densities. The resulting competitive panorama in fixed broadband technologies is a blend of infrastructure-based and service-based competition (alternative operators using the infrastructures of the incumbent) in urban areas and almost a lone presence of the incumbent in suburban and rural areas (with some interesting regional exceptions). As a consequence, facilities-based competition in the form of a duopoly is intense in those areas where cable is present, while in the remainder of the territory competition only happens through the incumbent's infrastructure. This has always called for considerable discussions in Spain on the benefits and drawbacks of this situation and consideration of potential remedies, either through market forces or of regulatory nature. In any

case, and as an overall result of these features of the market, broadband prices in Spain have been traditionally higher than the average in comparable EU countries[31] and the most frequently used data rates are also lower[32].

[31] The latest data available on broadband pricing in Spain covering 2013 (Digital Agenda Scoreboard – Broadband Internet Access Cost) indicate that the median offer for broadband at low data rates (8 Mbit/s to 12 Mbit/s) was EUR 30.10 at prices adjusted for purchasing power parity, slightly more expensive than the EUR 29.80 average for the EU. At data rates above 12 Mbit/s and below 30 Mbit/s, the difference was not significant in the median offer, and in the range of offers for data rates over 30 Mbit/s, the EUR 43.00 in Spain is well over the average in the EU (EUR 35.20).

[32] According to Digital Agenda Scoreboard data (as of December 2012), Spain had 54.2% of lines with a data rate above 10 Mbit/s (5% lower than the EU average and far from Bulgaria, the leading country with 92.2%) and only 10.2% with data rates above 30 Mbit/s (lower than the 14.8%

Another feature of broadband markets in Spain of particular interest is related to wireless technologies. With a similar competition structure to that of other EU countries, the coverage and penetration of mobile broadband, particularly the penetration of smartphones, is among the highest in Europe (and in the world)[33]. There is no obvious explanation of this fascinating result, although some available evidence point to specific features of Spanish demand and lifestyles.

A final relevant characteristic of broadband markets is linked to the structure of the actual competition and the three-layered public administration structure. This consists of the considerable involvement of some local and regional administrations in all forms of broadband encouragement and even deployment, to a certain extent irrespective of the economic crisis, and at the same time a number of relevant difficulties for deployment derived from lack of coordination and excessive red tape from these same three layers of government.

In summary, and from the particular perspective of broadband, Spain has a number of distinct features in comparison with similar countries: lower fixed broadband penetration, higher fixed broadband coverage, the pre-eminence of DSL technologies, delay in high-data rate broadband connections in both supply and demand, and higher mobile broadband coverage and penetration.

The market dynamics to arrive at this situation have been characterized by some particularities of the Spanish case: geographical elements (higher costs of deployment in rural areas); administrative features (three-layers of conflicting competences for network deployment on one side, but also the involvement of regional and local governments in broadband provision on the other); the socio-economic profile of Spanish customers (lower income but with a preference for mobile solutions); a mostly service-based competition on incumbent facilities in fixed broadband, but with an important role for cable operators as a key force for the provision of ultra-fast broadband services; the successful use of structural funding for the inclusion of (modest) broadband as a universal service; the general lack of achievement of more ambitious information society development plans; and relatively intense competition between mobile providers.

12.11 Reflections on the future

From this scenario, it is interesting to examine briefly the implications of the current situation when looking at the next steps in the evolution of broadband: the deployment of NGNs in Spain. In fact, the conditions for the deployment of the access part of NGNs (NGAN) are currently at the forefront of the debate about the role of telecommunication markets, the best regulations for them and the level and modes of potential public involvement (see Gómez-Barroso and Feijóo, 2009, for a discussion).

In the case of Spain, the uncertainties about NGNs are influenced by the diverging paths of industry technology roadmaps and possibly by some doubts about the implementation of the regulatory scenario, as well as, especially, by the economic uncertainties about return on investment.

First, and the datum is no less important despite being expected, it is clear that any NGN requires major investment. As a consequence, the general economic situation has a huge influence on deployment as well as uncertainties in demand. In addition, the recovery of these investments implies that the prices charged for access and usage of the services should not differ much from current prices. Every available study agrees on this point (Analysis Mason, 2008, 2009; De-Antonio, Feijóo, Gómez-Barroso, Rojo, and Marín, 2006; Jeanjean, 2010). In the words of Noam (2010):

> ...a competitive fiber-based network industry is potentially even more unstable than the preceding

average of the EU and far below the 58.4% of Belgium). Finally, only 1.9% of lines had a data rate of more than 100 Mbit/s, while the average in the EU was 3.4%, with Sweden the reference country with 24.6% of total lines above this data rate.

[33] In terms of the adoption rate of smartphones, Spain was only below Sweden, Norway and Denmark in 2012 with 44 smartphones per 100 inhabitants (Fundación Orange, 2013).

industry structure, since the ratio of fixed-to-variable cost is higher than before. Investors remember the calamitous impacts of the previous downturn [...] these factors are likely to reduce governments' previous emphasis on competition and lead to a greater emphasis on stabilization.

In addition, it is worth remembering that, should demand for large bandwidths appear, it could happen that no access technology by itself, at least with the technical and economic conditions expected today, could present the optimal characteristics for satisfying all the requirements demanded by users in every circumstance. Therefore, the various advantages and drawbacks for each technology, backed by the need to achieve a return on investment, lead operators to create platforms capable of integrating different access technologies over the same backbone network. The future market of the ICT sector, characterised by 'comprehensive' operators, would be quite different from the current one where there is clear separation between technologies.

However, the departure point for the different types of operators in Spain (historic, cable, wireless, alternative and even potential new agents) is not the same. These initial differences are conditioning the path followed for the transformation of their networks into NGNs and will continue to do so in the future. As a consequence, each operator has a different set of drivers for migrating to NGNs. These drivers are dictating their basic timeframes for investing in this advanced infrastructure and subsequently migrating services from existing networks.

In a previous study (Feijóo and Gómez-Barroso, 2013), the authors considered the scenario for ultra-fast broadband infrastructures and calculated in some detail the costs of deploying a NGN through the main technologies. This work, together with the previous discussion on the development of broadband in Spain, allows us to forecast a baseline for ultra-fast broadband market behaviour. Thus, by 2015 it would be relatively possible for Spain to enjoy a '2+' infrastructure-based competition (incumbent, cable operator and mobile operators) for NGNs at about 50% of premises: that is, roughly nine million households and businesses. Beyond this point, the required investment

would be much higher. The cheapest choice would be for a '1+' infrastructure-based competition (incumbent using VDSL-type technology plus mobile operators) for an additional 10% of the population. For the remainder of the population, the most probable option would be no access to NGNs except maybe some scattered local initiatives and mobile 4G deployments, very dependent on the conditions of spectrum licences. These figures seem to be lower than those stated in information society development plans. However, in general, no regulatory 'carrot' seems able to easily increase investment in the required zones, and a huge public effort to compensate for the lack of pure market action seems to be impossible under the current economic conditions.

Indeed, operators invest in areas that are profitable. As densely populated areas are more profitable than rural ones, dense areas will be served first. The available data on the NGNs roll-out in Spain confirm this hypothesis. If we consider geographic density as a continuum, there is a point where operators stop investing because it is no longer profitable. In fact, in most rural areas low population density and high deployment costs discourage private investment, creating negative feedback about limited capacity, high prices and low service demand. As a consequence, there is little or no commitment to connect areas that include smaller towns and rural villages (Pereira, 2007). In fact, the data collected by the OECD shows that among developed countries, those with a large urban population such as South Korea, Japan, France and the Netherlands are more likely to achieve a higher rate of broadband penetration than those with significant rural communities such as the US and Canada (Sherif and Maeda, 2010). In the case of Spain, the transition seems to happen between zones V[34] (zones I–V include 57% of the population and just 1.4% of the surface area) and VI (zones VI–X include the remaining 43% of population and 98.6% of the surface area). In other words, the discontinuity in potential profitability seems to be at the 500 inhabitants/km^2 population

[34] Zone V: 500–1000 inhabitants/km2; Zone VI: 100–500 inhabitants/km2.

density where the 'growth of costs overcomes the growth of the consumption of households in broadband communications' (Rupp and Selberherr, 2010). Thus, as the profitability of these areas depends on infrastructure costs, which tend to decrease slowly over time, there is some potential for less dense areas to become profitable over time. However, this effect could be too slow and would affect equity significantly in territorial terms for a potentially long period. However, the picture on the investments required to cover less dense zones looks rather different when just a small area is considered. It would be possible to deploy a NGN in a small town or village at an affordable cost, especially if the slow development of the market in these areas is taken into consideration. Therefore, we are confronted with a patchwork of local initiatives that aim to solve the market failures by their own means.

Some additional notes on this future baseline are discussed in the following. First, there are good chances of sharing infrastructure to reduce costs and accelerate roll-out. In fact, as discussed previously, during 2013 the main operators have announced their intentions to share network investments and deployment.

A second relevant feature is the role of copper lines. With new technological developments, copper lines will continue to be a strategic asset well into the mid-term. Not only are they able to provide data rates that would fall into the NGN category right now but, in addition, they also allow for a smoother and more scalable path in the transition from ADSL to FttH. In principle, in Spain the incumbent operator has favoured VDSL only for those customers close enough to local exchanges (about 20% of the total number of fixed telephone lines in Spain). However, it remains to be seen if the deployment of FttH exceeds the urban footprint.

The role of cable networks in Spain has been already stressed in this chapter, and they have proven to be the cheapest alternative for the rapid deployment of NGNs in Spain. Moreover, the authors consider, following Siciliani (2010), that 'the lack of actual competitive restraint from cable operators precludes the replication [in Europe] of US-like regulatory forbearance, as it might lead to

the (re-)monopolization of broadband markets by telecom incumbents'. However, cable operators in Spain have another highly relevant asset from the perspective of NGNs: almost 40% of premises have, in addition to coaxial cabling, a copper wire deployed in parallel with the former. Owing to the architecture of cable networks, this copper line typically runs for the last 500 m to user premises. Therefore, there would be (commercial and regulatory) possibilities to reuse this copper (using VDSL2, for instance) to provide an additional means of deploying NGN for interested parties. Thus far, no one has considered this possibility for increasing competition in Spain.

Wireless technologies (mainly 4G) could play a fundamental role in Spain: not only are they the cheapest solution for rural areas, but they can also complement or even replace fixed broadband in urban and suburban areas, especially as these technologies fit Spanish lifestyles better. Therefore, the usage of spectrum for wireless solutions seems to be a main element in configuring the future broadband landscape.

References

Analysis Mason (2008). The costs of deploying fibre-based next-generation broadband infrastructure. London: Final report for the Broadband Stakeholder Group. Retrieved from www.broadbanduk.org/component/option, com_docman/task,doc_view/gid,1036/Itemid,63/.

(2009). Competitive models in GPON. London: Ofcom. Retrieved from www.ofcom.org.uk/research/technology/research/emer_tech/sbt/Analysys_Mason_GPON_Final_R1.pdf.

CMT (2009). Informe final sobre los resultados del modelo de despliegue de redes FttH/GPON en España. Barcelona: Comisión del Mercado de las Telecomunicaciones. Retrieved from www.cmt.es/es/documentacion_de_referencia/redes_nueva_generacion/anexos/Informe_final_HE_1_2008_09_MDF.pdf.

(2010). Informe anual 2009. Barcelona: Comisión del Mercado de las Telecomunicaciones. Retrieved from www.cmt.es/es/publicaciones/anexos/20100705_IA09_CMT_INFORME_ANUAL_2009_SENCER_BAIXA.pdf.

(2013). *Informe económico sectorial 2012*. Barcelona: Comisión del Mercado de las Telecomunicaciones. Retrieved from www.cmt.ess.

De-Antonio, J., Feijóo, C., Gómez-Barroso, J. L., Rojo, D., and Marín, A. (2006). A European perspective on the deployment of next generation networks. *The Journal of the Communications Network*, **5**(2), 47–55.

EC (European Commission) (2009). Progress report on the single European electronic communications market 2008 (14th report). Brussels. Retrieved from http://ec.europa.eu/information_society/policy/ecomm/doc/implementation_enforcement/annualreports/14threport/commen.pdf.

EUROSTAT (2010). Urban-rural typology. Eurostat regional yearbook, Statistics Explained. Brussels: European Commission. Retrieved from http://epp.eurostat.ec.europa.eu/statistics_explained/index.php/Urban-rural_typology.

Feijóo, C, and Milne, C. (2008). Re-thinking universal policy for the digital era: setting the scene. *info*, **10**(5–6), 4–11.

Feijóo, C., and Gómez-Barroso, J.L. (2013). El despliegue de redes de acceso ultrarrápidas: un análisis prospectivo de los límites de mercado. *Papeles de Economía Española*, **136**, 116–130.

Fundación Orange. (2013). eEspaña. Informe anual 2013 sobre el desarrollo de la sociedad de la información en España. Madrid, Spain. Retrieved from www.proyectosfundacionorange.es/docs/eEspana_2013_web.pdf.

Gómez-Barroso, J.L., and Feijóo, C. (2009). Policy tools for public involvement in the deployment of next generation communications. *info*, **11**(6), 3–13.

Gómez-Barroso, J. L., and Feijóo, C. (2010). A conceptual framework for public-private interplay in the telecommunications sector. *Telecommunications Policy*, **34**(9), 487–495.

IDATE (2008) *Broadband coverage in Europe. Final Report*. Montpellier: DG INFSO, European Commission. Retrieved from http://ec.europa.eu/information_society/eeurope/i2010/docs/benchmarking/broadband_coverage_2008.pdf.

INE (Instituto Nacional de Estadística) (2010). *Cifras de población y censos demográficos*. www.ine.es. (2013). *Cifras de población y censos demográficos*. www.ine.es.

Jeanjean, F. (2010). Financing the next generation infrastructures. Consumer subsidies or infrastructure subsidies? EuroCPR 2010. Brussels.

Noam, E. (2010). Regulation 3.0 for telecom 3.0. *Telecommunications Policy*, **34**(1–2), 4–10.

Pereira, J. P. R. (2007). A cost model for broadband access networks: FttX versus WiMAX. Second International Conference on AccessNets '07. doi:10.1109/ACCESSNETS.2007.4447117

Ramos, S. (2005). Contribución al estudio, caracterización y desarrollo del sector europeo de comunicaciones móviles e Internet móvil. Doctoral dissertation. Universidad Politécnica de Madrid.

Ramos, S., Arcos, M., and Armuña, C. (2009). The role of public administrations in developing the electronic communications infrastructures in Spain. *info*, **11**(6), 69–81.

Rupp, K., and Selberherr, S. (2010). The economic limit to Moore's Law. *Proceedings of the IEEE*, **98**(3), 351–353.

Sherif, M. H., and Maeda, Y. (2010). Standards for broadband access and beyond. *IEEE Communications Magazine*, **48**(10), 136–138.

Siciliani, P. (2010). Access regulation on NGA – A financial, market-led solution to bridge the gap between US and European diverging regulatory approaches. *Telecommunications Policy*, **34**(5–6), 287–298.

Greece

ANASTASIA CONSTANTELOU

13.1 Introduction to the case study

Greece's programme for regulatory reform in the telecommunication sector has been guided by the principles prescribed by the European Union (EU) directives. However, its slow implementation of market liberalization in the voice segment occurred on 1 January 2001, several years after the target date of 1 January 1998. This late start allowed Greece to draw on the experiences of other countries regarding the actual pace and effects of regulatory reforms, as well as the policies pursued by member states regarding the development of advanced broadband networks and services, the so called next-generation networks (NGNs) – a major objective of the EU telecom policy for over a decade now.

Greece has been lagging behind in the availability of alternative infrastructures. This is partly due to the lack of a cable network and partly to the reluctance of alternative operators to invest in network infrastructure. This slowed down the development of access competition, in particular platform competition (i.e., the availability of different systems offering high speed access to the Internet). In many other countries, cable has been an important means of creating effective competition with technologies that function over the traditional public switched telephone network (PSTN), in particular xDSL. In the early 2000s it had become apparent to most Greek stakeholders (policy makers, academics and advisors to policy makers) that the lag in Greek telecoms, in both demand and supply, was there to stay unless a serious effort was made by all the actors involved. The intrinsic characteristics of the local market[1]

combined with the lack of serious competition in the access market (with the exception of mobile) did not allow for a rapid development of broadband access, as was happening in the other EU countries. In early 2000, Greece was the only country in the EU (among the fifteen member states at the time) where the spread of fast, always-on and cheap Internet access was close to 0%!

In the light of this situation, a major initiative took place under the auspices of the Ministry of Transport and Communications, with the involvement of the Greek Research and Technology Network (GRNET). The initiative was led by a Scientific Committee of academic researchers and its primary objective was to initiate a public consultation with all main stakeholders in order to propose a set of ambitious, albeit realistic and manageable, interventions that would enhance broadband in Greece. A starting point for the members of this initiative was the belief that the development of broadband networks and access to broadband services would not be a result of the telecommunications market's operation at the time. Rather, a new set of business models, tools and practices were required that would bring together, in an innovative way, private and public sector actors to realise a common objective. The initiative was well-timed, as Greek authorities were considering using European structural funds available under the 3rd Community Support Framework for Greece to improve broadband penetration in the country, and therefore were in need of concrete guidance and advice.

This chapter concentrates on broadband developments in Greece that have taken place since this

[1] The Greek market is small in size with a distinctive geographic landscape (many mountainous areas and dispersed islands). Moreover, at that time, there was a wide digital divide and a lack of a clear regulatory framework regarding access conditions.

initial consultation in 2000. The aim is to provide a detailed account of the broadband market dynamics over this period, highlighting the strategies and tactics of main actors involved (dominant players in the telecoms market, mobile operators, public entities, regulators, and policy makers), as well as their outcomes that influenced the course of events in the Greek broadband market up to mid-2013. To do so, information was retrieved and gathered primarily through desk-based research from a variety of sources, including:

- official web sites of major Greek telecommunications service providers;
- official public documents and Internet sites that relate to broadband in Greece;
- academic articles and publications as well as deliverables of specialized studies.

In addition, a number of interviews were conducted with key players involved in the conceptualization and design of relevant policies at the time.

Prior to this analysis, however, it is important to place the evolution of the telecommunications sector in Greece into a historical perspective. Thus, this chapter is structured as follows: Section 13.2 presents the historical background to the Greek telecommunications sector. First, it looks at the process of modernization of the telecommunications infrastructure led by the incumbent operator OTE. Next, it continues with an overview of the liberalization process and the role of regulation. The section also discusses the state-of-the-art in the Greek telecommunications market, including alternative operators and mobile service providers. Section 13.3 discusses the case focus of broadband. It starts with an overview of the recommendations of the early consultation process, which led to a number of broadband initiatives funded by public sources (Greek government funds and European structural funds). The section also discusses the implementation of these actions and provides an account of the early results. Section 13.4 discusses the case of municipal broadband networks in Greece and the prerequisites for their successful operation, which are currently scarce. Section 13.5 presents the more recent developments in broadband investments and infrastructure, as well as progress towards the realization of

the Digital Agenda targets. Finally, Section 13.6 concludes with an analysis of the main findings of the case.

13.2 Greek telecommunications in retrospect

13.2.1 Overview and milestones in the development of Greek telecommunications.

The first telecommunications operator in Greece, the Greek Telephone Company S.A. (GTC) was established in the early 1930s with Siemens-Halske as its main shareholder. GTC developed local networks in twenty-three Greek towns. In 1946, after the end of World War II, 75% of GTC's shares were handed over to the Greek state as a compensation for war damages. The Hellenic Telecommunications Organisation (OTE) was founded in 1949 and was given exclusive rights for the operation of telecommunication services in the country. In 1973, a Presidential Decree elucidated OTE's relationship with the state. In particular, it was clarified that: (a) the state should not interfere in OTE's management; (b) OTE's investment programmes should conform to the annual and five-year government investment programmes; and (c) OTE's agreements, contracts, and tariffs had to be approved by the Ministry of National Economy and the Ministry of Transport and Communications before their launch. Still, despite these clarifications, a period of intensive commingling between OTE and the state started. This was further intensified when Pasok's socialist government came to power in 1981. In 1985, OTE became a public utility company, which called for an increased representation of employees on its Board of Directors (Constantelou, 1998).

Until the late 1980s, the telecommunications sector in Greece operated as a natural monopoly. However, in the early 1990s the country's entry into the European Union and the deteriorating performance of the public network resulted in pressure for a shift towards a more liberalized market environment. At the same time, technological advances in communications systems and services offered 'windows of opportunity' for engagement in new service areas, which were attracting the interest of both Greek and international investors (OECD, 2001, p.10).

In their study on Greek telecommunications, Caloghirou and Darmaros (1994) identified three phases in the history of Greek telecommunicatiosn policy-making: The *first phase* (1949–1980) was characterized by massive investments in network infrastructure aiming to extend basic service provision across the country. During this time, OTE was purchasing switching and transmission equipment from a variety of vendors. This tactic resulted in OTE ending up with twelve different types of analogue switches which in the 1980s were becoming increasingly obsolete. The *second phase* (1981–1990), was initiated when the Socialists came to power and was characterized by an increased involvement of the state in OTE's affairs, leaving the organization with very little room for independence and autonomy in its organisation and management. A *third phase* in Greek telecoms history started in 1991 and lasted until the opening of the voice market to competition in 2001. During this time, a duopoly was introduced in the provision of digital mobile telephony whereas OTE's emphasis was on the modernization and digitalization of its fixed network infrastructure. This period was also characterized by significant delays in the formulation of policies and actual decisions that would prepare the ground for the upcoming liberalization of the sector. Towards the end of this period, OTE launched its ISDN service, at a time when all major operators in the EU had already moved into ADSL. Still, for OTE, which during the previous years had invested heavily in building intelligence into its network, skipping the ISDN phase and moving directly into ADSL seemed like the wrong decision at the time. Such a strategy would not allow for a payback of the investments made; moreover, it would make those investments obsolete, requiring extra financing for the new technology to be introduced.

The opening of the voice market to competition on 1 January 2001 marked the beginning of a fourth phase in Greek telecommunications development. In fact, in June 1996, the Greek state and OTE entered into negotiations with the European Commission for an extension of the EU's 1 January 1998 deadline for full liberalization to 1 January 2003. The arguments on the Greek side were that inherent national financial constraints, OTE's costly modernization program and the increased pressure of pending demand for basic service throughout the country had put extra burdens upon OTE. Therefore, full digitalization could only be achieved if OTE was further guaranteed sufficient revenues by maintaining exclusive rights for a longer period of time. The Commission rejected the arguments of the Greek side and granted OTE an extension only until 31 December 2000, to allow OTE sufficient time to rebalance its tariffs. The OECD was even stricter in its judgement of the situation: as OTE was making significant strategic investments in the Balkans throughout the 1990s, it seemed well positioned to bear the cost of universal service in Greece, given the resources available for foreign investment. To which it added: '*had OTE operated in a competitive environment, there would have been no reason to question its external investments*' (OECD, 2001, p.7).

The full opening of the Greek telecommunications market to competition made the 2000s a decade of rapid technological and institutional changes. These were also driven by the political will of the new Socialist government and the euphoria associated with the positive international financial climate and the prospective organisation of the 2004 Olympic Games in Athens. During this time, all actors involved were going through a learning process, each in its own domain; OTE was investing in its network, while defending its position as the incumbent operator, making life difficult for new entrants who were heavily depended on OTE to roll out their networks. At the same time, the national regulatory authority (NRA), EETT, began to take an open approach in decision-making by initiating public consultations on matters such as the unbundling of the local loop, the allocation of fixed-wireless access licenses, etc. Despite criticisms by some market participants that these processes were not managed properly and ended up being cumbersome and time-consuming, the need to catch-up after years of indecision and delay made an open and effective consultation procedure an indispensable part of the way forward.

It was in early 2000 that discussions on the creation of a strategic framework for the development of broadband started with great enthusiasm among industry experts and policy makers. The spirit in these discussions (and in the ones that followed) was always in favor of state involvement in network financing through national and/or European funds (e.g., EU structural funds). In contrast to the situation in other European countries (e.g., Denmark, see Chapter 6), the future of broadband in Greece has always been seen as a 'market failure' problem which demands state intervention in some form of public (co-)financing in the roll-out of infrastructure. In this vein, in 2010 the idea was put forward for the development of Fibre-to-the-Home (FttH) by creating an independent, passive fibre-optic network open and available on equal terms to all undertakings providing electronic communications services as an alternative to OTE's nationwide network. This next-generation access (NGA) network would be co-financed by public sources. The argument was that without public intervention (legislative and co-financing) no provider – not even OTE – would undertake the cost of developing such a network entirely on its own. To this end, a public-private partnership (PPP) agreement was proposed, in which private entities would undertake the cost and risk of the necessary investments in exchange for the commercial exploitation of the NGA network through the wholesaling of local loop fibre optic at affordable prices. However, as will be discussed later in this chapter, the financial crisis put these plans on hold for an undetermined period.

In the following sections developments in the Greek telecommunications market are discussed in more detail by theme: first the regulatory developments, followed by a discussion of the role of the operators. The section concludes with a discussion of the developments in the mobile sector.

13.2.2 Telecommunications policy and regulation in the 1990s and 2000s

In the 1990s, Greece derogated from nearly all deadlines set by the European Commission regarding the gradual opening of markets to competition. For example, value-added networks and services over leased lines appeared in Greece in the early 1990s, offering services to closed user groups and corporate customers. However, OTE was given special permission by the European Commission to maintain its exclusive rights over public data networks and services until 1997, whereas data and satellite communication markets in other EU countries had opened to competition as early as 1994. The use of alternative network infrastructure for the provision of data and other value-added services was liberalized in October 1997. Some utility companies, such as the National Railways and the Public Electricity Company, expressed interest in deploying dark fibre through their existing country-wide infrastructures. However, none of these companies went further to become an alternative network provider.

This situation should be seen in the light of the political climate of that period. For the most part of the 1990s, the Socialist government maintained a defensive and inactive stance to the structural changes to be introduced into the sector and it considered liberalization as a rather intrusive force to the established status-quo serving the interests of OTE, state authorities and OTE's main equipment suppliers. On its part, the European Commission exercised a carrot-and-stick policy towards Greek authorities. For example, in 1997, it suspended subsidies to OTE on the grounds that there were serious delays in the harmonization of Greek legislation to EC directives (OECD, 2001). Nonetheless, on the eve of opening the full market to competition in January 2001, the Greek authorities managed to put in place most of the key pieces of legislation required, including provisions for universal service obligations, draft licenses for alternative operators, and provisions for interconnection charges. OTE also adopted current, rather than historical, cost accounting principles, as a first step towards the adoption of the long-run incremental cost (LRIC) methodology for the calculation of interconnection charges to alternative operators.

On the regulatory front, the National Telecommunications Commission was established in 1995 as an independent regulatory authority for the sector. In 1998 the Commission took under its jurisdiction the supervision of the postal sector and was renamed National Commission for

Telecommunications and Posts (EETT). However, throughout the 1990s, government's sluggishness left EETT severely understaffed, with the majority of its personnel being seconded from OTE. In the 2000s, this situation gradually changed and EETT was in a position to recruit over 250 scientific staff and external associates as members of various working groups (EETT, 2006). In 2006 EETT assumed the role of the Competition Committee on issues pertaining to electronic communications.

EETT took regulatory measures on local loop unbundling (LLU) as early as 2002. However, over the period 2002–2006, the majority of alternative providers remained on the first and second rung of the 'ladder of investment'[2] providing services based on OTE's infrastructure, using either carrier pre-selection or bitstream access.[3] It was not until early 2007, with the enactment of Law 3431/2006, that actual unbundling of the local loop took place and alternative operators started to move to the third rung of the investment ladder. In 2007, Greece experienced for the first time an annual broadband growth rate higher than the EU average (EETT, 2008b). Furthermore, in 2009, following EETT's Decisions on OTE's Wholesale Line Rental Offer, wholesale leased lines (WLL) were introduced to the Greek market, permitting alternative providers to lease a subscriber line from OTE on wholesale terms and to resell it to the end-user, in combination with the Carrier Pre-selection service. Since that time, however, alternative operators have gradually abandoned reselling and have moved to investing in collocation infrastructure taking advantage of LLU regulation and reducing their dependence on OTE.

In the 2000s EETT also showed particular interest in wireless technology for enhancing broadband access. Fixed wireless access (FWA) networks in particular were regarded as a suitable alternative to copper wire or optical fibre networks in inaccessible or sparsely populated areas of the Greek territory, where the installation of wired networks was economically unattractive. Hence, EETT carried out an auction for the award of a FWA license of the 3.5 GHz band, which would enable deployment of a wireless access network based on WiMAX technology in August 2006. The license was granted to the highest bidder, Cosmotelco Telecommunications Services, for the amount of EUR 20,475,000. However, until March 2011 the bidder had neither taken any significant initiative for the installation of the WiMAX network nor had it paid a residual amount of 20% of its bid. Therefore, EETT revoked its license and the WiMAX network was never completed.

13.2.3 The role of telecom operators

As soon as the market for voice telephony was liberalized in 2001, a number of alternative operators entered the market aspiring to obtain a piece of OTE's market share. However, the large number of operators and their small size raised concerns about their future viability. These alternative operators mainly built their business on using OTE's network. During the first years of their operation their business model was based on the margin between the wholesale price they were paying for leasing lines from OTE – which has always been regulated – and the retail price they were charging their customers. As this practice was the norm for most of the 2000s, it did not lead to investments by alternative operators that would differentiate their network development strategy from OTE's.[4]

In 2001, apart from the four major market players (OTE and the three mobile operators), there were more than 200 telecommunication service providers operating in the Greek market. Most of them were active in the market for Internet services, while a significant number of companies offered the so-called 'value-added' services to closed user groups.

---

[2] The 'ladder of investment' concept was introduced by Cave (2006). The first rung can be perceived as pure resale using carrier pre-select, the second rung as using bitstream and the third rung as using unbundled local loop.

[3] According to EETT (2008a, p.8) in mid-2006, the number of unbundled local loops provided by OTE was almost 16,000. Of these, only one alternative operator had more than 2,000 local loops.

[4] It should be noted that OTE benefited from an extension of the deadline under EU regulations for the introduction of number portability and carrier selection and pre-selection to 1 January 2003.

Table 13.1: Licensed operators, Greece, 2001 and 2012

Activity	Number of operators in 2001	Number of operators in 2012
Fixed network development	1	64
Voice telephony and fixed network development	1	192
Voice services to closed user groups, pre-paid telephone cards	30	n.a.
Voice telephony	1	179
Audiotex	9	n.a.
Data services	17	n.a.
Fax services	17	n.a.
Resale of mobile services	6	n.a.
Internet access	143	n.a.
Satellite networks	n.a.	53
2G Mobile telephony	2	12
3G Mobile telephony	-	13
TETRA	n.a.	7
W-LAN	-	95

Data sources: OECD, 2001; EETT, 2012.

In 2012, the picture was completely different, as shown in Table 13.1. However, it should be noted that not all licensed operators in the voice telephony and fixed network segment provide commercial services to the public. Some of them are licensed to provide services to closed user groups and/or are corporate members who serve their own communication needs.

At the end of 2012, OTE had retained its dominant position in the fixed access market for the provision of public telephone services, albeit with a decline in market share from 72.7% in 2010, through 66% in 2011 to about 62.4% in 2012. The decline reflects the ongoing competitive pressure by alternative operators. However, the penetration rate of access lines in fixed telephony has been on a downward trend in recent years, from 46.7% in December 2010 to 43.4% in December 2012) This has been the result of increased substitution by mobile telephony and the gradual disconnection of telephone lines in resort homes around Greece.

OTE has been regarded as the leading integrated telecommunications operator in southeastern Europe, providing voice, mobile and broadband services in contiguous markets. More specifically,

since 1997, the OTE group of companies has been active in Romania (through its affiliates Romtelecom and COSMOTE Romania) and in Albania (through its affiliate AMC).[5] OTE is one of the five largest companies on the Athens Stock Exchange, with its shares also traded at the London International Stock Exchange. Since 1996 the Greek government has been gradually reducing its shareholding in OTE. On 14 May 2008 an agreement was signed between the Greek government and Deutsche Telekom (DT) on a major participation in OTE's share capital by DT. After additional sales of shares and voting rights by the Greek government, the stake of Deutsche Telekom in OTE reached 40% in July 2011, reducing the Greek government's participation to 10%. The remainder of OTE shares are held by Greek and international institutional investors.

Table 13.2 summarizes key events in OTE's broadband agenda for the period 2005–2012.

---

[5] OTE was also active in the Bulgarian market but on 26 April 2013 it announced the sale of its 100% subsidiaries Cosmo Bulgaria Mobile EAD (Globul) and Germanos Telecom Bulgaria (Germanos).

Table 13.2 Milestones in OTE's Broadband Agenda, 2005–2012

Date	Event
2005–2006	– The emphasis has been on the development and diffusion of broadband. OTE's initiatives ranked Greece as the fastest growing country in the world in terms of percentage growth of broadband connections (Point Topic, Research Global Broadband Statistics); – By the end of 2006, OTE exceeded 500,000 broadband connections, ten times higher than in 2005; – Access data rates doubled in 2006; – In summer 2006 OTE launched its two-year nationwide information campaign on broadband.
2007	– New access data rates of up to 24 Mbit/s became available; – Successful completion of OTE's two-year nationwide information campaign on broadband, having visited a total of 33 cities around the country.
2008	– OTE's broadband connections reached 970,000 in 1390 nationwide points of presence; – A new service, Hellas SAT net! Home of Hellas Sat, a subsidiary of OTE, enabled access to the Internet in areas where no terrestrial infrastructure or other means of telecommunication existed; – Commercial pilot launch of Conn-X TV, OTE's IPTV service.
2009	– Full commercial launch of Conn-X TV, through OTE's broadband ADSL lines; – OTE's ADSL lines exceeded 1.1 million. OTE maintained broadband connections in more than 1,500 points of presence nationwide (i.e., 95% of telephone connections in the country).
2010	– OTE developed a broadband fibre optic network of FttC/VDSL2 technologies in selected areas in the municipalities of Alexandroupoli, Komotini, Xanthi, Serres and Zografou (Attiki). – OTE upgraded its ADSL data rates nationwide with no additional cost for the customers. The new data rates offered were 2 Mbit/s downstream/512 kbit/s upstream and up to 24 Mbit/s downstream/1 Mbit/s upstream.
2011	– OTE presented its OTE TV Via Satellite and consolidated all of the pay-TV services offered under the common name OTE TV; – Since February 2011, OTE has been technically ready to provide ultra-high broadband speeds up of to 50 Mbit/s. However, at the end of 2011, the National Regulatory Authority had not yet allowed the commercial provision of these services to the public; – As part of the modernization of its access network, OTE launched pilot installations of Fibre-to-the-Building (FttB) mainly in industrial areas. The new access network uses a Point-to-MultiPoint architecture and is capable of providing data rates of up to 100 Mbit/s.
2012	– OTE made commercial VDSL available in late November offering data rates of upto 50 Mbit/s. This was the final result of a long negotiation process between OTE and the Greek Regulatory Authority, EETT. The case began with the provisional measures set by EETT in response to the attempted commercialization by OTE of VDSL services without price control. EETT then proceeded with a market analysis, the approval of commercial rates for wholesale VDSL, the publication of the Rules for Spectrum Management in the access network, the adoption of OTE's Reference Offer, a regulatory integration in September 2012 of the new wholesale product (to be offered by OTE), and the final approval of VDSL retail prices using EETT's cost model; – Regulatory approval of OTE's double-play bundled products in May 2012 narrowed OTE's competitive disadvantage compared to alternative carriers; – OTE TV subscriber base exceeded 100,000 subscribers in mid-October.

Data source: Compiled based on information on OTE website, 28/6/2013.

The backbone network of OTE is fully based on optical fibre, consisting of more than 35,000 kilometers of optical fibres, complemented with satellite, terrestrial and underwater links to connect to international networks.

The access network of OTE has been supporting the entire broadband development in Greece, as copper-based xDSL has been the major technology for broadband access in the country. Its access network is mostly copper-based (with over 5.3 million pairs) with optical fibres gradually and steadily replacing the copper network in the course of OTE's strategic investments in next-generation access (NGA).

In the beginning of the liberalization process, private companies were reluctant to invest in alternative technologies because of the high risk associated with such investments, the instabilities that prevailed in the market and competition from OTE. Instead, they tried to build their own clientele, offering phone

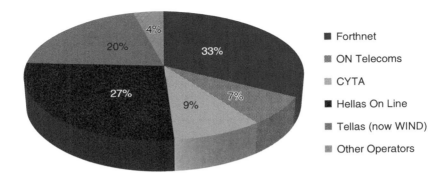

Figure 13.1 LLU-based market share of alternative operators (full and shared LLU), Greece, 1 January 2011 *Data source*: Observatory for the Information Society, 2011, *12th Semester Report for Broadband*, April.

services using infrastructure leased from OTE. In order to compete with OTE, they were leasing large-capacity circuits at wholesale prices controlled by the regulator. As prices for telephony services dropped significantly in recent years, a number of bankruptcies of and mergers between private telecommunications firms have taken place, thereby reducing the number of key players to around five. These alternative providers base their service offerings mainly on the use of local loop unbundling (LLU) rather than on other types of wholesale broadband access. See Figure 13.1 for the division of LLU market shares of the major players.

Initially, alternative service providers mainly offered broadband access services and no content services. The latter were limited and were offered by a minority of telecommunications services providers (mainly the bigger ones). Also, there was not a common pattern or business model in the provision of content service. As gradually significant investments in optical backbone infrastructures were made by the competing network operators to leverage the LLU regulation for broadband access, they are now able to offer and support innovative products such as double-play, triple-play, etc., at competitive prices.

13.2.4 *The mobile communications sector*

Following an international tender in 1992, a duopoly was established in 1993 between Panafon SA (today Vodafone) and STET Hellas

(later TIM, and today Wind) for the provision of GSM 900 services. In 1995 a third license was granted to OTE to install and operate its own GSM 1800 network through its subsidiary COSMOTE. The company started operations in April 1998.

In 2002 a fourth license was granted to Q Telecom, which in 2007 merged with Wind Hellas. Table 13.3 below summarizes milestone events of the last ten years in the Greek mobile sector. Of particular significance are the mergers and acquisitions that have taken place among operators, as well as the strategic alliances among different types of operators and service providers (mobile, alternative, ISPs, and TV platform providers).

The development of the mobile industry has been impressive. The Greek mobile industry has invested a total of EUR 7.012 billion in networks, base stations and telecommunications equipment over the period 1993–2012 and has contributed significantly to economic growth and public revenue of the country (Association of Mobile Communication Companies, 2013).[6]

From 1998 to 2002, the annual growth rate of mobile penetration was more than 10%, whereas in 2005 the penetration reached 100% of the population. By mid-2013, mobile penetration reached 141%, a figure which is close to the European

---

[6] This amount does not include the license fees paid for the allocation of frequency spectrum.

Table 13.3 Milestone events in the mobile sector, Greece, 2001–2012

Date	Event
2001	Award of 3G licenses to established players Vodafone, Cosmote, and TIM (today Wind)
2001	Launch of GPRS technology over the established 2.5G GSM networks marked the beginning of a new era in mobile data services.
2003	Mobile operators started to offer integrated service packages (including data services) to their customers (COSMOTE i-mode, Vodafone Live, Wind Plus).
2004	Launch of 3G UMTS technology allowed an increase in data rates and use of data services
2007	Launch of the first smartphones and mobile Internet services
2009	Strategic alliances, mergers and acquisitions: Mobile operators allied with alternative operators, Internet service providers and TV platforms to offer bundled service packages (known as double-play or triple-play). Examples include Vodafone's strategic alliance with the ISP Hellas-on-Line (HOL) and Forthnet's acquisition of NOVA, a Greek digital platform for subscribed satellite TV services.
2010	Launch of 3.5G HSPA Services
2010	First launch of integrated communication services (fixed-mobile-Internet) in the Greek market.
2011	Renewal of mobile operators' old licenses and acquisition of new rights in the frequency bands of 900 MHz and 1800 MHz until 2027. Old and new spectrum rights become technology neutral.
2012	Official launch of 4G/LTE services (high ultra high speed data services) by Vodafone and Cosmote.

Data source: Based on Association of Mobile Communication Companies, 2013.

average.[7] However, as Figure 13.2 suggests, there was a sharp drop in the total number of subscribers after 2009 which can be linked to the economic crisis. In 2012 the number of subscribers took an upward turn again.

The rapid growth of the sector during the first fifteen years of operation is reflected in the evolution of the sector's turnover. More specifically, the industry had a turnover of EUR 12 million in 1993 and reached EUR 4.5 billion in 2006. However, from 2008 onwards the saturation of the industry, combined with the economic downturn, reduced termination fees and tax increases led to a cumulative drop in turnover of 36%. At the European level a decline in revenues also can be observed – but this remains modest, at -1.9% per year from 2007 onwards reflecting losses being offset by the development of new services, including mobile broadband – whereas in Greece, the economic downturn and the delay in the take up of mobile data services have led to a more significant drop (-10.2% per year from 2007 onwards).

In November 2011 the mobile industry reinvested EUR 298 million in the renewal of mobile phone licenses and EUR 82 million for the acquisition of new rights in the frequency bands of 900 MHz and 1800 MHz.[8] Mobile broadband is the future of the sector, as the uninterrupted growth in mobile data services suggests: from 4.2 billion MB in 2009 to 10.8 billion MB in 2012 (EETT, 2012). Mobile operators in Greece continue to invest heavily to upgrade their networks even at the time of economic crisis. According to the Association of Mobile Communication Companies (2013), over the period 1995–2001 the sector invested approximately 30% of its revenues in building network infrastructure, whereas over the current maturity period

[7] A study funded by the Association of Mobile Operators published in September 2013, indicated that if the holders of two or more connections were counted as one, mobile penetration rate reached 84% of population, covering more than the entire adult population in the country.

[8] According to the Association of Mobile Operators (2013), mobile operators have not yet exploited the entire frequency band available to them due to problems they experience in the licensing procedures for the installation of antennas and base stations. According to the operators, Greece has the longest time-lag among all European countries and the highest number of interfering authorities during the consultation periods prior to the issue of a license.

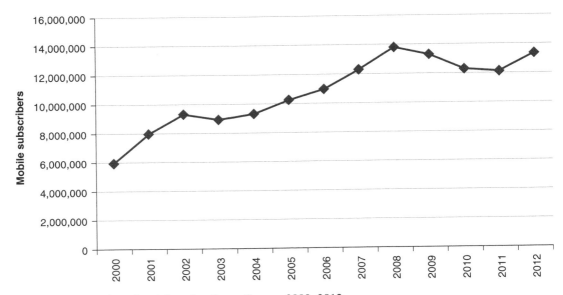

Figure 13.2 Number of mobile subscribers, Greece, 2000–2012
Data source: International Telecommunication Union, 2013.

(2002–2012) the sector managed to maintain investments at an average of 11%.

Today, the Greek mobile sector is a prime contributor to the achievement of the Digital Agenda targets, as it provides high data rate Internet access through its mobile broadband networks, including 4G LTE (long-term evolution).

13.3 Case focus: early public consultation on broadband, recommendations and actions

This section focuses on the public policy agenda for the development of broadband in Greece, which started soon after the publication of the White Paper 'Greece in the Information Society' in 1999. In early 2000 a consultation took place over the future of broadband in the country, led by a committee of experts. A number of similar initiatives and strategic documents prepared in other countries were reviewed and the committee reached a number of conclusions, the most important of which are summarized below:

- A need was identified for the state to set up an appropriate institutional, regulatory and business framework that would allow the exploitation of synergies between the public and private sectors, and develop a spirit of cooperation among providers;
- Participants expressed their concern over the price levels at which broadband services would become available in the future, and over the lack of 'broadband culture' among the majority of Greek citizens. A question was subsequently raised as to whether, and under which conditions, acceptance of and participation in those services could be foreseen;
- Providers in the market acknowledged OTE's position in the market as crucial for providing interconnection services at reasonable prices to other companies if the latter were to develop their services locally, and viewed positively actions for the development of common infrastructure (community broadband networks and condominium fibre);
- One in two participants believed that there should be financial support (in the form of

subsidies and/or tax benefits) from the state provided there were clear rules of operation and investment; and

• Participants strongly supported the view that demand for broadband services could be fueled primarily by the public sector, through initiatives that would enhance demand in the education and healthcare sectors, while further expansion could be achieved by training citizens in the new technologies.

All in all, the results of the consultation process strongly suggested a policy-making role for the state, setting the institutional and regulatory framework for the implementation of novel business models and practices, in which the private sector participates along with the state in the roll-out of broadband. The state should also act as a major user of network services, and as an enabler and manager of direct and indirect interventions in this area through programs which would anticipate and correct possible market failures.

These observations were in line with the best practices found in Europe and in other parts of the world. Normally, the role of central governments in broadband developments has been to set the framework within which public involvement could be achieved. This included: (a) ensuring broad social acceptance of the benefits and opportunities of the information economy, such that the allocation of significant public funds to build optical networks would become socially acceptable; (b) designing programs that help people gain skills, such that they could be successfully integrated into the digital economy; (c) encouraging entrepreneurial innovation in online services and applications which enhance demand for broadband connections and services; and (d) forming a clear framework of entrepreneurial activity that would guide telecommunications providers' strategies in the development of optical access networks.

In early 2000 the Greek telecommunications market depended on OTE's optical fibre backbone network, which was available and suitable for broadband development. However, the optical network arteries at the national and regional level and the availability of broadband infrastructure at the local access level were missing. The geography of the country has been a significant obstacle to the development of regional and municipal metropolitan networks in areas other than the densely populated economic centers of Athens and Thessaloniki. The mountainous terrain and the large number of islands make connectivity difficult and expensive. Due to the small population of towns and the small size of most business enterprises, only a limited number of cities present significant prospects for broadband. This is the main reason that the market for backhaul in Greece has remained monopolized by OTE. Even if the circumstances could justify investments in remote areas, such decisions were discouraged by the fact that the only option for investors to interconnect over long distances was through the dominant carrier. As a result, the provision of broadband connections outside the densely populated city-areas of Athens and Thessaloniki has remained very limited and broadband penetration extremely low.

Under these circumstances and in the light of the targets set in the eEurope 2005 Agenda, which was prepared at the time, the Scientific Committee made the recommendations to the State authorities shown in Table 13.4.

It is obvious that the best possibilities for high broadband penetration were to be expected in large metropolitan centres, whereas in most of the regions this would be unlikely. It was therefore of paramount importance that the state find ways to boost broadband evolution in these regions. The opportunity arrived through the "Information Society" Operational Programme. The Greek government, with support from the European Union through the 3rd Community Support Framework (CSF), set up an innovative, multi-sector and horizontal programme as a response to the attainment of eEurope objectives and the achievement of digital convergence with the rest of Europe. The programme ran over the period 2000–2006 and included a series of initiatives that targeted broadband penetration beyond the two main metropolitan centres of Athens and Thessaloniki. These initiatives can be grouped in three areas of intervention as follows (Troulos, 2012):

Table 13.4 Priorities and recommendations for the broadband era, Greece

Observations	Recommendations
Strong need for open and transparent government interventions in less privileged areas	– Develop optical fibre networks (Metropolitan Area Networks) at the regional level, which combined with other technologies (including wireless networks) could provide high data rate access to the last mile.
Need for exploitation of aggregated public sector demand for the creation of a competitive market	– Create a national network for the public administration by the end of 2003. This action is also aimed to boost wholesale infrastructure providers to become active at the national level; – Support services such as xDSL and LMDS, and create hotspots in locations with comparable business profiles. These measures should be combined with information and awareness-raising activities; – Use satellite infrastructure and provide satellite services to serve remote parts of the public administration (such as health, education, etc.).
Need to establish conditions for the development of a healthy and competitive marketplace in areas where the presence of multiple providers is foreseen	The Regulator should: – Address the issue of rights of way and one-stop shopping; – Accelerate and support local loop unbundling (LLU); – Clarify interconnection regulation among telecommunications providers. State Authorities should investigate the following: – Use of alternative infrastructures (e.g., electricity and water networks) for the development of broadband access; – Separation of services from infrastructure provision – Provisions for the roll-out of broadband infrastructure in road construction works (national and regional), water supply and drainage works, etc.; – Regulatory interventions for the collocation of facilities; – Costing arrangement for OTE's backbone network.

Source: Chiotis, 2002.

- Development of broadband infrastructure: This intervention was implemented through six separate actions;
- Development of broadband services: This intervention was implemented through five separate actions;
- Strengthening demand and 'broadband awareness' among the population: This area of intervention was implemented through three separate actions.

These areas of intervention had a total budget of over EUR 450 Million. In particular, the following fourteen actions targeted broadband development across the country. Each of these actions corresponds to a call for tenders issued by the Administrative Authority of the Information Society Programme, see Table 13.5.

Among these actions, the following are of particular interest for the current state of broadband in the country:

At the metropolitan level, the interest lies in the Calls for Proposals Nºs 93, 145 and 192 of the Operational Programme for the Information Society. These were intended to subsidize the construction (capital expenditure) and operation (operational expenditure) of metropolitan fibre networks (metropolitan access networks – MANs) during the early years of the investments in more than seventy Greek cities beyond Athens and Thessaloniki. The initial aim of the MANs was primarily to support the operation of public sector establishments, as this could guarantee their immediate deployment and use, as well as raise awareness and subsequent demand for broadband by

Table 13.5 Areas of intervention and proposed actions, Information Society Program, Greece

Areas of Intervention	Actions
Development of broadband infrastructure	1. Broadband metropolitan area networks in 75 municipalities; 2. Wireless broadband networks in 120 municipalities and 20 local communities; 3. Construction of 770 wireless hotspots in enterprises; 4. Exploitation of the broadband satellite capacity of HellasSAT; 5. Investment aid for broadband across peripheral regions; 6. New Investment Law: provisions for the development of broadband infrastructures.
Development of broadband services	1. Boost private investment in the development of broadband services; 2. Development of 'smart communities'; 3. Broadband services and digital television for people with special needs; 4. Development of digital services for the citizen; 5. New Investment Law: provisions for the development of broadband services.
Strengthening demand and 'broadband awareness' among the population	1. Raising awareness for broadband through the set up of 85 regional points across the country; 2. Strengthening demand for broadband services in peripheral regions; 3. Communication campaign for raising citizens' awareness and familiarity with broadband.

Source: Troulos, 2012.

citizens. Overall, seventy-five cities received the right to develop metropolitan networks in their territories. As the financing of these networks was through EU structural funds[9], the municipalities involved in the building of these MANs had (a) to comply with the European framework for public funding of telecommunications infrastructures, which requires that the networks co-financed by EU funds provide wholesale services only and are governed by clear rules of open access; and (b) set up detailed business plans which would comply with the respective guidelines and the regulatory framework of the European Union and would ensure a fair and adequate level of competition in the market and a viable future for these investments. The municipalities participating in these initiatives would become the legal owners of these infrastructures.

At the peripheral level, Call 105 was aiming to further promote the development of local access broadband networks in areas less populated than those covered by Call 93. The main beneficiaries of this Call were local unions of municipalities and small communities (LUMSCs) and the 'A' class of local government organizations (LGOs), as well as the operators of the Greek School Network. The implementation of Calls 105 and 93 were expected to dramatically change the broadband map of the country due to the construction of network infrastructure independent from that of the incumbent operator (OTE).

At the regional level, Call 157 'Enterprise financing for the development of broadband access in Greek regions' was mainly addressed to private telecommunication operators[10] and aimed at the development of DSL and Wi-Fi services to users in rural areas, possibly using the metropolitan fibre networks. The call also included provisions for high data rate Internet and advanced content services to end-users. It also provided for subsidies to end-users to further stimulate demand.

[9] 75% of the financing would come from European Union funding and 25% from national sources.

[10] OTE decided not to participate to this Call, although it was not formally excluded by the authorities issuing the Call.

It was envisaged that by the end of 2008 over 60% of the Greek territory would be covered by broadband networks which would serve over 90% of the population.

For the purposes of the action, the eligible areas of the country were divided into seven geographical areas. Four companies were awarded the contracts for the completion of projects (Hellas On Line (HOL) S.A., Forthnet S.A., Tellas S.A. (now Wind) and Cyta Hellas S.A.) with a total budget of EUR 206.6 million. In the beginning, most companies planned to use a combination of wired and wireless technologies, including Wi-Fi and mobile links. However, during the roll-out phase it became clear that this solution was not feasible due to deficiencies in the legal framework and bottlenecks in the licensing procedures set by regional authorities. As a result, the initial plan was replaced by optical networks only. These projects were completed by November 2009.

Most of the aforementioned actions were completed, in terms of installing the infrastructure, by the end of 2010. Meanwhile, in 2009, the Greek Ministry of Transport and Communications (MTC) announced an ambitious plan to build a Fibre-to-the-Home (FttH) network of 2,000,000 households. The project, with an initial budget of EUR 2.1 billion and a plan for completion in seven years, was expected to cover fifty-four large Greek cities, including Athens and Thessaloniki. However, the economic crisis in the country has put this plan on hold.

To summarize the outcomes of this development, it was obvious from the early start of the discussions on the Greek broadband agenda that because of the geography of the country several rural and scarcely populated areas would remain underserved. Thus, in line with the international experience, Greek policy makers considered public funding for infrastructure in these areas a remedy to resolve the anticipated market failure in the development of broadband across the country. By mid-2000, Greece had shown a significant increase in broadband penetration but retained the lowest position in Europe, exhibiting an overall 2.66% broadband penetration in July 2006, while the equivalent figure for the EU15 was 14.46% (Bouras, 2009).

By 2006, broadband infrastructure provision could be distinguished in three categories:

- Public broadband networks: These were the Greek Research and Technology Network (GRNET), the Greek Network of National Government ('Syzefxis'), which interconnects all ministries and public authorities, the Greek Universities Network (GUNET), and the Greek School Network (GSN). The last two networks interconnect research and academic institutes and public schools;
- Private broadband networks: Very limited new broadband infrastructures had been developed by alternative providers in only the two major cities of Athens and Thessaloniki; and
- Municipal optical networks, providing dark fibre in support of broadband access, were underway in the major cities, in small towns and in non-urban and remote areas of the country. The development of these infrastructures was guided by regional strategic objectives, taking into account the physical particularities and socio-economic conditions of the regions.

In the last case, policy makers adopted a model also found in other European countries (e.g., France, see Chapter 11) allowing municipalities to become telecommunications network providers, but not operators, in places where no private investments were to be expected. Thus, they assigned to local authorities the role of 'facilitators' in the deployment of Fibre-to-the-X (FttX) roll-out strategies (A. T. Kearney and Planning S.A., 2008).

However, this has not been an easy task for municipalities to handle. Several questions arose regarding the operations phase of these networks that demanded serious discussion. For example, what would be the role of the municipalities in these initiatives, to what extent should the central government bodies intervene, how could competition in the market be promoted, and – above all – how could the viability of the networks be ensured for the years to come? Thus, a key issue of concern for policy makers and local authorities since the late 2000s has been the selection of an appropriate business model to ensure the optimal exploitation of municipal optical networks. This issue is discussed in the following section.

13.4 Municipal optical networks: a Greek tragedy?

The use of optical MANs in the Greek periphery, exclusively by the public sector, raised a number of issues concerning the economic viability of these networks. As the cost per optical link was estimated to exceed EUR 500 per month, with a positive ROI to be achieved in 25 years, their economic viability would depend to a large extent upon their extension into the backbones of FttH networks and the provision of services to residential and business customers (Troulos, 2012).

The need for municipalities to take an active role in the operation of these networks was understood from the beginning. Prior to the implementation of a MAN in a particular city, a relevant study had to take place that would summarize the situation in the city and highlight all the challenging points that might require special attention. In addition, for each city, a business model for the efficient operation of the network had to be proposed that would take into account the possibility of providing optical fibre on cost-based prices, so as to cover the operational and maintenance costs of the infrastructure. Thus, two issues remained pending and demanded the attention of the technical consultants who were commissioned to provide their suggestions for:

a) the business model(s) for the optimal exploitation of the municipal optical networks; and
b) the appropriate management structure for the operations and management of the metropolitan networks on behalf of the municipal authorities.

Following Henderson and Ball (2005), the proposed business models had to take the following requirements into account (Bouras et.al, 2009):

- determine the role of the municipality and the region;
- ensure healthy competition;
- define the degree of involvement of the private sector;

- ensure the viability of the metropolitan community-owned optical network;
- secure the resources for its operation, maintenance and expansion;
- promote competition for offering better and cost effective services to the citizen.

The technical consultants in their studies of alternative business models considered the following characteristics and limitations of the Greek case (Bouras et. al. 2009):

- The majority of service providers were not in a position to build their own infrastructure as investment in telecommunications infrastructures in the periphery was not envisaged as being profitable;
- There has been a lack of a clear regulatory framework that would ensure equal treatment of the competitive alternative providers at any network level[11];
- Unbundling by OTE was proceeding slowly and competition in network infrastructures and services provision was limited;
- European regulations for structural funds state that beneficiary municipalities should offer open access, cost-based services and be prohibited from exercising monopoly powers over their infrastructures;
- Full state control (in all three layers of the network, from the infrastructures to the services level) would inhibit competition;
- Each telecommunications provider has its own active equipment that may be a source of competitive advantage.

As the MANs are owned by the municipalities, the prevalent approach that resulted from the studies was a 'passive infrastructure model' (Bouras, et. al. 2009; Kyriakidou, et.al. 2010). According to this approach, the passive network equipment (first network level) should be managed by a public

---

[11] The open access infrastructure can be modeled in three layers: the passive, the active and the service layers. The passive layer consists of the ducts, the microducts and the dark fibres. The active layer includes any type of active network equipment (switches, routers, modems, optical multiplexers, etc.). The service layer includes basic, advanced and value-added network services.

authority (at the municipal, regional or national level) and be offered in a cost-effective way to the telecommunication providers who would then make the investments to set up their own active equipment at the second network layer in order to provide different broadband services to the end-users (at the third network layer).

The next question that was raised concerned the management structure of these networks; i.e., who should manage, maintain, exploit and expand the passive infrastructure. Here, the technical consultants made a thorough review of prevalent models in order to inform the municipalities of the business practices and strategies available in Europe and elsewhere. The results indicated three prominent options: (a) establishment of a municipal enterprise to operate the business at the municipal/community level; (b) establishment of a regional enterprise to operate the business at the regional level, and (c) establishment of a centralized enterprise that would operate at the national level.

All three options were extensively discussed in the literature (Bouras, et. al. 2009; Troulos, et.al 2010, Troulos 2012). In particular, Troulos, et.al (2010: 81) summarized the disadvantages of establishing a municipal enterprise at one extreme of the spectrum and a national enterprise at the other as follows:

> Both approaches exhibit some limitations. The city-wide FttH network reaches a small market size making the effort financially risky; thus inhibiting private investments. Also, most municipalities do not have the human resources or experience for such endeavors, nor can they afford the management and operational overhead. On the other extreme, the case of the countrywide NetCo is marked by increased complexity to coordinate municipal efforts (especially in view of conflicting local priorities), and may result into increasing agency costs and bureaucracy. The efficiency of a centralized NetCo may be affected by the distance between its rigid planning center and the local communities' needs. Finally, this approach may be in conflict with European Union's and [the National Regulatory Authority's] EETT's policies that aim to reduce the national monopoly bottlenecks in electronic communications, i.e. the access networks.

To mitigate these drawbacks, the authors proposed the establishment of regional broadband companies (RBC) on a voluntary basis, where each participating municipality would contribute to the company's revenues and to the broadband development of the region according to its size and capacity.

In the light of these discussions, several municipalities and neighboring cities started to organize their next steps in terms of evaluating collective ways to offer fibre access and services to their citizens and leverage the already-installed municipal fibre MANs. To this end, by 2010 four regional groups had been formed (Troulos, 2012):

1. Digital Cities of Central Greece, led by the mainland city of Trikala;
2. Broadband Network of Southwest Greece, led by the city of Patras, the third largest city of Greece;
3. Ikaros Network, led by the city of Heraklion and municipalities of the Aegean Islands and Crete, and
4. Broadband Network of Northern Greece (covering the regions of Macedonia and Thrace), led by the municipality of Kavala.

However, the outbreak of the economic crisis in early 2010 and the political, administrative, and bureaucratic burdens that have been encountered in the formation of municipal network companies have put the commercial exploitation of these networks on hold. Despite the early euphoria regarding the prospects of municipal broadband throughout the 2000s, the situation today is almost stagnant and hardly shows signs of recovery. The initiative of setting up broadband companies at the regional level proved very demanding for the local and regional authorities. In the meantime, the economic and political priorities of the country have changed dramatically, as the financial crisis hit the public sector and imposed severe budget cuts across all sectors and regions. The current National Strategic Reference Framework (known as ESPA), which describes the strategic priorities of the country for the period 2007–2013 and which is co-funded by European Union funds (Cohesion Funds), has put digital convergence high on the political agenda. To this end, a new operational programme called 'Digital Convergence' has been

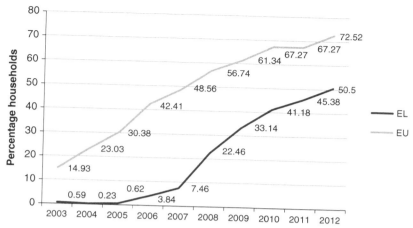

Figure 13.3 Households with a fixed broadband connection, Greece and EU, 2003–2012
Data source: European Commission, Digital Agenda Scoreboard, 2013.

running, but it mostly targets 'soft measures' which would enhance the use of ICTs within the public and private sectors, rather than the exploitation of broadband infrastructures.[12]

Whether there will be a *catharsis* in the modern municipal broadband drama that will relieve the tensions and agonies and provide policy makers and municipal authorities a clearer and renewed vision, as was the case in the ancient Greek tragedy, remains to be seen, ideally in the not-so-distant future.

13.5 Realizing the Digital Agenda targets

The Digital Agenda is one of the seven pillars of the Europe 2020 strategy of the European Commission, endorsed by the member state governments, and sets out the objectives for the optimal exploitation of Information and Communication Technologies (ICTs) to foster innovation, economic growth and progress in Europe. Initially,

the Digital Agenda identified seven priority areas where member states should concentrate their efforts in order to stimulate growth and competitiveness. One of these areas concerned the development of the financial, regulatory and technological environment for the development of broadband infrastructures across Europe.[13] This section reviews the progress made in Greece in the attainment of the Digital Agenda objectives, particularly with regard to the development of broadband infrastructure.

Overall, Greece has made significant progress but lags behind the EU average on important Digital Agenda indicators.[14] Although Greece, with 99.1% fixed broadband coverage, scores above the EU27 average of 95.5%, it is below European average in broadband penetration by households: the uptake was 24% compared to the European average of 28.8% at the end of 2012. See also Figure 13.3. Urban centers in Greece enjoy full broadband coverage, while in suburban and rural areas broadband coverage is 85% and 50%, respectively. This disparity also relates to

[12] The programme aims at promoting the use of ICTs in enterprises, business process re-engineering of the public sector, the promotion of entrepreneurship in ICT sectors, the development of digital public administration services for citizens, and the improvement of everyday life through ICTs.

[13] This is according to the new Digital Agenda priorities adopted in December 2012.
[14] See *Digital Agenda Scoreboard 2013*, available at https://ec.europa.eu/digital-agenda/en/scoreboard/greece   (last access November 2013).

the uneven distribution of population across the country, with more than 70% of the population living in the three major cities (Athens, Thessaloniki and Patras).

Next-generation access (NGA) networks were available to 21.9% of homes (as compared to 53.8% in the EU), whereas the uptake of high data rate connections was also low: 0.1% compared to 14.8% in the EU. Ultra-fast connections of at least 100 Mbit/s are not provided yet.

Nonetheless, there is significant progress, and the gap is closing. The total number of broadband lines reached 2.7 million in 2012, registering a 9.1% increase compared to 2011.

By December 2012, the incumbent operator OTE had a broadband market share just above the European average: 43.3% compared to 42.3%. Broadband is provided almost 100% on the basis of ADSL. The ADSL market share of OTE decreased from 55.4% in January 2009 to 43.4% in January 2012. The ADSL share by the OLOs is almost 100% based on LLU (European Commission, 2013). Unbundled broadband access is provided almost exclusively using fully unbundled access lines: 99.7% of the connections by December 2012, compared to 73.8% in the EU.

On the regulatory front, EETT took significant steps in the promotion of wireless broadband in 2012. Through its radio spectrum management policy, it conducted an auction of spectrum in the 900 and 1800 MHz bands and thereby opened the way to the development of 4G networks by mobile operators. Further auctions for spectrum licensing were expected in 2014. EETT also completed all preparations for the transition to VDSL. Following a decision by EETT, and soon after the launch of its own retail VDSL services, OTE was obliged to launch wholesale VDSL services to alternative operators as a 'fully functional' product at a standard quality of service, with established procedures for the recovery of failures, a clear and detailed pricelist, etc., in order for them to develop their own competitive VDSL offerings. This was the result of pressure exercised by alternative operators upon EETT to demand OTE make a similar wholesale product available to alternative operators.

Moreover, the regulatory framework for NGA is awaiting the full transposition of recent laws passed by the Greek parliament that address critical problems in the licensing procedures for new antenna installations.[15] Such a framework is necessary to further boost the development of mobile broadband. Other areas where public policy could enhance developments in broadband through regulatory interventions include: (a) strengthening the role of municipalities in the development of broadband; (b) encouraging the use of common public utility infrastructure; and (c) establishing standards and/or provisions regarding the internal wiring of buildings.

On the policy front, a new broadband development project was put to a public consultation in August 2013 aiming to reduce the 'broadband divide' and improve access to broadband in currently underserved rural areas. The project, with a budget of EUR 160 million co-financed by structural funds, will subsidize the development of broadband access networks by alternative operators in 6,145 remote rural villages. These represent 50% of the total rural area and correspond to 80% of the rural population. At the same time, it plans to enhance the level of competition among different operators in these areas which are currently served only by OTE. The project prescribes 30 Mbit/s services to villages with over 400 inhabitants using Fibre-to-the-Cabinet (FttC) technology, and 8 Mbit/s to villages with fewer inhabitants, with a capacity to increase to 30 Mbit/s by 2020. The technologies proposed for these purposes are FttC, fixed wireless access (P2P Ethernet links, P2MP WiMAX) and mobile networks (2G, 3G, LTE). For its part, OTE argues that the project is overpriced in providing broadband service in rural areas where little real added value is expected, and that the state could save public money and avoid duplication of investments if OTE was allowed to extend its broadband network to these remote areas under its universal service obligations. Although the result of the

---

[15] The new institutional framework introduces key elements for the simplification of the licensing procedures for new antennas and base stations by creating one-stop shopping processes at EETT.

consultation process was unknown at the time of completion of this chapter, it is unlikely that OTE's claims will be considered seriously.

On the mobile front, Greece performs above the European average in the availability of mobile broadband. At the end of 2012, third-generation mobile broadband was available to 99.4% of population, compared to 96.3% in the EU, whereas 4G availability reached 42.4% of the population (26.2% in the EU). However, the uptake rate of mobile broadband (subscriptions as a percentage of population) was 44.8%, a figure that is below the EU average of 54.5%. Driven by shrinking revenues, the two mobile operators Vodafone and Wind agreed to share equipment and network infrastructure for mobile 2G/3G, following approval by EETT.

13.6 Case analysis and concluding remarks

Greece has been a typical case of a country where state authorities, through the exercise of targeted subsidy programs, have advanced developments in broadband coverage and uptake. Unlike other EU member states, where the first priority has been to boost services and applications delivered over broadband, the Greek policy agenda concentrated on initiatives to foster actual infrastructure development and country-wide expansion. There has been a general consensus in the political system that such investments, if left to operators alone, would not materialize to the extent envisaged by European bodies, either because demand was not there yet or because the operators did not consider such investments to provide a sufficient financial return. Therefore, the expected market failure called for public money (national and European) to be used in building up the broadband infrastructure, mostly but not exclusively in remote and rural areas of the country.

The argument has been that the take-up of broadband would come as a natural next step as long as citizens were convinced of the benefits of high-speed Internet connections at their homes and businesses. However, to make this happen, the state had an important role to play, first in creating the conditions and providing the incentives to the (reluctant) market players to invest in infrastructure development; and, second, in making the state the primary user of services delivered over these networks. Thus, the main drive behind the development of MANs in major Greek cities was to support the operations of the public sector, in the provision of basic public services such as e-prescriptions, e-taxation, and the issue of electronic certificates and documents following citizens' on-line requests. Citizens were expected to go through a learning curve that would raise their demand for broadband and subsequently accelerate the take-up of services and applications. This 'adoption ladder' has proved itself in practice, despite not being as pronounced as operators might wish. Based on the data collected by OTE, it has been estimated that as soon as broadband is established in a region, about 20% of the population in the region take up the service within the first month of operation.[16]

By mid-2013, the main providers of broadband services in Greece have been: (a) the fixed line operators (including the incumbent OTE) who provide direct access to the Internet mainly through wired telephone lines; and (b) the mobile operators who provide wireless Internet access through their cellular networks. However, as is the case worldwide, such a distinction becomes increasingly blurred. On the one hand, fixed-line operators gradually adopt wireless technologies in order to reduce capital expenditure in fixed installation costs and, on the other hand, the popularity of smartphones, especially among the young ages, and the personalized nature of the service results in mobile broadband gradually overtaking wired connections at home. The municipal networks that were built by mid-2000 have not managed to become fully operational. Despite the early euphoria regarding their prospects, the majority remain inactive and their deployment remains in question. The initiative of setting up broadband companies at the regional level proved very demanding for the local and regional authorities.

---

[16] The source of information does not explicitly distinguish take up rate between urban and rural areas.

OTE has remained the dominant operator and is the sole provider of universal service in Greece. For over a decade OTE has invested heavily in broadband infrastructure by building up a network of 30,000 km of fibre across the country, putting an emphasis on urban areas where the take-up was expected to be more rapid. Following the state-led initiatives for building subsidized broadband infrastructure, and under the threat of being put at a disadvantage compared to the recipients of funds to implement these actions, OTE further accelerated investments in broadband in suburban and rural areas, thereby largely achieving the early targets set in terms of geographical and population coverage. With respect to FttH/B, some time will pass before OTE starts building an NGA network in a more systematic way. This delay is caused by: (a) the severe economic conditions the country is facing, which put into question the expected rate of return on investment in broadband access; (b) the economic vulnerability of households, which has put on hold domestic demand for broadband; and (c) the lack of any serious competitor in the fixed network market. Moreover, the unfavourable economic conditions in the country have made OTE change its investment preferences. Until 2010 OTE was investing heavily in fibre optics, whereas in recent years it shifted to deploying wireless systems because of the significantly lower installation costs compared to fixed infrastructure. In the case of Greece, with its particular geographical terrain, wireless technology is considered the most suitable option for inaccessible and/or geographically isolated areas and islands.

DSL has become the most popular technology for broadband access in Greece. As OTE dominates in the fixed network market, the majority of alternative operators have become dependent on OTE for their position in the market. This does not imply that alternative operators have not made their own investments in network infrastructure. The action plan Call 157, which was addressed to telecommunication operators and aimed at the development of DSL and Wi-Fi in rural areas, provided them an opportunity to develop subsidized infrastructure in the regions: i.e., in addition to the metropolitan centres where they had already established points of presence. This action plan changed the model by which these providers sought to compete with OTE. While by 2006 alternative operators were mainly relying on OTE's wholesale services, with their own minor infrastructure developed in the urban centers of Athens and Thessaloniki, the action plan subsidized the development of over 6,000 km of optical network in peripheral regions and prepared the ground for a change in the level of competition across the country. By setting up their own transmission infrastructure, alternative operators have been able to reduce their dependency on OTE. However, as OTE owns all local loops across the country, there are limits to their disengagement from OTE. On the other hand, this particular action plan made a model of cooperation among these alternative operators commercially and economically attractive. Given that each final recipient enjoyed the privilege of establishing subsidized infrastructure in specific parts of the Greek territory, the final recipient in one region could provide facilities to other operators in return for access to the infrastructures in the other areas. The result has been the creation of a number of subsidized networks by different operators, which may give rise to the prospect of their forming a single rival to OTE in the near future.

OTE has seen its share in the fixed broadband market shrinking over the last years. Hence, its strategy has been to concentrate on the upgrade of its DSL network to VDSL, increasing the data rates and thereby bringing it closer to the Digital Agenda targets. However, following EETT's decision of September 2012 to permit the launch of OTE's VDSL retail products into the Greek market on the condition that the respective wholesale product was also available to alternative operators, OTE's first-mover advantage was being challenged.

Mobile operators have become important players in broadband access, as their wireless infrastructure complements fixed broadband networks across the whole country. Although the take up of mobile broadband remains below the EU average, it is gaining momentum, and the mobile operators, with their ongoing investments in LTE networks, are expected to make a significant contribution to the attainment of Digital Agenda objectives. Given the difficult economic times and in an attempt to control costs, mobile operators have chosen the strategy of network sharing, a practice that is already implemented in other countries. Of crucial importance to the operation of mobile broadband, as to all wireless infrastructures, is the full transposition of recent laws regarding the simplification of licensing procedures for installation of mobile base stations and antennas (under the new one-stop-shopping licensing framework) and the acceleration of decisions on spectrum management. For example, as EETT has not yet assigned bands for P2MP fixed wireless access, OTE may face problems in its plans to use this technology for broadband connectivity in remote rural areas. These transpositions are expected to remove the barriers often raised by local community councils and the lobby of citizens against the installation of mobile infrastructure and will further accelerate developments in mobile broadband.

13.6.1 Reflections on expected future developments

Despite the severe economic crisis, Greece has made significant progress in its broadband agenda and is slowly but steadily catching up with respect to realizing the Digital Agenda targets. OTE started upgrading its network from ADSL to VDSL. Alternative operators are expected to increase competitive pressure, including areas outside the three main cities. The next phase will be the transition from FttC/FttB (Fibre to the Cabinet/Building) to FttH (Fibre to the Home), replacing the remaining copper access and ensuring high quality broadband services to households.

To this end, and given all the public financial support given to broadband, the next step in the policy agenda could be the creation of conditions for the effective combination of all forms of subsidized infrastructure. In this way, a new network infrastructure could emerge as a mix of all publicly subsidized networks including the metropolitan fiber networks (MANs) located in seventy-five municipalities and the fibre and wireless networks developed in the remote and rural areas of the country. Thus, MANs could safeguard their future viability through their evolution into FttH/B services to local communities.

This scenario, however, may not be as straightforward as one might expect. A number of important issues need to be considered including the following:

a) To what extent and under which terms and conditions can OTE's current fibre infrastructure (which stops at the local switch) be used for the roll-out of FttH?

b) What would be the ownership structure of a possible mix of all publicly subsidized networks? Who would manage such a network and under what conditions?

c) In the event of such a coalition among alternative operators, how would the terms of use and lease of OTE's infrastructure – upon which alternative operators have based their businesses – be affected?

d) How is the broadband market going to evolve? Is the current model of fully integrated companies (operators that provide both infrastructure and services) likely to be maintained in the future? Or will the open access model as part of the MAN deployments provide a window of opportunity for the separation of network and service provision, and become the new norm?

e) How will the evolution of mobile broadband affect developments in the fixed broadband market? At the moment, there is a general consensus that fixed and mobile broadband complement each other, especially in areas where fixed broadband is too costly and/or too risky to establish. With the rate of mobile broadband growth, however, will it soon evolve into a real competitor to fibre-based infrastructure?

f) Also, with network sharing becoming popular among mobile operators, how is competition in mobile broadband going to be protected?

It is too early to predict what the outcome of these debates will be or whether real infrastructure competition will eventually emerge. This is even more so given the current financial and social turmoil in the country, which makes any future predictions risky. What can safely be said is that the broadband era brings along new challenges for policy makers, regulators, and other stakeholders in the market that will demand their increasing attention in the years to come.

References

Association of Mobile Communication Companies (2013). 20 years of Mobile Telephony and the Greek Economy. Study conducted by the Athens University of Business and Economics, available at www.eekt.gr, (in Greek). Accessed on 30/10/2013.

A.T. Kearney and Planning S. A. (2008). Developing the Hellenic Ministry of Transport and Communications 5-year broadband strategy for Greece. Presentation of preliminary results on the development of strategy for electronic communications industry in Greece.

Bouras, C. (2003). White Bible for Broadband Networks in Greece: Design and Strategy. Presentation at ELECTRONICA Conference (available at www.broadband.cti.gr) (in Greek).

Bouras, C., Gkamas, A., Papagiannopoulos, J., Theophilopoulos, G. and Tsiatsos, T. (2009). Broadband municipal optical networks in Greece: a suitable business model. *Telematics and Informatics* **26** (4), 391–409.

Caloghirou, Y. and Darmaros T. (1994). Internationalisation of Telecommunication Service Provision and the Greek Privatisation Debate. In Bohlin, E. and Grandstrand O. (eds.) *The Race to European Eminence: Who are the coming tele-service multinationals?* Amsterdam: North Holland.

Cave, M. J. (2006). Encouraging infrastructure competition via the ladder of investment. *Telecommunications Policy*, **30**(3–4), 223–237.

Cava-Ferreruela, I. and A. Alabau-Munoz (2006). Broadband policy assessment: a cross national empirical analysis. Telecommunications Policy, **30**(3–8), 445–63.

Chiotis, T (2002). A strategic Document for Broadband development in Greece. Presentation in Greek, Rhodes, September 2002.

Constantelou, A. (1998). Transformation Dynamics in Southern and Eastern Europe: the Emergence of Advanced Communication Networks and Services. Unpublished PhD thesis, Science Policy Research Unit (SPRU), Sussex theses; S 4594, University of Sussex.

EETT (2006). The Profile of the Hellenic Telecommunications and Posts Commission. Available at www.eett.gr/opencms/opencms/EETT_EN/Publications/Publications/ Accessed on 30/10/2013.

(2008a). Two Years from the Enactment of the New Telecommunications Law. Available at www.eett.gr/opencms/opencms/EETT_EN/Publications/Publications/ Accessed on 30/10/2013.

(2008b). EETT Annual Report. Athens: EETT.

(2012). Report of the State of Broadband (3rd trimester 2012). Available at www.eett.gr (in Greek).

European Commission (2013). Digital Agenda Scoreboard. Available at https://ec.europa.eu/digital-agenda/en/scoreboard (last accessed, November 2013).

Hellenic Statistical Authority (ELSTAT) (2013). Greece in Figures 2013. Available at www.statistics.gr/portal/page/portal/.../ELLAS_IN_NUMBERS_EN.pdf (last accessed 30 October 2013).

Henderson, A. and Ball, E. (2005). WTO principles and telecommunications in developing nations: Challenges and consequences of accession. *Telecommunications Policy*. **29**(2-3), 205–221.

InformationSociety, 2007. Information Society. Managing Authority of Operational Program. The Official Greek Portal for the Information Society. www.infosociety.gr.

International Telecommunication Union (ITU) (2013). World Development Indicators.

Kanellos, L. (2009). *Fibre-to-the-Home Project – Greece*. Paper presented at the 4th Annual FttH Council Asia-Pacific Conference and Exhibition, Melbourne.

Kanellos L. (2012) Opening Speech at the Infocom Conference – Athens. 30.10.2012.

Kyriakidou, V., Katsianis, D., Orfanos, I., Chipouras, A., and Varoutas, D. (2010). Business modeling and financial analysis for metropolitan area networks: Evidence from Greece. *Telematics and Informatics*, **28**(2), 112–124.

Observatory for the Information Society (2006). Broadband in Greece: Situation and Prospects. Available at: www.observatory.gr (last accessed 30 September 2013).

(2011) 12th Semester Report for Broadband, April. Available at: www.observatory.gr (last accessed 30 September 2013).

OECD (2001) Regulatory Reform in Greece. Paris: OECD.

OTE (2013). Corporate Presentation Q4 2012, available at www.ote.gr.

Troulos, C., Merekoulias, V. and Maglaris, B. (2008). Broadband promotion policies by local municipal authorities in Greece. Paper presented at EETT's National Broadband Forum, Athens, available at: www.eett.gr.

Troulos, C., Merekoulias V. and Maglaris, B. (2010). A business model for municipal FttH/B networks: the case of rural Greece. lower case *info* **12**(3) 73–89.

Troulos, C., Primpas, D., Scopoulis, Y., Karounos, T., Kaloxylos, A. and Papadopulos, P. (2008b). Fiber to the Home/Fiber to the Building: developments and policy recommendations for Greece. FttH/FttB Workgroup Deliverable, available at: www.ebusinessforum.gr

Troulos, C., Merekoulias, V., Kastrinogiannis, T., Grammatikou, M., Kalogeras, D., Papavassiliou, S. and Maglaris, B. (2007). A business model for the operation of the fibre municipal MANs of Sterea Hellas. Project Deliverable 1.2 Call 93, available at: www.netmode.ntua.gr.

Toulos C. (2012). Fiber Optic Infrastructures for Next Generation Access Networks: Strategies for Municipal Intervention, Unpublished Phd Dissertation, National Technical University of Athens, School of Electrical and Computer Engineering.

Poland

IWONA WINDEKILDE AND PIOTR ŁADNY

14.1 Introduction to the case study

Following its return to independence in 1989, Poland joined the EU in 2004 and according to the January 2013 EC broadband scoreboard the country took sixth position in total number of broadband lines. However, in terms of penetration it still is one of Europe's least developed broadband markets. It stands second-to-last with a broadband penetration of 19.6% of population, followed by Romania at 16.6%. The good news is that in recent years the gap with the EU average has been reduced significantly. From a historical point of view, the functioning of the fixed telephony market, especially the persistence of a monopoly structure in this market, has been extremely important in explaining the development of the broadband market. The lack of effective competition over the years and the protective nature of state policy towards the incumbent operator Telekomunikacja Polska SA (trading as Orange Polska[1]; also known as TPSA or just TP), keeping its monopoly position in tact, allowed the company to set the pace of development to suit its own terms of business. This situation changed for the better in early 2006, with a change in the application of regulation.

14.1.1 Liberalization and regulation

Poland was the first Central European country to enact a competition law and establish a competition enforcement agency after the collapse of communism in the first half of 1987[2]. The first law concerning telecommunication regulation, in the context of Poland's restructuring toward a market economy, was adopted on 23 November 1990. The Communications Act of 1990 ended the state monopoly in domestic services, but it retained the state monopoly in international services and its control over domestic long-distance services. But the end to the monopoly on local lines did not mean the immediate emergence of competition, as telecom policy has taken many turns since 1990: starting from attempts to build a model based on free-market competition principles in the period 1990–1994, followed by a period of support for the monopoly of the dominant operator (1995–2000), which led to a period characterized by inefficient regulatory interventions (2001–2005), to be replaced by a period of strong and effective involvement by the telecommunications regulator with a clear focus on increasing service competition (2006–2009), which provided the basis for the current period characterized by stimulating the development of the market through the use of pro-investment stimuli, primarily aimed at increasing infrastructural penetration (2010–2013). These changes in telecommunications policy coincided with the changes in political leadership in the Parliament (*Sejm*).

The policy changes over the period 1990–2013 are reflected in a succession of regulatory organizations. The independent regulatory authority in the telecommunications business and radio frequency management was established by the Telecommunications Act and began its operation on 1 January 2001 under the name of Telecommunications

---

[1] Telekomunikacja Polska was renamed Orange Polska in April 2012, in line with France Télécom's international telecommunications branding.

[2] Act of 28 January 1987 Law on Counteracting Monopolistic Practices in the National Economy (Act on Combating Monopolistic Practices), Dz.U. 1987, Nr 3, poz. 18.

Regulatory Authority (*Urząd Regulacji Telekomunikacji* – URT)[3] – as required by European Union directives. With the establishment of URT, the National Radiocommunications Agency and the National Telecommunications and Postal Inspection were liquidated. On 1 April 2002 the URT was liquidated and, the Office of Telecommunications and Post Regulation (*Urząd Regulacji Telekomunikacji i Poczty* – URTiP) was created. URTiP took over all the tasks, powers and duties of the URT in the telecommunications field. This transformation took place under the Act of 1 March 2002 on changes in the organization and functioning of central government authorities and their subordinate units and the amendment of certain laws (Journal of Laws No 25, item 253 of 20 March 2002). Significant activity of the regulatory body has been noticeable only since January 2006, when UKE was set-up to replace URTiP, and the new President – Anna Streżyńska – took its helm.[4] (See Section 14.4 for a detailed discussion).

The replacement of the former President of URTiP by the new President of UKE following the 2006 elections cast doubts on the Polish NRA's political independence. In addition, as URTiP ceased to exist in January 2006 and the President of UKE was officially appointed only in May 2006, the legality of the decisions issued in the meantime have been questioned. The independence of the Polish regulator was further weakened when Poland adopted the law on state personnel resources and key state administration officials that entered into force on 26 October 2006. According to this law, the five-year term of office for the President of the NRA was repealed and the President of the Council of Ministers was granted an unlimited right to dismiss the President of the NRA at any time and without the necessity to indicate reasons. This raised the concern that the changes introduced might influence the impartiality of the NRA, given the state's holdings in various electronic communications operators.

The liberalization process initiated in 1990 with the local networks was followed in 2000 by the liberalization of inter-city networks and, finally, in 2003 the international networks. Hence, by January 2003, TP had formally lost its monopoly to provide telephone services on the fixed network.[5]

Figure 14.1 provides an overview of the most important events in the regulatory environment in Poland.

This case study is structured as follows: In Section 14.2 we discuss the historical developments of the telecommunciations sector. In Section 14.3 the focus turns to the development of broadband. Section 14.4 is dedicated to the regulatory intervention. Mobile broadband developments are covered in Section 14.5. Section 14.6 provides the broadband market overview as of 2013. Section 14.7 addresses the deployment of EU funds. Section 14.8 reflects on the realization of the Digital Agenda targets and Section 14.9 provides the case summary and conclusions.

14.2 History of telecommunications developments

14.2.1 Development of the fixed network

In 1990, the rural areas in Poland had fewer than 2.4 phones per 100 inhabitants, compared to 8.2 for the country at large, and new initiatives were needed to rectify forty years of neglect in bringing telephone service to rural areas. The post-communist reform government encouraged the formation of village telephone committees for self-help efforts to build rural systems. The idea to operate a public telecommunication network independently from the state was born in southeast Poland, where local governments and village-level telephone committees established two independent telephone operators: District Telephone Cooperatives (DTC) Tychy and WIST[6]. Within

---

[3] The establishment of an NRA was in anticipation of the joining the EU.
[4] Since 27 January 2012 the President of the Office of Electronic Communications (UKE) is Magdalena Gaj.

[5] It is important to point out that before the privatization process of TP started, the State Treasury tried to maximize the sales value of TP shares by maintaining TP as a monopoly for many years.
[6] Tyczyn and WIST received support from US-based National Telecommunications Cooperative Association (NTCA) volunteers who provided practical expertise in managerial, organizational and technical issues.

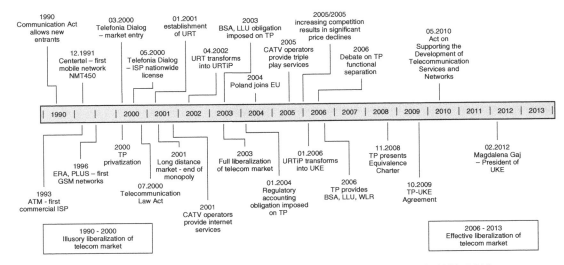

Figure 14.1 Timeline of most important events in telecom development, Poland, 1990–2013

3 years, both were profitable and able to pay back loans and finance additional equipment for expanding their network. This type of public-private partnership in financing was one of the most important innovations for the region and the country in the early 1990s and led the way for the development of forty-four other independent telecommunications systems of this kind[7],[8]. Moreover Tyczyn and WIST were pioneers in establishing interconnection and revenue sharing arrangements with TP, which was a precedent in the framework of Polish legislation. The telephone cooperatives served as a model for bringing telephone service to rural areas and as a model for member-owned, democratic business organizations.

In parallel, TP had expanded and improved its access network capacity and was in the process of digitalization of the switching systems, which meant that at the start of the full liberalization of the telecommunications market and the privatization of TP in 2000, TP had a reasonable budget and relatively modern facilities and modern technological infrastructure, able to provide services to a broad range of consumers. Despite the ongoing improvements, the problem that remained was the low capacity of the access network in the rural areas. Even by the end of 2000, in some rural areas telephone connections were still made using manual switchboards.

14.2.2 Development of the cable network

Similar to the telecommunication market, the television market in Poland was controlled by the state (i.e., the communist government) for many years. The first cable television networks began to appear at the local level (apartment buildings) and the municipal level by the end of the 1980s. Although the Polish government took no specific measures for the development of the cable television market in the period from 1990 to 2000, the number of CATV operators continued to grow strongly.

The process of consolidation of operators started in 1992 and is ongoing today. The largest acceleration of this process was evident in the period 1996–1999. Currently, the consolidation process has slowed down and takes place through the full acquisition of smaller operators, or through various forms of co-operation between operators. According to the Polish Chamber of Electronic Communication over 60 per cent of

[7] District Telephone Cooperative (DTC) Tyczyn: Partnership for Local Economic Development, United Nations Development Programme, September 2007.
[8] By 2003 the independent telecommunications companies were investor-owned, except for Tyczyn and WIST.

Table 14.1 Internet access by technology, fixed and mobile, Poland, 2005 and 2012

Access technology (%)	2005	2012
Dial-up	25	
xDSL	47	24
CATV	19	19
WLAN/LAN	8	20
Modem 2G/3G		35
Other	1	2

Source: Report on the telecommunication market in Poland in 2005, UKE, 2006. Report on the telecommunication market in Poland in 2012, UKE, 2013.

the market belongs to the three largest operators combined: UPC Telewizja Kablowa, Vectra and Multimedia Polska. The large cities have a high penetration, and competition between CATV operators takes place in particular local markets, not nationwide.

14.2.3 Development of wireless communication

PTK Centertel, as a subsidiary of TPSA, began to offer mobile services based on NMT450 in December 1991. In 1996 Centertel introduced GSM. The market was subject to significant changes in 1996, when the monopolist PTK Centertel was faced with two new GSM-based competitors: Polkomtel S.A. (using the trade name Plus GSM) and Polska Telefonia Cyfrowa S.A. (Era GSM)[9]. The first UMTS networks in Poland were launched in 2004–2005 by Plus GSM and Era GSM but coverage was limited to Warsaw. By January 2006 most of the major cities were covered by Era GSM, Plus GSM and PTK Centertel. At present, the Polish mobile market is well developed with seven mobile network operators, all operating at the national level.

The legacy of a very low teledensity resulted in mobile communications to substitute for fixed lines, resulting in fixed penetration reaching its peak at 31% in 2003.

14.2.4 Emergence of the Internet: narrowband developments

The Internet has been available in Poland since 1991. The first international link based on the TCP/IP protocol was established between Warsaw University (through NASK – Research and Academic Computer Network) and the Computer Centre of the University of Copenhagen in August 1991.

The first commercial Internet services were offered by the ATM Manufacturing Company in 1993. In 1994 the company was carrying out pioneer implementations of ATM (asynchronous transfer mode) technology. The launch of TP's dial-up access number (0–20 21 22) in 1996 was a crucial moment in the development of Polish Internet.

14.3 Development of fixed broadband

The first services of fast Internet access (using SDI[10]) ensuring data rates of up to 115 kbit/s were offered by TP in 1999. In 2002 TP extended its offer with a new Internet access service provided via ADSL modems. In the following years the broadband offer has been substantively extended. Two factors contributed to such a development: the digitalization of the TP network, which was completed in 2005, and the enhanced activity of cable operators, which also started to offer broadband Internet access. Table 14.1 provides an overview of Internet access by technology in 2005 and in 2012.

14.3.1 Initial development of competition in fixed broadband

Alternative operators have had the opportunity to develop their own access networks since 1990. However, achieving success has proven to be very difficult in practice. The investments by alternative operators could only become successful when aimed at those areas not yet served by the access network of TP, thereby capturing unserved

[9] ERA GSM – currently T-Mobile – the sole owner of PTC is the Deutsche Telekom (DT) Group.

[10] SDI – stały dostęp do Internetu (fixed Internet access)

Table 14.2 Wholesale price, LLU – Monthly rental, Poland, 2006–2011

LLU price (€)	2006	2007	2008	2009	2010	2011
Poland	13.86	8.60	5.25	5.25	5.25	5.25
EU	11.05	10.83	9.93	9.66	9.81	9.70

Data sources: Analysis and possible scenarios for the development of the telecommunications market in Poland. A.T. Kearney; Orange Poland, October 2012, http://blog.orange.pl/uploads/mail/raport_rozwoj_rynku_telekomunikacyjnego_w_polsce.pdf.

demand. Moreover, nascent success was hindered by TP imposing unfavorable settlement terms (interconnection rates) and using a series of monopolistic practices towards operators entering the market. This, along with the significant financial outlays necessary for the construction of their own networks, limited the activity of new entrants and thereby adversely affected the development of infrastructure and of infrastructure-based competition. Only a few companies succeeded in overcoming the barriers. In 2004 the telecommunications enterprises with the biggest DSL market share were TP with 91%, Netia S.A. and Telefonia Dialog S.A. each having 3%, Telenet with 1% and all others combined with 5%.[11]

Netia is the largest alternative operator in Poland. It operates on the basis of its own backbone network, connecting the largest Polish cities, and on the basis of local access networks. The operator provides a wide range of telecommunications services, including telephone services, Internet and data transmission services. Historically Netia has been an active acquirer and consolidator of local operators.[12] Netia made twenty-five acquisitions between mid-2007 and the end of 2009, of small local players specialized in FttX/Ethernet LAN services. In 2007 the company began to provide services on the basis of TP's infrastructure.

Telefonia Dialog S.A. was incorporated on 12 August 1997 under the name of Telefonia Lokalna S.A. The company pursued activity within the scope of fixed telephony services and Internet access. Telefonia Dialog S.A. also has been providing broadband Internet access services using its own network. Since mid-2007 the company has offered Internet services on the basis of TP S.A. infrastructure using bitstream access. In 2008 Telefonia Dialog began to provide wholesale line rental (WLR) services. In 2008 they started to offer IPTV as a new service.[13] Telefonia Dialog was acquired by Netia in 2011.

Wholesale broadband access

To stimulate competition the UKE introduced wholesale access, both bitstream (BSA) and wholesale line rental (WLR) in 2006. The pricing for the services was attractive – the BSA tariff was reduced from EUR 7.74 in 2006 to EUR 5.86 in 2007 – and the wholesale market developed reasonably well, reaching 15.8% of access lines for BSA and 19.5% for WLR, by the end of 2012.[14]

In 2005 unbundling was introduced. However, in the following years alternative operators did not migrate to LLU (unbundled local loop) on any significant scale, remaining focused on the use of BSA and WLR, which were more attractively priced than LLU and did not require any significant investment outlays. The situation changed when the price was reduced in 2006–2007 to below the EU average; see also Table 14.2. In 2012 the number of unbundled local loops had reached 5.9% of all access lines.

Cable-TV-based broadband

The development of cable TV towards broadband services can be observed from 2000 onward. The Telecommunications Law of 21 July 2000

[11] Source: Report on the telecommunication market, URTiP, 2005.
[12] In 2008 Netia acquired Tele2 and over the next few years it started buying up smaller, local ISPs. The acquisition of Dialog took place in 2011.
[13] http://en.uke.gov.pl/files/?id_plik=95.
[14] Source: Report by A.T. Kearney, October 2012.

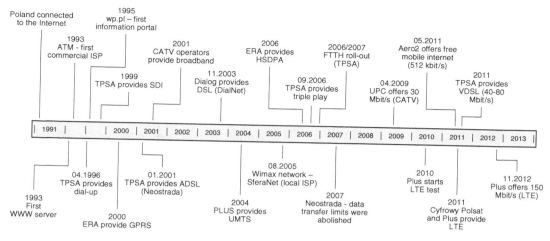

Figure 14.2 Timeline of most important events in broadband development, Poland, 1991–2013

had laid the foundations for increased liberalization of the sector and had removed the (formal) obstacles to entry by new operators. Cable-TV companies were allowed to compete with telecommunications operators for the provision of telecommunications services. The cable-TV and data communications (Internet access) markets were open for competition, but they did not have to provide access to other operators. Since then, the media market has gone through significant changes. Cable networks were consolidated and three large networks developed: (1) UPC Telewizja Kablowa Sp. z o.o.; (2) Telewizja Kablowa Vectra S.A.; and (3) Multimedia Polska S.A.

In 2001–2002 CATV operators started providing Internet access services. In 2005 cable television subscribers accounted for about one-third of the close to 1.6 million people who had broadband access to the Internet in Poland.

Multimedia Polska S.A. was the first operator in Poland which introduced the triple-play package service, namely cable TV, Internet and telephone on a commercial scale, under the trade name of 'multipack' in 2005. In 2006 TP also introduced triple-play. Triple-play services are now offered by CATV-based operators as well as by the PSTN-based operators.[15]

Figure 14.2 provides an overview of the most important events in broadband development in Poland.

14.4 Regulatory intervention

While market factors have been important, regulatory factors have played a decisive role in setting the competitive conditions and prospects for the development of the broadband market. These regulatory factors include:

- activities of UKE (*Urząd Komunikacji Elektronicznej* – Office of Electronic Communications), the national regulatory authority (NRA);
- legal acts that constitute principles of operation of the telecommunications market.

While predictability and stability of legislation and actions taken by the regulatory authority are of particular importance, the actions of UKE, which were associated with responding to problems in the market, have often led to lengthy disputes (including litigations). According to operators, uncertainty about the future actions of the regulator, prolonged disputes and problems with the enforcement of regulatory obligations imposed a significant increase in risks for entrepreneurial activities in the telecommunications market and thereby reduced their willingness to develop the broadband infrastructure.

---

[15] Poland's telecommunications industry, Polish Information and Foreign Investment Agency, 2006.

14.4.1 TP–UKE agreement

In 2006 the new President of UKE started a debate on the applicability of an extraordinary remedy in the form of functional separation of TP. The formal reason provided was the limited competition in the markets of fixed telephony and Internet access caused by the significant market power (SMP) of TP. The analysis conducted confirmed the existence of several barriers to the development of these markets, in particular:

- a strong market advantage of TP, resulting from its size and market share;
- anti-competitive behaviour of TP that hindered cooperation with alternative operators and the flow of information within the TP Group that facilitated and favoured such behaviours;
- poor quality of the access network;
- lack of appropriate price relationships between the charges for wholesale services (WLR, BSA and LLU) and retail services, which meant, for example, that provision of retail services based on LLU was not profitable for alternative operators (i.e., margin squeeze);[16]
- ineffectiveness of regulatory activities undertaken so far to eliminate market barriers and lack of prospects for their elimination.

Recognizing that the functional separation of the incumbent operator (IO) would eliminate a major barrier in the form of anti-competitive behavior by TP and would also reduce the negative effects on development of competition that result from the weakness of the legal system in Poland (including a change of TP's attitude, looking to exploit loopholes and weaknesses of the legal system), the President of UKE announced the initiation of functional separation proceedings: i.e., the creation of two companies, whereby one would be responsible for the provision of access to the infrastructure for all parties concerned and the other would focus on selling services to end customers, as of 15 December 2008.

However, the Telecommunications Law of 16 July 2004 (*Prawo telekomunikacyjne* – Pt) did not explicitly provide for dividing a telecommunications firm or arranging functional separation as a method of regulating the telecommunications market. Nor did the EU regulatory framework in force at that time bestow such rights on the national regulatory authorities.

The lack of clear rules on the separation meant that the UKE was criticized and that the proposal was treated reluctantly by TP. Nonetheless, recognizing that functional separation is a far-reaching regulatory measure, TP began negotiations with the participants in the telecommunications market to improve the conditions for cooperation. In November 2008, TP presented the President of UKE with proposals for actions aimed at reducing the market problems as indicated by the regulatory authority without the need for functional separation.

The proposal, entitled the Equivalence Charter (*Karta Równoważności*), assumed the resolution of the problems by voluntary actions and cooperation of TP with the regulatory authority and the alternative operators (AOs), thereby avoiding administrative orders. In addition, implementation of the Equivalence Charter would be less expensive and the effects were to be achieved within a shorter time frame than would be the case with functional separation. According to TP, the introduction of a comprehensive solution in the form of the Equivalence Charter was to ensure the stability of the telecommunications market in Poland and to be a starting point to improve cooperation amongst operators. The provisions of the Equivalence Charter assumed:[17]

---

[16] On 22 June 2011 the Commission imposed a fine of EUR 127.5 million on TP for refusing to supply wholesale broadband products to alternative operators. The decision found that TP's behaviour aimed at hindering alternative operators' access to TP's wholesale products applied at every stage of the process.

(Commission Decision of 22 June 2011 relating to a proceeding under Article 102 of the Treaty on the Functioning of the European Union, Case COMP/39.525 – Telekomunikacja Polska (notified under document C(2011) 4378).

[17] www.uke.gov.pl/uke/index.jsp?place=Lead24&news_cat_id=314&news_id=3980&layout=9&page=text.

Table 14.3 Wholesale prices of LLU, WLR and BSA for the three-year period, Poland (per month)

	PLN	EUR
LLU full	22.00	5.25
LLU partial	5.81	1.39
WLR	20.00	4.77
*BSA 1 Mbit/s	21.22	5.06
*BSA 10 Mbit/s	32.70	7.80

* price ceiling on BSA

Data source: www.netia.pl/files/inwestorzy/prezentacje/generic/generyczna_listopad_2013.pdf.

- implementation of rules of conduct that guarantee the same treatment to other operators as to the retail branch of TP;
- transparency of TP's actions in the sector of wholesale customer service, through a system of monitoring using key performance indicators (KPI);[18]
- implementation of a 'culture of non-discrimination' in the organization through comprehensive training of employees in the field of non-discriminatory treatment of operators and modification of the incentive system;
- improvement of the customer process with respect to alternative operators and of the quality of wholesale services (simplification, transparency, shortening of the process);
- development and implementation of regulated services, involving all stakeholders (regulatory authority, alternative operators and TP);
- the possibility of reaching agreement and looking for effective operational arrangements between the different stakeholders

in the market – by establishing the Telecommunications Forum.

After public consultation on the proposal submitted by TP, and gathering a series of opinions on the possibilities and consequences of functional separation, the President of UKE informally halted work on the functional separation of TP in August 2009. As a result of negotiations between the operator and the regulatory authority, an agreement was signed on 22 October 2009 in which TP committed itself to the proper performance of all regulatory duties imposed on it and to the implementation of a series of actions to ensure transparency and non-discrimination in its relations with other operators, in return for the withholding of measures undertaken by UKE towards functional separation of the company.[19] The main parts of the agreement included such issues as implementation of the Equivalence Charter, freezing the level of wholesale prices (only for LLU and WLR) for a period of three years[20] and signing bilateral agreements with operators. See Table 14.3 for the LLU price agreement.

Under the agreement, TP also committed to building and modernizing the fixed network infrastructure and to connecting at least 1.2 million new broadband lines (including one million lines with the capacity of at least 6 Mbit/s and two hundred thousand lines with the capacity of at least 2 Mbit/s) within three years (by 31 December 2012). During the first twenty-four months of the Agreement, TP built a total of 683,933 lines, including 100,700 in the so-called 'white areas' – locations where, due to the economic balance, the investment would not have been made by any other operator. In January 2012, the time frame for investments was extended from 31 December 2012 to 31 March 2013 in exchange for higher data rates (220,000 lines at 30 Mbit/s instead of 6 Mbit/s, including 70,000 fibre lines).

---

[18] KPIs – key performance indicators that enable assessment of the objectives' realization in areas such as finances, customer service, product quality. Analysis and publication of indicators developed by TP and concerning the quality of wholesale and retail services is to allow the statement whether the company discriminates against alternative operators. In a set approved by the President of UKE, 55 indicators have been defined along with their required level. See: Annex No. 5 to the Agreement. KPI List together with their reference level www.uke.gov.pl/uke/ redir.jsp?place = galleryStats & id = 23644.

[19] The agreement between TP and the President of UKE. Communication of 22 October 2009 www.uke.gov.pl/ uke / index.jsp?Lead02& place = new s_cat_id = 19& news_id = 4750&layout = 1&page = text.

[20] Wholesale prices of LLU, WLR and BSA have remained the same into 2013.

Under the agreement, TP committed to ensuring that, within its own organizational structure, a new branch would be created to be responsible for the provision of wholesale services. Under conditions of non-discrimination it would provide these services to the TP branch responsible for retail services, other companies of the TP Group (including PTK Centertel) and alternative operators. In addition, the incumbent operator would regularly provide the President of UKE with information on the degree of conformity to the non-discrimination principle in its organization, using indicators (KPIs) specially developed for this objective. Moreover, TP would provide quarterly reports to independent auditors.

Further measures to ensure equal treatment of all market participants by TP include diversification of the incentives system for employees involved in the provision of wholesale services and for employees who deal with retail services (salaries of employees of TP's wholesale branch would depend only on the results achieved by that branch, without taking into account the results of the retail branch or the results of the whole company) and the introduction of a new corporate culture for employees engaged in the provision of wholesale services, particularly in terms of application of the non-discrimination principle.

TP was also committed to reducing the flow of illicit information both within the company itself and between entities that belong to the TP Group. Limitation of the flow of information was to be achieved on the one hand by separating the workers engaged in the provision of wholesale services from those of the retail branch and through the introduction and application of rules of conduct (a new code of practice) and, on the other hand, by separation of information systems within TP.

As a result of the actions taken by TP, the incumbent operator's information systems are to operate in such a way as to ensure both transparency of the internal organization of TP and the companies belonging to the TP Group and equal access to information for all operators. They also prevent discriminatory flow of illicit information within the TP Group. Wholesale services are provided by the wholesale branch of TP using separate information systems, to which other branches of TP and the TP Group companies have no access.

Under the agreement, at the request of alternative operators, TP is obliged to conclude separate agreements to establish the conditions of cooperation between TP and other telecommunications entrepreneurs and help to reduce disputes that arise in this respect.

The agreement also regulates many other issues related to, *inter alia*, the resolution of almost 200 litigations between TP and the President of UKE and between TP and alternative operators, as well as monitoring the implementation of the commitments made by TP.

Effects of the TP–UKE Agreement and projected actions

Monitoring the implementation of commitments undertaken by TP in the Agreement is based on monthly reports by TP which include the status of implementation of measures, assessment of the risk of delays in the implementation schedule of individual solutions and any information about actual delays. So far, thirty eight reports have been presented and published on the website of UKE. Additionally TP submits a quarterly report which informs the President of UKE on the progress of investments in the network.

Verification of the information submitted by the operator is based on quarterly audits of the implementation of the Agreement. All reports and results of independent audits are publicly available on the web pages of UKE.

The UKE's report published in October 2011, summarizing the effects of two years of operation of the new regulatory measure, shows that there were still problems to be resolved and concerns associated with the level of implementation of some commitments TP had made. Among the indicated problems were:

- inadequate quality of data used to determine the expected throughput of the access lines in TP's network. For this reason, AOs are not able to determine which data rate they can offer to their customers;
- SLAs offered by TP to its own customers contain shorter damage repair times than those offered to AOs;

Table 14.4 Status of implementation, agreement between TP and UKE after two years, Poland

Area	Number of lines	Implementation
Rural	196,800	117%
Small/medium city	242,700	110%
Agglomeration	255,500	73%
Total	**695,000**	**98%**

Data source: The report on 2 years agreement between TP and UKE. The President of the Office of Electronic Communications, Warsaw, October 2009. www.uke.gov.pl/uke/index.jsp?place=Lead01& news_cat_id=168&news_id=7301&layout=3&page=text

- lack of full implementation of technical solutions in the field of remote diagnostics and reconfiguration of lines, such that AOs using infrastructure of TP could offer their customers support services comparable to those of TP; and
- protracted work on a new system of KPIs (key performance indicators) to be used to assess the quality of business processes provided by the wholesale branch of TP to AOs. Work on the new system of KPIs commenced in January 2011 and its completion was planned for September 2011.

It should be noted, that these problems are mainly technical in nature and their number has decreased gradually. Given all the goals and aspects of the Agreement, both the regulatory authority and AOs assess its implementation and effects on the market as positive.

One of the most important elements enabling the impact assessment of the Agreement is the state of implementation of TP's investment commitments associated with the development of broadband infrastructure. During the first twenty-four months of the Agreement, TP has built a total of 683,933 lines, including 100,700 in the so-called 'white areas'. The vast majority, 93%, are lines with a data rate exceeding 6 Mbit/s. A positive phenomenon is the fact that investment proceeds more quickly in the least cost-effective locations in rural areas.

Table 14.4 shows the schedule for development of broadband infrastructure and the status of its implementation as of 30 September 2011.

With respect to the competitiveness of the market, the improvement in KPIs showing the level of support for AOs by TP should be assessed very positively. The largest leap in quality took place in the first period after the signing of the Agreement – from November 2009 to September 2010, when the average score for selected KPIs improved by 4 percentage points, reaching a stable value of 96%. Currently, the average hovers around 97%.

Improvement of business processes involving the provision of services to AOs is confirmed by the results of a survey conducted by UKE among AOs. When asked for an overall assessment of the effectiveness of the agreement, most operators[21] reported that it was an effective solution. Giving examples of the effectiveness of the Agreement, the entrepreneurs indicated facilitating access to TP's infrastructure, greater promptness on the part of TP in the delivery of orders and more serious treatment of AOs by TP. However, according to AOs the most important positive effects of the Agreement are:

TP keeping (in most cases) to contract deadlines in RLLO (reference leased lines offer) and RIO (reference interconnect offer) services;
removal of illegal clauses from existing contracts;
TP's inability to refuse the lease of ducts if the technical conditions exist;
preventing TP from putting additional clauses in the contracts;
an easier process of concluding wholesale services contracts with TP; and
the development and implementation of good practices (so-called Chinese walls).

This created a positive environment for all players to compete in the market under the same,

[21] 49% of the operators agreed somewhat, 11% agreed completely, and only 4% of the operators disagreed, while 36% of the respondents said they did not have an opinion on this issue.

non-preferential conditions for development, as well as for the withdrawal by TP of appeals from decisions of the President of UKE, which has improved the legal certainty of wholesale services provided by TP.

The agreement also significantly improved the ability to perform public tasks in the field of telecommunications by local government entities. The local government, before planning its investments, may request access to information about infrastructure owned by TP. This information is very important in the context of obtaining EC approval for public intervention undertaken in the form of investment.

Despite the positive effects that have resulted from the agreement to date, it remains difficult to determine whether functional separation of TP would have been a better option and what further steps the regulatory authority might have taken.

14.4.2 Legal acts constituting principles of operation of the telecommunications market

On 7 May 2010 the Polish parliament passed the Act on Supporting the Development of Telecommunication Services and Networks[22]. The purpose of the Act was to facilitate investment related to telecommunications infrastructure roll-out and to help to achieve higher levels of competition. Due to the fact that accessibility and range of the telecommunications infrastructure were at a very low level, especially in comparison with the other member states of the EU, the President of UKE has created an administrative and legal framework to encourage local governments to invest in telecommunications infrastructure. The Act has introduced many changes in the field of preparing spatial development plans. The new rules authorize UKE to provide opinions on draft local plans and studies of conditions and directions of spatial development in the field of telecommunications.

Extremely important parts of the Act are the provisions regulating the access to buildings, cable

ducts and telecommunications cable. They aim to eliminate the phenomenon of monopolies in multi-family buildings. Three basic rules can be distinguished. First, the Act requires the owner, operator and property manager to provide a telecommunications entrepreneur access to the property and building, including the place in the building where the indoor cables are terminated. Secondly, the owner of cable ducts on the property is obliged to provide access to these ducts to any entrepreneur who has no alternative of using other (existing) cable ducts to provide telecommunications services. Thirdly, the owner of a telecommunications cable connected to a building or distributed in a building is required to provide access to any telecommunications entrepreneur to all or part of this cable if there is no possibility of connecting another telecommunications cable.

In the Act, in response to identified barriers to investment, amendments were made to the so-called rights of way. For new investments and new operators, in particular those building fibre-optic networks, access to existing ducts and dark fibres, as well as transparent and efficient conditions regulating laying one's own infrastructure on land owned by others, are a matter of vital importance. Until now, the problem in this area was that existing local plans contained numerous prohibitions and restrictions, often factually unjustified (e.g., prohibitions on an investment location just because it has been formally classified as a 'project likely to significantly affect the environment'), which thus form areas unavailable for the development of telecommunications networks. In addition, access to land of local government units and legal entities must be improved, in particular access to public roads which are administered by these entities. At the same time, it is necessary to open to investments those areas where disproportionate and inadequate restrictions and prohibitions were established by local plans, and also to establish the limits of freedom of planning with respect to telecommunications infrastructure.

When roads are built or upgraded, technology ducts will have to be made available for placing telecommunications cables. The Act imposes an obligation on road managers – the General Directorate for National Roads and Motorways

---

[22] The Act of 7 May 2010 on supporting the development of telecommunications services and networks, *Journal of Laws* No. 106, 2010.

and local governments – to construct such ducts. Moreover, municipalities will not be able to place prohibitions on telecommunications investments in their spatial development plans without providing a specific reason. Such a prohibition would have to be justified by specific regulations: e.g., on the protection of health or the environment.

Given the high level of investments required, the Act introduces an innovative solution for conducting joint investments by several operators and the establishment of separate ownership of individual optical fibres in fibre-optic cables, as well as wires in cables other than fibre-optic and ducts for laying telecommunications cables in multi-opening ducts.

New powers for local authorities in the field of telecommunications investment

The Act also introduced a new competence for local government entities. The Act stipulates that these entities may build as well as operate telecommunications networks, as part of their own public utility tasks. These tasks will be financed from the entities' own budgets. The entities may build telecommunications infrastructure, in particular its passive elements (cable ducts, cable collocation facilities, poles, masts, cables) and prepare them for use as a basic layer for telecommunications networks. They can also build telecommunications networks and operate such networks, as well as acquire the rights to already-existing infrastructure. Moreover, they can provide such infrastructure and telecommunications networks to other operators. To build a network, local government entities can also use facilities of electrical power, gas and sewage companies.

New regulations stipulate that local governments can provide telecommunications services to end-users. However, this is permitted only when local entrepreneurs are unable to meet the demand for the telecommunication services, especially Internet access. Moreover, the activities undertaken by local governments must be proportionate and non-discriminatory, so as not to undermine the principles of fair competition in the local telecommunications market. Provision of telecommunications services to residents may, in exceptional circumstances, be free of charge or at reduced

prices. However, each commencement of such activity requires the written approval of the President of UKE, expressed in the form of a decision. The decision of the President of UKE shall detail the conditions for the provision of services by the local government entity.

From the perspective of telecommunications companies, the guarantees of competitiveness of services provided by local government entities in the Act are of crucial importance. Under the Act, local governments can both create telecommunications infrastructure and provide access to the Internet. Moreover, the Act expressly provides that the activities of local governments in dealing with digital exclusion are not an economic activity – as a consequence of which local governments are not allowed to gain profit from their activities.

The Act introduces a number of conditions that are designed to preserve the principles of fair and free competition. The networks built by local governments must be compatible and interoperable with other networks, and telecommunications companies are granted the possibility to access and share the network. Compliance with specified requirements is controlled by the President of UKE and, in the case of failure to comply, the President of UKE may order rectification of the non-compliances, indicating the measures to be applied in order to implement this obligation.

The Act also allows local governments to work with telecommunications entrepreneurs. Provision of Internet access services using infrastructure financed by local governments may be entrusted to telecommunications entrepreneurs. If it is not possible for entrepreneurs to run a financially profitable telecommunications business in the area, local government entities may provide the infrastructure or telecommunications network to telecommunications operators for a fee lower than the direct cost of building that infrastructure or network, or co-finance the costs incurred in the provision of telecommunications services to end-users or telecommunications businesses for the provision of those services.

The local government entity is obliged to allow telecommunications companies to share or access telecommunications infrastructure in

Table 14.5 Number of alternative operators using TP infrastructure, Poland, 2006–2011

Operators	2006	2007	2008	2009	2010	2011
BSA	2	10	13	13	12	14
LLU	-	3	4	5	7	8 *
WLR	1	11	13	15	15	17

Data sources: Analysis and possible scenarios for the development of the telecommunications market in Poland. A.T. Kearney; Orange Poland, October 2012, http://blog.orange.pl/uploads/mail/raport_rozwoj_rynku_telekomunikacyjnego_w_polsce.pdf.

accordance with the principles of equal treatment and fair and free competition.

In practice, it is likely that both business models will be exercised by local governments – provision of Internet access services directly by local governments, as well as financing infrastructure and making it accessible to telecommunications companies. It seems that the Act is a reasonable attempt to deal with the problem of digital exclusion while keeping a guarantee of competitiveness of the telecommunications market.

14.4.3 Improved local loop unbundling

The market for local loop unbundling (LLU) in Poland started functioning in 2005, following the intervention by UKE.

Even though TP had been aware of upcoming access obligations for LLU, BSA and WLR since 2003 when the Polish Telecommunication Law identified TP as an SMP operator, until 2009 TP used various delaying tactics throughout the access negotiation process.

According to the European Commission, TP has been abusing its dominant position by refusing to provide access to its network and supply BSA and LLU wholesale products since 3 August 2005. TP rejected a high number of BSA and LLU requests on formal and technical grounds, at least until 2007. Furthermore, TP proposed unreasonable conditions governing alternative operators' access to the wholesale broadband product. For example, TP proposed exaggerated costs estimates for LLU collocation, which often resulted in a very high percentage of locations not being accessed by AOs despite the positive outcome of the technical verification. Moreover, TP delayed the

implementation of orders and executed certain collocation works with delays.[23]

As a result, for the first four years alternative operators did not use LLU on a large scale, remaining focused on the use of TP's infrastructure through bitstream access (BSA) and wholesale line rental (WLR) services, which were cheaper than LLU and did not require any investment outlays. (See also Section 14.3.1 Wholesale broadband access for detailed prices)

After changing the framework offer for LLU in 2008 and the signing of the Agreement between TP and UKE in October 2009, alternative operators, reassured by TPs changing approach to regulatory obligations and completion of actions that were blocking the development of wholesale markets, started using the wholesale LLU services more willingly. Due to this intervention the number of unbundled loops started to grow from 2009, to stabilize in 2011 and to reach 6.94% of total lines by 2012. See also Table 14.5 reflecting the number of alternative operators by (main) wholesale product of TP. Note that 99.6% of LLU lines are used by a single alternative operator – Netia.[24]

The development of services based on LLU has a negative impact on the size of BSA and WLR markets, mainly replacing BSA, while WLR still has the largest wholesale share. The investments by alternative operators in network elements necessary for the provision of LLU-based retail services

---

[23] Commission Decision of 22 June 2011 relating to a proceeding under Article 102 of the Treaty on the Functioning of the European Union, Case COMP/39.525 – Telekomunikacja Polska (notified under document C(2011) 4378.

[24] Source: The analysis of market development of LLU, The President of the Office of Electronic Communications, Warsaw, 2010 and KPI report, Q3 2012, Warsaw 2013.

reflect the next rung of the investment ladder. As WLR and BSA wholesale services introduced mechanisms for price competition, LLU-based service introduced mechanisms of competition that are also based on innovation. The strategy of the President of UKE in the period 2006–2009 was based on enabling service-based competition between telecommunications companies, so that benefits to consumers were both high and extremely quick. The current strategic objective is focused on service-based competition using LLU and infrastructure-based competition with the CATV-network operators.

However, the development and popularity of the LLU service depends on creating competitive offers through innovation, increasing the number and range of services. A lack of ability to offer advanced services (e.g., HDTV, VOD) due to low penetration and the long sections of TP's copper access network involved – limiting the data rates that can be offered – are major barriers to the purchases of LLU services.

Also TP is affected by the low quality of the copper network and limited in offering converged services: that is, bundles including TV. Therefore, TP is currently investing in the network in order to obtain higher data rates. The attractiveness of LLU-based services should increase after TP finishes its investments. The systematic modernization of the incumbent operator's network provides the possibility of offering more advanced services to its own customers and to wholesale buyers using the LLU service[25]. By the end of 2012 the TP share of DSL-lines was 71% and the share of alternative operators 29%. Of the DSL market of the alternative operators, 39.8% was provided based on their own networks, while 60.2% was based on wholesale, including 43.7% based on bitstream, 4.8% on shared access and 11.7% on full unbundling.[26]

14.5 Development of mobile broadband

On the broadband services market in Poland, the greatest dynamics of development are currently observed in the segment of mobile access. Since 2011, the role of mobile data transfer has been steadily increasing, driven by higher smartphone penetration. The penetration of mobile broadband continued to be slightly above the EU average with 10.36% for dedicated data cards and modems in January 2013, representing over 4.1 million users.[27]

Mobile broadband penetration, which refers to Internet access on third-generation technologies and higher data rate mobile technologies (i.e., HSPA or LTE), including modems and dongles reached 41.4% in 2012, only 1.7% below the EU average.

14.6 Broadband market overview: status in 2013

14.6.1 The supply side

The providers of broadband Internet access in Poland are fixed telephony operators, cable television operators and operators of GSM/UMTS mobile networks.

The largest fixed network operators are: TP and Netia SA. The network of TP covers an area of about 312,000 km^2, which means the coverage of almost the entire Polish territory. However, with PSTN penetration peaking at 31% the household coverage is approximately 85%. The coverage of the fixed networks of Netia SA is just over 30,000 km^2 and 2.9 million households or approximately 20% of households.

There are about 500 cable television operators, which serve about 4.6 million subscribers. The largest operators are: UPC Telewizja Kablowa Sp. z o.o., Telewizja Kablowa Vectra S.A. and Multimedia Polska S.A, which together account for about 67.5% of the cable television market.

---

[25] Analysis of the development of LLU service, Warsaw, October 2010, www.uke.gov.pl/uke/index.jsp?place=-Lead01&news_cat_id=188&news_id=5899&layout=3&page=text.

[26] Source: Report on the telecommunications market in Poland in 2012, UKE, 2013. Fast and ultra-fast Internet access – analysis and data, Broadband indicators, Digital Agenda Scoreboard key indicators 2013, http://ec.europa.

eu/digital-agenda/en/fast-and-ultra-fast-internet-access-analysis-and-data.

[27] Digital Agenda Scoreboard, January 2012. According to UKE mobile internet penetration is 8.64%.

Table 14.6 Overview of the largest cable network operators, Poland, 1Q 2013

	Operator	Number of subscribers	Number of cities	Market share
1	UPC Polska	1,466,100	119	31.87%
2	Vectra	813,200	164	18.13%
3	Multimedia Polska	812,559	2000	17.93%
4	TOYA	160,000	4	3.48%
5	INEA	159,000	7	3.48%
6	Petrus	50,000	11	1.09%
7	Promax	34,100	18	0.77%
8	Sat Film	25,000	1	0.54%
	Others	1,044,939		22.72%

Source: Polska Izba Komunikacji Elektronicznej, http://www.pike.org.pl/index/ranking.

Table 14.6 shows the largest cable network operators, the number of subscribers and market share.

Cable television networks are built and operated only in regions with a high density of inhabitants: i.e., primarily built-up urban areas consisting of multi-family buildings. A consequence of this is the low coverage of the geographical area of the country, with CATV networks reaching only about 8,000 km².

Mobile network operators include those which provide Internet access services via GSM/UMTS technologies. At the end of 2012, the shares of the operators in the total number of 2G/3G modem users were as follow: T-Mobile 29.3%, PTK Centertel 27.6%, Polkomtel 25.6%, P4 16.2% and others (MNOs and MVNOs) 1.3%.[28]

Among the alternative operators, the largest group are small local ISPs, of which there are about 8,500 (90% of which serve fewer than 1,000 subscribers). To provide broadband services to consumers, they primarily use LAN, Ethernet and WLAN technologies. For the backbone connections they make use of the infrastructure of other operators including TP.

Despite the ongoing convergence of services towards bundled offers such as triple-play, the traditional services remain fundamental in terms

of revenue for the major players in this market: i.e., fixed telephony services and cable television services, respectively.

By technology

On the retail market, broadband data transmission services are provided by telecommunications operators using different technologies or transmission media. The most popular of these by far in terms of revenues is the xDSL technology related to the strong position of TP, the former monopolist and largest telephone service provider. In 2012, TP had direct control of approximately 71.2%[29] of xDSL lines. The remaining 28.8% of the lines were operated by alternative operators, 11.5% directly owned and 17.3% through wholesale. xDSL technology held more than a 36.8% market share of total fixed broadband in 2012.[30]

The second most popular access technology is DOCSIS, used by the operators of cable TV networks.

---

[28] Report on the telecommunications market in Poland in 2012, The President of the Office of Electronic Communications, Warsaw, June 2013.

[29] Report on the telecommunications market in Poland in 2011, Office of Electronic Communications, The President of the Office of Electronic Communications, Warsaw, December 2011.

[30] Report on the telecommunications market in Poland in 2012, The President of the Office of Electronic Communications, UKE, 2013.

Table 14.7 Internet access technologies by number of subscriber lines, Poland, 2012

Internet access technology	Number of subscriber lines (millions)	%
xDSL	2.8	36.8%
CATV	2.2	28.9%
WLAN	1.6	21.1%
LAN	0.65	8.6%
Others	0.35	4.6%
Total	**7.6**	**100%**

Source: www.polskaszerokopasmowa.pl/artykuly/polska-kraj-wielu-malych-projektow-ftth-b.html.

The market structure of Internet access technologies in Poland in terms of the number of subscriber lines in the year 2012 is shown in Table 14.7.

Among the other technologies, a major role is played by wired LAN (Ethernet) and wireless LAN (WLAN) serving about 2.25 million people. These remaining technologies constitute 4.6 per cent in terms of market share. It is important to point out that by 2010, there were only 25,500 lines subscribed using optical fiber technology (FttH), which accounted for 0.4% of all fixed lines. The pace of deployment appears to be increasing, with the installed base nearly doubling by mid-2011. By 2013, FttH/B subscription was estimated at 100,000 lines.

In Poland as in other EU countries, there is a new trend in the Internet services market: the increasing market share held by local ISPs, cable TV operators and mobile operators. The reason for the migration of consumers between technologies is the ability to reduce charges for telecommunications services by combining them in a package of services (service bundling) from one operator. The report published by the President of the Office of Electronic Communications (UKE) in 2013 showed that the offer of cable television operators was always the cheapest. Subscribers who chose access through a CATV modem paid an average of 40–50% less than customers of Telekomunikacja Polska and other providers offering Internet through the infrastructure of the incumbent operator.

14.6.2 The demand side

Due to the increase in consumer interest in new services, and due to provision of bundled services which lowers the cost to consumers, the degree of market penetration of broadband services in Poland continues to grow. Figures 14.3 and 14.4 reflect the growth and penetration per 100 inhabitants of fixed and mobile broadband, respectively. At the end of the 2012, broadband access to the Internet was used by more than 11 million users – approximately 7.6 million connected via fixed lines and 4.1 million via wireless access using GSM/UMTS mobile phone networks (dedicated data service cards, modems and keys).

Usage

Analysis and research on the availability of the Internet in Poland indicate a continually growing number of Poles using the networks. It is estimated that in December 2012 the Internet was used by 62% of Poles aged over 15 years[31], which is 17.1 million Poles[32]. It is worth noting that the vast majority (69.4%) of the respondents declare that they use it daily or almost daily, and 21.3% use the Internet several times a week[33,34]

It should be noted, however, that despite the increase in Internet activities, there are still significant barriers which limit the demand for network access services in Poland. About 38% of Poles do not use the Internet, and half of them explain this fact by a lack of need and interest: 83% of people aged over 60 years do not use the Internet. This is true for both private individuals and entrepreneurs and does not result solely from financial or infrastructural obstacles but more from lack of motivation and from competence barriers. Social research shows that 38% of Poles are computer

---

[31] World Internet Project 2013.

[32] According to Internet World Stats percentage of Internet users in Poland in 2010 exceeded 58%, or more than 22 million people. www.internetworldstats.com/top25.htm.

[33] www.ekonomia.rp.pl/artykul/1028947.html.

[34] www.wirtualnemedia.pl/artykul/450-tys-polskich-internautow-wiecej-niz-przed-rokiem-58-proc-z-5-letnim-stazem.

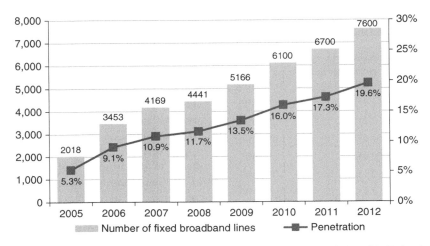

Figure 14.3 Fixed broadband lines (left axis in thousands) and penetration (right axis), Poland, 2005–2012
Source: UKE www.uke.gov.pl/_gAllery/39/18/39189/Projekt_decyzj_R5_TP_1_10.pdf.

illiterate.[35] An additional element that limits demand is a very weak level of development of public services in the area of e-administration and e-health. The implementation of such services and appropriate promotional and educational activities can significantly increase citizens' Internet activity as exemplified by the system initiated in 2008 to submit annual tax returns.[36] Unfortunately, such initiatives are still rare, both from the private sector and from public authorities. As a result, the demand for the digital economy offer is smaller than might be expected from the existing demographic potential in Poland.

14.6.3 Market drivers

A key factor in the growth of demand for Internet access services is an increase in the number of households equipped with computers. Their number is growing fastest among the wealthiest households and is the highest in families with children and in households of three or more people. The smallest increase in the number of computers is in single-person households without children. Fewer and fewer people indicate economic grounds as the reason for not having a computer and not having access to the Internet.

The survey conducted shows that the number of new connections implemented using DSL technology continues to grow, but the rate of growth is slowing. The shares of each fixed technology remain at a similar level. However, the share of mobile access soars as a result of, *inter alia*, aggressive marketing policy, an increasing perception by customers of mobile Internet access as being equal to fixed service, the increase in sales of portable computers and the fashion for mobility, especially among young people.

However, for many people, mobile broadband access is not so much the choice of a modern approach to the consumption of services but rather a necessity due to lack of alternative access technologies. The same was true of mobile telephony, which has become a substitute for fixed-lines for many subscribers in areas where a fixed line network has never been built.

Mobile broadband access is perceived by a significant proportion of Poles as a substitute for fixed broadband access, rather than as

---

[35] Narodowy Plan Szerokopasmowy, – perspektywa 2020 r., Warszawa 2012.
[36] The tax refund system was canceled in 2012, mainly due to budget constraints.

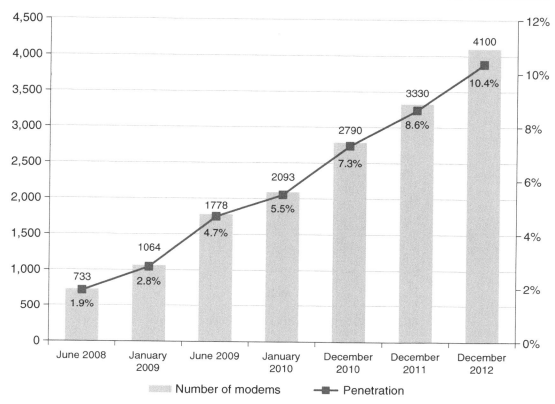

Figure 14.4 Mobile broadband modems (left axis in thousands) and penetration (right axis), Poland, 2008–2013
Source: UKE, 2013.

additional access. Depending on the profile of Internet use and household wealth, mobile broadband access can be complementary to fixed broadband access, or may be its substitute because of:

- growing number of mobile devices with access to the Internet (smartphones, tablets, PCs, notebooks, netbooks, etc.);
- greater difficulties in obtaining fixed broadband access in rural areas than in highly urbanized areas;
- low requirements for bandwidth and volume of data transmitted by most of the users, who almost exclusively take advantage of applications that do not require broadband (e-mail, text messaging, occasional web browsing without watching movies simultaneously);

- lower price of mobile access in relation to fixed access (subscription to fixed telephony is often perceived as unnecessary);
- increasingly better transmission performance in mobile networks.

The increase in revenues of mobile operators from mobile Internet is also the result of the emergence of new models of smartphones, tablets, and also of equipping mobile devices with 3G modems.

The increase in the number of mobile devices with network access is accompanied by a steady decline in the prices of mobile Internet access. The charges for domestic data transmission ranged from PLN 13.98 (EUR 3.33) to PLN 32.02 (EUR 7.62) per month for 2 GB. See also Figure 14.5.

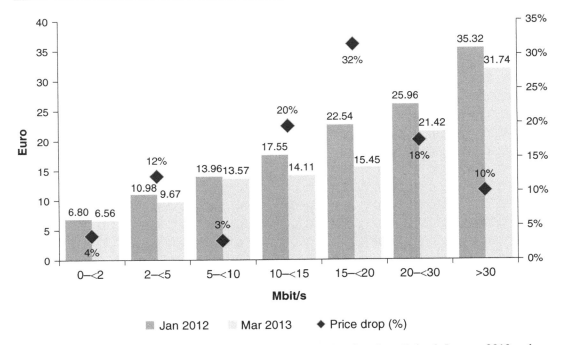

Figure 14.5 Average monthly cost of service and percentage drop in prices, Poland, January 2012 and March 2013
Source: UKE, Warsaw, April 2013.

All these factors lead to an increased demand for mobile data. The volume of traffic carried over the Polish mobile networks is increasing dramatically. In 2010, 37.3 billion MB of data was carried over the mobile networks. In 2011, it was already 73 billion MB, and in 2012 approximately 157 billion MB.

Bundled services market

In 2010, bundling services was one of the main trends in the Polish market. Its attractiveness results mainly from lower usage costs for the full bundle. The development of competition opened up the prospect of choosing an offer tailored to the users' individual needs. In 2013, a total of forty-one companies provided bundled offers from which about 2.6 million users benefited, generating revenues for operators at the level of PLN 3.8 billion (EUR 900 million). Double-play packages were the most popular: 79.5% of subscribers have chosen this option. Over 19.7% of consumers have chosen the variant of triple-play. The package of

four services was used by only 0.9% of users, which was associated with the small number of quadruple-play offers and less favorable conditions than in other packages for mobile phone services by mobile operators.

The solution combining Internet and cable TV was the most successful among the packages including two services. In 2012, more than 50 per cent of users decided on this package, whose popularity stemmed from the highly competitive offers of CATV operators that provide their services using high-bandwidth connections. The main actors in the market were TP, UPC and Vectra. See also Table 14.8 showing the demand for bundles in 2011 and 2012.

14.7 Deployment of EU funds

Until 2012 the level of absorption of EU funds for development of infrastructure for the Information Society under various programs left much to be

Table 14.8 Market share of bundles, Poland, 2011 and 2012

Bundle (%)	2011	2012
CATV+Internet	48.1	50.6
PSTN+Internet+CATV	16.4	24.2
PSTN+Internet	15.1	4.3
Mobile+Internet	10.0	12.8
PSTN+CATV	3.3	4.0
PSTN+Mobile	2.7	1.6
Others	4.3	2.3

Data source: The analysis of bundled services, The President of the Office of Electronic Communications, Warsaw, 2012.

desired. For example, out of PLN 2.3 billion (EUR 549 million) granted to Poland in 2007–2013 within the framework of sixteen regional programmes, only 8.8% of the funds available had been spent and cleared as of mid-2011.

Since 2012 there has been an increase in the utilization of the European Regional Development Fund. This is due to local authorities becoming involved in the implementation of projects aimed at the development of Information Society infrastructure. These projects seek to build modern fibre-optic networks for the provision of broadband services. In particular:

- Eastern Poland Broadband Network
- Broadband network project in Mazovia
- Lower Silesia broadband network

The Eastern Poland Broadband Network is the largest ICT investment in Europe funded by the European Union. Its value is more than PLN 1.4 billion (approximately EUR 300 million), of which EUR 255 million will come from the European Regional Development Fund. Other costs will be financed by the local governments of the voivodeships (provinces). Its aim is to increase access to broadband Internet in the macroregion of Eastern Poland consisting of: Lubelskie, Podkarpackie, Podlaskie, Swietokrzyskie and Warmia and Mazury. As a result of the project, fibre optic infrastructure will be deployed, allowing the development of telecommunications services including next-generation services.

The broadband network project in Mazovia is estimated at PLN 475.6 million (EUR 115.5 million) for the almost 3,700 km fibre optic network. A significant part of the funding will come from EU funds – PLN 340 million (EUR 82 million) – and the remaining amount will come from the budget of the Masovian voivodeship regional government. This project is interesting because it envisages the construction not only of transmission and distribution networks but also of an access network based on fibre-optic technologies (FttB).

The Lower Silesia broadband network project includes a 1,700 km fibre network, including 700 km of backbone, to be deployed in southwestern Poland. The total cost of the project is estimated at PLN 342 million (EUR 83 million).

Currently, broadband networks co-financed with the European funds are being deployed in many different regions of Poland, to close the broadband gap due to a lack of private investment in broadband network infrastructure.

14.8 Realization of the Digital Agenda targets

Regulatory actions taken by the President of UKE have increased the pace of development of the Polish telecommunications market. However, the low penetration of fixed networks and lack of investment in existing and new networks remain the most important barriers to the development of broadband networks.

Attempting to meet even the first of the Digital Agenda objectives – coverage of 100% of Europeans with conventional broadband by 2013 – has not been realized due to the low population density in rural areas (rural 50/km², urban 1105/km²; average 122/km²) and gaps in coverage by fixed networks in rural areas which are very expensive to cover. A report published by the European Commission has revealed that most of the unconnected households in rural areas in Europe are in Poland (37%), followed by Germany (9%) and Italy (6%).[37]

---

[37] Digital Agenda Scoreboard, January 2012

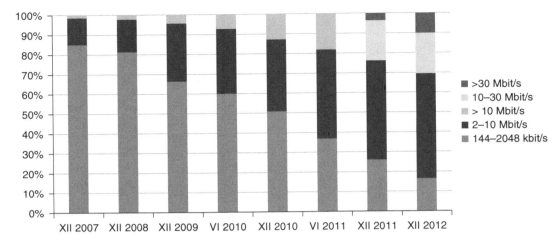

Figure 14.6 Downstream data rate trends, Poland, 2012
Note: From December 2011 the chart shows the share of broadband lines within the range 10–30 Mbit/s and >30 Mbit/s to replace the previously used >10 Mbit/s.
Source: UKE, 2013.

Broadband penetration (fixed plus mobile) per household shows a steady growth over the period 1H 2010 to 2H 2012, from 61.0% to 83.5%. The numbers per 100 inhabitants are 21.3% and 29.3%, respectively. As a result, according to data from the European Commission (January 2012), Poland assumes the antepenultimate place, with fixed broadband Internet penetration at 19.6% (the average for the EU27 is 28.8%).[38]

For many years, broadband lines in Poland were characterized by a much lower data rate than in other EU countries; the range of 144–2048 kbit/s being dominant until December 2010 (50.9%). In recent years this has improved significantly. By December 2012, more than 53% of broadband lines had download data rates in the range from 2 to 10 Mbit/s, while nearly one-third had 10 Mbit/s or more. See Figure 14.6 for the progression in data rates.

Even though broadband connections are becoming faster, ultrafast Internet access is still rare in Poland – only 8.8% of fixed broadband connections are above 30 Mbit/s and only 1.2% are above 100 Mbit/s. This indicates that Poland is still far away from achieving the high-end target of the Digital Agenda for Europe, which is 50% subscription of broadband access technologies with at least 100 Mbit/s in 2020.

The second, more qualitative factor in the development of this market is the growing competition in the market for broadband Internet access, understood as the increasing share of alternative operators. In recent years, the share of the incumbent operator TP in the total market for provision of Internet access has been decreasing. Cable television network operators achieved significantly greater penetration of broadband services in households than TP. This means that in Poland, in big cities where cable TV networks operate, penetration of broadband services is significantly higher as a result of infrastructure-based competition in those areas. However, in the medium-sized and small cities and suburban areas, there is only TP's infrastructure. This means that in non-urban areas, TP often remains the only operator, with a relatively modest level of service-based competition. Moreover, there are still 'white areas' where there is no or very limited potential to provide users with fixed access to the Internet. Often such areas are also not within the UMTS network coverage of mobile operators, which results in digital

[38] Digital Agenda Scoreboard, January 20123

exclusion. An important feature in these areas remains the local ISPs, providing services within a small area, responding to local demand. A further qualitative factor is the development of competitive retail markets for broadband services on the basis of BSA and LLU contracts. They provide great opportunities for alternative operators to compete with the incumbent operator for individual clients. Analysis of indicators of BSA and LLU penetration shows that in Poland this segment is still in early stages of development.

An important recent step towards removing barriers to broadband Internet access was the adoption of the 'Act on supporting the development of telecommunications networks and services.' The new regulations are expected to significantly accelerate the development of telecommunications investments and facilitate the process of disbursement of EU funds for development of broadband Internet access.

Even though, Poland is already working to close the rural gaps by creating an LTE network to deliver fourth-generation mobile broadband and using structural funds to finance the development of high-speed networks, the roll-out of ultra-fast broadband in Poland may take longer than desired.

Essential for further development of the market is for the regulatory authority to take significant steps to support the development of the broadband market in Poland. It is also important to stress the activities of the government in development of this market, especially during the economic downturn and while the incumbent operator is unwilling to invest in the development of the company and its infrastructure assets. The coming years should therefore be devoted to implementing the provisions of the Act on supporting with development of telecommunications networks and services, which condition the effective provision of access to modern infrastructure for clients. Continued support for the local authorities in the development of telecommunications networks will also play a major role in improving the climate for investments. By increasing the efforts of local governments in the acquisition and spending of EU funds for development of broadband infrastructure, it will be possible to implement not only small projects (hotspot access networks) but also the large investments associated with construction of fibre-optic NGA networks.

The initiative of local authorities may be an alternative way of influencing the level of development of broadband infrastructure. The growing number of projects involved in the construction of regional broadband networks in Poland, as well as the recent investment measures, appears to confirm this observation. However, most of these projects are currently in the early stages of implementation and at this stage it is difficult to determine the financial and market effects that will be achieved after they have been completed.

The involvement of local authorities in projects related to the construction of broadband networks presents an interesting topic for further research. Further research should also be done to investigate the possibilities of implementation of more flexible regulations that will facilitate and promote an appropriate environment for large-scale network investment in FttH technology. The Polish experience shows that at a very early stage of the development of FttH, the imposition of regulatory obligations on operators, and even fear of the imposition of such duties, might effectively discourage operators from building their own fibre-optic access networks. Analysis of the results of these changes could provide the most efficient tools to support the construction of fibre-optic networks.

14.9 Case summary and conclusions

The case summary is provided with reference to the research questions formulated in Chapter 2 – Research context and perspective.

14.9.1 Starting conditions

A highly relevant starting condition in terms of comparing broadband development in Poland with other member states of the European Union is the return to independence of the state in 1989. The starting position in 1989 was a teledensity of 8.2% on average and 2.4% in rural areas, on the low end of the spectrum compared to other East European countries (Hungary: 10%; Czech Republic: 16%; Latvia: 26%), and significantly lagging the West

European countries (e.g., Germany: 40%; UK: 44%; Sweden 68% as of 1990). (OECD, 1999).

14.9.2 Role of the central government

The liberalization of the telecommunications market started in 1990 with local access. The long-distance network was liberalized in 2000, to be followed by international networking in 2003.

Since 1990, the public telecommunications policy and regulations have reflected different objectives to be pursued: starting from attempts to build a model based on free-market competition principles in the period 1990–1994, followed by a period of support for the monopoly of the dominant operator (1995–2000), which led to a period characterized by inefficient regulatory interventions (2001–2005), to be replaced by a period of aggressive and effective involvement by the telecommunications regulator with a clear focus on increasing service competition (2006–2009), which provided the basis for the current period of stimulating development of the market through the use of pro-investment stimuli primarily aimed at increasing infrastructural penetration (2010–2013).

The Act of 2010 regulated the access to buildings, cable ducts and telecommunications cable, thereby making an end of the monopoly on indoor access.

14.9.3 Role of municipal government

The Act of 2010 allows local government entities to build and operate telecommunications networks as part of their public utility tasks. These tasks are to be financed from the entities' own budgets. However, this is permitted only when private operators will not be able to meet the demand for Internet access. Moreover, the activities undertaken must be proportionate and non-discriminatory so as not to undermine the principles of fair competition. The networks built by local governments must be compatible and interoperable with other networks, and telecommunications companies are granted the possibility to access and share the network. The Act provides

that the activities dealing with digital exclusion are not an economic activity – as a consequence of which local governments are not allowed to gain profit from these activities. The Act sets conditions designed to preserve the principles of fair and free competition.

14.9.4 Role of the regulator

Five years after full liberalization, no action had been forthcoming from the government on improving the conditions conducive to the development of effective competition. This situation changed in 2006, when Anna Streżyńska took the helm as the President of UKE (*Urząd Komunikacji Elektronicznej* – Office of Electronic Communications), the national regulatory agency, and challenged the monopoly position of TP. Due to her proceedings towards functional separation, TP changed its strategy from blocking entry to enabling entry and making a commitment to improve the PSTN infrastructure. In return the UKE promised not to reduce the wholesale rates for the next three years. In this way, the President of UKE initiated a new era in the relationship between the regulatory authority and the incumbent, an era of dialog formalized through the Equivalence Charter, with monitoring of TPs commitments based on KPIs.

14.9.5 Achieving the Digital Agenda targets

The low penetration of fixed networks and the lack of investment in existing and new networks remain the most important barriers to the development of broadband networks. As a result, Poland assumes the antepenultimate place, with fixed broadband penetration at 19.6% (the average for the EU27 is 27.7%).

The penetration of mobile broadband continues to be slightly above the EU average with 10.36% for dedicated cards and modems in January 2013, representing over 4.1 million users.

The deployment of high data rate broadband lines is still limited, with about 20.4% of fixed broadband lines providing more than 10 Mbit/s, and ultrafast Internet access is still rare in Poland – only 8.8% of fixed broadband connections are above 30 Mbit/s and only 1.2% are above 100 Mbit/s. This indicates that Poland is still far away from achieving the high-end targets of the Digital Agenda for Europe.

14.9.6 Salient items in this country case

The salient items in this case are:

- The reverse sequence of liberalization as compared to most other countries – first the local networks, followed by the inter-city network and finally the international network access – which may be explained by the importance of international settlements in hard currency;
- The frequent changes in objectives pursued through telecommunications policy and regulation, as a consequence of changing political forces in Parliament;
- The changes in the organization of the regulatory office, from its start in 2001 as URT, to URTiP in 2002 and in 2006 to UKE;
- The role given to municipalities as 'lenders of last resort' to build and operate telecom infrastructure in those areas that are not served by commercially oriented operators.
- Technology-based catch-up in mobile but not in fixed broadband. The substitution of mobile communications resulted in teledensity of fixed lines reaching its peak at 31% in 2003;
- Infrastructure-based competition limited to the major cities where CATV-cable is deployed;
- The lack of transition in access-based competition, from BSA and WLR to LLU, despite unbundling regulations in place;
- Leapfrogging technology, moving towards FttH/B without the interim solution of VDSL, of which deployment is hindered by the quality of the existing copper loops;
- The challenge of closing the gap between urban and rural developments, Poland representing 37% of unconnected households in rural areas in Europe.

14.9.7 Experiences that might benefit other member states in realizing the Digital Agenda for Europe targets

- The personal intervention of the president of the regulatory authority in achieving a change in the attitude of the incumbent operator towards its competitors;
- The role given to municipalities as 'lenders of last resort' to build and operate telecom infrastructure in those areas that are not served by commercially oriented operators. With the change of law in 2010, the role of municipalities is still in a very early stage;
- EU funding of NGA projects in sparsely populated regions.

References

A.T. Kearney (2012). The development of telecommunication market in Poland, Report. October 2012.

Babis, H. and Flaga-Gieruszyńska, K. (2011a). Regulacja rynku telekomunikacyjnego. Rozdział w publikacji "Rynek usług telekomunikacyjny" pod red. Warszaw: Wydawnictwo Wolters Kluwer.

Babis, H. and Flaga-Gieruszyńska, K. (2011b). Sieci telekomunikacyjne. Rozdział w publikacji "Rynek usług telekomunikacyjny" (wsp.) pod red. Warszaw: Wydawnictwo Wolters Kluwer.

District Telephone Cooperative (DTC) Tyczyn (2007). Partnership for Local Economic Development. United Nations Development Program, September 2007

European Commission (EC) (2010). Digital Agenda for Europe. Brussels, COM (2010) 245.
    (2012). Digital Agenda – Commission calls on Polish telecoms regulator to improve access to fibre network, August, 2012.
    (2013). Digital Agenda Scoreboard, June 2013. Brussels: EC.

European Union (EU) (2011). Broadband network project in Eastern Poland. Brussels, 10.11.2011.
    (2012). Fast and ultra-fast internet access, Digital Agenda Scoreboard 2012.

KPMG Advisory Sp. z Ograniczoną Odpowiedzialnością spÃ³łka komandytowa and

MDI Sp. z o.o (2008). *Report on the Condition of the Telecommunications infrastructure in Poland Telecommunications Policy – Investment – Competition*: a network of new opportunities, Warsaw: American Chamber of Commerce, November 2008. http://amcham.pl/file/pdf/lobbying/raport_telekom_en_2008_11_08.pdf.

Ładny, P. (2007). The Development of the Polish Mobile Phone Market. Zilina: Transcom.

(2012). Działalność organu regulacyjnego na polskim rynku telekomunikacyjnych w latach 2006–2011. Szczecin University.

(2013). Rozwój sieci nowej generacji w Polsce na tle Europejskiej Agendy Cyfrowej. Szczecin University.

NIK (Supreme Chamber of Control) (2012). Report on the Internet access and telecommunications services. www.nik.gov.pl, Warsaw, 20.06.2012.

OECD (1999). Communications Outlook 1999. Paris: Organisation for Economic Cooperation and Development.

Poland (1987). The Act of 7 June 1987 on the monopolistic practices counteractions in national economic (Act on Combating Monopolistic Practices Dz.U. 1987, Nr 3, poz. 18.

(2004). Telecommunications Act of 16 July 2004 (in force on 2 September 2004) (Ustawa z dnia 16 lipca 2004 r. Prawo Telekomunikacyjne, Dziennik Ustaw 2004 No 171, item 1800).

(2010). The Act of 7 May 2010 on supporting the development of telecommunications services and networks, *Journal of Laws No.* 106.

(2012). Narodowy Plan Szerokopasmowy, – perspektywa 2020 r. Warszawa: Ministerstwo administracji i Cyfryzacji (MAC).

Streżyńska, Anna (2011). Report on the Activities of the President of the UKE for 2010. Warsaw: UKE, April 2011.

UKE (Office of Electronic Communications) (2004) The Act of 16 July 2004 Telecommunications Law, Warsaw, UKE. (Unofficial English consolidation of amendments to June 2013: www.en.uke.gov.pl/files/?id_plik=41).

(2006) Report on the telecommunications market in Poland in 2005 Warsaw 4, June 2006.

(2008a). New Reference Interconnection Offer. Warsaw, April 2008.

(2008b) Bitstream Access reference offer. Warsaw, May 2008.

(2009) The agreement between TP SA and the President of UKE. Warsaw 22.10.2009.

(2011a) Market for wholesale broadband access in Poland. Warsaw, April 2011.

(2011b). Report on the coverage of the Republic of Poland with the existing telecommunications infrastructure, Warsaw, June 2011.

(2011c). Report on the telecommunications market in Poland in 2010. Warsaw, June 2011.

(2011d). Report of 2 years of TP-UKE Agreement, Warsaw, October 2011.

UKE, (Office of Electronic Communications), (2011e). Projekt_decyzj Audytel report, 2010–2011. Warsaw. www.uke.gov.pl/_gAllery/39/18/39189/Projekt_decyzj_R5_TP_1_10.pdf.Audytel report, 2010–2011.

(2011f). The analysis of bundled services, The President of the Office of Electronic Communications Warsaw.

(2011g). The analysis of market development of LLU, The President of the Office of Electronic Communications, Warsaw, 2011.

(2012a). Report on the telecommunications market in Poland in 2011. Warsaw, June 2012.

(2012b). The analysis of bundled services, The President of the Office of Electronic Communications, Warsaw, October 2012.

(2012c). Regulatory strategy to 2015, Warsaw, November 2012.

(2013). Report on the telecommunications market in Poland in 2012. Warsaw, June 2013.

Windekilde, I. (2005). Access to Internet – as a determining factor of the Information Society development in Poland, 16th European Regional Conference September 4–6, 2005, Porto, Portugal.

Windekilde, I. and Henten, A. (2006). Broadband development in Poland, 16th Biennial ITS conference, 12–16 June 2006, Beijing, China.

Windekilde, I. and Henten, A. (2012). Policy factors affecting broadband development in Poland. ITS 2012 Bangkok, 18–21 November 2012.

Latvia

ANDRIS VIRTMANIS AND EDVINS KARNITIS

15.1 Introduction to the case study

Latvia has a longstanding competence in tele-communications (telecom), producing telephone sets already before the First World War. More-over, the *VEF* factory (established in 1932) pro-duced 40% of local and regional telephone exchanges in the Soviet Union in the 1980s. The Riga Technical University was the only edu-cational institution in the Baltic area that trained telecom engineers. Hence, high skilled telecom professionals were available in the labour market in Latvia when independence was restored in 1991.

The major problem – as in other Eastern Euro-pean countries – was underinvestment in the net-work. Although the telephone density, with about 26 main lines per 100 population, was fairly high by Eastern European standards, the public network was based mainly on analogue technology. The telephone waiting list included more than 140,000 applications, with waiting times up to twenty years.

In this chapter we capture the quick catch-up that Latvia was able to realize. In this section the early developments are described, including the emergence of the Internet and the role of mobile communications. Section 15.2 is focused on the regulatory developments and Latvia joining the EU. The development of fixed broad-band is discussed in Section 15.3 and mobile broadband in Section 15.4. The realization of the Digital Agenda targets is the topic of discussion in Section 15.5. The quality of broadband service and broadband usage are covered in Section 15.6 and 15.7, respectively. Section 15.8 explores developments expected in the near future. Section 15.9 provides the case analysis and conclusions.

15.1.1 Basics of the normative and regulatory environment

In 1993 the Supreme Council of Latvia passed a comprehensive Law 'On Telecommunications', which established the basis of the legal framework for telecom activities in Latvia (Virtmanis, 1997a); see Figure 15.1 for a timeline of major events. According to the law, the Department of Communi-cations of the Ministry of Transport was responsible for the overall telecom policy in Latvia, including radio frequency management, mobile licensing and relations with international telecom organizations.

In the same year, the Telecommunications Tariff Council (TTC), the de facto regulatory body, was established. Its task was setting tariffs and rates for basic telecom services (moving to cost-based prices), as well as control of the quality of services.

The government established the national telecom company in 1992 (from 2006 called Lattelecom) according to the country's general political and economic transition strategy. The public telecom institutions and the whole infrastructure falling within the framework of the Ministry of Transpor-tation were placed under its responsibility. The law granted Lattelekom an exclusive right to provide the basic public voice services, as well as the leasing of circuits, for 20 years. The provision of 'universal service' was coupled with granting the monopoly to Lattelekom.

The market segments of mobile, satellite com-munications and paging (all under a licensing regime) as well as value-added services were opened to competition (under the responsibility of the Ministry). See Table 15.1 for an overview of the current major operating entities[1].

---

[1] SIA Baltcom TV and SIA IZZI finished a two-year-long M&A process in 2013.

Table 15.1 Main telecommunications operators and their shareholders, Latvia, 2013

Operators	Services	Shareholders (September 2013)	Shareholders ownership
SIA Lattelecom	Fixed (PSTN)	51% LV State 49% TILTS Communications	100% TeliaSonera AB from 2002
SIA Baltcom TV	Fixed (CATV)	0.04% LVRTC 99.96% offshore companies	100% LV State
SIA IZZI	Fixed (CATV)	100% SIA Baltcom TV (LV)	
SIA LMT	Mobile (GSM, UMTS, LTE)	5% LV State 23% LVRTC 23% SIA Lattelecom 24.5% Sonera Holding BV 24.5% TeliaSonera AB	100% LV State
SIA Tele2	Mobile (GSM, UMTS, LTE)	100% Tele2 AB	
SIA BITE Latvija	Mobile (GSM, UMTS, LTE)	100% Mid Europa Partners	
AS Telekom Baltija	Mobile (CDMA)	80.5% LV companies 19.5% offshore company	

Data source: PUC, 2013.

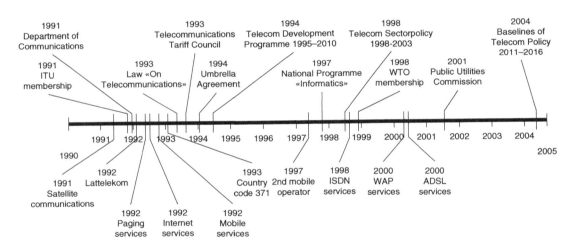

Figure 15.1 Formation of the normative, regulatory and technological environment

Starting from 1994 the state telecom policy was updated several times (Lauks & Berzins, 1998) in response to issues arising. Latvia joined the WTO in 1998 and the government already had signed the Association Agreement with the EU. Discussions with the European Commission (EC) on various levels were intensive in the second half of the nineties (Karnitis, 1999). Therefore it became necessary to harmonize the 20-years monopoly granted to Lattelekom with the general trend towards competition. On the other hand, because of a weak economy and low purchasing capacity, there was no place for another serious investor in the relatively small fixed market in Latvia. Modelling of the situation showed that opening-up the fixed market would have a significantly negative impact on the network upgrade plans.

15.1.2 Development of the fixed network

Modernization and upgrade of the Latvian fixed public telecom network was a critical precondition for the creation of an advanced infrastructure with independent access to international communications. The establishment of a full four-level hierarchy of the digital network, which is prescribed by international standards, was envisaged by the modernization project to replace the star-shaped centralized infrastructure of the analogue PSTN network[2].

A partial privatization of Lattelekom was chosen to ensure the necessary investments, to provide telecom modernization and stimulate rapid growth in the sector, to gain access to advanced technologies and services, to introduce private sector management practices, to improve network performance and the quality of services, and to make Latvia a major telecom hub on the eastern shore of the Baltic Sea (Karnitis 1996, Virtmanis 1996). The TILTS Communications consortium (70% Cable & Wireless, 30% Telecom Finland) was selected as Lattelekom's strategic investor because of a higher value bid, better inward investment, shorter time frame for implementation, lower tariff basket and equal priority to both corporate and technical modernization. The International Finance Corporation joined the TILTS with a 10 per cent stake in 1994. The Umbrella Agreement among shareholders defined their responsibilities as: technical network modernization, management of Lattelekom and its development, inward investments and principles of tariff setting. The Umbrella Agreement covered the period 1994–2013; to start market liberalization, the government shortened the monopoly to 2003, maintaining the validity of the agreement.

Lattelekom's obligations (bound by the Law and the Umbrella Agreement) did not allow it to act purely for profit: the company was required to digitalize the telecom system completely (including remote rural areas) and in the meantime to maintain the quality of the existing analogue network.

The construction of the fibre trunk network with international connections was the key element of the modernization. A western and an eastern optical loop were built; communications between Riga and all twenty-six district centres were provided using SDH multiplexing technology. The submarine cable connecting Latvia and Sweden, the microwave link between Riga and Tallinn and satellite communications via the EUTELSAT system (later connections to Lithuania, Belarus and Russia) provided reliable and sustainable international connections.

The OPGW (optical ground wire) technology[3] was chosen for development of the Western optical ring. For the implementation Lattelekom concluded a long-term agreement with energy company Latvenergo, which later was enabled to equip and explore a parallel nationwide optical trunk network. Another such network was constructed by the national railway company following railway tracks and connecting the capital with the country's larger cities. All-in-all, three competing fibre core network infrastructures were developed in the country.

In the first years of the modernization, some commitments were accomplished or even exceeded, while others remained unachieved. Lattelekom was successful in developing the digital access network in Riga, as well as in laying international fibre connections that sharply improved Latvia's capability of carrying transit traffic. The new fibre telecom backbone covered the major cities within the territory of Latvia.

1995 was the year when customers felt the impact of the benefits of the modernization of Lattelekom; thousands of them were connected to digital switches, including those from the waiting list. Half of Lattelekom customers were connected to digital switches by 2000; moreover, the people had the opportunity to use digital payphones.

At the same time a higher level of capital expenditures for the upgrading of local lines, combined with lower tariffs set by the TTC, resulted in the

---

[2] The kernel of the PSTN was the Moscow hub, which was connected by trunk-lines with second-level hubs in the capitals of the Republics and provinces. Long-distance calls were routed through the Moscow hub and international direct dialling was available only from the Moscow hub. Second-level hubs were connected with local hubs in the regional centres, which in turn were connected with local crossbar and step-by-step exchanges in towns and villages. Only local calls were routed directly; calls requiring settlement were routed through the star system.

[3] An optical ground wire, or in the IEEE standard an optical fibre composite overhead ground wire, is a type of cable that is used in the construction of electric power transmission and distribution lines. Such a cable combines the functions of grounding and communications.

delay of some capital expenditures: e.g., the extension of the eastern leg of fibre backbone, development of rural radio systems and payphones.

A significant growth of fixed phone density in Latvia was forecast; however, in practice it never happened and fixed phone density in Latvia never exceeded the 31% threshold. The main reason was the substitution of mobile for fixed lines, which happened in the country thanks to the successful roll-out of mobile networks, as well as changes in the pricing policy of the incumbent operator.

Before liberalization and interference by the regulator, the incumbent cross-subsidized domestic telecom services with revenue from international services; in addition, users of services on the analogue network historically paid only a fixed monthly fee. A huge customer loss resulted after setting new prices for local telecom services; the so-called tariff rebalancing was not completed in Latvia by the deadline because of the low purchasing power of consumers.

The full switchover of analogue customer lines to digital, as one of the modernization goals, was finalized by 2008.

15.1.3 Development of the cable TV network

The CATV segment developed rapidly in parallel with the modernization of Lattelekom. According to EU regulations, no classic CATV licence was granted to Lattelekom to stimulate infrastructure-based competition.

CATV provider Baltcom TV was established in 1991; another CATV company IZZI has existed since 1994, while the company's shareholders and name changed several times. In 2013 Baltcom TV acquired a 100% stake in IZZI, although the companies remain operating separately.

Both companies worked according to the Law on Radio and Television, without any further regulation during the 1990s. They were licensed by the NRA in 2003; currently both CATV companies have developed to become nation-wide providers of classic CATV services (digital since 2003). They could become strong competitors in the broadband market if the Cable-TV operators used more aggressive marketing of Internet services and could change the traditional Latvian perception of them solely as TV providers: currently less than 10% of CATV consumers are also using CATV-based Internet access services.

Furthermore, more than fifty firms are operating as city or local providers of CATV services, but their share in the telecom markets (both TV and broadband) remains quite marginal.

Lattelecom started to provide digital TV (Internet TV and interactive TV) in 2007. Currently more than 100 interactive TV programmes are offered, as well as virtual video rentals, time-shift service, choice of language and other services.

15.1.4 Emergence of the Internet: narrowband development

The academic community anticipated the necessity and advantages of information networks earlier and better than other specialists. As a result, the Latvian Academic Network was created; it started operations in 1992, when a 2.4 kbit/s connection to Tallinn (and further to NORDUNET) was constructed utilizing Lattelekom's network which reached 19.2 kbit/s from 1993 on. External access for academic, governmental and commercial institutions was organized immediately supporting e-mail, FTP, Gopher, Listserv, WWW, etc. services; the Latvian Academic Library was the first organization to be connected by means of a leased line in early 1993.

IP networking was spread to other centres in Latvia; some thirty-five Internet service providers (ISPs) operated in 1999 using Lattelekom's network according to special agreements on delegation of exclusivity rights to ISPs. Major providers were linked by fibre with the national Internet exchange centre GIX in Riga already before 2000. Handling international traffic was the main goal of the primary development of the Internet services. Due to its rapid growth a direct connection to Stockholm was created (at 128 kbit/s from 1995, 256 kbit/s from 1996). The gradual increase of total capacity of international connections to 60 Mbit/s in 2000 shows the unabated growth of the Internet traffic.

The major technologies applied initially for Internet access were 56 kbit/s dial-up and ISDN connections. Point-to-point radio-links (up to 11 Mbit/s) were popular Internet access channels when wired connections were not economically rational. Cable modems (64–256 kbit/s) were also introduced in the late 1990s by the CATV operators. Baltcom TV has developed an optical infrastructure in some districts of Riga, providing Internet services to its customers. It was estimated that the Internet was accessible to approximately ten per cent of the Latvian population by 2001; about one third of all businesses used the Internet.

Although the introduction of Information Society services started in the 1990s (Virtmanis 1998), the year 2000 may be considered as the start of e-commerce in Latvia, as the majority of Latvian commercial banks started to introduce Internet banking services then. The creation of public access points to the Internet in less-developed regions according to the Information Society targets started in late 1999. During the year 2000 an Internet connection was provided to every secondary school, and in the following years to local self-governments and public libraries, too. In 2000, ADSL technology (up to 2 Mbit/s) was offered in the market; marking the beginning of broadband development.

In less than a decade, Lattelekom had turned from a simple voice service operator into a provider of modern integrated telecom and information technology services.

15.1.5 Development of wireless communications

Satellite services became the first real international communications technology exploited by business and foreign embassies, the VSAT user-licenses being issued by the Ministry. Paging was also a progressively growing service in Latvia in the early 1990s. By 1994 four paging licenses had been issued, and the user base grew significantly by the end of 1995. Nevertheless, soon both services were overpowered by rapidly growing mobile communications.

Mobile services were introduced as an enhanced alternative to fixed network access. LMT (Latvijas Mobilais Telefons) – a consortium of domestic and foreign players – was the first NMT-450-based operator in Latvia, introduced in 1992. NMT offered coverage of mobile communications to up to 90% of the residents. There were roaming services for NMT customers through eleven NMT networks in ten countries.

The Ministry also issued LMT the first licence for GSM services. By the end of 2001, the LMT's GSM network covered more than three-quarters of the territory of Latvia, including all major economic and cultural centres, providing coverage to around 90% of the Latvian population. By that time LMT had entered into roaming agreements with more than 150 GSM operators in 83 countries. From 1999 LMT started to operate both GSM-900 and GSM-1800 networks. In addition to voice transmission LMT offered an extensive range of value-added services, including WAP services.

By 1995 Latvia remained the only Baltic state where a mobile monopoly existed. Therefore it became a natural decision to issue two more GSM licences. The company Baltcom GSM (now Tele2) won the international tender in 1997, and the company Bite Latvia won the tender in 2005. Competition in the Latvian mobile market prompted a considerable drop in tariffs; in addition, discounted handsets and mobile prepaid cards made mobile communications affordable for many Latvians.

Low data rate fixed wireless connections (up to 256 kbit/s) for customers in remote, sparsely populated rural areas to the basic network had been created in 2007–2009 using cellular technology – CDMA. This development is considered a very successful public-private partnership project of the Ministry of Transport and AS Telekom Baltija. Unfortunately, the latency in this case (up to 400 ms) is higher than when using a fixed connection.

15.2 Regulatory developments: joining the EU

Latvia – like other new EU member states – was expected to accept the *acquis*[4] before joining the

---

[4] The EU community *acquis* or *acquis communautaire*, sometimes called the EU *acquis* and often shortened to *acquis*, is the accumulated legislation, legal acts and court decisions which constitute the body of European Union law.

EU. In the case of telecom it was necessary to transpose the EU 1998 regulatory framework into national legislation (Virtmanis, 2002).

The liberalization date for the fixed telecom market in Latvia – 1 January 2003 – was set in the *Telecommunications Sector Policy* document (SM, 1998); the date was approved earlier by WTO agreement (Virtmanis 1997b) and through the pre-accession negotiations with the EU. The transition to a liberalized telecom market was envisaged by issuing a new telecom law and by the creation of a strong independent national regulatory authority (NRA) whose role would be market supervision, tariff and interconnection regulation and other functions, which later (in due time) would be replaced by supervision of the competition authority. The Ministry of Transport, besides the responsibility for policy and law-making tasks, would retain the licensing of undertakings and the granting of frequency usage rights, as well as the creation of a 'universal service' fund.

To improve the regulatory system, the regulatory model was reviewed in-depth. In 1997–2000 the global experience was analysed and the new multi-sector regulatory concept was elaborated in cooperation with World Bank experts. The concept is based on the idea that in essence the basic processes in all sectors providing services of general economic interest (with the corresponding regulatory activities) are similar. Taking into account these considerations, the multi-sector regulatory model was developed and the relevant NRA – the Public Utilities Commission (PUC) – was established in Latvia in 2001 by the Law on Regulators of Public Utilities (Karnitis, 2005; Karnitis & Virtmanis, 2011). By establishing a strong multi-sector NRA Latvia tried to avoid both the political influence of the government on regulatory procedures and the pressure of powerful utility companies that would result in regulatory capture.

Only a few arguments in favour of sector-specific regulation were provided, of which twelve-years of experience revealed their weakness.

Problems could arise due to differences in the legal frameworks for the sectors and in the policies of the sector ministries, as well as due to a lack of coordination among the DGs of the European Commission. Our experience shows that it is precisely the unified strategic approach of multi-sector regulation that to a great extent reduces those differences and facilitates the creation of a pan-sector harmonized business environment in the country.

Another set of arguments relates to potential lack of sector-specific competence in the multi-sector regulator that would result in a lower quality of regulation. There is some concern that regulatory failures in one sector could be transferred to other sectors. In reality Latvia's multi-sector experience shows inter-sector benefits and experience sharing. Harmonization problems of multi-sector regulation are much lower than those with a lot of uncoordinated sectoral regulations: e.g., the weaknesses of the unbundling strategy in the electricity market very much helped to fight against initiatives for a mandatory structural separation of integrated telecom companies.

In addition, some institutional aspects have to be mentioned: in order to better handle sector individualities, several sector departments were created in the organizational structure of the PUC, supported by common economic and legal services. The competence level achieved shows that unified regulation can be more competent and even cheaper than the alternative.

The status of PUC's institutional independence was defined by the law. The decision-making body of the PUC (the commissioners) has a strong mandate to make principled decisions. The five commissioners of the PUC are nominated by the parliament (*Saeima*) for five years; nobody (including the *Saeima*) can dismiss them prematurely. Although formally the PUC was operating under the supervision of the Ministry of Economy, the supervisor's power to affect PUC's decisions and activities was limited to the formal one mentioned in the law. The PUC's decisions become valid without requiring any approval from a minister or anyone else. At the same time, any decision of the PUC can be appealed in court within a defined time period.

This new approach of independence in the creation of the NRA was also the basis for regulation of the telecom sector in the new law 'On Telecommunications'. Unfortunately, the adoption of this new law was postponed several times; it became

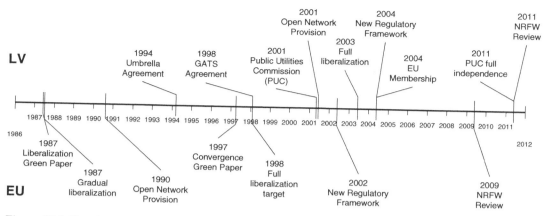

Figure 15.2 Development of the regulatory framework in the EU and in Latvia

valid only in late 2001. The reason was a request for arbitration against the government of Latvia submitted by TILTS in the international court in 2000 on the timing of Lattelekom's privatization, investments being compromised and dividend distribution (Dombrovskis et al. 2004). The case was resolved only in 2004, when the disputing parties came to an agreement.

The new law redistributed the regulatory functions between the Ministry of Transport and the PUC. The ministry was entrusted to elaborate policies for the development of the sector and to set out principles for the financing of universal telecom service; it was obliged to monitor radio frequencies and to elaborate new laws and regulations of the Cabinet of Ministers for the sector. The PUC was to be engaged in all practical aspects of regulation of the sector. The new law contained the basic principles for regulation of the telecom sector – competition where possible and regulation wherever and as much as necessary – that have been included in EU directives over the previous decade:

- establishment of a telecom licensing regime for the liberalized market;
- frequency and numbering planning to develop and optimize numbering resources as well as to manage frequencies that are available for telecom operations;
- elaboration of a proper methodology for setting telecom tariffs;

- establishment of a sector-wide interconnection regime;
- ensuring universal telecom service;
- quality-control functions, including the handling of complaints about poor quality of telecom services;
- avoiding potential conflicts of interests between licensed utility companies (especially publicly owned) and the government;
- representation in international telecom regulation organizations and working groups.

It was over a ten-year period that the older member states implemented the telecom market liberalization principles step-by-step; see Figure 15.2 for a timeline of events. This absolutely necessary, gradual market development (segment by segment) period was dramatically reduced in Latvia. The European Commission noted in 2002 that Latvia 'had made good progress' in aligning with the *acquis* in the area of telecom; nevertheless this did not mean full preparedness. Only a two-year transition period for the preparation of the secondary legislation was provided for the PUC by the law, while the density of secondary legislation in Latvia's normative system is high; nevertheless the market was liberalized on 1 January 2003, even without having a full legal environment in place.

Moreover, a reconsideration of the EU legislation was already under way: in 2002, the New Regulatory Framework of the EU (NRFW), which was based on competition law principles, was approved. The new member states were required to adapt their internal normative acts by the date of their entry in the EU – 1 May 2004.

In an extremely short period, significant efforts had been applied to open the market and to introduce as many rules as possible to favour competition. To transpose the NRFW's rules of the game, the PUC drafted around thirty secondary regulatory acts by the end of 2004. Of course this resulted in a high regulatory burden with a long list of related problems.

The EU 2002 regulatory framework was legally implemented in Latvia only sixteen months after market liberalization (SM, 2004). Due to the lack of time for the development of competition, the market was not fully prepared for this new framework which introduced more general rules on competition; the movement from a monopoly to true (not merely nominal) competition in any country requires more support than the simple establishment of a favourable legal framework. The market must inevitably go through a series of stages (allowing time for participants to develop business models according to the changing normative and regulatory environment) in which flexibility in implementation of the EU rules should increase, allowing for tactical diversity in the implementation of the EU regulations and directives according to particularities in the member state[5]; in our case the presence of a competent and strong NRA (see, e.g., Karnitis, Virtmanis 2011) and its active role stood out as a key factor.

In hindsight, the implementation of the 2002 package of regulatory directives in Latvian legislation by 1 May 2004 has to be appraised as a premature action, as it resulted in nine infringement procedures opened by the EC against Latvia in the period 2005–2011 over incorrect implementation of the framework; three of them concerned the PUC competence.

The revised EU telecom reform package adopted in 2009 was intended to ensure more effective competition and better rights for consumers. The revised framework was only partly transposed in Latvia by the deadline that was set in the directives (25 May 2011); therefore Latvia was one of the member states against which the EC opened an infringement procedure (in July 2011). The transposition measures (regulations by the Cabinet of Ministers and the PUC) were adopted in the following months and the EC notified, after which the various infringement proceedings against Latvia were closed in October 2011.

The amendments of 2011 to the 'Law on Regulators of Public Utilities' reinforced the independence of the PUC; particularly in budgetary matters and by eliminating the supervision of the Ministry of Economy. Due to demands of the 3rd Energy Regulatory Package, the telecom sector also obtained the advantages of a fully independent regulator: 11 August 2011 was the PUC's first Full Independence Day.

Twelve years of experience have shown the advantages of harmonized regulation for both service providers and consumers. With a number of sector-specific regulatory bodies, it would have been impossible to manage all the processes and to perform all activities, to achieve the current level of efficiency of regulation, as well as the current level of authority and competence (technological, economic, legal), nor the level of independence. The multi-sector model can be appraised as the most advanced and efficient one, especially for small and medium-sized countries (i.e., for the majority of EU member states). Also, recent global and European trends show a movement towards the harmonized multi-sector regulatory model.

15.3 Fixed broadband

15.3.1 Development of fixed broadband

A number of academic activities (e.g., the academic network LATNET since 1992) and corporative activities (e.g., a country-wide data network for the Latvian postal company since 1995), together with the governmental approval of political initiatives

---

[5] EU legislation is mainly directed at strategic issues (although sometimes it is too detailed and painstaking). Tactical activities and measures to implement strategic trends have to be chosen by the member states according to the real situation in the corresponding country as well as to the traditions and mentality of the people.

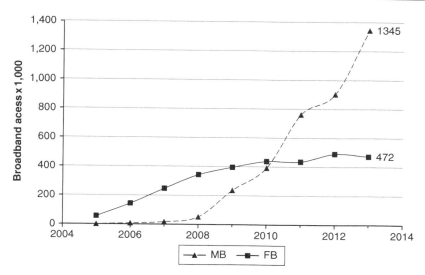

Figure 15.3 Uptake of fixed and mobile broadband, Latvia, 2004–2013
Data source: PUC, 2013.

(the National Informatics programme in 1999, the socio-economic e-Latvia programme in 2002) which led to budget co-financing of the ICT projects and development of ICT based applications (e.g., in education, banking, health care, library and many other sectors) were raising the overall demand for advanced data services.

In 1998 Lattelekom started to offer ISDN and LAN-to-LAN services to the business sector, which represented the first fixed broadband (FB) solutions. Co-operation agreements on Frame Relay service provision were concluded with the foreign partners in 2000. Internet access based on ADSL technology (up to 2 Mbit/s) was introduced by Lattelekom in spring 2000. Several new services were introduced subsequently – 'Ultra DSL' (up to 2 Mbit/s), 'Fast Data Net' (up to 1 Gbit/s, using Gigabit Ethernet technology), 'E-Call' (a service for owners of Internet home page) and the 'Unified Data Business Network' (a virtual private data transmission network service providing customers' transmissions at the IP level) together with service level agreements (SLAs).

In 2000 the overall demand for digital leased lines in the country grew by 44% and the number of dial-up users by 108%; the amount of time that dial-up customers spent on the Internet increased

by 128%. However, very high Internet access costs (the highest in peak time and the second highest in off-peak time among the EU candidate countries) were a significant barrier to further growth.

Lattelekiom introduced ADSL2 technology in 2005. Since 2007 Lattelecom's business model includes the active development of FttH (sometimes FttB) connections to all apartment buildings with more than twenty apartments. FttH is applied instead of intermediate VDSL to save on capital expenditures. GPON technology providing up to 1 Gbit/s access is available to 60% of households since October 2013. Lattelecom's middle-mile fibre network is also used; for the development of FttB + Ethernet connections, mostly by alternative operators. The result is a high penetration of very fast Internet: 50.8% of broadband lines at data rates at or above 30 Mbit/s and 35.6% above 100 Mbit/s (see also Table 1.3 in Chapter 1 Introduction). Lattelecom is also an active developer of Wi-Fi hotspots, many of them free of charge for everybody.

The development of mobile broadband (MB) has an impact on the development of fixed broadband (FB) (see Figure 15.3). The much higher penetration figures in comparison with PSTN and a high quality of basic voice (e.g., average unsuccessful call ratio 1.0–1.2%, call set-up time 6–7 sec) provided a good starting position for the introduction of mobile data transmission services in general and for 3G development in particular. The capacity of 3G for everyday use (e.g., 4–6 Mbit/s on the downlink) is good enough for many consumers, while the price is more affordable (see also Section 15.7.2) which is an important, if not the most critical, issue.

15.3.2 Infrastructure competition vs unbundling in the fixed broadband market

The opening of the market led to a significant increase in the number of service providers: around 200 providers were licensed by the PUC by the end of 2003, the majority of them for provision of Internet services. As of January 2013 a total of 415 firms were recorded in the PUC register as providers of telecom services; approximately 80% of them are active in the market; more than 240 firms provide broadband services. Hence, it is no surprise that mergers and acquisitions of telecom companies are ongoing; for instance, Baltcom TV acquired six smaller companies and its main competitor IZZI during 2013. More competent and more competitive providers with growing network capacity should be considered a positive factor for the market and for customers.

Infrastructure competition among 240 FB operators is typical of the Latvian market today. Local providers are competing with the main actors, as well as amongst themselves, mostly in limited areas, even within one apartment block. A number of technological platforms are used: see Table 15.2. The wide use of Ethernet technologies by small companies for last-mile broadband provision in apartment buildings remains habitual for Latvia even today. The broad introduction of NGA is expected to change the market situation, as providers will need to adapt their business models.

However, the introduction of bitstream access and unbundled local loop (ULL), as part of the market liberalization in 2003 did not raise the interest of potential access seekers, notwithstanding a price of around EUR 8.40 for full unbundling in 2005. The main reason was the ambition of Lattelekom to stay an exclusive provider. It was unwilling to accommodate retail competitors at

Table 15.2 Fixed broadband market shares by technology, Latvia, January 2013.

Access technology	Market share (%)
Fibre	47.3
xDSL	31.8
Ethernet	12.6
Cable	3.9
FWA	3.2
Other	1.2

Data source: PUC, 2013.

the wholesale level, trying to avoid the development of VoIP service using various tactics. Other reasons include the lack of legal requirements for the construction of communications networks, the sparsely populated countryside and the comparatively low quality of the legacy copper network. Market entrants preferred to use fixed wireless access based on the license-exempt use of the 2.4 GHz (later 5 GHz) spectrum (RLAN technology). Because competitive infrastructure was already developed (although not very solid in many cases), this approach continued even after 2007, when the PUC applied wholesale access obligations to Lattelecom, having concluded it had SMP in the first round of market analysis.

Infrastructure sharing among operators to reduce expenditures instead of infrastructure competition will have to be an important principle for realistic and profitable NGN developments in the coming years because of the weak purchasing power of consumers, hence a low average revenue per user (ARPU), as well as the EU's increasing demands to facilitate access to NGNs.

Lattelecom's share in the provision of DSL and FttH services is close to 100%, but the competing infrastructures using other technologies – Ethernet in the building connected to fibre (mostly that of Lattelecom) – captured more than half of the total broadband access market within a few years. Ethernet networking in apartment buildings and CATV network access (using the DOCSIS-3 standard) became widely used alternative fixed infrastructures as the demand for Internet services grew. The compound annual growth rate (CAGR)

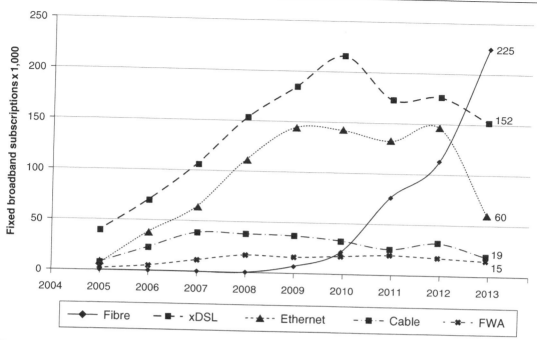

Figure 15.4 Fixed broadband market development by technology, Latvia, 2005–2013
Data source: PUC, 2013.

of the broadband market over the period 2008–2013 was 20.8%; see Figure 15.4 for the development and distribution of the technologies used in the period 2005–2013.

An interesting feature is the increasing FB market share (as well TV market share) of the incumbent Lattelecom since 2007 (see Figure 15.5) – i.e., since the implementation of its fibre-related strategy. As a result of these developments the concentration of the telecom market remained quite high: the Herfindahl-Hirschman Index (HHI) for the fixed voice market was 8067 in 2012, and for the mobile voice market 3607; only the Internet market is moderately concentrated with an HHI of 2111.

15.4 Mobile broadband

15.4.1 Mobile services

On the one hand, the mobile market development in Latvia is analogous to global and European trends (Cernakovs-Neimarks et al., 2013). Four

sequential generations of technology since 1992 have resulted in an evolution from a circuit-switched, low-quality analogue voice network to digital packet-switched broadband networks that ensure secure voice, messaging and data communication services. Following the global pioneers, LMT launched commercial LTE pilot projects in several major urban areas (Riga, Liepaja, Jurmala) using the 1800 MHz band in May 2011. Meanwhile, LTE/4G service provision had expanded to more than thirty-five cities by 2013.

More and more people are using mobile services. The CAGR of mobile subscriptions in the last decade was close to 14%, leading to an official penetration rate of 190% in 2012, which was the highest in the EU27 (see Table 15.3) and double the global level of 91%. However, growth by more than 20% was not a realistic figure in 2012, as recalculation of population by the Population Census has a direct impact of more than 10% on penetration. In addition, crisis-related emigrants and tourists do not close their prepaid SIM cards, which means more than 20% of additional

Table 15.3 Basic indicators, mobile market, Latvia and EU, 2012

| | Uptake,% of population | | | | |
	Mobile subscriptions, Dec 2012	Mobile broadband (3G, 4G), Dec 2012	Dongles, December 2012	M2M SIM cards, 2012	ARPU in mobile communications, 2011 (EUR)
Latvia	190.1%	50.5%	7.4%	2.0%	55.2
EU27	130.47%	54.1%	9.0%	5.0%	195.4

Data source: DA, 2013.

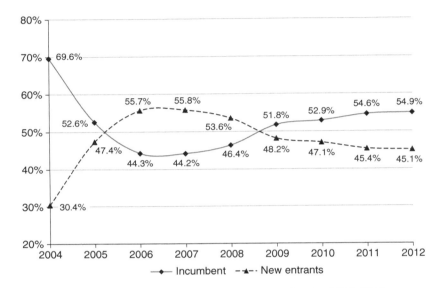

Figure 15.5 Fixed broadband market shares by type of operator, Latvia, 2004–2012
Data source: PUC, 2013.

subscribers are fictitious. Therefore, the actual mobile penetration level would be around 160–165%.

MB penetration in Latvia is lagging slightly behind the EU27 average. Nonetheless, mobile data traffic grows sharply; e.g., Tele2 stated that its total mobile data traffic exceeded mobile voice traffic for the first time in 2012.

At the same time the average revenue per user (ARPU) of mobile operators as well as their total revenues have declined since 2008. One of the reasons is the strong regulatory measures initiated by the EC: i.e., the gradual decrease of roaming and interconnection tariffs. It represents a serious risk factor for the development and sustainability

of mobile services in the future: it may result in scant investments in network infrastructure and a possible decrease of quality of communications and services.

On the other hand, there is a principal difference from Western European countries, where mobile services entered the market of voice services at a comparatively high fixed line penetration. In Latvia, as in other post-USSR countries and most Central and Eastern European countries, mobile services became available for users when the fixed telecom network was still underdeveloped. This was a significant accelerating and driving force for the development of mobile services during the 1990s; the connection of new consumers, who preferred mobile, was the basis for the rapid growth of mobile subscriptions.

One of the cellular operators, Telekom Baltija, has developed a country-wide MB network by exploiting CDMA2000 technology in the 450 MHz band; the quality of voice and data services using a lightly-loaded CDMA network is in between the average indicators of low data rate (GPRS, EDGE, UMTS) and high data rate (HSPA technologies) provisions of GSM-based operators (see also Section 15.7.3.). The CDMA service was the first form of MB Internet access in Latvia. Currently it is a complicated task for the company to compete with the strong GSM operators; there is a very limited CDMA handset range and the inter-connection with GSM subscribers is expensive. As a result there are only few CDMA consumers remaining and their share in the mobile market is marginal.

It is difficult to predict the future of CDMA services. Currently there are no signs of growth. A migration to LTE is unlikely. The company has invested to modernize the infrastructure in 2013, to upgrade all base stations towards using the advanced CDMA technology EV-DO Rev. B2. It is projected to achieve peak download data rates of up to 24.5 Mbit/s and peak upload rates up to 9 Mbit/s.

15.4.2 Drivers and risks

Generally accepted key factors influencing the development of mobile communications (e.g., increasing data rates, supply of advanced mobile devices, more and richer offer of media content and applications) are, of course, valid in Latvia, too. Nevertheless, a number of specific aspects apply.

The most critical driver from the demand side is a sharp increase in uptake and usage of mobile equipment – smartphones, media tablets, dongles (PCs, laptops, notebooks), and M2M devices. These advanced consumer devices are becoming available at affordable prices. In a pool of respondents, smartphones were used by 44% in Q3 2013; among the younger generation (15–29 years) smartphones are even more popular with 65% of respondents. Samsung and Nokia handsets are the most popular

in Latvia. The number of mobile-connected laptops and tablets in the LMT network, for instance, grew by 78% in 2012 and the amount of transferred data by 152%. M2M constituted 1.4% of all active mobile subscriptions in Latvia in 2011; LMT has noticed more than 50% growth in M2M applications for its business customers in 2011.

Leading Latvia's MB market for the foreseeable future will be the 3G and also 4G technologies. Strong market consolidation and/or arrival of new competitive local mobile players is neither observed nor expected. The impact of alternative mobile technologies (e.g., CDMA, WiMAX, satellite-based) is low. At the same time, social networking applications and the entry of global over-the-top content providers (OTTs) are changing the whole value chain and will have a significant impact on the MB market.

The impact of mobile communications at a macroeconomic level is a source of direct motiv-ation for the national and local governments to be interested in mobile roll-out (see, e.g., Van Ooter-ghem et al., 2009). The annual contribution of MB to the growth of GDP of Latvia was evaluated from the very beginning as being considerable at 0.29%: e.g., through business mobility, remote monitoring of processes, increased productivity due to time savings when information is searched or any Inter-net application is used (Gruber & Koutroumpis, 2011). Another conclusion is that municipalities are interested in supporting the deployment of MB suitable for the implementation of their public functions – smart transport management, utilities services, public safety, etc.

The ongoing parallel development of fixed fibre expansion has to be mentioned as a potential source of serious impact on the roll-out of mobile networks (Schejter et al., 2010; Thompson and Garbacz, 2011); this will be the case in Latvia, too. The EU broadband policy drives investments in optical access networks (FttH and FttB) and, in addition, requires the availability of unbundled metallic access lines. This takes place alongside the EU radio spectrum policy which supports high data rate MB through the roll-out of LTE. The continuing implementation of nationwide middle-mile optical network projects may cause different scenarios to unfold (from successful cooperation to

Table 15.4 Frequency bands assigned for wireless broadband services, Latvia, October 2013

Band	Available spectrum	Assigned spectrum	Beneficiaries
450 MHz	15 MHz	2×7.5 MHz	1 operator
800 MHz	60 MHz	60 MHz	3 operators
900 MHz	70 MHz	2×35 MHz	3 operators
1800 MHz	150 MHz	2×75 MHz	3 operators
2 GHz	120 MHz	2×60 MHz	3 operators
2.6 GHz	190 MHz	2×70 MHz FDD 50 MHz TDD	4 operators
3.4–3.8 GHz	400 MHz	28×14 MHz	6 operators

Data source: PUC, 2013.

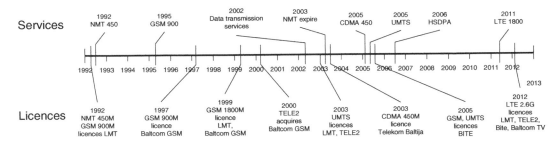

Figure 15.6 Development of mobile market: spectrum licences issued and services provided, Latvia, 1992–2012

strong competition in the use of fibre-to-the-base station); growing FB supply will affect mobile service demand and possible future investments in MB networks. At the same time, fixed network developments are not expected to become a real threat to the sustainability of Latvia's mobile market.

15.4.3 Radio spectrum policy and usage

An increase of demand is closely related to the qualitative improvement of the access to the network in terms of services and the quality of these services (EC, 2011). The trend of development of mobile networks in Latvia is a bright illustration: two decades of dynamic growth reflect two decades of new services being introduced, which in turn became possible after assigning new spectrum licences (see Figure 15.6). The availability of spectrum is the essential factor for development of all wireless broadband services; any delay in awarding licenses hinders the broadband roll-out.

The radio frequency assignment process in Latvia is realized according to the EU telecommunications policy (BEREC 2012) and in compliance with the National Development Plan. In this regard the PUC has created a favourable climate for development of broadband services – that is, the PUC has assigned all attractive spectrum allocated for wireless broadband networks in the EU (see also Table 15.4).

The last of the popular bands – the 800 MHz 'digital dividend' – was auctioned in October 2013; with a slight delay for a reason common to all countries bordering Russia and Belarus – the intended use of this band (preferred in sparsely populated rural areas) conflicts (especially in a 10–15 km border zone) with the use of these frequencies for radio navigation services (RNS) in Russia and Belarus until July 2015. It is hoped the migration of the RNS systems out of this part of the spectrum will happen, as according to an Analysys Mason study its use for mobile will provide an estimated benefit of EUR

19 billion for the Russian economy over the period 2015–2030.

Network development strategies and improvement of communications capacity are now the key challenges for operators to create a growth driver from the supply side.

Basic GSM and UMTS mobile communications frequency bands have been awarded to mobile operators in quite equal portions[6]. Moreover, single portions of bands are allocated, which is a significant precondition for the development of an optimum broadband network topology with increasing network efficiency and provision of broadband services. Smart network strategy and the upgrade of infrastructure are the basic tools to achieve efficient use of the allocated bands.

So far, consumers' uptake of the pilot LTE services (1800 MHz band) is quite low. Nevertheless, the current dynamics and the projections indicate that in 3–5 years the currently assigned spectrum bands will not be able to satisfy the growing MB traffic demand. This means that operators have to start network planning and make provisions for investments in infrastructure now; the PUC is convinced that having awarded spectrum licences is a prerequisite for the inception of these activities.

To achieve a return on their investments in LTE, spectrum licences operators are in the first place interested in covering areas with high potential traffic: i.e., with a large number of concentrated and solvent consumers. This is facilitated by the generally high urbanization level in Latvia, which is near the EU27 average, while gross income of urban households exceeds that of rural residents by 10–35%.

The majority of solvent consumers are concentrated in the seventeen major and medium-sized cities, with more than 10,000 residents and a population density higher than 1,000/km^2 (in total 56% of the population). These cities become the priority for LTE network deployment. Therefore it made sense to auction the 2.6 GHz band, a typically urban spectrum, first; this was done in the very beginning of 2012 (Karnitis et al., 2012). The auction was based on the following principles:

- to attract all three existing GSM/UMTS operators in order to ensure sustainability of mobile services provision;
- to provide three equal basic lots (defined frequency blocks) to guarantee an environment for fair competition in the future;
- to ensure space for additional bidders as local (niche) operators.

Three 20 MHz paired FDD blocks formed the auction kernel; in addition one 2x10 MHz FDD licence was successfully auctioned. The auction (based on the simultaneous multi-round auction format) included the requirement for operators to cover 55% of the population by 2018 (equivalent to covering the 17 cities mentioned above). The spectrum became available from 2014, because of its previous use for TV provision by Baltcom TV (using MMDS technology)[7].

In analysing the fiscal proceeds from the European 2.6 GHz auctions, we found a quite strong correlation between the ARPU and the number of MB subscriptions in the country (rather than the habitual number of population) on the one hand and, on the other, the amount that the bidders have invested in obtaining the licenses for the spectrum blocks (see Figure 15.7). Radio spectrum auction fees in Latvia reflect the current mobile market situation. The significant investment by Latvia's operators in spectrum licences is connected with serious competition among the bidders (as is the case in Sweden and Belgium).

15.5 Realizing the Digital Agenda targets

Despite the dynamics and prospects of mobile communications with LTE being launched, FB

---

[6] GSM bands were assigned to the LMT as an administrative decision, while the assignments to Tele2 and Bite were the result of auctions of previously-defined single spectrum blocks. UMTS and LTE spectrum blocks were fully auctioned.

[7] More than five years before the planned introduction of LTE, Baltcom TV was required to end its MMDS service. According to national law compensation for the move is not envisaged if changes in spectrum plans (refarming) are announced at least two years before the move. Instead of this band the company required a position at the 10.5 GHz band on FCFS base, which was granted by the PUC.

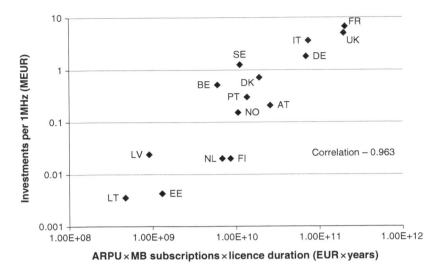

Figure 15.7 Investments in 2.6 GHz spectrum licences in relation to anticipated revenues, Europe
Source: Karnitis et al., 2012.

access is the key for the achievement of the Digital Agenda broadband policy targets – 'download rates of 30 Mbit/s for all citizens and at least 50% of European households subscribing to Internet connections above 100 Mbit/s by 2020'. Due to active deployment of fibre connections[8], Latvia is well ahead of the EU27 average and well on the way to the general availability target for very fast FB; Latvia occupies second place in the EU for share of FB subscriptions above 100 Mbit/s and fourth place for share of subscriptions above 30 Mbit/s in 2012. Table 15.5 shows the basic FB market indicators for Latvia and the EU27.

Coverage of the population (territory) continues to lag behind the EU27 average level; its increase is slow – the CAGR over the period 2005–2010 was only 0.8%. The major reason for the backwardness in FB is the low coverage of rural areas (39.8% of rural households by standard FB and 24.4% by NGA FB). The low general population density in Latvia combined with a quite high

urbanization level (68%, near the EU27 average) results in the population density in rural regions being much lower. The FB services are primarily viable in economically active and densely populated urban and suburban areas and therefore mostly supplied in these areas.

The detailed analysis of the situation showed that there is sufficient capacity in the optical trunk networks. The primary bottleneck is a lack of middle-mile networks in the rural areas for the provision of high speed broadband access, especially at data rates above 30 Mbit/s (SM, 2012). The fixed CDMA access mentioned above and some other low speed FB connections are currently the only real possibilities for the rural population. This is reflected by the Internet statistics on broadband uptake in the regions (Table 15.6). In addition, in these areas the access costs are high in comparison with the purchasing capacity of the population, becoming unaffordable for the majority of customers; these prices are a serious barrier to the use of the Internet.

In these areas, high data rate FB service provision will not be realized in the foreseeable future without public support (EU funds and/or public investments). Focused public intervention without giving any competitive advantage to any provider

[8] Lattelecom's strategy is to upgrade the existing copper networks by fibre in apartment buildings with twenty or more households (especially in the major cities and regional centres), while FttH (FttB) is used for connection of all new buildings.

Table 15.5. Digital Agenda indicators of the fixed broadband market, Latvia and EU27, 2012

	Total FB coverage (supply) % of households		FB uptake (demand) % of total population (% of households)		
	Standard	*NGA*	*Total*	*>30 Mbit/s*	*>100 Mbit/s*
Latvia	82.9%	78.5%	23.1% (55.4%)	10.0% (24.0%)	4.7% (11.3%)
EU27	95.5%	53.4%	28.8% (76.6%)	4.1% (11.2%)	0.9% (2.4%)

Data source: DA, 2013.

Table 15.6 Fixed broadband (>256 kbit/s) uptake in planning regions as percentage of households, Latvia, 2011

Region	Households (%)
Riga	65
Riga suburbs	69
Kurzeme	61
Latgale	45
Vidzeme	53
Zemgale	55

Data source: SM, 2012.

Table 15.7 Consumers' assessment of telecom services, Latvia and EU27, 2012

Service	Latvia	EU27
Fixed telephony	105.1	99.4
Mobile telephony	103.0	97.1
Internet	98.4	97.6

Data source: DG Health and Consumers, 2012.

(see more detail in Section 15.9) is a realistic tool to reduce the existing regional gap. In reality, it means the development of a form of 'universal service'.

Although broadband demand is more dynamic than supply, currently only around 30% of people with access to FB services have actually subscribed. (The EU27 average figure is not much better.) There is, of course, the impact of the economic crisis: where Latvia lagged behind the EU27 in FB penetration by 1.5 years in the period 2004–2007; the gap had become 4 years in 2011; fortunately, the after-crisis recovery has started. There are two other reasons for the low FB uptake: the inadequate supply of national content, as described in more detail in Section 15.7.1 and the higher prices of FB compared to MB offers, as shown in Section 15.7.2.

FB is and will be the base for achievement of Digital Agenda targets. The high data rate connections (> 30 Mbit/s) will have to be provided by fixed networks, as measurements show that under realistic operational conditions the download data rate of LTE will not reach 30 Mbit/s.

15.6 Quality of broadband services

Consumers' evaluation of the telecom market, in particular their satisfaction with the services provided, is a principal factor for the development of the demand for services.

The level of satisfaction of Latvian consumers ranks above the EU27 average (EC DG Health and Consumers, 2012); especially as it relates to telephone services (see Table 15.7). The comparatively lower uptake of Internet services is connected with the broadband coverage gap between major cities and rural areas mentioned above. In addition, when evaluating the services provided by mobile operators, only 11% of the users fully agreed that their Internet data rate corresponds to what the operators announced.

There are also significant technological peculiarities and differences between metallic and fibre solutions on the one hand and wireless broadband access to the Internet on the other hand. It is an extremely hard task for mobile access providers to compete with the quality provided by FB networks. Currently service providers do not explain the advantages and disadvantages of wire and wireless technologies to consumers; this will have to be done in the near future to avoid further confusion and increasing dissatisfaction. A critical mass of uneducated and unhappy customers could become a significant risk factor for mobile market development. Understanding how low the satisfaction of consumers is with mobile and Internet services in many EU countries provides a substantive indicator of the underlying problems.

15.6.1 Regulatory activities

There are several regular activities of the PUC directed towards control and improvement of the quality of telecom services – setting quality requirements for the 'universal service' provider, mandatory quality declarations for other providers and annual quality assessment reports. The PUC draws the attention of service providers to customer-oriented quality criteria. According to the 'General Authorisation Rules' issued by the PUC, from 2008 there has been a mandatory requirement to set the guaranteed Internet download and upload data rates in the customer's service contracts. From 2012 on, these guaranteed data rates cannot be less than 20% of the promised peak connection rates. A guaranteed minimum download rate of 144 kbit/s is also set for MB connections.

The PUC conducts regular quality control of the telecom services. An innovative system for measurement of quality was developed and introduced by specialists of the PUC to obtain objective, credible information on quality and to be able to inform providers and end-users accordingly. Since 2007 the testing of voice telephony quality parameters is performed by an automatic system, which includes fixed and mobile phone terminals serving as call simulators. The widely accepted PESQ[9] algorithm for end-to-end connections is used to

perform objective data measurements on voice telephony. The speech quality in mobile networks can also be verified during drive tests.

The Internet control system, called ITEST, has been used since 2007. This Internet access testing device also was provided to the service providers, permitting them to check the actual parameters of their customers' Internet connections. As of 2009 public access makes it possible for any consumer to test his or her Internet connection. The ITEST carries out measurements of quality (download and upload data rates, packet loss, jitter and latency) of data transmission between two points – the quality control server is connected directly to the national GIX and the consumer's terminal.

This system has become quite widely used: more than 3% of consumers tested their connections in 2012; operators tested more than 2% of their connections. Purposeful measurements have demonstrated their efficiency and have a positive impact, including increasing the discipline of operators. The quality control is continued and expanded for early detection of quality risks and for the promotion of sustainability of broadband services: e.g., 24-hour testing of MB access was started in 2012. Further improvement of the ITEST will include the possibility of measurement for smartphone users.

15.6.2 Quality of fixed services

The PUC's measurements show the splendid quality of emerging FB fibre networks; very high Internet data rates have been achieved with excellent latency (<10 ms) and jitter (<3 ms) levels.

The penetration of high data rate broadband lines is increasing more rapidly than the general broadband penetration rate; the number of existing subscribers who migrated to high-speed connections in 2011 was more than quadruple the number of new customers. For instance, Lattelecom regularly increases the data rate of the various connections for the same price: e.g., 50 Mbit/s instead of 20 Mbit/s was implemented in 2012.

International fixed broadband quality studies regularly rank Latvia among the global leaders (Oxford University, 2009; Akamai, 2012; Pando Networks, 2012: see also Table 15.8) Already in

---

[9] PESQ: Perceptual Evaluation of Speech Quality is a family of standards comprising a test methodology for automated assessment of the speech quality as experienced by a user of a telephony system.

Table 15.8 International evaluation of fixed broadband quality, Latvia, 2009 and 2012

Study performer	Year	Parameter	Global rank
Said Business school University of Oxford	2009	Broadband quality score (45% download + 32% upload + 23% latency)	6
		Broadband quality divide (between cities and rural areas)	3
Akamai Technologies Inc.	2012	Peak connection speed	5
		Average connection speed	4
Pando Networks Inc.	2012	Average download speed	5

Data sources: Oxford University, 2009; Akamai, 2012; Pando Networks, 2012.

2009, Oxford University researchers classified Latvia as a country 'already prepared for the Internet applications of tomorrow': e.g., for Internet TV and high-quality video communications. At the same time, the researchers identified the basic fixed Internet problem for Latvia: the third biggest quality gap between the major cities and the rest of the country. The middle-mile project mentioned in Section 15.8 is directed at closing this gap.

15.6.3 Quality of mobile services

The actual quality of mobile services in comparison with the advertised figures is one of the reasons for dissatisfaction of mobile consumers and is a key challenge for the operators. Only 20.7% of the tests performed by the PUC throughout territory of Latvia in 4Q 2012 (PUC, 2013) showed actual download data rates above 4 Mbit/s (see Figure 15.8). At the same time 55% of tests showed data rates below 2 Mbit/s. Moreover, the indicators for the three mobile operators were very different – 40%, 40% and 86%, respectively.

Operators, of course, pay more attention to the major cities where consumers' density and traffic is much more profitable. The rapid deployment of HSDPA technology in 2012 significantly improved the situation in the major cities: the measurements showed 91.7% above 2 Mbit/s and 68.6% above 4 Mbit/s (65.2% and 21.7% respectively in 2011). The supply of mobile broadband in medium-sized regional centres is on the level of the country's average, which is not adequate for these centres, which the National Development Plan for 2014–2020 defines as development centres (PKC, 2012), given their concentrated business entities as well as educational and public

institutions. All of the above applies equally to the upload data rates.

The measurements also confirm the efficiency of 4G technology – the download rates ensured by medium loaded cells are reaching 14–18 Mbit/s. Currently there are no indications on the possibility of realizing 100 Mbit/s.

These multi-annual measurements allow the early recognition of potential serious risks related to mobile service quality degradation in the near future.

An issue for the 3G MB supply is the sometimes very high level of latency (up to 500 ms) and especially jitter, which sometimes is up to 200–300 ms, depending on the traffic. The measurements of the CDMA network indicated a much lower jitter than the GSM network – 60 ms on average. This issue does not influence the quality of downloaded content from different sources or surfing on websites. Problems will occur with jitter over 50 ms for applications requiring correct sequencing of packets: e.g., still pictures or unsynchronised picture and sound as for using Skype or as part of IPTV, etc. (ITU 2008). This represents a serious risk, as according to LMT video applications already generate 30% of the total traffic.

The typical ratio between download and upload data rates for MB access is around 2–3 to 1, with a tendency to increase when the download rate is increasing. A characteristic problem is that mobile operators prefer to use the scarce frequency resource to connect as many customers as possible. Providers emphasise the high download data rates without providing for the adequate increase of upload rates; for example, some measurements show 4G upload rates lower than 1 Mbit/s, implying that the ratio in this case is more than 15 to 1.

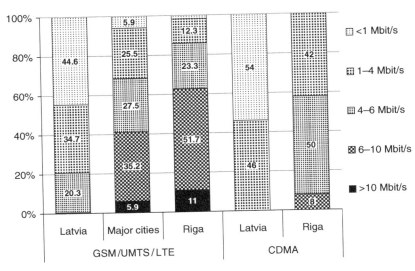

Figure 15.8 Mobile download data rates, Latvia, 4Q 2012
Source: PUC, 2013.

Such situations, with a high level of asymmetry between download and upload rates, become critical above all for content-creative applications: e.g., educational and health care services, social networking and online games.

15.7 Broadband usage

15.7.1 The practice

Latvia has defined the knowledge and wisdom of its inhabitants, and the ability of each individual to make use of them, as the basic resource for growth. The development of an innovative economy is a principal component of such a growth model. This means a radical increase of cooperation and sharing of information is required. These activities are supported by the active use of advanced telecom technologies in business. In this respect there are no notable particularities in broadband usage by enterprises in Latvia as compared to other EU countries (Karnitis 2008):

- a similar proportion of enterprises use FB connections – 85.6% in Latvia, 89.6% in EU27 (2012) and all basic services defined at the EU level for enterprises are available on-line;

- similar usage of FB and MB for various business transactions and activities in a networked environment within the enterprise and in co-operation with partners;
- large enterprises are the most active users of broadband, while smaller enterprises use it less and most micro enterprises are just beginning.

The residential segment is much more nuanced, although the indications of Internet usage and non-usage in Latvia are very similar to the EU27 average. All basic broadband e-services have been well developed in Latvia – e-governance, e-health-care, e-commerce, e-education, etc. Of the basic public services defined for citizens, 90% are available. In addition, specialized mobile applications are also used, some of them developed by Latvian specialists for general usage (e.g., m-parking) or corporative use (e.g., for banks, exchanges); several ideas are extremely innovative: for example, a patent was granted to a resident of Latvia in 2010 on a coffin equipped with mobile phone.

However, the usage patterns of individual Latvians are rather different from the EU27 average (see Figure 15.9). Latvian Internet users are recognized as very qualified ones: more than 60% of

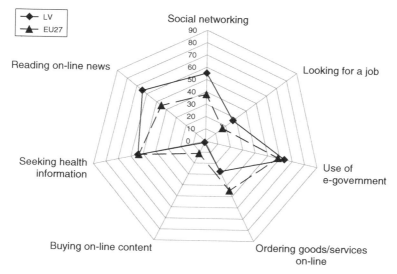

Figure 15.9 Usage of broadband services, % of individuals (age 16–74), Latvia and EU27, 2012 or last available
Source: DA, 2013

them have high-or medium-level skills, putting Latvia in second position in the EU27 in 2011. Evidently, services of general interest are therefore very popular. Social networking has become an attractive online activity. Latvians are among the most active participants in social networking in the EU: 90% of smartphones are regularly connected to one of the social networks. A Latvian phenomenon that should be mentioned is that the most-used social networking application on mobile phones is for the locally developed site *draugiem. lv* (57% of polled users) with Facebook in second (51%) and Twitter in third (25%) place. People over 50 years of age typically communicate in one social network only, while the younger generation is active in several of them.

Other popular online activities are reading news, job seeking, etc. The use of more specific services such as e-government and e-health services is on the EU27 average level.

However, the population of Latvia is much more cautious in use of the Internet for any purpose related to e-commerce and online payments (except e-banking). Some 67% of the polled users reported they are afraid of a possible leak of information and are concerned about the security of transactions. Obviously, there is an impact of the

still-fresh memory of widespread dishonesty and fraudulent e-commerce transactions in the 1990s (non-delivery of goods, defective goods, etc.).

Internet usage is strongly affected by the availability of local content in the national language. The lack of national content – such as e-books (including classics), e-periodicals, e-textbooks, digitized cultural heritage collections, and advanced applications (e.g., e-signature, e-voting, civil construction procedure, registration of cars) which are in high demand by the majority of users is a serious barrier to the further development of both FB and MB. The CAGR of Internet hosts in Latvia was 38% over the last four years; nevertheless, the number of local hosts (representing the availability of local content) remains quite low, with only 165 hosts per 1000 population in 2012 (compared to more than 300 hosts/1000 for the EU27).

Evaluation of content usage shows that current broadband networks are ready for much higher data flows. As the market for national content is small, public subsidies are necessary for the development of content in the national language.

When looking at the usage of MB, it is critical to evaluate the actual use of advanced MB applications and services. LMT reported that the number who used mobile Internet with smartphones grew by 55% in 2012, while the amount of data sent and received quadrupled. The amount of mobile data on the Tele2 network doubled every 8–12 months in recent years. In 2012, 72% of smartphones in Latvia were connected to the mobile Internet at least once a week. Smartphones, MP3 players and game consoles are popular in the group aged 15–24 and desktop computers and e-books with those aged 35–44 while low-end phones are most used by those aged 45–54 years.

Nonetheless, a lot of subscribers do not use the capacity of the devices in full. The younger generation is the most active user of new opportunities; for example, in the group aged up to 39 years, advanced applications are used by no less than 40% of the polled smartphone users; the number falls by more than half in older age groups. E-mail (40%) and Internet browsing (32%) remain the most popular activities among mobile Internet users. Around 30% of the smartphone users exploit only the basic functions such as voice calls, SMSs, address book and camera; the significance of these services remains high. Operators noted that the introduction of bundled mobile tariffs, which contain unlimited voice and messaging services, substantially increased the number of messages sent per subscriber: by 56% in the LMT network and by 23% in the Bite network in 2012.

Around two-thirds of users of mobile applications are exploring only the free applications and have never purchased one. The use of applications subject to a fee by one-third of mobile users is highly dependent on their income level: 15% of users in the income group up to EUR 200/month in comparison with 47% in the income group of EUR 600–850/month.

Regarding the prospect of network usage, several socio-economic factors constrain the demand for advanced mobile applications. Global and European economic prognoses are not optimistic yet, which is an alarming signal for Latvia's very small (GDP was only 0.17% of EU27 GDP in 2012) and very open economy (total export and import of goods and services was 126% of GDP). The purchasing capacity of users is an important factor, which of course influences the customers' willingness to pay for services and applications.

The impact of the economic crisis on the purchasing capacity of the population has been very strong, reducing it by 20–40%.

Demographic processes also have a strong impact. The level of emigration during recent years due to the economic crisis is a noteworthy characteristic of the Baltic states and especially of Latvia, which also has a low birth rate and an ageing population. According to official statistics Latvia has lost close to 12% of its population since 2005. Even more significant is the reduction in persons below or at the active working age – those being the most active users of advanced telecom services and applications.

15.7.2 Investments

There is a close relation between developments in the telecom sector and general economic development: economic growth means increasing investments in telecom services, which in turn strongly supports the rapid development of all economic sectors, an increase of productivity of businesses and capacity of administration, and gains in the strength and scope of competitiveness of enterprises and of the country as a whole. The telecom sector serves as a catalyst for economic and social activities (Dombrovskis et al. 2004). Both technological and financial accessibility of high-quality telecom services are also important for the quality of life – for health, even for life itself, as well as to eliminate social exclusion, which results in an increase of wellbeing (Karnitis 2006). In this sense there are specific national interests in the development of the sector (see also Lam & Shiu 2010).

The fundamental reorganization of the telecom sector after the restoration of independence, the full liberalization of the market and the change of several technological generations provided the potential to improve telecom services radically and to become an integrated part of the international telecom system. Huge investments were necessary to perform all the activities. Latvia's providers of telecom services are among the most active investors in the EU until today, with 15.8% of turnover (2.87% of GDP) against 12.8% for the EU27 (2.56% of GDP) in 2011 (DA, 2013). In

Table 15.9 Tariffs for broadband services, Latvia, 2013

Provider	Connection	Amount/month	Monthly tariff, EUR
Lattelecom	DSL 5 Mbit/s	Unlimited	10.90
	DSL 20 Mbit/s	Unlimited	24.90
	FttH 50 Mbit/s	Unlimited	14.90
	FttH 200 Mbit/s	Unlimited	28.90
Baltcom	Fibre 250 Mbit/s	Unlimited	12.95
IZZI	Cable 25 Mbit/s	Unlimited	15.55
LMT	3G	2 GB	7.05
	3G	Unlimited	16.95
	4G	Unlimited	26.85
Tele2	3G	500 MB	2.70
	3G	25 GB	25.30
Bite	3G	1 GB	2.80
	3G	Unlimited	20.65
Telekom Baltija	CDMA	3 GB	11.25
		Unlimited	26.90

Data sources: Company news.

2010 53.5% of total investments were devoted to fixed networks, 32.5% to mobile networks.

15.7.3 Tariffs

The level of revenues of the sector are determined by the tariffs. In Latvia the tariffs for fixed and mobile broadband services are in general approximately half of those in Western Europe for services of the same quality (see Table 15.9).

The usage of fixed, bundled offers (two or three services) stands at 30% of inhabitants in Q3 2012 and was slightly above the average in the EU27 with 28%. Prepaid mobile, with 50% of subscriptions, is also close to the average level in the EU27 of 48%.

Pilot tariffs for 4G connection are very high at present: TeliaSonera's partly owned operator LMT charges a flat rate that is 4.6 times higher than Telia/Sonera's tariff in Sweden. Such price levels are unaffordable for the majority of customers and will be a strong barrier for further development of 4G services.

Consumers looking for more appropriate services and tariffs can migrate to another provider using the number portability service. Porting subscriber numbers has become increasingly popular: during the last four years the CAGR of ported consumers was 41% for fixed and 35% for mobile services.

Real household spending for telecom services is not very high today. Nevertheless, the payments for services remain a significant share of consumers' budgets. The statistics show that low-income households (first and second quintiles) are limiting their use of services; in addition they are spending a larger share of their comparatively lower budgets (see Table 15.10). The average spending per capita for all telecom services combined (fixed, mobile, voice, data, TV, etc.) was EUR 13.00/month in 2012. This shows that only the mobile subscriptions with medium data rates and medium traffic are fully affordable for the majority of the population.

The attractiveness of, and therefore consumers' willingness to pay for, new advanced telecom services and applications is higher than the general decrease of tariffs. As a result, consumers' payments for services have increased by 33% since 2003. Combined with an increase in personal

Table 15.10 Usage of telecom services and payments by income quintile, Latvia, 2012

Income quintiles	Usage (relative to average)	Payment (% personal income)
1	70	5.66
2	85	5.23
3	93	4.55
4	116	4.65
5	148	3.73
Total/ Average	100	4.61

Data source: CSB, 2013.

income by 97%, the share of payments for telecom services in consumers' budgets has decreased from 6.84% to 4.61%.

Nonetheless, revenues in the telecom sector have decreased year over year since 2008; by 2011 revenues had dropped by more than 20% in comparison with 2008. Nearly all of the reduction relates to the voice market. As a result of low tariffs, Latvia has the lowest mobile ARPU in the EU and had the third-lowest mobile average revenue per minute (ARPM), in 2011.

Global and local socio-economic factors have a major impact on the demand-side, on the purchases of advanced applications. Although the general development trend will continue, lower-income consumers will economize on applications subject to fees and on films, video and music online; they will not require superfast FB nor 4G subscriptions.

At the same time, next-generation networks (NGNs) and the transition to 4G require huge investments. For instance a 100% deployment of the 4G network will require investments of nearly twice the turnover of a typical mobile provider in 2012. It is difficult to see how ARPUs which are less than EUR 100 per year can provide for sustainable development. How sustainable is the current investment rate? A slowing down in the growth of personal income and a lower willingness to spend more for telecom services represent a serious risk factor. The design and introduction of sustainable business models will be the big challenge for the mobile operators.

15.8 Reflections on the future

Projections of telecom market development have not always been fulfilled. For instance, as part of the sector policy the government forecasted a fixed penetration level of 65% and mobile penetration of 75% in 2008 (SM, 2005). In fact, fixed penetration reached only a 30% level, while mobile subscriptions exceeded 90%. Our assumptions will not be fully accurate either, due to the uncertainties around the economic developments (GDP and personal income level), because of demographic issues (emigration and aging society) and the effects of state aid for the development of telecom networks. Nevertheless, the general patterns and trends can be identified.[10]

FB coverage has grown slowly in recent years – 0.8% year over year; the early rapid-growth phase based on coverage of the cities is being replaced by coverage of sparsely populated areas which are inhabited mostly by low-income consumers.

In order to support the achievement of a more complete FB coverage, the Ministry of Transport has coordinated with the EC on state aid for the development of middle-mile fibre communications networks and optical access points up to 2018 (SM, 2011). These networks will be created step-by-step, in municipalities where none of the private providers is planning to create such connections in the next 3–4 years; scaling up from 38.8% of municipalities having high data rate connections to the trunk network in 2011, to 54.9% in 2016 and 100% in 2020. The program intends to provide the Internet backbone for last-mile operators which can use various wired and/or wireless technologies to ensure data transmission rates of at least 30 Mbit/s at

---

[10] There are several possibilities for modelling the development of telecom markets (see, e.g., Arvidsson, Hederstierna and Hellmer, 2007). We are using a sigmoid model for modelling the fixed and mobile penetration, as adoption of new technologies typically reflects the sigmoid (S-shaped) curve. The sigmoid model, based on the Gompertz function which can be appropriately parameterized, provides sufficient flexibility for predicting penetration (e.g., Rouvinen, 2006, Zheng Yan, 2009). Therefore, based on inputs from the study of past trends and market development scenarios, we are applying Gompertz distributions to forecast the subscription growth.

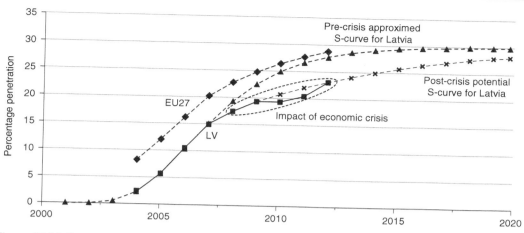

Figure 15.10 Forecast of fixed broadband penetration up to 2020, as % of population, Latvia

the subscribers' access channels. Installation of the middle-mile network was launched in Q2 2013 in the Latgale region – a region with the greatest amount of white areas. An important feature of the project is forbidding the middle-mile network owner to develop last-mile connections, thus ensuring equal possibilities for all last-mile competitors.

An immediate impact of the gradual state aid policy should not be expected, as the planned fibre connection to the trunk network is not a guarantee of last-mile coverage offers from any of the operators. The activities of the last-mile providers will be evaluated after a few years and a decision will be made on the need for state aid in development of the access networks. The PUC will also periodically evaluate the capacity of the trunk networks.

All in all, there is no reason to forecast a more rapid growth of coverage: it may increase by 3–4% until 2020 to reach 92–93%.

The analysis of development of the fixed market shows that the FB penetration trend corresponds surprisingly well to the ideal S-curve, especially in the pre-crisis period (see Figure 15.10). The slow-down since 2008 reflects the impact of the economic crisis. Approximation of the pre-crisis development trend with the ideal sigmoid function suggests that the FB penetration saturation level of around 30% will be achieved around 2017. The crisis has resulted in a delay of 3 years and slowed down further developments, too. The penetration level will increase by 4–6%, mainly due to the gradual

support for development in the rural areas, so we can predict an FB uptake of around 28% in 2020.

This forecast 30% FB penetration level will not be enough to achieve the Digital Agenda target. With the average size of the Latvian household at 2.4 members, it means that to reach the high data rate target, a penetration level of 42% is necessary for the coverage of all households. Adding the connections to businesses and educational and public institutions, a total penetration level closer to 60% would be necessary to achieve the target of 100% household coverage.

As reliable MB penetration statistics are available only for the last three crisis years, an indirect benchmarking is used, comparing the current MB penetration level in EU countries with the combined MB penetration and FB penetration as indicator (see for more detail Cernakovs-Neimarks et al., 2013)[11].

---

[11] Forecasting telecom markets has to be done regularly. It calls for reliable market data (see, e.g., Krizanovic, Zagar & Grgic, 2011; Zarmpou, Vlachopoulou & Patsioura, 2011). The problem is in the small number of reliable input values and the large number of output values (medium-term prediction is necessary to evaluate development trends) which can cause the over-learning effect of these models. Although a variety of institutions are publishing various statistical data on telecom development, official statistics have not stabilized yet. In addition, trends are typically distorted by an economic crisis. Therefore benchmarking is also applied to raise the credibility of the potential forecasts.

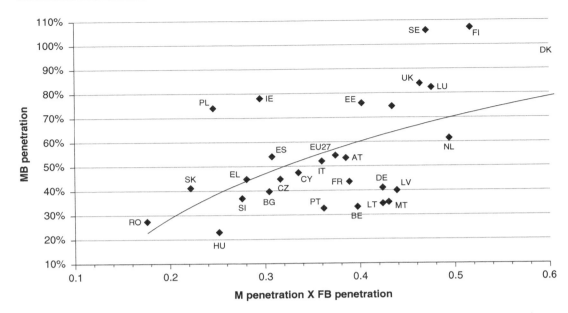

Figure 15.11 Mobile broadband penetration in relation to the combined mobile and fixed broadband penetration rates, EU countries, end of 2012
Data source: DA, 2013.

Such benchmarking gives a line of general relevance (see Figure 15.11). In this case, saturation is still far away: only Sweden, Finland and Denmark are already near saturation, while Latvia is still in the growth phase. Forecasts show that a MB penetration of around 60% will be achieved in 2020.

Mobile traffic trends show that the growth will continue. The various future projections differ as to growth rate (CAGR 60–90%) and factors that slow down growth are appearing but there are no signs of approaching the saturation phase.

The projected average monthly traffic per subscription would be around 4.0–4.2 GB/month in 2020, the total monthly mobile traffic volume in Latvia will grow to 14–16 PB/month.

15.9 Case summary and analysis

The case summary is provided with reference to the research questions formulated in Chapter 2 Research context and perspective.

15.9.1 Starting conditions

A highly relevant starting condition in terms of comparing broadband development in Latvia with other member states of the European Union is the return to independence of the state in 1991. For most economic sectors, it implied a catch-up process, which for telecommunications was completed in a relatively short time. The starting position was a teledensity of 26%, a position very favourable compared to other East European countries (Poland: 9%; Hungary: 10%; Czech Republic: 16%), but significantly lagging the major OECD countries (Germany: 40%; UK: 44%; USA 54%; Sweden 68% as of 1990). (OECD, 1999). The waiting list for a telephone included 140,000 applications, with waiting times up to 20 years.

15.9.2 Role of the central government

Recognizing the need for a catch-up in telecoms, the government decided on a strategic partnership to introduce private sector management practices and quality of services. This was enabled through a partial privatization (49%) of the incumbent operator Lattelekom. The incentive was the grant of a twenty-year monopoly on basic public voice and data services, including leased lines; the condition was the obligation to invest – reducing the waiting list – and modernize the network according to the Umbrella Agreement. Through a tender process, the consortium of Cable & Wireless (70%) and Telecom Finland (30%) was selected as the strategic partner. Tariffs were controlled through the Telecommunications Tariff Council, the *de facto*, partly independent regulatory body. By 2000 the waiting list had been reduced to zero and 50% of the subscribers were connected to digital switching systems. The highest level of teledensity reached, measured by fixed line connectivity, was 31%. The predicted growth of fixed lines was not realized as the success of mobile rapidly closed the connectivity gap, reaching a density of 190% of population.

The incumbent operator Lattelecom had turned from a simple voice service company to a provider of modern integrated telecom and information technology services in less than a decade.

15.9.3 Catch-up in next generation technologies

The catch-up process led to a leap-frog in technologies being deployed and to embracing new technologies as soon as these became available. The long distance and international connectivity was realized based on the construction of optical backbone networks.

In contrast to many other countries, the first mobile license was not granted to the fixed-line incumbent, but to LMT – a consortium of domestic and foreign players. The NMT-450 system introduced in 1992 – the 1G cellular system – was succeeded by GSM – the 2G cellular system – in 1992, the first license being granted to LMT. A second GSM license was granted in 1997 through a tender process to Baltcom GSM (now Tele2). WAP-based services were launched in 2000. ISDN was introduced in 1998 and ADSL in 2000. By that time the technology gap with the leading countries in the EU had disappeared. 3G

was introduced in 2005 and 4G is being deployed now, having started in 2011.

15.9.4 Cable network development

Cable networks had developed as city or local networks, with two providers (Baltcom TV and IZZI) being granted NRA licenses to operate telecommunications services throughout the country in 2003 at the time of market liberalization. Cable coverage is near 100% of urban households (70% of total). There was a significant mergers and acquisitions process among cable operators in 2009–2011. Nevertheless, with more than fifty city and local CATV operators remaining, it seems that a second consolidation wave has started in 2013.

15.9.5 Joining the European Union and the application of the Regulatory Framework

Leading up to the EU accession in 2004, an independent national regulatory authority was established in 2001 and the telecommunications market was liberalized in 2003. The incumbent operator was already partially privatized in 1993.

The twenty-year monopoly granted to Lattelekom was shortened at the time of implementing the EU Regulatory Framework and market liberalization. This led to court proceedings initiated by Lattelekom's owner TILTS in 2000, to be resolved by 2004.

The short interval available to transpose the EU regulation into national law led to nine infringement cases initiated by the European Commission in the period 2005–2011 referring to incorrect implementation of the Framework. The transposition of the New Regulatory Framework issued in 2009 was completed in 2011. In 2011, too, the PUC became fully independent as to budget matters and freed from supervision by the Ministry of Economy.

In 2007 wholesale access obligations were applied to Lattelecom, including local loop unbundling.

15.9.6 Narrowband developments

Access to the Internet was organized by the academic community in 1992 with a connection to NORDUNET; this was some five years after the first Internet connections were established by academic institutions in Western Europe. By 1999 some thirty-five ISPs served the Latvian population in the major cities, providing access to the global Internet via the Riga Internet Exchange (GIX) established in 1995. End-user access started with dial-up and ISDN-based access. In the late 1990s CATV – cable-based – Internet access was introduced. The year 2000 may be considered as the start of e-commerce in Latvia as the majority of Latvian commercial banks started to introduce Internet banking services. In 2000, ADSL was introduced by Lattelecom. This provided the basis for infrastructure-based competition in narrowband Internet access, albeit, given the limited coverage of the CATV networks, this competition was a practical reality in the cities only. Notwithstanding, cities represent 68 per cent of the population,

Reaching the remaining 30% of the population in the rural areas is the major network developmental bottleneck in Latvia, requiring state aid for its development.

The adoption of mobile technologies as a substitute for the lack of fixed connectivity also prompted the development of mobile Internet access. Tests executed by the PUC in 2012 showed that only 45% of the access tested had download rates of 2 Mbit/s or more. The rapid deployment of HSDPA technology in 2012 significantly improved the situation in the major cities; the measurements showed 91.7% over 2 Mbit/s and 68.6% over 4 Mbit/s (65.2% and 21.7%, respectively, in 2011). With these rates mobile Internet access provides an alternative to fixed access, as reflected by the development of broadband market shares over the years 2005–2013. Traditional fixed broadband is being marginalized by FttH and mobile, first reducing the role of cable and secondly the role of ADSL. With an average spending of EUR 13.00/month for all telecom services it appears that for most Latvians fixed and mobile are substitutes rather than complements.

15.9.7 Intensity of competition

The intensity of competition is very high, as reflected by the high churn rates: CAGR for the last four years of 41% for fixed and 35% for mobile. This may be explained by the relatively low willingness or ability to pay, indicated by relatively low average spending per month and the low uptake of applications subject to additional fees. Also the low teledensity rates when competition was introduced suggest that the number of captive users was relatively small from the outset. Hence, most end-users tend to search for the best value for money available.

15.9.8 Type of competition

At the time of independence, licenses to operate the cable network were granted to entities other than the PSTN incumbent. This enabled the competition for Internet access in the later part of the decade. However, with market liberalization in 2003 (shifted five years relative to old member states), the PSTN incumbent had a head start with ADSL and, as a consequence, infrastructure-based competition (PSTN vs cable) had a much smaller role to play.

The preference by alternative operators to invest in alternative wireless infrastructure can be explained first of all by the exclusivity ambitions of Lattelekom, as well as the lack of good quality PSTN lines and shortage of PSTN lines given a density of only 31%). Unbundling introduced in 2007 did not lead to any significant uptake of access-based service provision by alternative operators. This was despite an attractive wholesale price set at EUR 8.40 per month for full unbundling.

Infrastructure competition among 240 fixed broadband operators is a typical Latvian market characteristic: local providers are competing with the main actors as well as with one another, mostly in limited areas, even in one apartment block. Nevertheless the FB market share of Lattelecom was near 55% in 2012.

Mobile competition was introduced in 1997 with the tender and award of the second GSM license to Baltcom GSM (now Tele2). The third operator Bite entered the market in 2005 as a result of a radio spectrum auction.

The competition is both price based and based on increasingly higher data rates at roughly constant prices. The low price levels, typically half of the EU average, are a result of intense competition and facilitated by relatively low operating costs as well as lower construction costs, both due to lower labour costs.

The development of price levels should be considered in the context of the higher level of ARPU (up 33% since 2003) and higher personal income (up 97%). This has led to a decrease in the share of discretionary spending for telecommunication services from 6.84% to 4.619%.

15.9.9 Broadband developments

Standard fixed broadband coverage has reached 83% of households, some 10% below the EU average, with rural households as the main communication users lacking coverage. Uptake is at 55% of households, some 20% below the EU average. The low uptake is explained by strong competition from mobile, at least in the 2–5 Mbit/s data range.

Mobile broadband plays a major role in standard broadband supply; in 2013 it had a broadband market share near 74%. This is based mainly on 3G deployment with HSDPA. Deployment of LTE/4G reached all major cities in 2013.

NGA coverage leads the EU average by a wide margin, 79% of households against 53%. This also applies for the uptake of data rates of over 30 Mbit/s, 24% against 11%, and for data rates of over 100 Mbit/s, 11% against 2%.

NGA deployment consists of cable with DOCSIS-3 modems and FttH. There is no VDSL deployment, which can be explained by advanced business model of Lattelecom avoiding double investments in the infrastructure.

While new entrants had been able to grow and capture 55% of the broadband market by 2007, the roll-out of FttH/B by Lattelecom has allowed the incumbent to regain market share, which stands at 55% in 2012.

15.9.10 State aid

State aid and regional funds will be required to close the digital access gap in the rural areas. Hence, the dynamics of the broadband market in the rural areas is distinctly different from the dynamics that can be observed in the cities.

15.9.11 Other actors

While the case identified a large number of fixed broadband operators active in smaller parts of cities, no other – unconventional – actors have been identified as having contributed to the broadband dynamics in Latvia.

15.9.12 Achieving the Digital Agenda targets

Despite the need for a catch-up in the early 1990s Latvia is well positioned for achieving the Digital Agenda targets where they apply to the urban areas. The deployment of FttH/B with a current coverage of 90% of households in the cities (68% of household nationwide), to which we should add the non-overlapping DOCSIS-3 coverage, allows the uptake of data rates in excess of 100 Mbit/s. There is no technological barrier to the deployment of higher data rates, as no VDSL is deployed and the incumbent is leading in fibre deployment.

The tariffs set for NGAs (around EUR 15.00 for a range of 25–250 Mbit/s) are comparable with the current level of total telecommunications spending (on average EUR 13.00 per capita per month). There is no price barrier that prevents the migration towards higher data rates. However, the current spending level includes fixed and mobile and hence there is the question of how many people can afford to add a fixed NGA subscription to their mobile one. Given the current price levels, lower prices should not be expected; thus much will depend on the growth of income, which is very much subject to economic developments in the coming years.

While content is said to drive the need for higher data rates, the relatively low willingness and ability to pay for services and applications supplied for additional fees may reduce the demand-side pull of content.

For the rural areas, the situation is much less favourable. The costs of supplying high data rate access are much higher, while the income levels are lower. The realization of the 'middle mile' project with state aid may lead to last mile solutions being provided in the future. The 'middle mile' project will also facilitate mobile backhaul and hence 3G-based solutions may become viable, along with community-based Wi-Fi solutions with dedicated backhaul. With a longer horizon, and some favourable developments, the 2 Mbit/s target may be realized for all citizens and the 30 Mbit/s target may be realized for at least parts of the rural communities.

Based on performance measurement of 4G, medium-loaded cells provide for downlink data rates of 14–18 Mbit/s. This suggests that mobile broadband will not contribute materially to the realization of the two high-end targets of the Digital Agenda.

The modelling of developments suggests that the economic crisis has had a delaying effect of three years compared to the momentum observed in the period 2005–2007.

15.9.13 Salient items in this country case

The salient items in this case are:

- The catch-up process since independence in 1991;
- The accelerated adoption of mobile to compensate for the lagging development of the fixed network, where fixed never achieved more than 31% teledensity;
- The infrastructure-based competition among 240 fixed broadband operators is a typical Latvian market characteristic;
- The lack of any access-based competition, despite unbundling regulation being in place;
- Leapfrogging technology, moving towards FttH/B without taking the interim solution of VDSL;
- The challenge of closing the gap between urban and rural developments;
- The involvement of the state in the sector is still very high, with a 51% direct ownership of Lattelecom and approx. 40% (direct and indirectly) in mobile operator LMT.

15.9.14 Experiences that might benefit other member states in realizing the Digital Agenda for Europe targets

- Reasonable lead-times should be set for the process of transposing the EU Regulatory Framework. When starting from scratch, a two-year interval is too short to assure a good quality outcome.
- Public subsidies will be necessary for development of NGA networks in sparsely populated regions and also for development of content in national languages in small countries.
- To achieve more dynamic development and catch-up, and to save capital expenditures, some technological steps can be omitted: e.g., intermediate VDSL.
- Innovative Internet quality measurement systems can be recommended.
- A multi-sector NRA is more competent and authoritative than sector specific regulators, being more independent and less prone to political impact, regulatory capture and populism.
- Reliable statistical data on telecom markets are needed for more accurate analysis of trends, including the early identification of risks; it is in the common interest and a task of government, regulators and operators to achieve harmonized collection of data.

References

Akamai. (2012). The State of the Internet. Available from www.akamai.com/stateoftheinternet. [23 September 2013].

Analysis Mason Benefits of the digital dividend spectrum in Russia: Final report. Report for the GSM Association, 24 June 2010. Ref: 17193-255. www.gsma.com/spectrum/wp-content/uploads/2012/03/gsmadigitaldividendrussia.pdf.

Arvidsson A., Hederstierna, A. and Hellmer, S. (2007). Simple and Accurate Forecasting of the Market for Cellular Mobile Services, in: *Managing Traffic Performance in Converged Networks*, eds. Mason L., Drwiega T. & Yan J., Springer, Berlin-Heidelberg, pp. 690–706.

BEREC. (2012). Report on exploring the economic and social value of radio spectrum for certain electronic communications services with respect to the frequency assignment procedures. *BoR* (12) 15. Available from: http://berec.europa.eu/eng/document_register/subject_matter/berec/reports/61-joint-berecrspg-report-on-exploring-the-economic-and-social-value-of-radio-spectrum-for-certain-electronic-communications-services-with-respect-to-the-frequency-assignment-procedures. [23 September 2013].

Cernakovs-Neimarks, A., Karnitis, E., Rutka, G. and Virtmanis, A. (2013). Mobile Services in Baltic States: Development to Improve Sustainability and Quality. *Journal of Security and Sustainability Issues*, **2**(3), pp. 71–84.

CSB (2013). Database. Central Statistical Bureau of Latvia. Available from: www.csb.gov.lv/. [23 September 2013]

DA (2013). Digital Agenda Scoreboard Reports. European Commission. Available from: https://ec.europa.eu/digital-agenda/node/639. [23 September 2013].

Dombrovskis, A., Feijoo, C., Karnitis, E. and Ramos, S. (2004). Electronic communications sector and economic development in Latvia: regularities and individualities. *Communications & Strategies*, **56**(4), pp. 77–109.

EC (2011). Regional Policy, Guide to broadband investment. Available from: http://ec.europa.eu/regional_policy/newsroom/detail.cfm?LAN=EN&id=158&lang=en. [23 September 2013].

EC DG Health and Consumers. (2012). The Consumer Markets Scoreboard, 8th edition, European Commission. Available from: http://ec.europa.eu/consumers/consumer_research/editions/cms6_en.htm. [23 September 2013].

Gruber, H. and Koutroumpis, P. (2011). Mobile telecommunications and the impact on economic development. *Economic Policy*, **26**(67), pp. 387–426.

ITU (2008). Quality of experience requirements for IPTV services. G-1080. Available from: www.itu.int/rec/T-REC-G.1080-200812-I/en. [23 September 2013].

Karnitis, E. (1996). *Latvian information infrastructure; the present stage and trends of development*, Latvian Academic Library, Riga.

(1999). Latvia on the Way toward the Information Society: the International Context. *Baltic IT Review*, **1**(12), pp. 10–15.

(2005). Optimizing the Regulatory Environment in Emerging Economies in: *Creating an Enabling Environment; Toward the Millennium Development Goals*, ed. Gilhooly, The United Nations ICT Task Force, New York, pp. 29–40.

(2006). ICT Development, Inclusion and Sustainable Growth in: *Vit@l Society: the New Social Use of ICT*, ed. Mackie L., Apgads Imanta, Riga, pp. 48–59.

(2008). Business innovation and ICT in the Baltic region. *Connect-World, Europe Issue II*, pp. 15–16.

Karnitis, E. and Virtmanis, A. (2011), *Multi-sectoral regulation of services of general economic interest; ten-year experience of Latvia*, Academic Press of the University of Latvia, Riga.

Karnitis, E., Virtmanis, A., Rutka, G. and Jelinskis, J. (2012). LTE take-up in Baltic States and the European context: urban first. *Network Industries Quarterly*, **14**(2&3), pp. 31–34. Available from: http://mir.epfl.ch/Newsletter. [23 September 2013].

Krizanovic, V., Zagar, D. and Grgic, K. (2011). *Techno-economic analyses of wireline and wireless broadband access networks deployment in Croatian rural areas. Proceedings of the 2011 11th International Conference on Telecommunications (ConTEL)*, IEEE, Graz, pp. 265–272.

Lam, P.-L. and Shiu, A. (2010). Economic growth, telecommunications development and productivity growth of the telecommunications sector: evidence around the world. *Telecommunications Policy*, **34**(4), pp. 185–199.

Lauks, G. and Berzins, G. (1998). Towards Europe – a New Telecommunications Sector policy for Latvia. *Baltic IT Review*, **2**(9), pp. 54–58.

OECD (1999). *Communications Outlook 1999*. Paris: Organisation for Economic Cooperation and Development.

Oxford University. (2009). Global broadband quality study. Available from: www.sbs.ox.ac.uk/newsandevents/Documents/BQS%202009%20final.pdf. [23 September 2013].

Pando Networks (2012). Pando Networks Releases Global Internet Speed Study. www.pandonetworks.com//company/news/pando-networks-releases-global-internet-speed-study. [23 September 2013].

PKC (2012). Latvijas Nacionālais attīstības plāns 2014.-2020. gadam. Available from: www.nap.lv. [23 September 2013].

PUC (2013). Public Utilities Commission of Latvia, Market Information. Available from: www.sprk.gov.lv. [23 September 2013].

Rouvinen, P. (2006). Diffusion of digital mobile telephony: Are developing countries Different. *Telecommunications Policy*, **30**(1), pp. 46–63.

Schejter, A. M., Serenko, A., Turel, O. and Zahaf, M. (2010). Policy implications of market segmentation as a determinant of fixed-mobile service substitution: What it means for carriers and policy makers. *Telematics and Informatics*, **27**(1), pp. 90–102.

SM (1998). Latvijas Republikas telekomunikāciju sektorpolitika laika periodam no 1998. gada līdz 2003. gadam. Available from: www.sprk.gov.lv/index.php?sadala=280&id=347. [23 September 2013].

(2004). Latvijas Republikas elektronisko sakaru nozares politikas pamatnostādnes 2004.-2008. gadam. Available from: http://polsis.mk.gov.lv/LoadAtt/file40225.doc. [23 September 2013].

(2005). Par Latvijas Republikas elektronisko sakaru nozares politikas pamatnostādņu 2004.–2008.gadam īstenošanas programmu. Available from: www.likumi.lv/doc.php?id=106665. [23 September 2013].

(2011). Latvijas Republikas elektronisko sakaru nozares politikas pamatnostādnes 2011.-2016. gadam. Available from: http://polsis.mk.gov.lv/view.do?id=3625. [23 September 2013].

(2012). Nākamās paaudzes platjoslas elektronisko sakaru tīklu attīstības koncepcija 2013.-2020. gadam. Available from: http://polsis.mk.gov.lv/view.do?id=4164. [23 September 2013].

Thompson Jr., H. G. and Garbacz, Ch. (2011). Economic impacts of mobile versus fixed broadband. *Telecommunications Policy*, **35**(11), pp. 999–1009.

Van Ooterghem, J., Lannoo, B., Casier, K., Verbrugge, S., Tanghe, E., Joseph, W., Martens, L., Colle, D., Pickavet, M., Moerman, I. and Demeester, P. (2009). Municipalities as a Driver for Wireless Broadband Access. *Wireless Personal Communications*, **49**(3), pp. 391–414.

Virtmanis, A. (1996). Privatization of Telecommunications: Two Years of Experience in Latvia. *Baltic IT Review*, **2**, pp.25–28.

(1997a). The Route to the Information Society: Latvian Motivations. *Baltic IT Review*, **2**(5), pp. 20–23.

(1997b). Latvia's Participation in Negotiations with the World Trade Organization about Liberalization of the Telecommunications Market. *Baltic IT&T Review*, **3**(6), pp. 43–46.

(1998). Latvia's Informatics Policy: Results and Trends. *Baltic IT Review*, **2**(9), pp. 31–35.

(2002). Regulation in Telecommunications – Are We Ready for Competition. *Baltic IT Review*, **4**(27), pp. 50–56.

Zarmpou, T., Vlachopoulou, M. and Patsioura, F. (2011). *An Exploratory research for Mobile services Penetration in Greece. Proceedings of the 10th International Conference on Mobile Business (ICMB)*, Como: IEEE, pp. 136–143.

Zheng, Yan. (2009). Prediction model based on Gompertz function. *Proceedings of the 2nd IEEE International Conference on Broadband Network & Multimedia Technology, (IC-BNMT '09)*, Beijing: IEEE, pp. 893–898.

PART 3

Analysis

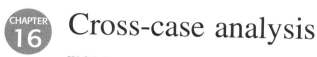

Cross-case analysis

WOLTER LEMSTRA AND WILLIAM H. MELODY

16.1 Introduction

This concluding chapter captures the insights obtained from the twelve country case studies and EU overview analysis and provides a synthesis of these findings to explain the broadband market dynamics in Europe. It builds upon the case material and the case analysis provided in the country case chapters. The analysis is facilitated by the common framework applied in the case studies and the EU policy framework that has guided developments in the countries that have been studied.

It should be noted that the authors of the case studies have placed emphasis on those topics that they considered most relevant in describing the broadband developments in their respective countries. This means that the references to and the quotes from the case studies are illustrative rather than exhaustive. No attempt is made to make statistical inferences. The emphasis in the analysis here is on the recognition of salient patterns, on exploring causal relationships, on trying to recognize the motivations and incentives of the actors involved. As such this chapter provides an analytical narrative.

The analytical narrative is provided by topic and is aimed at capturing the role of the most important actors and factors. Following a general, political framing of broadband developments, the analysis starts with the introduction of the Internet, the starting point for narrowband and later broadband developments. This is followed by those aspects that are least malleable, which are largely a given for policy makers. These are the infrastructure endowments upon which narrowband and broadband have developed (PSTN and CATV).

We then move to a remnant of the liberalization process – the attempt to create a level playing field – reviewing the application of functional separation. Subsequently, we move to exploring the role of alternative operators in broadband supply, including the role of unbundling and the progression following the 'ladder of investment' concept. In completing the view on market players, we cover next the private initiatives and the role of (relative) outsiders. The interplay in the market is addressed through a review of the role of competition.

This is followed by a review of the roles of governments, in stimulating demand, in removing barriers and as 'chief architect' in national broadband developments. This overview of government roles is concluded by reviewing the role of municipalities, and then the role of governments in closing the digital divide and the role of broadband in economic recovery. This is followed by observations on wireless broadband, the realization of the Digital Agenda and concluding remarks.

For the theoretical framing of this analytical narrative we apply the analysis frameworks as introduced in Chapter 2 Research approach and perspective. Those we have found particularly useful for the cross-case analysis are the framework for socio-technological systems as described by Koppenjan and Groenewegen, the role perception of governments as interpreted by Groenewegen, and the five-forces industry analysis framework by Porter and others. An application of the general conception of the production function also has been helpful.

In compiling the narrative, use is made of complementary research that has been executed in parallel to this project, in particular into the role of unbundling and the 'ladder of investment' concept (Lemstra and Van Gorp, 2013); and a quantitative exploration of broadband performance (Lemstra, Van Gorp and Voogt, 2013).[1]

As most of the case studies have been focusing on the development of fixed broadband, this is also the primary focus of this concluding chapter. But placing our analysis in a dynamic context, we recognize the increasing role of mobile with each new generation of technologies and users.

We start the cross-case analytical narrative with a general, political framing of broadband developments.

16.2 The policy context: the role perception of governments

Depending on the position taken by governments, there is a stronger reliance on either market forces or on governmental support, particularly for fixed broadband. In Japan, for instance, the government provided financial support for Fibre to the Home (FttH) deployment in the form of financing support and tax incentives. (Jaag, Lutzenberger and Trinkner, 2009). The Korean government made FttH roll-out a part of its industrial policy (Kushida and Oh, 2006; Oh and Larson, 2011). In Australia, New Zealand and Singapore, there has been significant government intervention, both in allocating subsidies for FttX roll-out and in determining the structure and ownership or shareholdings associated with companies supplying high speed broadband (see e.g.: Jaag, Lutzenberger and Trinkner, 2009; Australian Government, 2013; iDA, 2013; New Zealand Government, 2013). In these countries, the government has adopted strong industrial policies supported by the logic of the developmental state.

At the other end of the spectrum, in the USA, the Federal Communications Commission (FCC) declared forbearance on unbundling of FttH with the aim to stimulate fibre deployments by incumbent operators (Cornell, 2005; Washburn, 2005), although it has extended its universal service subsidy funding to include broadband development in rural areas. This could be characterized as an extensive reliance on 'market forces' for driving broadband development by a regulatory state.

In the European Union the approach towards the broadband market and the supply of next-generation access has been primarily 'market driven', but with major adjustments to the regulatory regime attempting to reduce roll-out costs (e.g., sharing of ducts and parts of the mobile/wireless infrastructure) and to incentivize roll-out in underserved areas through state aid. In addition, special considerations relating to the appropriate cost calculations and return on capital, believed necessary to stimulate investment in broadband, have been applied.

Within the market economy of the European Union, the roles that different governments assume will vary along a continuum between a primarily regulatory or a primarily developmental state. The EU broadband policy and programmes associated with the 2020 Digital Agenda have many strong developmental elements, but the EU contribution to achieving these goals is primarily by means of market regulation and the delegation of responsibility for implementation to the member states.

Whether the 2020 goals will be achieved will depend on the roles that the member states play. For the wealthier states with strong infrastructure endowments and a market orientation, an emphasis on regulatory state roles may be sufficient. The UK may be the best example of this, while France would be expected to incorporate more developmental roles alongside regulatory roles. For the new member states, much greater emphasis on developmental state roles will be necessary. Different state governments will sit at different points along the continuum between the regulatory and developmental state in fashioning their respective programs for implementing the 2020 Digital Agenda objectives. Making the distinction between regulatory and developmental roles facilitates the interpretation of the differences that can be observed across the twelve country case studies.

---

[1] This quantitative analysis derives from a research project aimed at explaining broadband performance in the EU member states executed at the Delft University of Technology in collaboration with Ecorys, an economics research institute, and co-funded by ECTA, the European Competitive Telecommunications operators Association.

Next to these differences in role perceptions of governments, one can observe further differences within the European Union. Historical developments, which have become engrained in the formal and informal institutional environment, provide for differences in national legal systems; differences in roles and responsibilities between national, sub-regional and city governments; differences in political orientations and preferences relating to the role of the market; and differences in the way conflicts are resolved.

16.3 Emergence of the Internet

As we address broadband developments, these are typically preceded by narrowband in providing access to the Internet.[2] As the Internet emerged from the development of computer communications using packet switching in universities and research centres in the United States, the university communities in Europe were the first to connect to the (pre-cursor of) the Internet in their respective countries.[3] From these activities evolved Internet access for business and for the private citizen.

The pattern that can be discerned is that access to the Internet was realized in the academic communities in the early 1990s, with access by the public at large from the mid-1990s. Typically alternative providers were the first ISPs, while the

---

[2] For the history of the Internet, see e.g., Hafner and Lyon (1996) and Abbate (2000).

[3] Four major events have been instrumental for the Internet to develop towards its current day popularity: (1) the creation of the TCP/IP protocol in 1972 under the personal leadership of Vint Cerf, to be used universally across the Internet for information exchange; (2) the creation of the World-Wide-Web using the principle of hypertext developed in 1989 by (Sir) Timothy Berners-Lee, the application (html) that would unlock information stored in computers on a worldwide basis; (3) the introduction of the first popular browser Mosaic by Marc Andreesen in 1993; and (4) the transition of the Internet in 1995 from the research and educational domain to the private domain. It should be noted that fundamental to the development of the Internet has been the popularization of computing through the invention of the microprocessor in 1971 and the introduction of the PC, notably the Apple (I) in 1977, followed by the IBM PC in 1981 (Lemstra, 2006).

incumbents followed, and began to dominate the markets within a few years. A similar pattern of development appears to be underway with respect to broadband at each level of capacity expansion.

The case study on the Netherlands describes the leading role provided by SURFnet, a foundation with universities and academic institutions as members, in providing leading-edge broadband connectivity to the academic research centres and assuming a leading role in Europe. This activity started as early as 1985 and continues today with the provision of 10 Gbit/s light-paths.

16.4 PSTN: the legacy telephone network

The first means of accessing the Internet involved dial-up connections using PSTN, which became the infrastructure endowment facilitating Internet access. As a consequence Internet coverage became equivalent to PSTN coverage. In 1995 PSTN penetration ranged from 68.4 per 100 inhabitants in Sweden to 14.9 in Poland (OECD, 1999).[4] While the data implied that most households in Western Europe had the ability to connect to the Internet, households in Central Europe were in a far less favourable position.

In the member states in Central Europe, universal telephone service coverage was largely realized through mobile communication. In Poland and Latvia PSTN penetration peaked in 2006 and 2000, respectively. By 2011 the penetration had declined to 17.8 per 100 inhabitants in Poland and 25.4 in Latvia. (See Chapter 1, Tables 1.2 and 1.3). By 2013 mobile was well established all across Europe. Penetration ranged from 190.1 in Latvia to 105.8 in France. This explains an important difference in the starting position for the introduction of broadband, as well as in the role of mobile communication in broadband development between Western and Central European member states.

---

[4] The more appropriate metric for penetration is access lines per household, as the entities being served. The per household data has been calculated using total population and total household data from the OECD reports.

While coverage provides the ability to subscribe to a particular service, it is affordability that allows the transformation into actual subscriptions and usage. In comparison with the USA, the adoption of Internet access was originally constrained by the use of metered tariffs for telephone services, while a flat calling fee applied in the USA and a flat Internet fee from 1996. As the operators established Internet access points in every local exchange area this alleviated this issue as only the local metered tariff applied.

Adoption is further influenced by income. The business and private spending on telecommunications moved from a plateau of just above 2% of GDP in the period 1985–1995 to a peak in 2001 above 3.5%, thereafter slowly declining toward a level just below 3% in 2011 (OECD, 2013). This links to the underlying increase in the proportion of disposable household expenditure on telecommunications. From an index of 100 in 1990 it increased to approximately 130 in 2003 and remained relatively flat in the later years (OECD, 2005, 2013).

This aggregate data does not recognize that there is a large difference in GDP per capita across EU member states. For instance, in 1995 Germany had a GDP per capita of USD 30,216 compared to Poland USD 3,527. By 2012 the gap had become smaller but still remained significant, with EUR 32,600 against EUR 9,900 (see Table 1.3). Differences in per capita income among countries are as significant for next generation broadband growth as they were for creating the original PSTN.

In addition, fixed broadband investments per household and mobile broadband investment per capita strongly correlate with GDP.[5] Quantitative analysis suggests that investment in turn is the most important driver of broadband performance, followed by competition (Lemstra, Van Gorp and Voogt, 2013).[6]

The evolution from narrowband to broadband began around 2000 with the introduction of ADSL, and the PSTN becoming the infrastructure endowment for broadband. With different infrastructure endowments come different starting points and different trajectories for realizing the Digital Agenda targets. Differences in GDP per capita identify different financial capabilities for taking up broadband and realizing the EU broadband targets. The strong correlation between GDP and investment suggests that broadband is an infrastructural enabler of GDP growth, but GDP first must enable the take up of broadband.

The pattern that emerges is the difference in PSTN endowment between Western and Central European member states: i.e., between coverage of close to 100% and to around a peak of 30%. It explains the importance of mobile communications in Central Europe and explains why fixed broadband was the default starting position in Western Europe and mobile broadband the default position in Central Europe. It is also a factor in explaining the bottom-up activities in Central Europe, where alternative providers are using broadband LANs and fibre based broadband.

However, as fixed penetration is linked to homes and mobile penetration to population, mobile broadband is leading in absolute numbers. At the end of the case study period, the ratio of mobile to fixed broadband ranges from 0.98 in Belgium, through 2.4 in Denmark and Italy to 3.9 in Poland (see Table 1.3).

16.5 CATV cable networks: the legacy content distribution network

Next to PSTN, in a number of EU member states another copper-based network has been deployed – the distribution network for radio and television (RTV) signals using coaxial cables (cable-TV; CATV). The presence of a CATV-network provides the opportunity for Internet access and hence

---

[5] Note that the difference becomes smaller when purchasing power parities are considered, which affects the labour component of infrastructural works more than the equipment component.

[6] In the quantitative analysis, fixed broadband performance is defined as a composite index including (1) uptake; (2)

price; and (3) download data rate (Lemstra, Van Gorp and Voogt, 2013). See also Appendix 2.

infrastructure-based competition in broadband services supply. As such, it represents another infrastructure endowment.

The joint reception and distribution of RTV signals in apartment buildings has provided the basis for the development of CATV-networks. As typically only one network served a particular apartment block, housing area or city, many non-competing systems have emerged. Moreover, cable coverage has been limited largely to urban areas. Free-to-air terrestrial broadcasting was the way universal service for broadcast content was realized.

Following changes in regulation that permitted expansion into telecommunications services supply, these (local) systems have become subject to consolidation, typically resulting in a few major regional suppliers and sometimes a number of smaller city suppliers. As part of the consolidation, the systems have become interconnected using optical fibre. To be able to provide telecommunication services, the networks had to be upgraded from one-way RTV signal distribution to two-way telecommunications. With the inherent larger bandwidth provided by coaxial cables, the CATV operators were favourably positioned vis-à-vis the PSTN-based operators to provide broadband Internet access. In many countries the CATV operators took the lead in broadband supply, using DOCSIS modems.[7]

Recognizing that infrastructure-based competition is generally preferred by policy makers over access-based competition in the development of broadband, the question to be raised is why have the development trajectories of cable been so different across the EU member states?

It appears that almost all case studies have a particular story to tell. Considering the importance of infrastructure-based competition, it is informative to recognize the wide diversity of experience. At one extreme we have Italy, where the absence of cable networks is explained by the early liberalization of the Free-to-Air (FTA) television market, also allowing foreign broadcasters to transmit from the Italian territory. This halted CATV in its infancy. Also an effort towards cable deployment in the mid-1990s failed. It concerned the broadcasting/broadband network platform project SOCRATE, which was aimed at deploying fibre-optic and coaxial cables in the nineteen biggest Italian cities, with the target to reach about ten million people by 2002. Right after the privatization of Telecom Italia had started in 1997, the SOCRATE project slowed down due to changes in Telecom Italia's governance structure and the focus turned to the deployment of ADSL.

In Latvia cable service is available in the major cities, but the platform does not have a strong appeal to consumers looking for fixed broadband connectivity. The case authors observe: 'They would become strong competitors in the broadband market if cable TV operators used more aggressive marketing of Internet services and were able to change the traditional position of the Latvian society in perceiving CATV providers as TV providers only: currently less than 10% of CATV consumers are using Internet access service.'

In Denmark an initiative was taken to build a so-called hybrid fibre network as a shared infrastructure to pave the way for a fully integrated broadband network in 1985. In 1995, the network was closed down. The most important remaining impact is that it allowed TDC as telecom operator to engage in the provision of cable-TV.

The UK is an example where an early role of cable can be observed. Following the UK government's review of the duopoly of BT and Mercury in 1991, the period of 'managed competition' drew to an end. Until then cable companies were permitted to offer telephony only in partnership with Mercury or BT. With the policy change they were allowed to enter the market, providing infrastructure-based competition to BT, which was the regulator's (Oftel's) preferred form of

---

[7] DOCSIS: Data Over Cable Service Interface Specification. DOCSIS was developed by CableLabs and contributing companies. The first specification, DOCSIS version 1.0, was issued in March 1997. DOCSIS 2.0 was released in December 2001 with enhanced upstream data rates. DOCSIS 3.0, was released in August 2006, increasing download data rates to 100^+ Mbit/s and to introduce support for Internet Protocol version 6 (IPv6). Cross-version compatibility has been maintained across all versions of DOCSIS, with the devices falling back to the highest supported version in common between both endpoints: the cable modem and the cable-modem termination system (CMTS).

competition. The role of cable has diminished in more recent years, in part through strong competition from (premium) content services provided through satellite by BskyB.

In Germany, as a result of the late divestiture of cable by incumbent operator Deutsche Telekom, the role of cable networks was small in the beginning, but has been growing in recent years through involvement of Kabel Deutschland Gruppe and Liberty Global.

In Spain, the first cable initiatives appeared in the early 1990s. In 1995, the Cable Telecommunications regulated the cable telecommunications service. The Act allowed two operators to provide services in each district: Telefónica Cable (a new branch of the incumbent) by default and the awardee of a public tender. Roll-out and service implementation started in 1999. However, Telefónica Cable had to comply with a moratorium of eighteen months, which became eternal, as Telefónica focused its strategy on developing ADSL and never used the cable license. Being CATV-cable-based, Retevisión became the second largest operator after Telefónica.

In France the cable networks were deployed mainly in cities in the 1980s and 1990s. Today, these networks are mainly managed by Numericable, which is the largest cable-TV operator and cable Internet provider in France. The company was founded in July 2007 through the merger of two competing networks, Noos and NC Numericable.

In Flanders, Belgium the 'Multimedia in Vlaanderen' project, initiated in 1996, included as an objective the conversion of the Flemish cable infrastructure into an interactive broadband network offering broadcast, telecommunication and multimedia services. The project resulted in the creation of Telenet, with close to 100% coverage in Flanders, as the major competitor for incumbent Belgacom, as the explicit aim of the policy intervention.

In the Netherlands, the municipal involvement has led to CATV networks reaching 95% of households. The market liberalization resulted in the consolidation of these local networks into two main regional networks and a few smaller city networks. Perhaps the final step is the January

2014 bid by Liberty Global, owner of UPC serving 1.7 million subscribers, to acquire Ziggo, with 2.8 million subscribers.

Factors that can be distinguished as having had an influence on the development of CATV-networks into competitive broadband platforms are: (1) the original ownership, either private firm, municipality or PSTN incumbent; (2) the presence of competition in RTV signal distribution, terrestrial or satellite based; (3) regulations – telecom, RTV and content related; and (4) public policy. Whether the CATV networks evolved into competing broadband platforms appears to have been influenced by: (1) ownership, private or incumbent; (2) degree of entrepreneurship, the means to invest and to compete; and (3) a helping hand from public policy.

Is cable all about legacy or should we still be concerned with the development of these networks? As the case studies illustrate, CATV cable networks can play an important role in infrastructure-based competition for broadband. The application of DOCSIS-3 modems allows data rates of 100 Mbit/s and more to be provided. As such it pushes the upgrade of the PSTN towards VDSL and ultimately to fibre deployments.[8] Hence, in the competition for increasingly higher data rates CATV-cable pushes development towards next-generation Access (NGA) – from realizing the 30 Mbit/s Digital Agenda target to realizing the 100 Mbit/s target.

This suggests that any remaining potential of cable networks to contribute to infrastructure-based competition should be exploited. However, it is unlikely that cable networks will extend their geographical coverage, as any new trenching opportunity will be used to deploy fibre rather than copper.

---

[8] Note that while coaxial cable has an inherently higher transmission bandwidth compared to twisted-pair copper, for RTV signal distribution the coax is shared by multiple homes. Hence, as a shared medium, the effective data rate available per home depends on the number of simultaneous users. As the data requirements per user increases, the ratio of sharing needs to be reduced. To increase the network capacity, fibre deployments have reached the distribution cabinets, hence, the reference to Hybrid Fibre Coax (HFC) networks.

An important feature shown in the cases of Italy, Denmark and the Netherlands are the early attempts to create a national broadband network for communications and broadcasting combined. These attempts have failed for political or competitive reasons.

16.6 Attempting to create a level playing field: institutions and actors

While infrastructure endowments allow particular forms of competition to develop, it is regulation and the regulator that attempt to assure that a level playing field is established as part of market liberalization and that access is provided to the legacy infrastructure of the PSTN operator.

While the monopoly position of the PSTN incumbent was a subject of investigation by some national governments in the early 1980s, it is the publication of the Green Paper by the European Commission in 1987 that set off an EU-wide program of liberalization, privatization and regulation (EC, 1987). As Cawley explains in Chapter 3 the initial objective concerned the break-up of the monopolies of the PSTN incumbents. While the resale of telephone services provided some degree of competition at the retail level, it is Internet access that allowed both access-based and infrastructure-based competition to develop, not only on price but also on the quality of the services – in particular relating to data communication.

However, as the incumbents were privatized, they became subject to the regime of financial markets – with expectations of increasing revenues and profits. It should not come as a surprise that incumbent operators reluctantly let go of their monopoly positions.[9] As the emerging competitors have been in many ways dependent on the network of the incumbent, both price based discrimination (margin squeeze) and non-price based discrimination (delays, unfavourable contract conditions, limited access to facilities, etc.) became common.

The more effective means to frustrate the development of effective competition appears to be non-price discrimination, as this is much more difficult to demonstrate in the form of hard evidence in cases brought before the regulator or in court cases. The allegations concerning these practices lead to intervention by regulators, in the extreme cases applying or threatening to apply the more intrusive remedy of functional separation.

The most salient case is that of the UK. The functional separation of BT with 'equivalence of inputs' is the main topic of the chapter on the UK. In Italy functional separation applied to Telecom Italia (TI), whereby the regulator decided to go one step further in applying 'structural separation'. The two key incentives for TI in proposing and accepting the Undertakings were: freezing (and ultimately avoiding) the potentially heavy sanctions for violation of fair business practices, and avoiding scrutiny by the Competition Authority.

In Poland a similar form of discontent with the behaviour of the incumbent had occurred. The remedy required the intervention of Anna Streżyńska, as the new President of the regulatory agency, in 2006. Ultimately, as a result of negotiations between the operator and the regulatory authority, an agreement was signed in 2009, in which TP committed to the proper performance of all regulatory duties imposed and to the implementation of a series of actions to ensure transparency and non-discrimination in the relations between operators, in return for the withholding of measures undertaken by UKE towards functional separation of the company.

The three cases on functional separation demonstrate the need for a strong NRA to guide the process from monopoly to effective competition. However, the strength of an NRA is not solely grounded in its institutional independence. Effective regulation requires a strong leader, able to face the strong (political) power of the incumbent operator.[10]

---

[9] This also leads to a wave of investments abroad, in other incumbents, and in new business opportunities: e.g., content; implying horizontal and vertical expansion of the firm (see e.g., Lemstra, 2006).

[10] Anecdotal evidence suggests that strong leadership at the introduction of the liberalization process has played an important role in the case of the Netherlands (Professor Dr Jens C. Arnbak) and in Denmark (Jørgen Abild Andersen, who currently holds the chair of the the Digital Economy Policy Committee at the OECD, formerly the ICCP).

The fact that in only three of the twelve cases the need to apply functional separation has proven to be necessary raises the question 'why not in the other countries?' One possible explanation is that the regulatory regime was effective from the start, the incumbent being more compliant; hence, there was no need to apply the more intrusive remedy of functional separation. An alternative explanation may be found in culture-related differences, whereby cultures (and political systems) have different approaches to resolving conflicts, some cultures being more focused on deliberations and others more on confrontation.

What can be concluded is that, where applied, the remedy appears to be having some success, given the absence of any (major) subsequent complaints from alternative operators. The fact that the remedies include the setting and monitoring of key performance indicators may contribute to the early detection and resolution of remaining issues.[11]

16.7 The role of alternative operators

After the liberalization of the market, attracted by the prospects of the Internet and fuelled by the financial sector, many alternative operators emerged in the late 1990s. Following the collapse of the Internet/telecom bubble, many entrants defaulted. The OECD reported 142 defaults and an amount of USD 183 billion for the period 1999–2003 (OECD, 2005).[12] In most member states a few main alternative operators remain, such as Jazztel in Spain and Tele2 in the Netherlands. Probably the best example of an early and ambitious entry was Fastweb in Italy in 1999. A very successful case is represented by Free in France, starting in 1999. Also the city carriers in Germany are a prime example of new broadband players.

Fastweb aimed to build a nation-wide network based on FttH, using regulatory-based access to the civil infrastructure coupled with an entrepreneurial vision. However, the price range of FttH services initially offered by Fastweb met with limited response (triple-play was offered at prices ranging between EUR 50–80 per month) and the company soon had to change its business model and try to profit from serving customers with LLU and other wholesale-based services. Today, Fastweb serves approximately 270,000 customers over FttH and has achieved coverage of more than two million residential or business units.

One of the most successful alternative operators has been Free/Iliad in France.[13] The company has been at the forefront of Internet access since its inception as an ISP in 1999. It launched its first 'broadband' offer (512 kbit/s downstream; 128 kbit/s upstream) for EUR 29.99 per month for unlimited use and a modem for free in 2002. Early in 2004 Free introduced an ADSL-based triple-play offer including a special modem – the 'Freebox' – without changing the price. In May 2004, making use of full local loop unbundling, Free offered Internet access at 2 Mbit/s, and access to more than 100 TV channels. In June it upgraded its offer to 5 Mbit/s downstream and 350 kbit/s upstream, always keeping its EUR 29.99 price.

By the end of 2007, Free/Iliad's customer base had grown to about 2.9 million ADSL subscribers, of which 81.5% was provided on the basis of unbundling. As the regulator ARCEP approved ADSL2+, Free started to offer 15 Mbit/s down and 1 Mbit/s up, again at EUR 29.99, including a new FreeBox version. In 2006, Free/Iliad joined the 'Paris-Digital City' initiative of the municipality, marking the start of fibre deployment in Paris. In July 2007 Free/Iliad announced its fibre service providing 50 Mbit/s (again) at EUR 29.99. In August, Free announced its 100/50 Mbit/s offer at EUR 29.99, with two FreeBox units, including

---

[11] In the UK case, an attempt has been made to assess the effect of functional separation on broadband market performance. However, the simultaneous lowering of local loop unbundling prices has made the separation of causes and effects difficult.

[12] See for a detailed discussion of the telecom developments before, during and after the bubble Lemstra (2006).

[13] This account is based on a research effort exploring the role of unbundling in Europe. The findings have been reported in a conference contribution at the Florence School of Regulation (Lemstra and Van Gorp, 2013).

router, Wi-Fi functionality and an HD-compatible digital video recorder. Although this has been an all-too-rare case of highly effective competition provided by a new entrant, it does demonstrate that the playing field can be made level in a supportive policy and regulatory environment.

A salient characteristic of competition in the telecommunications market in Germany illustrates the early uptake of unbundling. The regional and local carriers founded by the regional/local utilities in the mid-1990s anticipated the business opportunities that the introduction of competition would provide. These companies have been able to establish a firm foothold in their 'home' markets as a result of their ties with their parent companies and their knowledge of the specific needs of the regional/local retail and business customers. They have been able to exploit a strong brand awareness. Examples are Hansenet in Hamburg with a DSL market share of about 50%, M'net in Munich with a DSL market share of 20% and NetCologne in Cologne with a share of about 50%. Hansenet has, since it was established in 1995, expanded its network outside Hamburg to approximately 150 cities in Germany. Aside from its own infrastructure the company used bitstream services from DT and QSC.

In addition to these examples, alternative operators have emerged in every EU member state, some of them having (or having had) operations in multiple member states, such as Tele2 in Sweden, Belgium, France, Italy and the Netherlands. Also the private telecommunications infrastructures of utility companies have been the basis for entry into public broadband services supply, such as the networks exploited by the railway companies (NL: Telfort; ES: Adif; LV: Latvijas Dzelzcel); the energy companies (NL: Enertel; UK: Energis; DK: DONG, Syd Energi, Waoo!; ES: Albura; LV: Latvenergo; DE: swb AG, EWETEL) and by water/sanitation utilities (FR: Bouygues). These utility-based companies have the further benefit of rights-of-way, synergies in outside plant works and an existing customer base that can be leveraged. To this list we should add the incumbent operators going abroad, such as FT/Orange into Belgium and Denmark, TeliaSonera into Ireland and Denmark, KPN into Ireland and the Czech

Republic, etc. – a list that can be extended further when mobile interests also are included.

In the case of Denmark, it has been fibre deployment by the energy utilities that has boosted NGA deployment. DONG Energy (which has sold its fibre network facilities to the incumbent telecom operator TDC) and SE (Syd Energi), the electricity provider in South Jutland, serve approximately 200,000 customers. South Jutland is one of the least densely populated regions in Denmark, but is the region with the best coverage by optical fibres.

The case studies document that a wide variety of types of new entrants have been able to enter telecommunications markets as alternative operators in most countries. But only in a few cases have they been able to provide real competition to the incumbent operators. There are competitors, but relatively little effective competition. The necessary expansion of infrastructure networks to meet the goals of the 2020 Digital Agenda provides an opportunity for governments to apply regulatory state roles to enhance competition and use market forces as the primary vehicle for achieving those goals.

16.8 Unbundling and the 'ladder of investment'

Attempts by regulators to reduce the barriers to entry for competitors have focused on unbundling infrastructure access from services provision and establishing conditions where new entrants can grow into the market by climbing a 'ladder of investment'.

Various studies and reports have investigated the effects of local loop unbundling on the development of broadband markets. As Cawley reports in Chapter 3: 'On balance, the empirical literature is inconclusive about whether access regulation stimulates or harms long-term competition and infrastructure investments, including the development of broadband.' To this review of the literature we can now add the qualitative insights obtained from the country case studies, as well as the results of a parallel research effort using mini-case studies aimed at investigating the role of unbundling and the applicability of the 'ladder of investment' concept.

The principle behind the 'ladder of investment' concept is that at the lowest rung of the ladder the barrier to market entry is also the lowest: little investment is required from the alternative operator to enter the market. Having established a customer base of sufficient size using a wholesale product such as resale or bitstream, the alternative operator will be enticed to decrease the dependency on the incumbent and the fees to be paid to the incumbent by investing more and thereby increasing the degree of possible product differentiation. Theoretically, at the highest rung of the ladder, the alternative operator would use a business model that is fully facilities-based, essentially providing for inter-platform competition (Cave, 2004, 2006). This means that 'the degree of unbundling', the regulated wholesale prices and the 'ladder of investment' concept are closely related.

Analysts have argued that for the progression on the 'ladder of investment' to work it is imperative that the prices set for the wholesale products at the different rungs provide the appropriate incentives for alternative operators to invest. Some analyst have also argued that the access price needs to start low and increase over time, in order to 'burn' the bottom-most rung off the ladder. Assuring these conditions are realized is a prime task of the national regulators. Additional incentives to climb the ladder of investments stem from the ability for alternative operators to gain more control over the functionality they can offer to their customers.

Ten years following the introduction of unbundling in Europe, there has been a significant shift from resale forms of competition and bitstream towards unbundling. Moreover, the first cases of alternative operators transitioning to fibre-based access can be observed. The extent to which full facilities-based competition, including duplication of the access network, is achievable for competitors depends on the network economics.[14]

The developments in the UK are a good illustration of how unbundling affects broadband.[15] Unbundling and the provision of collocation came into force in August 2000 as an amendment of the license of BT. By January 2001 BT had published a reference offer for full, shared and sub-loop unbundling; the price was to be set by BT on the same terms as it offered its own service provider business. However, the uptake remained very small, By October 2001 only 137 lines were unbundled, growing to a total of 785 by July 2002. Resale and bitstream remained far more popular. See Figure 16.1.[16]

From March the momentum increased and by December 2002 the prices of the nine leading broadband providers had converged as the market matured. The range of the highest to the lowest price fell from more than £20 to less than £6. By the first quarter of 2005 broadband penetration had reached 7.2 million lines and 31% of households. Of these lines, 5.1 million were served through the PSTN and 2.1 through cable. Out of the 5.1 million lines ISPs served, 3.3 million customers were using bitstream products from BT (46% of the total). The penetration achieved was approximately two thirds of that achieved in leading countries, such as Sweden and the Netherlands.

In 2004–2005 Ofcom[17], the national regulatory agency, conducted a major review of the market (the Telecoms Strategic Review), which revealed

---

[14] See for instance the study by WIK Consult on viability of competition in NGA (2008).

[15] This description of the UK developments draws upon the Chapter 9 contribution on the UK by Richard Cadman; the book by Maldoom et al. (2005); a study by Analysys Mason (2010); OECD Communications Outlook (2001, 2003); EC Implementation Reports and related annexes (EC, 1998a, 1998b, 1999, 2000, 2001, 2002, 2003, 2004, 2006, 2007, 2008a, 2009, 2010a); the study on broadband internet access costs (Van Dijk, 2011); the COCOM report (EC, 2011); and company websites www.Netindex.com and www.akamai.com.

[16] The EC has applied different data collection moments: 2001–2003 October; 2004–2005 July; 2006 October; 2008–2010 January. This explains the absence of the year 2007. The data set is otherwise very complete, where necessary interpolation has been applied.

[17] In 2003, the activities of Oftel, the national regulatory agency, were merged with those of the Independent Television Commission, the Radiocommunications Agency, the Radio Authority and the Broadcasting Standards Commission to become Ofcom, the Office of Communications.

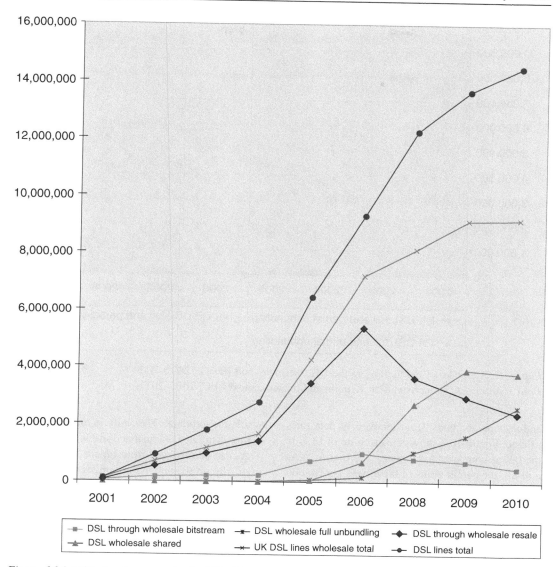

Figure 16.1 DSL developments in the UK, 2001–2010
Data sources: EC Implementation Reports and related annexes EC, 2001–2011.

some of the issues that providers depending on BT' services were experiencing. The Telecoms Strategic Review resulted in the functional separation of the incumbent BT with the provision of 'equivalence of inputs' (see Section 16.6). In a parallel effort, Ofcom began the market review of the wholesale local access market in line with the obligations under the Regulatory Framework.

Ofcom reviewed the cost orientation and concluded that a separate weighted average cost of capital for the low-risk local access network business was to be applied, resulting in a substantial price reduction. Prices for a fully unbundled line dropped from € 24.27 in 2003 through EUR 15.44 in 2004 to EUR 10.48 in 2005. Three effects resulted: (1) a catch-up in LLU; (2) a drop in

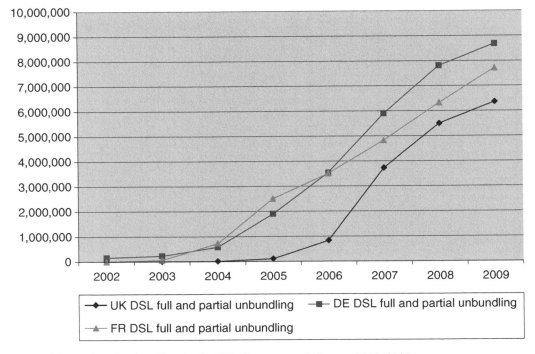

Figure 16.2 Uptake of unbundling in the UK, Germany and France, 2002–2009
Data sources: EC Implementation Reports and related annexes EC, 2001–2011.

end-user prices; and (3) an increase in data rates offered. Figure 16.2 shows the catch-up of LLU in the UK as compared to Germany and France.[18] As a result, the gap in terms of broadband penetration with the leading countries was reduced from approximately 33% to approximately 15%. As Cadman pointed out in his research, the quick catch-up was facilitated by the possibility of transferring the customer base from bitstream and resale to unbundling.

Figure 16.3 shows the composition of the DSL wholesale portfolio over time. The figure illustrates the change in the composition of the portfolio coinciding with the change in prices of the unbundling products. It shows the sensitivity of the alternative operators to price in their choice of

wholesale product. The shift in uptake towards higher data rates is illustrated in Figure 16.4.

As can be observed from Figure 16.5 Oftel had originally set the unbundling prices relatively high compared to other countries. This is probably linked to the early introduction of competition in the UK – the duopoly – aimed at creating an alternative infrastructure through the licensing of Mercury Communications. In pursuing this objective unbundling was at the time considered less desirable.[19]

The UK case shows that alternative operators do 'climb the ladder of investment' if the conditions are set to encourage it, at least for the lower rungs examined here – from resale and bitstream to unbundling (shared and full). In the UK the role of unbundling is significant and amounts to 70% of

---

[18] Note that partial unbundling refers to the situation whereby the incumbent continues to provide voice services, while an alternative operator provides Internet access using a higher frequency band on the same copper wire to the customer premises; also referred to as shared lines.

[19] At the time Oftel claimed that: 'the introduction of access to the copper loop would not do anything to promote local competition in the UK, and could jeopardize the development of competition already underway' (EC, 1997).

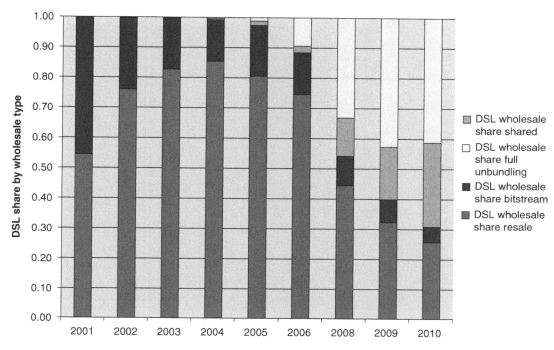

Figure 16.3 DSL share by wholesale type in the UK, 2001–2010
Data sources: EC Implementation Reports and related annexes EC, 2001–2011.

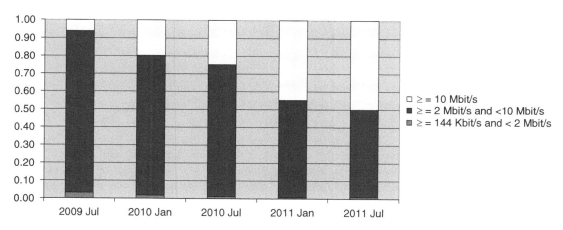

Figure 16.4 Developments in data rates in the UK, July 2009–July 2011
Data sources: EC Implementation Reports and related annexes EC, 2001–2011.

the total wholesale market in 2010. A similar account can be provided on the basis of the mini-case studies on France and Germany as part of the parallel research effort, with unbundling

having had a much earlier start and larger share in Germany.

The city operators in Germany also moved up the 'ladder of investment'. The majority of the

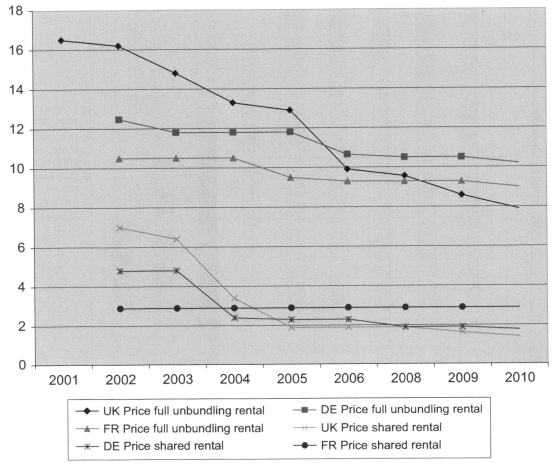

Figure 16.5 Comparison prices for unbundling in the UK, Germany and France, 2001–2010
Data sources: EC Implementation Reports and related annexes EC, 2001–2011.

investments in FttH/B are being made by city carriers and municipalities in their regions through the municipal public utilities companies (*Stadtwerke*). The reason is that the majority of the investment needed to deploy fibre is allocated to the passive infrastructure, and *Stadtwerke* and city carriers are the owners of this passive infrastructure. The *Stadtwerke* are public companies in charge of providing services such as energy and water and they are used to providing 'patient capital' investments that earn long term returns. This is significant as there are more than a thousand *Stadtwerke* in Germany.

The case of Free/Illiad is illustrative of the progression on the 'ladder of investment', a concept that the company has used explicitly in its communications with the market. In 2006, Free/Iliad joined the 'Paris-Digital City' initiative of the municipality, marking the start of fibre deployment in Paris. In July 2007, Free/Iliad announced its fibre service. The company planned to reach four million homes in Paris, Montpellier, Lyon and Valenciennes. The company has relied for its early fibre deployments on access to the Paris sewer system and on additional trenching.

Since a favourable ruling in September 2008 by ARCEP, Iliad now also makes use of the France Telecom ducts. To further reduce roll-out costs, use is made of aerial solutions and facilities belonging to the municipalities. To create a viable fibre-based business case, only those areas or neighbourhoods are targeted where the company has at least a market share of 15%, leveraging the density of existing subscribers. According to IDATE the fibre deployment by Free/Iliad had passed 450.000 homes by June 2011. This is comparable with the 550.000 homes passed by SFR. The deployment by the alternative operators now compares very favourably with the approximately 820,000 homes passed by the incumbent FT.

The pattern that the case studies reflect is that the progression on the 'ladder of investment' is very sensitive to the prices set for the wholesale products at the different rungs. The cases also show that unbundling is a necessary but not sufficient condition for moving to the 'final rung' of the ladder. Through the 'stepping stones' provided by resale, bitstream and unbundling, alternative operators must build a sufficiently large and dense customer base, upon which they can make an attractive business case for the transition to fibre-based access.

16.9 Private initiatives: grass-roots and leap-frogging

Next to municipalities getting involved in broadband supply, many private entities and citizens have become active in exploiting the broadband opportunities. This category of actors includes the many SME-ISPs in Latvia, as well as the fibre operators in Bulgaria.[20]

In Latvia some 240 fixed broadband service providers are competing with the main operators as well as one other, mostly in limited areas, even within one apartment block. There is a wide use of Ethernet technologies by these small companies in the provision of broadband in apartment buildings.

Although unique, the Bulgarian case is instructive, as Rood's research study shows:

In 2005, the broadband market in Bulgaria was almost non-existent, and broadband penetration stood at less than 1 percent of the population of 7.7 million. The steady growth of broadband subscriber lines and emergence of high-speed offerings can be mainly attributed to the efforts of local broadband LAN services providers. Their service answers the growing need among users for an affordable broadband product, with high speeds and quality of connections. In recent years, broadband LAN has developed into the dominant type of access technology in use. Today, about 91 percent of all fixed subscriber broadband lines offer service over 2 Mbit/s, and nearly 55 percent exceed data rates of 10 Mbit/s, making Bulgaria the leading member state in the EU regarding local penetration of over 10 Mbit/s lines [in 2008]. People were wiring up their neighbourhood without regulation by the (local) government(s), keeping building costs and operational costs low. These low costs have been a key driver for the fast increase in both the number of LAN operators and their subscribers. A typical 10 Mbit/s symmetric Broadband LAN subscription costs EUR 10.22 per month, a 50 Mbit/s subscription around EUR 22.50. [In 2010], there are nearly 670 official ISPs that provide broadband LAN Internet access throughout Bulgaria, but interviewed experts have indicated that the actual number is close to 2,000. These unregistered ISPs, however, mostly operate on a very local basis and usually do not serve more than a few dozen subscribers each. In 2008 ISP Cluster performed a survey among peer ISPs to assess the size of the area covered by an ISP and its subscribers: 55% covered a residential area in a city; 16% served one or several city districts; 7% served an entire city; 13% a town or city and its vicinity; and 9% provided regional coverage. (Rood, 2010).

These examples of 'grass roots' initiatives, largely of private citizens or single/few-person entities, occurring in the member states where PSTN is underdeveloped, are providing a leapfrog in technology – going straight to fibre. The Bulgarian case suggests this is made possible by the absence, or lax enforcement, of building codes and town regulations, which allows fibre to be

---

[20] The information on Bulgaria is derived from the TPRC conference contribution by Rood (2010).

'strung on facades of buildings'.[21] Compared to underground deployment – either fibre cables in ducts or cables being directly buried – these above ground deployments are significantly less expensive. The Analysys Mason report on the costs of deploying fibre-based broadband in the UK reflects £8 per metre in the case of aerial deployment against £100 per metre for fibre buried under road pavement (Analysys Mason for GBP, 2008).

Anecdotal evidence related to the Latvian case suggests that the many ISPs are a result of individual citizens' motivation to improve Internet access and their willingness to share the solution with neighbours and family in an apartment block. These small-scale entrepreneurial activities are executed as a side job. Not being listed at the stock exchange avoids the constant pressures of revenue and profit growth and may explain the endurance of these service offerings and the absence of any consolidation of these initiatives. As the case authors suggest, this situation may change when the incumbent Lattelecom progresses with rolling out fibre-based next-generation access.

The emerging pattern is that private and bottom-up initiatives emerge when the broadband supply from the operators is insufficient or lacking.

16.10 The role of relative outsiders: using demand aggregation

In Section 16.5 we observed that infrastructure-based competition can provide better broadband performance than access-based competition alone. In a duopolistic market of two incumbents, a PSTN and a CATV operator, this relative advantage may turn into a disadvantage when the transition to a new infrastructure is to be considered: i.e., the transition to FttH. Hence, some analysts suggest that 'two is not enough' for realizing full fibre-based next-generation access. The case of Belgium-Flanders points to this effect with hardly any deployment of fibre. The case of the

Netherlands appeared to be the same, until a third actor and relative outsider emerged: Reggefiber.

The intriguing questions the Netherlands account raises are: 'why did this 'third actor' emerge?' and: 'why did this type of third actor only emerge in the Netherlands?'

The opportunity for entry was provided by the housing corporation 'Portaal' wishing to enhance the value of its property by connecting its homes with fibre, providing ultra-fast Internet access to new residents. VolkerWessels Telecom was the designated contractor to execute the works. Wessels recognized a wider business opportunity to develop open-access fibre networks on the basis of demand aggregation, provided by, among others, the housing corporations. Private equity funding helped establish the firm Reggefiber for that purpose.

Demand aggregation using pre-subscription became the leading principle for fibre deployments. In that way the critical issue of assuring a minimum level of uptake to create a profitable business case was resolved. Even today, with KPN as Reggefiber's major shareholder, this remains the leading principle, with advertisements announcing 'fibre will come to your town if you wish'. Some business analysts have observed that the endgame has also played an important role in the venture being started and becoming successful: the prospect of being acquired by the incumbent operator.

The question why this 'third actor' only emerged in the Netherlands is more difficult to answer. Similar construction firms are likely present in all EU member states. A more detailed comparison of Belgium-Flanders and the Netherlands shows that the two countries had much in common, including a lack of fibre deployments, but differ in the absence of housing corporations in Belgium-Flanders. This means that a natural point of demand aggregation is missing.

16.11 Interpreting the role of competition

The liberalization process was aimed at ending the monopolies and introducing competitive markets. Internet access became the pre-eminent service that

---

[21] Anecdotal evidence suggests that the mayor of Budapest has announced that such 'façade installations' have to be replaced by underground deployment of fibre.

has benefitted from this change in regime. Regulation has enabled the change, by opening the PSTN network for access-based entry and by allowing the cable operators to provide telecommunications services. The current regulatory debate has become centred on the roles of inter-platform and intra-platform competition: i.e., access-based versus infrastructure-based competition.

There is little doubt that competition drives broadband performance – in line with economic theory – as illustrated by the structure-conduct-performance (SCP) paradigm. This paradigm has informed a quantitative research project into broadband performance in the EU, which has been executed in parallel to the qualitative research reported in the case studies in this book. (Lemstra, Van Gorp and Voogt, 2013).

The quantitative analysis reflected the variance in the mode and intensity of competition as exemplified by the case studies. The analysis reinforced the importance of wholesale pricing. It showed that the broadband market share of the PSTN incumbent is negatively related to broadband performance, irrespective of the type of competition: i.e., infrastructure-based or access-based. Where present, infrastructure-based competition has a stronger effect on performance than access-based competition only. Also, where there is strong competition between the PSTN and CATV-cable, access-based competition makes a relatively smaller contribution towards improving broadband performance.

However, drawing the conclusion that 'two is enough' for reaching optimal performance – i.e., infrastructure-based competition without access-based competition – is not correct. This is indicated by the important role that the LLU wholesale price level has on broadband performance. The analysis showed that the LLU wholesale price is the most important regulatory variable in explaining broadband performance. This is the second-largest driver of performance, after investments which are driven by GDP per household.

The study concluded that LLU serves as a 'catalyst' for competition, whereby LLU prices are important for LLU-based players to exert pressure on the incumbent players, PSTN and cable alike. Hence, on the basis of the analysis, we can conclude that a regulatory regime which favours only infrastructure competition is not enough to deliver strong broadband performance.

This econometric analysis identified the regularities in the data relating to broadband development and competition in Europe, and fits all the country case study experiences with the exception of Denmark, which ranks near the top in broadband penetration but near the bottom in terms of competition. The incumbent operator TDC dominates all technology platforms: PSTN, CATV, fibre and mobile. The driving force in Denmark seems to be its developmental state policies of allowing employers tax deductibility for the supply of PCs in their employees' homes, and activist government policies requiring that business with government be done electronically by both organizations and individuals. The data suggest this can be successful in a country with a high GDP per capita.

16.12 The role of government: setting the national Digital Agenda

In the previous sections we have discussed the role of private actors in the supply of broadband services in Europe, within a context where the government assumed responsibility for promoting competition as part of the market liberalization process. Beyond this regulatory role, we can observe different roles being assumed by local, regional and central governments in the provision of broadband services. This ranges from information supply by central governments, through a regional government shaping a competitive player, to municipalities declaring market failure and undertaking supply of broadband services. See for a theoretical framing Chapter 2 Research approach and perspective, Section 2.3.

The Lisbon Agenda and the Digital Agenda for Europe are examples where governments inform the market process. By setting goals they assist the market in developing in a certain direction. Consistency in the plans reduces the uncertainties related to government intervention in markets. The request from the European Commission to member state governments to develop plans for the realization of the Digital Agenda at the national level fits the subsidiarity principle, the idea that a central authority should have a subsidiary function, performing only those tasks which cannot be performed effectively at a more immediate or local level.

We can observe (formal) national broadband plans that were ahead of the EC plans (e.g., Spain), plans that were more ambitious, either in target and/or in timing (e.g., Denmark), plans that follow the Digital Agenda (e.g., the Netherlands), as well as plans that were more modest in the target setting (e.g., the United Kingdom). The national broadband plans were often followed by more specific initiatives facilitating broadband market development by sharing information, by bringing together the broadband actors, identifying the roles of private and government actors, sharing best practices, etc. (e.g., Germany, the Netherlands).

We should note that the publication of national Digital Agendas was not the first sign of governments developing ICT-oriented policies and broadband plans. It appears that the Lisbon Agenda and its successors have provided for convergence in the national policies and plans.

The emerging pattern is that Digital Agendas and broadband plans have been developed at the EU level and at the national level. Most of these agendas and plans have been adjusted as reality caught up with the plans, in particular the financial and later the economic crisis. The case study evidence is insufficient to determine to what degree the plans have contributed to broadband development. The case studies do suggest that the national broadband and related plans have contributed to the awareness of the importance of broadband for economic development. Moreover, the cases show that the various actors involved in broadband development have been brought together for information-sharing, planning and implementation purposes. A positive effect may be inferred.

A good illustration is the German administrative ruling which provides the *Bundesnetzagentur* with the possibility of expanding the market analysis period from three to a maximum of six years, to improve the consistency and predictability of regulation, as well as the security of planning and investment for undertakings, provided the European Commission has no objections to such prolongation.

16.13 The role of the government: stimulating the demand side

As reflected in many of the case studies, the role of government is primarily seen in stimulating broadband demand, while the role of the private actors is the supply of broadband networks and services. These two activities together should propel the 'virtuous circle of broadband', as positioned in the Digital Agenda for Europe. (EC, 2010b) For that to happen, the barriers identified should be resolved, see Figure 16.6. The research reported in this book is addressed primarily to 'lack of investment in networks', although resolution of this issue will have beneficial effects on several others, such as interoperability and fragmented markets.

This 'role division' is clearly reflected in the policy of national governments. Denmark's *The information society year 2000* report from 1994 reflects the understanding that infrastructure and service development initiatives are mutually interdependent. The Danish policy has been and is to intervene in this interdependent relationship by way of promoting the service side. This includes the promotion of e-government (G2G), as well as the promotion of electronic communications between public administrations and citizens and businesses (G2C and G2B).

In Germany initiatives for local governance started under the label MEDIA@KOMM, with the aim to develop and apply multimedia in towns and communities. Within the 'BundOnline 2005' initiative, a modernization of federal administration was carried out, whereby all governmental services suitable for such provision were transformed into online services. The currently ongoing MEDIA@KOMM-Innovation project aims to support the development of regional and local e-government networks and provides for the exchange of experience and best practices, as well as for harmonisation and standardisation of e-government solutions.

The case of the Netherlands provides for the creation of *Kenniswijk* ('Knowledge Quarter'): '...a real-life environment to 'test the consumer market of the future' aimed at (1) breaking the perceived deadlock between infrastructure development and service development; (2) improving the competitive

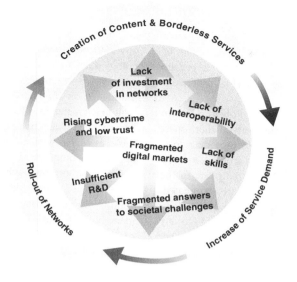

Figure 16.6 Digital Agenda virtuous circle
Source: EC COM(2010) 245 A digital agenda for Europe (2010b).

position of The Netherlands; (3) sharing the knowledge obtained through *Stedenlink* (City link); and (4) providing input for government policy.' The all-fibre pilot project in the city of Nuenen, involving 7,500 households in an area representative of the Dutch population, was set-up to develop and test new services and applications as part of the *Kenniswijk* project.

16.15 The role of regulation: removing barriers

Following the initial implementation of access regulation and the application of remedies to resolve the inappropriate use of market power that hinders entry, regulators are beginning to focus on removing barriers to broadband deployment, in particular the deployment of fibre to the premises. These measures largely relate to two categories of issues: (1) the access to apartment buildings; and (2) reducing the costs of fibre deployment.

Two case studies, of France and Poland, draw attention to the removal of barriers related to the in-building wiring. The French government proposed legislative measures that outline the principle of sharing the terminal section of optical fibre networks, and endowed the regulator ARCEP with regulatory powers in that area, notably for setting the technical and pricing terms for a system of infrastructure sharing. This requires an agreement between property (co)owners and a telecom operator providing the terminal part of the network – the 'building operator'.

To allow other operators to offer their services the 'building operator' must offer passive access at the point of sharing. Such access must allow operators to control the entire technical chain by installing their own equipment at the sharing point. Access can be realized in several ways: (1) co-financing offer: the operator participates in the financing of the shared network prior to its deployment by purchasing a usage right in the long term; (2) access offer: after the deployment of the network, the operator buys a long term usage right; and (3) offer comprising access to the leased line (on the model of the local loop unbundling).

Investment offers or access offers allow an operator to have a long term usage right on all or part of the fibre of the shared network. It also allows sharing of financial risk between the various oper- ators who will then use the shared network to provide high data rate services. These offers must be presented to other operators irrespective of whether the project is carried out by a private operator or a local authority as part of a network of public initiative.

Building access in the case of Poland refers to three basic rules. First, the property owner, oper- ator, and manager are required to provide a tele- communications entrepreneur access to the property and building, including the place in the building where the indoor cables are terminated. Secondly, the owner of cable ducts on the property is obliged to provide access to these ducts to any entrepreneur who has no alternative of using other (existing) cable ducts, in order to provide telecom- munications services. Thirdly, the owner of a tele- communications cable connected to a building or distributed within a building is required to provide access to any telecommunications entrepreneur to all or part of this cable, if there is no possibility of connecting another telecommunications cable.

In terms of reducing the deployment cost of fibre roll-out, the cases of France and Poland show clear examples of regulatory guidance. In France the regulation of Orange's civil engineering infrastruc- ture is considered essential for the deployment of an optical fibre local loop such that also alternative operators can supply end-users with ultra-fast broadband services. Orange is obliged to provide access to its ducts to other operators deploying FttH networks under transparent, non-discriminatory and cost-oriented conditions. The offer by Orange for that purpose is regulated by ARCEP, including its price. Orange must also provide access to its poles and air support to other operators deploying FttH networks. This infrastructure will therefore be leveraged, especially in rural areas, where it is expected to reduce deployment costs.

The case of Poland points to barriers formed by existing local plans containing numerous prohib- itions and restrictions, often factually unjustified (e.g., prohibitions on an investment location just because it has been formally classified as a 'project likely to significantly affect the environment'), which thus create areas unavailable for the develop- ment of telecommunications networks. The Act of 2010, addressing the rights of way, imposes an obligation on road managers – the General Director- ate for National Roads and Motorways and local governments – requiring the construction of tech- nology ducts for placing telecommunications cables when roads are built or upgraded. The Act also introduced an innovative solution for conducting joint investments in cables and ducts, in addition to the separate ownership of individual optic fibres in a cable, as well as wires in cables and individual ducts in multi-opening ducts.

The case of the Netherlands shows how the NRA can use market developments in setting the appropriate conditions for a viable fibre deploy- ment business case. Triggered by the emergence of Reggefiber deploying open access fibre net- works, OPTA has issued a new wholesale price regulation. It has based its analysis on the real-life business case presented by Reggefiber.

The German telecom law also allows the collo- cation of telecommunications infrastructure with other facilities (water, gas pipes, power lines) to further minimize the costs of the development of new broadband networks: Upon a written request from an interested provider of public telecommuni- cations networks, undertakings and legal persons of public law in possession of facilities that can be used for the development and laying of next gen- eration networks are obliged to make an offer to share such facilities. Additionally, the Telecom Law of 2012 provides for the sharing of roads, waterways and railway infrastructure belonging to the German federal government.

Case studies executed by researchers in the field of techno-economic analysis at the University of Ghent suggest that the total gains of combining the broadband trenching with utilities can yield total FttH project cost savings of up to 7% (Tahon, 2013).

16.16 The role of governments: removing barriers

The role of the central government in facilitating the competitive development of broadband markets is largely enacted through regulation. The local gov- ernments have an important role in the deployment of broadband, through urban planning and implementing rights-of-ways by issuing building and excavation permits; as well as any coordination of civil works between utility firms. At the implementation level, local governments can remove very practical but important barriers. Maintaining a register of cable routes is another activity in which municipalities play an important role, although the register may be retained at regional or national level.

An example is the city of Almere in the Netherlands. Recognizing the importance of fibre for the development of the ICT infrastructure for the city government and fibre to the home, it adjusted its planning and right-of-way procedures, creating a one-stop shop, whereby implementation approvals can be obtained in one to two weeks rather than the usual thirteen weeks. This should facilitate the connection of 60,000 homes with fibre within two years.

The case of France illustrates how the local authorities can play a decisive role in furthering regional development by enabling operators' roll-outs through measures that encourage them to share their resources. They can also provide local information on underground infrastructure, help coordinate civil engineering works, install ducts for future use, authorize less costly civil engineering infrastructure or wiring on building facades, and encourage the pre-installation of fibre in new buildings and in buildings undergoing major renovations.

In Germany the respective local authorities or associations thereof may apply for financing through subsidies, grants or loans from the federal government. With these means they can complement private and communal investments in projects for infrastructure roll-out and accompanying activities (planning, consulting, informational events, etc.). In the new framework, the laying of empty ducts has been rendered eligible for financing and the federal subsidy ceiling has been increased from 60% to 90% with the remainder provided by the *Länder*.

These cases appear to suggest that a closer involvement of municipalities in the deployment of broadband tends to increase the awareness of their role and hence a higher interest in removing any remaining barriers. (See Section 16.18 on the role of municipalities).

16.17 The role of government: as chief architect

A typical example of market failure is the lack of supply of broadband in rural areas. In most of the case studies, there is attention to closing the coverage gaps, largely through subsidies targeted at the so-called white areas. Often the incumbent, as sole supplier in these areas, is the recipient of these subsidies. The case of France is an example of a more holistic approach and reflects the developmental role of governments. The case shows the vision of the government in recognizing the differences between high urban, urban, regional and rural areas, and it differentiates its broadband policies accordingly. In the highly developed urban areas the policy calls for private supply in competition. Regulation is tuned toward facilitating deployments through, for example, sharing of ducts. In the deep rural areas it is recognized that private supply is not economically feasible and hence a strong role is assigned to the municipal government to coordinate the roll-out of broadband using public funding.

The case describes the 'implementation vision' for the rural area as follows:

> First, very early, [the local authorities] develop, usually at the Departmental level, the digital territorial development master plan ... These indicative documents are essential. They make an inventory of digital coverage and existing networks and identify projects in progress or planned. They also give the vision of the territory in matters of digital coverage and action scenarios and how to achieve it according to a strategy to promote consistency between private investment and public intervention. Then local authorities are consulted by operators while they are deploying their networks. Finally local authorities may decide to make public initiative networks such as the law allows in accordance with the regulatory framework.

See also the next section addressing the role of municipalities as the 'lender of last resort'.

16.18 The role of municipalities: market failure to lender of last resort

Probably the most prominent government actors in the field of infrastructure supply are the municipalities. Historically they have assumed the prime responsibility for the supply of a range of infrastructures, including road works, sanitation, the distribution of water, gas and electricity, and sometimes also their supply (Millward, 2005; Van der Woud, 2007). In the early days these activities were wholly owned and operated by the municipalities. The German *Stadtwerke* are a good example. In more recent times semi-governmental and private firms have become responsible for the infrastructure supply, but municipalities remain important actors in terms of coordinating the works, both maintenance and repair, as well as new builds.

In line with these developments it should not come as a surprise that municipalities have played an important role in telecommunications supply, although their role has varied across EU member states, from very strong involvement (e.g., NL), through involvement in rural areas only (e.g., PL, and very recently FR) to no involvement at all (e.g., BE). National governments have played an important role in the provision of long-distance connectivity, a service transcending the interests of a single municipality. The collection of country case studies provides many examples of municipal involvement, suggesting that a pattern is emerging.

In Poland new initiatives to rectify forty years of neglect in bringing telephone service to the rural areas were very much needed. The idea to operate a public telecommunication network independently from the state emerged in southeast Poland, where local governments and village-level telephone committees established two independent telephone operators. Within three years, both were profitable and able to pay back loans and finance expansion of their networks. This type of public-private partnership in financing was one of the most important innovations for the region and the country in the early 1990s and led the way for the development of forty-four other independent telecommunications systems of this kind.

A renewed involvement of the municipalities in the Netherlands started in the beginning of the new millennium and created a wave of municipal activity across the country. In 2001 the City Council of Amsterdam placed the topic of fibre networking on the political agenda, being concerned about a possible 'digital divide' emerging in the city, which was and is considered economically and socially undesirable. In the Dutch tradition of broad consultations a series of studies was executed which ultimately led to a public-private partnership for the implementation of an open access passive network infrastructure, supporting service-level competition. For the purpose a foundation was established in which the municipality participated for 1/3, the four housing corporations for 1/3, and investors for another 1/3; each party contributing EUR 6 million. This enabled the first phase of implementation – 40,000 connections – to start in 2006, subject to approval by the European Commission, which was granted in December 2007.

The early and widely cited example of early fibre networking is the city of Stockholm, established in 1994 under the name of Stokab. Stockholm city's basic idea was that the IT infrastructure should be available to the whole society, public sector, telecom operators, and other businesses alike. To realize that vision Stokab was established to own and operate a passive optical fibre network, to be used by all market players in delivering services to residents and business. About 90% of households and almost 100% of enterprises are covered and an extensive backbone network connects industrial areas, all major healthcare facilities and urban centres in the region. In 2012, Stokab served over 100 telecom operators and more than 700 companies and organizations as customers.

The more recent and much broader set of initiatives involves half of all municipalities in Sweden, including the much more rural ones. One of the most compelling reasons for municipalities to become involved is a saving of 30% to 50% of the total municipal data and telecommunication costs. This is partly due to increased efficiency and partly due to the fact that the fibre network allows for more competition. An important indirect effect being observed is reduced migration, a problem among rural municipalities in Sweden. The availability of a very high quality ICT infrastructure prevents businesses from moving to the cities, creates new business opportunities and allows people to stay or move to the rural areas, combining a high quality of life with distance working.

What explains the differences in municipal involvement? Is this past involvement and past experience? It is questionable whether the 'municipal memory' can bridge a gap of sixty years in the case of the Netherlands. Should this be explained based on enduring influence of the 'informal institutional environment' – the norms, value orientations and codes – Layer 4 as depicted in the model for socio-technological institutional analysis? (see Chapter 2, Figure 2.1) A detailed comparison of the Dutch and Flemish cases, which have many aspects in common, suggests that there is a noticeable difference in the role of municipalities, with the regional government having become much stronger in Flanders. The role of the *Stadtwerke* in Germany, being the basis of many city networks, appears to support the notion of a historical 'golden thread'.

The German case provides a very pragmatic reason for municipal involvement:

'...the majority of the investments in FttH/B are being made by city carriers and municipalities in their regions through the municipal public utilities companies (Stadtwerke). The reason is that the majority of the investment needed to deploy fibre is allocated to the passive infrastructure, and Stadtwerke and city carriers are the owners of passive infrastructure.'

In the light of these developments, it is interesting to observe a renewed call by the politicians, supported by regulators, for municipalities to become involved in telecommunications supply, in particular in areas where it is less profitable for private firms to engage in the supply of broadband. As such, the municipalities are being assigned the role of 'lender of last resort', using public means when private ones fall short. This is a role that has become part of legislation in, for instance, France and Poland.

In France the role of local governments in broadband supply is developed in great detail, including the implementation process and funding, see Section 16.16. The salient fact is that, since 2004, the French legislative framework allows communities to act as operators in the electronic communications sector. This has never been the case before. Twenty projects of ultra-fast public-initiative networks have already been built or are being defined. Some of them are conducted on a departmental or regional scale and deal with more than 100,000 lines each.

The Polish case describes the enactment of the municipalities as 'lender of last resort'. The Act of 2010 introduced a new competence for local government entities: these entities may build as well as operate telecommunications networks, in particular its passive elements, which are to be financed from the entities' own budgets. The local government entities can also use the facilities of electrical power, gas and sewage companies. The provision of telecommunications services to end-users is permitted only when local entrepreneurs will not be able to meet the demand for Internet access. Moreover, the activities undertaken by local governments must be proportionate and non-discriminatory, so as not to undermine the principles of fair competition in the local telecommunications market.

A call upon municipalities for assistance in closing first the 'analogue divide' and now the 'digital divide' is not surprising considering the expanse of rural areas in these countries. About 37% of the of the unconnected households in the European Union are in the rural areas of Poland. France can be characterized by an 'urban divide', with Paris as the largest metropolis on the one hand and vast rural areas on the other.

Given the large amounts of investments required – rural connectivity being the most expensive – and considering the economic crises having resulted in severely distressed government budgets, the question is how effective the designated 'lender of last resort' can become. At least the appropriate regulation is in place: the EC *State Aid Guidelines* have been clarified, uncertainties should have diminished (EC, 2013). The largest uncertainty remaining is probably the uncertainty around the level of demand. France provides probably the best example of how municipalities can be assisted in the implementation and funding of broadband. See also Section 16.16 on the government as 'chief architect'.

16.18 The role of government: in bridging the digital divide

As illustrated in the previous sections, central, regional and local governments have assumed an important role in bridging the digital divide. A consistent pattern is emerging.

In France, the law on the fight against the digital divide (Pintat Act) of December 17, 2009 aims to prevent the emergence of a new digital divide. It has defined the digital territorial coverage master plan and created the digital development fund to finance deployment in areas not covered by private initiative.

As Spain is one of the most mountainous countries in Europe, universal service for voice telephony was only completed in the 1980s, through the use of wireless solutions. When Internet access was included as a universal service in the early 2000s, this system was upgraded using GPRS and also some LMDS, providing narrowband in the rural areas. In 2004 a plan for broadband extension in rural areas was started using regional funding to update local exchanges to provide DSL services based upon public-private cooperation models. By 2008, when the program concluded, low data rate broadband coverage had reached 98% of the population.

In Germany the *Länder* play an important role in addressing the digital divide. In 2008 the financing of broadband infrastructure roll-out became possible for eligible rural areas within the Joint Task for the Improvement of Agrarian Structures and Coast Protection of the federal Ministry for Food, Agriculture and Consumer Protection. The *Länder* can propose their own measures and the local authorities may apply for financing through subsidies, grants or loans from the federal government. With these means they can complement private and communal investments in projects and the accompanying activities (planning, consulting, informational events, etc.).

In Latvia, in order to support the achievement of a more complete fixed broadband coverage, the Ministry of Transport has coordinated with the EC a state aid program for the development of middle-mile fibre communications networks and optical access points up to 2018.

The case of Poland shows as a salient item the discrepancy between the availability of funds to close the digital divide and their application. Out of PLN 2.3 billion granted to Poland in 2007–2013 within the framework of sixteen regional programs, only 8.8% of the funds had been spent or cleared as of mid-2011. However, since 2012 there has been an increase in utilization of the European Regional Development Fund. This is in part the result of local authorities becoming involved in the implementation of the projects.

In Greece EU funding played an important role in the development of broadband in the regions. Calls for proposals were issued for the subsidized construction of metropolitan fibre networks in more than seventy cities beyond Athens and Thessaloniki. Given that the financing of these networks was through EU structural funds, these metropolitan area networks should provide wholesale services only and be governed by clear rules of open access.

The case studies on Sweden and Greece show that pursuing a successful fibre project is not a simple affair; moreover, running a communications network requires a specialized set of skills, different from what is required for running a municipality. Outsourcing to a specialized firm is one of the options being applied.

The case on Greece also showed the vulnerability of these projects in the broader context of an economic crisis. The whole initiative of setting up broadband companies at the regional level came to a halt. Although the current National Strategic Reference Framework has placed digital convergence high on the political agenda, the new operational programme mostly targets 'soft measures' to enhance the use of ICTs within the public and private sectors, rather than the deployment of broadband infrastructures.

16.19 Broadband and economic recovery

Considering the importance of broadband for economic and social activity, investments in broadband have become part of the economic recovery plans in the wake of the recent financial/economic crisis. The emphasis of the European Commission, in particular DG Connect, on investment in electronic communications provides a clear example.

Also, the case study on Germany points to this role of broadband: Under the second recovery package, which expired at the end of 2010, additional financing was made available for the cases not falling under the Joint Tasks. The attractive features of this mechanism were the absence of the subsidy limit per project and the possibility to apply for regional projects not being carried out by local authorities. Another source of financing was made available directly for undertakings: according to the Law on Future Investments the *Länder* can provide local authorities with finances which, in their turn, can be made available to undertakings developing or operating broadband networks. Undertakings may apply to the federal government and/or Länder for guarantees that assume a default risk of up to 90%.

16.20 Wireless broadband

The critical role of wireless communication is illustrated by the cases of Poland, Latvia and Spain. As noted in Section 16.4, the PSTN fixed line penetration in Poland and Latvia has peaked at around 30%, with mobile/cellular becoming the default means of communication. The Latvian case shows how this narrowband phenomenon influences broadband developments; here again, mobile broadband is the first choice. The case on Spain clearly shows that wireless is the only means of reaching deep rural areas.

The case of Spain points to a change in broadband market dynamics that is applied generally. The succession of next-generation technologies, from 1G analogue through 2G digital to 3G broadband reflects a virtuous cycle of infrastructure investment and innovation, followed by the adoption of new services and new devices. However, with the next generation of 4G – LTE this cycle has been broken. It is replaced by a cycle that runs in the opposite direction. Today, innovation at the device, service and application level drives adoption and requires investments by mobile operators in expanding the capacity of mobile networks to support the higher data rates and volumes required.

However, these investments will not necessarily lead to increase in revenues.

The case of Belgium provides for a salient item, whereby a device manufacturer holds the use of the next generation technology hostage. By initially blocking the use of 4G on its smartphones it delays the adoption of a next generation of technology.

16.21 Realizing the Digital Agenda: measuring broadband performance

Once targets are set, there is a need to measure achievement. In assessing the performance of the broadband market, league tables play an important role. These tables typically reflect rankings based on broadband penetration in terms of the number of broadband lines per capita. While these tables are readily accessible, this is a very coarse and imprecise way of presenting broadband performance (see e.g., the critique by Cawley in Chapter 3). In a series of reports, Ford and associates move from the development of a Broadband Performance Index, through a Broadband Efficiency Index to a Broadband Adoption Index (Ford, Koutsky and Spiwak, 2007, 2008; Beard, Ford and Spiwak, 2009). The common theme among the papers is the critique of simplistic and often erroneous representation of performance. They emphasize that performance is about the efficiency of translating inputs into outputs: that is, relating input factors such as income, income inequality, education, population age and population density to broadband lines per household. Thereby they strip away many factors over which telecom policymakers have very little influence or control. A primary finding of their studies is that a country's demographic and economic endowments explain the vast majority of the variations in broadband subscriptions across the OECD. Moreover, they conclude on the basis of their index that Korea and Japan are not broadband 'miracles" but like the USA they are 'average performers' in translating their available endowments into broadband lines (2007).

These studies focus on the number of broadband lines as the explanandum and use as explanans the factors derived from studies into consumer buying behaviour. These studies do not explore, at least not explicitly, the role of telecommunications policy or regulation.

As broadband has evolved and is impacting the economy and society more broadly, so has the scope of measurements expand. In 2003 the ITU developed the Digital Access Index (DAI), which was presented later in the year at the World Summit on the Information Society (WSIS). The DAI was to measure the overall ability of individuals to access and use ICTs, using five categories: infrastructure, affordability, knowledge, quality and usage. In 2005 the index was merged with the Orbicom Infostate Index aimed at monitoring the digital divide.

Following the Geneva Plan of Action, work started on the Digital Opportunity Index to be presented at WSIS 2005, targeted at capturing the potential of countries to benefit from access to ICTs. In 2006, the ITU Plenipotentiary Conference mandated that the work should converge towards a single index, which culminated in the ICT Development index (IDI). This effort captured the inputs (ICT readiness, ICT use and ICT capability) towards the realization of the Information Society and has been updated regularly (ITU, 2012).

In 2008, the European Commission took the initiative for 'Indexing Broadband Performance' in a joint development effort with the national regulatory authorities to establish the Broadband Performance Index (BPI) (EC, 2008b). The BPI captures as dimensions: rural broadband coverage; competition by coverage; price; quality in terms of data rates; uptake of advanced services; and the socio-economic context. As such, the index captured both input and output variables.

Next to the choice of the variables to be included under the heading of performance (number of lines, data rate, price, e-readiness, etc.), the various studies that aim to create a composite index highlight the issue of assigning the appropriate weight to each variable. Badasyan et al. (2011) therefore proposed that as policy priorities differ across constituencies [in their case US states] 'each state should be granted leeway for deciding how to weigh its own indicators ...'.

Moreover, broadband is not a uniform product, which increases the complexity of measurement. This is compounded by technical measurement issues related to the use of the underlying communication infrastructure. Bauer et al. (2010) and Lehr et al. (2013) provide insight into the complexity of the measurement of data rates and compare the quality of the various sources of information, including Speedtest/Ookla, Akamai and Youtube.

Hence, the primary objective of the research project that has run in parallel to the research reported in this book was to obtain deeper insights into what explains broadband performance in general and what explains the difference in performance across the EU member states in particular.[22] Having observed the difference in broadband outcomes and, through the case study research, the large variance in broadband market dynamics, an exploratory approach was considered most appropriate – allowing the 'factors and actors' that determine the outcome to emerge, rather than be predefined. The research started with defining broadband performance as output, and identified and tested which variables as inputs are statistically significant in explaining broadband performance. See the Appendix and, for more details, Lemstra, Van Gorp and Voogt (2013).

Based on data from sixteen EU Member States over the period 2008–2011, a composite performance index (PI) for fixed broadband has been determined that best captures the difference in level of performance across the EU member states, considering the various attributes that constitute broadband performance. From the wide range of attributes, such as coverage, uptake, downstream data rate, upstream data rate, prices, latency, jitter, packet loss, etc., three attributes capture the differences best: broadband uptake (as percentage of households); broadband revenues; and the percentage of lines with a download data rate above 10 Mbit/s.

For each of these three parameters the weight has been established. The interpretation of the derived weights is as follows:

- one extra percentage point in broadband uptake increases the PI score by 0.410 points;

---

[22] See note 1 and Appendix 2.

- a revenue increase of EUR 1.0 per connection decreases the PI score by 1.81;
- a 1% increase in broadband lines having a data rate greater than 10 Mbit/s) increases the PI score by 0.03 points.

The performance index values for the EU countries included in the study are reflected in Table 8.1.

16.22 Concluding remarks

Reflecting on the trigger for this project, the concern for diversity against a drive for uniformity, the results of the twelve case studies show much more diversity than was anticipated. They strengthen the notion of a 'common market' in the European Union, rather than a 'single market'. They reflect common, shared objectives – the Digital Agenda for Europe – with varying ways of reaching these objectives. While all member states have a tele-communications regulatory framework in common and all industry actors have access to the same communication network technologies, the trajectory along which the DAE targets may be reached is to a large extent determined by the legacy situation, which is highly diverse.

The usual starting assumption is that all households are connected to the telephone network. While largely valid for the EU15 in the early days, today this assumption is wrong, as network developments in the new member states have followed a different trajectory and pace. The developments in the member states in Central Europe show that PSTN peaked at a density of approximately 30 lines per 100 inhabitants. In these countries mobile connectivity has become the default means of communication; this now also holds for broadband.

The concept of infrastructure-based competition suggest a straightforward competitive model being applicable. However, in practice the competitive pressure from CATV-cable varies widely. In some countries CATV is associated with viewing television, not as a means for Internet access. In other countries the (former) ownership by the PSTN incumbent explains the late start of the transition towards a broadband platform. In another case,

Table 16.1 Fixed broadband performance index by country, 2009–2011

Country	PI 2009	PI 2010	PI 2011
AT	94*	94	94
BE	106	108	110
BG	79	86	89
CY	97	102	111
CZ	79*	83	87
DE	99	100	102
DK	119	120	119
EE	90	94	96
EL	94	100	103
ES	100	104	106
FI	101*	99*	93*
FR	109*	111	112
HU	85*	88	89
IE	110	112	116
IT	95	98	99
LT	72	75	77
LU	115	114	117**
NL	121*	121*	123*
PL	81*	83*	84*
PT	92*	92*	94
RO	79	79	78
SE	106	107	106
SI	100	101	99
SK	69	73	75
UK	112*	112*	115*

Legend:
* Missing one data point, which is estimated within the model;
** Using the retail price level of 2010.
Source: Lemstra, Van Gorp and Voogt, 2013.

where infrastructure-based competition resulted in intense rivalry, the cable network has been an instrument of regional policy to create a powerful competitor, able to challenge the PSTN-incumbent in the broadband market. The outlook for CATV-based competition is limited in terms of coverage, which is not expected to grow, but the outlook in terms of increasing data rates is still significant. The PSTN and CATV networks represent clear cases of path dependency.

The purpose of the liberalization process was to unleash competitive market forces. As former monopolists, the incumbents were bestowed with significant market power, which they could apply to hinder market entrants. It appears that the stance taken by the NRAs in the early days of the liberalization process is indicative for the degree of success in creating a level playing field. This includes the stature of the persons appointed as the heads of the NRAs. In a few cases the NRAs were – in later years – forced to apply or threaten to apply one of the more intrusive remedies: namely, functional separation. In some cases the European Commission considered that the NRA was too lenient towards the incumbent. This suggests diversity in the attitude of the incumbent players towards the competitive market, which the common regulatory framework allowed to be addressed in different ways.

The liberalization initiatives achieved a degree of success in the early days as many firms entered the market attracted by the new possibilities, the growth of demand for Internet access and ample funding being provided by the financial sector. This included incumbents going abroad and taking shareholdings in other incumbents that were being privatized.

In the aftermath of the telecom/Internet bubble, firms had to consolidate and those firms unable to establish a positive cash-flow had difficulties surviving. The incumbents changed their strategies and re-focused on domestic operations. Consolidation of the industry with fewer players was the outcome, but not necessarily a lower intensity of rivalry. This development could be observed across the EU. However, the ultimate aim of moving from access-based to infrastructure-based competition has varied across the EU in terms of timing and the degree of success. This is largely the result of regulatory action and firm strategy.

Both qualitative and quantitative analysis suggest that setting the appropriate wholesale price for unbundled local loops determines whether the alternative operator moves up the 'ladder of investment', shifting from buying bitstream products from the incumbent to buying unbundled products. Whether the alternative operator reaches the final rung of the ladder – building its own (fibre-based)

infrastructure – depends also on the deployment strategy the alternative operator has applied. Climbing the 'final rung' appears to happen only in those cases where a sufficiently dense customer base has been built and access to passive infrastructure is made available, which together make the business case for the transition to fibre viable. The individuality of circumstances across European cities explains the great variety in fibre deployments.

Adding to the wide diversity of broadband development are the 'grassroots' fibre deployments as a result of entrepreneurial activity in some member states that recently joined the EU. A lack of broadband supply by the incumbent combined with significantly lower installation costs as a result of aerial/façade deployment explains the 'leapfrog' in fibre-based rankings of some countries in Central Europe.

With fibre holding the promise of being the 'ultimate' infrastructure – virtually unlimited in data rates that can be supplied – and operators moving slowly in its deployment, it is not a surprise that certain actors, such as municipalities, have started to take initiatives of their own. As municipalities compete on the basis of infrastructure supply to attract business and citizens and start to recognize the socio-economic benefits, being dependent on third parties for the telecom infrastructure can be frustrating. These new actors add to the dynamics of the broadband market. Following a steep learning curve in terms of what is (or is not) allowed by (European) law and regulation, municipalities have become important new actors, which can affect both supply and demand conditions.

It is interesting to observe that central governments call upon municipalities as the 'lender of last resort' in those circumstances where private firms operating in competitive markets fail to invest. Apparently, the municipality is the right level for intervention. It is the place where the 'rubber meets the road'.

This also applies to housing corporations, where property value is not only driven by location, but also determined by being connected to the appropriate infrastructures. As such, history repeats itself. As a natural point for demand aggregation, housing corporations can positively and significantly influence the viability of the fibre business case. This also applies for the open access model used by alternative fibre network providers, which shifts the competitive model from infrastructure-based competition to services-based competition, channelling the total demand onto one network.

While infrastructure-based competition has served us well in the transition from narrowband to broadband, and through technological enhancements of the legacy networks, this preferred model will not be able to realize the high-end targets of the Digital Agenda everywhere, in particular in the sparsely populated areas and areas without legacy networks.

The French government is most explicit in acknowledging this fact and translating this into regulation that differentiates between areas that are suitable for competition between infrastructures, areas that can only be served in an economically viable manner using one infrastructure which is shared, and areas that need governmental support for the business case to become viable. And in all three cases, complementary actions are needed to optimize the business case, through removing remaining barriers, such as open access to the passive infrastructures of the incumbent, the sharing of passive infrastructures across utilities, and sharing the access into buildings.

The German government acknowledged the role of wireless solutions in bringing broadband to remote areas by making rural roll-out a first-priority obligation as part of a recent radio spectrum license award process. As we approach 2020, wireless solutions are likely to become a more significant contributor to broadband development as demands for mobile access continue to expand.

Opening the black box of the country cases has provided some profound insights, rich in detail, on the dynamics of broadband markets in Europe. Measuring competition by focusing only on the number of players in the broadband market fails to expose the many dimensions of competition in reality. In each country that has been covered, public and private actors collaborate and compete in different settings, largely determined by the legacy infrastructures.

The cases show that we share common objectives in terms of broadband developments and we act based on a common regulatory framework. We can observe that competition among operators is the leading principle, but that the development of the market can be supported by other private and public actors. Depending on political preferences and market circumstances, the interventions can follow a top-down approach or be based on bottom-up initiatives.

Notwithstanding the importance of policy and regulation, the quantitative analysis confirmed the importance of economic, demographic and topographical factors in driving broadband development.

Compared to the development of mobile communications, with a neat succession of generations of mobile/cellular technologies being deployed in infrastructure-based competition by three to five operators, of which some are operating on a pan-European basis, fixed broadband market dynamics appear to be much more complicated. But also in mobile, market dynamics have become more complicated; the mobile industry's virtuous cycle of innovation, infrastructure investment and adoption of services having been broken, presents new investment challenges.

The case studies confirm a clear momentum in all countries toward achieving the broadband targets set in the Digital Agenda for Europe. The targets are necessarily ambitious, to encourage the broadband developments in all member states. They will not all reach the finish line at the same time; some member states may have moved beyond the targets by 2020; others may still be on their way. With the diversity made visible through the country case studies, this reflects reality.

The case studies show clearly that progress in Europe is not only dependent on Pillar IV: Fast and ultra-fast Internet access. There is a strong interdependency among the Pillars. The cases point to Pillar VI: Enhancing digital literacy, skills and inclusion, while news reports clearly point to the importance of Pillar III: Trust & Security.

The country case studies have come a long way to answering the research questions raised in the introductory chapter:

- *Set 1*: What have been the trajectories for broadband development (fixed and/or mobile); which actors have been instrumental in these broadband developments and how; and to what degree have competition in and regulation of broadband markets played a role in the provision and uptake of broadband?
- *Set 2*: What are the (anticipated) trajectories towards the next generation of broadband networking (fixed and/or mobile) and the realization of the Digital Agenda targets; which actors are instrumental in the transition and how; and how and to what degree should competition between infrastructures and the regulation of infrastructures play a role in the provision and uptake of next generation broadband?

The charter for the case study authors has been to respond to the framework and bring to the forefront those phenomena that, in their perspective, are salient to the development of the broadband market in their country. As such, we have been able to observe interesting commonalities and differences across the twelve case studies. This research has shed light on the role of private and public actors. Foremost it has shown the role of path dependence. It informed us on the broad scope of solutions to the problems observed. It showed the importance of looking beyond the traditional actors, operators and regulators. It showed top-down and bottom-up approaches to resolving issues. More specific questions will require more detailed and focused case work, for which the current set of cases may provide a good starting point.

References

Abbate, J. (2000). *Inventing the internet*. Cambridge, MA: MIT Press.

Analysys Mason (2010). Europe's digital deficit: revitalising the market in electronic communications. London: Analysys Mason.

Analysys Mason for GBP (2008). The costs of deploying fibre-based next-generation broadband infrastructure. Cambridge, UK.

Australian Government (2013). National Broadband Network.

Badasyan, N., D. Shideler and S. Silva (2011). Broadband achievement index: Moving beyond availability. *Telecommunications Policy* **35**(11): 933–950.

Bauer, S., D. D. Clark and W. Lehr (2010). Understanding broadband speed measurements. 38th Research Conference on Communication, Information and Internet Policy (TPRC), Arlington, VA: George Mason University.

Beard, T. R., G. S. Ford and L. J. Spiwak (2009). The broadband adoption index: Improving measurements and comparisons of broadband deployment and adoption. Washington, DC: Phoenix Center for Advanced Legal & Economic Public Policy Studies.

Cave, M. (2004). Making the ladder of investment operational. Brussels: European Commission.

(2006). Encouraging infrastructure competition via the ladder of investment. *Telecommunications Policy* **30**(3–4): 223–237.

Cornell (2005). National Cable & Telecommunications Assn. v. Brand X Internet Services (04–277) 545 U.S. 967 (200). *Supreme Court Collection*. Retrieved 2009-01019, from www.law.cornell.edu/supct/html/o4-277.ZS. html.

EC (1987). COM(87)2 290: Green paper on the development of the common market for telecommunications services and equipment. Brussels: European Commission.

(1997). COM(97)236 First Implementation Report. Brussels: Eurpean Commission, DG XIII and DG IV.

(1998a). COM(1998)80 final Third Implementation Report. Brussels: European Commission.

(1998b). Fourth Implementation Report. Brussels: European Commission.

(1999). Fifth Implementation Report. Brussels: European Commission.

(2000). COM(2000)814 Sixth Implementation Report. Brussels: European Commission.

(2001). COM(2001)706 Seventh Implementation Report. Brussels: European Commission.

(2002). COM(2002)695 final Eighth Implementation Report. Brussels: European Commission.

(2003). COM(2003)715 final Ninth Implementation Report. Brussels: European Commission.

(2004). COM(2004)759 final Tenth Implementation Report. Briussels: European Commission.

(2006). COM(2006)68 final Eleventh Implementation Report. Brussels: European Commission.

(2007). COM(2006)155 final Twelfth Implementation Report. Brussels: European Commission.

(2008a). COM(2008)153 Thirteenth Implementation Report. Brussels: European Commission.

(2008b). SEC(2008) 2507 Staff Working Document – Indexing broadband performance. Brussels: European Commission.

(2009). COM(2009)140 final Fourteenth Implementation Report. Brussels: European Commission.

(2010a). COM(2010)253 final Fifteenth Implementation Report. Brussels: European Commission.

(2010b). COM(2010) 245 A digital agenda for Europe. Brussels: European Commission.

(2011). COCOM11–24 Broadband access in the EU: situation at 1 July 2011. Brussels: European Commission.

(2013). 2013/C 25/01 EU Guidelines for the application of State aid rules in relation to the rapid deployment of broadband networks. Brussels: European Commission.

Ford, G. S., T. M. Koutsky and L. J. Spiwak (2007). The broadband performance index: A policy-relevant method of comparing broadband adoption among countries. Washington, DC: Phoenix Center for Advanced Legal & Economic Studies, p 32–.?

(2008). The broadband efficiency index: What realy drives broadband adoption across the OECD? Washington, DC: Phoenix Center for Advanced Legal & Economic Public Policy Studies, p 26–.?

Hafner, K. and M. Lyon (1996). *Where wizards stay up late: The origins of the Internet.* New York: Simon & Schuster.

iDA (2013). Next Generation Broadband Network. Retrieved 2013-08-02, from www.ida.gov.sg/Infocomm-Landscape/Infrastructure/Wired/What-is-Next-Gen-NBN.

ITU (2012). Measuring the information society 2012. Geneva: International Telecommunicatiosn Union.

Jaag, C., M. Lutzenberger and U. Trinkner (2009). Approaches to FttH-regulation: An international comparison. Second Annual Conference on Competition and Regulation in Network Industries, Brussels: CRNI.

Kushida, K. and S.-Y. Oh (2006). Understanding South Korea and Japan's spectacular broadband development: Strategic liberalization of the telecommunications sectors – BRIE Working Paper 175. Berkeley, CA: University of California at Berkeley.

Lehr, W., S. Bauer and D. D. Clark (2013). Measuring performance when broadband is the new PSTN. *Journal of Information Policy* 2013 (3): 411–441.

Lemstra, W. (2006). Dissertation: *The Internet bubble and the impact on the development path of the telecommunication sector. Department* of *Technology, Policy and Management* Delft, The Netherlands: TUDelft.

Lemstra, W., A. van Gorp and B. Voogt (2013). Explaining broadband performance across the EU. Delft University of Technology Delft: p 63.

Lemstra, W. and N. Van Gorp (2013). Unbundling: Regulation is a necessary, but not sufficient conditions to reach the final rung of the investment ladder. Second Annual Conference on the Regulation of Infrastructure Industries in an Age of Convergence. Florence, Italy: Florence School of Regulation.

Maldoom, D., R. A. D. Marsden, J. G. Sidak and H. J. Singer (2005). Broadband in Europe – How Brussels can wire the Information Society. New York: Springer.

Millward, R. (2005). *Private and public enterprise in Europe – Energy, telecommunications and transport 1830–1990.* Cambridge, UK: Cambridge University Press.

New Zealand Government (2013) Ultra-Fast Broadband Initiative.

OECD (1999). Communications Outlook 1999. Paris: Organisation for Economic Cooperation and Development.

(2001). Communications Outlook 2001. Paris: Organisation for Economic Cooperation and Development.

(2003). Communications Outlook 2003. Paris: Organisation for Economic Cooperation and Development.

(2005). Communications Outlook 2005. Paris: Organisation for Economic Cooperation and Development.

(2013). Communications Outlook 2013. Paris: OECD Publishing.

Oh, M. and J. F. Larson (2011). Digital development in Korea: Building an information society. Abingdon, UK: Routledge.

Rood, H. (2010). Very high speed broadband deployment in Europe: The Netherlands and Bulgaria compared. Telecom Policy Research Conference, Arlington, VA: TPRC.

Tahon, M. (2013). *Dissertation: Flexibility, competitive and cooperative interaction in telecommunications networks: a model for extended techno-economic evaluation. Ingenieurswetenschappen en architectuur.* Ghent, Belgium: Universiteit Ghent.

Van der Woud, A. (2007). *Een nieuwe wereld – Het ontstaan van het moderne Nederland (A new world – The emergence of the modern Netherlands).* Amsterdam: Prometheus – Bert Bakker.

Van Dijk (2011). Broadband internet access cost. Brussels: Van Dijk Management Consultants.

Washburn, B. (2005). The FCC eliminates DSL internet sharing, handling RBOCs freedom over broadband resale: CurrentAnalysis.

WIK Consult (2008). The economics of next generation access – Final report. Bad Honnef, Germany: WIK Consult.

PART 4

Appendices

Glossary

Note: Acronyms specific to a single chapter and acronyms denoting a corporation or an organization are not included in the list.

Acronym:	Meaning:	Remarks:
2G	Second-generation cellular communications systems	E.g., GSM: Provides voice and low data rate services, based on circuit switching
2.5G	Stepping-stone from 2G to 3G	E.g., GPRS: Provides packet data services
3G	Third-generation GSM	E.g., UMTS: Provides voice and broadband data communication services
3.5G	Stepping-stone from 3G to 4G	E.g., HSPA$^+$
3GPP	3G Partnership Project	Industry standards group
4G	Fourth-generation cellular communications systems	E.g., LTE: high data rate/broadband communication services, all-IP, end-to-end and adaptive QoS
AD	Access Directive	
ADSL	Asymmetrical digital subscriber line	ADSL2 and ADSL2$^+$ are ADSL upgrades
altnets	Alternative network operators	
AMS-IX	Amsterdam Internet eXchange	
AO	Alternative operator	
ARPM	Average revenue per minute	
ARPU	Average revenue per user	
AT	Austria	
ATM	Asynchronous transfer mode	
BBS	Bulletin board system	
BCD	Basic conditions demand	
BCS	Basic conditions supply	
BE	Belgium	
BEREC	Body of European Regulators of Electronic Communications	
BG	Bulgaria	
BPI	Broadband Performance Index	
BSA	Bitstream Access	
BU-LRIC	Bottom-up long-run incremental costs	
CAGR	Cumulative average growth rate	
CAI	Central antenna installation	

(cont.)

Acronym:	Meaning:	Remarks:
cap	capita	
CAPEX	Capital expenditures	
CAS	Central antenna system	
CATV	Cable TV	Originally coaxial cable based
CCITT	International Telegraph and Telephone Consultative Committee	the predecessor of the ITU-T
CDMA	Code division multiple access	CDMA-450: operating in the 450 MHz band
CDMA EV-DO	CDMA Evolution data-optimized	
CEC	Commission of the European Communities	
CEO	Chief Executive Officer	
CEPT	Conférence des administrations européennes des postes et télécommunications	Association of European Postal and Telecommunications Administrations (PTTs)
CERN	Centre européenne pour la recherche nucléaire	
CFA	Confirmatory factor analysis	
CH	Switzerland	
CI	Conduct Index	
CMTS	Cable modem termination system	
CP	Communications provider	
CPE	Customer premises equipment	
CRF	Common regulatory framework	
CRM	Customer relationship management	
CY	Cyprus	
CZ	Czech Republic	
DCS	Digital communications system	
DAE	Digital Agenda for Europe	
DAI	Digital Access Index	
DE	Germany	
DG	Directorate-General	
DK	Denmark	
DOCAT	Digital optical community antenna trunk	
DOCSIS	Data Over Cable Service Interface Specification	
DSL	Digital subscriber line	xDSL any type of DSL
DSLAM	Digital subscriber line access multiplexer	
DTT	Digital terrestrial television	
DVB	Digital video broadcasting	
DVB-H	Digital video broadcasting – handheld	
DVB-T	Digital video broadcasting – terrestrial	

(cont.)

Acronym:	Meaning:	Remarks:
EBITDA	Earnings before interest, tax, depreciation and amortization	
EC	European Commission	
ECTA	European Competitive Telecommunications Association	
EDGE	Enhanced data rate for GSM evolution	
EE	Estonia	
EEC	European Economic Community	
EFA	Exploratory factor analysis	
EL	Greece	
EoA	Equivalence of access	
EoI	Equivalence of input	
EoO	Equivalence of output	
ES	Spain	
ETNO	European Telecommunications Network Operators Association	
ETSI	European Telecommunication Standards Institute	
EU	European Union	EUxx: the number of member states constituting the EU at a certain point in time
EUR	Euro	€
FB	Fixed broadband	
FCC	Federal Communications Commission	US regulatory authority
FDD	Frequency division duplex	
FI	Finland	
FR	France	
FTA	Free-to-air	
FTP	File transfer protocol	
FttA	Fibre to the amplifier	In Cable-TV networks
FttB	Fibre to the business/building	
FttC	Fibre to the curb/cabinet	
FttCab	Fibre to the cabinet	
FttCurb	Fibre to the curb	
FttdP	Fibre to the distribution point	
FttH	Fibre to the home	
FttLA	Fibre to the last amplifier	In Cable-TV networks
FttN	Fibre to the node	
FttX	Fibre to the X (all types included)	
FWA	Fixed wireless access	
G2B	Government to business	
G2C	Government to citizens	

(cont.)

Acronym:	Meaning:	Remarks:
G2G	Government to government	
GATS	General Agreement on Trade and Services	
GB	Gigabytes	
GDP	Gross Domestic Product	
GHz	Giga Hertz	
GIX	riGa Internet eXchange	
GPON	Gigabit-capable passive optical network	
GPRS	General packet radio service	
GSM	Groupe Spéciale Mobile, later to be known as Global System for Mobile Communications	Working party of CEPT; GSM-900: operating in the 900 MHz band; GSM-1800: operating in the 1800 MHz band
GSMA	GSM Association	
HD	High Definition	
HDTV	High-definition television	
HFC	Hybrid fibre-coax	As used in CATV networks
HH	Households	
HHI	Herfindahl-Hirschman Index	HHI* modified HHI
HIPERLAN	Wireless access standard by ETSI	
HSCSD	High-speed circuit-switched data	
HSDPA	High-speed downlink packet access	
HSPA	High-speed packet access	HSPA^{+} upgrade of HSPA
HSUPA	High-speed uplink packet access	
HTML	Hypertext mark-up language	
HU	Hungary	
ICT	Information and communication technology	
IDI	ICT development index	
IDN	Integrated digital network	
IE	Ireland	
IEEE	Institute of Electrical and Electronic Engineers	
IETF	Internet Engineering Task Force	
IMT	International mobile telecommunications	
IP	Internet protocol	
IPO	Initial public offering	
IPTV	Internet-protocol television	
IRU	Indefeasible right of use	
ISDN	Integrated services digital network	
ISOC	Internet Society	
ISP	Internet service provider	
IT	Italy	

(cont.)

Acronym:	Meaning:	Remarks:
IT	Information technology	
ITU	International Telecommunications Union	Part of the United Nations organisation
ITU-T	ITU-Telecommunication Sector	
IX	Internet eXchange	
kbit/s	kilobits per second	
KPI	Key performance indicator	
LAN	Local area network	
LBO	Leveraged buyout	
LLU	Local loop unbundling	
LRAIC	Long-run average incremental costs	
LRIC	Long-run incremental costs	
LT	Lithuania	
LTE	Long-term evolution	As related to cellular communication, also denoted as 4G, fourth-generation; LTE Advanced upgrade of LTE
LU	Luxembourg	
LV	Latvia	
M2M	Machine-to-machine	
MAN	Metropolitan area network	
MB	Megabytes	
MB	Mobile broadband	
Mbit/s	Megabits per second	
MDF	Main distribution frame	
MDU	Multi-dwelling unit	
MHz	Mega Hertz	
MMDS	Multichannel multipoint distribution service	
MMS	Multimedia message service	
MNO	Mobile network operator	
MVNO	Mobile virtual network operator	
NCA	National competition authority	
NCC	Network coordination centre	
NGA	Next-generation access	
NGAN	Next-generation access network	
NGN	Next-generation network	
NL	Netherlands	
NMT	Nordic Mobile Telephone system	NMT-450: operating in the 450 MHz band
NP	Network provider	
NRA	National regulatory authority	
NRFW	New regulatory framework	
O/E	Optical to electrical	

(cont.)

Acronym:	Meaning:	Remarks:
OECD	Organization for Economic Cooperation and Development	
OLO	Other licensed operator	
ONP	Open network provision	
OPEX	Operational expenditures	
OPGW	Optical ground wire	
OPTA	Onafhankelijke Post en Telecommunicatie Autoriteit	National Regulatory Authority, now part of Authoriteit Consument en Markt (ACM)
OTT	Over-the-top (services)	
P2P	Point-to-point	
P2MP	Point-to-Multi-point	
PA	Public administration	
PB	Petabytes	1000 billion bytes
PBX	Private branch exchange	
PC	Personal computer	
PCMCIA	Personal Computer Memory Card International Association	Referring to the card or card slot for credit-card-sized peripheral devices such as modems
PE	Private equity	
PESQ	Perceptual evaluation of speech quality	
PI	Performance index	
PIP	Physical infrastructure provider	
PL	Poland	
PM	Prime Minister	
PoP/POP	Point of presence	
PPP	Public-private partnership	
PPP	Purchasing power parity	
PSTN	Public switched telephone network	Originally twisted copper pair based
PT	Portugal	
PTT	Post, Telegraph and Telephone administration	
PUC	Public Utility Commission	Multi-sector NRA
Q	Quarter	1Q: first quarter
QoS	Quality of Service	
R&D	Research and development	
RACE	Research and Development in Advanced Communications Technologies for Europe	
RII	Regulatory Institutional Index	
RIPE	Réseaux IP Européens	
RLAN	Radio local area network	
RNS	Radio navigation services	
RO	Romania	

(cont.)

Acronym:	Meaning:	Remarks:
ROI	Return on investment	
ROIC	Regulatory outcome index – Conduct	
ROIS	Regulatory outcome index – Structure	
RTV	Radio and television	
SA	Service area	
SCP	Structure conduct performance	
SDH	Synchronous digital hierarchy	
SDI	Serial digital interface	
SDLC	Synchronous data link control	
SDSL	Symmetric DSL	
SE	Sweden	
SEM	Structural equations modelling	
SL	Slovenia	
SI	Structure index	
SK	Slovakia	
SIM	Subscriber identity module	
SLA	Service level agreement	
SLU	Sub-loop unbundling	
SME	Small and medium-sized enterprise	
SMP	Significant market power	
SMS	Short message service	
SP	Service provider	
TACS	Total access communication system	
TDD	Time division duplex	
TCP	Transmission control protocol	
TPRC	Telecommunications Policy Research Conference	
TU	Technical University	
TV	Television	
ULL	Unbundled local loop	Also LLU
UK	United Kingdom	
UMTS	Universal mobile telephony service	Also denoted as 3G, third-generation mobile
US	United States	
USA	United States of America	
USSR	Union of Soviet Socialist Republics	
VAN	Value-added network	
VCR	Videocassette recorder	
VDSL	Very high data-rate DSL	Also VDSL2/VDSL2$^+$ as next generation
VLAN	Virtual local area network	
VoIP	Voice over IP	

(cont.)

Acronym:	Meaning:	Remarks:
VSAT	Very small aperture terminal	
VULA	Virtual unbundled local access	
WACC	Weighted average cost of capital	
WAP	Wireless application protocol	
WBA	Wholesale broadband access	
WDM	Wavelength division multiplexing	
WE	West European	
Wi-Fi	Certification mark for interoperability between IEEE 802.11 conformant WLAN devices	
WiMAX	Worldwide interoperability for microwave access	
WISP	Wireless Internet service provider	
WLAN	Wireless local area network	
WLL	Wholesale leased line	
WLL	Wireless local loop	
WLR	Wholesale line rental	
WMN	Wireless mesh network	
WSIS	World Summit on the Information Society	
WTO	World Trade Organization	
WWW	World Wide Web	
X.25	Denotation for packet switched data networking protocol	
xDSL	Any type of DSL	
YoY	Year-ove-year	

Quantitative analysis of broadband performance

WOLTER LEMSTRA

There is little doubt that competition drives broadband performance – in line with economic theory – as illustrated by the Structure-Conduct-Performance (SCP) paradigm. This paradigm has informed a quantitative research project into broadband performance in the EU, which has been executed in parallel to the qualitative research reported in the case studies in this book.

Given the difference in broadband outcomes and the large variance in broadband market dynamics observed through the case study research, an exploratory approach was considered most appropriate – that is, allowing the 'factors and actors' that determine the outcome to emerge, rather than be predefined. The research started by defining broadband performance as output and identified and tested which input variables are statistically significant in explaining broadband performance. The exploratory effort was guided by the stylized model of industry performance: the SCP paradigm, adapted for regulation, see Figure Annex 2.1.[1]

First, it was necessary to determine what actually constitutes broadband performance. Furthermore, we needed to tackle how to measure the level of competition as well as the other elements in the SCP-framework. Finally, we needed to determine the direct and indirect relationships among all these elements (performance, structure, etc.). Considering this analytical challenge, the multivariate data analysis technique applied was structural equations modelling (SEM) (Hair et al., 2006; Schumacker and Lomax, 2010)[2] This technique facilitates the detection of patterns within a large set of variables. Within SEM, exploratory factor analysis (EFA) is used to detect general patterns among a large set of variables. EFA is an unrestricted model in which relationships between factors are not pre-set. As such, it provides directions for assigning variables to certain factors and the number of factors that are underlying the data. In developing a parsimonious model, an iterative process is applied, moving from exploratory factor analysis to confirmatory factor analysis to test the hypothesized model, and vice versa. In each iteration cycle a new variable is added and evaluated in terms of its effect on the construct and on the model.

In the rudimentary path model, we started with the Herfindahl Hirschman Index (HHI) measuring the concentration of suppliers as the initial single variable specification for the structure index. The initial findings suggested a positive relationship, which would imply that less competition would lead to higher performance; a rather surprising result. Detailed analysis of the components constituting the HHI suggested a combined effect of inter- and intra-platform competition. It appeared that the presence and size of a competing cable network has a strong positive effect on broadband

---

[1] We recognize and acknowledge the critique of the SCP model and the difficulties in interpreting the regularities that have been found in the context of identifying and measuring market power (see e.g., Church and Ware, 2000). It is not our objective to apply more recent approaches of analytical and game theoretical models for that purpose. Our objective is to identify and measure, based on empirical data, which factors can be said to influence performance in a statistically significant manner. With this objective the SCP paradigm is considered to provide useful guidance in identifying the candidate variables to be explored in this research. Moreover, structured equations modeling – the statistical technique applied – does not depend on causal relationships between structure and conduct and between conduct and performance being assumed *ex-ante*.

[2] SEM is the only statistical technique that allows for the simultaneous analysis of variables that are dependent in one relation and independent in another relation.

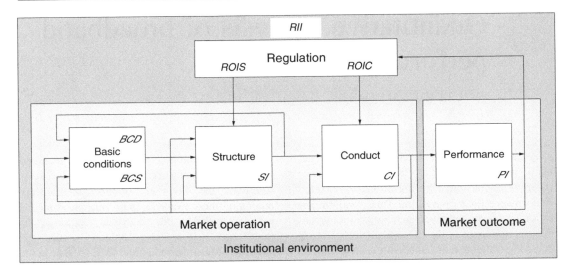

Appendix 2.1 SCP model, extended with regulation
Source: Lemstra, Van Gorp and Voogt, 2013.

uptake and on data rates and a negative effect on prices. At the same time the contribution of DSL-based intra-platform competition is weaker in the presence of cable. Further analysis suggested that a general HHI of the broadband market, taking broadband shares irrespective of technology platform, needed to be replaced by a HHI* reflecting the competition between platforms rather than between firms, essentially reflecting the HHI of technologies deployed. The HHI* being adopted is the sum of squares of the broadband market share of: (1) the incumbent operator's xDSL plus cable (and fibre) where applicable; (2) the cable operator(s)'s DOCSIS-3, exclusive of incumbent's share; (3) the full plus shared local loop unbundling; (4) the share of bitstream plus resale; and (5) the share of fibre plus other technologies.

We also tested other variants of a concentration ratio, but the HHI* provided overall the best model fit. Market structure – and thereby the HHI* – is also influenced by the cost structure, largely as a 'basic condition of supply'. The variable 'degree of urbanization' has been analysed as a proxy for differences in the cost structure. This variable has a significant effect. Furthermore, we analysed two regulatory instruments which might affect the

HHI*: (1) rights of way, which affects the degree of infrastructure competition; and (2) local loop access (unbundling), which affects the degree of access-based competition. Both the wholesale price for full unbundled loops and that for shared loops have been evaluated (corrected for purchasing power parity). Once the price for full unbundling was factored in, the price of shared unbundling did not add significant explanatory power. Considering the period of analysis (2008–2011) the role of LLU has become leading compared to alternative access products, such as resale and bitstream; hence, the prices for resale and bitstream were not analysed. Rights of way and related variables such as duct access did not appear to be statistically significant for inclusion in the Structure Index in the period analysed.

The most important element of the Conduct Index is the average investments in the fixed market per household. GDP per capita, corrected for purchasing power, has been identified as the major, statistically significant factor that influences the Conduct Index.

For more details on this quantitative analysis, see the report *Explaining Broadband Performance across the EU* (Lemstra, Van Gorp and Voogt, 2013).

References

Church, J. R. and R. Ware (2000). *Industrial Organization: A strategic approach*. New York: McGraw-Hill.

Hair Jr., J. F., W. C. Black, B. J. Babin, R. E. Anderson and R. L. Tatham (2006). *Multivariate data analysis*. Upper Saddle River, NJ: Pearson Prentice Hall.

Lemstra, W., A. van Gorp and B. Voogt (2013). Explaining broadband performance across the EU. Delft University of Technology Delft: 63.

Schumacker, R. E. and R. G. Lomax (2010). *Structural equations modeling*. New York: Routledge.

Index